THE BOOK OF ACTS IN ITS FIRST CENTURY SETTING

Bruce W. Winter

Series Editor

I. Howard Marshall • David W. J. Gill

Consulting Editors

THE BOOK OF ACTS IN ITS FIRST CENTURY SETTING

VOLUME 3

The Book of Acts and Paul in Roman Custody

by

Brian Rapske

WILLIAM B. EERDMANS PUBLISHING COMPANY
GRAND RAPIDS, MICHIGAN

THE PATERNOSTER PRESS
CARLISLE

© 1994 Wm. B. Eerdmans Publishing Company

255 Jefferson Ave. S,E., Grand Rapids, Michigan 49503

First published 1994 jointly
in the United States by
Wm. B. Eerdmans Publishing Company
and in the U.K. by
The Paternoster Press,
P.O. Box 300, Carlisle, Cumbria CA3 0QS

Printed in the United States of America

09 08 07 06 05 04   7 6 5 4 3 2 1

Library of Congress Cataloging-in-Publication Data

Rapske, Brian.
The book of Acts and Paul in Roman custody / by Brian Rapske.
p.   cm.   — (The book of Acts in its first century setting; v. 3)
Includes bibliographical references and indexes.
ISBN 0-8028-2912-0
1. Bible. N.T. Acts — Criticism, interpretation, etc.
2. Paul, the Apostle, Saint — Imprisonment.
3. Imprisonment — Rome — History.
I. Title.   II. Series.
BS2625.2.R37   1994
226.6'067 — dc20   94-34745
                                            CIP

British Library Cataloguing in Publication Data

Rapske, Brian
Book of Acts and Paul in Roman Custody. —
(Book of Acts in Its First Century Setting series; Vol. 3)
I. Title   II. Series
226.606

ISBN 0-85364-565-5

TABLE OF CONTENTS

ACKNOWLEDGEMENTS

The writing of such volumes as this are initially solitary labours. Their preparation for general publication, however, draws in many more individuals and, with that progress, the author's indebtedness grows. There are a number of individuals to whom I owe much and would like to express thanks.

Dr Ruth B. Edwards advised me along the way to this work's first presentation for the PhD at the University of Aberdeen. Latterly, Drs Conrad Gempf and Philip Kern rendered invaluable assistance in reducing the dissertation to a publishable size. The consulting editors, Professor I. Howard Marshall and Dr David W.J. Gill, read the work as it was being revised and made many helpful recommendations. I am also grateful to Dr Andrew Clarke and a team of workers at Tyndale House who were recruited to assist in the preparation of camera ready copy and the indexes.

Special thanks must go to the series editor, Dr Bruce W. Winter. He generously made the facilities and resources of Tyndale House, Cambridge available to me and extended the kind invitation to include my work as the third volume of *The Book of Acts in Its First Century Setting*.

The encouragement of my family has been considerable, but especially that of my father Robert Rapske. This volume is dedicated to his memory.

Brian M. Rapske
July, 1994

CHAPTER 1

INTRODUCTION

Luke devoted much space to the prisoner Paul. Nearly 25% of Acts concerns Paul's final arrest and imprisonment.[1] When the twenty-four verses of the earlier Philippian arrest and imprisonment are included, the proportion of Acts devoted to Pauline imprisonments approaches 30%. The reader's interest in Luke's intention is heightened when the amount of space devoted to the free and the imprisoned Paul is compared. The last section on Paul's arrest and incarceration 'is slightly longer than that describing his mission'.[2] Maddox has suggested that 'when we read Acts as a whole, rather than selectively, it is Paul the prisoner even more than Paul the missionary whom we are meant to remember'.[3]

This is volume three in the series *The Book of Acts in its First Century Setting*. It is hoped that it rectifies the concerns expressed when W.C. van Unnik said, 'I am becoming more and more convinced that much critical study of Acts has been done at a distance from, or even without *living* contact with, Luke's world'.[4] This observation applies particularly to the study of Paul's experiences of custody in Acts. In the past, questions relating to the impact of imprisonment upon Paul and his mission have not concerned scholars. Profound differences between modern and ancient penal practices have not been appreciated, and as a result insights into Luke's intention(s) may well have been overlooked.

In the course of this study it will be shown that imprisonment in the ancient world posed practical problems even apart from stigmatising individuals. Luke's description of Paul's experiences can be firmly placed in their first century context of Roman custody, prison environment and subculture, and contemporary social perceptions. It will be further argued that Luke was keenly aware of the practical and theological threat that imprisonment posed for Paul, and addresses these difficulties. In the light of what may be known about the ancient world, one of Luke's primary objectives in Acts was to defend or justify the prisoner missionary Paul to the reader.

---

[1]Weighed in the overall scheme of Luke-Acts, this amounts to 12% of the text. See R. Maddox, *The Purpose of Luke-Acts* (FRLANT 126; Göttingen: Vandenhoeck und Ruprecht, 1982), 66. *Cf.* H.J. Cadbury, 'Note 26. Roman Law and the Trial of Paul', in *BC*, vol. 5, 297.

[2]Maddox, *Purpose*, 66.

[3]*Ibid.*, 67.

[4]W.C. van Unnik, 'Luke's Second Book and the Rules of Hellenistic Historiography', in *Les Actes des Apôtres: Traditions, Rédaction, Théologie*, ed. J. Kremer (Gembloux: J. Duculot/Leuven: LUP, 1979), 60.

I. The Primary Sources

The method of reading Acts from a vantage point informed by ancient sources has received new life and can now take us beyond previous studies. Because of recent technological advances, the present writer had immediate access to nearly all the known Greek and Latin literature of the ancient world and was able to access it with an ease which could have never been imagined even a decade ago[5] Laser data bank discs exist which contain some 8,000 Greek works from 2,900 writers from Homer to 600 AD,[6] some 268 volumes of papyri,[7] and the works of over forty major Latin authors.[8] The information harvested with these tools allows for a reading of Acts which manifests a nuance and depth where previous efforts were limited.

Imprisonment, its consequences, and the reactions it sparked in others and in Paul are more fully appreciated against the backdrop of ancient sources. Roman evidence dating to the century before and the century of Christ's birth is important to our study, particularly passages in which, for example, judicial procedures and prison administration are discussed. Evidence from a broader time frame also illustrates important issues, and thus reference will be made to that material in the text or footnotes. In matters pertaining to prison life more generally—prison appointments, the social, psychological and economic impact of imprisonment, and such—Roman and Greek evidence across a broader time frame is apposite to this study.

Archaeological evidence; classical authors; ancient novels; NT apocrypha; Christian and pagan martyr literature; the writings of the Apostolic and early post-Apostolic Fathers; Jewish literature; Latin juridical texts; inscriptional evidence; and the papyri all contain a wealth of data which would have contributed much to the main studies previously undertaken on our subject. An example of a successful study

---

[5]The present writer had access to much of the vast literature using the IBYCUS computer facilities made available through the generosity of Tyndale House, Cambridge. Relevant literature and papyri not yet available in computer-readable media were of course also consulted.

[6]*Thesaurus Linguae Graecae Pilot CD ROM #C*, © Thesaurus Linguae Graecae, University of California, Irvine 1987 [*Cf*. L. Berkowitz *et al.*, *Thesaurus Linguae Graecae: Canon of Greek Authors and Works* (2nd. ed.; New York/Oxford: OUP, 1986)].

[7]*PHI Demonstration ROM #2*, © The Packard Humanities Institute, 1988 [Contents: Data Bank of Documentary Papyri, Duke University].

[8]*PHI Demonstration CD ROM #1*, © The Packard Humanities Institute, University of Pennsylvania, 1987 [Contents: (1) PHI Latin Texts (partially corrected); (2) CCAT Biblical Materials, University of Pennsylvania].

is F. Millar's more recent analysis of the second-century novel, Apuleius' *Golden Ass*. He allows ancient novels, plays and the NT apocrypha to shed light on his subject and Millar is able, as a result, to suggest that such sources

> may extend beyond purely physical descriptions, to realistic images of social and economic relations, the framework of communal life in a Roman province and even, here and there, to the wider context of what it meant to be a subject of the Roman Empire.[9]

Millar's helpful observations regarding policing and the administration of justice in provincial cities and towns confirm his contention that a variety of sources helps us obtain a picture of life in the early days of the empire.[10]

The electronic innovations already alluded to represent a watershed, for they allow us to adopt a method similar to Millar's while moving us, at least with respect to the primary sources, beyond even the best of the previous studies of Luke's discussion of Paul in prison.[11]

II. Plan of the Current Study

What follows can be divided into three major sections. The first part (chapters 2-4), entitled, 'Custody, the Legal System and Status in the Roman World', deals with custodial deliberations in the ancient world and for Paul in Acts. It is concerned with exploring the impact of legal and social factors upon official Roman deliberations in determining the treatment and custody of accused persons and drawing together what is disclosed of the Pauline legal and social *persona* in Acts. Then Acts as viewed through the social/juridical template is analysed for in-

---

[9]F. Millar, 'The World of the Golden Ass', *JRS* 71 (1981), 63

[10]For three uses to which such writers of fiction can be put, see Millar, 'The World', 66.

[11]Three important works are F.A.K. Krauss, 'Die Gefangenen und die Verbrecher unter dem Einflusse des Christenthums', *Blätter für Gefängnisskunde* 25 (1889-90), 1-95; T.R. Coleman, *Paul's Prison Life* (Southern Baptist Theological Seminary, Louisville: Unpublished PhD. Dissertation, 1939); and, most recently J.C. Lentz, Jr., *Luke's Portrayal of St. Paul as a Man of High Social Status and Moral Virtue in the Concluding Chapters of Acts* (University of Edinburgh: PhD. Dissertation, 1988), and published as *Luke's Portrait of Paul* (SNTSMS 77; Cambridge: CUP, 1993). I interact more fully with Lentz's monograph in a review to appear in *EvQ* in 1994.

dications of sensitivity to status, offence and other influences as Paul goes before Roman magistrates and officials on the way to custody

Part two (chapters 5-8), 'Paul on Trial in Acts', examines data relevant to Paul's four major Lukan encounters with authority. Events in Philippi, Jerusalem, Caesarea, and Rome are discussed in the light of part 1, allowing for detailed interaction with the various groups and magistrates who play a determinative role in Paul's imprisonments.

Part three (chapters 9-15), 'Paul in Prison in Acts', interacts with Luke's handling of a missionary who spent so much time in custody. The thesis of a Lukan defence or justification of the prisoner missionary Paul will be elaborated along three lines. The activities of Paul will be compared with what can be known about activities undertaken by prisoners, arguing that Luke describes a Paul who is not crippled by the constraints of imprisonment, but who remains active for his Lord. Next, we will describe what relations could be like between Graeco-Roman prisoners and those 'on the outside', and what Luke tells us of Paul's own prison helpers. Finally, we will consider indications of divine help for prisoners in antiquity and the ends which that help served.

Incarceration constituted a serious threat to Paul's mission. At a personal level, what sorts of distress would prison have brought? How would his labours have been curtailed beyond preventing him from free travel, removing him from the usual preaching venues, and separating him from churches he had founded? Having lost his freedom, what would have been the consequences of dependence upon others? Further, did the fact and nature of Paul's incarcerations in some way reflect an official assessment of his status and social worth? At the level of interpersonal relations in ministry, would not extended incarceration constitute a frontal assault upon Paul's status, credibility and vocation? In what ways might co-workers, helpers, and churches—both those of his own mission and those outside of it—view differently the missionary now become a prisoner? How would interested unbelievers have viewed his predicament?

PART 1

CUSTODY, THE LEGAL SYSTEM AND STATUS IN THE ROMAN WORLD

CHAPTER 2

THE PURPOSES AND VARIETIES OF CUSTODY IN THE ROMAN WORLD

Accepted inequalities before the Roman law played a significant role both when individuals were being imprisoned and when they stood in a court of law. Such influences frequently intruded into the setting of custody. Imprisonment served several purposes. Custody could be to protect, to assure the accused person's appearance in court, to compel recalcitrant individuals to obedience, and to await the execution of sentence, including death. Punitive incarceration became increasingly common over time.

The severity of one's imprisonment depended on the prison into which one was cast and also on the part of that prison. In Rome the worst place was the state prison, and the worst place within that structure was the Tullianum or death cell. More tolerable was confinement in the Roman quarry prison. Whether one was chained or not was a further indication of the severity of one's imprisonment. Custodia libera denotes a less harsh type of imprisonment. Military custody was another less severe form of confinement: a barracks venue was generally most harsh; a private house, much less so. Less severe still than military custody was entrustment to sureties. The accused resided in the house of the one charged with his or her care. A later development was more consultative and limited the liability of the one giving the undertaking. Release on one's own recognizances was the least severe custodial option.

9

I. Purposes of Custody

C.F.D. Moule has written concerning Paul's circumstances that 'it would not be without theological significance if one could distinguish between punitive and protective arrest in antiquity'.[1] To do this requires discussion not only of the purposes imprisonment served, but also of the places and types of custody and their relative severity. Private and unofficial confinement existed in the Roman world. Our principal concern here, however, is to describe those forms which fall within the pale of official judicial and extra-judicial process.

1. Protection

A less common purpose of confinement was protection. Confinement might buy time for the accused, as when the emperors Vitellius and Otho imprisoned individuals whose lives were threatened by fellow soldiers[2] or when Vitellius himself begged 'that he be confined for a time, even in the prison',[3] on the pretext of having something important to say to Vespasian. A rescript of Marcus and Commodus held that criminally insane persons were to be confined to protect themselves and the community.[4]

2. Remand

Much more common was the practice of imprisonment on remand. This was 'a precautionary measure to secure the appearance of the *reus* [accused] at the trial'.[5] From very early times, this was a recourse taken by the Romans.[6] Garnsey notes, however, that

---

[1] Cited in G. Bertram, 'φυλάσσω κτλ.', *TDNT*, vol. 9, 242.
[2] Tacitus, *Hist.* 1.58, 71.
[3] Suetonius, *Vit.* 7.17.1. For other examples of 'witness protection', see Livy 32.26; 39.14.2f.
[4] *Dig.* 1.18.13f.; 48.9.9.
[5] P.D.A. Garnsey, 'The *Lex Julia* and Appeal Under the Empire', *JRS* 56 (1966), 171.
[6] See F.H. Hitzig, 'Carcer', *PW*, vol. 3, 1576. *Cf.* S. Arbandt, W. Macheiner and C. Colpe, 'Gefangenschaft', *RAC* 9 (1976), 324.

in the early days of the Republic, this practice was already being superseded by that of giving bail (*uades* or *uadimonium*). This in turn had practically disappeared by the late Republic, and in the criminal procedure of the *quaestiones perpetuae* the *reus* [accused] is left free in the interval between the *nominis receptio* [initial hearing] and the actual trial.[7]

A number of instances where a choice was given between bail or being remanded in prison may be cited, including the case of Caesar's accuser Vettius (63 BC).[8] Remand in prison without the option of bail might be preferred where condemnation was considered the likely outcome of the trial. Cicero mentions certain pirates who were held in the house of Verres at first and then later, on Cicero's orders, in the prison (70 BC).[9] The Catilinarian conspirators (63 BC) were lodged in the houses of the urban praetors while the Senate decided their fate.[10]

In the Imperial period, imprisonment on remand once again came into vogue and lighter forms and gradations of remand outside prison also appeared.[11] These developments are indicated in Ulpian's remand legislation[12] and the rescript of Antoninus Pius (138-161 AD); the latter affirming that, where an accused can furnish sureties, custody in a prison ought not to be used.[13] The elder Seneca states that the unconvicted should neither be remanded in a prison nor abused there.[14] However, defendants—whether of high or low station—do await their trials in prison during this period as well. The concern of Tiberius (14-37 AD) for his own safety, coupled with his laxness in conducting trials, saw many remanded for long periods before the final disposition of their cases.[15] Sejanus (31 AD) was jailed briefly while he awaited the determination of his fate by the senators who gathered in the temple of Concord.[16] John the Baptist (Mark 6:14-29) and Peter (Acts 12:3ff.) may constitute two early NT examples of Roman impris-

---

[7]Garnsey, '*Lex Julia*', 171. So also Arbandt *et al.*, 'Gefangenschaft', 325.
[8]Suetonius, *Jul.* 17.2. See also Arbandt *et al.*, 'Gefangenschaft', 325 and Livy 25.4.7-11
[9]Cicero, *Verr.* 2.5.76.
[10]Appian, *BCiv.* 2.1.6.19.
[11]Arbandt *et al.*, 'Gefangenschaft', 325.
[12]*Dig.* 48.3.1.
[13]*Ibid.* 48.3.3.
[14]Seneca, *Con.* 9.4.21.
[15]Dio Cassius 58.15.3f. Josephus writes that he was not only 'negligent about hearing trials of prisoners' (*AJ* 18.170 [18.6.5]), but that in this regard 'no king or tyrant was ever more given to procrastination' (*AJ* 18.169 [18.6.5]).
[16]Dio Cassius 58.11.1-3.

onment on remand in the Provinces. The philosopher Apollonius and his cellmates were similarly detained before trial during the reign of the emperor Domitian (81-96 AD).[17] The practice of remanding prisoners pending trial in the later Empire can also be attested.[18]

3. Awaiting Sentence

Prison was also the place where one awaited the execution of sentence. There were several ways in which this might take place. The jurist Venuleius Saturninus (2nd cent. AD) states: 'Should the accused confess, he shall be thrown into a public prison until sentence is passed on him'.[19] Vettius (63 BC) is imprisoned for admitting to having carried a weapon.[20] Demetrius of Sunium (162 AD), on incriminating himself in the temple theft for which his friend Antiphilus had been falsely convicted, 'was haled straight to prison...'.[21] The Christian martyrs are also legally deemed to have confessed as they freely admit their faith and will not abjure during examination or torture.[22]

The confinement of a convicted and charged person might last only a few days.[23] It might, on the other hand, be much longer where this suited other purposes. The jurist Gaius (2nd cent. AD) writes:

> Those condemned to the extreme penalty immediately lose their citizenship and their freedom. This fate therefore anticipates their death, sometimes by a long period, as happens in the persons of those who are condemned to the beasts. Again, it is often the custom for them to be kept [alive] after their condemnation, so that they may be interrogated under torture against others.[24]

Many other examples of prison as the place for the condemned occur in the available literature.[25]

---

[17]Philostratus, VA 7.21f. et passim.
[18]Cf. Lucian, Asin. 45f. and Achilles Tatius, Clit.& Leuc. 6.5.3.
[19]Dig. 48.3.5.
[20]Cicero, Att. 2.24.
[21]Lucian, Tox. 31f.
[22]E.g., Mart. Ptol. & Luc. 11; Mart. Let. Lyons & Vienne 1.7-10; Mart. Perp. & Felic. 5.6-6.2; Mart. Mar. & James 9.1, 5; Mart. Let. Phil. 11.
[23]See Dio Cassius 58.27.5; Seneca, Tranq. 14.6f.
[24]Dig. 48.19.29. Examples of damnatio ad bestias: Mart. Let. Lyons & Vienne 1.42; Mart. Perp.& Felic. 19.5f.).

Courts and magistrates might in some cases be competent to try and sentence an accused person but not carry out the sentence apart from ratification by a higher authority. Caesar refers the matter of executing certain pirates whom he captured to Junius who, as governor of Asia, had jurisdiction (77 BC). Going to Junius in person, Caesar arranges for the pirates to await their death in the prison at Pergamum.[26] Similarly, the magistrates of Cirta bring a number of Christian confessors to a certain point in their condemnation and then refer the case to the prefect at Lambesa (259 AD). The confessors are held in various prisons pending the final determination.[27] Where the convict claimed Roman citizenship or was a decurion, governors themselves might need to delay execution of sentence pending confirmation or, at a later time, to refer the case even higher.[28]

4. Execution

For those condemned to death, prison could also be the place of execution. Such execution is even described euphemistically in some sources simply as going to or being cast into prison.[29] Carried out within the confines of the prison, it constituted a concession to the dignity or status of the malefactors[30] who might be highborn Roman men[31] and women[32] or noteworthy non-Romans:[33] It was out of public view and to some extent minimized the shame to the accused while they lived.

---

[25]E.g., Cicero, *Verr.* 2.5.72, 112; Suetonius, *Jul.* 17.2; Seneca, *Con.*1.3.2, 9.4.21; Josephus, *AJ* 18.178 [18.6.5]; Suetonius, *Tib.* 61.5; Dio Cassius 58.3.3-6, 59.6.2, 59.13.2; *Mart. Perp. & Felic.* 6.6-8; Achilles Tatius, *Clit. & Leuc.* 8.8.4.

[26]Plutarch, *Caes.* 2.3f.

[27]*Mart. Mar. & James* 9.1, 5.

[28]The governor's sentence against a Roman citizen or a decurion (or his near male blood relatives) must be ratified by the emperor before its execution. While awaiting ratification, writes Ulpian, the accused remains in prison. See *Dig.* 28.3.7; 48.22.6.1f. Cf. *Mart. Let. Lyons & Vienne* 1.43f.

[29]See the discussion of J.L. Strachan-Davidson, *Problems of the Roman Criminal Law* (Oxford: Clarendon, 1912), vol. 1, 164; A.W. Lintott, 'Provocatio': From the Struggle of the Orders to the Principate', *ANRW* I/2 (1972), 260.

[30]So T. Mommsen, *Le Droit Pénal Romain*, tr. J. Duquesne (Manuel des Antiquités Romaines 19; Paris: Albert Fontemoing, 1907), vol. 3, 268 and n. 5; Hitzig, 'Carcer', 1577. *Contra* Strachan-Davidson, *Problems*, 145.

[31]E.g.: Cicero, *Verr.* 2.1.14; 2.5.149; Dio Cassius 46.20.5 (≈ Plutarch, *Cic.* 20.3; 22.1f.; Sallust, *Cat.* 55.1f., 5f.; Appian, *BCiv.* 2.1.6.19); Appian, *BCiv.* 2.2.12; Sallust, *Jug.* 31.7.

[32]E.g.: Tacitus, *Ann.* 5.9; Dio Cassius 60.16.1.

Generally, following execution in the state prison at Rome, malefactors' bodies were flung out onto the nearby *Scalae Gemoniae*, a flight of steps leading up the Capitoline.[34] The bodies were then dragged to the Forum with large hooks and thrown into the Tiber river.[35] Scourging might precede execution.[36] Josephus describes the pattern for conquered non-Romans on the day of a Triumph in the capital city as follows:

> The triumphal procession ended at the temple of Jupiter Capitolinus, on reaching which they halted; for it was a time-honoured custom to wait there until the execution of the enemy's general was announced. This was Simon, son of Gioras, who had just figured in the pageant among the prisoners, and then, with a halter thrown over him and scourged meanwhile by his conductors, had been haled to the spot abutting on the Forum, where Roman law requires that malefactors condemned to death should be executed.[37]

As to the means of death, Roman execution in prison seems usually to have been by strangulation.[38] The Numidian king Jugurtha is said to have died of starvation and cold in the *Tullianum* (104 BC)[39] and Marius (87 BC) was under threat of the Cimbrian executioner's sword at Minturnae.[40]

5. Prison and Coercion

Prison could also serve as an instrument of coercion. The term *coercitio*, from which the word coercion derives, generally describes

> the special instrument of enforcement which a magistrate had at hand. *Coercitio* (hardly a technical term down to the Late Republic)

---

[33]E.g.: Polybius 16.23.6f.; Strabo 14.1.38; Plutarch, *Mar.* 12 (≈ Livy *Ep.* 67); Dio Cassius 40.41, 43.19; Josephus, *BJ* 7.153 [7.5.6].

[34]See Fig. 1 and discussion in S.B. Platner and T. Ashby, *A Topographical Dictionary of Ancient Rome* (Oxford: OUP/London: Humphrey Milford, 1929), 466.

[35]Ovid, *Ars* [*Consolatio ad Liuiam*] 271-82; Pliny, *Nat.* 8.145; Dio Cassius 58.1.3, 58.11.3f., 59.18.3, 60.16.1, 61.35.4; Seneca, *Con.* 9.2.2f.; Valerius Maximus 6.9.13.

[36]See Livy 8.20.7; Seneca, *Con.* 9.2.6, 21; Dio Cassius 78.9; 79.9.4.

[37]Josephus, *BJ* 7.153 [7.5.6].

[38]E.g., Cicero, *Verr.* 2.5.147; Sallust, *Cat.* 55.5f.; Tacitus, *Ann.* 5.9; 6.39f., 6.58; Suetonius, *Tib.* 61.4-6; Pliny, *Ep.* 2.11.

[39]Plutarch, *Mar.* 12.

[40]Lucan 2.76-81.

should be understood as the general term for a number of measures a magistrate could use to enforce obedience without instituting legal proceedings.[41]

He had this recourse not because he was a judge, but by virtue of his holding the executive authority. The objective of *coercitio* was to compel reluctant or recalcitrant individuals—particularly those of the ruling class—to obey the magistrate's orders. The means employed included the power to arrest and carry a disobedient person to prison.[42] The duration of imprisonment was determined by the magistrate; it ended when the magistrate's authority expired, but only if his successor did not issue a new decree.[43]

Since legal provisions kept magistrates from using the most severe forms of *coercitio* upon citizens, imprisonment was used instead. Republican examples show that coercion was a recourse of tribunes faced with rebellious censors and consuls.[44] The writer Naevius (*fl.* 270-206 BC), however, was imprisoned by the superintendent of prisons, but released by the tribunes of the commons after he apologized for insulting the leading men of Rome.[45] In the Imperial period, Tiberius threatened the knight Pompeius with prison to suppress his opposition in the Senate.[46]

It was also a recourse of magistrates to compel the obedience of individuals of lesser stature in Roman eyes—namely, foreigners, slaves and women.[47] The Roman people, for example, called for their magistrates to imprison Jugurtha (104 BC) to compel him to reveal his co-conspirators.[48] Ulpian advises provincial governors in the Imperial period to jail those who harbour blasphemers, robbers, hijackers and thieves 'without whose help a robber cannot lie hidden for too long'.[49] Prison thus serves the dual purposes of loosening tongues and keeping the malefactor from those who might give him aid. The imprisonment

---

[41]W. Nippel, 'Policing Rome', *JRS* 74 (1984), 22.
[42]Other means included scourging (*uerbera*) and execution (*supplicia*), imposition of fines up to a *multa maxima*, seizure of pledge (*pignoris capio*), confiscation of property (*consecratio*) or sale into slavery.
[43]Hitzig, 'Carcer', 1576; Arbandt *et al.*, 'Gefangenschaft', 323.
[44]See Dio Cassius 37.50.1f., 38.3.2; Sallust, *Cat.* 48.6; Cicero, *Att.* 2.1, Plutarch, *Cat. Mi.* 33.1f., *ibid.*, *Caes.* 14.7; Suetonius, *Jul.* 20.4.
[45]Aulus Gellius 3.3.15.
[46]Suetonius, *Tib.* 57.2.
[47]A. Berger and B. Nicholas, 'Law and Procedure, Roman'. *OCD'*, 589.
[48]Sallust, *Jug.* 33.3.
[49]*Dig.* 1.18.13.

of the Christian martyrs in many cases can be accounted instances of coercion in the face of stubbornness.[50]

6. Prison and Punishment

It is difficult to determine if prolonged imprisonment was a recognized punishment for Roman citizens. An investigation must consider both the matter of legal warrant and actual practice. The elder Pliny relates two Republican cases of punitive confinement (c. 218-201 BC) where citizens were found guilty of inappropriately wearing chaplets of flowers.[51] Certain of the Bacchanalian conspirators (186 BC) appear also to have been punished with imprisonment. Livy writes:

> Those who had merely been initiated with the ritual formula, the priest dictating the words, in which the wicked conspiracy to all vice and lust was contained, but had committed none of the acts of which they were bound by the oath against either themselves or others, they left in chains; upon those who had permitted themselves to be defiled by debauchery or murder, who had polluted themselves by false testimony, forged seals, substitution of wills or other frauds, they inflicted capital punishment. More were killed than were thrown into prison.[52]

As von Eisenhut indicates, Livy distinguishes two types of delict, for which two different punishments are meted out; imprisonment for those convicted of being initiates and execution for those found guilty of overt expressions of membership in the Bacchanalia.[53]

Additional insight into practices during the Republican era may be gained from the trial of the Catilinarian conspirators (63 BC). Caesar proposed as an alternative to the death penalty or exile that the malefactors should have their goods confiscated and be confined under guard in a strong free town.[54] If a town allowed its prisoner to escape it would be subject to a heavy penalty.[55] The local citizenry were not to attempt to mitigate the penalty by moving a decree in the Senate or by a vote of the people on pain of being reckoned to be co-conspira-

---

[50]E.g., *Mart. Felix* 23-28; *Mart. Iren.* 3.5.
[51]Pliny, *Nat.* 21.8f.
[52]Livy 39.18.3-5.
[53]W. von Eisenhut, 'Die römische Gefängnisstrafe', *ANRW* I/2 (1972), 274.
[54]Sallust, *Cat.* 51.43; Suetonius, *Jul.* 14.1.
[55]Cicero, *Cat.* 4.8.

tors.[56] These arrangements can hardly amount to a case of indefinitely-postponed execution or quasi-pardon[57] despite Plutarch's comment that the confinement was to last 'until Catiline should be defeated'.[58] Both the provisions set forth by Caesar and the fact that Cicero himself describes the confinement as 'lifelong'[59] prevent such an interpretation.

Was Caesar's recommendation illegal? Cicero suggests that the proposals involve injustice and difficulty. But this 'difficulty' is most likely to be that felt by the towns, since the requirements and provisions presented them with such an onerous burden.[60] Caesar's recommendation was favoured by some and swayed still others in the Senate. This may, however, have been simply because senators perceived it to be politically advantageous to the powerful Cicero.[61] In the end the death penalty is preferred over life imprisonment and Cicero duly orders it for the Catilinarians.[62] While von Eisenhut correctly concludes that at the time of Cicero's consulship life imprisonment was a legitimate alternative to execution or exile,[63] Cicero's statement that it 'is an exemplary punishment indeed for a heinous crime',[64] casts doubt upon von Eisenhut's further characterization of it as customary.[65] Compared to the many other reasons for confinement, punitive custody in the Republican period is relatively rare; especially because it arises principally out of senatorial action.[66]

Berger asserts that 'Roman criminal law did not recognize the imprisonment of free persons as a form of punishment'.[67] Whether temporary or lifelong, it is nowhere actually threatened in Republican legislation and no legal provisions for it seem to have been made.[68]

---

[56]*Ibid.*; Sallust, *Cat.* 51.43.

[57]So von Eisenhut, 'Gefängnisstrafe', 272; Strachan-Davidson, *Problems*, 165f.

[58]Plutarch, *Cic.* 21.1.

[59]Cicero, *Cat.* 4.7, 10.

[60]*Ibid.*

[61]*Cf.* Plutarch, *Cic.* 20.3; 21.2f.

[62]Appian, *BCiv.* 2.1.6.19.

[63]von Eisenhut, 'Gefängnisstrafe', 272.

[64]Cicero, *Cat.* 4.7.

[65]von Eisenhut, 'Gefängnisstrafe', 272.

[66]So Hitzig, 'Carcer', 1578; F.A.K. Krauss, *Im Kerker vor und nach Christus. Schatten und Licht aus den profanen und kirchlichen Culture = und Rechtsleben vergang. Zeiten. In 3 Büchern* (Tübingen: J.C.B. Mohr, 1897) 70.

[67]Berger, 'Prison', 731. *Cf.* Mommsen, *Droit Pénal*, vol. 1, 351.

[68]Hitzig, 'Carcer', 1578. So also Arbandt *et al.*, 'Gefangenschaft', 329.

The closest one comes to an indication that punitive confinement was legally sanctioned is when Cicero states:

> ... in no statute of ours will you find, as you will in the laws of other states, that exile figures as the punishment for any crime at all; but people seeking to avoid imprisonment, death, or dishonour, when imposed upon them by our laws, take refuge in exile as in a sanctuary.[69]

Lucretius' (95-55 BC) listing of imprisonment with other punishments commonly meted out also implies as much.[70]

This juridical silence is broken during the Imperial period, but *not* by the formal endorsement of punitive confinement. Rather, confinement is explicitly prohibited as a punishment for citizens. Ulpian writes concerning its use: 'punishments of this type are forbidden. Prison indeed ought to be employed for confining men, not for punishing them'.[71] Callistratus, in the first half of the 3rd century AD, indicates that 'in the mandates given by the emperors to provincial governors, it is provided that no one is to be condemned to permanent imprisonment; and the deified Hadrian [117-35 AD] also wrote a rescript to this effect'.[72] The prefatory comment to Ulpian's finding, however, explains his and others' vigorous restatements of the official position in law. He writes that 'Governors are in the habit of condemning men to be kept in prison or in chains'.[73] Ulpian's opinion appears to be an attempt to reverse a general trend with a considerable history.[74] In using confinement thus, these governors and judges whom Ulpian has in view could, in Garnsey's words, 'be said to have shown a fuller understanding of the direction in which the penal system was evolving'.[75]

There was much moving them in this direction, both contemporary to and well before their time. Statutes providing for the public chaining of slaves would certainly have been influential.[76] Provisions

---

[69]Cicero, *Caecin.* 100. *Cf. ibid., Rep.* 3.34; Augustine, *C.D.* 21.11
[70]E.g., Lucretius 3.1014-17.
[71]*Dig.* 48.19.8.9.
[72]*Dig.* 48.19.35.
[73]*Dig.* 48.19.8.9.
[74]E.g., Josephus, *AJ* 20.215 [20.9.5] on Albinus' practice.
[75]P.D.A. Garnsey, *Social Status and Legal Privilege in the Roman Empire* (Oxford: Clarendon, 1970), 149.
[76]Ulpian, *Dig.* 48.19.8.13 (*in perpetua uincula*); Papinian, *Dig.* 48.19.33 (*in temporaria uincula damnatos*). *Cf.* Garnsey, '*Lex Julia*', 171 n. 38, for additional examples.

for chaining free men lacking status also had a significant effect[77] as would their appearance in lists of punishments[78] and as a legal punishment for specific crimes without apparent regard to status.[79] Finally, the example of the Emperor would have had considerable impact: first in Rome and then also in the provinces.

On the last point, the reign of Tiberius furnishes many instructive examples of the use of confinement for punishment.[80] Junius Gallio (32 AD) was 'dragged back to the capital [i.e., from exile on Lesbos] and detained under the roof of various magistrates'.[81] Tiberius sentenced most of the populace of Pollentia and their leaders to life imprisonment.[82] Delays in trials and sentencing could also serve the purpose of punishment. Tiberius' propensity in this regard has already been mentioned;[83] he also delayed indefinitely dates of executions for dark motives. Legally, prisoners in this situation were simply awaiting death; practically speaking, they were suffering punishment. Postponement could effectively constitute a commutation of the death penalty to a life sentence. Having procured the death sentence of Asinius Gallus (30 AD), for example, Tiberius permitted him neither execution nor suicide. His object was the misery of the condemned.[84] Gallus, according to Dio Cassius,

> was kept under the eyes of the consuls of each year, except when Tiberius held the office, in which case he was guarded by the praetors; and this was done, not to prevent his escape, but to prevent his death. He had no companion or servant with him, spoke to no one, and saw no one, except when he was compelled to take food. And the food was of such a quality and amount as neither to afford him any satisfaction or strength nor yet to allow him to die. This was, in fact, the most terrible part of his imprisonment. Tiberius did the same thing in the case of several others.[85]

Suetonius writes that when Tiberius 'was inspecting the prisons and a man begged for a speedy death, he replied: "I have not yet become

---

[77]For examples, see Garnsey, 'Lex Julia', 171 n. 38; ibid., Social Status, 150 and n. 1.
[78]See Seneca, de Ira 1.16.1f.; Sent. 5.17.2.
[79]E.g., Tacitus, Ann. 3.36; Dig. 11.5.1.4, 47.10.38, 48.19.28.7; Sent. 5.21.1.
[80]B.M. Levick, Tiberius the Politician (Aspects of Greek and Roman Life; London: Thames and Hudson, 1976), 188.
[81]Tacitus, Ann. 6.3.
[82]Suetonius, Tib. 37.3.
[83]Cf. Mommsen, Droit Pénal, vol. 1, 355 n. 5 for other examples.
[84]Dio Cassius 58.3.3-5.
[85]Ibid. 58.3.5f. For examples later in his Principate, cf. ibid. 59.13.2.

your friend.'"[86] After Tiberius' death (37 AD), Caligula 'freed those
who were in prison, among them Quintus Pomponius, who for seven
whole years after his consulship had been kept in jail and maltreated'.[87]

It is hardly a surprise, then, that one finds magistrates sentencing
persons to imprisonment. In cases dealing with individuals of status or
where the judges' own safety was at issue, contrived delays in trial,[88]
sentence, and execution[89] might achieve the unstated purpose of punishment. Magistrates found ample precedent both in law and in practice as shown above despite juridical attempts to restrict the practice.

II. The Severity of Custody

Dig. 48.3.1 furnishes a helpful categorization of forms and degrees of
custody. There, the jurist Ulpian indicates a progression from custody
in a prison through military custody to entrustment to sureties and finally release on one's own recognizance. The sequence clearly runs
from most to least severe. Severity is distinguished both in terms of
places (the first) and types (the latter three) of confinement. The examples canvassed below reveal distinctions by categories, but also indicate distinctions in severity *within* each of the categories specified by
Ulpian.

1. Prison

Ulpian identifies confinement in a prison as the most severe type of
custody. The maintenance of public structures which existed for the
confinement of persons was necessary. Buildings might be converted
for such use,[90] but more usually—and especially in the larger cities—
they were specifically designed and constructed as prisons. The archi-
tect Vitruvius (*c.* reign of Augustus) indicates that 'the treasury, pris-

---

[86]Suetonius, *Tib.* 61.5. Dio Cassius 58.3.6, probably referring to the same incident,
notes that the prisoner who pleaded was one of Tiberius' friends (τινα τῶν ἑταίρ-
ων).
[87]Dio Cassius 59.6.2. *Cf.* Tacitus, *Ann.* 5.8.2.
[88]Strachan-Davidson, *Problems*, 165.
[89]Mommsen, *Droit Pénal*, vol. 3, 306.
[90]See the following discussion on the original use of the *Tullianum* and Quarries
and *cf.* Pausanius, *Testimonium* 6.13.1.

on, and senate-house are to adjoin the forum but in such a way that their scale and proportion answers to that of the forum'.[91]

Juvenal (1st to 2nd cent. AD), asserted, '... happy the days of old which under the Kings and Tribunes beheld Rome satisfied with a single gaol!'[92] This first and oldest place of confinement was the state prison of Rome,[93] whose construction was attributed to king Ancus Martius (640-616 BC) by Livy.[94] Literary sources locate it to the NE. of the Roman Forum, at the base of the Capitoline Hill between the Temple of Concord and the Senate House along the Silversmith's Rise (Fig. 1).[95] Two surviving cells of the prison (Figs. 2f.) support the ancient evidence for its location. The dates of the archaeological remains of the upper cell (late 2nd or early 1st cent. BC)[96] do not, however, accord with Livy's attribution of its construction to Martius. Grant writes:

> The upper cell, which was originally one of a number, possesses a rounded vault of the tunnel or barrel variety,[97] constructed with the help of concrete. The far end of the chamber is walled in by the rock of the Capitoline Hill, and at the side runs a transverse wall cutting into the vault.[98]

The lower cell (Figs. 3-5), called the *Tullianum*[99] and falsely attributed by ancient historians and etymologists to king Servius Tullius (578-534 BC),[100] pre-dates the existing upper structure by only a century or so.[101] The earliest form of its construction consisted of a circular cell having rows of unmortared stones rising in ever smaller circles, thus giving it the shape of a beehive. Slots (now bricked in) originally held support beams for a wooden roof. Later, the wooden roof was replaced by a domically constructed horizontal stone ceiling with a circular hole for access. The fact that even today a small spring rises from the floor and is connected by an ancient channel to the Great Drain

---

[91]Vitruvius 5.2.1.
[92]Juvenal 4.313f.
[93]*Carcer*: Livy 34.22.10; 34.44.7; Sallust, *Cat.* 55.2. This is the term used by Ulpian at *Dig.* 48.3.1. The name *carcer Mamertinus*, arose much later.
[94]Livy 1.33.8.
[95]E.g., Plutarch, *Cic.* 22.1f.; Livy 29.22; Dio Cassius 58.11.4.
[96]M. Grant, *The Roman Forum* (London: Weidenfeld and Nicolson, 1970), 127.
[97]Sallust, *Cat.* 55.3 speaks of this cell as 'a chamber with a vaulted roof of stone'.
[98]Grant, *Roman Forum*, 127.
[99]Called by Plutarch, *Mar.* 12, the abyss (τὸ βάραθρον) and by Ovid, *Consolatio ad Liuiam* 278, the gloomy cell (*maestus carcer*).
[100]Varro, *L.* 5.151. *Cf.* Livy 29.22; Dio Cassius 46.20.5.
[101]Grant, *Roman Forum*, 127; Platner and Ashby, *Topographical Dictionary*, 99.

suggests that it probably first served as a water catchment.[102] Sallust
describes this subterranean cell in the following terms:

> In the prison ... there is a place called the Tullianum, about twelve feet
> below the surface of the ground. It is enclosed on all sides by walls,
> and above it is a chamber with a vaulted roof of stone. Neglect, dark-
> ness, and stench make it hideous and fearsome to behold.[103]

The state prison (*carcer*) was held to be the most severe form of
imprisonment, first of all because it was for the most unsavoury malefactors. For Livy it is the place of 'thieves of the night and brigands'
and for Calenus a place for 'the basest criminals', Sejanus is dragged
there 'as if no better than the worst', and with deep irony, Asilius Sabinus complains, 'I haven't yet been convicted—yet I have to ask parricides for bread to keep me alive'.[104] Later Ulpian will indicate that the
state prison was only for 'those of humble birth; for I do not think that
those who have been placed in some position of rank ought to be confined in the state prison'.[105]

Second, the general conditions of the state prison were more severe than other places of confinement. Sabinus himself, asking to be
transferred to the stone-quarries, joked: 'None of you need be deceived
by the word stone-quarry [*lautumia*]: the actual thing is far from cushy
[*lauta*]'.[106] According to his witticism, the quarries were bad, but certainly not as bad as the state prison. This relative assessment stands in
the classical jurist Sextus Pomponius who sets a sequence—fine, quarry prison, state prison[107]—which is clearly intended to represent a progression from least to most severe.

Jones writes that 'every city had its jail'.[108] The state prison of
Athens was constructed about the middle of the 5th century BC. There
is considerable confidence that it should be identified with ruins locat-

---

[102]The suggested derivation of the name *Tullianum* from *tullius*, meaning 'spring',
is the more likely.

[103]Sallust, *Cat.* 55.3. The existing cell is six feet high. Grant, *Roman Forum*, 127, explains that 'the discrepancy can be accounted for by a subsequent raising of the
floor level, under which the three lowest rows of blocks may be hidden (the
present floor dates from 1665)'. (Figs. 3f.)

[104]Livy 3.58.2 (*cf.* 38.59.10); Dio Cassius 46.20.3 (*cf.* 58.11.1); and Seneca, *Con.*
9.4.20f. respectively.

[105]*Dig.* 26.10.3.17.

[106]Seneca, *Con.*9.4.21.

[107]*Dig.* 11.5.1.4.

[108]A.H.M. Jones, *The Greek City from Alexander to Justinian* (Oxford: Clarendon,
1940), 213.

ed a short distance SW. of the Agora where the Street of the Marble Workers and the road to the Piraeus Gate intersect (Figs. 6f.) in part because of this building's large size (*c.* 40 x 17 meters) and its close proximity to the Agora and to the law court (the Heliaia).[109] What may be a bathing room to the NW. (room 5W in Fig. 7), the discovery there of 13 small terracotta drug vials (probably for hemlock) in the cistern at room A3, and a small marble portrait of Socrates who died in the state prison by taking hemlock after first bathing, may reasonably be thought to strengthen the identification.

The appointments of the prison suggest security without apparent severity (Fig. 8). The structure consisted of

> two rows of square rooms, five in one, three in the other, separated and served by a corridor which led south to a large unroofed courtyard. Incorporated in the northeast corner of the building is a semi-detached unit consisting of four rooms on the ground floor; there was probably a second storey over this part.[110]

Camp offers that 'the square rooms would serve as cells, the large courtyard for multiple arrests, and the single entrance is controlled by the complex of four rooms that could be the guard's quarters'.[111] Large numbers—both men and women—could be housed there at one time if necessary.[112] Plutarch's remark concerning the relative status of Andocides and Timaeus suggests that, while in prison even on the same charges, it might be expected that one 'keep to one's own'.[113]

The city of Alba Fucens, a Roman colony from 304 BC and situated 67 miles from Rome, was often used to confine Rome's enemies honourably because it was remote and well-walled.[114] The city did, however, have a one-room prison and it is described thus by Diodorus Siculus:

---

[109]See J.M.Camp, *The Athenian Agora: Excavations in the Heart of Classical Athens* (New Aspects of Antiquity; London: Thames and Hudson, 1986), 113; H.A. Thompson, ed., *The Athenian Agora: A Guide to the Excavation and Museum* (1954; 3rd edn.; Athens: American School of Classical Studies at Athens, 1976), 174; and *cf.* Plutarch, *Phoc.* 37.1.

[110]Thompson, *Athenian Agora*, 174.

[111]Camp, *Athenian Agora*, 116.

[112]See Thucydides 5.18.7; *Andokides on the Mysteries*, ed. D.M. MacDowell (Oxford: Clarendon, 1962), 47f. [≈ Plutarch, *Alc.* 20.2-21.4]; Plutarch, *Phoc.* 36.

[113]Plutarch, *Alc.* 21.2.

[114]Strabo, *Geog.* 5.3.13.

> This prison is a deep underground dungeon, no larger than a nine-couch room, dark, and noisome from the large numbers committed to the place, who were men under condemnation on capital charges, for most of this category were incarcerated there at that period.[115]

This prison was for common rather than high status criminals. The Macedonian king Perseus was first imprisoned there, apparently without the knowledge of the Roman Senate. Later, he was placed 'in more suitable custody' when the leader of the Senate, 'to maintain both his own principles and his country's code of equity, indignantly admonished the senate, even if they had nothing to fear from men, at least to respect the Nemesis that dogs those who arrogantly abuse their power'.[116] Other such city prisons, some less well documented, could be mentioned and these appear to have been, almost uniformly, harsh and forbidding structures in which to be confined.

Turning back to Rome again, the next most severe form of custody, as already indicated, was placement in the Roman quarry prison.The quarries were located on the slope of the Capitoline near the prison and it is possible that some unexcavated chambers next to the jail may belong to this complex.[117] Varro indicates that the inspiration for using this quarry as a prison came from Syracuse where quarries had previously thus been used.[118]

The quarry prison of Rome could hold a considerable number of prisoners. Used in Republican times for prisoners-of-war and noble hostages, eventually it housed offenders of all kinds—including Roman citizens.[119] The slaves of these prisoners could apparently move in and out of the prison quite freely in 198 BC—that is, until the prison administrators were instructed to clamp down owing to suspicions of conspiracy against the government.[120] Diodorus describes the horrors of life and labour experienced by some of its first prisoners—Athenian prisoners-of-war in 413 BC—and Plautus relates more generally the plight of slaves in such prison quarries, digging out eight blocks of stone a day underground while heavily shackled and then being fur-

---

[115]Diodorus Siculus 31.9.2.

[116]*Ibid.* 31.9.4f. For further discussion of the site of this prison, see F. de Visscher and F. de Ruyt, 'Les Fouilles d'Alba Fucens', *L'Antiquité Classique* 20 (1951), 72-74.

[117]Varro, *L.* 5.151; Livy 26.27.1-3. *Cf.* Seneca, *Con.9.4.20f.*; Platner and Ashby, *Topographical Dictionary*, 316.

[118]Varro, *L.* 5.151.

[119]Livy 32.26.17f.; 37.3.8. See also Krauss, *Im Kerker*, 64; Arbandt *et al.*, 'Gefangenschaft', 320.

[120]Livy 32.26.17f.

ther chained in a dark cell at night.[121] In Cicero's day it was to have served for 'persons officially sentenced to imprisonment ... not only from Syracuse but from all the other towns of Sicily', whom he later catalogues more specifically as foreign criminals, scoundrels, pirates and public enemies.[122] The use of quarries as prisons, and prisoners for quarry work, can be shown for other locales as well.[123]

Little early information exists concerning the Prison of the Hundred (*carcer centumuiralis*) in Rome. The late 4th century AD historians Sextus Rufus Festus and P. Victor indicate that it stood in Region IX to the NW. of the Capitoline and near the Circus Flaminius.[124] It is possible that this is the prison which Appius Claudius built (*c.* 450 BC) and in which he himself was eventually imprisoned.[125] Others, however, suggest that the prison of Appius may in fact be the quarry-prison.[126] The evidence is inconclusive. Mention might also be made of the ancient prison on the site of the Theatre of Marcellus and of the prison cells in the various regional fire-stations under the jurisdiction of the quasi-military police/fire brigade known as the *vigiles*.[127]

There are also indications of the existence of smaller prisons in towns and municipalities away from the great cities. Sources for the Republican period either assert or assume the existence of such structures.[128] Their presence is also attested in the Imperial period.[129] These prisons generally served as places of light punishment or transient confinement for the accused pending transfer to the provincial headquarters.[130]

Whether one was chained or not further indicates the severity of one's imprisonment. There are difficulties associated with making firm statements in all instances in this regard because of the metonymic usage of some Greek terms and the lack of a helpful general rule with respect to the relationship in usage between τὰ δεσμά and οἱ δεσμοί. Similar difficulty exists with the Latin term *vincula* which can mean 'bond'/'chain' or, by metonymy, 'prison'.[131] Add to this the fact

---

[121]Diodorus Siculus 13.19.4 (*cf. ibid.* 13.33; Thucydides 7.86f.) and Plautus, *Capt.* 722-26, 729-31 respectively.
[122]Cicero, *Verr.* 2.5.68, 144.
[123]*P Cair Zen.* 2:59296 and see the notes and additional sources there cited (p. 164).
[124]Cited in Krauss, *Im Kerker*, 64 and 352 n. 47.
[125]Livy 3.57.4-6.
[126]R. Whiston and W. Wayte, 'Carcer', *DGRA* 1:363.
[127]See Pliny, *Nat.* 7.121 on the Theatre of Marcellus site.
[128]E.g., Cicero, *Verr.* 2.5.68; Dionysius Halicarnassensis, *Ant. Rom.* 15.3.15.
[129]E.g., Pliny, *Ep.* 10.19 and *cf. Dig.* 47.2.52.12.
[130]So Krauss, *Im Kerker*, 67.

that chaining is not always necessarily connected with incarceration.[132] Some precision, however, may be obtainable in discerning the circumstances of chaining by virtue, not only of a number of clear examples in history, but also of the manner in which prison and chaining are juridically intertwined.[133]

Imperial legal sources usually give the broadest definition to being in bonds.[134] Helpful information, however, is discernable from Callistratus who writes:

> Help is also given to one who was in bonds. This applies not only to a person kept in public confinement but also to one who has been forcibly overcome and kept in bonds by robbers or bandits or someone more powerful. Moreover, the word 'bonds' is interpreted widely. For it is settled that even those who have been shut up, for example, in a stone quarry, are held to be bound, because it makes no difference whether a person is confined by walls or fetters.[135]

Two things may be observed here: First, Callistratus associates physical binding with *public* confinement. Second, those in the stone quarry, while deemed in law to be bound, are in fact not thus restrained.[136] This probably accounts, in part, for the earlier-noted ancient assessment that the quarry prison is judged to be less severe than the state prison. That this linkage of chaining with the public or state prison was not a recent development can be seen from Livy's account of the praetor's instructions to the cities of the Latin confederacy in 198 BC that prisoners-of-war be 'loaded with chains of not less than ten pounds' weight, not otherwise than if they were confined in a public prison'.[137]

Additional examples may be cited which support equating chains with the state prison. Captive kings and generals are conducted in Roman Triumphs to the prison and enter it bound with chains, as do Romans destined for capital punishment.[138] Frequent instances of

---

[131]Arbandt *et al.*, 'Gefangenschaft', 319. *Dig.* 4.6.23 illustrates the possibilities for confusion.
[132]*Dig.* 50.16.216. See further, Hitzig, 'Carcer', 1581.
[133]Mommsen, *Droit Pénal*, vol. 3, 304.
[134]E.g., *Dig.* 50.16.48 and *cf. ibid.* 4.6.23.
[135]*Ibid.* 4.6.9. *Cf. ibid.* 4.6.10.
[136]We may exclude from consideration the case of slaves sentenced to work there in chains.
[137]Livy 32.26.18.
[138]Foreigners: Ovid, *Consolatio ad Liuiam* 273; Sallust, *Jug.* 64.5; Josephus, *BJ* 3.409 [3.8.9], 628f. [3.10.7] (≈ Suetonius, *Ves.* 8.5.6), 7.36 [7.2.2]. Romans: Dio Cassius 58.3.3; 58.11.1. *Cf.* Lucian, *Tox.* 32; Achilles Tatius, *Clit. & Leuc.* 7.15.2; 8.8.4.

prisoners being sent to Rome to plead their cases in chains would also seem to indicate that, until the actual trial, the accused remained chained in the prison.[139] The jurist Julius Paulus advises, 'If the officer in charge of a prison [*carcer*] is bribed to keep someone in custody without chains [*sine vinculis*] ... he must be punished by the court'.[140]

Finally, a particularly interesting instance of the *vincula-carcer* connection is found in the experiences of Apollonius of Tyana at Rome. First ordered 'into the prison, where the captives were not bound'[141] by Domitian (81-96 AD), the Emperor after a short while insults the philosopher by removing him to another prison, 'confining him among the vilest felons'.[142] In that second prison, an informer placed there by the state asks the philosopher: '... who would ever have thought of Apollonius being thrown into chains'? ... and how can your leg endure the weight of the fetters?'[143] Some time thereafter an official comes to Apollonius saying, 'The Emperor, Apollonius, releases you from these fetters'.[144]

Other examples where chains and prison standing in close proximity[145] suggest that the connection may not necessarily be as formal as in those cases cited above. Hitzig indicates that methods of chaining prisoners varied in large part according to the risk of escape, the dangerousness of the criminal, the number of visitors, and the rather broad discretionary powers of magistrates and prison officials.[146] These cannot be quantified except where there is sufficient information in the individual case.

Were individuals confined in prison without chains? Based upon the fact that 'custody' [*custodia*] is frequently distinguished from 'in chains' [*vincula*] in the legal sources,[147] some maintain that *custodia* generally denotes confinement without chains.[148] In the absence of further qualifying information, however, the term says nothing about the place of confinement. The same may be said of the designations

---

[139]Livy 29.19.5 (≈ Diodorus Siculus 27.4.6f.). See also Josephus, *AJ* 19.131 [19.6.2]; Suetonius, *Nero* 6.36.2; ibid., *Dom.* 8.14.4; Tacitus, *Ann.* 4.28; *Apocr. Acts Thom.*, 12.140; *Mart. Felix* 26; *Dig.* 48.3.2.
[140]*Dig.* 48.3.8.
[141]Philostratus, *VA* 5.22. *Cf. ibid.* 7.40.
[142]*Ibid.* 7.34.
[143]*Ibid.* 7.36.
[144]*Ibid.* 7.40.
[145]E.g., Livy 39.52.8; Cicero, *Verr.* 2.3.59; 2.5.106; Seneca, *Ad Lucilium Ep.* 26.10.
[146]Hitzig, 'Carcer', 1581. So also Mommsen, *Droit Pénal*, vol. 3, 304 n. 1.
[147]*Dig.* 4.6.28.1.
[148]Arbandt *et al.*, 'Gefangenschaft', 319.

custodia libera and φυλακὴ ἄδεσμος which, Mommsen writes, ordinarily indicate at least that the prisoner is not chained, indeed, that whoever is responsible for the prisoner assures that his detention is sufficient to prevent escape.[149] These expressions, therefore, denote a less harsh type of imprisonment irrespective of place.

It is not legitimate, however, to characterize the terms as 'signifying that a person was under strict surveillance and guard, though not confined within the walls of a prison'.[150] A prison did exist in Rome where prisoners were not bound. Philostratus calls it the ἐλευθέριον δεσμωτήριον at three places.[151] This prison may be the same as the Roman quarry-prison. If not, at least two prison locations existed in Rome where individuals could be confined without chains. Somewhat later, Tertullian (195 AD) mentions the morally corrupting conditions of the *libera custodia* that some alleged Christian confessors experienced.[152]

Imprisonment without chains was a concession to high status.[153] Apollonius' unchained fellow-prisoners possessed considerable status and wealth. Among their number—some fifty according to the text— were a Cilician whose fortune had become the cause of his imprisonment, and a man with property near Acarnania who apparently owned an island.[154] Most other examples of unchained detention cited above, whether indicating confinement in a prison or not, suggest the same relationship to status.

2. Military Custody

Less severe than confinement in prison is the handing over of the accused into the care of the military.[155] This was a development of the Imperial period.[156] Military custody could be employed in a variety of contexts: 1) within a barracks or camp;[157] 2) within one's own home;[158]

---

[149]Mommsen, *Droit Pénal*, vol. 1, 357

[150]Whiston and Wayte, 'Carcer', 363.

[151]Philostratus, *VA* 7.22, 40 (2x).

[152]Tertullian, *de ieiun.* 12.

[153]Arbandt *et al.*, 'Gefangenschaft', 326.

[154]Philostratus, *VA* 7.23, 25.

[155]*Dig.* 48.3.1. *Cf. ibid.* 48.3.12, 14; 48.22.7.1; and the comparative assessment given by F.H. Hitzig, 'Custodia', *PW*, vol. 4, 1898.

[156]So Hitzig, 'Custodia', 1898; Arbandt *et al.*, 'Gefangenschaft', 320, 327; R. Raber, 'Coercitio'. *KP*, vol. 1, 1352.

[157]E.g., Tacitus, *Ann.* 1.21, 12.66, 13.15.

3) when prisoners were sent on to provincial capitals or to Rome for trial; and finally, 4) where watch was kept over those sentenced to exile or relegation.[159] Military custody ought not, however, to be confused with that form of detention in the public prison where soldiers were employed as guards.[160]

Among the static forms of military custody, confinement in the camp was usually the most severe. In fact, the experiences of the Jewish prince Agrippa demonstrate that it might be scarcely better than confinement in a public prison. Thanks to the empress Antonia's influence, the severity of Agrippa's imprisonment in the camp was considerably lightened.[161] Details of the easing of his imprisonment suggest, by implication, that normally a prisoner in these situations might expect hostile treatment from his guards. He was not permitted to go outside the camp;[162] free access by and help from friends and servants, if permitted at all, were severely limited. Poor sleeping conditions and prison food could also be expected. Despite the concessions secretly granted Agrippa during this phase of his imprisonment, Josephus— himself not unfamiliar with Roman custody—still asserts that Agrippa was 'under rigorous treatment'.[163] The Christian confessor Perpetua and her associates suffered miserably under rigorous constraint in the Carthaginian military camp in 203 AD because the tribune feared that they might escape.[164]

Military custody in a private house was much less severe than in the military camp. Josephus writes that when Tiberius died, Gaius removed Agrippa 'from the camp to the house where he had lived before his imprisonment. After that he had no hardship to fear, for though he was still guarded and watched, yet the watch on his daily activities was relaxed'.[165] The level of creature comfort was apparently limited only by the prisoner's own resources and the constraints of security.

Prisoners processing to Rome and elsewhere for trial or into exile under military guard no doubt had varied experiences. Ignatius was

---

[158]E.g., Josephus, *AJ* 18.235, 237 [18.6.10]); Tacitus, *Ann.* 3.22.

[159]E.g., Suetonius, *Aug.* 65.4; Dio Cassius 59.8.8; Tacitus, *Ann.* 14.60. See *Dig.* 48.22.7.1 on *custodia militaria* prior to relegation and the comment in Dio Cassius 55.20.5.

[160]So Hitzig, 'Custodia', 1898.

[161]Josephus, *AJ* 18.203f. [18.6.7].

[162]Though Agrippa's daily bath assumes freedom to go out of the camp to the bath (Josephus, *AJ* 18.203 [18.6.7], 228 [18.6.10]).

[163]Josephus, *BJ* 2.180 [2.9.5]. Cf. *ibid.*, *AJ* 18.235 [18.6.10].

[164]*Mart. Perp. & Felic.* 16.2-4.

[165]Josephus, *AJ* 18.235 [18.6.10].

harshly treated by his keepers along the way to Rome and so too was the Christian martyr Phileas as he went from Thmuis to Alexandria.[166] Others, however, fare better. Gaius Calpurnius Piso went into exile with slaves and attendants in tow.[167] Bassus was first 'taken to Ardia with an escort of light vessels under an honourable guard'. Arriving there, 'he was put in chains' but then was 'at once released through the intervention of Hormus, a freedman of Vespasian'.[168] The examples suggest again that higher status often ensured better treatment.

The principal objective of military custody was to ensure the production of the prisoner, whether for trial, sentencing, or execution of sentence.[169] In order to ensure the security of the prisoner, the jurist Modestinus indicates that custody was to be given to experienced persons and that two soldiers ought to be responsible for each prisoner.[170] Concerns of this sort are evident in the case of the Jewish prince Agrippa and his German fellow prisoner. The latter is apparently guarded by an ordinary footsoldier while Agrippa is in the care of a centurion and other soldiers under the centurion's authority.[171] In this case, the rank and experience of the soldier assigned, and the number of co-watchers, correspond to the importance of the prisoner. The Emperor Gaius shows his concern for security when, having permitted Gaius Calpurnius Piso to take ten slaves with him into exile, he indicates that Piso can have even more slaves if he wishes but, 'You will have just so many soldiers, too, with you'.[172]

From the early days of the Empire, a penalty system ranging from corporal punishment without loss of rank to the death penalty was in force for guards who permitted the release or escape of their prisoners through neglect, drunkenness, sloth, avarice, or sympathy.[173] Penalties were graduated on the basis of the degree of culpability of the guard and the importance or numbers of prisoners who had escaped. Where the prisoner was a fugitive slave, the guard might simply be expected to compensate the master for loss.[174] Release or escape

---

[166]Ignatius, *Rom.* 5.1 and *Mart. Phil.* A col. 1 respectively.
[167]Dio Cassius 59.8.8.
[168]Tacitus, *Hist.* 3.12.
[169]So Hitzig, 'Custodia', 1898.
[170]*Dig.* 48.3.14. prol.
[171]Josephus, *AJ* 18.195f., 203 [18.6.7].
[172]Dio Cassius 59.8.8.
[173]*Dig.* 48.3.12, 14. Cf. Petronius, *Sat.* 112; *Cod. Theod.* 9.3.5; 9.21.2.2.
[174]*Dig.* 48.3.14.7.

by mischance or another soldier's collusion or neglect was, however, not punishable.[175]

Beyond simple vigilance, physical restraints were employed. Prisoners and their guards were often manacled together. The usual practice was for the prisoner to be chained by his right wrist to the soldier's left, thus giving the latter the advantage should force be required to either subdue or protect the prisoner.[176] Agrippa and his fellow prisoner were thus kept. In order to converse with Agrippa, his companion had first to ask 'the soldier to whom he was handcuffed',[177] for permission. It is uncertain from Josephus' words whether the requests were directed to Agrippa's guard or to his own. The text indicates that Agrippa himself was earlier chained; he may have simply worn a set of manacles on both wrists.[178] The long term arrangements indicate, however, that Agrippa was to be bound to the centurion who had charge of him.[179] In any event, the need for permission from one's soldier-guard to move, to approach others, or to be approached, shows how restricted prisoners might be. Agrippa is later, and for some time, free of manacles. The circumstances of his re-chaining,[180] however, suggest that being unchained was illegal and that wearing chains was the required and usual pattern. That this was not only the case for prisoners in the military camp but also those guarded by soldiers in their own homes would seem to be implied by the fact that only at Agrippa's audience with Gaius and after a period of house arrest is his iron chain removed and exchanged for an ornamental chain of gold of equal weight.[181]

Chaining also ensured the prisoner's secure transit to the assize city or the Imperial capital. Ignatius emphasizes the discomfort and hostility that such close chaining often engendered. He writes: 'From Syria to Rome I am fighting with wild beasts, by land and sea, by night and day, bound to ten "leopards" (that is, a company of soldiers)'.[182] Other cases of transfer in chains in the literature almost certainly occurred in a similar manner.

---

[175]Ibid. 48.3.12; 48.3.14.2.
[176]See Seneca, Ep. 5.7; ibid., Tranq. 10.3.
[177]Josephus, AJ 18.196 [18.6.7].
[178]Ibid. 18.189f. [18.6.6].
[179]Ibid. 18.203 [18.6.8].
[180]Ibid. 18.233 [18.6.10].
[181]Ibid. 18.237 [18.6.10].
[182]Ignatius, Rom. 5.1.

If security was a concern of military custody, so also was safety. Modestinus enacts the following provisions: 'If a prisoner kills himself or throws himself down from a height, this shall be held to be the soldier's fault, that is, he shall be corporally punished. If the guard himself kills his prisoner, he is guilty of homicide'.[183] Furthermore, 'if the prisoner is said to have died by accident, this must be proved by the evidence of witnesses, and thus a pardon will be given'.[184] This concern for safety probably explains why Agrippa was permitted a haircut only at the point of his summons before Gaius.[185] Military security lapses comparable to those evident in the civilian guarding of Vitellius which allowed him to open his veins with a pen knife would have been severely punishable.[186]

3. Entrustment to Sureties

Less severe than military custody is entrustment to sureties (*fideiussoribus committenda*).[187] This form of confinement was an Imperial development which blended the provisions of *custodia libera* with the furnishing of sureties.[188] *Custodia libera*, as seen earlier in the discussion, can have the general sense of confinement without chains, whether within or outside a prison. It has, however, a more formalized sense. It can designate the judicially ordered transfer of an accused person into the private care and safekeeping of a magistrate or notable citizen pending the trial outcome.[189] It is clear that there is some overlap with cases already discussed.

Beyond certain earlier Republican examples of formal *custodia libera*,[190] mention might be made of Verres (70 BC), who while governor of Sicily, kept certain prisoners in his own house.[191] The Catilinarian conspirators (63 BC) were detained in the houses of the praetors pending the final disposition of their case by the Senate.[192] In the Im-

---

[183]*Dig.* 48.3.14.3f. *Cf. ibid.* 48.3.8.

[184]*Ibid.* 48.3.14.5. *Cf.* the official death notice of a prisoner at *P Oxy.* 43:3104 (228 AD).

[185]Josephus, *AJ* 18.237 [18.6.10].

[186]Suetonius, *Vit.* 7.2.3.; Tacitus, *Ann.* 6.5.8.

[187]*Dig.* 48.3.1. *Cf. ibid.* 4.6.28.1; 48.21.3.7.

[188]Hitzig, 'Custodia', 1899.

[189]Krauss, *Im Kerker*, 72; Mommsen, *Droit Pénal*, vol. 1, 357f.; E.A. Whittuck, 'Custodia', *DGRA*, vol. 1, 589.

[190]E.g.: Livy 39.14.1-3,9; Dio Cassius 20.66.4

[191]Cicero, *Verr.* 2.5.68,76f.

perial period, the citizen Gallus (30 AD), a friend of Tiberius, was thus kept by the consuls. When Tiberius himself held the consulship, Gallus was lodged in the houses of the praetors.[193] Additional examples include Junius Gallio (32 AD) who was lodged in the houses of magistrates, and the slaves of Lepida who, after a time in military custody, were kept by the consuls in Rome.[194]

Persons ordered or permitted by magistrates into the care of their own families may similarly be thus designated. Publius Vitellius (31 AD) was put into the care of his brother and Aelius Priscus (reign of Marcus and Commodus) into the care of his relatives.[195] In the later Empire (303 AD), one even finds the assigning of a Christian bishop to the care of a senator of Tibuica for transport to Carthage.[196]

Our examples indicate that this form of custody was the nearly exclusive preserve of high-ranking persons, particularly those possessing the Roman citizenship.[197] Cicero's outrage at the way Verres kept a pirate emphasizes this: he writes that Verres 'preferred the innovation of keeping this pirate captain a prisoner to the regular practice of having him executed; and I now ask, what was the imprisonment like? among whom was the man kept, and in what fashion?'[198] The pirate, a *non-Roman*, was being kept in the governor's own house while *Roman citizens* were languishing in the Syracusan stone-quarries. Incensed by such arrangements, Cicero ordered Manius Glabrio to lodge the pirate and his cronies in a prison where they belonged.[199] Provisions for keeping the insane parricide Aelius Priscus, over a century later, carry the same emphasis. Priscus, the emperors asserted, was of sufficient position and rank to be guarded privately.[200]

Raber speaks of entrustment to surety as being a 'near relative' to the much older *custodia libera*.[201] Though the actual form of custody—i.e., in the house of a citizen—was the same for both, arrangements and assurances were different. Entrustment to a surety was

[192]Sallust, *Cat.* 47.2-4.

[193]Dio Cassius, 58.3.5.

[194]Tacitus, *Ann.* 6.3.3 and *ibid.* 3.22 respectively.

[195]Suetonius, *Vit.* 7.2.3 and *Dig.* 1.18.14 respectively.

[196]*Mart. Felix* 22.

[197]See Krauss, *Im Kerker*, 72; Whittuck, 'Custodia', 589; Raber, 'Coercitio', 1352; E.Brewer, 'Roman Citizenship and Its Bearing on the Book of Acts', *ResQ* 4 (1960), 216.

[198]Cicero, *Verr.* 2.5.68.

[199]*Ibid.* 2.5.76.

[200]*Dig.* 1.18.14. *Cf.* Garnsey, *Social Status* 149.

[201]Raber, 'Coercitio', 1352.

probably much more a consultative process between magistrate and prisoner than *custodia libera*. True, Catiline does make some attempt to arrange privately for *custodia libera* with associates and friends,[202] but this appears to be unusual, especially since, as the cases cited above indicate, that custody was assigned by magisterial or senatorial order. The advantage of assignment over voluntarism was that it protected the keeper from any association with the malefactor's crime. The prisoner might have better prospects for securing a sympathetic keeper, and potential keepers knew that their liability was not unlimited. Collusion by a surety in facilitating a prisoner's escape was a different matter and could trigger, according to Ulpian, both a fine and severe condemnation.[203] Securing sureties could be available over a much broader social spectrum than the older *custodia libera*. The direction of individual appeals for such custodial assistance would certainly be upward:[204] i.e., from slave to master, client to patron, or notable to more notable.

Mommsen writes that the person responsible for the prisoner had absolute control over the manner of detention and its modalities.[205] Conditions could be comfortable: roomy living quarters furnished from the prisoners own resources, and the retention of personal possessions including slaves, might be permitted.[206] Sometimes, however, conditions were miserable. Gallus, kept by consuls and praetors for some time, 'had no companion or servant with him, spoke to no one, and saw no one, except when he was compelled to take food. And the food was of such a quality and amount as neither to afford him any satisfaction or strength nor yet to allow him to die'.[207] These provisions were specifically arranged for by Tiberius. Moreover, from what Dio indicates, these were not singular arrangements. While conditions of custody might vary considerably, the cases of Hispala, Gallus and others[208] indicate that security and safety were paramount.

---

[202]Cicero, *Cat.* 1.19.

[203]*Dig.* 48.3.4. *Cf. P Oxy.* 2:259.

[204]*Dig.* 48.3.4. *Cf. Ibid.* 48.3.2.

[205]Mommsen, *Droit Pénal*, vol. 1, 357.

[206]E.g., the provisions for Hispala Faecenia (Livy 39.14.2f.) and king Perseus (*ibid.* 45.42.4; Dio Cassius 20.66.4). *Cf.* Flavius Arrianus, *An.* 7.24.2

[207]Dio Cassius 58.3.5f.

[208]*Cf.* the provisions for Minius Cerrinius (Livy 39.19.2) and the serious security lapse in the case of Vitellius (Tacitus, *Ann.* 6.5.8).

4. Release with Conditions

The final custodial option was release of the accused on his own recognizance. For whatever reason, the magistrate might have sufficient confidence to permit the accused to retain his liberty.[209] This sometimes might not be considered custody; when, however, an accused was barred from public appearance or travel outside of the assize city, it more clearly shows itself to be a true form of custody.

---

[209]Hitzig, 'Custodia', 1897.

CHAPTER 3

THE ROLE OF THE MAGISTRATE IN SENDING PEOPLE INTO CUSTODY

Modern notions of 'fairness' or 'justice' do not figure in the Roman process of setting custody. Magistrates were expected to be impressed not only by the gravity of the crime alleged, but also by the relative status of the defendant and the plaintiff. There were also sinister factors which could adversely affect the process.

Treason, fomenting war or rebellion, participation in civil disturbance, the practice of philosophy, astrology or magical arts, the taking of life and theft were all generally considered to be prisonable offences. A disparate collection of other prisonable crimes existed, including the practice of Christianity. The severity of an offence was, additionally, a measure of who had offended and against whom the offence had been committed.

Magistrates also took careful account of the respective personae of the litigants. Roman citizenship conferred the right to appeal to the people or their tribunes in the first instance, and later to the emperor himself, when incarceration or other harsh actions were threatened. There was also a strong emphasis placed upon background and social status. Defendants possessing citizen status and a high social standing enjoyed the greatest advantages and was extended the most lenient custodial treatment. If the accuser had the higher status, however, the whole picture could change in the estimation of the magistrate.

Power, influence, and bribery frequently played a part in the process. They together with the powers, immunities and protections granted to magistrates explain the degree to which judicial corruption flourished its provinces—notably, in Judea.

The figure of Justice is a familiar one, representing the highest ideals of jurisprudence. She holds in one hand the scales upon which facts and evidence from plaintiff and defendant are placed. In the other she holds an unsheathed sword, representing the power and will to punish the lawbreaker and defend the victim. The most riveting aspect of this figure is that she is blindfolded: she does not see those who come before her. Hence she renders judgement without considering the estate of the litigants: all are treated equally.

While this notion of a system of equitable law commends itself as a fitting ideal, it is most emphatically not the system at work in the world of the New Testament. Garnsey writes,

> The Romans saw men as subordinate to or raised up above one another by their involvement in conventional social relationships (so a father was placed above a son, a patron above a freedman, and a master above a slave); by their involvement in the political relationship (the magistrate was placed above the private citizen); and by their respective positions in society.[1]

This structure and ethos of Roman society remained constant despite remarkable political changes from Republic to Principate.[2] When persons came before the bar of Justice, her discerning eyes saw the estate of plaintiff, defendant, and even their respective agents, when weighing facts, rendering verdicts, and handing out punishments. Garnsey's study of social status and legal privilege indicates that inequality before the law was the norm as a direct result of the 'acceptable' prejudice and partiality of Roman judges and officials. High and low status defendants went to different courts and received different punishments. In fact, high status defendants were frequently immune from prosecution 'from below'.[3] Further support comes from Pliny's advice to Calestrius Tiro that nothing could be more unequal than the state of affairs that exists where one ignores distinctions of rank and status.[4] Inequality was also the reality in that 'the legal procedures themselves, independently of interference of judicial officials, constituted barriers to the enjoyment of theoretical legal remedies'.[5] Garnsey continues:

---

[1] Garnsey, *Social Status*, 1f.
[2] *Ibid.*, 3.
[3] *Ibid.*, 277. *Cf.* A.H.M. Jones, 'I Appeal Unto Caesar', in *Studies in Roman Government and Law*, (Oxford: Basil Blackwell, 1960), 64, on the growth in such discrimination.
[4] Pliny, *Ep.* 9.5.
[5] Garnsey, *Social Status*, 277.

'Wealth, influence, and knowledge of the law prevented the lower classes from making full use of the legal system, and neither the formulary system nor the officials presiding over it made allowances for this fact'.[6]

Two implications follow for our consideration of Paul's circumstances in Acts: first, we should expect Acts—a document fully embedded in the Roman context—to disclose indications of sensitivity to rank and status in contexts where Paul finds himself embroiled in judicial proceedings. Second, and more important for this study, it is virtually certain that matters of status and legal privilege helped determine the sorts of imprisonment Paul would undergo. This raises important questions: What specific factors would have been considered in Paul's case? How does he, when subjected to such treatment, fare in terms of social and ministry implications? Before analysing Paul's progress to his various imprisonments, we need to understand the factors which would influence magistrates in assigning different types of custody.

I. Factors in Assigning Custody

Ulpian (*fl.*170-228 AD), arguably the most celebrated classical Roman jurist next to Papinian, deals with the matter of determining the custody of accused persons. He writes:

> The proconsul normally determines the custody of accused persons, whether someone is to be lodged in prison, handed over to the military, entrusted to sureties, or even on his own recognizances. He normally does this by reference to the nature of the charge brought, the honourable status, or the great wealth, or the harmlessness, or the rank of the accused.[7]

This text clearly confirms that the process of determining custody was complex. Moreover, it furnishes a list of some of the factors which a magistrate might consider and thus serves as a means by which a discussion of Paul's own custodial experiences may be organized and analysed.

The following observations may be made regarding Ulpian's text. First, there are degrees of confinement. Second, custody is partly

---

[6]Ibid.
[7]*Dig.* 48.3.1. *Cf. ibid.* 48.3.3; *Cod. Theod.* 9.2.2.

determined by the nature of the crime. Third, custody depends in part upon the identity of the accused. We may add two further matters not explicitly commented upon in Ulpian's text. Fourth, if the *persona* of the accused is given careful attention, we may be sure that the *persona* of the accuser or his agents is not ignored. Finally, the official who sets the custodial arrangements does not stand outside the process. Whether a city magistrate, a proconsul, or even the Emperor himself, he might personally be the object not only of positive but also negative influences.

The deliberative process may helpfully be represented by a diagram (Fig. 9). It is the magistrate's business to ensure that accused persons appear for trial. In order to do this the accused must be 'propelled' through a deliberative process (left to right on Fig. 9), the end result of which is to place him or her in an appropriate form of custody. A serious charge, when viewed independently of other considerations, would probably result in heavier custody; a less serious charge, if it merited confinement at all, might call for lighter custody. Similarly, the higher the status of the accused, the lighter the custody, while the lower the status, the heavier the custody. Finally, the same proportional relationship exists where the status of the accuser is considered: i.e., the higher the status, the heavier the custody, and *vice versa*.

A worst case situation would exist where a low status accused person was brought before a magistrate by a high status accuser on a serious charge. We might represent this by a line consistently 'pulled' downward and progressing along the very bottom of Fig. 9 towards a heavier form of custody. The line running along the top of Fig. 9 represents the best case scenario for an accused. Other lines, showing different configurations of 'pulls' or deflections, might be drawn which indicate a variety of situations between these two extremes. The matter of sinister influences upon the magistrate must also not be forgotten. A magistrate might be induced (or even compelled) to be 'blind' to some factors or to highlight others to the detriment or advantage of one or another of the parties as he propels the accused through the deliberative process.

In order for this model to be most helpful in elaborating and understanding Paul's own experiences of custody, several issues must be considered. We have treated the purposes of imprisonment, and discussed the severity of custody partially in terms of the place of incarceration, in the last chapter. It now remains for us to canvass the literature in an attempt to discover which charges were deemed less serious and which were serious and therefore eminently prisonable (section II); to discuss 'status' and related notions to learn what a Roman magistrate would understand by 'high' and 'low' (section III); and finally, to clarify the matter of negative 'inducements' or 'compulsions' to which a magistrate might be exposed (section IV).

II. Prisonable Charges

Ulpian states that custody of an accused person was in part determined by 'the nature of the charge brought'.[8] It is unlikely that he envisages a precise hierarchy of crimes such that one crime is more severe than another, but less so than a third. Rather, he seems to assume that some crimes are inherently prisonable,[9] while others are not. What follows is a general classification of cases of imprisonment on the basis of the charges brought.

The first category of prisonable crime might be placed under the heading of war, rebellion and civil disturbance. Foreign kings or leaders who determined to wage war against Rome or break free from the Roman yoke, if conquered and captured, might expect to be reserved in custody. Royal pretenders fared little better. Andriscus (149/8 BC), claiming to be the son of the deceased Macedonian king Perseus, sparked enough popular interest and enough official concern to earn a stay in the prison of Miletus. He was later released, following consultations with representatives from Rome, as a harmless oddity.[10] Those who moved men to concerted and violent action, however, were treated as a real threat. Varus the legate of Syria, punished the supporters of the would-be Jewish king Judas (c. 4 BC) with great violence. 'Those who appeared to be the less turbulent individuals he imprisoned; the most culpable, in number about two thousand, he crucified'.[11] For his kingly pretensions during the Jewish revolt of 66-70 AD, Simon ben Gioras was reserved in chains, made the set piece of Vespasian's and Titus' Triumph in Rome, and died in prison.[12]

Civil unrest or riot among subject peoples was also something not tolerated by the Roman government or its representatives. Jewish examples are again useful. The disturbances between Jews and Samar-

---

[8]*Dig.* 48.3.1.
[9]*Cf. ibid.* 48.3.3 and comments in E.A. Whittuck, 'Custodia', *DGRA*, vol. 1, 589.
[10]Diodorus Siculus 32.15.3f.
[11]Josephus, *BJ* 2.71-75 [2.5.1f.].
[12]*Ibid. BJ* 7.36 [7.2.2.], 153 [7.5.6].

itans in Palestine during the procuratorship of Cumanus (48-52 AD) resulted in some of the principals being sent to Rome in chains.[13] The ringleaders in the Jewish-Syrian feuding at Caesarea in 59 and 60 AD became the objects of a preventative program of scourging and imprisonment.[14] Rioting in Alexandria between Jews and Greeks (115-17 AD) resulted in the jailing of sixty belligerents together with some of their slaves.[15]

The crime of 'high treason' (*maiestas minuta* = ἀσέβεια) and the much older 'treason' (*perduellio*) applied to a number of actions which might be summarized under the general category heading of treason. High treason was any conduct which directly or indirectly diminished or endangered the dignity, grandeur or power of the Roman people, its agents, or the emperor.[16] Chilton writes that 'no fewer than four laws *de maiestate* ... were passed in the seventy years before the reign of Augustus. But it is clear that for all practical purposes these laws were comprehended and superseded by the Lex Julia of Augustus'.[17] Along the way, the legislation progressively absorbed the much older provisions against the crime of *perduellio*, i.e., the betrayal of Rome or any individual Roman into the hands of an enemy (*perduellis*). It furnished permanent courts or improved upon their predecessors, and gathered in an ever-broader collection of specific treasonable acts. Gradually encompassed within the scope of these crimes were such actions as

> the misconduct of magistrates and pro-magistrates, especially unauthorized warfare and departure from a province, military failures, cowardice, ill-treatment of allies and enemy prisoners, disregard of the auspices, and unfair division of booty; retention of office beyond the due term; bias in the administration of justice; neglect of sacral duties; misuse of public funds; the misconduct of censors, tribunes, and inferior magistrates; and breaches of duty by legates, senators, and private individuals who undertook services on behalf of the State.[18]

---

[13]*Ibid. BJ* 2.241-44 [2.7.6]; *AJ* 20.131 [20.6.2]. *Cf. ibid., BJ* 2.232-40 [2.12.3-5]; *AJ* 20.118-24 [2.6.1].

[14]*Ibid. BJ* 2.269 [2.13.7].

[15]H.A. Musurillo, *Acts of the Pagan Martyrs: Acta Alexandrinorum* (Oxford: Clarendon, 1954), 184.

[16]*Cf.* Cicero, *Inv. Rhet.* 2.17.53; *Dig.* 47.10.38; 48.4.1.1; 48.4.5f., 7.4.

[17]C.W. Chilton, 'The Roman Law of Treason Under the Early Principate', *JRS* 45 (1955), 73.

[18]R.A. Bauman,*The Crimen Maiestatis in the Roman Republic and Augustan Principate* (Johannesburg: Witwatersrand University Press, 1967) 21f.

With the full flowering of the Empire, it became possible to prosecute someone on the charge of treason for publishing or uttering libels against the Emperor, his forebears or his relations,[19] committing adultery with his female relatives,[20] or showing disrespect for his image.[21]

It is clear from the sources that the criminal offences countenanced under treason were prisonable. Apollonius (70 BC), the Catilinarians (63 BC), and certain supporters of Julius Caesar (46 BC) are Republican examples in which custody was employed. The statutory penalty in the very earliest treason legislation seems to have been death, but accused persons were usually expected to flee into exile. Flight was deemed an admission of guilt and led to exile with loss of citizenship, partial or total confiscation of property, and the prohibition of drafting a will. Later, the legally mandated maximum penalty was exile.

In some sense, the category of offences related to philosophy and/or the occult is connected with treason, for it encompasses actions which might unravel the fabric of the State or threaten its representatives. Official concern regarding philosophers had to do with the influence of Greek thought, manners, and morals even from early times.[22] The philosopher's vocation, in keeping with the Greek pattern, often entailed heaping abuse upon the State, its leaders or its sovereign.[23] However, philosophy was not entirely divorced from prophecy or the practice of magical arts and this was often of even greater concern.[24] These factors account for the measures enacted against lampooners and astrologers by the emperor Vitellius (69 AD) and explain why philosophers were banned from Rome and throughout Italy by Domitian (81–96 AD).[25] For their disregard of imperial proscriptions and for their speech and actions, philosophers like Musonius of Babylon[26] and Apollonius of Tyana,[27] Otho's astrologer Ptolemy,[28] and others in the provinces,[29] were imprisoned, some for considerable periods of time.

---

[19]E.g., Suetonius, *Vit.* 7.14.4; Tacitus, *Ann.* 6.39.

[20]E.g., Dio Cassius 59.8.8.

[21]*Dig.* 48.4.5f. *Cf. ibid.* 48.5.4.4.1.

[22]*Cf.* the senatorial decree of 161 BC and editorial notes in *ARS* 34.

[23]Suetonius, *Tib.* 11.3. *Cf.* Diogenes Laertius, *De clarorum philosophorum uitis* 2.131.

[24]Bauman, *Crimen Maiestatis*, 292.

[25]Suetonius, *Vitel.* 7.14.4 and *ibid., Dom.* 8.10.3 respectively.

[26]Philostratus, *VA* 4.35.

[27]*Ibid.* 4.44.

[28]Juvenal 6.560-64.

[29]E.g., Dio Cassius 59.20.4, 67.16.2. See *P Coll Youtie* 1:30 and discussion in *New Docs.*, vol. 1, no. 12.

John the Baptist may be placed within this group, for his prophetic vocation threatened the stability of one of Rome's client kings.[30] For his 'ministry', John was sent in chains to the fortress of Machaerus and there, after some time in prison, was beheaded.

Murder and poisoning were also prisonable crimes. Laws issued by Sulla dating to 81 BC concern those who take others' lives. Making, selling, possessing, or administering poison for the purpose of homicide was a capital crime and prisonable.[31] The military commander Pansa's physician was arrested on suspicion of having applied poison to his battle wound.[32] The famed poisoner Locusta spent time in military custody from Nero's reign until Galba's.[33]

Theft, brigandage, piracy and sacrilege may be gathered into the next category of prisonable offences. The state prison at Rome is described in Livy as the place of thieves of the night and brigands.[34] A special case of theft punishable under the Julian laws of sacrilege related to individuals who, either individually or in bands, gained access to temples by stealth or violence and carried off the deities' offerings, articles used for worship, or the deities themselves.[35] This could be construed both as theft and sacrilege since temples served as public treasuries.[36]

Quite clearly, the above mentioned crimes are not the only ones that merit custody. Rather, they represent cases in the literature which can be placed into specific categories. Other examples of prisonable offences are fiscal mismanagement and debt,[37] wearing chaplets during a time of war,[38] violating the prerogatives of rank,[39] sexual impurity,[40] and assault on dead Romans for the purpose of defrauding their es-

---

[30]Matt. 14:5-11; Mark 6:14-18; Josephus, *AJ* 18.116-19 [18.5.2]. For further discussion, *cf.* R.A. Horsley and J.S. Hanson,*Bandits, Prophets and Messiahs: Popular Movements at the Time of Jesus* (New Voices in Biblical Studies; San Fransico: Harper and Row, 1985), 180f.

[31]Cicero, *Clu.* 54.148; 57.157; *Dig.* 48.8.1.1; 48.8.3; 50.16.236; *Sent.* 5.23.1, 14, 19.

[32]Suetonius, *Aug.* 11.

[33]Tacitus, *Ann.* 12.66; 13.15; Dio Cassius 63.3.4.

[34]Livy 38.59.10.

[35]*Dig.* 48.13.4.2; 48.13.7 (6), 11-13 (9-11).

[36]See Lucian, *Asin.* 41f.; *Tox.* 27f., 31f; and B.D. Shaw, 'Bandits in the Roman Empire', *Past and Present* 105 (1984), 3-52.

[37]Seneca, *Con.* 9 pref. 5.; Livy 37.59.1-6; 38.59f. (possibly also a case of treason?); Matt. 18:21-35; *P Oxy.* 2:259; *Dig.* 26.10.3; *P Oxy.* 43:3104.

[38]In Pliny, *Nat.* 21.8f., the offence may relate to striking a celebrative stance in time of national distress caused by war. In Suetonius, *Jul.* 1.79, the near imprisonment of a man for placing on Caesar's head a wreath with a white fillet—the fillet being emblematic of royalty—may suggest an offence closer to *maiestas minuta*.

tate.[41] Other prisonable crimes from the later period of Roman law could also be mentioned.[42]

Included in this final category is imprisonment for being a Christian. The actual crime for which Christians were tried varied during the different phases in early Christianity's development. In the period to just before 64 AD, Christians were the targets of private accusations, mostly Jewish, but increasingly in the latter decades Roman as well. Even before the conflagration of Rome in 64 AD, Christians were generally perceived to be lawbreakers. de Ste. Croix writes:

> Tacitus, like his friend Pliny and their contemporary Suetonius, detested the Christians; and although he did not believe they caused the fire he does say they were 'hated for their abominations' ('flagitia') and he calls them 'criminals deserving exemplary punishment'. The Christians were picked on as scapegoats, then, because they were already believed by the populace to be capable of horrid crimes, *flagitia*...[43]

The crimes alleged are identified by de Ste. Croix as cannibalism and incest.[44] The next phase, from 64 AD to 250 AD, begins with Christians being charged with arson. While not widely believed, it was significant that the charges against Christians came from Nero himself. de Ste. Croix offers that this opened the way for their official prosecution as a class of dangerous criminals; i.e., for simply being Christians.[45] 'Being a Christian' is the charge under which believers are prosecuted in both the second and the final (i.e., 250-313 AD) phases.[46] The charge is gradually emptied of its original rumour-inspired content (*flagitia*) and is replaced by 'atheism'.[47]

---

[39]A common soldier is thought to have been jailed for occupying a knight's place in the Colosseum during the time of Octavian (41 BC?). (Appian, *BCiv.* 5.2.15.)

[40]Seneca, *Con.* 1.3.2; Dio Cassius 79.9.4; *Dig.* 4.7.1; *cf.* Achilles Tatius, *Clit. & Leuc.* 6.5.3

[41]*Dig.* 47.10.4, 6; Suetonius, *Tib.* 37.3.

[42]*Cf. Cod. Theod.* 9.38; *Sirm.* 7f.

[43]G.E.M. de Ste. Croix, 'Why Were the Early Christians Persecuted?' *Past and Present* 26 (1963), 8, citing Tacitus, *Ann.* 15.44.3-5, 8; *Hist.* 5.5; Suetonius, *Nero* 16.2.

[44]de Ste. Croix, 'Early Christians', 20, and the many sources cited at 36 n. 109. *Cf. Mart. Let. Lyons & Vienne* 26, 52. Further, A.N. Sherwin-White, 'The Early Persecutions and Roman Law Again', *JTS* n.s. 3 (1952), 199-201; and 'The Charge of Immorality and Cannibalism', in *Pagan Rome and the Early Christians*, S. Benko (London: B.T. Batsford, 1984), 54-78.

[45]de Ste. Croix, 'Early Christians', 8.

[46]See *ibid.*, 9f. for a discussion of the Pliny-Trajan correspondence (*Ep.* 10.96f.) and its implications.

Except for manifest 'offences', prosecution of Christians was a matter not of imperial edict or police action in the first two phases; it was localized, isolated and 'from below'. Studied official indifference, the restriction of prosecutions to cases brought by private individuals, and the fact that Christian complaints are usually not against inquisition but prosecution, characterize the first two periods.[48] From 250 until 313 AD, however, prosecution 'for the Name' is sanctioned by imperial edict and is thus generalized and 'from above'.[49] It will suffice to say that the charge of Christianity, under any guise, contributed to the filling of jails and prisons in the Empire during the first three centuries AD.

III. The Status of the Parties

'Who stands before me?' is perhaps the first question a Roman magistrate would have asked himself when accuser and accused came to his tribunal. The question was not unimportant, and arriving at an answer could be extremely difficult. Garnsey's study demonstrates that a number of social measures worked together: 'In Roman society legal and political capacity depended, not only upon the *persona* or character of the individual as defined or recognized by the civil law (free or slave, citizen or alien), but also upon his background or status'.[50] What Garnsey calls the *honestiores/humiliores* distinction,[51] which embraces the matter of background and status, 'cuts across the citizen/alien distinction: there were citizens (and aliens) on both sides of the dividing line'.[52] T.W. Marshall's discussion of citizen status and social status helpfully elucidates the possibilities for upset or disturbance:

> Citizenship is a status bestowed on those who are full members of a community. All who possess the status are equal with respect to the rights and the duties with which the status is endowed. ... Social status, on the other hand, is a system of inequality. And it too, like citi-

---

[47]See de Ste. Croix, 'Early Christians', 25 and sources there cited.
[48]Sherwin-White, 'Early Persecutions', 204f.
[49]de Ste. Croix, 'Early Christians', 26f.; D.W. Riddle, *The Martyrs: A Study in Social Control* (Chicago: UCP, 1931), 11 indicates this for the emperors Decius, Valerian and Diocletian.
[50]Garnsey, *Social Status*, 271.
[51]*Honestiores* and *humiliores* mean something like 'upper-' and 'lower-class' respectively. *Ibid.*, 280.
[52]*Ibid.*, 266.

zenship, can be based on a set of ideals, beliefs and values. It is therefore reasonable to expect that the impact of citizenship on social class should take the form of a conflict between opposing principles.[53]

We note the conflicting claims to citizenship and social status as critical to Paul as he is dragged before Roman magistrates and placed into custody.

1. Citizen Status

We have seen that Ulpian elaborates the *persona* of the accused in terms of social status but not (overtly) in terms of citizenship.[54] The value of citizenship was thought by some to have declined over time, perhaps because of the increase in the number of citizens.[55] This must be weighted against clear indications of 'the eagerness of individuals and whole communities to obtain Roman status in the second century, as well as in the first'.[56] Its continuing desirability lay in the fact that it conferred, even during Rome's gradual decline, significant advantages to the holder. Ball writes that citizenship was

> much more than a mere social distinction. It was accompanied by incidents which affected every relation of life. In the routine of business, in the making of contracts, in the payment of taxes, in the commonest details of domestic management, in the whole field of litigation, in testamentary dispositions and the succession of inheritances, the Roman citizen was confronted with technical distinctions between his position and that of the Roman subject who had not received the franchise.[57]

When penalties were assessed, a citizen expected milder treatment than his non-citizen counterpart.[58]

---

[53]T.W. Marshall, *Citizenship and Social Class and Other Essays* (Cambridge: CUP, 1950) 28f. The factors of equity and inequity are discussed by E.A. Judge, *Rank and Status in the World of the Caesars and St. Paul* (1981 Broadhead Memorial Lecture/ucp 29; Christchurch, Nz: University Of Canterbury, 1982), 9.

[54]*Dig.* 48.3.1.

[55]See P. Garnsey, 'Legal Privilege in the Roman Empire', in *Studies in Ancient Society*, ed. M.I. Finley (Past and Present Series 2; London/Boston: Routledge and Kegan Paul, 1974), 165 and n. 86 and his analysis of Tacitus, *Ann.* 3.40.2.

[56]Garnsey, *Social Status*, 270.

[57]W.E. Ball, *St. Paul and the Roman Law and Other Studies on the Origin of the Form of Doctrine* (Edinburgh: T. and T. Clark, 1901) 2.

Of particular interest to the present discussion, however, is the right of citizens to appeal in the Republican period to the *plebs* (*provocatio*) or their tribunes (*appellatio*), and in the Imperial period to the Emperor himself for protection from the capital jurisdiction or violent discipline of magistrates.[59] How the appeal worked in the face of judicial abuse or heavy-handedness is helpfully explained by Lintott in terms of self-help:

> *Provocare* was probably in origin to call citizens out into the street to witness an outrage and to afford assistance. It is easy to see why the word came to refer to appeals of citizens against the actions of magistrates, since, even if the crowd was already in the street, the cry *Pro (porro), Quirites* might be used, as on any occasion when the protection of the community was sought. It is difficult to be sure what the meaning of *Pro* as an interjection was, but it seems to me likely that *Pro, Quirites* meant 'Out! citizens' in view of analogous cries used for the same purpose in other societies. ... We cannot tell whether in early Rome *provocatio* took the form *provoco ad populum, provoco* (as on the coins) or *pro fidem, Quirites*. At all events I would suggest that at that time *provoco* meant 'I call "Out" to the people'.[60]

Particular attention in the discussion below will be given to those instances where citizens appealed flogging and/or imprisonment.

The *Lex Valeria* was the earliest legislation on record to codify support for this citizen right to appeal.[61] Livy writes: 'The Valerian law, having forbidden that he who had appealed should be scourged with rods or be beheaded, merely provided that if anyone should disregard these injunctions it should be deemed a wicked act'.[62] It may have been possible to prosecute offending magistrates[63] though the legislation, so far as Livy indicates,[64] had no teeth. Lintott doubts that the law, no matter its shortcomings, would have induced many to abandon their right to appeal—whether to their peers or to *plebeian* representatives in the persons of the tribunes.[65] Republican examples from this period[66] generally confirm Lintott's conclusion that

---

[58]Garnsey, 'Legal Privilege', 261 for examples.
[59]A.W. Lintott, 'Provocatio. From the Struggle of the Orders to the Principate', *ANRW* I/2 (1972), 234.
[60]*Ibid.*, 232f.
[61]Livy 10.9.3.
[62]*Ibid.* 10.9.5.
[63]Lintott, 'Provocatio', 238.
[64]Livy 10.9.6.
[65]Lintott, 'Provocatio', 238.

provocatio in the classical period remained an appeal to the people, not just to the *provocatio* laws, and in two ways. It always was an appeal to bystanders to witness what was happening and to offer assistance, and now by a process of evolution *provocatio* became an appeal in the last resort to the will of the assembly expressed in a vote.[67]

Whereas the Valerian law furnished no concrete sanctions against magistrates who disregarded *provocatio*, a law sponsored by the elder Cato *c.* 198 BC did. Livy writes that 'the Porcian law alone seems to have been passed to protect the persons of the citizens, imposing, as it did, a heavy penalty if anyone should scourge or put to death a Roman citizen'.[68] While we do not know if this penalty was capital or financial, the law helped rein in unbridled magisterial action and offered a means of redress for aggrieved citizens or the witnessing body politic. Cicero refers to the Porcian law in his scathing censure of the tribune Labienus.[69]

This law and its provisions are celebrated on coins (Fig. 10) minted by P. Porcius Laeca.[70] Above the head of Roma on the obverse side is the word ROMA; behind the head, P • LÆCA; below the chin, X. The three figures on the coin's reverse side are from left to right, a citizen wearing a toga, a magistrate wearing military cuirass and sword with right arm upraised, and a lictor approaching with rods in hand. The legend below these figures reads PROVOCO. The scene depicts the moment in a trial just after the magistrate has ordered his lictor to administer a beating. As the lictor approaches with rod drawn from the bundle in his left hand,[71] the citizen defendant cries out '*Provoco!*' (I appeal). The magistrate extends his right hand to the citizen in a gesture of intervention and the proceedings immediately stop. It is signif-

---

[66]Roman and Campanian rebels (Valerius Maximus 2.7.15; Polybius 1.7.7-11; Dionysius Halicarnassensis, *Ant. Rom.* 20.16.1f.; *cf.* Lintott, 'Provocatio', 241); Q. Pleminius (Lintott, 'Provocatio', 241-43); Munatius (Pliny, *Nat.* 21.8f.).
[67]Lintott, 'Provocatio', 246.
[68]Livy 10.9.4. *Cf.* Cicero, *Rep.* 2.31.
[69]Cicero, *Rab. Post.* 4.12.
[70]H.A. Grueber, *Coins of the Roman Republic in the British Museum* (London: British Museum Publications, 1910), vol. 2, 301 and vol. 3, Plate XCV.13 is dated *c.* 91-89 BC. The same coin is also presented in R.A.G. Carson, *Principal Coins of the Romans. Volume 1: The Republic c. 290-31 BC* (London: British Museum Publication, 1978), 38 and dated *c.* 105 AD. A coin minted from a different die and found in M.H. Crawford, *Roman Republican Coinage* (Cambridge: CUP, 1974), vol. 1, 313-14 and vol. 2, Plate XL.301/1 is dated *c.* 110-109 BC.
[71]The 'bundle' consists of two rods, shortened because of their placement at the edge of the coin. See Crawford, *Coinage*, vol. 1, 314.

icant that the magistrate in the coin is dressed as a military commander. 'The scene', writes Lintott, 'therefore, is outside the *po-moerium* [boundary] and the coin probably commemorates the right of Roman citizens to appeal against flogging even when out of range of the immediate *auxilium* [assistance] of the tribunes'.[72] Lodging such an appeal outside the jurisdiction of the tribunes perhaps also implies a partial shift to a greater dependence upon the legislation itself rather than the self-help principle it sought to codify.

There are indications that in this period such an appeal was employed to avoid not only flogging or the death penalty, but also incarceration. Cicero, nearing the end of his oration against Verres, asserts: 'To bind a Roman citizen is a crime, to flog him is an abomination, to slay him is almost an act of murder: to crucify him is—what? There is no fitting word that can possibly describe so horrible a deed'.[73] These words, though crafted for maximum effect, are certainly not a gross or obvious exaggeration.[74] Verres' crimes were the flogging and even execution of Romans without regard for their repeated cries of citizen status.[75] Though Cicero does not object to imprisonment *per se*,[76] he decries not only the cruel and violent killing of citizens, but also the fact that Verres turned the quarries into 'the home of Roman citizens' where they ought not to have been.[77] The cry 'I am a Roman citizen!' might well have prevented such abuse under a less harsh governor and a more militant Roman citizenry. In the case of the citizen Gavius, it inspired only 'the loud groans of the Roman citizens who then stood by'as he was being flogged.[78]

There are other examples which indicate or imply that one might appeal against imprisonment. Where a citizen enjoyed good standing with the populace and Senate, recourse to appeal, while possible, might not be necessary. Caesar, when he imprisoned the younger Cato for opposing his legislation (59 BC), hoped that Cato would appeal to

---

[72]So Lintott, 'Provocatio', 250; Grueber, *Coins*, vol. 2, 301 n. 1; and *cf.* Garnsey, '*Lex Julia*', 168 n. 13. Confirming that *provocatio* functioned outside Rome, see Cicero, *Verr.* 2.5.63. For a different interpretation, A.H.J. Greenidge, 'The Porcian Coin and the Porcian Laws', *Class Rev.* 11 (1897), 440 and see *infra*, 67-68 on why it is unconvincing.

[73]Cicero, *Verr.* 2.5.170.

[74]L.H.G. Greenwood puts this point very strongly in Cicero, *Ver.*, LCL, vol. 2, 654 n. *a*.

[75]Cicero, *Verr.* 2.1.7, 13f.; 2.5.140-42, 161-63.

[76]*Ibid.* 2.5.149.

[77]*Ibid.* 2.1.7, 14; 2.5.143, 147-49, 160.

[78]*Ibid.* 2.5.163.

the tribunes, which would have effectively amounted to a climb-down and an admission of Caesar's superiority. Cato's refusal was founded on an awareness of popular sympathy for his stand—sympathy demonstrated by the host of senators and supporters who attended him as he was taken to confinement. Concerned by Cato's popularity, Caesar privately arranged for a tribune to obtain Cato's release, falsely claiming that Cato had called for assistance.[79] The prospect for appeal against coercive imprisonment, though not taken, was a live option for Metellus (60 BC) and, a second time, for Cato (55 BC).[80]

Early Republican examples of unmade or failed appeals[81] include the already cited Catilinarian (63 BC) trials in Rome in which there is no indication that appeal was even contemplated as a recourse to imprisoned defendants. The open and formal character of these trials suggests an official approval that either discouraged or actively blocked the opportunity to appeal. The evolution of juridical arrangements in the late Republic, writes Lintott, 'rendered helpless the man who wanted to appeal, partly because in the intense political struggles the Senate was reluctant to give its political opponents the benefit of it'.[82]

Perhaps to revive the weakened protections of appeal for a growing population comprising not only citizens travelling abroad but also citizens newly-made by generous imperial and military grants, the provisions are once again heralded in the Julian laws concerning public violence some time between 23 and 19 BC.[83] What survives of its provisions can be found in three texts; a mid-2nd century fragment from the jurist Maecianus, the late-2nd century reference of Ulpian, and a segment of the mid-4th century compendium known as the *Sententiae Pauli*. These are cited in the above-noted order below:

> It is provided in the *lex Julia* on public violence that no one is to bind or hinder an accused so as to prevent his attending at Rome within the fixed period.[84]

---

[79]Plutarch, *Cato Mi.* 33.1f.; *Caes.* 14.7; Dio Cassius 38.3.2.
[80]Dio Cassius 37.50.1f. and Plutarch, *Cat. Mi.* 43.3 respectively.
[81]Scipio (187 BC: Livy 37.59.1-6; 38.58-60 and discussed in Lintott, 'Provocatio', 255); the Bacchanalian conspiracy (186 BC: Livy 39.14.9; 39.18.3-5 and discussed in W. von Eisenhut, 'Gefängnisstrafe', ANRW I/2 (1972), 274 and Lintott, 'Coercitio', 244).
[82]Lintott, 'Coercitio', 262.
[83]A.H.M. Jones, 'Imperial and Senatorial Jurisdiction in the Early Principate', in *Studies in Roman Government and Law*, A.H.M. Jones (Oxford: Basil Blackwell, 1960), 97f.

Also liable under the *Lex Julia* on public violence is anyone who, while holding *imperium* or office, puts to death or flogs a Roman citizen contrary to his [right of] appeal or orders any of the aforementioned things to be done, or puts [a yoke] on his neck so that he may be tortured.[85]

Anyone invested with authority who puts to death or orders to be put to death, tortures, scourges, condemns, or directs a Roman citizen who first appealed to the people, and now has appealed to the Emperor to be placed in chains, shall be condemned under the *Lex Julia* relating to public violence. The punishment of this crime is death, where the parties are of inferior station; deportation to an island, where they are of superior rank.[86]

According to Garnsey, the *Lex Julia* as originally drafted would probably not have contained all the elements nor all the phrasing found in the above-noted texts. The dual penalty provision and the development of the phrasing in the *Sententiae* [87]represent a later effort to contemporise the legislation.[88] Garnsey indicates, however, that by analogy to the Republican legislation, the prohibitions against murder and assault would certainly have stood in the *Lex*. Comparing Ulpian with the *Sententiae* suggests that the prohibitions against torture and imprisonment—not previously indicated in any known appeal-related legislation—also stood in the original *Lex Julia*.[89] The phrase *condemnaverit inve publica vincula duci iusserit* is awkward. Having considered the several other options put forward, Garnsey offers that '"Condemnaverit" … shares with "duci iusserit" the common predicate "in vincula publica"'.[90] Assuming that this is correct, the first member would then ban the penalty of sentencing a citizen to imprisonment; the second would ban imprisonment of a citizen as an act of *coercitio*.[91]

---

[84]Maecian in *Dig.* 48.6.8.

[85]Ulpian in *Dig.* 48.6.7.

[86]*Sent.* 5.26.1;*cf. Sent.* 5.26.2 and discussion in Garnsey, 'Lex Julia', 173f. and A.N. Sherwin-White, *Roman Society and Roman Law in the New Testament* (Sarum Lectures 1961-62; Oxford: Clarendon, 1963), 58.

[87]The phrase *antea ad populum, nunc imperatorem appellantem* replaces an older expression like *adversus provocationem*?

[88]Garnsey, 'Lex Julia', 169.

[89]See ibid., 169.

[90]*Ibid.*, 170. He argues that this is a loose parallel to the construction *necaverit necari iusserit*.

[91]*Ibid.*, 170f.

Examples can be found where individuals under threat of harsh treatment were specially regarded for their citizenship. Antipater (6-4 BC) is probably a special case as he was both a citizen and a prince. Found guilty on charges of plotting to take the Jewish throne for himself, Antipater is confined while his father the king awaits Caesar's pleasure in the matter.[92] The proconsul of Asia in 64 AD sends on to the capital the Roman citizen Claudius Demianus to stand before Nero's tribunal.[93] The younger Pliny sends certain condemned Bithynian Christians who are citizens on to the emperor Trajan in Rome.[94] Pliny elsewhere notes the appearance of an Ephesian nobleman named Claudius Aristion before Trajan. Falsely accused by certain local opponents, Aristion had apparently appealed to Caesar.[95] Deinias, arraigned on murder charges in Lucian's mid-2nd century AD *Friendship (Toxaris)*, is tried by the governor of Asia and then sent along to the Emperor.[96] The Christian confessor Attalus (177 AD) is kept with other Roman citizens in prison as the governor 'had sent an inquiry concerning them to the emperor and was waiting for his decision'.[97] Finally, when ordered by Tiberius (37 AD) to bind the Jewish prince Agrippa, Macro, the successor to Sejanus, 'partly because he was not quite sure whom he meant and partly because he would not have expected him to plan such treatment for Agrippa, waited to get the exact intent of the order'.[98] Tiberius has to order Macro a second and even a third time before he acts.[99] At least part of Macro's uncertainty arises from the fact that chaining a Roman citizen, and especially one of royal status, was undertaken only in extreme circumstances. An error might be extremely costly to the one doing the arresting or chaining.

Citizenship was, in other cases, disregarded both by individuals and by communities. As governor, Galba (60-68 AD) sentenced a man to crucifixion for poisoning his ward. Suetonius writes that

> when the man invoked the law and declared that he was a Roman citizen, Galba, pretending to lighten his punishment by some consolation and honour, ordered that a cross much higher than the rest and painted white be set up, and the man transferred to it.[100]

---

[92]Josephus, *BJ* 1.640, 661 [1.32.5, 7]. Further, Sherwin-White, *Roman Society*, 63f.
[93]Tacitus, *Ann.* 16.10.
[94]Pliny, *Ep.* 10.96.
[95]*Ibid.* 6.31.
[96]Lucian, *Tox.* 17.
[97]*Mart. Let. Lyons & Vienne* 1.44.
[98]Josephus, *AJ* 18.189 [18.6.6]. The instructions to bind Agrippa are vague.
[99]*Ibid.* 18.190 [18.6.6].

Gessius Florus (64-66 AD), while governor of Palestine, did there 'what none had ever done before, namely, to scourge before his tribunal and nail to the cross men of equestrian rank, men who, if Jews by birth, were at least invested with that Roman dignity'.[101] When a man appealed a case from Capito's (68 AD) jurisdiction, Capito 'changed his seat to a high chair and then said: "Now plead your case before Caesar." He then passed sentence and put the man to death'.[102] Vibennius Rufinus, the prefect of cavalry in Adria in 69 AD, put the naval commander Lucilius Bassus in chains without regard for his citizenship or military rank, only relenting at the intervention of Hormus, a freedman of Vespasian.[103] The younger Pliny (c. 98 AD) writes of the exile, flogging, condemnation to the mines, and strangulation in prison of certain Roman knights in the province of Africa during the governorship of Marius Priscus.[104] A deposition of 153 AD records the following abusive treatment of a Roman citizen in Egypt:

> … we in this way beheld Gaius Maevius Apellas, veteran of the *ala Apriana*, being flogged at the order of the strategus Hierax by two guards with rods and scourgings. Wherefore we in good faith testify that we beheld him being scourged in the village of Philadelphia.[105]

Originally kept with other Roman citizens from a servile punishment, the previously mentioned Christian confessor Attalus is offered to the beasts by the governor to please the mob, despite imperial instructions that citizens should be beheaded.[106] Peasant citizens on an Imperial estate in Burunitanus, Africa lodge a protest with the Emperor Commodus (180-83 AD), complaining that they have been chained and beaten by a procurator and various estate overseers despite their possession of Roman citizenship.[107] Whole communities also are known to have abused the rights of citizens. The people of Cyzicus, during the course of factious quarrelling in 20 BC, 'had flogged and put to death some Romans.'[108] Once again in 25 AD they came under Imperial cen-

---

[100]Suetonius, *Gal.* 9.1.
[101]Josephus, *BJ* 2.308 [2.14.9].
[102]Dio Cassius 64.2.3.
[103]Tacitus, *Hist.* 3.12.
[104]Pliny, *Ep.* 2.11.
[105]*Sel Pap.* 2:25.
[106]*Mart. Let. Lyons & Vienne* 1.50.
[107]*FIRA* 1:103 which is discussed in Garnsey, 'Legal Privilege', 160 and L. Wenger, 'Vinctus', *Zeitschrift der Savingny-Stiftung für Rechtsgeschichte* 61 (1941), 363.
[108]Dio Cassius 54.7.6.

sure 'because they had imprisoned some Romans and because they had not completed the shrine to Augustus which they had begun to build'.[109] In 44 AD, the Rhodians killed a number of Romans by impaling them.[110]

This disregard for citizen rights was not because there was no resolve to punish offenders. While it is doubtful that Capito lost his head for his audacious conduct,[111] the communities of Cyzicus (on both occasions noted above), Rhodes, and perhaps also Miletus, are said to have lost their freedom for their violent treatment of Roman citizens.[112] The documents sent on behalf of the veteran Apellas and the Burunitanian peasant citizens also indicate that at the very least a hope was cherished, even as late as the mid 2nd century AD, that Roman officialdom would punish wrongdoers and perhaps secure some compensation for victims.

The advantages of appealing to the Emperor against a penalty threatening one's person might be considerable: it could interrupt what might otherwise be an inexorable progress to personal disaster, remove one from a biased or hostile court and, finally, perhaps put the defendant before a more favourably inclined tribunal. However, beyond the press of an ever-increasing citizen population, there were practical hindrances to an appellant's being granted a personal hearing before the Emperor's tribunal. Appeal was a costly business. The appellant might need to personally undertake the costs of travel to Rome, the living costs while there awaiting what could be a distant trial date, and perhaps the cost of actually litigating the case. Sherwin-White notes these concerns, adding that the appellant might face the additional cost of bringing along and supporting witnesses.[113] The status which granted the citizen the right of appeal never implied the means to carry it out.

Citizens in the provinces who had 'friends and connections in high places in Rome'[114] might feel assured of gaining access to the Imperial tribunal and of having success in their appeal. The 'average' citizen, however, was probably without such connections and hence would probably think twice about appealing. Success depended, in the first instance, upon the governor's sense of legal propriety and discre-

---

[109]*Ibid.* 57.24.6. *Cf.* Tacitus, *Ann.* 4.36; Suetonius, *Tib.* 37.3.
[110]Dio Cassius 60.24.4.
[111]*Ibid.* 64.2.3 suggests this. However, *cf.* Garnsey, *Social Status*, 268.
[112]Regarding Miletus see Garnsey, *Social Status*, 268 and n. 1.
[113]Sherwin-White, *Roman Society*, 62f. *Cf.* Garnsey, *Social Status*, 66.
[114]Garnsey, *Social Status*, 85.

tion in permitting the appeal. Suffice it to say that bare citizenship might not move a governor to respond as favourably to an appeal as he might to a citizenship augmented in other compelling ways.

When such hindrances to appeal were present, a citizen under threat might, rather than appealing, either quietly submit to the determination of the local magistrate as the less costly course and/or—as did Domitius Silvanus, Apellas and the Burunitanian peasants[115]— send a written appeal to the Emperor seeking justice *after* flogging, imprisonment etc. had taken place.

Several of the examples cited above indicate that the denial of a person's citizen appeal was illegal and was to be punished as such. However, interspersed through the examples are others where the denial, while legal, is irregular or harsh.[116] In some of the earliest examples, when violations occurred, the cause for remark was not the matter of the victims' citizenship (which was certain) so much as the additional entitlements or advantages.[117] Persons with a bare citizen status were increasingly treated as though they did not have it and that despite their protests. Violations, while potentially dangerous, were in many cases the expression of a ruthless pragmatism which was eventually translated into legal pronouncements such as that of Callistratus: 'It is not the custom for all persons to be beaten with rods, but only freemen of the poorer classes; men of higher status are not subject to beating with rods, as is specifically laid down in imperial rescripts'.[118] The above matters already begin to touch upon the next area for consideration; the social status of individuals.

2. Social Status

Garnsey writes: 'Judges and juries (where there were juries) were easily impressed by qualities such as social prominence, wealth and good character, and this was thought perfectly proper'.[119] Ulpian advised that the *persona* of the accused, measured in terms of honour, great wealth (*amplissimae facultates*), dignity, and integrity, was to be scruti-

---

[115]For Domitius Silvanus, *cf. Dig.* 48.6.6.
[116]Sherwin-White, *Roman Society*, 60f., speaks of these cases as ones that have 'long troubled historians because it is difficult to explain them all away as the abuse of power'.
[117]Cf. Josephus, *BJ* 2.308 [2.14.9] and Pliny, *Ep.* 2.11.
[118]*Dig.* 48.19.28.
[119]Garnsey, 'Legal Privilege', 148.

nized before custody was set. These terms are part of what Garnsey has called the vocabulary of privilege.[120]

Honour can denote the regard, respect or esteem in which an individual is held and the underlying reasons for that high esteem. These reasons might include high public or political office, or an award such as the granting of a triumph.[121] When the jurist Marcian writes that 'veterans and their children have the same honourable status [*honor*] as decurions',[122] it is clear that *honor* is both apportioned on the basis of social position relative to others and inheritable.[123] To be *honestus* is to be morally worthy of respect and, hence, honourable.[124] Garnsey assesses the term in Ulpian's custody text thus: 'The reference is apparently to the "honour" or esteem which attaches to a member of the higher orders, whether for offices held or for high social standing'.[125] *Honestiores* is the designation for those having the above-noted entitlements in sufficient measure.

Dignitas 'connotes a man's place in the queue within the Roman body politic'.[126] It is, according to Cicero, 'the possession of a distinguished office which merits respect, honour, and reverence'.[127] Of Cicero's definition, Garnsey writes:

> In this heavily loaded sentence, the emphasis is placed on moral qualities, manner of life, and the esteem which these evoke—or rather command, for *auctoritas* is a full-blooded word, meaning influence or power, the authority which in the Roman context is derived from political leadership. The word *dignitas* may stand for a particular office, and in this sense it is found in both the singular and the plural.[128]

This closely interrelated complex of ideas is elsewhere given expression in an opinion of Ulpian concerning the granting of a legal action:

---

[120]*Ibid., Social Status*, 221-33.

[121]See OLD, 801f.; LD, 861f. and entries for the words *honoro, honoratus* and *honestus*.

[122]*Dig.* 49.18.3 cited in Garnsey, *Social Status* 223.

[123]The words *honestiores* and *honestus* are appropriately rendered 'men of noble birth' and 'well-born' respectively. *Cf.* OLD, 801 (2).

[124]OLD, 801 (3). Garnsey, *Social Status*, 223, indicates a close linkage between political and social prominence with moral ascendancy.

[125]Garnsey, *Social Status* 223.

[126]Bauman, *Crimen Maiestatis*, 10.

[127]Cicero, *Inv. Rhet.* 2.166.

[128]Garnsey, *Social Status* 224.

> Nor ought it [i.e., the legal action] to be given to a man of low rank
> against someone of higher rank, for example, to a plebeian against a
> man of consular rank possessing acknowledged authority or to a man
> of licentious or spendthrift or other worthless habits against a man of
> more correct behavior.[129]

Dignitas is here characterized in its possessors by exemplary or virtu-
ous lives which are contrasted with the man whose life is wanton,
wasteful, or otherwise worthless. *Dignitas*, like *honor*, also connotes the
position which confers rank or the dignity which honourable official
public employment brings,[130] and is evidenced in the contrast drawn
between the consular (*consularis*) and the common person (*plebeius*).
Furthermore, the mention of reputation or authority indicates that *dignitas* also relates to the regard accorded by the community.[131] Garnsey
indicates that *dignitas* too is 'non-transient and inheritable'.[132] The plural *dignitates* designates persons whose life, influence and/or offices
have enfranchised them.[133] Garnsey comments, in his analysis, that 'it
is often impossible to separate the various shades of meaning possessed by the word: the office itself, the prestige that is acquired
through office, the rank in society that an office holder attains to, the
quality of his life'.[134]

The expression *facultas* in the plural denotes goods, riches, property and such.[135] The superlative *amplissimus* indicates abundance or
even superabundance of such wealth. Garnsey writes:

> *Amplissimae facultates* might keep a man out of prison. A wealthy de-
> fendant could be entrusted to *fideiussores*, no doubt partly because he
> would be less inclined to run away and abandon his estate. Again, a
> rich man could expect not to be beaten. This exemption was not grant-
> ed simply because he could pay damages; it was a prerogative accord-
> ed to status.[136]

---

[129]*Dig.* 4.3.11.1.

[130]OLD, 542 (3b); LD, 578 (II.Bα,β). E.g., the position (*dignitas*) of *tutores* at *Dig.*
26.10.3.17.

[131]OLD, 542 (4b); LD, 578 (II). PS 5.4.10 cited in Garnsey, *Social Status*, 227, where
senators, knights, decurions and others are identified as possessing *auctoritas*—the
'others' probably includes such individuals as magistrates, aediles, and judges.

[132]Garnsey, *Social Status*, 224.

[133]OLD, 542 (3.2).

[134]Garnsey, *Social Status*, 224.

[135]LD, 719 (II). *Cf.* OLD, 671 (5b).

[136]Garnsey, *Social Status*, 232.

Wealth also often generated influential connections from business and/or political relationships with both foreign and Roman élites. Through financial largesse directed downward as well, considerable goodwill could be accumulated from the general populace. All of this would merit careful consideration when it came to assigning custody or dispensing punishment.

Finally, the term *innocentia*, rendered 'harmlessness' in the English translation of Ulpian's custody text, can also mean innocence, inoffensiveness, uprightness, disinterestedness or integrity in various contexts.[137] As actual guilt would be formally undetermined at this point, 'innocence' may be an inappropriate rendering. Standing as it does with other terms which indicate moral ascendency, virtue, or noble character, however, *innocentia* may relate to the *presumption* of innocence; that is, Ulpian may be advising the proconsul to consider, based upon an awareness of the conduct and life of the accused, whether he or she is likely to have committed the crime alleged.

The following examples clearly indicate that the measure of one's birth, social standing, office and honours, wealth, and the style of life they were presumed to engender, figured prominently in cases where individuals were alleged to have run afoul of the law. Those who possess such advantages might expect (sometimes wrongly) a more delicate treatment. Livy writes that Appius Claudius (450 BC), 'a man whose portrait-mask would be held in the highest honour by coming generations, the framer of statutes and the founder of Roman law, lay in prison among night-prowling thieves and banditti'.[138] Publius Scipio Nasica, in contesting L. Scipio's (187 BC) imprisonment,

> delivered a speech full of deserved tributes, not only to the Cornelian *gens* as a whole, but specifically to his own family. The fathers, he said, both of himself and of Publius Africanus and the Lucius Scipio who was being imprisoned, were Gnaeus and Publius Scipio, men of the highest distinction [*clarissimos uiros*].[139]

L. Scipio's plight is drawn in similar terms by Livy who describes him as a most distinguished man.[140]

Apollonius of Panhormus is fined without trial by the governor Verres on the false charge of conspiring to foment a slave rebellion and

---

137OLD, 916; *LD*, 958.
138Livy 3.58.2.
139*Ibid.* 38.58.3f.
140*Ibid.* 38.59.9f.

is imprisoned until he pays. At the trial of Verres (70 BC), Cicero refers repeatedly to Apollonius' faultless *persona*. Apollonius is 'a wealthy man who would lose all if a slave rebellion took place in Sicily'.[141] Cicero describes him as a man of honesty, excellence, and industry, honourable and from an honourable community, and decries the fact that such a worthy man lay in appalling prison conditions, denied even the comfort of visits from his aged father and youthful son.[142] Cicero also notes the sympathy of community leaders who time and again petitioned Verres for Apollonius' release.[143]

Several of the status features noted above figure in accounts of the imprisonment and death of the Catilinarian conspirator Lentulus (63 BC). Sallust notes them to emphasize the magnitude of Lentulus' fall: 'Thus that patrician, of the illustrious stock of the Cornelii, who had held consular authority at Rome, ended his life in a manner befitting his character and his crime'.[144] Those same remarks are later marshalled by Calenus in his criticism of Cicero (43 BC) for having imprisoned and put to death Lentulus, whom he lionizes as 'a man respectable and aged, who could furnish in his ancestors abundant and weighty guarantees of his devotion to his country, and by reason of his age and his character had no power to incite a revolution' and later describes as 'a man who had been consul and was then praetor'.[145] Lentulus' social *persona*, Calenus indicates, should have cast doubt upon the truthfulness of the crimes alleged, or at least warranted for him a more respectful treatment.

While Metellus (60 BC) and the younger Cato (59 and 55 BC) could have appealed against the orders to imprison them, they do not explicitly do so.[146] Confident of their political and social position, they trust in the high regard in which both Senate and people hold them. Their *honor* and *dignitas* can be said to have prevented them from stooping, as it were, to protect themselves by relying on their citizen status. Indeed, Dio writes that no one believed the report that Metellus had appealed, as Metellus' pride was well known to all.[147]

---

[141]Cicero, *Verr.* 2.5.18. On *locuples/locupletior, cf.* Garnsey, *Social Status* 232f.
[142]Cicero, *Verr.* 2.5.20f.
[143]*Ibid.,* 2.5.21.
[144]Sallust, *Cat.* 55.5f.
[145]Dio Cassius 46.20.3.
[146]*Supra,* 44f. Cato could, in the second case, be construed to have appealed to the people for assistance, but perhaps not in the more strict sense of *provocatio.*
[147]Dio Cassius 37.50.2.

Perhaps, in a way similar to Sallust's record of Lentulus' demise, the mention of how highly Sejanus had been regarded, of Vitellius' praetorship, and of Agrippa's royal garb,[148] is intended to heighten the contrast between status and treatment. In other cases, however, the manner in which the political or social status of certain individuals is mentioned appears to suggest that this should have influenced their treatment. Josephus' account of the scourging and crucifixion of Jews having equestrian status (c. 62-64 AD) is one such case; the younger Pliny's mention that victims of the governor Marius Priscus and his co-conspirators (c. 98 AD) were knights may be another.[149] That a distinguished military career also ought to have won an exemption from certain kinds of treatment is suggested by the case of Gaius Maevius Apellus (153 AD).[150]

Clinging to the hope epitomized long before by Cicero that the citizenship of 'poor men of humble birth'[151] should be sufficient to merit them honourable treatment, the Burunitanian peasants protested against the abuses they had suffered. Their admission to being lowly country folk,[152] however, in the face of the movement of legislation to exclude unimportant men from protection,[153] suggests that the hope for redress may have been naive.

The features of citizen and social status which meant so much for the defendant were also vital for the plaintiff. It was very unlikely that an action would even be granted to a low status accuser against his or her social betters. Were such an action granted, the court tended to favour the higher status party.[154] A compensation existed in cases where a powerful agent or witness weighed in on the plaintiff's behalf.[155] Where the plaintiff had a higher relative status, the consequences for the defendant might be grave for other reasons. Hunter notes that a

---

[148]*Ibid.* 58.11.f.; Suetonius, *Vit.* 7.2.3; and Josephus, *AJ* 18.191, 197 [18.6.6f.] respectively.

[149]Josephus, *BJ* 2.308 [2.14.9] and Pliny, *Ep.* 2.11 respectively.

[150]*Sel Pap.* 2:25. Further on the impact of veteran status, the cases of Gavius of Consa and Fadius.

[151]Cicero, *Verr.* 2.5.167.

[152]*FIRA* 1:130.

[153]Callistratus in *Dig.* 47.21.2. *Cf.* Garnsey, *Social Status*, 222f. on *tenuiores*.

[154]Garnsey, *Social Status*, 99f.

[155]*Ibid.*, 'Legal Privilege', 148. Citing Dionysius Halicarnassensis, *Ant. Rom.* 2.10.1, J.M. Kelly, *Roman Litigation* (Oxford: Clarendon, 1966), 27 notes that though legal advice might be the sole benefit of the client/patron relationship, patrons might also be expected to take up the cases of their wronged clients. On witnesses, *cf. Sent.* 5.15.1.

wrong against a person was held to be aggravated not only because of the nature of the act, the place of its commission, and the severity of the damage done, but also the *persona* of the plaintiff.[156] Injury done to a slave was not considered assault but merely property damage. Where, however, a parent was struck by a child, a patron by his freedmen,[157] or where the injured person was a senator, knight, decurion, or some other prestige,[158] the injury was held to be aggravated and hence more severely punishable.

IV. The Role of the Magistrate

It was, therefore, not only acceptable but even expected that magistrates would have regard for the citizen and social status of litigants. Judicial favouritism, however, also had a sinister and unacceptable face which showed itself in a triad of unfair influences that were gradually compounded by the granting to magistrates of extensive but unchecked powers.

1. General Negative Influences

Cicero enumerates the three influences perverting the equitable function of law in answer to the question, 'What is the civil law?': '... that which influence cannot bend, nor power break, nor wealth corrupt'.[159] Favour, influence and money (*Gratia, potentia* and *pecunia*) are, writes Kelly,

> peculiarly united, because in human societies any one or two of the three tend both to produce the other one or two and to be produced by them. In fact, the three ideas belong closely together, and are merely different normal aspects of social superiority in the broad sense.[160]

Power, sway or influence are possible renderings of the term *potentia*.[161] In juridical contexts it can denote the unofficial and sinister

---

[156]W.A. Hunter, *Introduction to Roman Law* (London: William Maxwell and Son, 1885), 137f.
[157]*Ibid.*, 138.
[158]*PS* 5.4.10 cited by Garnsey, *Social Status*, 227.
[159]Cicero, *Caecin.* 73.
[160]Kelly, *Roman Litigation*, 33. *Cf.* Garnsey, *Social Status*, 207.
[161]OLD, 1416 (1); *LD*, 1408.

exercise of one's power and control over others. Cicero confirms this sense when he writes that 'power [*potentia*] is the possession of resources sufficient for preserving one's self and weakening another'.[162] *Gratia* can have the sense of partiality, favouritism or indulgence.[163] It indicates '"excessive favour". In the judicial context, it is the favourable response in a judge or jury to *potentia*, to the pressure applied by men of influence'.[164] The above two definitions might suggest that the terms are clearly separable. Kelly writes, however, that

> a large number of texts treat *potentia* and *gratia* as a natural pair, by coupling them in phrases, and use them, if not as synonyms, at any rate as only vaguely differentiated ideas. If one were to juxtapose the most mutually distant meanings of *potentia* and *gratia* as forces in legal proceedings, one would have on the one side an influence consisting in an immediate threat of physical force if the wishes of the *potens* [i.e., the one with power] are not respected, on the other side an influence consisting only in the mind of the person influenced, in other words an unwillingness for any reason to offend the *gratiosus* [i.e., the favoured one], or a desire to please him.[165]

While power and influence could rebound against its holder in the judicial context,[166] they frequently conferred a distinct advantage as Kelly has shown in a number of examples. Augustus is said to have chided the traitor Cinna that he was not fit to be guardian of the Empire as he could not guard his own house, remarking that 'just lately the influence [*gratia*] of a mere freedman defeated you in a private suit'.[167] Tacitus expresses surprise at the indictment of Agrippina's champion Vitellius who seemed unassailable; yet he, while 'at the height of his influence, and in the extremity of his age—so precarious are the fortunes of the mighty—was brought to trial upon an indictment laid by the senator Junius Lupus'.[168] Kelly notes in another case,

> Under Tiberius, we are told, Lucius Piso was thought extremely bold to summon in civil proceeding Urgulania, whom friendship with the empress Livia had raised above the law (*quam supra leges amicitia Augustae extulerat*). Livia took the summons as an insult to herself, and

---

[162]Cicero, *Inv. Rhet.* 2.56.169.
[163]OLD, 773 (3).
[164]Garnsey, *Social Status*, 209.
[165]Kelly, *Roman Litigation*, 42.
[166]So *ibid.*, 53f. and *cf.* Tacitus, *Hist.* 1.2; 2.10.
[167]Seneca, *Cl.* 1.9.10.
[168]Tacitus, *Ann.* 12.43 cited by Kelly, *Roman Litigation*, 51.

only with reluctance advised Urgulania in the end to pay the money claimed. Would anyone less noble and powerful than Piso have got away with this?[169]

Litigants who failed to observe the measure of the opponent's relative status and influence had little chance in court. Kelly illustrates that 'measuring up' took place as a matter of course: in Terence's *Eunuchus*, Chremes is urged to summon a soldier (Thraso) to law in the event of trouble, since he is 'a foreigner, not so influential as you, not so well known, not possessed of so many friends in Athens'.[170] Citing Plautus' *Poenulus*, Kelly observes that 'already in Republican comedy some passages illustrate the position of a wronged *peregrinus* [foreigner] seeking justice; friendless, unknown, the stranger is the extreme example of the man with neither *potentia* nor *gratia*'.[171]

Advocates saw the fear inspired by the influence of clients as a boon to their pocketbooks.[172] Their own effectiveness, however, might be compromised by these influences. The advocate Tuscilius Nominatus failed to appear on behalf of his clients and later confessed that he had been terrified by the warnings of his friends not to enter into a contest with the senator and ex-praetor Sollers owing to the *gratia*, *fama* and *dignitas* he commanded in the Senate.[173] Pliny, though formally elected a state prosecutor, felt keenly the *potentia* and *gratia* of the ex-governor Marius Priscus (*c*. 98 AD) who, despite his obvious guilt, his repugnant crimes, and his already having been deprived of his status, still commanded the sympathy of the Senate.[174] Ulpian (*fl*.170-228 AD) directs praetors to assign an advocate to the litigant who, owing to 'either intrigues or duress on the part of his opponent, has not found an advocate'.[175]

Juries and magistrates were no less prone to render verdicts on the basis of these negative influences. Citing Suetonius, Kelly notes that 'Augustus was anxious that no one should have an advantage at law through friendship with the princeps; the clear implication is that abject magistrates and judges were ready to concede such an advan-

---

[169]Kelly, *Roman Litigation*, 52, citing Tacitus, *Ann.* 4.21.
[170]Terence, *Eu.* 759f.
[171]Kelly, *Roman Litigation*, 44, citing Plautus, *Poen.* 1403ff. *Cf.* also Terence, *An.* 810-12 on the difficulty of coming to one's rights in a strange town.
[172]Kelly, *Roman Litigation*, 53, citing Tacitus, *Ann.* 11.7 and 4.10.
[173]Pliny, *Ep.* 5.4; 5.13.
[174]Pliny, *Ep.* 2.11, analysed in P.A. Brunt, 'Charges of Provincial Maladministration', *Historia* 10 (1961), 217.
[175]*Dig.* 3.1.1.4. *Cf. ibid.* 1.16.9.4.

tage'.[176] Tiberius intervened to prevent such influence from determining the outcome of criminal cases:

> ... if it was rumoured that any of the accused were being acquitted through influence, he would suddenly appear, and either from the floor or from the judge's tribunal remind the jurors of the laws and of their oath, as well as of the nature of the crime on which they were sitting in judgment.[177]

Tiberius' interest in and frequent presence at trials, according to Tacitus, was responsible for many decisions being given 'in opposition to the influence and solicitation of important personages'.[178] Tacitus' report is significant only if the powerful normally got what they wanted.[179] Ironically, Tiberius' own influence generated effects similar to those he sought to prevent. The cost to a magistrate for failing to have regard for such factors might be considerable. Caesar was named by Vettius as an accomplice of Catiline before the quaestor Novius Niger. Having ignored the potential consequences of 'allowing an official of superior rank to be arraigned before his tribunal' and the action having failed, Novius falls to the defendant's influence—Caesar throws Novius into the prison![180] This illustrates that the magistrate's job was a high wire act requiring consummate balancing skill. Pliny makes the point to Tiro when he writes that 'many men, in their anxiety to avoid seeming to show excessive favour to men of influence, succeed only in gaining a reputation for perversity and malice' and encourages Tiro to continue treading 'the middle course'.[181]

In juridical contexts where it has a negative sense, *pecunia* means 'judicial bribery'—it is wealth used to pervert justice, whether through buying off witnesses, an opponent's counsel, the jury, the judge, or any several of the above together.[182] As to witnesses, Cicero discounts their testimony as they 'can be corrupted by bribery, or partiality, or intimidation, or animosity'.[183] The *lex Julia* disqualifies witnesses 'liable or found guilty of taking money for giving or not giving evidence'.[184] Julius Tarentinus enters a written complaint to Hadrian

---

[176]Kelly, *Roman Litigation*, 51, citing Suetonius, *Aug.* 56.
[177]Suetonius, *Tib.* 33.
[178]Tacitus, *Ann.* 1.75.
[179]Kelly, *Roman Litigation*, 51.
[180]Suetonius, *Jul.* 17.2.
[181]Pliny, *Ep.* 9.5.
[182]See Kelly, *Roman Litigation*, 40f.
[183]Cicero, *Ad C. Herennium* 2.11.

alleging 'that the judge in his case had been deceived by false evidence through a conspiracy of his opponents, who had bribed the witnesses'. Hadrian instructed that the charge be explored; if found to be true, the witnesses were to be punished.[185]

There exist traces in the literature 'of the practice of bribing one's adversary's counsel (presumably to "throw" the contest, like a jockey)'.[186] The tribune Nigrinus publicly condemns the practice and Ulpian later makes provision for suing anyone who bribes 'the advocate of another party or any of those to whom he had entrusted his case'.[187]

A number of laws were enacted to provide for the punishment of those who corrupted magistrates or juries and to punish magistrates who permitted themselves to be corrupted. According to the XII Tables 'a judex or an arbiter legally appointed who has been convicted of receiving money for declaring a decision shall be punished capitally'.[188] The Julian law on extortion, writes Macer,

> lays down that no one shall take anything for the purpose of providing a judge or *arbiter*, or changing him, or ordering him to give judgement; nor for not providing, not changing, or not ordering him to give judgment; nor for throwing a man into the public prison, binding him, or ordering him to be bound, or releasing him from his chains; nor for condemning or acquitting any man; nor for assessing damages, or giving or not giving a judgment involving status or money.[189]

Such bribery, however, remained a problem. First, while the laws against it are clear, they are few. Second, sources indicate that despite the legislation, bribery was prevalent. Apuleius, whose life spans a significant portion of the period in which we are interested, gives a sour assessment of the extent of the problem. One of his characters asks, 'Why are you so surprised … if nowadays all jurors hawk their verdicts for a price?'[190]

The sale of condemnations, acquittals, confinement and freedom can also be demonstrated. Verres cast the wealthy Apollonius into

---

[184]*Dig.* 22.5.3.5.
[185]*Ibid.* 42.1.33. *Cf. ibid.* 48.10.1.2 on the punishment of witnesses who take bribes.
[186]Kelly, *Roman Litigation*, 41.
[187]Pliny, *Ep.* 5.13 and *Dig.* 4.8.31 respectively.
[188]*ARS* 8—XII Tables: IX.3.
[189]*Dig.* 48.11.7.*prol.* For other indications of the problem and provisions and punishments of it, *cf. ibid.* 4.6.26.4, 4.8.31, 12.5.2.2, 48.3.6, 48.10.1.2, 48.11.3-5; *Sent.* 5.23.10, 5.25.2.
[190]Apuleius, *Met.* 10.33, noted in Kelly, *Roman Litigation*, 40.

prison until he paid the illegally levied fine; thus he actually purchased his release from jail.[191] Such official corruption was also rife in 1st century AD Judea. Albinus (62-64 AD) accepted ransoms from individuals to release relatives who had been imprisoned for trifling and commonplace offences. Josephus caustically remarks that the land once again became infested with brigands and the prisons were emptied of all occupants except those who could not pay the price of their release.[192] Florus (64-66 AD) was no less predatory and equally heedless of potential consequences.[193] Following his term as proconsul of Africa, Marius Priscus (c. 98 AD), was charged with taking bribes: 300,000 HS to exile a Roman knight and execute seven of his friends; 700,000 HS to beat, condemn to the mines and eventually strangle in prison another equestrian.[194]

   Some emperors were themselves no less guilty. Galba allowed 'his friends and freedmen to sell at a price or bestow as a favour, taxes and freedom from taxation, the punishment of the guiltless and impunity for the guilty' and Vespasian made no bones of selling 'acquittals to men under prosecution, whether innocent or guilty'.[195] If governors and emperors were influenced by bribes, it is unlikely that lesser magistrates were immune from their power inside and outside the courtroom. We may conclude the present discussion with Kelly's remark that such bribery 'was an apparently constant factor in Roman life, and is evidenced both by the ineffectual legislative measures enacted from time to time to punish it, and by the complaints ranging from loud invective to a cynical satirizing of an accepted evil'.[196]

2. Unchecked Judicial Power

Magistrates had considerable power and wide discretion in its exercise. Where the praetor had charge of a jury court, it was his responsibility to chair the proceedings. The jury's verdict, however, was final and he was bound by it. Trials before a judge, common during the Em-

---

[191]Cicero, Verr. 2.5.23f. Cicero writes that 'others who bought freedom from such injuries, were assuredly numerous'.
[192]Josephus, AJ 20.215 [20.9.5]; ibid., BJ 2.273 [2.14.1].
[193]Ibid., BJ 2.284-308 [2.14.4-9].
[194]Pliny, Ep. 2.11.
[195]Suetonius, Gal. 7.15.2 and ibid., Ves. 8.16.2 respectively.
[196]Kelly, Roman Litigation, 33. Cf. R. MacMullen, Roman Social Relations, 50 B.C. to A.D. 284 (New Haven: Yale University Press, 1974), 118.

pire, left both the procedure and the matter of sentencing in the hands of the praetor. He might solicit advice but he had the final and determinative say in the case.[197]

Those given the 'power of the sword' (*ius gladii*) held a capital jurisdiction in criminal cases. Emblems of this power were the right to wear a military uniform and to carry a sword.[198] This right was conferred upon governors (whether proconsuls, propraetors or procurators) from at least the Julio-Claudian period (but probably much earlier) to the 3rd century AD and could not be delegated.[199] The unfettered right to execute citizen soldiers was one aspect of the *ius gladii*; it may have also included the right to execute civilian citizens.[200] Garnsey presents a convincing case that it did include the right to execute citizens, whether civilians or military personnel. He concedes, however, that 'while it is true that governors were not permitted to execute citizens *summarily*, they were certainly able to execute them *judicially*. That is to say, they could try, condemn and execute citizens, provided that an appeal did not reverse the sentence'.[201] Successful appeal, however, depended in large part upon how governors used their extensive discretionary powers.

Laws such as those concerning the right to appeal were enacted primarily to curb the abuse of these powers.[202] Brunt has shown, however, that unfettered power, including the ability to frustrate negative consequences, encouraged abuse. Governors were immune from prosecution during their term of office. Only in the year following their return to Rome, when they were not eligible for new offices, could they be prosecuted. Normally appointed to hold office for a three year term, however, governors, if required, could do so for much longer. *Equites* were frequently moved from post to post and, in consequence, would have their immunity extended as well.[203] Brunt concludes: 'From such officials the provincials might suffer long, if they had no means of

---

[197]Sherwin-White, *Roman Society*, 23; Garnsey, 'Legal Privilege', 151, 163.
[198]Dio Cassius 52.22; 53.13.6f.; 53.14.5.
[199]Sherwin-White, *Roman Society*, 6-9.
[200]See M. Stern, 'Chapter 6. The Province of Judaea', *Compendia*, vol. 1, 339f.; E. Schürer, *The History of the Jewish People in the Age of Jesus Christ (175 BC-AD 135)*, ed. tr. rev. G. Vermes, F. Millar, M. Goodman (Edinburgh: T. and T. Clark, 1973), vol. 1, 368 n. 73.
[201]P. Garnsey, 'The Criminal Jurisdiction of Governors'. *JRS* 58 (1966), 54. See particularly his case analyses.
[202]Ulpian, *Dig.* 3.3.19, allows for procurators being of doubtful character or in prison.
[203]Brunt, 'Charges', 189-227.

making their grievances known to the Emperor, before they had the right to prefer formal charges.'[204] Cicero asks Verres at his trial, 'Did no thought of your trial ever enter your mind?'[205] Apparently, the immediacy of illicit satisfaction and material enrichment and the distance from the day of reckoning outweighed any dangers in throwing Romans into the Syracusan quarry prison. Governors during the Principate were seldom deposed or punished for crimes against their subjects.[206]

Distance from the imperial capital also encouraged the abuse of power. Brunt observes: 'Josephus makes king Agrippa tell the Jews that it was not by Rome's command that a governor was oppressive but that what occurred in Palestine could not be seen or easily heard of at Rome (BJ ii 353)'.[207] The distance of governors had similar effects upon municipal magistrates in outlying districts.[208]

Where a defendant (in the Antonian and Severan periods at least) wished to appeal against the decision of the governor in a civil or criminal case, he was required to lodge a formal written appeal with the governor within two or three days of sentencing. If accepted at all, the written appeal was sent on with the governor's accompanying letter. An appeal which promised to embarrass or threaten the governor in any way could be neutralized by misstatement, distortion of facts, or outright lying in the cover letter.[209] Occasionally governors, having granted leave to plead a case in Rome, felt so threatened that they confined the appellants to prevent or delay departure.[210] Brunt indicates that corporate appeals against a governor by cities and even whole provinces also needed approval,[211] since unsanctioned embassies from cities or provinces had little effect. Factionalised communities were open to the most severe predations as governors could benefit by playing the sides against one another.[212] Brunt illustrates that the quarrels between Jews and Greeks and the factions among the Jews

---

[204]*Ibid.*, 206.
[205]Cicero, *Verr.* 2.5.144.
[206]Brunt, 'Charges', 209.
[207]*Ibid.*, 207.
[208]F. Millar, 'The World of the *Golden Ass*', *JRS* 71 (1981), 69-72.
[209]Garnsey, *Social Status*, 70f., 82f.
[210]*Dig.* 49.1.25. *Cf. ibid.* 48.6.8.
[211]Brunt, 'Charges', 208: '... the Jews of Palestine needed the consent of the procurator, or of the legate of Syria who had some supervision over him, to approach the Emperor (Philo *Leg.* 247; Josephus, *AJ* xx 7; 193-4)'.
[212]Brunt, 'Charges', 214.

themselves in Palestine 'permitted Felix, Albinus and Florus a harvest of plunder'.[213]

Having got their man to court, the prospect of a conviction might still be remote. Brunt writes that

> The course a trial took often depended, whatever the issue, on factors wholly irrelevant to the conduct of the accused in his province. Thus prosecution often resulted in unjustified acquittals or in penalties unduly light or soon remitted, of little deterrent force; at worst, it was dangerous.[214]

Governors and judges received their mandate from the highest powers in Rome. Their careers were often personally sponsored by those who might one day judge them. Even those who were hostile to an accused governor had to consider, before rendering a verdict or voting a sentence, the political implications of their action—the 'rebound effect' which would become a factor were they themselves ever hauled before a tribunal.

---

[213]*Ibid.* and see too Brunt's comments upon Cumanus and the Samaritans.
[214]*Ibid.*, 220.

CHAPTER 4

PAUL'S CITIZENSHIP AND STATUS

The previous chapter has demonstrated that one's legal and social persona were of great interest to magistrates when custody was being decided. How one fared depended largely upon who one was as measured by ancient criteria. The importance of the prisoner's identity can hardly be overestimated.

Before looking at custodial arrangements for Paul in Acts, it must be asked, 'Who was Paul?' Simply put, he is presented in Acts as a Tarsian, a Roman, and a Jew possessing significant social/religious credentials. The historical probability of Paul's actually possessing such a triple identity has come into severe criticism and some are prepared to conclude that the identity of Paul in Acts is a Lukan creation.

This chapter argues that the probability of such a Paul is hardly so slim as recently made out. Moreover, the disparate aspects of Paul's triple identity, far from needing modern resolution, may actually help to explain what happens to Paul in crises and custody.

I. Paul's Status as a Citizen of Tarsus

Paul appears to be legally classifiable on the basis of citizenship claims he makes for himself in the book of Acts; he is a 'citizen' (πολίτης) of Tarsus in Cilicia according to Acts 21:39, and asserts that he is a Roman citizen at Acts 16:38 and 22:25. Some, however, see impediments to the acceptance of these designations.[1] Paul and his forebears, as Jews, would have felt hindered, or even have been officially prevented, from attaining to citizenship except at the cost of giving up their religious exclusivism. Paul's claims of Roman citizenship in Acts come at suspiciously 'un-Roman' moments. Rather than revealing his citizenship well before he can be mistreated, Acts portrays Paul as making his claims at the point of or after punitive actions, chaining, or incarceration. Moreover, the Pauline epistles are silent concerning the apostle's Roman citizenship. Instead, these letters imply such troubles in his coming to his rights (viz., 2 Cor. 11:25; cf. 6:5, 9; 11:23 [!], 24) that one wonders if the real Paul possessed such citizenship! These concerns must be addressed.

Citizenship—and particularly the Roman citizenship—could and often did put a significant 'spin' upon the working of the law, either impairing litigants or conferring advantage upon them, as has already been seen. One ought not to underestimate its impact upon a person's prospects. The previous chapter serves well, however, to caution that neither ought one to *overestimate* it as some have done.[2] One's status as a citizen did not count for everything and social status for nothing. A skewed assessment of the significance of Paul's citizenship in turn distorts modern assessments of the extent and timing of Paul's self-disclosures when in trouble. It also distorts the reading of Luke's record of the ancient perceptions of and responses to Paul. A more nuanced approach, it will be argued, discloses that many aspects of the text deemed problematic actually have the ring of authenticity.

Paul tells the Tribune that he is a Tarsian of Cilicia; a citizen 'of no ordinary city' (Acts 21:39). Williams writes that the litotes suggests 'a Greek sense of superiority'.[3] Paul betrays pride in his civic status and probably expects some token of recognition from the Tribune.

---

[1]E.g., W.W. Tarn and G.T. Griffith, *Hellenistic Civilisation* (3rd. edn.; London: Edward Arnold, 1952), 221f.; W. Stegemann, 'War der Apostel Paulus ein römischer Bürger?', ZNW 87 (1987), 200-29; J.C. Lentz, Jr., *Luke's Portrayal of Paul* (SNTSMS 77; Cambridge: CUP, 1993), 23-61.

[2]See H.W. Tajra, *The Trial of St. Paul: Juridical Exegesis of the Second Half of the Acts of the Apostles* (WUNT 2/35; Tübingen: Mohr-Siebeck, 1989), 77.

Tarsus did indeed seem to some a worthy object of 1st century civic pride in respect of its political, economic and intellectual prominence. An inscription proclaims: 'Tarsus, the first and greatest and most beautiful metropolis'.[4] Little is known of the founding of this city, though it is thought to have been a site of very early Ionian Greek colonization efforts.[5] An on-going Roman presence in Cilicia began about 104 BC with the establishment of a provincial interest which excluded Tarsus and the Cilician plain.[6] The Cilicia of the 60's BC, whose initial area was secured as part of an extensive campaign to clear the coast of Cilicia Tracheia of pirates, extended from the Chelidonian Isles to the Gulf of Issus with Tarsus as its capital. In 58 BC Cyprus was added.[7] The constantly varying borders of the province from 104 to 49 BC highlight the uncertainty of Roman aims, particularly during the turmoil of the Civil War.[8] In the struggle to Empire, Tarsus sided with Julius Caesar rather than Pompey and for its support was honoured by a brief visit from Caesar in 47 BC. It renamed itself Juliopolis[9] and continued to be well disposed to Caesar's nephew, the future Emperor Augustus. At the hands of the anti-Caesarean Cassius, Tarsus was subjected in 42 BC to severe financial predation,[10] but its pro-Caesarean sympathies were eventually rewarded by M. Antony later that year.[11] These privileges were later confirmed by Augustus in 31 BC.[12] The memory of services rendered to the Julians created a feeling of superiority which was quite strong even in Dio Chrysostom's day nearly a century later.[13]

---

[3]C.S.C. Williams, *A Commentary on the Acts of the Apostles* (BNTC 5; London: A. and C. Black, 1964), 243.

[4]See H. Conzelmann, *Acts of the Apostles: A Commentary on the Acts of the Apostles*, tr. J. Limburg *et al.* (Hermeneia; 2nd ed. 1972; Philadelphia: Fortress, 1987), 184, citing *OGIS* 578.7f.

[5]Further on Cilicia's pre-Roman history, see W.M. Ramsay, *The Cities of St. Paul: Their Influence on His Life and Thought* (Dale Memorial Lectures; London: Hodder and Stoughton, 1907), 116-31; E.M. Blaiklock, 'Tarsus', *IllBibD*, vol. 3, 1519. *Cf.* Strabo 14.5.12; Xenophon, *An.* 1.2.26; 2 Macc. 4:30-36.

[6]Ramsay, *The Cities of St. Paul*, 191.

[7]T.B. Mitford, 'Roman Rough Cilicia'. *ANRW* II/7.2 (1980), 1234f. Dio Chrysostom, *Orationes* 34.7f. notes Tarsus as capital from the very institution of the province.

[8]So Ramsay, *The Cities of St. Paul*, 193.

[9]Dio Cassius 47.26.2.

[10]*Ibid.* 47.30f.; Dio Chrysostom, *Orationes* 34.7f. It was forced to pay to him a 1500 talent levy.

[11]Ramsay, *The Cities of St. Paul*, 197. *Cf.* Dio Cassius 47.31; Appian, *BCiv.* 5.7.

[12]Ramsay, *The Cities of St. Paul*, 197.

While special favours and tax concessions granted by Antony and Augustus certainly improved the economy of Tarsus,[14] this in no way suggests that the city had until then been disadvantaged.[15] Its constitution in the Imperial period favoured land owners, a property-qualification of 500 drachmæ being the test of citizenship.[16] The fourteen year old Neo-Pythagorean Apollonius is said to have criticized Tarsus for its citizens' zeal for luxury and sloth, charging that these fostered an atmosphere of philosophic indolence.[17] Strabo wrote of the Tarsus of Paul's youth that 'in general it not only has a flourishing population but also is most powerful, thus keeping up the reputation of the mother-city'.[18] Dio Chrysostom described it as the greatest of the cities of Cilicia, possessed of size and splendour.[19]

Tarsus was in its intellectual prime about the time of the apostle Paul, which may well have figured prominently in his mind when he described it as 'not ordinary' (οὐκ ἄσημος). In fact it was governed by philosophers of some note from about 29 BC until the first decades of the 1st century AD.[20] Strabo speaks of the Tarsians' unrivalled devotion to learning.[21] The city also possessed 'all kinds of schools of rhetoric'.[22] However, its 'differentness' (διάφορος) from other centres of learning—perhaps the ambience created over time by the mixing of Oriental and Hellenistic cultures—was problematic, according to Strabo. He writes:

> ...it is so different from other cities that there the men who are fond of learning are all natives, and foreigners are not inclined to sojourn there; neither do these natives stay there, but they complete their education abroad; and when they have completed it they are pleased to live abroad, and but few go back home.[23]

Strabo states that 'it is Rome that is best able to tell us the number of learned men from this city; for it is full of Tarsians'.[24]

---

[13]Dio Chrysostom, *Orationes* 34.25.

[14]*Ibid.* 34.8.

[15]See Ramsay, *The Cities of St. Paul*, 132 and Xenophon, *An.* 1.2.23.

[16]Dio Chrysostom *Orationes* 34.23.

[17]Philostratus, *VA* 1.7; *cf.* 6.34.

[18]Strabo 14.5.13. *Cf.* Ramsay, *The Cities of St. Paul*, 97 on its population at that time.

[19]Dio Chrysostom, *Orationes* 33.17, 28; 34.7f., 37.

[20]Strabo 14.5.14; Dio Cassius 56.43.2; Dio Chrysostom, *Orationes* 33.48. *Cf.* Ramsay, *The Cities of St. Paul*, 228-35 for a description of the city's administration.

[21]Strabo 14.5.13. *Cf.* Dio Chrysostom, *Orationes* 33.6.

[22]Strabo 14.5.13.

[23]*Ibid.*

The Tarsus some years after Paul's death, while still a centre of higher learning, presents a somewhat less attractive picture. Apollonius of Tyana went there to study under the Phoenician rhetor Euthydemus, only to leave with his instructor shortly thereafter. It was not conducive to philosophical enquiry.[25] Dio Chrysostom hints that its glory days, characterized by the philosophical virtues of 'orderliness and sobriety',[26] were past. Tarsus now bristled at the criticisms of philosophers and nursed grievances against them.[27]

If Paul had been born in Cilicia only to move away and never return, his Tarsian origin might not have been worth noting. This is, however, how he is often identified in his adult life. He is called a Tarsian (Acts 9:11) and he reinforces the Tarsian/Cilician connection with vigour at several places (Acts 21:39; 22:3). Both Acts and Galatians indicate that Paul was domiciled in Tarsus/Cilicia for some time (Acts 9:30; 11:25; Gal. 1:21) and that his place of origin figured in the sphere of his apostolic ministry (Acts 15:23, 41). Paul's connections with Tarsus and Cilicia, we may conclude, are neither tenuous nor expressions of an antiquarian interest; they possess a current social, missiological, and legal significance for him.

Paul also asserts that he was a 'citizen' (πολίτης) of Tarsus (Acts 21:39). 'Citizen' can have a political and juridical sense to it. Tajra writes in this regard,

> Strictly speaking the word πολίτης refers to a citizen of a town or state, a member of the πόλις as a political entity, someone who participates actively in the city's civic and religious life and who shares in the privileges, but also the duties, of the πόλις in its political quality. Finally the πολίτης is completely distinct on the juridical plane from a resident alien or slave.[28]

Tajra demonstrates that 'citizenship' allows for a broader set of interpretations. He illustrates this from the LXX, Maccabean literature, Philo, Josephus, and three other NT instances (Luke 15:15; 19:19; Heb. 8:11),[29] concluding that Acts 21:39

---

[24]*Ibid.* 14.5.15.
[25]Philostratus, *VA* 1.7.
[26]Dio Chrysostom, *Orationes* 33.48.
[27]*Ibid.* 34.3. *Cf.* Philostratus, *VA* 6.34 which says that Tarsus hated Apollonius for this reason.
[28]Tajra, *The Trial of St. Paul*, 79.
[29]*Ibid.*, 79f.

... most likely refers to Paul's membership in the resident Jewish community at Tarsus rather than to any citizenship in the Greek πόλις. His mention of Tarsus in this verse is a statement of domicile and not a proclamation of citizenship.[30]

But this is doubtful for several reasons. First, Luke clearly represents Paul's predicament as political and juridical. Paul's precise legal identity is therefore at issue here. Second, while Tajra notes that the juridical/political sense of πολίτης is distinctively Greek,[31] he overlooks the Greek character of Acts 21:37-39. Paul addresses the Tribune in surprisingly good Greek as we have already seen. Third, it is interesting that, whereas Paul is very Greek to the Tribune, he adopts an obviously Jewish (and selective!) manner when addressing the crowd. Paul's salutation is distinctly Jewish, he speaks in Aramaic and he refers only to his having been *born* in Tarsus, but not being a *citizen* from there (Acts 22:1-3). Full legal self-disclosure to the Jews would hardly have served the interest of conciliation. Finally, it may be that the D-text, by replacing 'citizen of' with 'born in' at Acts 21:39, is not so much emphasizing Tarsus as his birthplace,[32] as confirming a sensitivity to the political/juridical sense of the term and the difficulties raised. We take it then that the text is in fact recording Paul's claim to a legally valid Tarsian citizenship; that Paul was on the city's roll'.[33]

Neither Paul nor his forbears would have received Tarsian citizenship either by individual[34] or *en bloc* grant if this meant joining in the religious practices of a Hellenistic tribe.[35] The only conceivable circumstances in which a Jew could obtain such citizenship without apostatising were where religious concessions had been granted by the tribal unit or where the tribal unit was Jewish.

Hemer notes that 'the possibility of Jewish citizenship in a Greek city has sometimes been denied absolutely because of the religious difficulty'.[36] Any such denial flies in the face of several examples where

---

[30]*Ibid.*, 80.

[31]*Ibid.*, 79.

[32]So *ibid.*

[33]A.D. Nock, '*Isopoliteia* and the Jews', in *Essays on Religion and the Ancient World*, ed. Z. Stewart (Oxford: Clarendon, 1972), vol. 2, 961.

[34]On the individual grant in Alexandria, see V. Tcherikover *Hellenistic Civilization and the Jews*. tr. S. Applebaum (Philadelphia: Jewish Publication Society of America/Jerusalem: Magnes, 1961), 327.

[35]See Ramsay, *The Cities of St. Paul*, 176.

[36]C.J. Hemer, *The Book of Acts in the Setting of Hellenistic History*, ed. C.H. Gempf (WUNT 49; Tübingen: J.C.B. Mohr [Paul Siebeck], 1989), 127 n. 75

Jews appear to have been granted Greek citizenship without apostatising. Josephus and Philo note Jews who are both members of the Jewish commonwealth, and, by virtue of their holding Greek municipal offices, are known to hold another citizenship:

> Philo's brother Alexander was alabarch (customs official) in the 30s A.D., and another Jew, Demetrius (otherwise unknown) held the same post late in Claudius' principate; neither case excites comment from Josephus as unusual. And a sentence in Philo, though vague and allusive, speaking of people, apparently quite numerous, who not only resided in the city (presumably Alexandria) but also sat in the assembly, acted as councillors and jurymen, and on occasion held Greek municipal offices, is credibly interpreted as referring to the Jews.[37]

Nock furnishes an example from Antioch 'in the statement of Malalas (290.14 ff.) that under Didius Julianus [193 AD] the Plethri(o)n was built on the site of the house of "Asabinus of the Council (πολι–τευομένου), a Jew by religion"'.[38] Nock continues,

> One cannot imagine why this should have been invented. May it not be that a rich and acceptable Jew who had inherited or acquired Antiochene citizenship was by tacit consent allowed to absent himself from such parts of Council business as would be against his scruples?[39]

The epigraphic evidence from Synagogue excavations in Sardis also suggests that citizenship and Jewish religiosity were not mutually exclusive. Of the eighty inscriptions, more than thirty refer to donors. Seager and Kraabel note that

> many donors proudly identify themselves as *Sardianoi*, 'citizens of Sardis,' and no less than nine may use the privileged title *bouleutes*, 'member of the city council'; perhaps because of their wealth, the latter must have possessed considerable social status.[40]

---

[37]E.M. Smallwood, *The Jews Under Roman Rule: From Pompey to Diocletian* (Studies in Judaism in Late Antiquity 29; Leiden: Brill, 1976), 227. The final case in Smallwood depends upon a loose reading of Philo, *Prob.* 6. *Cf.* Nock, '*Isopoliteia*', 961 n. 5.

[38]Nock, '*Isopoliteia*', 961.

[39]*Ibid.*

[40]A.R. Seager and A.T. Kraabel, 'IX. The Synagogue and the Jewish Community', in *Sardis From Prehistoric to Roman Times: Results of the Archaeological Exploration of Sardis 1958-1975*, ed. G.M.A. Hanfmann (Cambridge/London: Harvard University Press, 1983), 184. *Cf.* P.R. Trebilco, *Jewish Communities in Asia Minor* (SNTSMS 69; Cambridge/New York: CUP, 1991), 46ff.

Lentz is inclined to discount this evidence, noting that it is both late and unique. Moreover, the names need not all represent Jews—there were pious non-Jews who contributed. Finally, the evidence suggests to him a Jewish community so highly integrated with its Hellenistic environment that its brand of Judaism can hardly be compared with that practised by a Pharisaic family such as Paul's.[41]

The Sardis evidence, it must be admitted, appears to be late. Coins under the mosaic floor inscriptions in the main hall of the synagogue are datable to the middle decades of the 4th century and in the forecourt to the second half of the 4th century AD.[42] But this may be undercut somewhat. First, it is possible that these are earlier inscriptions that have been carefully saved and reinstalled.[43] Second, the privileged status of the Jewish community at Sardis did not leap from nothing. The antiquity of the Jewish community in Sardis and the character of its history must not be forgotten. Jews lived in Sardis as early as the 6th century BC, and more were formally settled there in the late 3rd century BC. Josephus attests to a thriving community in the 1st century BC. Some of its members had received Roman citizenship yet remained committed to traditional religious practices. Jewish wealth and religious commitment were undiminished through the first centuries AD despite the fall of Jerusalem and the growing influence of the church. The existence of at least two synagogue buildings prior to that discussed above is probable.[44] We therefore conclude that the Sardis evidence provides a precedent for a secularly privileged and conservative Judaism.

The unusualness of the Sardis material suggests to Seager and Kraabel not the need to discount its significance, but to carefully reassess the other evidence which touches on Judaism's relationship to its Diaspora environment.[45] It is possible, as Lentz suggests, that not all those noted as benefactors were in fact Jews. But again, the Jewish community had long been settled and boasted families of considerable distinction by the mid-1st century BC. The dearth of Hebrew names among the donor inscriptions (there are only two) is hardly unusual when compared with Jewish catacomb inscriptions found in Rome.[46] Moreover, the two inscriptions which distinguish the donors as God-

---

[41]Lentz, *Luke's Portrait of Paul*, 34-36.
[42]Trebilco, *Jewish Communities*, 43f.
[43]*Ibid.*, 44.
[44]For details of this summary, *cf.* Seager and Kraabel, 'The Synagogue', 178f. and 284 nn.
[45]Seager and Kraabel, 'The Synagogue', 178.

fearers[47] suggest that the other donors were in fact full Jews. Lentz' final objection depends on the premise that Pharisaism was at its root radically separatist. Our discussion of Paul's Pharisaism will question this characterization. Seager and Kraabel's sketch of the Sardian evidence is a fitting conclusion: 'The Sardis synagogue shows unmistakably that these Jews did not abandon their ancestral heritage, but affirmed it and gloried in it; at the same time they flourished among gentile neighbours who greatly outnumbered them'.[48]

In Philostratus' *Life of Apollonius* certain Jews appear to stand as part of the citizen body of Tarsus. Philostratus records that

> on one occasion the Emperor [i.e., Titus] was offering a sacrifice in public, when the whole body of citizens met and presented a petition to him asking for certain great favours; and he replied that he would mention the matter to his father, and be himself their ambassador to procure them what they wanted; whereupon Apollonius stepped forward and said: 'Supposing I convicted some who are standing here of being your own and your father's enemies, and of having sent legates to Jerusalem to excite a rebellion, and of being the secret allies of your most open enemies, what would happen to them?'[49]

The context and the dilemma put by Apollonius to Titus assumes that the company is a formal gathering of the citizenry represented by chosen ambassadors. The phrase 'when the whole body of citizens met' thus appears accurate.[50] The Tarsian Jews had strong nationalistic sympathies and had taken action by sending envoys to Jerusalem to promote the insurrection. Apollonius appears quite easily to have been able to identify them.[51]

A question left unanswered by the above examples is whether citizenship is by individual or by *en bloc* grant. Greek citizenship to Jews *en bloc*—i.e., by constituting them a Jewish tribe[52] within the po-

---

[46]*Ibid.*, 184 and H.J. Leon, *The Jews in Ancient Rome* (Morris Loeb Series 5; Philadelphia: Jewish Publication Society of America, 1960), 93-121.

[47]The 'Godfearers' (θεοσεβεῖς) were religiously inferior to full Jews in the synagogue community (Trebilco, *Jewish Communities*, 153).

[48]Seager and Kraabel, 'The Synagogue', 178.

[49]Philostratus, *VA* 6.34.

[50]*Cf.* Ramsay, *The Cities of St. Paul*, 178; Hemer, *The Book of Acts*, 127 n. 75.

[51]Would they have been identifiable by their clothing? *Cf.* J. Milgrom, 'Of Hems and Tassels', *BAR* 9 (1983), 61-65; *b. Mo'ed* VII: *Ta'an.* 22a on such distinctions.

[52]In most cities the citizens were divided into tribes (φυλή). Our use of this standard term is not related to the twelve tribes of Israel, but to groups that possess citizenship.

litical structure of the city—is the only available means for a serious Jew according to Ramsay.[53] He asserts that in Tarsus, a city of mixed Hellenic and Oriental origin, 'the Jews would have been regarded in a less degree than elsewhere as an alien element'.[54] He offers that Paul might have sprung from one of the families receiving Greek citizenship in 171 BC, properly rejecting Jerome's theory that Paul or his parents emigrated from Gischala in Palestine following its capture by the Romans (c. 4 BC).[55]

Hemer suggests that the Jewish citizen indications of the Sardian synagogue inscriptions are likely to have arisen out of a Seleucid constitution.[56] But is there evidence of a Jewish tribe? The lion, a powerful and prevalent Greek symbol associated with Sardis from the time of Herodotus, appears to have been a part of the Jewish identity there as well. A large Lydian lion figure was found just outside the synagogue and carved lions dating from the Persian period bracket the great Eagle Table at the front of the synagogue. Of particular interest, however, is the following inscription found within the synagogue precincts: 'Aurelius Olympius, of the tribe of Leontioi, with my wife and my children, I have fulfilled my vow'.[57] Is it possible that this is a reference to a tribe to which Jews possessing the citizenship belonged in Sardis? The use of this image, write Seager and Kraabel,[58] would have been an inspired one as it married the lion's prominence in Sardian Greek thinking to ancient Jewish descriptive and identificational uses in biblical and extra-biblical texts (e.g., Gen. 49:9; Deut. 33:22; Num. 23:24; 24:9; 1 Macc. 3:4-6; Micah 5:8; 4 Ezra 11:37-12:34). The statues, they contend, suggest an association with the symbol rather than a simple re-using of the lion statues. Sardian Jews, it is observed from other inscriptional evidence, even adopted the name 'Leo'.[59] Seager and Kraabel are prepared to leave the question open, while others confidently assert that the reference is only to a group within the Jewish community.[60]

---

[53]Ramsay, *The Cities of St. Paul*, 176f., 180 and *cf.* 2 Macc. 4:30-36.
[54]Ramsay, *The Cities of St. Paul*, 139.
[55]*Ibid.*, 185. *Cf.* C.J. Hemer, 'Tarsus', *ISBE*, vol. 4, 735f.; S. Applebaum, 'Chapter 8. The Legal Status of the Jewish Communities in the Diaspora', In *Compendia*, vol. 1, 440f.; Th. Mommsen, 'Die Rechtsverhältnisse des Apostels Paulus', *ZNW* 2 (1901), 82f. n. 4.
[56]Hemer, *The Book of Acts*, 127 and n. 75.
[57]Trebilco, *Jewish Communities*, 44.
[58]Summary of Seager and Kraabel, 'The Synagogue', 184.
[59]*Cf. ibid.*, 184f.; Trebilco, *Jewish Communities*, 44f., on the graffito 'ben Leho'.

The claim of Tarsian citizenship for Jews as a body has been made in the past on the basis of Josephus' assertions that similar conditions of grant existed for Alexandria, Antioch, and the cities of Ionia.[61] The results of more recent analysis, however, do not inspire great confidence in assertions for Alexandria. That Jews as a body had significant political clout and aspired to Greek citizenship in Alexandria are beyond doubt. But Josephus' and Philo's blending of the legal and popular senses of 'citizenship', 'citizen' and even 'Alexandrian', when taken together with the letter of Claudius to the Alexandrians in late 41 AD, seems to disqualify Josephus' indications for the Alexandrian Jews.[62]

A similar judgement is passed on Josephus' reliability concerning Jewish claims at Antioch on the Orontes. The Jews experienced serious problems with the dominant populace despite being called citizens by Josephus.[63] Abusive treatment by known citizens should not automatically call into doubt Josephus' accuracy,[64] but his imprecise terminology hardly strengthens the Antiochene case.

In another account, Josephus states that Ephesian Greeks appeared before M. Agrippa to contest the Jewish right to citizenship because the Jews did not worship their gods.[65] Agrippa, in response, confirmed the *status quo* which, Applebaum states,

> referred to Jewish rights in matters of religious practice and jurisdiction (to use their own customs)—not to citizenship. But if Josephus' phrase συνηγορήσαντος Νικολάου ('their defence-counsel being Nicholas') is accurate, the Greeks were the plaintiffs, hence the assumption is that they were attacking Jewish *politeia* which, by virtue of their

---

[60]See, e.g. L. Robert, *Nouvelles inscriptions de Sardes* (Paris: Librairie D'Amérique et D'Orient, 1964), 45f. 5.

[61]Josephus, *Ap.* 2.38f. *et passim* as well as in *AJ* and *BJ*.

[62]See V. Tcherikover, *Hellenistic Civilization and the Jews*, tr. S. Applebaum (Philadelphia: Jewish Publication Society of America/Jerusalem: Magnes, 1961), 309-32; Smallwood, *The Jews Under Roman Rule*, 224-35; R.D. Sullivan, 'The Dynasty of Judaea in the First Century', *ANRW* II/8 (1977), 348; and the discussion and text of Claudius' letter to Alexandria in H.I. Bell, *Jews and Christians in Egypt*. (Greek Papyri in the British Museum 6; London: British Museum, 1924) 10-21, 23-9

[63]For discussion, *cf.* W.A. Meeks and R.L. Wilken, *Jews and Christians in Antioch in the First Four Centuries of the Common Era* (SBLSBS 13; Missoula: Scholars, 1978), 2-5, 37 nn. 3, 5; Sullivan, 'The Dynasty of Judaea', 350. *Cf.* Applebaum, 'Legal Status', 440f.

[64]*Cf.* the case of Tarsian linen workers at Dio Chrysostom, *Orationes* 34.23.

[65]Josephus, *AJ* 12.125f. [12.3.2].

argument on difference of religion, must be membership of the polis.[66]

The Jewish community in this account appears to have sufficient power not only to assert Greek citizenship but also to make political and social inroads without conceding its religious distinctiveness. Josephus' second account of this dispute, however, relates that *the Jews* approached Herod and M. Agrippa, complaining of mistreatment, and were affirmed in the right to practice their religion freely.[67] There is no mention of citizenship. The outcome in both accounts tends to confirm the opposite case—i.e., that if there was a Jewish assertion of an ancient *en bloc* grant, however successfully maintained in the initial stages, it was denied when tested in law.

Tarn and Griffith generalize from the evidence available to them that the Jews in a Greek city were only ever able to 'call themselves a racial unit (*laos*), and never (apparently) an enfranchised people (*demos*)'.[68] They explain Paul's claim to be a citizen of Tarsus in the following manner:

> Where the kings had power, as they had in new foundations like Alexandria or Antioch or in cities where, like Ephesus, the Seleucids restored democracy and could make terms, they gave the Jewish settlers isopolity [ἰσοπολιτεία], *potential* citizenship…; that is, a Jew could become a citizen on demand, provided of course that he apostatised by worshipping the city gods.[69]

Nock disputes the notion that apostasy was a prerequisite to receiving Greek citizenship by means of this 'isopolity'. He writes that from what is known of inscriptions, this 'potential' citizenship, whether granted by one city to another or by a city to individuals, was fully activated with only the one condition of taking up residence. 3 Macc. 2:30 (*cf.* 3:21) actually implies that the grant to Jews of isopolity had not previously been made available and that those Jews who did apostatise were slaughtered on the permission of Philopater. Finally, Nock cites a number of examples, including Paul's claim of Greek citizenship at

---

[66]Applebaum, 'Legal Status', 442. *Cf.* W.M. Ramsay, 'Tarsus', *Exp* VII/2 (1906), 41.
[67]Josephus, *AJ* 16.27-61 [16.2.3-5]. For discussion, Trebilco, *Jewish Communities*, 168-72.
[68]Tarn and Griffith, *Hellenistic Civilisation*, 221. So also M. Grant, *The Jews in the Roman World* (London: Weidenfeld and Nicolson, 1973), 118.
[69]Tarn and Griffith, *Hellenistic Civilisation*, 222. Stegemann, 'War der Apostel Paulus', 220f.

Acts 21:39, which undermine the assertion of a basic incompatibility between Greek citizenship and Jewish faith. Nock states that conditional isopolity is an unnecessary modern theoretical construct.[70] We may add Applebaum's observations: First, one can hardly imagine any Jewish community drafting such a formal arrangement of conditional 'potential citizenship' with a Greek city on the ground of its inciting individual Jews to break the second commandment. Second, whereas some Jews might prefer citizenship to Jewish faith and identity, 'they neither needed (nor would have obtained) their community's formal consent, nor asked it' if the grant came at the cost of apostasy.[71]

Textually and contextually, then, Paul should be understood to declare his full Tarsian citizenship at Acts 21:39. The evidence above, whatever the actual circumstances or means of grant, shows the declaration to be credible even for a Jew zealous for his faith.

II. Paul as a Roman Citizen

The Paul of Acts claims to possess both Roman and Tarsian citizenship from birth. It had not earlier been generally possible to maintain dual or multiple citizenship because of the Roman 'rule of incompatibility'.[72] The difficulties and disadvantages in maintaining the rule were eventually mitigated by its less restrictive use[73] until the practice of possessing full dual citizenship was thoroughly established about the reign of Claudius.[74]

While the fact of Paul's dual citizenship claim cannot be contested, the circumstances of acquisition—i.e., from birth—require that precedents be at least as early as the turn of the century and, if his forbears possessed it too, earlier still. Precedents going as far back as Augustus can be found,[75] and even before the Julian period, isolated

---

[70]Nock, 'Isopoliteia', 960f.

[71]Applebaum, 'Legal Status', 438.

[72]So called by A.N. Sherwin-White, 'The Roman Citizenship. A Survey of Its Development Into a World Franchise', ANRW I/2 (1972), 46. The rule is indicated in Cicero, Balb. 28; Caec.100; Leg. 2.2.5.

[73]Sherwin-White, 'Roman Citizenship', 46, 53.

[74]See ibid., 51f.

[75]See FIRA 1:55 (= ARS 128 [36/30 BC]), 68 (= ARS 148 [6/4 BC]). See Sherwin-White, 'Roman Citizenship', 50f.; E. Schürer, History of the Jewish People, rev. ed. G. Vermes et al. (Edinburgh: T. and T. Clark, 1986), vol. 3.1, 134, esp. n. 31; Conzelmann, Acts, 184; H.J. Cadbury, TheBook of Acts In History (London: A and C. Black, 1955) 81.

instances are noted. The legitimacy of the claim for both Paul and his forbears is therefore probable despite occasional denials of the practice's legality.[76]

The explicit indications of Paul's Roman citizenship in the text of Acts are several. Paul asserts it on one occasion (Acts 16:37f.) and on another first intimates it and then elaborates upon the claim in subsequent discussion (Acts 22:25-29). In both instances, the disclosure of Roman citizenship occurs in the presence of Roman officials. The Tribune Claudius Lysias also notes it in his letter to Felix (Acts 23:27). Finally, it is the basis of Paul's appeal to Caesar (Acts 25:10-12). Whether Paul was schooled in Latin and made use of it or ever wore a Roman toga[77] cannot be certainly determined from the NT documents.

Ramsay writes that

> no one could be a Roman citizen without having a Roman name; and, though he might never bear it in ordinary Hellenic society, yet as soon as he came in contact with the law and wished to claim his legal rights, he must assume his proper and full Roman designation.[78]

Citizens had three names: a 'personal name' (*praenomen*) of which there were only about fifteen possibilities; a 'surname' (*nomen* or *gentilicium*), associating one with the largest number of relatives; and a 'family name' (*cognomen*) which was more often than not used alone for the individual.[79] Latin 'personal names' by themselves are unhelpful as indicators of Roman citizenship because 'they had long been domesticated in Greek usage, and one may guess that most people would scarcely be conscious of their Latin origin'.[80] The use of 'personal names' or 'surnames' and 'personal names' together can be helpful beyond securing the fact of citizenship, as Hemer indicates:

---

[76]So M. Hammond and L.J. Bartson, *The City in the Ancient World* (Harvard Studies in Urban History; Cambridge, Mass.: HUP, 1972), 272f. for Italy. *Cf.* further Cicero, *Leg.* 2.2.5; *Balb.* 30 and comments by Sherwin-White, 'Roman Citizenship', 49.

[77]The impact of Paul's wearing a toga during clashes with Romans and Roman officials in Acts would have been profound. The mistreatment of Paul, however, makes it clear that he was not thus clad.

[78]Ramsay, 'Tarsus', 155.

[79]C.E.B. Cranfield, *A Critical and Exegetical Commentary on the Epistle to the Romans* (ICC; Edinburgh: T. and T. Clark, 1975), vol. 1, 49. *Cf.* Cadbury, *Book of Acts*, 69.

[80]E.A. Judge, *Rank and Status in the World of the Caesars and St. Paul* (1981 Broadhead Memorial Lecture/ucp 29; Christchurch, Nz: University Of Canterbury, 1982), 13. *Cf.* Cadbury, *Book of Acts*, 69.

When a provincial was enfranchised, as when a slave was freed, he automatically assumed the *praenomen* and *nomen* of his patron and transmitted it to his descendants. This is a valuable principle of epigraphic dating, for the mention of persons named 'Ti. Claudius' or 'T. Flavius' immediately sets a *terminus a quo* in the time of Claudius or of Vespasian.[81]

The 'family name' can also be quite informative if the citizen grant had been given after birth. Slaves and free-born provincials took the personal name and surname of the one granting the citizenship but retained their native name as family name. Their children often were given, instead of a native family name, a full Roman name.[82]

Roman citizenship would be incontestably indicated for Paul had his full Roman name, or even surname and family name alone, been disclosed somewhere in the NT. Its absence, particularly from the letter of Claudius Lysias to Felix at Acts 23:26-30,[83] is disappointing. However, this must be balanced by the fact that nowhere in the NT is an individual known by all of his or her three names.[84] The reader of the NT has only the names 'Saul' and 'Paul'[85] to evaluate. The unofficial name, known as a *signum* or *supernomen*, could be indicated 'by the term *signo* or, most commonly, by the expression 'who is also' (ὁ καί) rendered in Latin as *qui et*'.[86] The names 'Paul' and 'Saul' appear in this configuration at Acts 13:9: 'Saul, who is also Paul' (Vg.: *Saulus … qui et Paulus*). Several points may be made in favour of the view that 'Paul' is the apostle's family name and 'Saul' his *signum* rather than the other way around: First, there is no convention forbidding this way of construing the names. It should be observed that 'the *signum* may either follow or precede the other name, being separated from it by the ὁ καί.'[87] Second, it is more probable that the author is making an impor-

---

[81]C.J. Hemer, 'The Name of Paul', *TB* 36 (1985), 179.

[82]Cranfield, *A Critical and Exegetical Commentary*, 49f. n. 5. This practice may be illustrated from Josephus (*Vit.* 5f. [1]; 422, 427 [76]).

[83]The expression 'having this pattern' (ἔχουσαν τὸν τύπον τοῦτον: Acts 23:25) should probably be taken as a disclaimer that the letter is a verbatim copy, but that the facsimile gives more than the letter's general purport. For similar prefatory phrasing using τύπος in Hellenistic-Jewish letters, see 1 Macc. 11:29; 25:2; Josephus, *AJ* 11.215 [11.6.6]; 3 Macc. 3:30; and Aristides 34.

[84]Hemer, 'The Name', 182f.; Cadbury, *Book of Acts*, 69.

[85]Σαούλ (=שָׁאוּל): Acts 9:4, 17; 22:7, 13; 26:14. Παῦλος: Acts 9, 13-28 and the Pauline epistles *passim*.

[86]Leon, *The Jews in Ancient Rome*, 117.

[87]Cranfield, *A Critical and Exegetical Commentary*, 49 n. 4. *Cf.* the Sardian inscription 'Samuel, known also as Julian' in Seager and Kraabel, 'The Synagogue', 184.

tant rather than a trivial observation; i.e., that Sergius Paulus and the apostle had the same official 'family name', rather than that Paul's *signum* (or personal name for that matter) was the same as the family name of the proconsul.[88] Third, as the apostle was citizen-*born* according to Acts 22:28, it is likely that his 'native *cognomen* would be exchanged for a regular Roman or Italian name'.[89] The final observation is related to the second that identity of family names is most probably being noted. While 'one or two examples of "Paullus" serving as a *praenomen* are known … they are so rare that we scarcely need to reckon seriously with the possibility of its being the apostle's *praenomen*'.[90]

Some Latin family names, like certain Latin personal names, had currency as Greek names. Judge notes, however, that the high level of correspondence between the Pauline list of family names and the popular family names of Roman soldiers suggests citizenship and also that the name *Paulus* rates as the most respectable.[91]

How might Paul have obtained the Roman franchise? People individually or collectively might obtain Roman citizenship in several ways: 1) by being citizen-born; 2) by manumission; 3) on completion of military service; 4) by reward;[92] 5) by *en bloc* grant;[93] or 6) for financial considerations. It is recorded in Acts that Paul obtained his citizenship by the first means noted above: he was citizen-born[94] (Acts 22:28; *cf.* 22:3). Some explanations of how Paul's family received the citizenship are less plausible than others.[95] All, however, are speculative. The warm relations between Tarsus and Pompey, Caesar, Antony, and Augustus permit Hemer to venture 'there is then the possibility—we can say no more—that Paul might have been Cn. Pompeius Paulus, C. Julius Paulus or M. Antonius Paulus'.[96]

---

[88]*Pace* A.N. Sherwin-White, *Roman Society and Roman Law in the New Testament* (Sarum Lectures 1961-62; Oxford, Clarendon, 1963), 152.

[89]*Cf.* Cranfield, *A Critical and Exegetical Commentary*, 50 n. 5.

[90]*Ibid.* Hemer, 'The Name', 183.

[91]Judge, *Rank and Status*, 13, 36 n. 20. H. Dessau, 'Der Name des Apostels Paulus'. *Hermes* 45 (1910), 351f., describes the apostle's name as uncommon and aristocratic. Further on Paul's name, see A. Nobbs, 'Cyprus', in *The Book of Acts in its Graeco-Roman Setting*, ed. D.W.J. Gill and C. Gempf (A1CS 2; Grand Rapids:Eerdmans/ Carlisle: Paternoster, 1994), 279-89.

[92]*Cf. ARS* 60 n. 1; 128 [= *FIRA* 1:55]; Strabo, *Geog.* 5.1.6; Cicero, *Balb.* 8.19.

[93]*Cf.* Strabo, *Geog.* 5.1.6; Suetonius, *Jul.* 28. See further, E. Brewer, 'Roman Citizenship and Its Bearing on the Book of Acts', *ResQ* 4, 207f.; Sherwin-White, 'Roman Citizenship', 40-45.

[94]Cadbury, *Book of Acts*, 68, indicates that the Greek γεγγέννημαι 'suggests plainly the Latin word *ingenuus*, the technical term for a birthright citizen. For once here I think it cannot be said, "The Greeks have a word for it."'

Even a desperate person could scarcely have risked two citizenship claims and an appeal to Caesar without the right to do so. Latin personal and family names could be used by non-Romans in Paul's day, but surnames were tightly restricted. Suetonius writes that Claudius executed those who usurped the privileges of Roman citizenship.[97] Epictetus (c. 50-120 AD) observes that 'those who falsely claim Roman citizenship are severely punished'.[98] Even an unsatisfactorily proven citizenship could result in prosecution or death.[99]

Thus, far from having nothing to say on the matter, both Paul's family name itself and the manner of its mention at Acts 13:9 may be taken to indicate his Roman citizenship, even if the circumstances of how his forbears obtained their Roman citizenship remain unknown. The presence of Roman officials in Tarsus and Cilicia in the 1st century BC with discretionary power to grant citizenship certainly allows for its reception by Paul's family.

Pairing a serious Judaism with Roman citizenship caused undeniable tensions. It may thus have been relatively rare for Jews to obtain the franchise. But this hardly effects the probability of individual cases. Obtaining citizenship through military service was scarcely possible for a religious Jew: though Jewish troops were found in the Seleucid and Ptolemaic armies, they were rare in the Roman forces of the first and second centuries AD.[100] Applebaum explains:

> ...Roman army life revolved extensively round the ruler-cult, the consecrated standards and the *auguria*; this and the constant tension between the Jews and the Roman power more particularly in Judaea during the first century of the current era, made Jews as reluctant to enlist as it made the authorities reluctant to accept them. Exceptions of course occur, and more may be found in the future.[101]

---

[95]Jerome's theory (*Lives of Illustrious Men* [NPNF] 5) that Paul and his parents were moved from Gischala to Tarsus as prisoners-of-war by M. Antony is flawed at several points. *Cf.* K. Lake and H.J. Cadbury, in *The Acts of the Apostles: English Translation and Commentary*, in *BC*, vol. 4,284f.; Sherwin-White, *Roman Society*, 152. That his father was not a non-observant Jew serving in the Roman army as a leatherworker is supported by Paul's boast that he was a son of a Pharisee (Acts 23:6).
[96]Hemer, 'The Name', 179. *Cf.* Ramsay, 'Tarsus', 144f.
[97]Suetonius, *Claud.* 25.3.
[98]Arrianus, *Epict.* 3.24.41. *Cf.* also *Seut.* 5.25.11 and *Cod. Theod.* 9.2.2 on false claims.
[99]See Cicero, *Arch.* 4.7, and *idemVer.* 2.5.169.
[100]Applebaum, 'Legal Status', 429-32. *Cf.* Trebilco, *Jewish Communities*, 197f. n. 58 and sources cited there.

Roman sensitivity to this religious conflict is reflected in several documents from the mid-1st century BC which exempt Jews from conscription.[102] How many Jews would this affect? Smallwood thinks that the numbers were trivial,[103] but such documents would hardly have merited publication had not the issue touched a significant number of individuals.[104] In any event, the phrases 'Jews who are Roman citizens' and 'Jewish citizens of ours'[105] in these documents confirm the simultaneous possession of Jewish religious sensibilities and Roman citizenship.[106]

Jewish possession of Roman citizenship in the civilian context posed fewer problems than in the military. Citizenship required inclusion in a 'tribe' (gens), but unlike Greek tribal membership, the Roman tribal connection was a political and legal fiction requiring no religious bond of union as membership was comprised of disparate peoples scattered throughout the Roman world. Religious practice might be expected where tribal members lived near enough to Rome and desired to vote.[107] Jews nevertheless exerted great effort publicly and in their religious observances to show their loyalty to the Roman State and its Sovereign.[108]

---

[101]Applebaum, 'Legal Status', 459. For a vivid illustration of apostasy resulting from the upwardly-mobile military/political career of a Jew, see E.G. Turner, 'TIBERIVS IVLIVS ALEXANDER', *JRS* 44 (1954), 54-64

[102]Josephus records three consular edicts of Lucius Cornelius Lentulus Crus (*AJ* 14.228f. [14.10.13]; 14.234 [14.10.16]; 14.237-40 [14.10.19]); a letter of M. Antony (*AJ* 14.235 [14.10.17]); and a letter of Titus Ampius Balbus (*AJ* 14.230 [14.10.13]); and the letter of the Syrian governor Publius Cornelius Dolabella on Jewish privileges in 43 BC (*AJ* 14.225-27 [14.10.12]).

[103]Smallwood, *The Jews Under Roman Rule*, 127f.

[104]See M. Stern, 'Chapter 3: The Jewish Diaspora', in *Compendia*, vol. 1, 152; Schürer, *History*, vol. 3.1, 120.

[105]If the reading is ὑμέτεροι at *AJ* 14.235 [14.10.17], Jewish citizens of Sardis alone would be intended. Comparison for date, form and content with the other documents *supra*, 88 n.102, disposes this writer to prefer ἡμέτεροι *contra* Trebilco, *Jewish Communities*, 169.

[106]See the details of the exemptions in the above-noted documents. Applebaum, 'Legal Status', 459 and A.M. Rabello, 'The Legal Condition of the Jews in the Roman Empire', *ANRW* II/13 (1980), 692, explain the exemptions and subsequent Roman practice.

[107]Ramsay, 'Tarsus', 156.

[108]See V.M. Scramuzza, 'Note 25. The Policy of the Early Roman Emperors Towards Judaism', in *BC*, vol. 5, 284. On the Hebrew dedicatory inscriptions at Sardis honouring the co-emperor Lucius Verus (*c.* 166 AD), see Trebilco, *Jewish Communities*, 44, 176 and 208 n. 23.

That Roman citizenship and participation in the Jewish faith were not mutually exclusive is also evident from the inscriptional evidence. Schürer mentions the Roman citizen Marcus Laelius Onasion who 'appears among the *archontes* [rulers] of the Jewish *politeuma* of Berenice in Asia Minor in a decree of (probably) AD 24'.[109] Far from being an honorary title or one that a Godfearer could possess, the office of ruler designated the chief leaders of Jewish Diaspora congregations. The rulers had responsibility for the community's general direction and were distinct from the synagogue-ruler whose functions were more religious.[110] The advantages to a Jewish community of having a congregational leader who possessed not only religious sensitivity but also Roman citizenship are obvious.

An inscription from Berenice of Cyrenaica, dated to the end of the 1st century BC or beginning of the 1st century AD, records the unanimous vote of honours to the Roman citizen Dec(i)mus Valerius Dionysios by the Jewish community and 'exemption from liturgies of every kind' which would otherwise need to be fulfilled.[111] Citizenship and active participation in the Jewish community go hand in glove.

Several relevant inscriptions have been unearthed in the city of Acmonia. A dedicatory inscription indicates that the synagogue there was built by the influential and sympathetic Gentile patroness Julia Severa who was active in the mid-1st century AD.[112] Mentioned also is the citizen P(ublius) Tyrronius Klados, who, with two others,[113] restored the synagogue from his own and the Jewish community's funds and donated items which further beautified it (*c.* 80-90 AD?). Klados is noted as 'the head for life of the synagogue'. The title 'head of the synagogue' (ἀρχισυνάγωγος) is the designation for the chief officer who supervised worship and synagogue business.[114] Once again, religious commitment and Roman citizenship stand together without apparent inconsistency.

---

[109]Schürer, *History*, vol. 3.1, 133 and 61.

[110]*Ibid.*, vol. 2, 435; H. Maccoby, *Judaism in the First Century* (Issues in Religious Studies; London: Sheldon, 1989), 60. *Contra* Lentz, *Luke's Portrait of Paul*, 46. Jairus in Luke 8:41 is one such ἄρχων (*cf.* Luke 12:11).

[111]*New Docs.*, vol. 4, #111 and see the extended discussion of R. Tracey there (pp. 203-9).

[112]See for the full text, Trebilco, *Jewish Communities*, 58f. and *cf.* Applebaum, 'Legal Status', 443; Ramsay, 'Tarsus', 157. A priestess of the Imperial cult and *agonothete*, it is very unlikely that Julia Severa was a Jew, or even an ex-Jew.

[113]They are the ἀρχισυνάγωγος Lucius and the ἄρχων Publius Zotikos.

[114]Acts 18:8; Schürer, *History*, vol. 2, 434-36 and nn. 26-31; Trebilco, *Jewish Communities*, 104-26; Maccoby, *Judaism*, 60f.

An Acmonian tomb inscription dating to 243/4 AD mentions one T(itus) Fl(avius) Alexandros who was 'a member of the Council' and 'Archon', having also been 'Warden of the Peace—Corn Purchaser. President of the Council—Clerk of the Market. Chief Magistrate—Corn Purchaser'.[115] The legislation would have permitted him to attain to these positions of civic responsibility without compromising his Jewish faith. The inscription's use of Deuteronomy shows that the family were practising Jews. Yet the name Titus Flavius is a quite clear indication that the family had possessed 'Roman citizenship for some 150 years and at least for the first 100 years were members of the privileged small minority of those who held the citizenship'.[116]

Evidence from inscriptions could be added, but the above suffice to demonstrate that one could maintain a strong Jewish faith alongside Roman citizenship. Our discussion, however, has not dealt with all the objections raised against Paul's citizenship. His frequent beatings and bonds and the lateness of his citizen appeals are discussed in the following chapters. The contention that Paul's Pharisaism casts doubt on his Hellenistic and Roman citizenship next occupies our attention.

III. Paul's Social Status as a Jew

The portrait that emerges from the NT documents[117] in terms of Paul's birth, social standing, offices, honours, wealth, character, moral uprightness, and education is primarily, though not exclusively, Jewish and religious. For three reasons it must be considered. First, in a significant portion of Acts (viz.: 21:30-26:32) the contexts of Roman judgements have a distinctively Jewish/religious aspect. Second, the claim

---

[115]Trebilco, *Jewish Communities*, 62f.

[116]*Ibid.*, 64.

[117]This section gathers information from both Acts and the generally acknowledged Pauline epistles. That 'the essential Paul', who lived in such variety of contexts, was complex, and that this is witnessed by the apparently disparate images found in our documents, has been forcefully argued by J. Jervell, *The Unknown Paul: Essays on Luke-Acts and Early Christian History* (Minneapolis: Augsburg, 1984), 52-76. For a survey of recent scholarship, A.J. Mattill Jr., 'The Value of Acts as a Source for the Study of Paul', in *Perspectives on Luke-Acts*, ed. C.H. Talbert (Edinburgh: T. and T. Clark, 1978), 76-98. Further, P. Vielhauer, 'On the "Paulinism" of Acts', in *Studies in Luke-Acts*, ed. L.E. Keck and J.L. Martyn (Nashville/New York: Abingdon, 1966), 33-50; M.S. Enslin, 'Once Again, Luke and Paul', *ZNW* 61 (1970), 253-71; F.F. Bruce, 'Is the Paul of Acts the Real Paul?' *BJRL* 59 (1976), 282-305.

to or imputation of religious power or prestige must certainly figure in any discussion of class, status and power.[118] Finally, this study is concerned to show the impact of variable weighting of aspects of Paul's social identity in different contexts when custody is being determined.

1. Birth Credentials

Paul asserts in Acts, 'I am a Jew' (Acts 21:39; 22:3). The epistles, consistent with this assertion, are even more emphatic concerning his pristine lineage in Judaism and its continuing significance: he is a descendant of Abraham (Rom: 11:1; 2 Cor. 11:22), an Israelite (Rom. 11:1; 2 Cor. 11:22; Phil. 3:5), and a member of the tribe of Benjamin (Rom. 11:1; Phil. 3:5). He asserts that he was circumcised on the eighth day (Phil. 3:5) and is a Hebrew of Hebrews[119] (Phil. 3:5; cf. 2 Cor. 11:22). Paul had impeccable birth credentials.

2. Educational Credentials

Though born in Tarsus, Paul's earliest upbringing and education probably took place in Jerusalem. Van Unnik has argued persuasively that the intent of Acts 22:3 is to convey the following information:

> 'I am a Jew, born at Tarsus in Cilicia, but my parental home, where I received my early upbringing, was in this city (Jerusalem); and under Gamaliel, a person well-known to you, I received a strict training as a Pharisee, so that I was a zealot for God's cause as ye all are to-day'....[120]

It is improbable that the phrase 'In my own country' at Acts 26:4 should be interpreted as a reference to Paul's early life in Cilicia. The term 'country' (ἔθνος) can hardly indicate the Jewish community there;[121] even less so can it refer to the Gentile nation of the Cilicians.[122] Harrison observes concerning the former notion:

---

[118]*Cf.* W.G. Runciman, 'Class, Status and Power?' in *Social Stratification*, ed. J.A. Jackson (Sociological Studies 1; Cambridge: CUP, 1968), 39.

[119]Probably a reference to Paul's facility in Hebrew/Aramaic (Acts 26:4; 21:40; 22:2; 26:14). So Bruce, 'The Real Paul', 285.

[120]W.C. van Unnik, *Tarsus or Jerusalem: The City of Paul's Youth*, tr. G. Ogg (London: Epworth, 1962), 44f.

If v. 4 depicts two separate stages; one covering Paul's life in Tarsus, indicated by ἐν τῷ ἔθνει μου, and the other a later stage expressly stated to have occurred in Jerusalem, then one is at a loss to understand how the words τὴν ἀπ᾿ ἀρχῆς γενομένην [from the beginning] can properly apply to both periods.[123]

He continues, 'It is also hard to understand how all Jews could have known of his life in a place as far removed as Tarsus'.[124] Paul would not seek to prove his Jewish orthodoxy by referring to an undifferentiated body of Cilician witnesses. The phrase designates co-religionists in Judaea ('my country'; ἔθνος μου) who can be called as witnesses to the character of his early life; particularly (τε) certain individuals in Jerusalem.[125]

Is rearing and education in Jerusalem consistent with those elements in his thought and manner of writing which indicate a Hellenistic background and education?[126] Some reject van Unnik's thesis because of a perceived inconsistency.[127] The underlying assumption is that Tarsus and not Jerusalem would have furnished such influences, but the dichotomy is probably false. Judge writes:

> To have been brought up in Tarsus need not have committed Paul to a full rhetorical education, let alone a philosophical one (both of which were a matter of tertiary training involving much time and money), while being brought up in Jerusalem need not have excluded

---

[121]So e.g., W. Neil, *The Acts of the Apostles* (NCB 42; London: Oliphants/Greenwood: Attic, 1973), 242. J. Munck, *The Acts of the Apostles*, tr. W.F. Albright and C.S. Mann (AB 31; Garden City: Doubleday, 1967), 241, allows this as a possibility.

[122]So e.g., N. Turner, *Grammatical Insights Into the New Testament*, (Edinburgh: T. and T. Clark, 1965), 84f., taking τε as a copula meaning no more than 'and'. Neil, *The Acts*, 242 allows this as a possibility.

[123]E.F. Harrison, 'Acts 22:3—A Test Case for Luke's Reliability', in *New Dimensions in New Testament Study*, ed. R.N. Longenecker and M.C. Tenney (Grand Rapids: Zondervan, 1974), 252.

[124]*Ibid.* Cf. van Unnik, *Tarsus or Jerusalem*, 46-48; R.P.C. Hanson, *The Acts in the Revised Standard Version* (New Clarendon Bible; Oxford: Clarendon, 1967), 237.

[125]So, e.g., G. Schneider, *Die Apostelgeschichte: II Teil* (HTKNT 5.2; Freiburg: Herders, 1982), vol. 2, 371; R. Pesch, *Die Apostelgeschichte* (EKKNT 5; Zurich: Benziger, 1986), vol. 2, 276.

[126]C. Forbes, 'Comparison, Self-Praise and Irony: Paul's Boasting and the Conventions of Hellenistic Rhetoric', *NTS* 32 (1986), 23, writes regarding the Corinthian correspondence: Paul's rhetoric possesses 'a mastery and an assurance unlikely to have been gained without long practice, and possibly long study as well'. Cf. B. Winter, 'The Importance of the *Captatio Beneuolentiae* in the Speeches of Tertullus and Paul in Acts 24:1-21', *JTS* 42 (1991), 505-31, for similar conclusions.

[127]E.g., Turner, *Grammatical Insights*, 83; Neil, *The Acts*, 223.

him from at least a general acquaintance with the Greek cultural tradition.[128]

It was possible to obtain in Jerusalem a religiously acceptable Jewish education informed by 'Greek elements'. The Diaspora synagogues of Jerusalem (Acts 6:9) were one means,[129] being the educational environment in which Paul and perhaps other NT authors grew up. Knowledge of Greek generally 'was no less established among the leading families of Jerusalem than in the scriptoria and the bazaars of the city or at the tables of the money changers in the temple forecourt'.[130] It was 'a prerequisite for upward social mobility, both in crafts and trade and in the service of the political powers, the Herodian rulers, the cities, the temple administration, and the other Jewish authorities and even more in the service of Rome'.[131]

Even orthodox Pharisaic educators were touched by Hellenism. Hengel and Markschies write: '...the multiform "Hellenistic" influence on the rabbis is manifest, and the early Pharisees were evidently more open to their "Hellenistic" environment than the rigoristic Essenes'.[132] The Talmud, discussing 'Grecian Wisdom', records:

> Did not Rab Judah say that Samuel stated in the name of R. Simeon b. Gamaliel: '[The words] *Mine eye affected my soul because of all the daughters of my city* [could very well be applied to the] thousand youths who were in my father's house; five hundred of them learned Torah and the other five hundred learned Grecian Wisdom, and out of all of them there remain only I here and the son of my father's brother in Asia'?—It may, however, be said that the family of R. Gamaliel was an exception, as they had associations with the government....[133]

Whether the above reference relates to Gamaliel I or to Gamaliel II,[134] a broader, more pragmatic and accommodating educational ex-

---

[128]E.A. Judge, 'St. Paul and Classical Society', *JAC* 15 (1972), 29. *Cf.* W.D. Davies, *Paul and Rabbinic Judaism: Some Rabbinic Elements in Pauline Theology* (1948; rev. ed., London: SPCK, 1955), 1-16.

[129]M. Hengel and C. Markschies, *The 'Hellenization' of Judaea in the First Century After Christ*, tr. J. Bowden (London: SCM/Philadelphia: Trinity, 1989), 13.

[130]*Ibid.*, 14. *Cf.* the comments in Sullivan, 'The Dynasty of Judaea', 346f. on Greek inscriptions found at Beth-Shearim.

[131]Hengel and Markschies, *The 'Hellenization'*, 17. *Cf. ibid.*, 26 on Tertullus

[132]*Ibid.*, 29. On the question of Pharisees in Galilee, see J.D.G. Dunn, 'Pharisees, Sinners, and Jesus', in *The Social World of Formative Christianity and Judaism: Essays in Tribute to Howard Clark Kee*, ed. J. Neusner *et al.* (Philadelphia: Fortress, 1988), 280f.

[133]b. B. Qam. 83a.

perience for Paul is certainly within the realm of 1st century AD Pharisaic possibility.

It was a logical choice for the young Paul's family to send him to Gamaliel for a thorough education in the Law (Acts 22:3). In the first instance, Gamaliel himself was, like Paul, a Benjaminite.[135] In the second, Gamaliel was arguably the most significant and influential Pharisaic educator in the early 1st century AD.[136] Third, Gamaliel had breadth of popular impact. The certain Gamaliel I traditions, according to Neusner,

> pertain to matters of common, and not merely sectarian, concern, such as exchanges of property in connection with inheritance, marriage and divorce, rules of evidence, witnesses in the Temple calendar process, and other public issues. The legal agenda of the Gamaliel-traditions conforms to that of a public official, rather than of a sectarian authority within Pharisaism. I therefore take it for granted that Gamaliel was both a Temple-council member, as Acts alleges [i.e., 5:34-40], and leader within the Pharisaic sect, as the rabbinic traditions hold.[137]

Gamaliel's enactments in the later tradition accord well with his speech in Acts in that they are consistently liberalizing and humanitarian.[138] It was later said of him: 'When Rabban Gamaliel the Elder died, the glory of the Torah ceased and purity and abstinence died'.[139]

Most objections to Paul's education at the feet of Gamaliel are more apparent than real.[140] Of the two more serious objections, the assertion that Paul's doctrine of Law could not have come from Palestine (i.e., from Gamaliel) because of its joylessness is founded upon the artificial characterizations of Palestinian and Diaspora Judaism critiqued elsewhere.[141] Those who question whether Paul's epistles demon-

---

[134]Gamaliel I; Judge, 'St. Paul', 29 (?). Gamaliel II; Forbes, 'Comparison', 23.

[135]J. Jeremias, *Jerusalem in the Time of Jesus*, tr. F.H. and C.H. Cave (London: SCM, 1969), 278 and n. 13 and 287.

[136]M. Stern, 'Chapter 11: Aspects of Jewish Society: The Priesthood and Other Classes', in *Compendia*, vol. 2, 618; J. Neusner, *The Rabbinic Traditions About the Pharisees Before 70: Part I—The Masters* (Leiden: Brill, 1971), vol. 1, 376.

[137]*Ibid.*, 376. See Neusner's compilation *ibid.*, 342-73.

[138]See W. White, 'Gamaliel', *ZPEB*, vol. 2, 649.

[139]*m. Sotie* 9.15. 'Abstinence', from the root פרשׁ, may be translated 'separateness' and suggests some relation to his Pharisaic vocation. See Neusner, *The Rabbinic Traditions*, 351f.; D.A. Hagner, 'Pharisees', *ZPEB*, vol. 4, 745.

[140]For a full discussion, see Harrison, 'Acts 22:3', 254f.

[141]Further, Davies, *Paul and Rabbinic Judaism*, 1-16; Harrison, 'Acts 22:3', 255-59.

strate sufficient technical sophistication to confirm rabbinic training under someone such as Gamaliel[142] have been answered by Jeremias. He notes striking similarities between Paul and the school of Rabban Hillel,[143] who may well have been the father or grandfather of Gamaliel I.[144]

Paul asserts that he is a Pharisee, a son of Pharisees (Acts 23:6). Many contend that Paul means an attachment to Pharisaism that is 'not merely a personal affair, but an ancient family tradition'.[145] Lentz, who adopts this interpretation, has argued that it raises two 'highly problematic questions: (1) were Pharisees found in the Diaspora? (2) how probable is it that Pharisees would also be citizens of a Greek city?'[146] He cites a personal communication from Neusner to the effect that Pharisees born overseas would, by definition, be unclean; that Pharisees would be frustrated in the drive to achieve cultic cleanness outside of the Holy Land; and that Paul is the sole case he can recall of a Pharisee in the further reaches of the Diaspora. Jeremias generally agrees.[147] The NT indicates that Pharisees were found in the cities of Galilee and Judaea, but evidence for Pharisee schools or communities in the Diaspora is scarce. Jesus speaks at Matt. 23:15 of the Pharisees who travel 'over land and sea' to make converts; but travel throughout the Diaspora, if this is intended, does not constitute settlement. It is possible that Eleazer, who lived in the kingdom of Adiabene on the boundaries of the Roman and Parthian states, was a Pharisee.[148] The Pharisee Hillel (fl. c. 20 BC) is called 'the Babylonian' and is said in rabbinic tradition to have come from Babylon.[149] He was well-trained prior to coming to Jerusalem and his purpose in coming, the traditions assert, was to resolve disputed points of Law. That he served an ap-

---

[142]E.g., M.S. Enslin, 'Paul and Gamaliel', *JRelS* 7 (1927), 360-75.

[143]J. Jeremias, 'Paulus als Hillelit', in *Neotestamentica et Semitica: Studies in Honour of Matthew Black*, ed. E.E. Ellis and M. Wilcox (Edinburgh: T. and T. Clark, 1969), 88-94.

[144]Jeremias, *Jerusalem*, 255 n. 32. *Contra* Neusner, *The Rabbinic Traditions*, vol. 1, 294f.

[145]Tajra, *The Trial of St. Paul*, 95. So also e.g., F.F. Bruce, *The Book of the Acts* (NICNT; 1954; rev. ed. Grand Rapids: Eerdmans, 1988), 427; G.A. Kroedel, *Acts* (Augsburg Commentary on the New Testament; Minneapolis: Augsburg, 1986), 425; H.F. Weiss, 'Φαρισαῖος', *TDNT*, vol. 9, 46 and n. 215.

[146]Lentz, *Luke's Portrait of Paul*, 54.

[147]Jeremias, *Jerusalem*, 252 n. 26.

[148]If ἀκρίβης means Pharisee; Josephus, *AJ* 20.38-41 [20.9.4].

[149]See the traditions and commentary in Neusner, *The Rabbinic Traditions*, 214, 220f., 242f., 246f., 254, 266f., 270, 273, 275.

prenticeship or immediately attained to a position of authority in Jerusalem cannot be determined and there is no explicit indication that he was a Pharisee in Babylon. Lentz concludes that, given the lack of further evidence, 'the suggestion that Paul was from a Pharisaic family from Tarsus can hardly be accepted without serious reservations'.[150]

It must be asked whether the text has been correctly construed in the first instance and, in the second, whether the problem Lentz identifies concerning Pharisees in the Diaspora is relevant in the case of Paul and his parents. Both questions would seem to demand a negative answer. Jeremias suggested that the phrase 'son of a pharisee' could equally be taken to mean that Paul 'was a pupil of Pharisaic teachers or a member of a Pharisaic association'.[151] This rendering, which connects Paul with a Pharisaic body, seems preferable on contextual grounds. Paul's purpose at Acts 23:6 is to identify himself with some of his hearers. It is surely more probable that he is claiming ties to this particular group of Pharisees within the Sanhedrin than telling them about the purity of his Pharisaic lineage (however true this last point might be). Regarding this second question, for Paul to claim a pristine Pharisaism from his earliest youth, his parents would need to make a commitment concerning both faith and practice in the home. But these claims can be encompassed within the Jerusalem phase of Paul's life without regard to Tarsus, as Acts 22:3 indicates. An increasing earnestness in the pursuit of the ideals of Pharisaism must be allowed for Paul during his Jerusalem phase; and it should not be denied to his parents as the family moves to Jerusalem. Such a move would surely eliminate the difficulties associated with practising Pharisaic Judaism in the Diaspora. Moreover, the inability to identify with certainty Pharisaic communities in the Diaspora need not force us to deny the pursuit of a less rigorous form of Pharisaism there. A rabbinic tradition of particular relevance describes how Gamaliel I directed that letters be written to 'our brethren' in Upper and Lower Galilee, in the Upper and Lower South, and in the Exile of Babylon, Media and 'the rest of all the Exiles of Israel'.[152] The burden of the letters is to inform these brethren of the times for collecting tithes of olives and wheat and to convey news of the sacrifices and intercalated month. Neusner indicates that the letters were probably not intended for all the Jews of the Land and the Diaspora, for this would usurp the authority of the Tem-

---

[150]Lentz, *Luke's Portrait of Paul*, 54.
[151]Jeremias, *Jerusalem*, 252 n. 26. *Cf. ibid.*, 177; Weiss, 'Φαρισαῖος', 46 and n. 215.
[152]Neusner, *The Rabbinic Traditions*, 356f., and *cf.* 360.

ple officials. He does, however, allow that 'it would be plausible to suggest that the Pharisees wrote to their *brethren*, as the letters specify, and that the concern of the party for proper tithing is herein reflected'.[153] At the very least, then, this reveals a geographically extended Pharisaic interest in the regulation of religious practices. The kind of Judaism practised in the Diaspora, Maccoby writes, was 'of the Palestinian type, i.e. Pharisaic on the whole (although there is evidence of a Samaritan Diaspora too), but modified by Hellenistic culture, as in Alexandria'.[154] These points should be considered alongside our previous observations concerning committed Diaspora Jews possessing Greek and Roman citizenship and the variable character of Palestinian Judaism, particularly the existence of a more relaxed Pharisaic Judaism than is usually allowed. This picture, when viewed as a whole, suggests that Lentz' questions are answerable.

The claim to have studied under Gamaliel I would, in itself, have been impressive. But Paul asserts further that he excelled in study and practice. He asserts at Acts 22:3, 'I ... was just as zealous for God as any of you are today'. His proof is the vigour with which he persecuted the followers of the Way. A widespread Jewish knowledge of the duration, vigour and purity of Paul's religious praxis is also asserted at Acts 26:5 (*cf.* 28:17): 'They have known me for a long time and can testify, if they are willing, that according to the strictest sect of our religion, I lived as a Pharisee'. The epistles give a similar impression.[155]

While Paul points to his life in Pharisaism without reference to his current status at Acts 26:5 ('I lived': ἔζησα), it is clear from Acts 23:6 that he is able to assert long after his conversion to Christianity, 'I am (εἰμί) a Pharisee'. Schneider claims that this can hardly be reconciled with Phil. 3:5-11,[156] but his assertion may be questioned. First, Paul is not unique in this respect: there were other believers in the church who were Pharisees (Acts 15:5).[157] Luke-Acts appears to make distinctions among the Pharisees, according to Sanders: some are favourably in-

---

[153]*Ibid.*, 357. Neusner will allow this explanation only to account for the brothers of the North and South, but not for the near and more distant Diaspora.

[154]Maccoby, *Judaism*, 33.

[155]Gal.1:14; Phil. 3:5.

[156]Schneider, *Die Apostelgeschichte*, 332.

[157]J.T. Sanders, 'Chapter 10. The Pharisees in Luke-Acts', in *The Living Text: Essays in Honor of Ernest W. Saunders*, ed. D.E. Groh and R. Jewett (Lanham/New York/London: University Press of America, 1985), 143 n. 7, indicates that while Luke's syntax makes it possible that the reference is here to ex-Pharisees, 'he apparently thinks rather of Christians who are also Pharisees...—or in any case, if they are somehow no longer Pharisees, the "no longer" is of little moment'.

clined to Jesus and the church, others are not. 'Paul's Pharisaism is, indeed, different from that of the Pharisaic Christians of Acts 15:5 as well as from that of the non-Christian friendly Pharisees; for Paul is a Pharisee *mutatis mutandis*—that is, he is a Christianized Pharisee, not a Pharisaic Christian'.[158] To say as Sanders does, however, that Paul is 'not affirming in any serious way his Pharisaic beliefs, he is just playing a trick on his audience'[159] at Acts 23:6 does not properly take into account the substantial compatibility of Pharisaism with Christianity.[160] Above all stands belief in resurrection. It is disingenuous to suggest that Paul's assertion of a Pharisaic commitment to the resurrection at Acts 23:6 is wholly explainable as rhetorical manipulation,[161] especially in light of Paul's reference to it in a later juridical context (*viz.*, Acts 24:21; *cf.* 26:7f.) and its centrality to his preaching and teaching in both the Acts and the Pauline epistles.

Second, Phil. 3:4-11 may be more nuanced than Schneider implies. Hawthorne writes that when Paul at Phil. 3:4

> proceeds to disparage personal assets which can make one proud and self-reliant, he does so not because he is a 'have-not,' a frustrated person lashing out in envy due to his own lack of resources or achievements, but because he is one who, although having everything, learned he had nothing, not having Christ.[162]

Paul admits in this passage to the real prospect of a present claim to distinction based upon his Pharisaism. It is not proper to weaken or explain away the force of the expression 'having confidence' (ἔχων πεποίθησιν) at Phil. 3:4; it is not that Paul 'might have confidence' or 'could have confidence' but that 'Paul fully intends to say that he does indeed (καί) have whatever it takes to boast in or rely upon himself'.[163] When he tells his readers that he can now claim Pharisaism as a basis for self-recommendation before God, 'Paul does not use the name Pharisee as a reproach, but as a title of honour'.[164] Paul's Phari-

---

[158] *Ibid.*, 166.

[159] *Ibid.*, 165.

[160] See A. Wikenhauser, *Die Apostelgeschichte* (RNT 5; 4th ed.; Regensburg: Friedrich Pustet, 1961), 251.

[161] As does Sanders, 'The Pharisees', 165. Cf., Hanson, *The Acts*, 165.

[162] G.F. Hawthorne, *Philippians* (Word Biblical Commentary 43; Waco: Word, 1983), 130.

[163] *Ibid.*, 131. So also J.B. Lightfoot, *Saint Paul's Epistle to the Philippians* (London/New York: Macmillan, 1900), 145.

[164] F.W. Beare, *The Epistle to the Philippians* (BNTC; 3rd ed.; London: A. and C. Black, 1973), 107.

saism, however, like all the other advantages of birth and voluntary choice which make him quintessentially Jewish, is entirely deficient as a basis for confidence before God. While it emphatically cannot save, Paul's Pharisaism nevertheless has a present significance and poses a present threat if not properly valued. Just as Paul at some point in the past (his conversion?) had settled in his own mind (Phil. 3:7) that his Pharisaic credentials as advantage were in reality a loss in the light of Christ, so he continues to count them thus (Phil. 3:8) and makes them, along with other advantages (and disadvantages such as being a persecutor!), an ongoing matter of forgetfulness (ἐπιλανθανόμενος: Phil. 3:13). This past and present transvaluation must inform our understanding of Paul's assertion that, 'I have lost all things'[165] (Phil. 3:8).

The above discussion supports Jervell's comment that Acts presents a Paul 'who remains a Pharisee after his conversion and never becomes an ex-Pharisee',[166] which is again confirmed by what Paul writes to the Philippians.[167] All that Christianity affirmed of his Pharisaism, Paul continued to embrace; all that in Pharisaism threatened the exclusiveness of Christ's salvific provision, he emphatically rejected. In this sense only can Paul be said to remain a Pharisee according to Philippians. He elsewhere does not deny his Jewish birth or circumcision (Rom. 3:1f.) and he apparently does not resist synagogal discipline despite its wrongful application (2 Cor. 11:24).[168] Hence, phrases such as 'Paul's renunciation of Judaism'[169] hardly describe what is taking place at Phil. 3:2-16.

---

[165]Would Paul *continue* counting his Pharisaism a loss if he had been disenfranchised? Voluntary renunciation makes better sense of the context.

[166]Jervell, *The Unknown Paul*, 71.

[167]So also Hanson, *The Acts*, 221; Neil, *The Acts*, 228.

[168]The forty lashes minus one was a disciplinary measure meant to restore one to brotherhood in the community and to spare one from capital punishment. Rabbis could be scourged for persistent obstinacy over points of law. This implies that during Paul's lifetime, Christianity and its leaders were looked upon by Jewish officials as still standing within Judaism, even in regard to the mission to the Gentiles. *Cf.* in this regard *m. Mak.* 2.15 and the discussion in A.J. Hultgren, 'Paul's Pre-Christian Persecutions of the Church: Their Purpose, Locale, and Nature', *JBL* 95 (1976), 101-4 and R.A. Stewart, 'Judicial Procedure in New Testament Times', *EvQ* 47 (1975), 99f.

[169]Beare, *The Epistle to the Philippians*, 102. See the contrasting position of H. Räisänen, *Paul and the Law* (WUNT 29; Tübingen: J.C.B. Mohr [Paul Siebeck], 1983), 175f. *Cf.* also Dunn, 'Pharisees', 271f. on blamelessness.

3. Political Credentials

The pre-Christian Paul's zeal for his ancestral traditions found expression in violent persecution of the Church. Luke portrays Paul not only seeking the followers of the Way in Jerusalem (Acts 7:58; 8:1-3; 9:1, 21; 22:2-4; 26:10) but also in foreign cities (Acts 9:1f., 14, 21; 22:5; 26:11f.). He pursues them in the synagogues and from house to house, beating them and trying to make them blaspheme (Acts 22:19; 26:11), imprisoning them (Acts 8:3; 9:21; 22:19; 26:10), and seeing to their conviction on capital charges in Jerusalem (Acts 9:1; 22:4; 26:10).

This portrayal of Paul the persecutor indicates something of his social standing and office. He is connected with the Sanhedrin, the principal juridical body of the ruling élite in Jerusalem. First, he is familiar with, and has access to, the highest levels of Jewish officialdom. He is able to obtain letters authorizing the pursuit of Christians in cities outside of Jerusalem from the high priest(s) (Acts 9:1; 22:5; cf. 9:15; 26:10) and the Sanhedrin (Acts 22:5; cf. Luke 22:66).[170] Second, Paul's persuasiveness before the ruling élite is seen in his personal initiation of at least part of the 'Diaspora' phase of the persecution. He secures authorization to persecute by personal petition to the high priest (Acts 9:1f.). This was not his first such mission: he states at Acts 26:11 that he went to 'foreign cities'. In the 'Jerusalem' phase of the persecution Paul was, at the very least, a major authorized force (Acts 8:1-3; 9:1, 21). Third, Paul's ability to secure such significant disciplinary and punitive powers over other Jews (Acts 26:12; cf. 9:14; 26:10) from the high priests and Sanhedrin is a significant measure of the official confidence placed in him.

Finally, Paul is, in some sense, an official agent of the Sanhedrin. One's understanding of the capacity in which he serves depends upon how one evaluates the letters. These letters are not addressed to the local officials of Damascus or the Romans but 'to the synagogues of Damascus' (Acts 9:2) and more specifically, 'to their [i.e., to the Jerusalem Sanhedrin's] brothers in Damascus' (Acts 22:5). More than mere letters of commendation, they authorize the use of punitive measures to dissuade Jews from following the Way and specifically mandate the ex-

---

[170]The fact that Paul recounts the authorization differently before different authorities is not problematic. This rather emphasizes the degree of co-operation and unanimity in the action. So G. Stählin, *Die Apostelgeschichte*, (NTD 5; 4th ed.; Göttingen: Vandenhoeck und Ruprecht, 1970), 134. *Cf.* R.N. Longenecker, 'The Acts of the Apostles', in *ExpBibCom*, vol. 9, 372; I.H. Marshall, *The Acts of the Apostles* (TNTC 5; Grand Rapids: Eerdmans, 1980), 215.

tradition of individuals to answer charges before the chief priests in
Jerusalem (Acts 9:2, 21; 22:5). The central question here is whether the
Jerusalem religious authorities could exercise jurisdiction over Jews
outside of Palestine. The case for such arrangements being based upon
the reciprocal extradition treaty between Simeon and Rome (1 Macc.
15:15-24) is weak owing to this document's distance in time and circumstances from Paul.[171] However, to argue in consequence of this
that the letters must be taken as an authorization to compel local Jewish co-operation in surreptitious extraditions[172] may also be misleading. Several factors indicate that the extraditions in Acts should be
construed as legal. Drawing commentary from mid- to late-1st century
AD rabbinic witnesses and set in the context of a discussion of capital
prosecutions, the Mishnah on the matter of jurisdiction states: 'The
Sanhedrin may conduct its office either within the Land [of Israel] or
outside the Land [of Israel]'.[173] Concerning Damascus,

> owing to the absence of any coins bearing the imperial impress be-
> tween the years 33-34 and 62-63, ... [it can be argued] that during this
> period Aretas and his successors held sway over the city and that it
> would have been to his advantage to afford Paul, as the agent of the
> Jerusalem Sanhedrin, power over such Jewish citizens in Damascus as
> were not Roman.[174]

Damascus had a large and powerful Jewish community,[175] and it is
reasonable to assume, therefore, that the secular authority would have
shown at least some regard for the legal claims of the Sanhedrin. According to Acts 9:23-25 and 2 Cor. 11:32f. Paul, after his conversion,
was the object of a city-wide manhunt sponsored by the governor of
Damascus under King Aretas and aided by the Jews. The good relations indicated by this level of co-operation increase the probability
that the extradition of Christians was legal and officially sanctioned.
We might add, in conclusion, that those who accompany Paul to Damascus (Acts 9:7f.; 22:9, 11; 26:14)—hardly just 'other members of the

---

[171]For discussion on this and other documents, see Rabello, 'The Legal Condition',
681-83; E. Haenchen, *The Acts of the Apostles: A Commentary*, ed. tr. B. Noble *et al.*
(Oxford, Basil Blackwell 1971), 320f. n. 2; Marshall, *The Acts*, 168.
[172]Hanson, *The Acts*, 112, offers that 'Paul was armed with official authorization
from the Sanhedrin to injure and even kidnap leading Christians, *if he could with
impunity*'. So also Marshall, *The Acts*, 168; Neil, *The Acts*, 127.
[173]*m. Mak.* 1:10.
[174]Enslin, 'Paul and Gamaliel', 374 n. 49, referring to Knox.
[175]Josephus, *BJ* 2.561 [2. 20.2]; 7.368 [7.8.7].

caravan'[176]—are probably Temple police[177] assigned by the high priests and Sanhedrin not only to lend dignity to Paul's mission but physically to enforce the punitive or custodial actions which Paul might call for. This further reinforces the impression that Paul's mission was public and official rather than clandestine. Regardless of the technical details of his commission, Paul clearly functions according to Acts as an agent of the Jerusalem Sanhedrin.

Paul's involvement in formal Sanhedral proceedings also appears to be indicated. Uncertainties surround the legality of the proceedings which culminate in the death of Stephen (Acts 7f.)[178] as well as Paul's part in them.[179] At the least, the text puts Paul in close proximity with Sanhedral actions and shows him approving of (Acts 8:1) Stephen's death. Acts 26:10, however, is quite clear on Paul's participation in Sanhedral proceedings against Christians. There Paul is recorded as having said that when Christians (note that Paul refers to more than just Stephen's case) were found liable to the death penalty,[180] 'I cast a vote against' them (κατήνεγκα ψῆφον). Taken in conjunction with 'vote' (ψῆφος), a word which can denote the pebble 'used in voting, in juries and elsewh., a black one for conviction, a white one for acquittal'[181] and by metonymy signifying the vote cast, the verb in question (καταφέρω) denotes not bringing a charge (Acts 25:7) but casting a vote against. A similar expression is used in Josephus' record of Jeremiah's troubles with the Jewish leadership.[182] The clearly juridical context of Acts 22:6 (and the fact that Paul speaks in Roman hear-

---

[176]Munck, The Acts, 81.

[177]See the comment of Stählin, Die Apostelgeschichte, 134.

[178]Mention of witnesses indicates that the trial itself was legally conducted (Acts 6:11, 13f.; 7:58). It is suggested, however, that if so, the mourning of the men who buried Stephen (Acts 8:2) would have been forbidden. Note the stoning procedure and the part played by the witnesses at m. Sanh. 6.4. Cf. Enslin, 'Paul and Gamaliel', 373 n. 47; Hanson, The Acts, 103; Neil, The Acts, 120; C.S.C. Williams, A Commentary on the Acts, 112; Schneider, Die Apostelgeschichte, vol. 1, 477.

[179]For discussion see Enslin, 'Paul and Gamaliel', 373 n. 47; Williams, Commentary on the Acts of the Apostles, (BNTC 5; London: A. and C. Black, 1964), 112; Longenecker, 'The Acts', 352.

[180]This does not necessarily preclude the involvement of the Roman authorities in subsequently ratifying such death sentences. On Jewish capital jurisdiction, see discussion in K. Lake and H.J. Cadbury, The Acts of the Apostles: English Translation and Commentary, in BC, 4: 317; Hanson, The Acts, 238; Marshall, The Acts, 393; Rabello, 'The Legal Condition', 737f.; Schürer, History, vol. 2, 206.

[181]For examples, see BAGD, 892; LSJ, 2023 [II.5.a].

[182]Josephus, AJ 10.92f. [10.6.2]. Cf. Aristotle, Rh. Al. 1437a.19f.; Josephus, AJ 10.60 [10.4.2].

ing!) hardly commends the notion that this is a figure of speech denoting unofficial action.[183] On this evidence it appears that Paul was a full member of the Sanhedrin.[184]

Paul's awareness of the Sadduceean and Pharisaic make-up of the Sanhedrin (Acts 23:6),[185] the evident familiarity of his salutation to its members (Acts 23:1), and the fact that he can appeal to its collective memory of his past faithfulness (Acts 22:5), also suggest a long-standing and close past connection with the Sanhedrin. The Lukan evidence shows Paul to be both a prominent Pharisee and a full member of the Sanhedrin.

A number of observations concerning the make-up and means of preferment in the Sanhedrin give further insight into Paul's political credentials. The Sanhedrin was tripartite. The monarchy having disappeared, the Sanhedrin initially grew out of the union of the non-priestly heads of families in Jerusalem—the 'secular nobility'—with the priestly aristocracy. About the mid-1st century BC, under Queen Alexandra, who held Pharisaic convictions, scribes of the Pharisees began to be admitted.[186] The Sadduceean theological perspective was typically embraced by the heads of the chief priestly families and the leaders of the lay aristocracy,[187] except where Pharisaism was politically expedient.[188] The lay aristocracy who enjoyed membership in the Sanhedrin were from among the wealthiest families of Jerusalem.[189] The Pharisees, on the other hand, were originally more a religious party. They numbered about 6,000 in Josephus' day.[190] Apart from the chief priests and members of patrician families, only scribes could become members of the Sanhedrin. As such, the Pharisaic party in the Sanhedrin was composed entirely of scribes.[191] That Paul excelled in the Law

---

[183]*Contra* Lake and Cadbury, *BC*, 317.

[184]He would not have been only a zealous student; students could only speak for acquittal and not for condemnation.

[185]See Pesch, *Die Apostelgeschichte*, 243. Paul's ignorance concerning the identity of the acting high priest (Acts 23:4f.) is explained, according to Hemer, *The Book of Acts*, 192f., by the fact that Paul 'had not been physically present in Jerusalem for some five years, and that his preceding visits as a Christian had probably been discrete and private, even if he participated unobtrusively in the crowded festivals'.

[186]Jeremias, *Jerusalem*, 222f.

[187]*Ibid.*, 225, writes that in the pre-70 AD period, this group 'formed a small close circle'.

[188]See *ibid.*, 265 and the passages in Josephus Jeremias cites there.

[189]*Ibid.*, 228.

[190]Josephus, *AJ* 17.42 [17.2.4].

[191]Jeremias, *Jerusalem*, 236.

beyond his peers would have strongly recommended him as a candidate.

Jeremias asserts that 'sociologically speaking, there is no question of including the Pharisees among the upper classes'.[192] Black has indicated that by the 1st century AD Pharisaism generally had become a bourgeois rather than a popular movement.[193] If wealth was increasingly a hallmark of the Pharisees, one might expect them to furnish the most intelligent and wealthy of their members to the Sanhedrin. It is of more than passing interest that Josephus refers to the Pharisees in the Sanhedrin at one place as the 'most notable' (γνώριμος),[194] which often denotes the wealthy.[195] While one cannot state categorically that only the wealthiest Pharisees were accepted into the Sanhedrin, wealthy Pharisees are nevertheless identifiable.[196] Keeping in mind what has already been said concerning indications of wealth in the family of Paul, this may well have been another factor recommending Paul above others.

Finally, it helped to have connections with powerful individuals in the Sanhedrin. Seating, as indicated in *m. Sanh.* 4.3f., was arranged according to seniority. Selection was undertaken with a view to the relative merits of the candidates. Before the seventy-one judges, *m. Sanh.* continues,

> sat three rows of disciples of the Sages, and each knew his proper place. If they needed to appoint [another as a judge], they appointed him from the first row, and one from the second row came into the first row, and one from the third row came into the second; and they chose yet another from the congregation and set him in the third row. He did not sit in the place of the former, but he sat in the place that was proper for him.[197]

---

[192]*Ibid.*, 246.

[193]M. Black, 'Pharisees', *IDB*, vol. 3, 781.

[194]Josephus, *BJ* 2.411 [2.17.3].

[195]Josephus uses both adjective and substantive. Note also particularly *AJ* 2.214 [2.9.3] where Jacob's γνώριμος is fully attributable to his great εὐδαιμονία; and *AJ* 8.172 [8.6.5] where the Queen of Sheba, seeing all the tangible results of Solomon's wisdom, speaks of 'the dignity [γνώριμος] of your state'. *Cf.* LSJ, 355.

[196]*E.g.* Nicodemus (John 3:1, 10; 19:39). Simeon, 'a native of Jerusalem, of a very illustrious family, and of the sect of the Pharisees' is extremely wealthy (he bribes the high priest and his party) and can be safely adjudged a member of the Sanhedrin based his actions in Josephus, *Vita* 189-203 [38-40]. Two Pharisees from 'the lower ranks' (οἱ δημοτικοί) also appear in this text.

We can assume from the aristocratic character of the Sanhedrin that membership did not change yearly and election was not by the populace, as in the democratic councils of the Greek cities. Offices were held for a longer period; perhaps for life. New members were appointed by existing members, by the secular political authorities, or by some combination of these two.[198] The Pharisees generally appear to have had the great power in the Sanhedrin. Whether or not Gamaliel I was president of the Sanhedrin,[199] his considerable influence in that body and among his own Pharisee brethren as indicated in the NT and Tannaitic traditions is indisputable. As such, he could have readily promoted a star pupil such as Paul. Moreover, Paul could be expected to have quickly progressed through the ranks of the disciples of the Sages.

4. Occupation and Indications of Wealth

While we have no explicit indication of Paul's financial resources in Tarsus, the implicit evidence suggests that they were significant. He appears to have been a man of means in the Jerusalem context as well. On his return to Jerusalem, James and the elders of the church suggest that he personally assist four Jewish Christians in fulfilling their Nazarite vows (Acts 21:23f.).[200] This would demonstrate Jewish loyal-

---

[197]The manner of the Great Sanhedrin's seating may be diagrammed as follows:

```
                President (P)                    X  P  X
Sanhedrin:      The Seventy (X)          X                      X
                Scribes (S)          X       s        s             X
                Highest Rank (D)     DDDDDDDDDDDDDDDDDDDDDDDDD
Disciples of Sages:  Middle Rank (d)   dddddddddddddddddddddddddddddddddd
                Lowest Rank (d)       dddddddddddddddddddddddddddddddddddddd
Congregation (c):                     ccccccccccccccccccccccccccccccccccccccccccc
```

Stewart, 'Judicial Procedure', 95, writes: 'Criminal cases in general required a Lesser Sanhedrin of twenty-three—the Talmud [t. Sanh. 17ᵇ] further demands two reporting clerks and two ushers, who also had to administer any necessary scourgings. These courts were free and mobile, whereas the Great Sanhedrin of seventy-one was tied to Jerusalem'.

[198]So Schürer, History, vol. 2, 211.

[199]S. Safrai, 'Chapter 7: Jewish Self-Government', in Compendia, vol. 1, 386-89, allows that Gamaliel I and other Pharisees did at various times lead the Sanhedrin in the capacity of president. Neusner, The Rabbinic Traditions, vol. 1, 375, expresses considerable doubt.

[200]For a discussion of how to construe the Lukan report in light of legislation on the circumstances of Nazarite vows (m. Nazir passim; m. Ker. 2.1) and Paul's ceremonial uncleanness in having been abroad, see Haenchen, The Acts, 611f.; Conzelmann, Acts, 180; Hanson, The Acts, 211.

ties to a suspicious Jewish Christian church. To pay a Nazarite's expenses expressed great piety. Significant examples can be found in Alexander Jannaeus (103-76 BC) who yielded to the encouragements of Simeon ben Shetah and paid the expenses of 150 Nazarites. Agrippa I, at the celebration of his accession in 41 AD, also showed his piety in this way.[201] The individual who paid the vow incurred a considerable expense (cf. Num. 6:13-21; m. Nazir 6.6-11), Paul must therefore have had considerable personal means in Jerusalem with which to render such assistance.

Paul's ability to keep himself for two years in Caesarea, his standing and entourage as a prisoner to Rome, his occupation of private lodgings in Rome, and Felix' hoped-for bribe are all additional indicators of Paul's financially privileged position,[202] but their significance can only be assessed after considering Paul's encounter with ancient custodial deliberations and prison life. Discussion is therefore reserved until later.

Paul's epistles, aside from referring to working with his hands and celebrating the freedom won thereby (1 Cor. 4:12; 2 Cor. 11:27; 1 Thess. 2:9; 2 Thess. 3:6-10), say nothing of his specific occupation. Acts, however, affirms that he plied a trade (Acts 20:33-35) and specifies that he was a σκηνοποιός (Acts 18:3). This term, appearing only this once in the NT, is also rare in non-NT sources. Michaelis writes:

> ...one cannot rule out the possibility that σκηνοποιός is used for the trade of "tent-maker." For one thing this meaning is wholly within the range allowed by the etymology and it is indeed the most natural, since a construct with –ποιός can hardly denote a casual and not a permanent activity.[203]

It has become popular to explain that Paul was a weaver of tent-cloth made either 1) from goat's hair (cilicium) which had associations with his home province of Cilicia,[204] or 2) from linen, weavers being subsidiary to the linen industry based in Tarsus.[205] The points against these explanations, however, are weighty. In the first instance, the principal objective behind the assertion that Paul was a weaver is to connect him with materials from Tarsus and Cilicia. But cilicium was

---

[201]On Alexander, see Schürer, History, vol. 1, 221f.; on Agrippa, see Josephus, AJ 19.294 [19.6.1].

[202]Cf. Hemer, The Book of Acts, 192; Neil, The Acts, 220; and many others.

[203]W. Michaelis, 'σκηνή κτλ.', TDNT, vol. 7, 393.

[204]Cf. R.F. Hock, The Social Context of Paul's Ministry: Tentmaking and Apostleship (Philadelphia: Fortress, 1980) 72f. n. 9 for those subscribing to this view.

used neither exclusively nor principally for the manufacture of tents and the same can be said of linen. Trying to connect Paul with Tarsus/ Cilicia in this way is irrelevant. He moved to Jerusalem while still very young and he is unlikely to have learned a trade until he began his formal theological training there (Acts 22:3). The fact that the same occupation is ascribed to Aquila and Priscilla though they are from Pontus shows the link to be unnecessary. Second, weaving is clearly indicated as a task for women which, when undertaken by men, became a despised trade. Men who engaged in this trade were disqualified from the high priesthood; their quarter in Jerusalem was the neighbourhood of the Dung Gate; and they were often considered unreliable witnesses. It is therefore highly improbable that Paul would have chosen to be, or have been trained as, a weaver by profession. Finally, the notion of Paul the weaver raises practical difficulties. Tools and equipment for weaving were quite inconvenient in size, weight and shape.[206] They do not match the highly mobile Paul portrayed in Acts.

It seems best to understand that Paul was a leather-worker. First, tents during the period with which we are concerned were usually made of leather and not textiles.[207] Second, the earliest versional renderings noted above by and large presume that Paul's trade, whatever it actually entailed, had something to do with working leather. Third, while tanning was considered an unclean trade,[208] no stigma attached to the Jew who worked already-prepared leather. Finally, the tools needed to work leather, certainly less onerous a burden to carry from place to place than weaver's equipment, lend themselves well to the picture of Paul found in Acts.[209] We may cite Hock's comments in summary:

---

[205]Lampe, 'Paulus—Zeltmacher', BZ 31 (1987), 256-61; S. Applebaum, 'Chapter 13: The Social and Economic Status of the Jews in the Diaspora', in Compendia, vol. 2, 717. Jeremias, Jerusalem, 5 and n. 2, 66 and n. 8, however, presents convincing arguments that the rationale for the synagogue of the Tarsians was not guild/artisan- but civic/national/linguistic-based.

[206]For pictures of Egyptian and Greek weavers' looms and equipment, see illustrations found in H.L. Roth, Ancient Egyptian and Greek Looms (Bankfield Museum Notes 2/2; Halifax: F. King and Sons, 1913), 41.

[207]So Applebaum, 'Social and Economic Status', 716 and n. 7; Hock, Social Context, 21 and sources cited 73 n. 16; Haenchen, The Acts, 534 n. 3.

[208]Lake and Cadbury, BC, 111f.; Jeremias, Jerusalem, 5f. A. Burford, Craftsmen in Greek and Roman Society (Aspects of Greek and Roman Life; London: Thames and Hudson, 1972), 77f., writes that the Greeks and Romans also excluded tanneries from the city and the smell of the tanner and the stench of his establishment were frequently the butt of cruel joking.

Leatherworking, then, was Paul's trade; the specialized title 'tentmaker' reflects a widespread tendency among artisans to use specialized titles, even though they made more products than their titles would suggest. We may thus picture Paul as making tents and other products from leather.[210]

IV. The Implications

The evidence discussed above shows that apostasy was not a *sine qua non* for Jewish acquisition of Greek citizenship, and religious Diaspora Jews did not inevitably remain completely aloof from political life in the Hellenistic city. Nor did Mediterranean society invariably demand uniformity of religious praxis. It is therefore unnecessary to reduce Paul's claim in Acts to something less than full citizenship or to suggest that Paul clothed himself (or was clothed by Luke!) in the prestige of a falsely claimed Tarsian citizenship.

This is not, however, to rule out of hand the possibility that the Jewish faith of Paul and his forbears may, in some Tarsian eyes, have been considered an impediment to be counterbalanced before Greek citizenship could be granted. A wealthy and supportive Jewish community in which Paul's family was a member would certainly have helped, on the understanding of an *en bloc* citizen grant. It will also be recalled that Tarsian citizenship on the basis of land ownership was set up some time before Paul's birth. Material recommendations and generosity to civic enterprises from Paul's family may have been needed in even greater measure if one assumes the acquisition of Greek citizenship by means of an individual or family grant.[211]

Our evidence does not permit us to say that Jewish acquisition of Roman citizenship was common. But even saying that it was rare hardly denies Roman citizenship to Paul. His claim in Acts to a dual citizenship from birth is entirely defensible. The apostle's Roman family name and the context and manner of its first appearance suggest that we are dealing with a citizen. Some assert that Roman citizenship and a serious Jewish faith are mutually incompatible and hence Paul could not have been a citizen. The evidence cited above has demonstrated

---

[209]So Hock, *Social Context*, 33 and 25, who notes the knives, awls, sharpening stones, and oil and blacking of the shoemaker's shop. For illustrations of Greek and Roman shoemakers' shops and instruments, see Burford, *Craftsmen, figs.* 3-7.

[210]Hock, *Social Context*, 21.

[211]*Cf.* Bruce, *The Book of Acts,* 432 and n. 40; Tcherikover, *Hellenistic Civilization,* 327.

that, while tensions invariably arose, simultaneous possession of a vigorous Jewish faith and the Roman franchise was indeed possible.

Paul, born to a dual citizenship, was no doubt unusual. With such significant and official stamps of approval upon him he was also privileged. His Hellenistic citizenship would have garnered great legal and financial advantages in Cilicia, and particularly in Tarsus. It is small wonder that he is found in Tarsus and in Cilicia from time to time in Acts. What of the impact of his Hellenistic citizenship outside of his home province? We have seen that the Tarsus of Paul's boast was politically, economically and intellectually a worthy object of pride and that it had a good reputation and influence abroad. As such, Paul might reasonably have expected the Tribune to be sufficiently impressed with this element of his identity to accord him a more respectful treatment. Properly revealed, Paul's Roman citizen birth-status would have opened to him legal and social advantages in many places in the Empire.

By every social measure which a Jew might use, Paul possessed great advantages. His birth credentials were impeccable. He also possessed pristine educational credentials. Not only had he studied with one of the greatest and most influential Pharisees of the century in the Holy city, he had distinguished himself. The political credentials of his pre-Christian years were also significant. Familiar with and having ease of access to the highest levels of Jewish leadership, Paul exercised a persuasive power and inspired sufficient confidence to merit the responsibilities of an authorized agent of the Sanhedrin. An individual coming from a family of some means, a student of one of the Sanhedrin's most august members, and distinguished as he was in learning, Paul would have been a full voting member of the Sanhedrin—numbered among the seventy-one.

The estimations we have noted above, however, are all Jewish. Outside of the conflict and animosity which Paul's commitment to Jesus brought him, it would be safe to say that in Jerusalem and Judaea, as well as the Jewish communities of the Diaspora, Paul would have counted as a man of high social status. The non-Jewish assessment of Paul, however, would have been very different. Rokeah indicates that

> the attitude of writers from the middle of the second century B.C.E. onwards, such as Lysimachus, Apollonius Molon and Poseidonius, seems to be one of 'hostile misunderstanding'. An anti-Semitic literature along the line of the *Acts of the Alexandrian Martyrs* and the invectives of Apion emerged gradually against the backdrop of the

struggle between the Jews and the Greeks in Egypt for privileges and social and political status in the first centuries of Roman rule. As for Cicero and Tacitus, one may perhaps include their views in the category of 'hostile misunderstanding'.[212]

Greek and Roman sources clearly show that Jewish monotheism, with its contempt for idolatry and idolaters, insistence upon a strict adherence to Sabbath observance, food laws and circumcision, and the evident success that it had in proselytism among polytheists, was a cause of anti-Semitism.[213] While Gentile officials in Jerusalem might have some regard for Jewish social credentials, officials in a predominantly or exclusively Gentile context would hardly have been impressed. Status, as we have argued previously, is measured on a shifting scale; it is a matter of both perspective and context.

The social implications of Paul's being a manual worker, a labourer who exploited a skill or craft to maintain himself, are significant—even if his financial circumstances in Jerusalem and Tarsus were quite comfortable. While such a labourer might generally share with others of his kind a positive attitude towards his profession, while his handiwork might be greatly admired for its quality or beauty, and while he himself might become wealthy from his labour or as a businessman with labourers in his employ, he was, to the eyes of better Greeks and Romans, a figure to be despised.[214] Small towns and cities might possess a higher regard, but in the bigger cities the prejudice would have been more constantly present. Beyond the stigma of working with one's hands can also be placed the stigma of rootlessness which this often implied. The labourer might have the advantages of freedom from some civic duties in the cities where he plied his trade, and of being able to remove himself from civic misfortunes. However justice, owing to the double stigma, might be uncertain if he were ac-

---

[212]D. Rokeah, *Jews, Pagans and Christians in Conflict* (Studia Post-Biblica 33; Jerusalem: Magnes/Leiden: Brill, 1982) 56f. *Cf.* W. Wiefel, 'The Jewish Community in Ancient Rome and the Origins of Roman Christianity', in *The Romans Debate*, ed. K.P. Donfried (Minneapolis: Augsburg, 1977), 102-5.

[213]See the sources cited and commented upon by M. Whittaker, *Jews and Christians: Graeco-Roman Views* (Cambridge Commentaries on Writings of the Jewish and Christian World 6; Cambridge: CUP, 1984), 3-134; M. Stern, 'Chapter 24: The Jews in Greek and Latin Literature', in *Compendia*, vol. 2, 1101-59.

[214]Burford, *Craftsmen*, 12f., 27, 157 *et passim* who cites Cicero, *Off.* 1.150 as one of many ancient sources expressing such negative sentiments. *Cf.* M. Maxey, *Occupations of the Lower Classes in Roman Society* (Chicago: CUP, 1938) in *Two Studies on the Roman Lower Classes*, M.E. Park and M. Maxey (Roman History; New York: Arno, 1975).

cused of transgressing the law, and any share in the city's good fortune would almost certainly be denied him.

Hock observes that the negative assessment of such workers was not only common to the secular view but also appears in ancient Christian discussions of Paul: 'Chrysostom concluded from Acts 18:3 that Paul "was not from a distinguished family. For how is that possible, if he had such an occupation?" Rather, Paul was just a "common man" (ἀγοραῖος) (*De laud. S. Pauli* 4.494 [PG 50:491])'.[215] Modern attempts to resolve the social tension of an apostle who was at once a man possessing dual citizenship and a 'common labourer' have been varied: emphasizing the importance of the status implications of his dual citizenship,[216] expunging from the text the offending low status indication,[217] or, as Chrysostom did, simply consigning Paul to the lower orders.[218] Paul's tentmaking skills may well have been learned as a necessary part of rabbinic training[219] or as a part of his parental upbringing.[220] In Jewish eyes, Paul the manual labourer was probably beyond reproach. He is at home with the more prosperous levels of society, and his aristocratic origin and 'self perception' may well be discernible in the terminology he uses to refer to his trade and its conditions.[221]

To one extent or another, all of the above studies attempt to resolve the tension in favour of a single-status Paul either by emphasis, explanation, or subtraction. A strong possibility, however, is that indications of status tension—described elsewhere as 'status dissonance' or 'low status crystallization'[222]—far from needing resolution, must be

---

[215]R.F. Hock, 'Paul's Tentmaking and the Problem of His Social Class', *JBL* 97 (1978), 556 n. 11 and note other citations there.

[216]See those cited by Hock, 'Paul's Tentmaking', 557.

[217]So Lentz, *Luke's Portrait of Paul*, 102f., who nevertheless is confronted with the fact that Paul attests in Acts (20:34) and epistles (1 Cor. 4:12; 2 Cor. 11:27; 1 Thess. 2:9; 2 Thess. 3:7f.) to his manual labour.

[218]See the simple journeyman picture described by A. Deissmann, *Paul: A Study in Social and Religious History*, tr. W.E. Wilson (London: Hodder and Stoughton, 1926), 48-51. *Cf.* Stegemann, 'War der Apostel Paulus', 226-28.

[219]Argued, for example, by Jeremias, *Jerusalem*, 112f.; M. Dibelius and W. Kümmel, *Paul*, tr. F. Clark (London/New York/Toronto: Longmans Green, 1953), 37. *Contra* Hock, *Social Context*, 22f.

[220]So Hock, *Social Context*, 23-25.

[221]Hock, 'Paul's Tentmaking', 558-64.

[222]G.E. Lenski, 'Status Crystallization: A Non-Vertical Dimension of Social Status', *American Sociological Review* 19 (1954), 405-13; W.A. Meeks, *The First Urban Christians: The Social World of the Apostle Paul* (New Haven/London: Yale University Press, 1983), 22f.

appreciated in terms of the extent to which they can account for Paul's treatment; particularly how he fares in crisis situations and resultant custodial evaluations.

PART 2

PAUL ON TRIAL IN ACTS

CHAPTER 5

PHILIPPI

The trial account in Acts 16 is realistic: the magistrates do not show undue favour, the 'crowd' plays a juridically legitimate role and the actions taken against Paul and Silas are legal. This reassessment depends on a recognition of the influence of social status on legal privilege in Roman law and on a closer scrutiny of Paul's behaviour.

The charges of disturbing the peace and proselytism had merit from the magistrates' perspective. The accused, presented as disenfranchised Jews and strangers to the community, were of no account. The accusers, on the other hand, were Romans and hence merited greater consideration. The Philippian magistrates' mandate is entirely consistent with the information provided them. Kept ignorant of Paul's and Silas' Roman identities, the magistrates have acted 'fairly'.

Paul's failure to assert his citizenship at the earliest possible time is the surface cause of the negative assessment of the magistrates. To declare his citizenship then would compromise his Jewishness, his Gospel message, and the fledgling Philippian church; to submit would, though preserving his religious integrity, give a false impression of his status and result in a public physical and social assault. Paul chose the latter course because, though a Roman, he had resolved to honour his religious and missiological commitments.

Uncharacteristically, Luke goes out of his way to introduce the legal/technical status of Philippi, clearly warning his reader that Paul and Silas run into trouble in a thoroughly Roman context. Philippi was both a leading city of the district of Macedonia and a Roman colony. Its dominant Roman minority—initially veterans and displaced Italians[1]—possessed the right of self-government structured and operated according to Roman law, freedom from tribute and taxation, and, by a fiction, the same personal legal position as those living on Italian soil.[2] Latin was the official spoken language and the language of administrative enactments.[3]

I. The Charges

The triggering event of the troubles at Philippi was Paul's exorcism of the python spirit from a slave girl. With its departure went the girl's fortune-telling ability and any income she might have generated for her owners. Paul and Silas were subsequently dragged before the authorities and charged.

As the aggrieved owners of the girl could hardly make a case by alleging property damage, they constructed other charges. How would they have known the apostles were Jews and the purpose of their stay in Philippi? Acts 16:17 indicates that the slave girl cried out that the apostles were servants of the 'highest God'. OT and extra-biblical literary sources as well as inscriptional materials show that the title 'Highest' and 'Highest God' were used by Jews for Jahweh and were also found on the lips of pagans. The examples do not, however, hark back 'above all to the religious speech of the Jews' as often claimed,[4] but describe Zeus or other pagan deities.[5] The *pagan* connotation of this title accounts for Paul's disquiet and the exorcism and renders more likely the prospect of the slave girl's actually having

---

[1]P. Lemerle, *Philippes et la Macédoine orientale à l'époque chrétienne et byzantine. Recherches d'histoire et d'archéologie* (Bibliothèque des Écoles françaises d'Athènes et de Rome 158; Paris: E. de Boccard, 1945), 13; Lake and Cadbury, *BC*, vol. 4, 187.

[2]*Dig.* 50.15.6: 'Colonia Philippensis iuris Italici est'. Further, Lake and Cadbury, *BC*, 190; E. Haenchen, *The Acts of the Apostles: A Commentary*, ed. tr. B. Noble *et al.* (Oxford: Basil Blackwell, 1971), 494 n. 2 and sources there cited.

[3]Lemerle, *Philippes*, 13. Further on Philippi, see D.W.J. Gill, 'Macedonia', in *The Book of Acts in Its Graeco-Roman Setting*, ed. D.W.J. Gill and C. Gempf (A1CS 2; Grand Rapids: Eerdmans/Carlisle: Paternoster, 1994), 411-13.

[4]BAGD, 850. For further examples, see P.R. Trebilco, 'Paul and Silas—"Servants of the Most High God" (Acts 16.16-18)', *JSNT* 36 (1989), 63 and 72 n. 69.

used this expression.[6] Luke, Trebilco argues, is sensitive to the pagan usage.[7] But would most pagans, on hearing this title, have thought exclusively in terms of Zeus or some other pagan deity as Trebilco claims?[8] Would the pagans have been ignorant of the title's Jewish usage? This seems unlikely. There is some evidence for a 'non-Jewish' use of the expression which is either influenced by Judaism or shows an awareness that a title such as this was used for the God of the Jews.[9] Horsley's suggestion that Acts 16:17 may show an 'overlapping of the Jewish and Greek influences'[10] commends itself. It is at least as likely that Paul's concern and the resulting exorcism arose from the threat of Philippian confusion as that he was upset by outright misunderstanding. The owners' knowledge of the apostles' Jewish identity could then have arisen, if not entirely, then at least in part,[11] from the girl's rantings regarding their connection with 'the highest God'

No Gentile mission had been initiated in Philippi by the apostles at the point of the uproar—only godfearers had been converted according to the text.[12] This fits Paul's usual pattern according to which only when Jews (and godfearers) had refused the Gospel did he proselytize among the Gentiles. The deduction of proselytizing among the populace of Philippi may also in part have arisen from the girl's assertion that Paul and Silas were announcing a 'way to be saved' (Acts 16:17).[13]

Two distinct yet related charges were constructed in order to do maximum damage to the apostles. First, they were accused of seriously upsetting (Acts 16:20) the city. Bringing together the charge of fostering civil disturbance with the apostles' Jewishness may reflect an

---

[5]P.R. Trebilco, *Jewish Communities in Asia Minor* (SNTSMS 69; Cambridge/New York: CUP, 1991), 127-44, opposes the notion that most pagan instances of this title in Asia Minor and elsewhere derive from Jewish influence.

[6]Trebilco, 'Paul and Silas', 51-73 and particularly 58.

[7]Trebilco, *Jewish Communities*, 130f.

[8]*Ibid.*, 144.

[9]*Ibid.*, 137-40. For additional examples showing some Jewish influence, see *New Docs.*, vol. 1, # 5 [pp. 25f.].

[10]Horsley, *New Docs.*, vol. 1, # 5 [p. 28].

[11]Would their mode of dress and/or the fact that the confrontation occurs on the Sabbath identify them as Jews?

[12]W.C. van Unnik, 'Die Anklage gegen die Apostel in Philippi', in *Sparsa Collecta: W.C. van Unnik*, (Leiden: Brill, 1973), vol. 1, 378. So also D.R. Schwartz, 'The Accusation and the Accusers at Philippi (Acts 16.20-21)', *Bib* 65 (1984), 362 and sources n. 28.

[13]This writer concurs with Trebilco, 'Paul and Silas', 64f. that the girl was implicitly denying an exclusive way of salvation.

awareness of Claudius' recent (c. 49/50 AD) and what must have been well-publicized efforts to quell riots in the city of Rome by expelling the Jews.[14] Bearing the responsibility of maintaining the peace and the city's good reputation (cf. Acts 17:5-9; 19:38-40), the magistrates would certainly have been levered to act on such charges.[15] Breach of the peace could lead to beating and imprisonment.[16]

The second charge, perhaps the ostensible cause of the alleged disturbance of the city, was the Jewish advocacy of customs (Acts 16:21) which were not lawful for Romans to receive or practice. Reviewing Josephus' use of the term 'customs', van Unnik indicates that to a Jew the term designates the impossibility of Roman military service, the requirements of Sabbath observance, food regulations and sending offerings to Jerusalem, recourse to special legal jurisdiction and, in general, a life according to the Jewish law.[17] We may add further monotheism and circumcision. Despite Gentile misunderstanding and antipathy toward Jews caused by these 'customs', their practice *by Jews* did not constitute a chargeable offence in Roman law. Proselytism, however, was a different matter. The serious adoption of the customs of Judaism by a Roman invariably required, if not the complete abandonment of the ancient customs, then at least a substantial movement away from them. The Jewish customs threatened effectively to destroy the web of conventions which represented the Roman cultural order and social relations and the Roman religion which preserved and sanctified them. Judaism, as Christianity after it, was popularly considered for such reasons to be atheistic and misanthropic.[18] In law, Roman conversion to Judaism was a punishable offence.[19] But the law was not rigidly enforced. A general laxity towards the Roman practice of foreign cults characterised the Julio-Claudian period except, of course, where such practice posed a serious threat to the welfare of the state.[20] In the latter instance, such practice could be a prisonable or even capital offence.[21] At Philippi, charges were brought privately *by*

---

[14]Sherwin-White, *Roman Society*, 81, citing Acts 18:2 and Suetonius, *Cl.* 25.4.

[15]*Cf.*.Tajra, *The Trial of St. Paul*, 14 and T.D. Barnes, 'Legislation Against the Christians', *JRS* 58 (1968), 48f.

[16]It could even result in death. *Dig.* 48.19.38.2; 48.19.28.3.

[17]van Unnik, 'Die Anklage', 381. I am unconvinced by the argument of Schwartz, 'The Accusation', 375-62, that Roman *Jews* are accusing Paul and Silas of teaching *not Judaism but Christianity* in Philippi.

[18]See, for example, Acts 19:23-27; Dio Cassius, *Ep.* 57.14; Tacitus, *Ann.* 15.44 and the discussion *supra*, 45f.

[19]Cicero, *Leg.* 2.8.19 indicates the boundaries.

[20]See Sherwin-White, *Roman Society*, 79.

Romans. The magistrates, as guardians of Roman religion in the colony,[22] were also bound to enquire after this charge.

II. The Accusers

The accusers are described to the reader as the Roman owners (Acts 16:21) of the slave girl (Acts 16:16, 19). These two points of identification, together with certain inferences derivative of them, carry implications significant to the magistrates' evaluation. As part of the privileged Roman minority in Philippi, they had legal advantages over the native Greek and Thracian populace.

If they were themselves Roman veterans or, as is probably more likely, had sprung from veteran stock, they would have possessed property.[23] Up until 13 BC pensioned soldiers, as a part of their settlement in the colonies, were allotted parcels of land.[24]

The accusers were also the owners of the slave girl. Whether she possessed the fortune-telling spirit before or after her purchase, she figured as a considerable business asset (Acts 16:19; *cf.* 19:24f.). The plural κύριοι may simply indicate that the slave girl was owned by a husband and wife.[25] But, if she was the joint property of a corporation of priests or a business syndicate as some suggest,[26] the combined legal/social status of the accusers would have carried even greater weight in the magistrates' assessment.

Finally, previous discussion suggests quite strongly that it would be significant that the accusers, as long-standing residents in

---

[21]See as a possible example Dio Cassius 67.14. Legislation enacted by Antoninus (138-61 AD) prohibited Jewish circumcision of anyone, save Jewish males, on pain of death (*Dig.* 48.8.11.1). For further discussion, *cf. supra,* 43f.

[22]So J.L. Kelso, 'Paul's Roman Citizenship as Reflected in His Missionary Experiences and His Letters', *BSac* 79 (1922), 175. *Cf.* Barnes, 'Legislation', 49 on the sense of religious duty in provincial governors.

[23]*Cf.* E.T. Salmon, *Roman Colonization Under the Republic* (Aspects of Greek and Roman Life; London: Thames and Hudson, 1969), 15.

[24]Their legal standing would therefore have been augmented by a measure of *facultates*; perhaps even *amplissimae facultates*. See Salmon, *Roman Colonization*, 18 on the range of allotments. G.R. Watson, *The Roman Soldier* (Aspects of Greek and Roman Life; London: Thames and Hudson, 1969), 147, writes that after 13 BC cash payments replaced land grants.

[25]So e.g., A. Souter, 'Interpretations of Certain New Testament Passages', *Exp* VIII/8 (1914), 94f, and BAGD, 459 for examples of this use.

[26]Noted as other possibilities by Lake and Cadbury, *BC*, 194.

Philippi, were locally known. Roman citizen status, military service/ family heritage, material wealth and past civic offices/contributions (if any), meant that they were well known.

III. The Accused

Paul and Silas are legally and socially identified with devastating economy at Acts 16:20—they are Jews. Paul's Jewish credentials, however advantageous in a Jewish environment, constituted a severe liability in this latently anti-Semitic context. The location of the Jewish place of worship (probably not a structure) on the banks of the river Gangites about 1.5 miles west of Philippi near a gate marking the border of that city[27] and the fact that no male Philippian residents appear to have been present on the Sabbath (Acts 16:13f.) suggest that the 'Jewish community', if it had a formal existence at all, was small and neither warmly received nor encouraged.[28] The contrastive phrasing 'being Jews' and 'who are Romans' emphasizes the accusers' assumed legal and social superiority in comparison with the accused. A hostile juridical assessment is clearly being encouraged on this basis. Without the citizenship, the apostles' blameworthiness was all the more likely.[29] Poverty would count against them as well.[30] Again, whereas the accusers would have been known to the magistrates, Paul and Silas were recently-arrived strangers: footloose vagrants unknown to the community or its officials. Xenophobia would have assured that no one of standing would vouch for them.[31]

---

[27]For discussion, see H. Conzelmann, *Acts of the Apostles: A Commentary on the Acts of the Apostles*, tr. J. Limburg et al. (Hermeneia; tr. 2nd ed. 1972; Philadelphia: Fortress, 1987), 130.

[28]For discussion of synagogue locations, see S. Safrai, 'Chapter 18: The Synagogue', in *Compendia*, vol. 2, 937-42; Schürer, *The History*, vol. 2, 440f.

[29]Codex Bezae at Acts 16:39 shows that the mere fact of the citizenship of Paul and Silas is sufficient to indicate to the officials that the apostles are 'innocent' or 'just' according to É. Delebecque, 'L'Art du Conte et la Faute du Tribun Lysias selon les deux Versions des Actes (22,22-30)', *Laval Théologique et Philosophique* 40 (1984), 222. Romans are not culpable; foreigners are.

[30]On the *prima facie* connection between poverty and criminality, see the example of Athenaeus, *Deip.* 6.227.d-e. See also J.M. Kelly, *Roman Litigation*, (Oxford: Clarendon, 1966), 69; Sherwin-White, *Roman Society*, 82 n. 2.

[31]J. Westbury-Jones, *Roman and Christian Imperialism* (1939; rpt., New York/London: Kennikat, 1971), 114, writes: 'No stranger had a *locus standi* before a Roman tribunal; he could not hold property or make a contract, or even sue when he was wronged'.

The social disadvantage of Paul's being an artisan may also have figured in the evaluation, though this is not mentioned in the text. Magistrates, one of whose qualifications for office was never to have been 'brought into disrepute by following an ignoble trade',[32] would certainly have allowed an 'upper crust' attitude to influence their evaluation of the litigants who came before them.

Kelly's description of the wronged foreigner, though drawn from comedies, suitably characterizes the position Paul and Silas find themselves in: '...friendless, unknown, the *peregrinus* [stranger] is the extreme example of the man with neither *potentia* [power] nor *gratia* [favour]'.[33]

IV. The Orderly Crowd

The function and behaviour of the crowd at Acts 16 is often treated dismissively in modern discussions, receiving no mention in the commentaries of Lake and Cadbury, Neil, Conzelmann and C.S.C. Williams. Others note in general terms that it bullied the magistrates into drastic and illegal action.[34] For some, the characterization of the mob is an artificial literary construction.[35] A closer examination of Acts 16:22, however, and a review of the function of the 'crowd' in law, suggest that a different assessment is in order.

Expressions such as 'rowdiness in the streets and the intensity of tumult'[36] and 'mob riot',[37] may accurately summarize the physical disturbance and general disorder at places such as Ephesus (Acts 19) and Jerusalem (Acts 21f.). However, the Philippian scene is not described by Luke as a riot; Acts 16:22 indicates only that the crowd 'joined in the attack' of the plaintiffs. What was the nature of that attack? The charg-

---

[32]F.F. Abbott and A.C. Johnson, *Municipal Administration in the Roman Empire* (Princeton: PUP, 1926), 59.

[33]Kelly, *Roman Litigation*, 44.

[34]*Cf.* W.M. Ramsay, *St. Paul the Traveller and the Roman Citizen* (London: Hodder and Stoughton, 1895), 219; B. Reese, 'The Apostle Paul's Exercise of His Rights as a Roman Citizen as Recorded in the Book of Acts', *EvQ* 47 (1975), 140f.

[35]R.I. Pervo, *Profit With Delight: The Literary Genre of the Acts of the Apostles* (Philadelphia: Fortress, 1987), 35.

[36]Tajra, *The Trial of St. Paul*, 9. *Cf.* R.J. Knowling, 'The Acts of the Apostles', in *Expositor's Greek Testament*, ed. W.R. Nicoll (1901; rpt., Grand Rapids: Eerdmans, 1983), vol. 2, 350.

[37]D.J. Williams, *Acts* (San Francisco: Harper and Row, 1985), 195. *Cf.* Ramsay, *St. Paul the Traveller*, 219.

es, we observed, were carefully constructed by the plaintiffs. The juridical context demanded this. The support of the crowd would have been
similarly articulate and orderly. Acts 24, also a Roman juridical scene,
supports this contention. At Acts 24:9, after the rhetor Tertullus had
presented the charges before Felix, Luke records that the company of
Jewish plaintiffs joined in the accusation. The character of the 'joining
in' expressed by the συν– compound must indicate a degree of articu-
lateness and orderliness in keeping with both the juridical context and
the character of the rhetor's presentation of the case. It cannot be denied that the accusations brought by the plaintiffs and assented to by
their supporters would have been made forcefully. But it is misleading
to assert that the scene was one of chaos and near riot.

R.F. Stoops, in a comparison of Acts 19 with a number of secular
examples of riot and assembly, asserts at one point in his discussion
that 'the story of the riot in Ephesus is more than stage dressing for favourable remarks from important officials'.[38] The same verdict is appropriate for the crowd at Acts 16. Ancient sources indicate that
watching *and participating* assemblies were not unusual in informal or
legal proceedings.[39] They could even fulfil, in the latter case, mandatory functions.

Roman jurisprudence showed an awareness of the assembly, as
evidenced by the impact of the presence and action of the people in
cases where one's Roman citizenship might be appealed. Appius Claudius' imprisonment and the vicious beating and crucifixion of Gavius
of Consa testify to the consequences of the people's acquiescence to official action.[40] The sympathy of the people, expressed in lending a willing ear or showing vocal or even physical solidarity, could protect a
Volero Publilius, Metellus or Cato from even the most threatening
magisterial intentions.[41] The crowd's unified opposition to the accused might dash any hopes of favour from the magistrates and effectively silence the accused who might otherwise have claimed what
protections Roman citizenship could afford. F. Millar's description of

---

[38]R.F. Stoops, 'Riot and Assembly: The Social Context of Acts 19:23-41', *JBL* 108
(1989), 89.

[39]For the Greek context, see the comment of J. Colin as cited by E.A. Judge, 'St Paul
and Classical Society', *JAC* 15 (1972), 27 and n. 44. *Cf.* Diodorus Siculus 18.67.3.

[40]Appius Claudius (Livy 3.56.5ff.; Dionysius Halicarnassensis, *Ant. Rom.* 9-11);
Gavius (Cicero, *Ver.* 2.5.163).

[41]Volero Publilius (Livy 2.55.4ff.); Q. Maximus Rullianus (Livy 8.34f.); Metellus
(Dio Cassius 37.50.1f.); Cato (Plutarch, *Cat. Mi.* 33.1f.; 43.3; *Caes.* 14.7; Dio Cassius
38.3.2).

how public order was maintained in the Roman provinces is consistent with these observations:

> ...in most places the governor was not present (obviously enough); and nor—which is perhaps not so obvious—were any forces, officials or representatives sent by him. The cities ran themselves. Or rather—and this is one of the most vivid impressions left by the novel—they were run by a network of local aristocratic families, whose doings, public and private, were the subject of intense observer participation—approbation, curiosity, indignation, incipient violence—on the part of the lower classes of the towns.[42]

It would probably not be anachronistic to take Lintott's assertion, made in respect of a specific and early Roman case, as a generally appropriate comment: '...the presence of the crowd is of immense importance'.[43]

While these observations are not intended as an argument that only Romans are present in the crowd at Acts 16 or that the assembly was entirely well-behaved, the evidence marshalled above suggests that it was not an illegal mob and probably contained a substantial number of Romans. Luke's emphasis upon the Roman character of Philippi and the distinctively Roman quality and Roman appeal of the charges as voiced by the accusers further confirms this assessment. The Philippian magistrates, being Romans chosen from among their fellow citizens to discharge the duties of governance, would formally have had an eye on those assembled and their general demeanour, attending particularly to Romans who could corroborate the truth (or falsehood!) of the charges. The assembly in this case, whether in knowledge or simply out of Roman sentiment and solidarity, sided with the accusers and against the accused—an expression of the plaintiffs' power.

V. Punishment and Custody

The magistrates of Philippi had the official title of *duoviri* (lit.: 'two men').[44] The literal translation δυανδρικοί being rough and un-Greek,

---

[42]F. Millar, 'The World of the *Golden Ass*', *JRS* 71 (1981), 69.

[43]A.W. Lintott, 'Provocatio. From the Struggle of the Orders to the Principate', *ANRW* I/2 (1972), 237.

[44]Abbott and Johnson, *Municipal Administration*, 56, 59; Lake and Cadbury, *BC*, 194.

the more general title ἄρχοντες was first used at Acts 16:19 and there-after the more specific στρατηγοί (Acts 16:20, 22, 26, 38).[45] They could judge cases privately and serve as public prosecutors in both civil and criminal matters in the colony. Each was attended by two *lictores* (= ῥαβδοῦχοι: Acts 16:35, 38 and *cf.* 22) who carried bundles of rods called *virgae* (Fig. 11). These symbolized their right to use physical co-ercion or corporal punishment.[46]

Non-citizen residents and aliens at Philippi stood under threat if they broke the law; the backs of Roman citizens, however, were pro-tected.[47] Corrective beating had been applied from earliest times in various forms to both slaves and free men. The beating of citizens was eventually forbidden by the provisions of the Valerian, Porcian and Ju-lian laws.[48] As with other punishments, there were degrees of severity. Garnsey notes three distinct contrasts in later legal texts: 1) between *fustigatio* and *flagellatio*—the former applied to free civilians and so-called because the instrument used was the military staff (*fustis*) which had replaced the rod (*virga*),[49] and the latter employing the scourge (*flagellum/flagrum*) and intended for slaves;[50] 2) between *admonitio/cas-tigatio* and *verberatio*—the former a light corrective beating employing the *fustis* or *flagrum*,[51] the latter using the *fustis* and invariably heavy;[52] and 3) between *pulsatio* and *verberatio*—the first originally employing the fist (*pugnus*) and the second a rod or thong,[53] though fists and chains are also noted.[54] Thus the *fustis* and *virga* could be used for ei-ther light or severe punishment. The bloody process and lethal result of the heavy beating with rods is graphically illustrated in the case of

---

[45]So e.g. W.M. Ramsay, 'Notes: The Philippians and Their Magistrates', *JTS* 1 (1899-1900), 114f.; C.J. Hemer, *The Book of Acts*, 115. *Cf.* Gill, 'Macedonia', 412.

[46]The absence of the axe (*securis*) from the *fasces* indicated that serious (i.e., capital-ly punishable) crimes were not within a magistrate's remit. *Cf. Mart. Pion.* 10.4; A.S. Wilkins, 'Colonia. II. Roman', *DGRA*, vol. 1, 483.

[47]Tajra, *The Trial of St. Paul*, 11 and sources there cited. Generally, *supra*, 48-52.

[48]T. Mommsen, *Le Droit Pénal Romain*, tr. J. Duquesne (Manuel des Antiquités Ro-maines 19; Paris: Ancienne Librairie Thorin et Fils, Albert Fontemoing, 1907), vol. 1, 52f. and vol. 3, 333.

[49]P.D.A. Garnsey, *Social Status*, 137; *idem.*, 'The *Lex Julia* and Appeal Under the Em-pire', *JRS* 56 (1966), 170 n. 29.

[50]See the sources cited by Garnsey, *Social Status*, 137 n. 4. Mommsen, *Le Droit*, vol. 3, 333, notes that this punishment was aggravated by the addition of balls of lead (*plumbatae*) to the thongs.

[51]See the sources cited by Garnsey, *Social Status*, 137 n. 3.

[52]*Ibid.*.

[53]Garnsey, 'The *Lex Julia*', 170 n. 29. *Cf. Dig.* 47.10.5*prol*-1.

[54]*Dig.* 47.10.15.40; 48.19.7.

Gaius Servilius.[55] It was considered an appropriate punishment for those causing civic disturbances.[56]

Paul and Silas were stripped of their garments[57] and 'severely flogged' (πολλὰς δὲ ἐπιθέντες αὐτοῖς πληγάς: Acts 16:22). The beating, severe enough to open wounds needing cleansing (Acts 16:33),[58] suggests *verberatio*. The treatment is consistent with the juridical and social assessment of the apostles as noted above; i.e., that Paul and Silas were low-status individuals safely presumed by accusation alone to be guilty of criminal behaviour.[59]

Beating was considered a sufficient punishment in many instances. In the case of Paul and Silas, however, additional action is taken. They are thrown into prison and guarded carefully (Acts 16:23). One would expect, by analogy to such places as Rome and Athens and in keeping with long-standing architectural practice, that the prison at Philippi would be located near the court, perhaps even adjoining the *forum*. The excavated remains of the Philippian *forum*, dating to the time of Marcus Aurelius (161-80 AD), show the outlines of various public buildings. Among and perhaps beneath these would probably have been found the 1st century AD facilities to which Paul and Silas were taken. While D.J. Williams writes that one can see 'the city jail and public buildings bordering it',[60] he neither indicates the exact location of the prison nor defends his identification. Does he mean the small crypt discovered in 1876 to the right of the entrance stairway of the Church of the Terrace (Basilica A) and popularly known as 'St. Paul's Prison?' Its location very near the NW corner of the *forum* (Fig.

---

[55]Cicero, *Ver.* 2.5.142. Gaius Servilius was savagely beaten 'till finally the senior lictor Sextius ... took the butt end of his stick, and began to strike the poor man violently across the eyes, so that he fell helpless to the ground, his face and eyes streaming with blood. Even then his assailants continued to rain blows on his prostrate body, till at last he consented to accept the challenge. Such was the treatment he then received; and having been carried off for dead at the time, very soon afterwards he died'. *Cf. m. Mak.* 3.11-13 on the method and vigour of the Jewish 40 stripes less one.

[56]Callistratus, *Dig.* 48.19.28.3; Tacitus, *Ann.* 1.77; Suetonius, *Aug.* 45.3; and *cf.* Josephus, *BJ* 2.269 [2.13.7].

[57]The pattern of commands given by magistrates to their lictors is found in Seneca, *Con.* 9.2.21 (*cf.* LCL nn.).

[58]The word πληγή can be rendered by either 'bruise' or 'wound' according to BAGD, 668. *Cf.* M. Zerwick and M. Grosvenor, *Grammatical Analysis of the Greek New Testament* (Rome: Biblical Institute, 1974), vol. 1, 406 renders ἔλουσεν ἀπὸ τῶν πληγῶν washing '(*sic.* the blood) from' the wounds.

[59]*Dig.* 48.19.10; *cf.* Garnsey, *Social Status*, 136.

[60]C.S.C. Williams, *Acts*, 278f.

12a) and the fact that this room was originally a cistern[61] might commend it. The smallness of this subterranean chamber, however, argues against this identification. The frescos depicting scenes from Paul's experience are no earlier than the 10th century AD.[62] Another structure, lying under the atrium of Basilica A (Fig. 12b), must also be considered. On the orientation of the *forum*, it originated as a Roman building (a prison?) but was later used as a cistern.[63] No certainty attends either conjecture.

Something can be learned of the prison's structure from Luke's record. The abrupt appearance of the members of the jailer's household at Acts 16:31-34 suggests that his quarters were within or near the prison precincts.[64] Some infer a prison courtyard and fresh water source from the washing and baptisms at Acts 16:30, 33f.[65]

Paul and Silas are cast into the inner[66] cell (Acts 16:24). We have seen that such places as the *Tullianum* in the Roman state prison, were not only the worst places to be because they were death cells, but also because they were where those who had committed the most serious crimes and who occupied the lowest levels of society were placed. Security may not have been the sole purpose of the command if the experience of the Christian prisoners in the *Martyrdom of Pionius* is any indication. Originally in less severe custody elsewhere in the prison, these later Christian martyrs were cast by their guards into the inner part of the prison.[67] The context indicates that this was intended to demoralize, humiliate and punish them. Paul and Silas are therefore shut up in a place reserved for dangerous low class felons.

Finally, the apostles' feet were fastened in stocks (Acts 16:24). These could be of several kinds.[68] They often consisted of a long piece

---

[61]The *Tullianum* in Rome is one example of the conversion of a cistern into a prison. See F.A.K. Krauss, *Im Kerker*, 45, 57.

[62]So P.E. Davies, 'The Macedonian Scene of Paul's Journeys', *BA* 26 (1963), 100f.; Lemerle, *Philippes*, 36, 59f., 296f.

[63]*Archaeological Reports* 12 (1985/86) 69. For a description, *cf.* M. Séve and P. Weber, 'Le Côté Nord du Forum de Philippes', *Bulletin de Correspondance Hellénique* 110 (1986), 531-81.

[64]A. Wikenhauser, *Die Apostelgeschichte*, 191; F.F. Bruce, *The Book of Acts*, (NICNT; 1954; rev. ed. Grand Rapids: Eerdmans, 1988), 318 n. 73; Williams, *Acts*, 282.

[65]So e.g., Haenchen, *The Acts*, 498; Neil, *The Acts*, 185.

[66] Ἐσωτέρος may serve as superlative, meaning 'innermost',

[67]*Mart. Pion.* 11.3f.

[68]For discussion, Krauss, *Im Kerker*, 50; G.E. Marindin, 'Nervus', *DGRA*, vol. 2, 228f. On other instruments of restraint, J.H. Flather, 'Compes', *DGRA*, vol. 1, 523 and illustration; L. Wenger, 'Vinctus', *Zeitschrift der Savigny-Stiftung für Rechtsgeschichte* 61 (1941), 367.

of wood pierced at regular intervals with notches or holes and split along the length so that the feet of the prisoner could be set in and secured.[69] In 1766 a metal 'rod through comb' type of these stocks was found in a guard house/prison in the Gladiators Barracks at Pompeii (Fig. 13). Prisoners' legs were set in the spaces between the teeth and a movable iron rod was run through the holes in the top of each tooth. The whole contraption was anchored to the floor.[70]

The employment of such restraint overnight could be a normal security precaution if Lucian's *Toxaris* is any indication.[71] If the Philippian jailer placed the apostles in stocks *immediately*, as seems the case, more than security may have been in mind. The stocks normally caused extreme discomfort as the prisoner had to sleep either in a sitting position or lying down on the floor. Changing position to avoid cramping was nearly impossible.[72] The discomfort of a prisoner could be turned to excruciating pain by increasing the distance between the left and right feet.[73] The use of stocks as a security measure was a grave indignity at the least, but it could also be a form of torture, and torture was legally forbidden to all but the lowest individuals; i.e., slaves, debtors and freeborn felons.[74]

The command of the Philippian magistrates to keep the apostles in prison suggests that the accused were considered wrongdoers entirely lacking legal and social merit. The fact of their secure keeping in the inner cell with feet in stocks would only reinforce this assessment. If the command was announced publicly, as seems likely, the legal and social assessment of the apostles would have been apparent to both accusers and interested bystanders.

---

[69]E. Le Blant, *Les Persécuteurs et Les Martyrs Aux Premiers Siècles de Notre `Ere* (Paris: Ernest Leroux, 1893), 282.

[70]*Ibid.*, 283. LeBlant notes that when discovered, this *nervus* was holding the leg bones of two skeletons. Thus prevented from fleeing, the two prisoners perished when Vesuvius erupted. *Cf.* P. Gusman, *Pompei: The City, Its Life and Art*, tr. F. Simmonds and M. Jourdain (London: William Heinemann, 1900), 153; L. Richardson, Jr., *Pompeii: An Architectural History* (Baltimore/London: Johns Hopkins University, 1988), 85. Fig. 14 shows a circular version of these stocks.

[71]Lucian, *Tox.* 150f.

[72]*Ibid.*

[73]*Mart. Let. Lyons & Vienne* 27 (177 AD).

[74]Marindin, 'Nervus', 229.

VI. Fair Magistrates

The evaluative procedure previously indicated was presumed to be able to generate results which were both equitable and legal *by Roman standards*. How did it do in the case of Paul and Silas? The answer depends upon how one construes the record of the events. A number of commentators assert that the apostles declared their Roman citizenship, but were either not heard[75] or ignored.[76] Several objections may be raised to such assessments. First is the tendency to exaggerate the crowd's behaviour out of all proportion to the evidence as has been shown above. Second is the unlikelihood that the Philippian magistrates or their lictors would have disregarded a claim of citizenship. Power, together with protections and precedents, could tempt mighty men to abuse Roman citizens. But the Philippian magistrates were not Emperors, tribunes or provincial governors; they were relatively unimportant and would thus be expected (and feel the need) to stay well within the law. To suggest that these were 'high-handed' and 'stuffy' magistrates who gave a 'sort of command, a wink, a nod, or a hint', or knowingly abused self-declared citizens, is therefore unconvincing.[77] Third, the text provides no warrant for asserting that the magistrates, taking the earthquake to be a sign of divine displeasure[78] or simply recognizing their own illegal conduct,[79] released Paul and Silas. The text shows that the magistrates' first indication of the apostles' Roman citizenship comes at Acts 16:38; only then do they become alarmed. Finally, had Paul and Silas really wished to assert their citizen rights, they could have done so, notwithstanding the wild disorder of the crowd which some improbably allege.[80] A single cry of Roman citizenship, if unheard or unheeded in the first instance, could have been shouted repeatedly as the cases of Gaius Servilius and Gavius of Consa

---

[75]So e.g., Reese, 'The Apostle Paul's Exercise of His Rights', 141f.

[76]So e.g., Ramsay, *St. Paul the Traveller*, 219; Knowling, 'The Acts', 350; H.J. Cadbury, *The Book of Acts in History*, (London: A. and C. Black, 1955), 77.

[77]*Contra* Cadbury, *The Book of Acts*, 77; J.C. Lentz, Jr., *Luke's Portrait of Paul*, (SNTSMS 77; Cambridge: CUP, 1993), 127, 130-38.

[78]G. Schille, *Die Apostelgeschichte des Lukas* (THNT 5; Berlin: Evangelische Verlagsanstalt, 1984), 348; R.B. Rackham, *The Acts of the Apostles* (WC 41; 7th ed 1913; London: Methuen, 1951), 290. The popularity of this view is due to the Western text.

[79]So Stählin, *Die Apostelgeschichte*, 220; G.T. Stokes, *The Acts of the Apostles* (Expositor's Bible n. ed.; London: Hodder and Stoughton, 1915), 220. *Cf.* F.J. Foakes-Jackson, *The Acts of the Apostles* (MNTC 5; London: Hodder and Stoughton, 1948), 156.

[80]D.O. Bauernfeind, *Kommentar und Studien zur Apostelgeschichte*, ed. V. Metelmann (WUNT 22; 1939; rv. com. Tübingen: Mohr, 1980), 210.

well illustrate.[81] Moreover, the apostles could effectively have disclosed their true legal standing at any time from their arrest to their imprisonment.[82]

Kelly has observed that Roman law 'can be applied only to a set of facts; and if the wrong facts are established, the law will be wrongly applied'.[83] If the apostles' citizenship was not asserted—and nothing in the text indicates that it was disclosed any earlier than Acts 16:37—then the evaluative procedure, though unfair to modern eyes, would from the magistrates' perspective seem legally proper. Sherwin-White writes that the events of Acts 16 follow a legally acceptable course to the point that they are taken.[84] The rationale for 'abandonment' or interruption of formal proceedings in favour of speedy punishment is equally in order. To have dignified a case where the accused were of no account by spending time on it or referring it upward would have insulted the higher class accusers and annoyed the provincial authority. Immediate and severe corporal punishment and imprisonment of such characters after simply hearing the accusation was fully within the remit of the magistrates. The punishment showed the accused their proper place, appeased the injured parties and gratified the offended populace. Taking all the above factors into consideration, it seems clear that the Philippian magistrates did not consciously pervert the law.[85]

VII. Paul's 'Un-Roman' Behaviour

A timely disclosure of Roman citizenship could have had far-reaching effects for Paul and Silas: legal proceedings, if not suspended entirely, would at least have proceeded on the basis of a different assessment of the relative weight of status factors. Assuming the accurate portrayal of formal and popular sensitivity to Roman proprieties in Philippi, official recourse to such abuse and humiliation as Paul and Silas suffered would have been unthinkable.

---

[81]Cicero, *Ver.* 2.5.142 (Gaius Servius); 2.5.62, 163 (Gavius).

[82]R.J. Cassidy, *Society and Politics in the Acts of the Apostles* (Maryknoll, NY: Orbis, 1987), 101.

[83]Kelly, *Roman Litigation*, 33.

[84]Sherwin-White, *Roman Society*, 82f.

[85]Even the assertion of Krodel, *Acts*, 314f., that *'for Luke* ... the Philippian magistrates perverted the law' [*my italics*] is quite doubtful. *Cf.* Cassidy, *Society and Politics*, 88.

Paul's disclosure of his and Silas' Roman citizenship is troubling because its lateness is so 'un-Roman'. Any citizen could be expected to preserve both self and dignity by the earliest, most favourable, and most forceful presentation of his legal and social status possible. The late disclosure here, when taken with Paul's own reference to at least two other occasions when he was officially (and severely!) beaten by Romans (2 Cor. 11:25; cf. 6:5, 9; 11:23), suggests to some that Paul's Roman citizenship is a fiction.[86]

Surely Paul's conduct raised questions in the minds of Luke's Roman readers.[87] Indeed, a reader would have asked not only why Paul did not disclose fully his legal *persona* at the 'Roman' time, but also why he did so when he did. Only the first of these two questions will occupy our attention at this point.

Distinct disadvantages to an appeal at the 'Roman' time indicate that Lukan invention is not the most convincing explanation of the record at Acts 16. First, an early citizenship claim would probably have resulted in legal entanglements and, hence, unwanted delays. How would Paul have proven his citizenship? Bruce writes:

> Each legitimately born child of a Roman citizen had to be registered within (it appears) thirty days of his birth. If he lived in the provinces, his father, or some duly appointed agent, made a declaration (*professio*) before the provincial governor (*praeses prouinciae*) at the public record-office (*tabularium publicum*). In the course of his *professio* the father or his agent declared that the child was a Roman citizen; the *professio* was entered in the register of declarations (*album professionum*)....[88]

While some such formal procedure was probably followed at the time of Paul's birth, the legislation for registration noted above was relatively recent.[89] At regular intervals when the Roman census was taken, Paul's name, status, age and property holdings would be duly recorded. Near their place of birth, most citizens could without difficulty prove their citizenship—one need merely go to the public record office

---

[86]E.g., W. Stegemann, 'War der Apostel Paulus ein römischer Bürger?', 223f.; Lentz, *Luke's Portrait of Paul*, 131, 133 who assert that Paul's citizenship is a Lukan creation.

[87]Cassidy, *Society and Politics*, 100 and 150.

[88]F.F. Bruce, *Paul: Apostle of the Free Spirit* (Exeter: Paternoster, 1977), 39.

[89]Bruce, *Paul*, 40, cites these as the *lex Aelia Sentia* (4 AD) and the *lex Papia Poppaea* (9 AD) and asks, 'If Paul was born even a year or two before the earlier of these enactments, would he necessarily have been registered in this way?'

or summon witnesses. For Paul at Philippi, some 700 miles away from home by land, it might be much more difficult.

It was possible to use a certified private copy of the record of the *professio*—called a *testatio*—as a kind of birth certificate or passport, though this kind of document was usually kept in the family archive.[90] The *testatio* was inscribed on the waxed surfaces of a small wooden diptych having a stereotypic five part form.[91] It included the names of witnesses (usually seven) and concluded with the abbreviation, *q. p. f. c. r. e. ad k.* The letters *c. r. e.*, representing *c(iuem) r(omanam/um) e(xscripsi/t)*,[92] clearly indicated the possession of Roman citizenship. Schulz notes that *testationes* such as these were widely used in the courts from Republican times and had considerable importance.

The *diploma militaris* (or *instrumentum*) given to pensioned-off auxiliary soldiers was related to the *testatio* in that it also confirmed the citizen franchise and carried the names of seven witnesses.[93] *Diplomata*, diptychs fashioned in bronze, were both more permanent and travelled better. The inner 'pages', containing the certified copy, were sealed. The outer 'pages' duplicated the inner contents for convenience so that the seals did not have to be broken to consult the document.[94] A civilian type of *diploma* conferring citizenship is also noted in the sources. The Emperor Nero gave such diplomas of citizenship to Greek youths to reward the quality of their performance in Pyrrhic dances he had sponsored.[95] We further read of travel documents, also called *diplomata*, which were obtainable on request by enfranchised individuals. Atticus (16 May 49 BC) had arranged for one for his sons. Cicero, his friend, furnished Atticus himself with one also, though it had not been requested. Hoping that no offence would be taken, Cicero asserted that it was indispensable for (trouble-free) travel.[96]

---

[90]F. Schulz, 'Roman Registers of Births and Birth Certificates: Part II', *JRS* 33 (1943), 58. For examples, H.A. Sanders, 'The Birth Certificate of a Roman Citizen', *CP* 22 (1927), 409-13; F. Schulz, 'Roman Registers of Births and Birth Certificates', *JRS* 32 (1942), 78-91.

[91]Schulz, 'Roman Registers: Part II', 58f.

[92]Sanders, 'The Birth Certificate', 410, offers this rendering. Schulz, 'Roman Registers: Part II', 56, ventures the rendering '*c(iuem) R(omanum) e(sse)*, so that this clause also depends on the implied verb *professus est*'.

[93]Sherwin-White, *Roman Society*, 146.

[94]*ARS* 184 [71 AD] introduction. For additional examples, *cf. ARS* 186 [76 AD]; 189 [79? AD] and M.M. Roxan, *Roman Military Diplomas 1954-1977* (Occasional Publication # 2; London: University of London Institute of Archaeology, 1978), *passim*.

[95]Suetonius, *Nero* 12.

[96]Cicero, *Att.* 10.17.

Magistrates could give *testationes* and military and civilian *diplomata* full credit, but they were not bound by law to do so as such documents furnished only presumptive proof of identity.[97] If there were doubts regarding either the bearer or the document, witnesses had to be called. It was Verres' right in 70 BC to question Gavius' citizenship claim. Cicero records that Gavius 'cried out that he was a Roman citizen, a burgess of Consa; that he had served in the army under the distinguished Roman knight Lucius Raecius, who was in business at Panhormus and could assure Verres of the truth of his story'.[98] Cicero criticizes Verres' haste, stating that if no remission was possible, at least a postponement of the execution was in order:

> ...when Gavius named the Roman knight Lucius Raecius, who was in Sicily at the time-might you not at least have written to him at Panhormus? Your Messanian friends would have kept your man in safe custody, you would have had him chained and locked up, till Raecius arrived from Panhormus.[99]

Cicero laments the implications of such haste for poor Romans of humble birth who find trouble in foreign places; they 'cannot always have with them acquaintances to vouch for them'.[100] He is elsewhere quite clear that the testimony of witnesses ought to be considered compelling.[101] A document of 92 AD records the oath of Titus Flavius Longus, deputy to the centurion of the legion III Cyrenaica stationed in Egypt, giving several names of soldiers as guarantors 'that he was freeborn, a Roman citizen and had the right of serving in a legion'.[102] If Longus possessed documentation, it was apparently considered suspect. To satisfy doubts, three guarantors had to swear by Jupiter Best and Greatest and by the divine spirit of Domitian that Longus' status and entitlement were authentic.

Would Paul have had a citizenship document? He would not, of course, have possessed a *diploma* as the conditions of grant bore no relation to the circumstances under which Luke indicates Paul received the citizenship. A *testatio*, however, is within the realm of possibility.[103] Without such a document, delay would have been almost cer-

---

[97]See in this regard, the remarks of Schulz, 'Roman Registers: Part II', 63.
[98]Cicero, *Ver.* 2.5.161.
[99]*Ibid.* 2.5.168.
[100]*Ibid.* 2.5.167.
[101]*Ibid.* 2.1.13-14.
[102]B.W. Jones and R.D. Milns, *The Use of Documentary Evidence in the Study of Roman Imperial History* (1984), 137f.

tain. Even if he did possess one, the weight attached to it would be influenced by the circumstances of its production. Displayed by a Jew in the thick of anti-Jewish trouble, it might only have invited a prolonged stay of proceedings until Paul's identity could be confirmed by the arrival of distant witnesses.

Even an uncontested citizenship appeal would have meant delay. The case, if pursued through the courts, would have likely had to be settled by the provincial governor. The wait for a governor's visit to a regional capital of the province could be a long one,[104] and travelling to the provincial capital to settle the matter might reduce the delay only a little. Haenchen writes that 'the appeal would have entangled him in a protracted trial with an uncertain outcome'.[105]

The financial burden of awaiting trial might also influence a litigant determining whether to claim the citizen right or not.[106] Would a travelling stranger, as Paul was, far away from the material resources and connections of home and in quite serious trouble, whose manual labour served the purpose not of accumulating great wealth but providing basic sustenance, think it prudent to court the potentially onerous costs of an appeal? Perhaps not.

Second and probably more significant of the potential disadvantages of an early citizenship claim were those we may call religious. It was argued earlier that we should expect to find clear indications of status tension or dissonance in the Pauline status; that in specific contexts Paul will need to contend with the practical implications of low status crystallization. His status is made up of elements which may be either advantageous or detrimental, depending upon who is evaluating him.

At Acts 16, one element is negatively exploited in the almost exclusively Gentile context—i.e., Paul is a Jew. Paul's Jewishness is both emphasized and inextricably intertwined with the charges in the text, figuring against him in the accusation phase, in the evaluation of the magistrates and in the punishments handed out. The terms Ἰουδαῖος and Ῥωμαῖος in the accusation are presented by the accusers as mutually exclusive; to be a Jew is *not* to be a Roman and *vice versa*. An early citizenship claim in the face of this contrast would reflect negatively upon Paul's Jewishness. The assertion 'I am a Roman citizen' would

---

[103]Schulz, 'Roman Registers: Part II', 63f.; Tajra, *The Trial of St. Paul*, 85.
[104]A.N. Sherwin-White, 'The Early Persecutions and Roman Law Again', *JTS* n.s. 3 (1952), 212.
[105]Haenchen, *The Acts*, 504.
[106]*Supra*, 55.

imply, if not 'I am not Jewish', then something close to it. Highlighting his 'Romanness' could only have compounded the damage to his 'Jewishness'.

An early claim would also have had profound negative missiological consequences. Even if Paul and Silas had not already begun evangelizing the Roman citizens of Philippi before the levelling of the charges, they could not in good conscience have denied that such activity fittedtheir ultimate missionary objectives. Moreover, the self-defence of an early citizenship claim would probably have been construed by the magistrates and populace as an assertion of commitment to the primacy of Roman, over against Jewish (i.e., Christian), customs. The signals sent would also have put the church at risk of dissolution if the new Philippian converts did not possess the Roman franchise. At the least, there would have been uncertainty surrounding Paul's commitment to his message. Converts might wonder whether only those suitably protected (i.e., by Roman citizenship) should become believers in Christ and they might think it disingenuous for Paul and Silas to ask others to suffer what they themselves were able to avoid. Missiological concerns might well also stand behind a desire not to become entangled in protracted litigation.

Each of these potential religious costs suggests the greater probability that Paul's earlier silence concerning his citizenship reflects a carefully considered choice rather than a novelistic dramatization or the expression of Luke's juridical naivete.

CHAPTER 6

JERUSALEM

The conditions of Paul's custody in Jerusalem improve considerably as the Tribune Claudius Lysias subjects Paul and the case against him to continuing scrutiny. The earliest treatment is the most harsh and least appropriate, reflecting Lysias' difficulties in securing a clear picture of the events. External indications suggested that a serious crime had been committed but no one would state what it was and there were no identifiable accusers. The disclosure that Paul was both Jewish and a Tarsian citizen had emerged as a cultured and forceful rebuttal to the social slur of Lysias' hopeful guess that Paul was a certain known Egyptian revolutionary. His attempts at discovery foiled, Lysias removed Paul to the Fortress Antonia where he determined to subject him to inquisitorial torture. Judged by the little he was able to discover and the little that had been volunteered to him, Lysias' action in manacling Paul with two chains and using torture is understandable from the Roman perspective. He does not know that Paul is a Roman citizen. Moreover, Lysias' use of other means of enquiry before resorting to the whip actually shows a high regard for the counsel of Roman law and demonstrates admirable restraint.

Jerusalem is the next locale for custodial deliberations. Whereas the magistrates at Philippi press for rapid closure of the deliberations, the process in Jerusalem is slower, going through a number of phases as the Tribune Claudius Lysias presses for clarification. On Paul's arrest at the Temple, the Tribune demands to know the identity of the accused and his crime (Acts 21:33b). Acts relates that 'some in the crowd shouted one thing and some another', and with such confusion the commander 'could not get at the truth' (Acts 21:34).[1] The first phase of the deliberations must progress without precise information.

I. Initial Enquiries

The Levites, who closed the gates leading to the Court of the Gentiles when the riot occurred, formed the Temple's police force. They may also have been responsible for dragging Paul from the Court of Women,[2] though the fact that Paul was being severely abused suggests that he came eventually to be in the hands of the crowd. There were no specific accusers; the Asian Jews who initiated the disturbance did not formally present themselves to the Tribune. Despite this, the breadth of antipathy still suggested to him that Paul had committed some serious crime against the body politic. Luke emphasizes the crowd's physical violence, volubility, and extent. Paul is in actual danger of lynch justice.[3] Finally, the crowd's shouts suggests that a capital offence has been committed.[4]

Though he lacked concrete information, Lysias did not shrink from forming an opinion about the identity of the accused and his offence. Lysias at first thought he had captured a real prize—the Egyptian revolutionary who had recently slipped Felix' grasp after organizing and leading a revolt (Acts 21:37f.).[5] We have argued that Paul's response to the Tribune's question had a clearly positive and in-

---

[1]*Contra* the insistence of Tajra, *The Trial of St. Paul*, 69, that Lysias took Paul into custody on the basis of *the oral denunciation* of the rioters.

[2]J. Jeremias, *Jerusalem*, 209f.

[3]Acts 21:31 (ζητούντων τε αὐτὸν ἀποκτεῖναι), 32 (τύπτω).

[4]Acts 21:36 (αἶρε αὐτόν); 22:22 (αἶρε ἀπὸ τῆς γῆς τὸν τοιοῦτον/οὐ γὰρ καθῆκεν αὐτὸν ζῆν).

[5]Josephus, *BJ* 2.261-63 [2.13.5]. If the numbers were expressed by Greek letters, the discrepancy between Luke's reference to 4,000 followers (= Δ) and Josephus' reference to 30,000 (= Λ) might be accounted for according to F.F. Bruce, *New Testament History* (London: Thomas Nelson, 1969), 322.

formative thrust: when he said he was a Tarsian, he did so in a proud
and most overtly Hellenistic way. But Paul's assertion that he was both
a Jew and a Tarsian was probably more than simply a legal self-de-
scription. It may also have amounted to an offended rebuttal. To be
mistaken for an Egyptian was a social slur of no small degree. Jews
who lived in Alexandria resented being identified as Egyptians.[6] The
offensiveness of the designation would have been compounded if, as
in this case, a Jew who boasted his religious faithfulness was identified
as an Egyptian false-prophet.[7]

The Tribune was still under pressure to discover the nature of
Paul's offence and prefer charges against him. If he hoped for clarification by permitting Paul to address the mob, he was disappointed. Paul,
speaking in Aramaic (Acts 22:2) addressed religious issues, touching
only obtusely upon the reason for the blow up (Acts 22:21). Being no
better informed, and with the crowd once again in a frenzy, the Tribune resolved to examine Paul privately.

II. The Fortress Antonia

While there were probably other prisons in Jerusalem,[8] K. Lake indicates that only three are mentioned in Acts. The first two—the prison
of the Sanhedrin, located 'either in the Temple, or in, probably below,
the Gazith'[9] and the prison of Herod, 'probably in the Praetorium, or
Palace, on the west side of the city'[10]—need not detain us. The location
of Paul's imprisonment in Jerusalem, called the 'barracks' (παρεμ–
βολή: Acts 21:34, 37; 22:24; 23:10, 16, 32),[11] must be the Fortress Antonia. This Fortress, adjoining the northwest corner of the Temple area
(Fig. 15) and originally called Baris, was extensively rebuilt and improved by Herod the Great and renamed Antonia in honour of Mark
Antony (pre-Actium, 31 BC).[12] Its strategic importance for the protec-

---

[6]Lentz, *Luke's Portrait of Paul*, 28-30.

[7]Josephus, *BJ* 2.261 [2.13.5].

[8]This may be assumed on the basis of Josephus' mention of δεσμωτήρια and the
astonishingly large numbers of prisoners kept in confinement (*BJ* 4.353
[4.6.1],4.385 [4.6.3]; 5.526 [5.12.4]).

[9]K. Lake, 'Note 35. Localities In and Near Jerusalem Mentioned in Acts', in *BC*, vol.
5, 478.

[10]Lake, 'Localities', 478. A few locate Peter's place of imprisonment at Acts 12 here.
Cf. Matt. 27:27; Mark 15:16; John 18:28 (x2), 33; 19:9)

[11]BAGD, 625; LSJ, 1335.

tion and defence of the city and Temple was realized by Herod and by those who eventually stormed and razed it in August of 66 AD.[13] Herod spared no expense in its construction: externally, it had the appearance of a tower with other towers at its four corners—three being fifty cubits high and the fourth on the southeast angle rising to seventy cubits.[14] Internally it was furnished 'with apartments of every description and for every purpose, including cloisters, baths and broad courtyards for the accommodation of troops; so that from its possession of all conveniences it seemed a town, from its magnificence a palace'.[15] It could garrison a full Roman cohort as Acts intimates.[16] A place where heavy armaments were kept, it had also for a time housed the high priestly vestments under the control of the Romans.[17] About 70/69 BC, Alexandra held Aristobulus' wife and children there.[18]

A part of Herod's reconstruction included the building of ornate roofed colonnades or stoae which ran around the perimeter of the Temple area and connected with the Antonia. The posting of Roman sentries on these stoae permitted an excellent view of religious celebrants and rapid communication with the Antonia in case of trouble.[19] This probably accounts for the fact that news (Acts 21:31) of Paul's trouble reached the Tribune as quickly as it did. Mention of the steps (Acts 21:35, 40) up which Paul had to be carried and from which he spoke fits well with Josephus' description of how access from Temple area to Antonia was obtained: 'At the point where it [i.e., the Antonia] impinged upon the porticoes of the temple, there were stairs leading down to both of them, by which the guards descended'.[20] The use of the verbs ἀνέβη (Acts 21:31), κατέδραμεν (Acts 21:32) and possibly καταβάν (Acts 23:10)[21] also suggest the relation of the Antonia to the Temple area.

---

[12]Josephus, AJ 15.409 [15.11.4]; BJ 1.75 [1.3.5.], 1.118 [1.5.4], 1.401 [1.21.1]; 5.238 [5.5.8]. *Contra* P. Benoit, 'The Archaeological Reconstruction of the Antonia Fortress', in *Jerusalem Revealed: Archaeology in the Holy City 1968-1974*, tr. R. Grafman (Jerusalem: Israel Exploration Society/Shikmona, 1975), 89.

[13]Josephus, AJ 15.292 [15.8.5], 15.409 [15.11.4]; BJ 2.328f. [2.15.5], 2.430 [2.17.7]; 5.183 [5.4.4], 5.238-45 [5.5.8], 5.267 [5.6.2], 5.356 [5.9.2]; 6.45 [6.1.5].

[14]*Ibid.*, BJ 5.242 [5.5.8]. See also Benoit, 'The Archaeological Reconstruction', 87-89.

[15]Josephus, BJ 1.401 [1.21.1].

[16]*Ibid.*,5.244 [5.5.8].

[17]*Ibid.*, 5.267 [5.6.2]; AJ 15.407 [15.11.4].

[18]*Ibid.*, BJ 1.118 [1.5.4].

[19]*Ibid.* 5.244 [5.5.8].

[20]*Ibid.*, BJ 5.243 [5.5.8].

[21]See Lake, 'Localities', 477f. on the Courtroom of the Sanhedrin.

III. Custody and Inquisition

Once Paul was inside the Antonia, the Tribune directed that he be interrogated with scourges (Acts 22:24). The μάστιξ (Lat.: *flagrum*) was a fearsome inquisitorial instrument. While it sometimes consisted of a handle on which were fixed leather straps, it was often an instrument of brutal innovation (Fig. 16). The lashes could be knotted cords or wire having bristled ends or be strung with knucklebones and lead pellets.[22] This method of interrogation, though never overtly construed as punitive, could nevertheless result in crippling or even death before the truth had been arrived at.[23]

Paul's assertion of his Tarsian citizenship did not dissuade the Tribune from initiating such enquiry. Lentz' assertion that 'this is only an indication of the Tribune's boorishness'[24] is entirely wrong. Torture was recommended only after other forms of enquiry had been exhausted or frustrated[25] and Acts is clear (Acts 21:33f., 39f.) that the Tribune had used all the non-coercive means. Persons taken into custody without accusers were not to be subjected to torture unless there were suspicions strongly attaching to them.[26] Serious wrong-doing *was* suspected of Paul. While Roman citizens might be scourged after conviction on capital charges and before execution, they were exempted by law from such treatment before trial.[27] Even if one's citizen status were declared but in doubt, enquiry by torture was not in order.[28] When the soldiers stretched Paul out for beating, he had not yet indicated his Roman citizenship. Known only as a Jew withTarsian citizenship, Paul hardly merited special protection. Torture was permitted in Roman law for the examination of slaves and non-Romans.[29] The Tribune, when judged by his knowledge of the situation, the extent of Paul's self-disclosure, and Roman law, therefore acted correctly.[30]

---

[22]J. Yates and W. Wayte, 'Flagrum', *DGRA*, vol. 1, 864 and sources there cited.
[23]*Dig.* 48.19.8.3; *Mart. Pol.* 2.1 (155/7 AD); *Mart. Justin & Co.* 5.1 (*recensio C*).
[24]Lentz, *Luke's Portrait of Paul*, 30.
[25]*Dig.* 48.18 *prol.*, 1.
[26]*Ibid.* 48.18.22.
[27]*Supra*, ch. 3, section III.1. Garnsey, 'Legal Privilege in the Roman Empire', 154 n. 37; Bruce, *The Book of Acts*, 421.
[28]*Cf. Dig.* 48.18.10.6; 48.18.12.
[29]*Ibid.* 48.2.6; 48.18; 48.19.10, 28; Juvenal 6.474-85; Horace, *Sat.* 1.3.119; and *cf.* Yates and Wayte, 'Flagrum', 864.
[30]Reference here to the cruelty of the Romans (*cf.* G. Lüdemann,*Early Christianity, Early Christianity According to the Traditions in Acts: A Commentary* [tr. J. Bowden. London: SCM, 1989] 238f.) obscures this fact.

How was Paul bound? Luke indicates that 'the commander came up and arrested him and ordered him to be bound with two chains' (Acts 21:33). The excessive disorder, lynch behaviour and mis-identification of Paul with the Egyptian insurrectionist all demand that he be heavily bound. Knowling indicates that the expression here for arrest (ἐπελάβετο αὐτοῦ; cf. Acts 17:19) suggests a hostile intention.[31] If the two chains are manacles rather than manacles and fetters (πέδαι), Paul has been bound not to one but two soldiers.[32] If, however, Agabus' prophetic action in binding himself at Acts 21:11 is an accurate depiction of Paul's later experience, then the two chains might indicate leg irons and manacles. It may be imprudent to take Agabus' prophecy so literally for two reasons. First, when Luke elsewhere wishes to indicate binding of hands and feet he is more specific (Luke 8:29; cf. Mark 5:4). Second, Acts 21:35 implies that after being bound Paul was still able to walk. Thus a very secure military custody is indicated, however one construes Paul to have been bound. Acts 22:25, if it indicates a further binding with thongs,[33] does not appreciably alter this assessment. The binding is consistent with the information the Tribune possesses.

IV. More 'Un-Roman' Behaviour

What is astonishing in all this is that Paul was a Roman citizen. The treatment he received was not only avoidable, it was illegal. Paul was treated in a manner far below his station and entirely out of keeping with his dignity. Paul silently allowed himself to be roughly arrested, clapped in irons and whisked into the prison of the Antonia like a common criminal for an interrogation which often conferred upon the slave and the low-born in Greek and Roman society that mocking and contemptuous title μαστιγίας.[34] Again, one is confronted with the two questions a Roman would ask: why did Paul not disclose his Roman citizenship at the 'Roman' time, and why did he do so only as he was stretched out?

---

[31]Knowling, 'The Acts', 453.
[32]So e.g, Tajra, The Trial of St. Paul, 68; Williams, Acts, 366; Cassidy, Society and Politics, 97f.
[33]For discussion, see R.H. Connolly, 'Syricisms in St. Luke', JTS 37 (1936), 383f.; Bruce, The Book of Acts, 419 n. 29, 421 and n. 38.
[34]Plautus, Capt. 558: 'Clap handcuffs on this rogue [mastigia]'. Yates and Wayte, 'Flagrum', 864.

The appearance of Tarsian citizenship prior to Roman citizenship in the text may appear somehow unnatural or simply wrong. Cassidy puts the point most dramatically:

> Given that Paul's standing as a Roman citizen would have supreme significance for the tribune and given that virtually no other piece of information could be so helpful to Paul's cause at this point, readers of Acts can only be astounded by Luke's report that Paul said nothing about his Roman citizenship at this juncture but emphasized instead his pride at being a citizen of Tarsus![35]

The priority given to Tarsian over Roman citizenship, however, has an ancient logic to it. Ramsay indicates that there is a modern tendency to underestimate the intensity of municipal patriotism among citizens of the ancient city because modern patriotism finds its near exclusive focus in country and/or race. He continues: '...to the ancient Greek citizen his city absorbed all his patriotism. His city, not his country as a whole, was his "fatherland"'.[36] Hanson's comment that pride in one's native city was still at the time of Paul a 'noticeable feature of city life'[37] must be considered something of an understatement. L.C.A. Alexander, in contextualising the Pauline political metaphors of exile and statehood, indicates that pride in, association with and relationship to the city continued a pervasive concern in the 1st century AD. There was in the cities a passionate interest in citizen status, a careful delineation of non-citizen rights, a studied retention of connections with the mother-city, and a concern on the part of outsiders to seek the advantages of the city through the protection and legitimacy afforded by patrons and parasitic associations.[38] The disposition to think of one's identity principally in terms of relationship to one's mother-city did not begin to abate until well into the 2nd century AD, only then giving way to a sense of Romanness as 'national identity'.[39] When one adds to this the fact already noted that Tarsus was a worthy object of 1st century AD civic pride in respect of its political, economic and intellectual prominence it is hardly surprising that Paul at once identifies himself

---

[35]Cassidy, *Society and Politics*, 101. *Cf.* Hanson, *The Acts*, 213.
[36]W.M. Ramsay, *The Cities of Saint Paul: Their Influence on His Life and Thought* (Dale Memorial Lectures; London: Hodder and Stoughton, 1907), 90.
[37]Hanson, *The Acts*, 213.
[38]L.C.A. Alexander, 'Christians as Outsiders: Some Functions of a Political Metaphor' (Sheffield: British New Testament Conference, 13 Sept. 1991) [Lecture].
[39]Comment of E.A. Judge during discussion of Alexander, 'Christians as Outsiders'.

in terms of his mother-city. Wrongly thought to be a revolutionary from the Roman province of Egypt, Paul discloses his identity in terms of adherence to Judaism and citizenship of the principal city of the Roman province of Cilicia. The temptation to judge the claim of Tarsian before Roman citizenship a blunder or narrative device to evoke suspense[40] is best resisted. One should also resist the temptation to see in the assertion of Tarsian citizenship a low view of Roman citizenship.[41]

Protection from the Jews and a dignified treatment at the hands of the Roman soldiery would not have been Paul's sole concern. Perhaps even more than at Acts 16, there are at Acts 21 religious disadvantages to an early disclosure of Roman citizenship. The Jerusalem context is predominantly Jewish and Paul's loyalty to Judaism is the issue. He is publicly accused to Jews by other Jews of profaning the geographic and religious heart of Judaism—bringing a Gentile into a forbidden area of the Temple. One should expect Paul to want, as at Acts 16, strongly to affirm both his loyalty to Judaism and the truth of his message. A claim of Roman citizenship, if not interpreted by the Jews (and perhaps even by the Tribune!) as conceding the truth of the charges, would nevertheless have evoked highly destructive distinctions between himself and his Jewish hearers. In such a context as this, 'Jew' and 'Roman' are strictly antithetic. That Paul would not have been so careless of such consequences as to disclose publicly his Roman citizenship is even confirmed by the manner of his Tarsian citizenship disclosure at Acts 22. We have already noted that, whereas Paul presents himself *in Greek* to the Tribune as a *Jew* who is a *citizen* of Tarsus, to the Jews Paul presents himself *in Aramaic* as a *zealous Jew* who, though born in Tarsus, was raised in Jerusalem.

Only at Acts 21:25 does Paul's Roman citizenship become a matter of record. Modern commentators, however, improperly assess this disclosure when they describe Paul as here 'appealing',[42] 'claiming',[43] 'pleading',[44] 'protesting',[45] 'affirming',[46] or 'asserting'[47] his citizenship/rights or 'suddenly and abruptly decrying'[48] the potential viola-

---

[40]So Haenchen, *The Acts*, 635; Conzelmann, *Acts*, 189f.; Schille, *Die Apostelgeschichte*, 424.

[41]So Cassidy, *Society and Politics*, 199 n. 17.

[42]So Haenchen, *The Acts*, 632; Lüdemann, *Early Christianity*, 237, and others.

[43]E.g., Longenecker, 'The Acts', 527; Lake and Cadbury, *BC*, 283.

[44]E.g., Foakes-Jackson, *The Acts*, 157.

[45]E.g., G.H.C. Macgregor and T.P. Ferris, *The Acts of the Apostles* (IB 9; New York: Abingdon, 1954), p 297; Munck, *The Acts*, 220; Neil, *The Acts*, 225.

[46]E.g., H.S. Songer, 'Paul's Mission to Jerusalem: Acts 20-28', *RevExp* 71 (1974), 505.

[47]E.g., H.J. Cadbury, 'Note 26. Roman Law and the Trial of Paul', in *BC*, vol. 5, 305.

tion of them. Bruce comes closest to an accurate description when he simply writes that Paul 'reveals'[49] his citizenship. In fact, Paul only *insinuates* it. This would surely have been a matter of surprise to a Roman reader. Paul does not cry out 'I am a Roman'.[50] Rather, he poses a hypothetical (εἰ) in the second person (ἄνθρωπον) for clarification on a question of Roman trial procedure (Is it legal for you to scourge a Roman, an uncondemned man?[51] Acts 22:25). The character of Paul's disclosure must be taken into account when the second question above, 'Why here?', is considered. One might expect that Paul, now out of the temple context where Jewish misunderstanding would almost surely have arisen and in the exclusively Roman context of the Antonia, would effect a more conventional Roman stance. Paul's insinuation of, rather than insistence upon, his rights encourages two conclusions: first, Paul will not so stridently insist upon his Roman rights as to undercut his religious commitment to Judaism before Roman eyes. In other words, the fact that he is a Christian Jew affects the way he claims his Roman rights. This is not to say, however, that Paul puts little stock in or is ambivalent about his Roman citizenship.[52] Second, while his self-disclosure indicates that he has some confidence that his Roman citizenship may make a difference in his treatment, its manner suggests that Paul is still prepared to suffer or even die without complaint (*cf.* Acts 21:13) if it is disregarded. The oft-suggested motive of simple avoidance of the μάστιξ/*flagrum*, while probably true, hardly exhausts the text's message.

V. Social/Juridical Damage Assessment

The indirect indication of his Roman citizenship falls upon sensitive ears. The centurion charged with the interrogation immediately warns the Tribune. When questioned directly by the Tribune, Paul confirms the fact with alacrity. We may doubt that Luke's intention in recording the disclosure and subsequent comparison of citizenships is 'to criticize the Roman system'.[53] The Tribune acts according to his knowl-

---

[48]Cassidy, *Society and Politics*, 101.

[49]Bruce, *The Book of Acts*, 419, though in earlier commentaries he speaks of Paul's 'protest'.

[50]*Contra* Tajra, *The Trial of St. Paul*, 91.

[51]*Infra*, ch. 12.

[52]*Contra* Cassidy, *Society and Politics*, 101.*Cf.* also Haenchen, *The Acts*, 635.

[53]A. Ehrhardt, *The Acts of the Apostles: Ten Lectures* (Manchester: MUP, 1969), 111.

edge and in keeping with Roman law and, when appraised of Paul's status, he demonstrates sensitivity. Neither is it the case that the comparison of citizenships is superfluous, adding 'nothing to Luke's purpose (except light relief)'.[54] When seen in the light of status comparisons in the custodial deliberative process, its inclusion makes great sense.

The Tribune was the highest ranking officer in Jerusalem and an important man. He was commissioned to lead a double cohort of 760 infantry and 240 cavalry troops as the title χιλίαρχος (Acts 21:31)[55] suggests. Sherwin-White ventures that he 'had worked his way up through the ranks and the centurionate of the auxiliary army of Syria, and bought his way into the citizenship—and the equestrian status and a military tribunate too—with his personal savings'.[56] His name Claudius Lysias (Acts 23:26; 24:22) and the cost of his citizenship (Acts 22:28) indicate that he was probably Greek and had received the franchise early in the Emperor Claudius' reign.[57]

The Tribune is keenly aware that he stands in some peril for having mistreated a fellow Roman. That he discloses the circumstances of his own acquisition of the citizenship should hardly be construed as a cynical jibe or irrelevant small talk.[58] It is much more appropriately read as a study in social/juridical damage assessment. The Tribune is drawing Paul into disclosing more personal information for the purpose of comparison. Discussion in the previous chapter has indicated that the harm done to a plaintiff was judged more serious and worthy of a more harsh penalty where the plaintiff was the defendant's better. The same principle held where a magistrate or official was guilty of arraigning or punishing a social superior. Caesar threw the quaestor Novius Niger into the prison for arraigning him, an official of superior rank, before his tribunal.[59] Lysias may have hoped that Paul's was an even more recently-granted citizenship under less auspicious circumstances than his own, rightly thinking that one might only lightly punish or even forgive the mistreatment by a superior of his social inferior.

---

[54]Marshall, *The Acts*, 360.

[55]*Cf.* John 18:12. The same position may be indicated by Josephus' φρούραρχος (*AJ* 15.408 [15.11.4];18.93f. [18.4.3].

[56]Sherwin-White, *Roman Society*, 155f. *Cf.* A.H.M. Jones, *A History of Rome Through the Fifth Century. Volume III: Empire* (The Documentary History of Western Civilization; London/Melbourne: Macmillan, 1970), 288.

[57]Dio Cassius 60.17.5f.

[58]See Marshall, *The Acts*, 359; Bruce, *The Book of Acts*, 421; E.M. Blaiklock, *The Acts of the Apostles* (TNTC; Grand Rapids: Eerdmans, 1959), 174.

[59]Suetonius, *Jul.* 17.2.

That Paul was a citizen from birth, however, threatened great damage to Claudius Lysias' person and career. Not only had the Tribune broken the law prohibiting the binding and torture of citizens, he had abused a Roman possessing by far a better quality of citizenship than his own. Long-standing prejudice would favour Paul above Lysias in the event of a formal complaint. Small wonder that the soldiers detailed to interrogate Paul withdrew immediately—perhaps even unbidden—and that the Tribune was seriously shaken by the disclosure (Acts 22:29).[60]

VI. Indications of Lightened Custody

The Tribune's discovery pressed him to do an immediate and radical reappraisal of the arrangements for Paul's keeping. However, the extent of the change at this point is debated because the text indicates that the Tribune, while fearful because he had bound Paul (Acts 22:29), apparently released him only the next day (Acts 22:30). What was the character of Paul's release? Finding support in MSS H L P, which add 'from the bonds' after 'he released him', some indicate that λύω only at this point signifies a release from chains and allege a contradiction in the Tribune's behaviour.[61] References to the citizen Paul's being in chains at Acts 26:29 and 28:20, it is alleged, only emphasize the contradiction.[62] Others attempt to resolve the apparent contradiction by linking only the desire to learn more with 'the next day' and not the release.[63] Finally, some have suggested that a change from heavier to lighter chains would allow Paul to remain in chains overnight, yet satisfy his aggrieved citizen rights.[64]

Several observations should be made: First, the MS evidence cited above is quite late. Second, references to Paul's chains at Acts 26:29 and 28:20 hardly figure in the present discussion as they describe the conditions of Paul's keeping ordered by other and higher officials at a

---

[60]Scepticism regarding the Tribune's fear is generated by the unfair comparison of the Tribune with unconcerned governors (so Haenchen, *The Acts*, 634). The Tribune's powers and protections do not match those afforded governors. *Cf.* Josephus, *BJ* 2.246 [2.12.7]).
[61]Conzelmann, *Acts*, 191; Haenchen, *The Acts*, 637, 639; and others.
[62]E.g., Krodel, *Acts*, 420; Haenchen, *The Acts*, 639.
[63]Holtzmann cited in Haenchen, *The Acts*, 639.
[64]Indicated in Tajra, *The Trial of St. Paul*, 91; Wikenhauser, *Die Apostelgeschichte*, 248.

later time. Third, there is no hint of a change in the heaviness of Paul's chaining. Most importantly, it is hardly conceivable that Luke means to suggest that Paul was left in any type of bonds, having just indicated both the Tribune's discovery of the superiority of Paul's citizenship to his own and the Tribune's fear at having bound Paul. This assessment is supported by the reading δεδεκὼς καὶ παραχρῆμα ἔλυσεν αὐτόν in MSS 614 syh** sa at Acts 22:29 which, while not original because it makes the textually secure ἔλυσεν αὐτὸν καί at Acts 22:30 otiose,[65] certainly represents a more legally- and contextually-informed early attempt at resolving the uncertainty in favour of Paul's immediate release from bonds.

The change of custody appears to have run as follows: whereas Paul's full identity was not earlier known to the Tribune, it is now. Out of his fear at having maltreated someone possessing a better citizenship than his own and in order to scotch the continuing offence, the Tribune removes the chains from Paul. The Tribune, however, still has a problem: the specific identity of Paul's accusers and the charges against him remain unknown. Indications that a serious offence has been committed are still of great concern to the Tribune as keeper of the peace because he still lacks the facts (Acts 22:30); and so Paul is kept, albeit in some comfort, in the Antonia overnight. In terms of the custodial determination diagram (Fig. 1), Paul's *persona* has intruded into the prior assessment, pushing him 'upward' from a harsh military custody with bonds and a close brush with inquisitorial torture to a much lighter and more dignified military custody without bonds.

The Tribune had, the day before, wrongly ordered Paul publicly chained and nearly flogged. He would hardly now either continue or renew the abuse, which would again violate the *leges Porcia* and *Iulia*, by publicly conducting Paul in bonds before a non-Roman official gathering. The term ἔλυσεν at Acts 22:30 must therefore be taken to indicate at least a further slackening of custodial arrangements for Paul. In fact, Acts 22:30-23:10 indicates that Paul is for a short time entirely free of Roman custody. This concession to Paul's Roman status, moreover, has confusing effects upon the Jewish proceedings which actually answer a number of puzzling aspects in Luke's account.[66] Acts 22:30 indicates that the Tribune personally escorted Paul to the venue of the enquiry and made him stand before the Sanhedrin. Otherwise, Paul is

---

[65]J.H. Ropes, *The Text*, in *BC*, vol. 3, 215.

[66]Hanson, *The Acts*, 247 and Conzelmann, *Acts*, 191f. discuss the problems involved.

unattended. The fact that the Tribune has to command his troops to come to Paul when trouble erupts indicates their distance, perhaps even considerable distance, from the proceedings. The Tribune apparently is sensitive enough not to intrude and unduly influence the proceedings by insisting upon a significant Roman military presence there. The verb καταβάν (Acts 23:10) is unhelpful in determining the Tribune's exact physical location during the investigation.[67] The Tribune's principal objective in convening the gathering is auditory and he need not be among the Sanhedrin, much less chairing it. The high priest's liberty to order Paul struck on the face (Acts 23:2f.) and the absence of Roman intervention when this occurs suggests that the Tribune (and his guards) not only stood at a distance but had also temporarily given up Paul to his own recognisances.[68] Such signals as these may explain the differences in perception evident in the text concerning the nature of the investigation. Quite clearly, Lysias did not construe the gathering as a trial (Acts 22:30; 23:28);[69] however, the ambiguities inherent in the Romans' behaviour in freeing Paul and standing away from him and the subsequently emboldened conduct of the Sanhedrin—particularly their unopposed physical abuse of Paul—account well for Paul's perception that he was tried by the Sanhedrin (Acts 23:3, 6; cf. 24:21).[70]

Rescued, Paul was returned to the Antonia. Some wrongly assume that Paul is now rechained.[71] He is a prisoner—he is called ὁ δέσμιος at Acts 23:18. But the conclusion that he is chained can hardly be drawn from Acts 26:29 and 28:16, 20, as we have already seen. Moreover, the immediate context will not support this interpretation. In fact, a number of indicators suggest that he is not only unchained, but even granted some dignity in the Antonia.

The letter (Acts 23:25; cf. 25:26f.) sent with Paul to the governor Felix in Caesarea shows the Tribune to have 'filled in' the missing information in the deliberative process to his personal satisfaction. The Tribune was already aware of Paul's Roman citizenship (Acts 23:27). The information concerning Paul's Tarsian citizenship is not deemed

---

[67]Contra Tajra, The Trial of St. Paul, 97.

[68]This fact must soften the objection that the Tribune was unclean and would have been prohibited from meeting with the Sanhedrin.

[69]There are problems in the Tribune's calling a formal gathering of the Sanhedrin (e.g.: Haenchen, The Acts, 640; Krodel, Acts, 421f.

[70]It is entirely unnecessary to claim that the text is inconsistent (e.g.: Krodel, Acts, 421f.; Stählin, Die Apostelgeschichte, 288).

[71]E.g., Cassidy, Society and Politics, 98.

worth mentioning and his religious commitment and indications of honourable status and rank in Judaism are apparently a matter of ambivalence (does αὐτῶν at Acts 23:29 include Paul?). There is no indication that the Tribune is aware that Paul has 'very considerable skills'. The Tribune is prepared now, however, to identify (or perhaps even nominate), because of their hostility, certain members of the Sanhedrin (Acts 23:28; cf. 24:1) as Paul's accusers (κατήγοροις: Acts 23:30).[72] He has also determined, according to Acts 23:29, that the charge against Paul relates to Jewish law, but from the Roman perspective calls for neither death nor chains. In terms of the custodial deliberation diagram (Fig. 9), outside of the troubling point that Paul's accusers have been identified as the powerful provincial élite, the Tribune has progressively replaced his initial 'worst possible case' assessment of Paul with a 'best possible case' assessment. The Tribune can hardly therefore mean by μηδὲν ἄξιον δεσμῶν that Paul does not deserve 'imprisonment' (NIV; NEB). After all, why then is Paul kept in the Antonia, called a prisoner, and sent along to Felix with his accusers ordered shortly thereafter to follow? Rather, in keeping with the above assessment and the Tribune's fear at having been earlier caught out in the matter of chaining a citizen, he is asserting that Paul has done nothing deserving 'chains'. An emphasis upon secrecy at Acts 23:16-22 also strongly suggests that Paul is not bound. When Paul's nephew relates the plot to Paul and this information is then conveyed to the Tribune, it seems that Paul is neither manacled to a soldier[73] nor attended so closely that he and his nephew cannot communicate privately.

It is also clear that Paul is not confined to some unsavoury cell or dungeon in either solitary confinement or with other malefactors in the Antonia. When Paul calls 'one of the centurions' (Acts 23:17), this indicates that there are several readily at hand. He is being kept in the senior officers' quarters at the fortress. His freedom to summon a centurion and tell him to take his nephew to the Tribune (apparently without resistance or questioning; Acts 23:17f.) suggests that the officers have orders to accommodate him and grant his reasonable requests.

Because Paul's nephew came to him (Acts 23:16-22), it has been suggested that Paul received visitors quite freely as a further concession to his dignity as a Roman. How was Paul's nephew able to gain access? Some assume that it was because he was a relative,[74] but this is

---

[72]Cf. Ulpian in Dig. 48.2.7.prol. and 1.
[73]Haenchen, The Acts, 646 states this as an assumption of the text.

probably wrong. The text notes that the youth is the son of Paul's sister (Acts 23:26), but it appears that the identification is for Luke's readers' benefit. He is identified only as a 'young man' by Paul to the centurion (Acts 23:17) and by the centurion to the Tribune (Acts 23:18; *cf.* v. 22). Apparently, the boy's relationship to Paul was kept a secret from the Romans. This being the case, might one then be justified in assuming, as some do, that other visitors were permitted him?[75] Given his several brushes with death it seems highly improbable. The nephew's access appears in several respects to be noted in the text as unusual and individual. To construe the nephew as 'visiting' Paul and to compare it with other examples of family/friend visits is inappropriate; his is an urgent coming motivated by the awareness that Paul is in mortal danger (Acts 23:12-16). His coming, moreover, is personally motivated; no one else apparently knows of it (Acts 23:16, 22). The nephew's relative ease of access to the inner Antonia, it seems from the emphasis of the text, is due to his youth.[76] Being so young, Paul's nephew was deemed entirely harmless by the soldiers. Other adult males would probably have been denied access for security reasons—Paul was as much in protective custody at this point as he was a remand prisoner.

---

[74]E.g., Schille, *Die Apostelgeschichte*, 429. For patterns of help and kinds of helpers, see *infra*.

[75]G. Clark, 'The Social Status of Paul', *ExpTim* 96 (1984/5), 111. *Cf.* Marshall, *The Acts*, 368.

[76]Twice the diminutive νεανίσκος is used in the text (Acts 23:18, 22) and the Tribune takes Paul's nephew by the hand (Acts 23:19).

CHAPTER 7

CAESAREA

During Paul's trial Felix obtained information which resulted in lighter custody for Paul. This reassessment considered the following matters: a charge of factionalism had been made, appealing to Roman political and administrative interests. The charge was rebutted on factual and procedural grounds by Paul. Felix was impressed, as the record of the motives for the adjournment seems to indicate, with the complexity of the case and the contradictions between the presentations of the plaintiffs and the defendant.

The matter of relative status between accusers and accused was equally important to Felix. The greater native social status of the accusers would have outweighed whatever he discerned concerning Paul. Paul's accusers were politically significant and by couching their charge in political terms thrust their status before Felix. Felix would have seen in Paul's leadership of a subgroup within Judaism a degree of influence, but he was more inclined to show regard for the representatives of the Jewish establishment.

The assignment of Paul to a centurion can in this context be considered the expression of Felix' desire to preserve Paul for his own possible political and monetary advantage. The vigilance was relaxed, though it is unlikely that Paul was unchained. Owing, among other things, to threats on Paul's life and the ethnic instability of the community, Paul probably remained in Herod's praetorium in a lightened military custody.

I. The First Phase

Paul is the object of two separate custodial deliberations in Caesarea. The first, of quite short duration, sets Paul's custody for the five days prior to his trial (Acts 23:31-24:1). During the second, which is ostensibly the trial itself, Paul's custodial arrangements are set for the next two years (Acts 24:1-27). Paul's custody in the first phase is determined by several means; the Tribune's letter, a personal interview, and perhaps the manner of Paul's arrival. We shall consider the relative influence of each.

1. The Tribune's Letter

The Tribune's message is hardly intended solely to inform Felix concerning the details of Paul's case. To be sure, the basic details are there: The accused standing before Felix is a Roman citizen rescued at the point of nearly being killed by the Jews. The only charges disclosed during subsequent enquiry before the Sanhedrin were Jewish in nature and not serious from the Roman point of view. A subsequent plot against the life of the accused was foiled by his immediate extradition to Caesarea. Sanhedral plaintiffs had been ordered to appear before Felix to accuse the defendant directly.

The Tribune also wishes to portray his own behaviour in the events in the most favourable light. One would certainly not expect to hear a whisper from the Tribune that he had, contrary to law, publicly chained a Roman citizen and nearly flogged him. The Tribune's assertion that he rescued Paul from certain death at the hands of the Jews because he had become aware of Paul's Roman citizenship (Acts 23:27), however, is both astonishing and amusing. Lysias shows amazing audacity in trying to benefit from the situation by portraying himself to Felix as not simply blameless but positively praiseworthy: he is the protector of a Roman citizen fallen into murderous provincial clutches. Such an exuberant but gross exaggeration risks rankling the citizen whom he had in fact abused.

Would Paul have officially contested the facts as represented? The letter seems to have been drafted to silence any protest and to evoke gratitude. Cassidy writes that Lysias' words at Acts 23:29 are almost too exonerating of Paul. Lysias reports not that Paul is innocent of the charges (there are Jewish charges) but that *no* substantive charges (from the Roman perspective) have been preferred against him.[1]

Paul could hardly fail to appreciate that, while the Tribune is building 'deniability' into the document, he has also been extremely helpful to Paul's case. The letter amounts, moreover, to a virtual recommendation to Felix that Paul's custody be honourable, i.e., without chains.

Lysias may be protecting himself even further when he writes that he has ordered Paul's accusers to appear before Felix (Acts 23:30). As Caesarea was the administrative and judicial centre for Judea, Paul might despair of a speedy hearing. The case load there would be particularly heavy.[2] It might therefore have been considered an additional favour to Paul that Lysias orders the accusers to appear at Caesarea post-haste to present their case before Felix. They are not to await a summons. This would presumably pre-empt the governor's trial calendar.

The letter, as analysed above, shows an awareness of the damage that Paul's influence might do to the Tribune. It also subtly displays favour toward Paul. While certainly not an explicit letter of recommendation,[3] it is more than a mere letter of report. Luke's perception of the letter's purpose is summarized by Cassidy as follows:

> ...Luke understands Lysias' letter to be an adroitly political move: Lysias is sending the governor a prisoner who is not only a Roman citizen, but a highly articulate one; and, to the degree possible, he wishes the 'prisoner' as well as the governor to have a positive estimation of the way he has handled the matter.[4]

2. Paul's Arrival

Paul has just arrived with a military contingent of some 70 *equites*. Would the manner of his arrival have influenced the custodial deliberations? Luke's reference to the dispatch of some 470 troops[5] to escort

---

[1]Cassidy, *Society and Politics*, 100.
[2]The matter of trial delays, touched upon already will be discussed more fully *infra*.
[3]For examples of the not too subtle use of *gratia* and *potentia* in letters see the examples from Cicero [50 B.C.] and M. Cornelius Fronto [c. 157-161 A.D.] given in Kelly, *Roman Litigation*, 56-60.
[4]Cassidy, *Society and Politics*, 100.
[5]Luke mentions 70 horse, 200 infantry and 200 δεξιολάβοι. Δεξιολάβοι probably means 'spearmen' (lit.: 'taking in the right hand') rather than the more popular 'led horses' (which cuts the numbers of troops and renders the distances travelled more credible as all have mounts. See Kilpatrick, 'Acts XXIII. 23', 393-96

one man has been called by some a fantasy intended to emphasize the importance of the prisoner, the enormity of the danger, and the quality of the measures taken by Roman military officials.[6] Were we ignorant of Roman-Jewish relations during this period, the numbers might seem inflated. The growing general unrest in Judaea, however, suggests that the numbers are realistic. Josephus records a number of acts by individuals which touched off explosive and devastating general uprisings calling for military intervention.[7] It would have been a wise senior officer who heeded trustworthy warnings and anticipated the level of popular animosity toward a prisoner in his care by taking swift and sufficient measures. The large numbers indicated at Acts 23:23 would discourage any attempt to assassinate his prisoner. The more general risk to troops of ambush and slaughter due to the fewness of their numbers would also thus be avoided. Failure to anticipate these risks could incur serious punishment.[8] The textual details concerning the third hour, the provision of mounts, and the numbers involved in Paul's transport, because of their precision and because they are not strictly material to the text, suggest accurate reporting rather than Lukan romancing. The same may be said of the fitness of the route taken by Paul and his guards,[9] the logic underlying the stopover at Antipatris and the return of the footsoldiers to Jerusalem from somewhere near that town.[10]

We conclude, therefore, that the measures taken for Paul's transport are not a Lukan indication of the high esteem in which the Tribune holds Paul the Roman citizen, but simply an adequate preparation which wisely avoided the very real perils of travel. Nor, additionally, would the 70 *equites* be interpreted by Felix as an indication of the prisoner's superior status or importance. The footsoldiers at Acts 23:31f. must include the two centurions mentioned at Acts 23:23. The expressions κατὰ τὸ διατεταγμένον, ἐάσαντες and ὑπέστρεψαν indicate the presence of those who have been put in charge of the operation. Paul would then appear before Felix in the company of cavalry soldiers be-

---

[6]So e.g., Conzelmann, *Acts*, 194; Lentz, *Luke's Portrayal*, 332.

[7]See e.g., Josephus, *AJ* 20.108-12 [20.5.3] ≈ *BJ* 2.224-27 [2.12.1]; *AJ* 20.113-16 [20.5.4] ≈ *BJ* 2.228-31 [2.12.2].

[8]Military incompetence was a *crimen maiestas minuta*. Cf. 42.

[9]This route was taken by Cestius Gallus and his army in October of 66 AD (Josephus, *BJ* 2.515f., 2.546-55 [2.19.1, 8f.]; cf. 2.228 [2.12.2]).

[10]After Antipatris the journey would not require such heavy security as the country was more open and largely populated by Gentiles according to F.F. Bruce, *The Acts of the Apostles: Greek Text with Introduction and Commentary* (1951; Grand Rapids: Eerdmans, 1990), 473 and Neil, *The Acts*, 232.

low the rank of centurion. Under normal circumstances, prisoners in transit would be chained for security.[11] It is very unlikely, however, given Lysias' alarm at having bound Paul in the first instance and the letter's assertion that Paul has done nothing deserving chains, that Paul would have so appeared before Felix. In this last respect only would there have been any 'influence' in the manner of Paul's appearance upon Felix.

3. The Interview

The brief personal interview consists in Felix asking Paul what province he is from (Acts 23:34). The question is jurisdictional and suggests that Felix might have avoided trying the case. An accused could be tried in his own home province, the province in which he had allegedly committed the crime, or in the province where he had been apprehended.[12] The discovery that Paul was from Cilicia foreclosed the option of a transfer as Cilicia was at this time under the authority of the Legate of Syria to whom Felix was responsible. A refusal to try the case in these circumstances would probably have been read as an annoying avoidance tactic by the Legate. A sudden change of trial venue would also strain relations with the members of the Jewish supreme court who were soon to arrive in Caesarea to accuse Paul. Felix was boxed into handling the case.

4. Custody in the Praetorium of Herod

Caesarea, built on a grand scale by Herod the Great (22-10/9 BC) upon the site of the coastal structure known as Strato's Tower, was the administrative seat of the Roman procurators of Palestine.[13] It became, in the time of the Flavians, a Roman colony. As cases for Roman determination were often referred there[14] it would have had ample facilities for imprisoning individuals. Citing Josephus, Haefeli writes:

---

[11]Cf. supra, 31.

[12]Dig. 48.3.7, 11.Cf. Mart. Pion. 9.1; Mart. Let. Lyons & Vienne 1.20.

[13]On the procurators and the powers of their office, cf. Sherwin-White, Roman Society, 6-10; H.O.A. Keinath, 'The Contacts of the Book of Acts With Roman Political Institutions', CTM 1 (1930), 197.

[14]Josephus, BJ 2.271-73 [2.14.1].

The last procurators in Judaea held a vast number of prisoners in custody in Caesarea. Upon recall from their posts they nearly all bequeathed prisons full of people to their successors, e.g. (A XVIII 4, 1), Cuspius Fadus (A XX 5, 2), Cumanus (A XX 6, 1; B II 12, 2), Felix (B II 13, 7), Albinus and Florus (A XX 9,5).[15]

The outbreak of war swelled the numbers of prisoners sent on to Caesarea.[16] Josephus speaks of Albinus emptying *the prisons*.[17] He elsewhere notes that civil magistrates in Caesarea had the power to incarcerate individuals in Caesarea—presumably in holding facilities not connected with the Roman military.[18]

Felix ordered that Paul be kept under guard in Herod's *praetorium* (Acts 23:35b). Πραιτώριον, borrowed from Latin, can signify, '(1) the general's tent or headquarters in a Roman camp; (2) the residence of a governor or prince...; (3) a spacious villa; (4) the *praetorium* or camp of the praetorian cohorts in Rome'. Meanings (1) and (2) seem most appropriate. Acts refers to the palace built by Herod the Great at Caesarea[19] which, after the usual pattern of expropriations, became the official residence of the Roman governors of Judaea.

A number of significant structures have been unearthed on the 164 acre site of the city, and its famous harbour facilities have been recently explored and reported. Successive destructions of the city by invading forces and the fact that its marble walls and statuary were burned by farmers for lime and its ruined buildings were quarried for ready-cut marble and granite to build cities elsewhere might leave doubt that anything of the *praetorium* has survived. Recently, however, the foundations of an opulent palace, replete with dining room facing a near olympic size pool and called by the excavators the Promontory Palace, have been offered as the remains of the *praetorium* in question (Fig. 17).[20] Pottery and lamps found where ancient renovations had occurred suggest that the palace was constructed when Herod rebuilt

---

[15]Tr. from L. Haefeli, 'Cäsarea am Meer. Topographie und Geschichte der Stadt nach Josephus und Apostelgeschichte', *NA* 10 (1923), 5. Heft, 22.

[16]Josephus, *BJ* 7.20 [7.1.3], 37.37-40 [7.3.1]. Josephus states that he himself was held there (*BJ* 3.410 [3.9.1]; 4.622-29 [4.10.7]; *Vit.* 414 [75]).

[17]*BJ* 2.273 [2.14.1].

[18]*Ibid.* 2.269 [2.13.7]. Cf. *AJ* 17.175, 178 [17.8.2]; *BJ* 1.659 [1.32.6].

[19]Josephus, *AJ* 15. 331 [15.9.6]; *BJ* 1.617 [1.21.5]; 2.17 [2.2.2]. Note, however, the use of the plural 'palaces' in the first and third texts. Would the *praetorium* have been part of a larger complex?

[20]B. Burrell, K. Gleason and E. Netzer, 'Uncovering Herod's Seaside Palace', *BAR* 19³ (1993), 50-57, 76.

Caesarea.[21] Two column-shaped pedestals were found on the site
bearing six inscriptions; the earliest in Greek dates after 71 AD and the
latest in Latin dates to 293-305 AD.

> Caesarea has produced other columnar pedestals, several inscribed
> and reinscribed like these, but none with so many inscriptions of ac-
> tual governors of the province. It would be natural for such inscrip-
> tions to be set up in some official yet public locale, such as (but not
> limited to) the *praetorium* at Caesarea, formerly Herod's palace.[22]

If the Promontory Palace is indeed the structure referred to at Acts
23:35, Paul would have been confined in one of its many rooms.[23]
Josephus indicates that Antipater (*c.* 6-4 BC) was incarcerated within
the palace. There was, moreover, sufficient proximity to Herod's own
quarters that when, at the king's attempted suicide, the sound of loud
lamentation was made, Antipater heard it. Believing his father to be
dead, Antipater tried unsuccessfully to negotiate his immediate and
complete release with the jailer.[24]

It seems that Felix was not overly impressed by the letter or by
Paul himself at this stage and that we should probably take 'to be
guarded' (φυλάσσεσθαι) at Acts 23:35 as indication that Paul was
placed under strict restraint, perhaps even in bonds in a cell. Bruce
writes that the expression ἔχειν τε ἄνεσιν [to have some freedom[25]] at
Acts 24:23 'is the only occurrence of ἄνεσις in the NT outside the
Pauline letters, where a contrast with θλίψις [tribulation] is regularly
implied if not expressed'.[26] If the term itself suggests something like a
freer form of military custody by implication the guards' constraints
on Paul in the first five days of Caesarean custody would have been severe. Paul would be closely watched and virtually immobile. Furthermore, the later command that visitors not be forbidden him (Acts
24:23) suggests that the first phase of his Caesarean imprisonment involved complete isolation from friends and associates and from the
help they might provide.

This first phase of Paul's Caesarean imprisonment was inappropriate to his station and the known facts of his case. It is unlikely, how-

---

[21]*Ibid.*, 54.

[22]*Ibid.*, 57.

[23]If, however, Paul is kept in a cell or a prison structure that is part of a Herodian
palace complex, we may need to look elsewhere for the *praetorium*.

[24]Josephus, *AJ* 17.182-87[17.7]. *Cf. ibid.*, *BJ* 1.617 [1.31.5]; 1.663 [1.32.7].

[25]BAGD, 65.

[26]Bruce, *The Acts of the Apostles*, 482.

ever palatial the *praetorium* was, that Felix' command put Paul in
officers' quarters as at Jerusalem. There are no centurions among the
soldiers with whom Paul has arrived as has been argued above.[27]
Moreover, if not directed to these soldiers, Felix is unlikely to have
commanded a centurion personally to keep Paul in light custody on
such slight information as he has thus far received. The command is
probably fulfilled by military personnel below the grade of centurion.[28] Outside of his being confined in Herod's *praetorium*, then, Paul
appears to have been treated in a rather routine and unexceptional
way.

II. Caesarea: The Second Phase

Five days after Paul's arrival, his accusers came before Felix. The trial
followed the 'judicial enquiry' (*cognitio*) procedure; though Felix had
immense power as judge, he played a merely inquisitorial role.[29] The
plaintiffs were required to prosecute in the presence of the accused (*cf.*
Acts 25:16),[30] and the accused had the opportunity to defend himself.
The judge, perhaps after consulting with his council, would then declare 'his verdict after considering the status of the parties as well as
the facts of the case'.[31]

1. The Accusers and Accused

Paul's accusers present to the Roman governor Felix imposing political, social, and economic Jewish status credentials. As 'rulers and
elders' (Acts 24:1) they represent the high priestly family and the leaders of the lay aristocracy respectively. Their birth credentials were superior, and they possessed offices and honours which put them at the
pinnacle of religious and political power in Judaism. They would have
been heads of some of the wealthiest families in Judaea.[32] As high as

---

[27]*Supra*, 154f.

[28]*Cf. Mart. Mont. & Luc.* 4.1f.

[29]J. Dauvillier, 'A propos de la venue de Saint Paul à Rome. Notes sur son procès
et son voyage maritime', *BLE* 61 (1960), 6f. and note the term *cognoscere* at Acts 24:8
(Vg). *Cf.* Garnsey, *Social Status*, 6, and on *extra ordinem* trial procedure, see Sherwin-White, *Roman Society*, 17f.; and Tajra, *The Trial of St. Paul*, 115f.

[30]See Tacitus, *Hist.* 1.6; Appian, *BCiv.* 3.54; *Dig.* 48.17.1.

[31]Garnsey, *Social Status*, 98.

Paul's status was[33] his accusers were superior. In one respect only
would they be at a disadvantage: Paul was a Roman citizen. Roman
prejudice would lean toward Paul's innocence and this would need to
be adroitly attacked.

We have indicated that retaining an advocate was a frequent resort of defendants and plaintiffs who felt vulnerable to the strength of
an opponent's case, juridical acumen or superior status.[34] It is probably the measure of their sense of disadvantage in prosecuting a Roman
citizen that Paul's accusers retained the services of the orator Tertullus
(Acts 24:1).[35] Hengel and Markschies write that the Jewish leaders
'brought a real expert with them'[36] and Winter's analysis of Tertullus'
opening comments corroborates this.[37] Far from being a rather artless
and insincere attempt by Tertullus at flattering Felix[38] (or by Luke at
mimicking the forensic form for that matter!), it follows closely the
conventional advice of the forensic handbooks. Winter concludes that
Tertullus 'was an able professional rhetor, whose *captatio benevolentiae*
was carefully linked to his accusations in the hope of mounting a formidable case against Paul'.[39] Well schooled in rhetoric and sensitive to
Roman provincial governance, he was perfectly fit to cross swords
with Paul. Retaining him probably conferred an additional advantage
because Tertullus was a familiar face to the governor. Tertullus would
undoubtedly have represented other clients before Felix.

Might Tertullus also have been a Roman citizen? This would
help minimize any disadvantage his clients might have had relative to
Paul in Felix' court. The name Tertullus (diminutive of Tertius) is unhelpful in making a determination in this regard. It probably indicates
that he was a Hellene but not necessarily that he was a Roman. Tertul-

---

[32]Further *supra*, 103f.

[33]See *supra*, ch. 4 on the indicators.

[34]For examples of the use of rhetors in the papyri, *cf.* R. Taubenschlag, '63. L'Emprisonnement dans le Droit Gréco-Égyptien'. *Opera Minora: II Band Spezieller Teil*
(Warszawa: Pánstwowe Wydawnictwo Naukowe, 1959), 725.

[35]See A. Steinsaltz, *The Essential Talmud*, tr. C. Galai (London: Weidenfeld and
Nicolson, 1976), 171, for the usual Jewish attitude toward legal counsel.

[36]M. Hengel and C. Markschies, *The 'Hellenization' of Judaea*, 26.

[37] Winter, 'The Importance', 505-31. We use Winter's analysis of the speech in what
follows. For Tertullus: vv. 2b-3 *exordium*; v. 5 *narratio*; vv. 6-8 *confirmatio* including
peroratio at v. 8. For Paul: v. 10b. *exordium*; v. 11 *narratio*; vv. 12f. *probatio* or *confirmatio*; vv. 14-18 *refutatio*; vv. 19-21 *peroratio*.

[38]Similarly, Paul's *exordium* at Acts 24:10b, for all its terseness, cannot be a cynical
attempt at flattery. *Cf.* Winter, 'The Importance', 508; Kelly, *Roman Litigation*, 53f.

[39]Winter, 'The Importance', 521. *Cf.* Cassidy, *Society and Politics*, 198.

lus might have been a Jew as he pleads his clients' case in the first person plural.[40] This would not be surprising. The presentation of the
accusers' case would have been helped immensely by a rhetor who
himself had, beyond his expertise, eloquence and the goodwill he
might inspire, strong and clear sympathies with Judaism. In keeping
with previous argument, Jewishness would hardly rule out the possibility that Tertullus also possessed the Roman citizenship. In the absence of more definite information, however, the tantalizing prospect
of Tertullus' being a Roman Jew must remain but a prospect.

When the Jews enter into the accusation phase of the trial (Acts
24:9), it is doubtful that they add materially to the charges. In fact, this
might have diminished the strength of the case already made. What is
probably happening instead is a kind of formal 'weighing in' of the accusers by their assertion of the truth of the charges as well as the non-
verbal marking of their status for the magistrate's consideration.

2. The Charges

The charge brought against Paul was very serious. Winter writes, 'According to the rhetorical handbooks, agitation or sedition, στάσις, was
the right charge to bring against an opponent in criminal proceedings'.[41] Related to war, rebellion and civil disturbance, στάσις was a
capital crime and pre-eminently prisonable as well. Thanks to Tertullus' masterful presentation, the charge and its proofs appear to have
been stripped of much of their distinctively Jewish or theological character and reconstructed in such a way as to appeal to Roman legal sensibilities and administrative concerns. Tertullus began his narratio by
accusing Paul of being pestilential; a troublemaker or scoundrel
(λοιμόν: Acts 24:5).[42] It is unlikely that this term deliberately recalls
the decree of the Roman Senate in which the alliance between Rome
and Simon Maccabeus was guaranteed,[43] as this enactment was over a
century old. The term is, rather, a general character assessment; Paul is
a troublemaker and dangerous to the public welfare as he has been
'stirring up riots among the Jews all over the world' (Acts 24:5). Sherwin-White indicates that the charge has a strikingly Roman flavour to

---

[40]Esp. Acts 24:3. Note also the phrase 'according to our law' (κατὰ τὸν ἡμέτερον
νόμον) in the Western text.
[41]Winter, 'The Importance', 518.
[42]Cf. the sources in BAGD, 479; LSJ, 1060.
[43]Contra Tajra, The Trial of St. Paul, 121. See 1 Macc. 15:21.

it. Claudius, in his letter to the Alexandrians in 41 AD, 'sums up his objection to certain political actions of the Jews as: "stirring up a universal plague throughout the world", κοινήν τινα τῆς οἰκουμένης νόσον ἐξεγείροντας' and refers to its 'startling' similarity to the charges against Paul, noting that it is 'precisely the one to bring against a Jew during the Principate of Claudius or the early years of Nero'.[44] The imperial measures taken against Jewish disturbers of the peace in Rome, most recently by Claudius in 49/50 AD, would also very likely have been recalled by such a charge.[45]

Paul was also identified as 'a ringleader of the Nazarene sect' (Acts 24:5). The term 'sect' (αἵρεσις) does not automatically have a negative connotation,[46] but here on the lips of an accusing advocate it surely does.[47] It implies a distinct group, but not necessarily one standing outside Judaism.[48] The intention was not to show that Paul was drawing the faithful away from Judaism into a religiously questionable sect but that the Nazarenes as a group were politically dangerous. Tertullus wished to remind Felix of earlier troubles associated with the Nazarenes in Judaea and abroad which indicated that it was 'a worldwide Jewish anti-Roman movement'.[49] By calling Paul a 'ringleader', Tertullus ascribes to him full responsibility for the troubles.

Winter's analysis draws the point of the accusation even more sharply.[50] Tertullus indicated at Acts 24:2f. his clients' general support for Felix' administration, praising him for the exercise of his *imperium* on behalf of the Jewish nation in the interests of public order and legal reform. Winter suggests that the first part of this praise would recall to Felix how he had recently quelled the rebellion of the Egyptian false prophet and his forces.[51] The second part would affirm, in addition to his judicial competence[52], Jewish appreciation of the helpfulness of Felix' legislative acts. Among them may have been Felix' inclusion in Judaean legislation of the specific provisions of the Claudian expulsion edict of 49/50 AD and the sanctions of the Claudian findings for the

---

[44]Sherwin-White, *Roman Society*, 51. *Cf.* J.J. Kilgallen, 'Paul Before Agrippa (Acts 26:2-23): Some Considerations', *Bib* 69 (1988), 173.

[45]*Supra*, 157.

[46]As in Josephus, *BJ* 2.119 [2.8.2].

[47]Lake and Cadbury, *BC*, 298. *Cf.* Acts 24:14; 28:22.

[48]*Contra* J.M. Gilchrist, 'On What Charge was St. Paul Brought to Rome?' *ExpTim* 78 (1966/67), 265f.

[49]Winter, 'The Importance', 520.

[50]Winter, 'The Importance', 516-19.

[51]Acts 21:38; Josephus, *BJ* 2.261-63 [2.13.5].

[52]*Cf.* Tacitus, *Ann.* 12.54; Josephus, *AJ* 20.162 [20.8.5].

Alexandrian situation.[53] Whatever the case, Tertullus accuses Paul of offending pragmatic and legislative efforts to maintain the peace, a matter concerning which Felix has a stake and thus will wish to act; i.e., to render a judgement favourable to the plaintiffs.

Acts 24:6-8 constitutes the *confirmatio* to the charge made. The assertion that Paul had 'even tried to desecrate the temple' (Acts 24:6) is probably intended to recall the prohibition publicized on plaques in Greek and Latin around this area against unclean persons entering the Temple enclosure.[54] Even the right of appeal could not protect a Roman offender from suffering the death penalty.[55] The force of the allegation, however, is blunted by several factors: First, as a ritually clean Jew, Paul was himself not liable to the penalty; his non-Jewish friends alone—had there been any with him (*cf.* Acts 21:28f.)—would have been. Second, while the word βεβηλῶσαι is fittingly chosen as it is more broadly secular,[56] Tertullus failed to explain what he meant. Such brevity was probably prudent as the explicit mention of Gentile uncleanness might have offended the governor. Third, though Acts 21:28 indicates that Paul was accused on the scene of *actually* profaning the temple, at Acts 24:6 the charge is weakened to the *attempt* (ἐπ-είρασεν) to do so. The distinction would not have been lost upon Felix.

If Tertullus was an expert at forensic discourse, Paul's own defence showed him to be equally well-equipped. The Pauline *captatio benevolentiae* at Acts 24:10b expresses confidence in Felix' juridical expertise in Jewish matters: Felix had been a judge over the Jewish nation for many years—the period which Paul had in mind could be as long as eight or nine years (ἐκ πολλῶν ἐτῶν[57]).

Paul's *narratio* and *probatio/confirmatio* assert his innocent purpose in being at Jerusalem and deny involvement in any disruptive ac-

---

[53]See esp. Winter, 'The Importance', 518f.

[54]For further discussion and photographs of these plaques, see A. Deissmann, *Light from the Ancient East*, tr. L.R.M. Strachan (London: Hodder and Stoughton, 1927), 80; R.J. McKelvey, 'Temple', *IllBibD*, vol. 3, 1528f. Ancient reference: Josephus, *AJ* 12.145 [12.3.4]; 15.417 [15.11.5]; *BJ* 5.193f. [5.5.2]; 6.124-26 [6.2.4]; Philo, *De Legatione ad Gaium* 212 [31]; Eph. 2:14; *m. Kelim* 1.8.

[55]Josephus, *BJ* 6.124 [6.2.4].

[56]At Acts 21:28, where Jews are addressed, the charge of bringing Greeks into the temple is described by the word κοινοῦν.

[57]Felix had occupied a subordinate office in Samaria from 48 AD in the procuratorship of Cumanus and received that procuratorship on the latter's removal in 52 AD (Tacitus, *Ann.* 12.54; Suetonius, *Cl.* 5.38; Josephus, *BJ* 2.223-47 [2.12.1-8]; *AJ* 20.137 [20.7.1], 20.162f. [20.8.5]; *cf.* Brunt, 'Charges of Provincial Maladministration', 214 n. 78) and Krodel, *Acts*, 435.

tivities in the temple or the Jerusalem environs. His accusers, he contends, are unable to furnish proof of their allegations. As to his involvement with the Nazarenes, Paul in the *refutatio* admits (Acts 24:14) to being a follower of the Way but denies that it is a αἵρεσις in the sense that his accusers intend. He stresses at Acts 24:14-16 not only his clear Jewish identity as a follower of the Way but also that his opponents at law have similar beliefs. Concerning his alleged defilement of the temple, Paul responds at Acts 24:17f. that his motives for being in Jerusalem are beneficent,[58] demonstrating good faith and solidarity with his people and the Jewish religion. He denies ceremonial uncleanness, accompaniment by a crowd or involvement in any disturbance.

Moving to an offensive stance in the *peroratio*, Paul asserts that the accusers are acting improperly on juridical grounds. This opportunity for a Pauline attack is the fruit of Claudius Lysias' action in nominating and ordering the Sanhedrin to appear before Felix to present charges against Paul. We have noted above that plaintiffs must be present to accuse. Paul states that the proper bringers of the charges of which he is accused ought to be certain Jews from the province of Asia; the accusers present are disqualified on this account. This is noted as a valid technical objection by Sherwin-White.[59] The only possible charge that the accusers present might legally bring by Paul's reckoning at Acts 24:21, pertain to his belief in the resurrection (a belief which some of them share). His description fits what is stated in Lysias' letter (Acts 23:29) and confirms that the case had to do with Jewish theology upon which Felix, competent as he was to judge, might not wish to make a determination. One of the distinctive attainments of the life characterized by honour, dignity and great wealth' (*honor, dignitas* and *amplissimae facultates*) was the possession of a high level of education. Felix was probably as impressed by Paul's learning and rhetorical ability as he was by Tertullus'.[60]

---

[58]The 'gifts' (ἐλεημοσύναι) probably alludes to the Jerusalem collection (K.F. Nickle, *The Collection* [London: SCM, 1966], 148 and nn. 27f.) and 'offerings' (προσφοραί) to the costs related to the four Nazarite vows (*cf.* Acts 21:24, 26 and *supra*, 105-108).

[59]Sherwin-White, *Roman Society*, 52.

[60]Festus similarly assesses Paul's intellectual abilities though this is stated negatively at Acts 26:24: *viz.*, 'Your great learning [τὰ πολλὰ ... γράμματα: lit. 'the many ... letters'] is driving you insane'. Festus' exclamation may reflect his own assessment, but one cannot exclude the possibility that Felix suggested as much in a written record left at his departure.

3. The Magistrate

Felix 'adjourned the proceedings' (ἀνεβάλετο: Acts 24:22) without condemning or acquitting. This was within his rights and neither party could force his hand to reintroduce proceedings.[61] Two motives for adjournment may be indicated in the text: First, Felix 'was well acquainted with the Way' (ἀκριβέστερον εἰδὼς τὰ περὶ τῆς ὁδοῦ: Acts 24:22). The emphasis of the comparative ἀκριβέστερον, here serving in place of the superlative or elative,[62] is upon the considerable certainty, definiteness, or accuracy of this knowledge. While Felix may have gained it through his Jewish wife Drusilla (Acts 24:24),[63] it was more probably the result of Felix' ongoing political and administrative interest. Acts 24:24 shows him, even after the first phase of the trial, continuing to gather information on the Way. It was well worth closely watching as it had existed for nearly 25 years to this point and currently consisted of many thousands (Acts 21:20) of Jewish adherents in Jerusalem. Felix would have known that, beyond this, the Way's adherents were also dispersed throughout the Empire, particularly in Caesarea (Acts 8:1ff.; 21:8f.) and even within the Roman armed forces (Acts 10:1ff.).[64] Luke may be indicating here that Felix' knowledge had given the lie to at least part of the plaintiffs' case against Paul. If this is so, there was in fact no case against him and the reason for the delay falls outside of legal considerations.[65]

The second motive, recorded at Acts 24:22, was Felix' desire to confer with Lysias when the latter came to Caesarea. Tertullus' accusations and Paul's defence went beyond the contents of Lysias' message. Serious contradictions had emerged concerning the facts of the case and on these a decision having wide-ranging implications might turn. An interview with the Tribune could be helpful. Lysias was, from the Roman perspective, the only independent witness.[66] The text is silent

---

[61]Sherwin-White, *Roman Society*, 53; Cadbury, 'Roman Law', 307; Tajra, *The Trial of St. Paul*, 129.

[62]M. Zerwick, *Biblical Greek*, tr. J. Smith (Rome: Scripta Pontificii Instituti Biblici, 1963) § 148. *Cf.* also Acts 18:26; 23:15, 20 and note especially Luke 1:3 (ἀκριβῶς).

[63]So e.g., Knowling, 'The Acts', 486; Neil, *The Acts*, 235; von Harnack, *The Acts of the Apostles* (London'; Williams and Norgate, 1909), 210; Wikenhauser, *Die Apostelgeschichte*, 260.

[64]For discussion of the Christian community in Caesarea, *cf.* L.I. Levine, *Caesarea Under Roman Rule* (Studies in Judaism in Late Antiquity 7; Leiden: Brill, 1975), 24-26.

[65]See Bauernfeind, *Kommentar*, 263; Knowling, 'The Acts', 486; Marshall, *The Acts*, 380. *Contra* Munck, *The Acts*, 231.

as to whether this meeting ever occurred. Either it never took place,[67] or it was of little help if it did.

The significance of the parties and their potentially negative political influence (*potentia*) suggest a third motive in favouring neither immediate condemnation nor acquittal. Garnsey writes that

> even those governors who emphasized the traditional subservience and inferiority of provincials could not be ignorant of the fact that the provincial aristocracy was a force to be reckoned with in their own provinces. Any governor who had been at all exposed to local power struggles, as had most governors, was aware of this. It was well within the capabilities of individuals or factions to create trouble for a governor both during and after his term of office, and often this could be avoided only by skilful diplomacy.[68]

Acquitting Paul could raise great political trouble for Felix with the plaintiffs. They were the indigenous spiritual and political powerbrokers of his province. Their co-operation was essential to a relatively smooth Roman overlordship. Moreover, Felix need not have strained himself to think of specific instances of compelling Jewish political pressure[69] and of the disaster that the Jewish leadership, despite Roman legal obstacles,[70] could bring upon the heads of provincial procurators who failed to administer the law with sympathy to the Jewish point of view. His immediate predecessor, the convicted and exiled Ventidius Cumanus, was a case in point.[71] Had Felix been tempted to forget, Tertullus' opening remarks reminded him of the link between responsible administration of law and Jewish gratitude and passivity. Felix' awareness of the Jews' power to do him well or ill as he left office compelled him to do them the favour of leaving Paul incarcerated.

Condemning Paul, however, might raise yet another set of problems for Felix. He had discovered during the trial that Paul was one of the ringleaders of a popular Jewish movement based in Judaea but also widely scattered abroad. As a leader, Paul too had a measure of political power. Felix might have thought that punishing Paul could spark

---

[66]Sherwin-White, *Roman Society*, 53; Rackham, *The Acts*, 448.

[67]So von Harnack, *The Acts*, 210.

[68]Garnsey, *Social Status*, 78. *Cf.* Rackham, *The Acts*, 448; E. Springer, 'Der Prozess des Apostels Paulus', *Preussische Jahrbücher* 218 (1929), 193; Longenecker, 'The Acts', 541.

[69]See, e.g. Josephus, *AJ* 20.114-17 [20.5.4] ≈ *BJ* 2.228-31 [2.12.2].

[70]*Supra*, 67-69.

[71]Josephus, *AJ* 20.118-36 [20.6.1-3].

internecine conflict among the provincial populace or at least raise the
tension to a less comfortable level.[72] Then there was the fact of Paul's
Roman citizenship and the legal protections which would probably be
invoked if Felix decided for punishment.

The logic behind an adjournment in such a potentially explosive
atmosphere was that it effectively removed Felix from the necessity of
having to take unpopular action. Such a response was apparently neither unusual for him nor for those prior to or following him in office.
Josephus attests to the fact that Albinus' ransom-motivated prison
clearances resulted in the release of many incarcerated 'by former
procurators'.[73] If the plural here is an accurate indication, this would
certainly have included individuals imprisoned by Felix. Additionally,
Festus' vigorous emphasis upon the prompt dispatch with which he
had handled Paul's case (Acts 25:17; cf. v. 6) may carry an implied criticism of the procrastinating tendencies of Felix.[74] The pattern of delay,
with its varied motivations, had precedents in the imperial capital as
well.[75]

Then there was the matter of procuratorial venality. We have
seen that despite the various legal provisions against it, the corrupting
influence of bribery could be significant and, in some cases, lethal. It
could effect juridical and custodial deliberations, whether conducted
by a lesser magistrate or by the emperor himself.[76] Far from the imperial capital and covered by protective legislation during a governor's
term of office, extortionate behaviour was often irresistible.[77] The
prospects for personal enrichment by a delay of proceedings were sufficiently evident for Felix to see. He was certainly well aware of the fact
that Paul's accusers, as members of the ruling Jewish aristocracy, possessed great wealth(amplissimae facultates). While they clearly desired
(viz., the fact of their having hired a rhetor) to do Paul mortal harm, the
text says nothing of a play for financial consideration from them. Perhaps their political 'clout' was a sufficient inducement to Felix' initial
cooperation. In the matter of Paul, however, the text is clear. During

---

[72]Marshall, The Acts, 377.

[73]Josephus, BJ 2.273 [2.14.1]; cf. AJ 20.215 [20.9.5].

[74]Haenchen, The Acts, 672; Marshall, The Acts, 388. Cf., however, Schille, Die Apostelgeschichte, 444.

[75]Cf. further the comments upon prisoners held beyond the terms of imprisoning
magistrates in cases of coercitio (supra, 14-16) and the review of Tiberius' behaviour
with respect to accused and condemned men (supra, 16-20).

[76]For sample cases see Brunt, 'Charges', 224-27.

[77]The corrupting climate in which Felix would have risen to his responsibilities is
well described by Brunt, 'Charges', 222.

the trial proceedings it had emerged that Paul had come to Jerusalem bearing substantial gifts for the poor. Felix may at first have thought, based upon Paul's freedom to travel extensively (Acts 24:5) and his apparent failure to indicate that these were communal gifts (Acts 24:17), that the funds were personal.[78] Paul's desire to present offerings at the temple would also not have gone unnoticed. Felix would have been right to assume that Paul was materially well off,[79] or at least that Paul could gain access, as leader of an Empire-wide Jewish movement based in Jerusalem, to considerable financial resources.

Felix' character and his later behaviour toward Paul do not discourage the view that bribery was on his mind at this earliest stage in the proceedings. Felix would have been encouraged to make the most of his procuratorship financially owing to the fact that the emperor had appointed him at the request of the Jewish leadership and he could count on the protection of his wealthy brother Pallas.[80] In an epigrammatic assessment, Tacitus wrote that Felix 'practised every kind of cruelty and lust, wielding the power of a king with all the instincts of a slave'.[81] Factionalism in Judaea would only have encouraged his rapacity.[82] Further, it is indicated at Acts 24:26 that from the very first interview, a short time following the trial, and at frequent[83] interviews thereafter Felix was hoping that Paul would offer him a bribe, whether to reinstitute proceedings or to secure his outright release. This series of plays for the contents of Paul's purse suggests that money played a key role in the deliberations.

4. Lightened Custody

The above-noted factors would also have influenced later custodial arrangements made for Paul at Acts 24:23. It was earlier observed that when responsibility for the custody of prisoners was assigned, the guards' experience, rank and numbers were considered. Experienced soldiers were preferred over inexperienced ones and the more impor-

---

[78]See further the discussion of Nickle, *The Collection*, 70, 148, 150.

[79]*Supra*, 105-108. *Contra* Munck, *The Acts*, 231.

[80]Tacitus, *Ann.* 12.54.

[81]*Ibid., Hist.* 5.9.

[82]Brunt, 'Charges', 214 and n. 79.

[83]The comparative adjective πυκνότερον, if it means '*all the more* often' rather than '*fairly* often', further emphasizes Felix' predatory character. *Cf.* BDF, §244 (1); Zerwick and Grosvenor, *Grammatical Analysis*, vol. 1, 439.

tant the prisoner, whether because of his or her status or the seriousness of the crime, the higher the rank of the soldier charged with
guarding and the greater the number of co-watchers. The first thing to
note concerning the change of arrangements is that Paul is assigned to
the personal care of a centurion rather than to a lower-ranking soldier
or, for that matter, to the general care of a military prison system and
its personnel.[84] Whether the centurion actually headed a century or
was an officer in the headquarters staff without full centurial responsibility cannot be certainly determined, though the latter, on balance,
would perhaps have been the more efficient and hence more probable
arrangement. As such, this assignment was probably not so much a token of the higher esteem in which Paul was held by Felix as an indication that Felix wished Paul to be healthily preserved for the longer
term from the predictable vagaries of military custody[85] in the hope of
exploiting him to his own political and monetary advantage.

Beyond the charge to keep Paul (Acts 24:23), the centurion is
commanded to give him some freedom (ἔχειν τε ἄνεσιν), ἄνεσις indicating some sort of loosening or relaxation.[86] The context of the term's
occurrence at several other places is helpful in appreciating its sense
here. At 2 Chron. 23:15 it probably indicates that queen Athaliah's
guards were to relax their close restraint of her so that she might remove herself from the house of the Lord before she was slain.[87] The account of the military custody of prince Agrippa, who like Paul was
both a Jew and a Roman citizen, is also helpful. Josephus writes that
after Agrippa's transfer from the camp to his own residence at the
death of Tiberius, 'though he was still guarded and watched, yet the
watch on his daily activities was relaxed'.[88] As in the previous examples, it is the level of the guards' vigilance which is emphasized here
rather than physical or material concessions. The watch on Agrippa's
every movement while in camp custody has been earlier described.[89]
Prisoners in the camp system were apparently closely watched even
when their assigned keepers were favourably disposed to them.
Agrippa's attendants needed, in the earlier phase of his incarceration,
to resort to deception to mitigate the prison conditions and that in col-

---

[84]See on the different rankings of prison personnel in the Roman army, Watson,
The Roman Soldier, 75-88, 126, 205 nn. 410-13.
[85]We shall detail these at some length in *infra*, ch. 9.
[86]LSJ, 135; BAGD, 65.
[87]A.C. Hervey, *The Acts of the Apostles*, 233.
[88]Josephus, *AJ* 18.235 [18.6.10].
[89]*Supra*, 30.

lusion with the centurion and soldiers assigned by the urban prefect Macro at the request of the empress Antonia.[90] Second, it is an important point that the relaxation does not mean that Agrippa was unchained. Josephus records that only during the audience with the Emperor Gaius at the end of the period of his house arrest was Agrippa's iron chain removed and exchanged for a golden ornamental chain of equal weight.[91]

The relaxation in Paul's custody, by analogy to Agrippa, probably meant that, while guarded, Paul would not be dependent upon his keeper(s) to sanction his every activity. There would be no oppressively close guarding. We have seen that it was normally expected that prisoners in military custody were manacled; typically to their soldier-guards and especially when they were in open places. There is nothing in Acts 24 to indicate whether Paul was simply manacled, chained to his centurion, or chained to other co-keepers. In light of the pattern, such prospects would seem neither unusual nor unreasonable. In fact, the lower level of vigilance implied by the term ἄνεσις would, as in the case of Agrippa, almost require Paul to be chained for proper security.[92] The later indication at Acts 26:29 that Paul wore chains as he stood before Agrippa is then not a recent innovation in Paul's custody brought on by his appeal or required by the audience. Rather, it is better understood to be the continued condition of his keeping while in Caesarea.

Where would Paul be kept? Rackham suggests that Paul occupied lodgings of his own in Caesarea.[93] This, however, is unlikely on three counts: First, the expression ἄνεσις, as indicated above, says nothing of the venue of the second phase of Paul's Caesarean imprisonment. Second, Felix would know from the mention of a Jewish assassination plot in Lysias' letter and the continuing animosity (later measurable to the newly-arrived Festus by the vigorous official representations and hostile public demonstrations in Jerusalem and Caesarea against Paul [Acts 25:2f., 15, 24]) that such a potentially lucrative prisoner was in considerable danger and would be vulnerable if lodged in the suburbs. For this reason alone such arrangements would have been ill-advised.

---

[90]Josephus, AJ 18.203f. [18.6.7].

[91]Ibid. 18.237 [18.6.10].

[92]Contra Mommsen, 'Die Rechtsverhältnisse des Apostels Paulus', 93f. and n. 3, who cites the Constantinian provisions (320 AD!) on 'free and open military custody [aperta et libra ...custodia militaris]' in Cod. Theod. 11.7.3.

[93]Rackham, The Acts, 450.

Third, the general climate of declining Jewish/Gentile relations in Caesarea would hardly have permitted Paul's safe incarceration in the suburbs. As at cities such as Azotus and Jamnia, Caesarea was frequently seized with conflict because of its mixed population.[94] From earliest times until its refounding by Herod the Great, Jewish settlement at Caesarea had been either non-existent or minimal. By the mid-1st century AD, however, there was an economically prosperous Jewish community, constituting nearly half the population—perhaps the fifth largest Jewish city population in the Empire.[95] The Jews claimed equal civic rights (ἰσοπολιτεία) and consideration on the basis of the city's founding by a Jewish king. The Gentile population, resentful of Jewish wealth and influence, countered the claim by reference to Caesarea's earlier Greek founding.[96] While Herod the Great was nominally Jewish, the character of his refounding activities actually supported the Gentile denial.[97] In the late 50s AD, the period of Paul's stay there, Jew-Gentile relations in Caesarea were in a steep decline for which Felix shared much blame[98] and which would eventually lead to disaster.[99] In such a religiously and politically fragmented context, the open presence of a figure charged with factionalism would be provocative, destabilising and administratively foolish in the extreme. Paul was probably kept in Herod's palace.

It is not a serious objection to the above suggestion that Paul and the centurion would hardly have been under the same roof as the procurator of Judaea. First, Herod's palace at Caesarea would undoubtedly have been large enough. Second, the apparent ease with which Paul was frequently sent for and dismissed by Felix who resided in the palace (Acts 24:24-6) would also seem to support Paul's having been lodged in secure quarters there. Finally, if the centurion to whom Paul was assigned was a member of the general staff, as has been suggested, it would be more likely that the centurion resided in praetorian rather than other military quarters.

---

[94]M. Hengel, *Between Jesus and Paul: Studies in the Earliest History of Christianity*, tr. J. Bowden (London: SCM, 1983), 113f.

[95]Levine, *Caesarea*, 20; Haefeli, 'Cäsarea am Meer'.

[96]Josephus, *AJ* 19.173f. [19.8.7].

[97]*Ibid.* 15.339 [15.9.6]; *BJ* 1.414f. [1.21.7f.]; cf. Levine, *Caesarea*, 17, 27; S.E. Johnson, 'Caesarea Maritima', *LTQ* 20 (1985), 29f.; Bruce, *New Testament History*, 246.

[98]See Josephus, *AJ* 19.182f. [19.8.8].

[99]Josephus, *BJ* 2.257-96 [2.14.1-6], 2.457f. [2.18.1]; 3.409 [3.9.1]. *Cf.* V.M. Scramuzza, 'Note 25. The Policy of the Early Roman Emperors Towards Judaism', *BC*, vol. 5, 287; Schürer, *The History*, vol. 1, 467

The centurion is finally instructed to 'permit [Paul's] friends to take care of his needs' (Acts 24:23). The NIV rendering 'permit' is misleading as μηδένα κωλύειν is actually negative; the centurion is commanded not to hinder, to prevent or to forbid individuals.[100] Κωλύει in this context probably denotes restricting access to the prisoner, whether out of duty or animosity. This command pertains to Paul's ἴδιοι who could be members of his immediate family or relatives.[101] However, if Luke's use of the term at Acts 4:23 can be taken as determinative, it here describes a larger group, including supportive or friendly co-religionists.[102] We agree with Haenchen that Felix could not very well have designated the Christians otherwise.[103] Presumably, those not identifiable (by Paul?) as his ἴδιοι would have been barred from access to him. They are mandated by the governor's order to 'take care' of Paul. The service, attention or helpfulness denoted by ὑπηρετέω must, coming from Felix, relate to Paul's basic needs for physical sustenance while in prison—to food and clothing. Far from being an exceptional privilege as many would argue, such a provision relieved the prison system of responsibility for Paul's ongoing physical maintenance and care and could even be considered the usual arrangement.[104] It may also have hinted at Felix' intention to keep Paul incarcerated for a longer rather than shorter period of time.

It would be inaccurate to take these arrangements to be an instance of free or open custody (*custodia libera*).[105] If the argument that Paul was kept in chains in Caesarea is correct, the general sense of *custodia libera* as confinement without chains is incorrect. Moreover, the formalized sense of *custodia libera*, the judicially ordered transfer of an accused person into the private care and safekeeping of a magistrate or notable citizen pending the trial outcome, is not strictly applicable. Paul is, technically speaking, in the chief magistrate's residence. However, this is a military context and a centurion is given full responsibility for Paul's custody. This hardly suggests personal or private care. Those who use the expression *custodia liberior*, which does not have the technical connotations noted above but refers only to a *lighter/lightened*

---

[100]BAGD, 461.

[101]On this and other possibilities, *cf.* BAGD, 370; LSJ, 818; Moulton, *Grammar*, vol. 1, 90.

[102]So, e.g., Lake and Cadbury, *BC*, 304; Haenchen, *The Acts*, 656.

[103]Haenchen, *The Acts*, 656 n. 5.

[104]We shall discuss this matter of Paul's helpers *infra*.

[105]*Contra* Williams, *Acts*, 402; J.V. Bartlet, *The Acts*, Century Bible [NT] 5 (Edinburgh: T.C. and E.C. Clark, 1901) 356; Rackham, *The Acts*, 448.

custody, are on much safer ground.[106] Paul is in a lightened form of military custody.

---

[106]So Haenchen, *The Acts*, 656 n. 4; Schille, *Die Apostelgeschichte*, 435.

CHAPTER 8

ROME

Paul was probably held initially within, and later in the vicinity of, the Praetorian barracks at Rome. He would be a complete stranger to the man setting his custody. The deliberations would probably then have been formal and dispassionate. Paul was permitted to live by himself with unrestricted access in private rented accommodation. Security provisions included the permanent presence of a soldier guard to whom, it seems, Paul was regularly though lightly chained.

Paul was held in remarkably light confinement—an extremely casual form of military custody. Since this probably did not result from his high status, its explanation must lie in the contents of the dossier sent along with Paul, including Festus' letter. The collected documents—Lysias' letter, the trial transcript from Felix' enquiry, the transcript from Festus' enquiry and probably the record of Paul's presentation and the conciliar findings during the audience before Agrippa—would have contained no evidence seriously threatening to Paul. In fact, they show a progressive deterioration in the case against him. The contents of Festus' letters, which draws from the collected documents, must be more in the nature of a factual report, indicating that while no serious Roman charges stood against him, Paul's request that the emperor hear his case, made in the face of continuing Jewish clamour for his prosecution and death, was duly granted.

The last evaluation of Paul in Acts is at Rome. Nothing is overtly stated in the text of Acts 28 concerning any of the usual influences. The description of the custodial arrangements for Paul at the close of Acts, however, is fairly detailed. Working backwards from the custodial arrangements and incorporating what information would have been available to the officials for their deliberation thus allows for an overall assessment.

I. The Official

The record of the custodial deliberation at Rome is found at Acts 28:16. Nothing of the identity of the official(s) who made the determination can be known from the preferred reading there (ἐπετράπη τῷ Παύλῳ) owing both to its brevity and its employment of the aorist passive. The expanded reading of the later Western text (ὁ ἑκατόνταρχος παρέδ-ωκε τοὺς δεσμίους τῷ στρατοπεδάρχῳ, τῷ δὲ Παύλῳ ἐπτράπη), however, is more helpful. Favourable assessments of the information contained in the latter reading[1] suggest that examining it may be profitable.

There are four potential identifications of the στρατοπεδάρχης (var. in -ος) who assigns Paul to custody in this reading: Least likely is view 1) which identifies him with the *praefectus urbi* in command of the urban cohorts of Rome. Sherwin-White writes that this official was concerned exclusively with urban police matters and the custody of local malefactors.[2] View 2) identifies the στρατοπέδαρχης with the *princeps peregrinorum*, an officer of centurial rank having charge of a force of soldiers of centurial rank. This force carried out special missions chiefly, though not exclusively, associated with provisioning the Empire with corn.[3] The reading *centurio tradidit custodias principi peregrinorum* of the 13th century MS *gigas* (a witness to the OL of *c.* 2nd to 4th cent. AD), and the fact that the ship in Acts 27 which foundered off Malta transported grain are taken to support this identification. If correct, this would put Paul in and later near the camp of the *peregrini* on the Caelian Hill in Rome (Fig. 18).

---

[1] E.g., Lightfoot, *Saint Paul's Epistle*, 8 n. 4, who considers the Western text 'a genuine tradition, even if it was no part of the original text'.

[2] Sherwin-White, *Roman Society*, 108f.

[3] Among the most influential, Mommsen, *Droit Pénal*, vol. 1, 370f.; Hitzig, 'Carcer', 1579; H.O. Fiebiger, 'Frumentarii', PW, vol. 7, 123; and many recent commentators.

Objections to identification 2), however, are several and serious: First, *princeps peregrinorum* in MS *gigas* 'is an interpretation, not an accurate rendering of στρατοπέδαρχος',[4] and a 2nd century one at that. Second, the excavated ruins where the camp was situated can be certainly dated only to the reign of Vespasian (69-79 AD) on the basis of stamped bricks found there.[5] In the absence of clear military evidence, however, one is only permitted the inference that the site was occupied in Vespasian's day, but not that it was occupied as the *castra peregrinorum*. The evidence of five coins dating to the early first century—particularly since the nature of the digging did not permit stratigraphic observation[6]—does not push the date back. Even if military occupation were conceded for Vespasian's reign, the suggestion that Paul was in the military custody of the *peregrini* there somewhere between nine and nineteen years earlier is hardly therefore proven.[7] A third objection is that there is no evidence earlier than Trajan that the duties of the corn merchants included policing and prisoner transport.[8] Sinnigen, who has researched the origins of the corn merchants, puts the case forcefully.[9] Fourth, the confident identification of the centurion Julius as a corn merchant based upon his official designation and alleged formal connections with the grain carrier traffic is not supported by a careful reading of Luke's text (Acts 27:1-28:16).[10] There are, finally, practical difficulties associated with the notion that Paul was kept in the care of soldiers of the camp of the *peregrini*. The centurial rank of the *princeps peregrinorum* together with the smallness of the permanent barracks staff—there were only three men: *the princeps*, the *subprinceps* and the *optio*—indicates to Reynolds that 'the number of troops there was not large'.[11] Numbered among them were three officer groups:

---

[4]T.R.S. Broughton, 'Note 33: The Roman Army', in *BC*, vol. 5, 444.

[5]*Cf.* T. Ashby and P.K.B. Reynolds, 'The Castra Peregrinorum', *JRS* 13 (1923), 159, 165f.; M. Grant, *The Armies of the Caesars* (London: Weidenfeld and Nicholson, 1974), 230.

[6]Ashby and Reynolds, 'The Castra Peregrinorum', 159 and 165—the coins noted as one each of Agrippa, Tiberius and Caligula and two of Claudius in the table.

[7]See Grant, *The Armies*, 230.

[8]Thus Sherwin-White, *Roman Society*, 109; Grant, *The Armies*, 230.

[9]W.G. Sinnigen, 'The Origins of the *frumentarii*', *Memoirs of the American Academy in Rome* 27 (1962), 213-24.

[10]See the discussion in B.M. Rapske, 'The Importance of Helpers to the Imprisoned Paul in the Book of Acts', *TynBul* 42.1 (1991), 9-12; *idem*, 'Acts, Travel and Shipwreck' in *The Book of Acts in Its Graeco-Roman Setting*, ed. D.W.J. Gill and C. Gempf (A1CS 2; Grand Rapids: Eerdmans/Carlisle: Paternoster, 1994), 22-46.

[11]Reynolds, 'The Troops', 177. He suggests a number no higher than 300 or 400 men.

centuriones deputati, centuriones supernumerarii and *centuriones frumentarii*.[12] This automatically eliminates a number of individuals in the camp from candidacy to guard Paul and the many others referred from the provinces.[13] Luke indicates that Paul was able to stay by himself 'with the soldier guarding him' at Acts 28:16. As Luke is normally quite careful to distinguish between the ranks of military personnel,[14] when he refers to the στρατιώτη here, he probably does not intend the reader to understand by it ἑκατοντάρχης. The remainder of the camp consisted of NCO's—corn merchants and watchmen.[15] It is doubtful that these soldiers or even the officer groups mentioned above would have been suitable for such a guard as Paul was put under—i.e., round the clock, for two years and outside the camp. They were together a constantly fluctuating and transient military population, having to remain free to their overriding duty as messengers who peregrinated to foreign parts of the Empire (hence the term *peregrini*).[16]

For view 3) a number of scholars[17] associate the στρατοπέδαρχης with the *praefectus praetorii* into whose care prisoners from without the immediate precincts of Rome and from the provinces were placed.[18] It is argued that the singular title in the Western text shows attention to accuracy as Afranius Burrus (51-62 AD) held this post by himself, whereas before and after him there were two *praefecti praetorii*.[19] It is a fair objection to this proposal, however, that the *praefectus praetorii* would hardly have troubled himself with such a mundane duty as setting custody for prisoners.[20]

View 4), in recognition of the objection to view 3), holds the term στρατοπέδαρχης to designate a subordinate of the *praefectus praetorii*. Sherwin-White has proposed that this officer was the *princeps castrorum* or *princeps praetorii*; 'the head administrator of the *officium* of the Pra-

---

[12]*Ibid.*, 175-77.

[13]*Contra* Neil, *The Acts*, 249; Haenchen, *The Acts*, 697f. n. 5.

[14]See the occurrences of 'centurion' (Luke 7:6; 23:47; Acts 10:1, 22; 21:32; 22:25f. [2x]; 24:23; 27:1, 6, 11, 31, 43 [28:16,*v.l.*]) and 'soldier' (Luke 3:14; 7:8; 23:36; 12:4, 6, 18; 21:32 (2x), 35; 23:10, 23, 31; 27:31, 32, 42); particularly where they appear in close proximity.

[15]Reynolds, 'The Troops', 177-79.

[16]*Cf. ibid.*, 168-70.

[17]E.g., Conzelmann, *Acts*, 224; Lightfoot, *Saint Paul's Epistle*, 7f. and n. 4; Broughton, 'The Roman Army', 444; E.M. Blaiklock, *The Acts of the Apostles* (TNTC; Grand Rapids: Eerdmans, 1959) 197 and others.

[18]Tacitus, *Ann.* 11.1. *Cf.* Trajan, *Ep.* 10.5.7.

[19]Wikenhauser, *Die Apostelgeschichte*, 286; Lightfoot, *Saint Paul's Epistle*, 7f.

[20]Voiced by Ramsay, *St. Paul the Traveller*, 347f.; and others.

etorian Guard'.[21] Such camp officers were known in the legionary armies from as early as the reign of Claudius. On balance, this last option seems the more likely of the latter two alternatives. Assuming the accuracy of this identification, then, Paul would have been in and later near the Praetorian barracks located at the Porta Viminalis just beyond the walls to the NE of the city (Fig. 18).[22] Clearly the determining official would have had no personal knowledge of or connections with Paul or his accusers. His deliberations might therefore be expected to be dispassionate.

II. The Custody

Acts 28 implies that Paul is permitted a remarkably light remand custody. First is the matter of his accommodation. The phrase 'to remain by himself (μενειν καθ ἑαυτον)at Acts 28:16 clearly indicates that Paul was able to occupy private lodgings in Rome. Hauser notes that

> In Acts the verb stem μεν– is quite frequent: μένειν (Matt. 3x; Mark 2x; Luke 7x; John 40x; Acts 13x), ἐμμένειν (only 2x in Acts), προσμέ-νειν (Matt 1x; Mark 1x; Acts 3x), ἐπιμένειν (Gospels 0x; Acts 1x). Where these verbs refer to a residence at a place (Acts 1;13; 9:43; 10:48; 16:15; 18:3, 8, 20; 21:4, 7, 8, 10; 27:31; 28:12, 14, 16, 30), they are practically synonymous with 'stayed, lived'. Words of similar meaning are διατρίβειν (Acts 12:19; 14:3, 28; 15:35; 16:12; 20:6; 25:6, 14), καθίζειν (Acts 18:11), ξενίζεσθαι (Acts 21:16) and συναχθῆναι (Acts 11:26).[23]

The expression καθ' ἑαυτόν is properly rendered 'by himself', 'privately', or even 'in his own quarters'[24] and can hardly be taken to designate solitary confinement in the camp. This would be incompatible with the degree of Paul's discretion and control in arranging meetings with individuals and the increasing size of the delegations indicated at Acts 28:17, 23 and 30. The Western text is still clearer, adding the phrase 'outside the camp'.

Cadbury asserts that while 'by himself' (καθ' ἑαυτόν) raises no lexical difficulties in that it clearly indicates private lodging, the same

---

[21]Sherwin-White, *Roman Society*, 110.
[22]Tacitus, *Hist.* 1.31.
[23]H.J. Hauser, *Strukturen der Abschlusserzahlung der Apostelgeschichte (Apg 28, 16-31)* (AnBib 86; Rome: Biblical Institute, 1979), 156.
[24]BAGD, 370, 503; LSJ, 818. *Cf.* κατ' ἰδίαν: Luke 9:10; 10:23; Acts 23:19.

cannot be said of the terms ξενίαν and μισθώματι at Acts 28:23 and 30 respectively:

> Either we must give each of these nouns its more regular meaning and then omit these passages from the list of examples of Luke's interest in lodging, or else we must suppose that precisely that interest has led the author to use concretely of a room or apartment at Rome two words of rather different and less tangible meaning.[25]

The second option, it will be argued, is the more probable. The expression ἐν ἰδίῳ μισθώματι at Acts 28:30 is rendered in one of two ways; either 'at his own expense',[26] indicating Paul's personal attention to living costs in Rome, or, focusing upon the type of accommodation retained, 'in his own hired dwelling/lodging'.[27] The sense of the term μίσθωμα in its many other contexts is of money paid to or by a person, and is appropriately rendered 'contract price', 'contract', or 'rent'.[28] Mealand, after an extensive survey, concludes that at Acts 28:30 it is a technical legal term which relates to Paul's expenses in paying rent.[29] Luke's comment would then deal only with accommodation costs.

While the most serious objection to μίσθωμα as hired lodging is that nowhere else do we find such a usage, Moulton and Milligan must confess that despite the clear strength of μίσθωμα as 'rent' or 'hire', 'there seems to be no exact parallel to the usage in Acts 28:30'.[30] The weakness in the former rendering is evident when it is observed that Hansack must argue its case from 4th through 10th century AD sources and the general Pauline pattern of self-support while resisting the pressure to take ἐνέμεινεν ἐν as locative and spatial by assuming that Luke's readers would understand the words 'in Rome' before 'at his own expense'.[31]

---

[25]H.J. Cadbury, 'Lexical Notes on Luke—Acts III. Luke's Interest in Lodging', *JBL* 45 (1926), 319f.

[26]So, e.g., Tajra, *The Trial of St. Paul*, 191; Bruce, *The Book of Acts*, 509; *ibid.*, *The Acts of the Apostles*, 542; Marshall, *The Acts*, 425.

[27]So, e.g., KJV; NIV; RSV; BAGD, 523; LSJ, 1137; Krodel, *Acts*, 483; Munck, *The Acts*, 260.

[28]LSJ, 1137.

[29]D.L. Mealand, 'The Close of Acts and Its Hellenistic Greek Vocabulary', *NTS* 36 (1990), 584-87.

[30]J.H. Moulton and G. Milligan, *The Vocabulary of the Greek Testament Illustrated from the Papyri and Other Non-Literary Sources* (London, Hodder and Stoughton 1930), 414.

[31]E. Hansack, 'Er lebte ... von seinem eigenen Einkommen (Apg 28,30)'. *BZ* 19 (1975),250-53.

There are significant reasons why μίσθωμα should be read in this context as the thing rented; i.e., a hired lodging. Luke presses the unusual term into service as the usual terms would have been misleading. Οἴκησις, οἶκος, οἰκια/οἰκία and οἰκιστήριον—as the Latin *domicilium, domus, aedes, sedes, aedificium* and *habitatio*—indicate the wrong type of accommodation (*viz.*, non-rental), whereas Paul, particularly in his circumstance as a prisoner, would have made lodging arrangements typical of the great majority of the Roman populace—*viz.*, rented accommodation.[32] An eye to the Vg. reading, *in suo conducto*, suggests the appropriate living arrangements: *conductum* can mean a hired apartment or house.[33] Verses 16 and 30 are so closely related that one can read from one to the other without logical or grammatical break according to Dupont and Hauser. The verb ἐνέμεινεν which begins verse 30 is evidently an echo of μένειν at verse 16. The two verses form an *inclusio* for the account of the Jewish meetings with verse 30 developing the description of arrangements for Paul from verse 16.[34] Beyond Luke's use of μεν– stem verbs in Acts with a spatial sense, the verbs ἀπεδέχετο and εἰσπορευομένους and the time and preaching indications at verses 30f. quite naturally encourage one to see μίσθωμα in a locative/spatial rather than financial sense.[35]

ξενία is taken in the older classical sense to mean 'hospitality'[36] or in the newer sense of place of residence/hospitality,[37] whether in the latter instance a 'guest room', 'reception hall', or 'shelter/lodging' at Acts 28:23. Its only other occurrence in the NT is at Phm 22 (*cf.* however, ξενίζω: Acts 10:32; 20:23; 21:16). 'Place of residence' must, at least in the first instance, be the intended meaning. It is questionable whether ἐλθεῖν (to come) followed by a personal pronominal place indication (πρὸς αὐτόν; *cf.* Acts 28:30) would here be tied with an abstract noun (ξενίαν). Possessing the definite article but without the personal pronoun, ξενίαν is more naturally taken as a strengthening of the earlier place indication.[38] There are, it is true, a few indications of the ab-

---

[32]F. Saum, '«Er lebte ...von seinem eigenen Einkommen» (Apg 28,30)', *BZ* 20 (1976), 226f.; Hauser, *Strukturen*, 156f.

[33]Knowling, 'The Acts', 552.

[34]J. Dupont, 'La conclusion des Actes et son rapport à l'ensemble de l'ouvrage de Luc', in *Les Actes des Apôtres: Traditions, Redaction, Theologie*, ed. J. Kremer (BETL 48; Gemloux: Duculot, 1979), 363 followed by Hauser, *Strukturen*, 13.

[35]Saum, 'Er lebte', 228f.; Hauser, *Strukturen*, 156f.

[36]So, e.g., MM, 433; Marshall, *The Acts*, 423.

[37]So, e.g., Stählin, 'ξένος', *TDNT*, 5:19 and n. 137; Haenchen, *The Acts*, 723; Conzelmann, *Acts*, 227. *Cf.* Stählin, 'ξένος', 19 nn. 135f. on πανδοχεῖον (Luke 10:34) and κατάλυμα (Luke 2:7), words Luke uses to describe an inn or public caravanserai.

stract ξενία with εἰς and with ἔρχομαι.[39] To insist, however, that Paul is inviting the Jewish leaders to a meal does not fit; the principal purpose of the invitation, as the context makes quite clear, is an interview or preaching of the gospel. Only by an inference from the phrase 'from morning until evening' might one assume that food was shared. This is certainly not supplied by the text.

The expressions 'by himself', 'to his lodgings', and 'in his own hired lodgings' are all, therefore, more or less synonymous,[40] indicating the one place where Paul lived in Rome; in particular, the expression at verse 30 serves to notify to the reader that Paul continued to live in the manner described at verse 16. The accommodation indicated is of the rental variety and Paul had to contract for it personally. That it was a single unit and that he lived alone is emphasized at Acts 28:16, 23 and 30 by the individualizing expressions 'by himself', 'to him' (2x) and 'in his own'.[41]

The text tells nothing of the size of Paul's quarters except to imply that the meeting place used was sufficient to accommodate the Jewish leaders 'in even larger numbers' (πλείονες: Acts 28:23; cf. πάντας: 28:30) at the second gathering. The number of synagogues in Rome (inscriptions for eleven so far, at least four of which definitely date to the early Empire) and the size of the oldest Jewish community located in the Transtiberinum (= Augustus' Region XIV)[42] suggest that the number who visited Paul at one time could have been considerable. Precision, however, eludes us.[43] One should not, moreover, presume a high quality of life in rented accommodation at Rome in this time.[44] If Paul's dwelling was near the Castra Praetoria as suggested above, the Jewish leaders would have had to travel as far as three kilometres across the city to meet him (Fig. 18).

We have seen that Luke intends his readers to understand that Paul was in the care of a soldier (στρατιώτης), not a centurion (ἑκατοντάρχης). The significance of this datum transcends the issue of

---

[38]See Hauser, *Strukturen*, 134f. *Cf.* Dupont, 'La conclusion', 374f.

[39]Cadbury, 'Lexical Notes', 320 n. 28; MM, 433.

[40]See further on the relation between the terms B.-J. Koet, 'Paul in Rome (Acts 28,16-31): A Farewell to Judaism?' *Bijdragen, Tijdschrift voor Filosofie en Theologie* 28 (1987), 408.

[41]The contrast is more than simply that Paul did not live in communal prison quarters.

[42]See Philo, *De Legatione ad Gaium* 155f. and the discussions of R. Penna, 'Les Juifs a Rome en Temps de l'Apotre Paul', *NTS* 28 (1982), 321-47 (esp. 327f.).

[43]*Contra* Tajra, *The Trial of St. Paul* who is prepared to suggest 40-50 persons.

[44]*Infra*, ch. 10.

which camp had custody of Paul. To this point, and outside of the hiatus of the first Caesarean custody arrangements, Paul was overseen by centurions. Now, when Paul arrives at Rome, he is placed in the care of a regular soldier and *not* a centurion. It will be recalled that, generally, the more important the prisoner was, the higher ranking and more experienced the soldier assigned to him and the greater the number of co-watchers. The implication of Paul's being placed in the care of a regular soldier—and a solitary one at that (two was the rule)[45]—would seem to oppose the notion that Paul was granted lighter custody because of his high status. Paul, now at the heart of the Empire and no longer unusual in his possession of citizenship, has entered a social environment with a rank and status register which extended well-beyond his own placement. We do not deny that status and wealth generally encouraged more lenient custody or even that Paul's means opened up this option; we are arguing, rather, that Paul's status and wealth did not *require* such keeping[46] and do not satisfactorily account for it here. Hence other reasons, unrelated to status, for Paul's custodial arrangements, must have been found in the reports received by the official who set custody. We shall turn to this matter shortly.

Security against escape in light custody conditions usually called for a chain which, in keeping with the pattern, would bind the prisoner by the wrist to his soldier guard. Such was the case for Paul, who asserts at Acts 28:20, that 'it is because of the hope of Israel that I am bound with this chain [τὴν ἅλυσιν[47] ταύτην περίκειμαι]'.

One might expect restricted access to offset the more lenient security of his suburban rather than military-camp incarceration with just one guard. To the contrary, Paul was granted considerable ease in this respect. First, he apparently has discretion to encourage and receive visits. This is indicated when he summons individuals to himself (Acts 28:17), when arrangements are made with him for an additional meeting (Acts 28:23) and when, in the two years following, he is able to indiscriminately receive individuals (Acts 28:30). Second, individuals and groups have considerable access to him; there is 'a constant flow of visitors'.[48] After three days in the city, some of the Roman Jewish 'leaders' (πρώτους Acts 28:17) are invited to meet Paul; they return for a second meeting 'in even larger numbers' (πλείονες: Acts 28:23); finally, in the extended period of time following these first meetings,

---

[45]Cf. Acts 12:6.
[46]Cf. Mealand, 'The Close of Acts', 586.
[47]This would probably have been a light chain rather than a heavy one.
[48]Tr. Hauser, *Strukturen*, 46.

'all' (πάντας: Acts 28:30) wishing to come to him may do so. Third, the closing words of Acts also reinforce the notion of considerable ease of access. Paul is able to proclaim the kingdom of God and teach the things concerning the Lord Jesus Christ unhindered (Acts 28:31). While we must agree with Moulton and Milligan that 'unhindered' (ἀκωλύτως) is 'legal to the last',[49] it is hardly the case that Luke is redeploying a commercial term denoting the unrestricted use of leased or rented property to the service of a literary and theological aim as Mealand suggests.[50] Delling asserts that the term probably denotes the official expressed permission of freedom to act in the religious sphere.[51] That Roman tolerance of the preaching and teaching of the kingdom and of Christ are in view can hardly be doubted. But the receiving of individuals in the first part of the sentence must surely also be intended. Recall the command of Felix to the centurion at Acts 24:23 not to hinder Paul's access to (and help from) friends. 'Unhindered' then denotes Roman tolerance generally,[52] but more specifically, as Stählin asserts,[53] the official leniency of the soldier who guarded the apostle during his imprisonment in Rome.

III. Litigants and Charges

Apart from his momentary freedom in Jerusalem before the Sanhedrin, Paul's custody in Rome is the least severe of all the imprisonments Luke reports. He undergoes not restricted freedom (*custodia libera*) as some assert,[54] but a very light form of military custody:[55] that in a private domicile. According to the pattern elaborated and discussed above, the imprisoning official in Rome would have considered the charges, the status of the accused and accusers, and any other relevant information furnished by Festus before setting Paul's custody. The fact that Paul was guarded by a single lower-ranking soldier suggests, as argued above, that Paul was not deemed as 'important' in the status context of the capital of the Empire as he was in Judea. The sta-

---

[49]MM, 20.

[50]Mealand, 'The Close of Acts', 590f. but see 591-93 for examples.

[51]G. Delling, 'Das Letzte Wort der Apostelgeschichte', *NovT* 15 (1973), 202f.

[52]Tajra, *The Trial of St. Paul*, 192f.; Haenchen, *The Acts*, 726.

[53]Stählin, *Die Apostelgeschichte*, 329.

[54]*Contra*, e.g., T. Zahn, *Die Apostelgeschichte des Lukas* (KNT 5.1/2; Leipzig: A. Deichert [Werner Scholl], 1919, 1921), 853.

[55]So, e.g., Lightfoot, *Saint Paul's Epistle*, 7 n. 2; Hervey, *The Acts*, 322f.

tus of Paul's accusers, who reside at such a great distance from Rome, apparently had no significant influence upon the custody arrangements either.

Failing a status explanation, the only other rationale for such a light custody must be found in the weakness of the case against Paul as indicated in the documentation sent with him to Rome.[56] The dossier Festus would utilize in formulating his *litterae dimissoriae* and which he would send along probably included a certified copy of Lysias' letter. The Lysias document recorded quite clearly that the charges against Paul related to matters of Jewish law not deemed, from the Roman perspective, to be either capital or worthy of chains (Acts 23:29). An extract of the trial proceedings under Felix would have shown a charge of factionalism with supporting allegations brought by a professional rhetor on behalf of Jewish plaintiffs, but an equally professional defence and rebuttal by the Roman defendant. The magistrate's adjournment in favour of securing additional information would also probably have been noted. Macgregor's assertion that Felix left Festus 'a report hostile to Paul'[57] hardly convinces in light of the available information. The former procurator's frequent interviews with Paul and his failure to proceed with the trial for two years argue, if not for a positive attitude, at least for official caution because insufficient evidence had been collected to secure a conviction. Acts 25:26ff., which thrice emphasizes that Festus was under pressure to memorandise the charges for the emperor[58] but had nothing of Roman juridical substance to write, also implies that there was nothing seriously threatening to Paul in Felix' records. Festus' awareness of Paul's great learning (Acts 26:24) may also argue that Felix left a positive account of Paul.

If Festus' perusal of the documents concerning Paul's case did not give sufficient information to secure a conviction or even to draft adequate and convincing charges, neither did his own trial of Paul. There are several indications that the Jewish leaders' case against Paul, if it did not collapse entirely, was seriously weakened. Frustrated in their attempt to have Paul brought to Jerusalem or condemned outright (Acts 25:3, 15f., 24), the Jews were granted leave by Festus to press charges against Paul in Caesarea. Perhaps emboldened by this concession and the mutual exchange of goodwill during the time spent

---

[56]Winter, 'The Importance', 528.
[57]Macgregor and Ferris, *The Acts*, 315.
[58]*Dig.* 49.6.1 notes the necessity of this practice, which must have gone back at least to the 1st century AD according to Dauvillier, 'A propos', 10.

in one another's company before the trial,[59] the Jewish leaders allowed the method and substance of their formal accusation to vary markedly from the earlier trial before Felix.

The Jewish leaders apparently were represented by neither a professional rhetor nor a nominated spokesman. Rather, they prosecuted their case against Paul directly before Festus. They stood around Paul (περιέστησαν αὐτόν: Acts 25:7), accusing him. Festus' report to Agrippa also emphasizes that the accusation phase was corporately brought (Acts 25:18). This concerted and hence more forceful display of political status was obviously successful to the extent that Festus was prepared to show the Jews favour (Acts 25:9; cf. 24:27; 25:3) by pressing Paul to accept a change of trial venue. Whatever the advantage in this method, it was apparently undone by a serious lack of discipline and focus in developing the case against Paul. This lack is hinted at in Luke's reference to the Jews 'bringing many serious charges against him, which they could not prove' (Acts 25:7). It appears more explicitly in Festus' surprise that the Jews 'did not charge him with any of the crimes I had expected' (Acts 25:18). The sense of the words 'which I expected' (ὧν ἐγὼ ὑπενόουν) here may indicate more than simple expectation or suspicion.[60] Sherwin-White writes that the verb ὑπονοέω

> is pejorative, and at its strongest means 'suspect'. This phrase may well correspond to the formula 'any act of which I was prepared to take cognizance', 'de quibus cognoscere uolebam'. Claudius, in his well-known letter to the people of Alexandria, uses the term in the sentence: 'Let them not do things compelling me to take serious notice'. Perhaps animaduersio in the judicial sense is the nearest equivalent.[61]

Sherwin-White's interpretation may be confirmed in the next verse. In contrast to the way in which the rhetor Tertullus earlier crafted the Jewish charges so as to appeal strongly to Roman administrative and legal interests, the Jews, according to Acts 25:19, leave the impression in Festus' mind that their case against Paul rested on 'some points of dispute with him about their own religion and about a dead man named Jesus who Paul claimed was alive'. Festus is, therefore, at a loss as to how to proceed (Acts 25:20; cf. Gallio's response at 18:14-16).

---

[59]εν αὐτοῖς: Acts 25:6.
[60]Cf. BAGD, 846; MM, 659; Acts 25:18 (Vg.): suspicor.
[61]Sherwin-White, Roman Society, 50.

Festus' final attempt to break the impasse was similarly frustrated. The thrice indicated objective in setting up the grand audience described at Acts 25:23-26:32 is to clarify the case against Paul in Roman
terms so as clearly to formulate charges for inclusion in the *litterae dimissoriae*. The words, 'I have brought him before all of you, and especially you, King Agrippa' (Acts 25:26), emphasize Festus' regard for the
combined expertise of those gathered to assess the matter. Paul's
speech too would have been taken in written evidence in the case.[62] In
it, he exudes great confidence that he will receive a fair hearing and he
acknowledges Agrippa's expertise in Jewish matters (Acts 26:2f.).
These indications only sharpen the dilemma for Festus because the audience ends with the council and Agrippa officially reaffirming the accuracy of the first Roman assessments (Acts 23:29; 25:25); *viz.*, that
Paul's actions were neither capital nor worthy of chains (Acts 26:31f.).
Songer writes: 'The concluding conference leaves Festus with the
problem with which he began'.[63]

The evidence cited above hardly suggests that charges of factionalism were specified after the Roman pattern or, even if they had been
recorded as Jewish claims, that this would have been done in a manner
suggesting that Festus believed them to be true.[64] In fact, inclusion of
information from any one or several of the Roman trial documents or
conciliary findings in Festus' letters or their inclusion in any dossier
that he might have collected and sent along would only have served to
exonerate Paul. While he had nothing to write against Paul, however,
Festus still had to explain why, rather than dismissing the case, he had
in fact referred it. Failure to do so would have been an annoyance at
least; at worst it would have raised questions concerning his competence. What, then, was in the *litterae dimissoriae* to the emperor? It is a
reasonable hypothesis that Festus included, to justify his referral, some
description of Paul's appeal in the face of the unrelenting and murderous ferocity of the Jewish leadership against him despite the weakness
of their case. Hence, it would chronicle the legal and religio-political
aspects of the case for the emperor or his agents in Rome.

---

[62]The comments of Winter, 'The Importance', 526-31 on the likelihood of Luke's
use of trial documentation and forensic speeches as sources for Acts 24 must equally apply in the case of Acts 25:23-26:29.
[63]Songer, 'Paul's Mission', 507.
[64]*Contra* H.J. Cadbury, 'Note 26. Roman Law and the Trial of Paul'. In *BC*, vol. 5,
318 n. 2 and A.H.M. Jones, *The Criminal Courts of the Roman Republic and Principate*,
ed. J.A. Crook (Oxford: Blackwell, 1972), 102.

The fact of Paul's appeal to the emperor at Acts 25:11 and its fourfold repetition (*cf.* Acts 25:12, 21, 25; 26:32; 28:19) suggests that it was essential in Luke's eyes to explain the referral of Paul's case to Rome. Some record of Paul's action must surely have been included in Festus' written explanation. The context of Paul's cry is Festus' question whether Paul is prepared to stand trial in Jerusalem rather than Caesarea. It is hardly the case that Festus was asking Paul at Acts 25:9 whether he would submit to the unfettered jurisdiction of a Sanhedral court rather than a Roman tribunal,[65] or even whether, Festus having dismissed the Roman political charges, Paul would submit to the Sanhedrin on Jewish religious charges.[66] Such interpretations falter on the words 'to be judged by me' at Acts 25:9, which clearly indicate a Roman rather than Jewish court.[67]

Paul's declaration that 'no one has the right to hand me over to them [i.e., the Jews]' (Acts 25:11) does not rule out a real Roman handling of Paul's case in Jerusalem. 'Handing over', as Acts 3:14 and 25:16 clearly indicate, can be either positive or negative; but it occurs, as both contexts show, after due Roman legal process. It is unknown whether Paul feared that qualified Jews sympathetic to the accusers would be pressed into service as legal advisors by Festus,[68] or whether he was expressing the conviction that Festus would cave in to the more generalized influence of Jewish political sway.[69] Whatever the means, Paul apparently asserted his conviction that the outcome of a Roman trial in Jerusalem would surely be his death by the agency of the Jews.

Space does not permit a full discussion of the difficulties in specifying exactly what principle in Roman law Paul was enacting when he called out his appeal to Caesar at Acts 25:11. To this point, his action has been designated a 'call' or 'request'. The question whether Paul's action can be traced back to either *provocatio* or *appellatio* presumes a high degree of specificity and distinctiveness in these terms. In many discussions *provocatio* is identified as 'to the people' (*ad populum*) and against the verdict/action of a magistrate (mainly the *consul*) in criminal cases calling for capital, corporal or economic punishment; *appella-*

---

[65]So, e.g., Dauvillier, 'A propos', 8f.; Tajra, *The Trial of St. Paul*, 140-42, 154; Schürer, *The History*, vol. 1, 378.

[66]So, e.g., Blaiklock, *The Acts*, 182; Macgregor and Ferris, *The Acts*, 315; Neil, *The Acts*, 238;

[67]So, e.g., A. Schalit, 'Zu AG 25,9', *ASTI* 6 (1968), 112; Garnsey, 'The *Lex Julia*', 184 n. 168; Haenchen, *The Acts*, 666; Bruce, *The Book of Acts*, 452.

[68]So, e.g., Garnsey, 'The *Lex Julia*', 184 n. 170; Sherwin-White, *Roman Society*, 67.

[69]Jones, *The Criminal Courts*, 102; Wikenhauser, *Die Apostelgeschichte*, 264.

tio is identified as 'to a magisterial senior' (usually *ad tribunum*) against the action of his colleague or subordinate either before or after his verdict.[70] In this context, Paul's 'appeal' at Acts 25:11 is often discussed in terms of *provocatio*. Lentz observes, however, that Paul's case does not follow the pattern because Paul does not appeal for protection or against a specific punishment; rather, 'Paul "appeals" *before* the sentence has been handed down'.[71] Maintaining the strict distinctions noted above drives scholars to assert either that Paul's appeal was a special case of *provocatio* before sentence,[72] presuming an even greater specificity, or to entertain the modern conceit that Acts is so 'very confused' that 'one is led to suspect that neither Paul nor his biographer understood the legal position'.[73]

Garnsey, in contrast, argues that Paul does not launch an appeal but invokes the principle of 'rejection' (*reiectio*) whereby a defendant rejects a judge, plan, or tribunal as hostile or unjust.[74] He writes: 'St. Paul requested a trial before Nero at Rome because he knew that he would leave himself no chance if he agreed to go before the procurator's tribunal at Jerusalem'.[75] This solution creates its own problems in that it turns 'a little-used if not virtually obsolete prerogative of provincial citizens'[76] into a generally applicable principle.[77] While it does account for Paul's concern that hostile Jews might have a hand, directly or indirectly, in helping Festus to a verdict, 'this is only one aspect of Paul's act. The other is that he was appealing to the emperor in order to achieve this'.[78]

Lintott's solution is to question the strictness of the definitions for *appellatio* and *provocatio*. He is not hindered, owing to 1) the close relationship between *appellatio* and *provocatio* in their single underlying principle, 2) the employment of the terms *appellatio* and *provocatio* in various places without apparent distinction, and 3) the granting of full tribunician powers to Augustus, from designating Paul's appeal

---

[70]Cadbury, 'Roman Law', 313-15.

[71]Lentz, *Luke's Portrait of Paul*, 144-55 for discussion.

[72]Sherwin-White, *Roman Society*, 57-68 Jones, 'I Appeal', 57-65. Garnsey, *Social Status*, 75 n. 4, states that this would then be a unique case in the available literature.

[73]Jones, *The Criminal Courts*, 101. So also P.W. Walaskay, *'And So We Came to Rome', The Political Perspective of St Luke* (SNTSMS 49; CUP, 1983), 56.

[74]P. Garnsey, 'The Criminal Jurisdiction of Governors', *JRS* 58 (1968), 51-59 but esp. 56f.

[75]*Ibid.*, 57.

[76]Garnsey, *Social Status*, 76 and *cf.* 263f.

[77]Lintott, 'Provocatio', 265.

[78]*Ibid.*, 264.

an example of 'one form of recourse to the tribune's *auxilium*'.[79] While the problems associated with Paul's legal recourse are in no way entirely resolved, Lintott's 'solution' is perhaps the most satisfactory to date.

As Paul's 'appeal' in the circumstances was highly unusual, it is doubtful that Festus was bound or compelled at that moment to grant a referral though Roman law counselled strongly that he do so. The text of Acts indicates that Festus had discretion either to grant or deny Paul's request.[80] A real choice is indicated by Festus' need for consultation (Acts 25:12) and juridical discretion is evident in the use of the verbs of command (Acts 25:12) and decision (Acts 25:25). Agrippa's comment at Acts 26:32 is not necessarily inconsistent with the above-noted indications. It may reasonably be taken to show not compulsion for Festus to comply with Paul's request, but compulsion to carry through on the grant of that request. After seeking advice and then publicly and officially committing himself to refer the case, Festus would effectively diminish the authority of the emperor if he took it up again.[81] Concern for his reputation as a competent governor in the eyes of local Romans as well as Gentile and Jewish notables might also have figured prominently in effectively blocking a dismissal at this point.

Despite his having had a choice to grant or deny Paul's request in these unusual circumstances, the fact of Festus' dilemma springs in part from a high regard for Roman citizenship and the laws which protected the one possessing it. Ample evidence from the various documents could be drawn upon to demonstrate the Jewish ruling élite's unrelenting pursuit of Paul and their insistence upon his execution despite the increasing weakness of their case against him. Paul's own summary to the Jewish leaders in Rome of how he had come to arrive as a prisoner in chains (Acts 28:18f.) adds confidence to this hypothesis. First, it is recorded that Paul told his Jewish auditors about the Roman desire to acquit him of capital charges, about Jewish objections to his release and about his need to appeal to Caesar. These points, as we have argued above, are essentially what would have been in Festus' letter. He must have been able to confirm his account by referring to the Roman trial documents he possessed. Second, Paul's denial that he had any charge to bring (Acts 28:19) against his people—a statement

---

[79] *Ibid.*, 265. Lintott calls it a case of *appellatio*.
[80] So, e.g., Haenchen, *The Acts*, 667 n. 2; Garnsey, 'The *Lex Julia*', 177, 179, 182, 184.
[81] Sherwin-White, *Roman Society*, 65.

surely calculated to allay Roman Jewish concerns—makes little or no sense unless it is assumed that behind it lies something more than mere bravado or a simple moral conviction of innocence. Rather, what seems to be present is the real prospect of Paul's doing serious damage to his countrymen in a Roman court of law. Paul is implying that he could launch a successful countersuit,[82] perhaps charging that his opponents were guilty of malicious prosecution.[83] Whatever the specific charge, the statement must surely presuppose the general strength of Paul's own case and the weakness of his opponents' case, but also and more specifically that Pauline countercharges were capable of proof on the strength of the facts and the witness of available Roman documents.

Conclusions to Part 2

We may draw several conclusions from the preceding analyses. First, the Lukan accounts of Paul's progress into various experiences of custody in Acts acquit themselves well as records sensitive to Roman official concerns. Both overtly and in a number of subtle ways the seriousness of the charges, the relative status of accused and accusers and the pressures of such other factors as the presence of the crowd and the negative influences of social and financial pressures of power, favour, and money were shown to effect the custody Paul experienced.

Second, Paul's dissonance-laden status frequently caused him suffering which, from a Roman perspective, could have been moderated or avoided. He experienced disadvantage in deliberations and endured harsher penalties than necessary because some litigants and officials judged him to be of lower status than he actually was. Paul's disclosures of his Roman citizenship demonstrate the high value that he attached to it; the 'un-Roman' aspects of these various disclosures, of which Luke is aware and does not shrink from recording, also demonstrate a disclosure strategy.

Third, Paul's disclosure strategy was governed by premeditated and consciously embraced priorities; viz., that Paul's religious identity as a Jew, the integrity of his missionary message, and the faith of his converts should never be compromised. These priorities account not only for when Paul disclosed or did not disclose his Roman citizen-

---

[82]Cf. Dig. 48.1.5
[83]Ibid. 48.16.1, 3. Cf. Cod. Theod. 9.39.1-3.

ship, but also where, before whom, and even how he disclosed it. When properly appreciated, the disclosures do not question Paul's possession of the Roman citizenship. Rather, they define the parameters within which Paul let his citizenship serve him.

Two implications from this third point are intended by Luke. The first, having an apologetic thrust, is that Paul was a faithful Jew and Christian missionary not only because he preached but also because he kept his mouth shut concerning his Roman identity at certain times. When he did disclose it, he did so with great care. This ties in with the record of Paul's more overt assertions of Jewish and Christian faithfulness. The second implication is didactic. Marshall's comment on Acts 22:29 that 'Luke takes the opportunity to underline that Christians who were Roman citizens could claim their rights as such'[84] can be taken as generally true of the other instances of disclosure. Our study, however, encourages some nuancing. The Roman reader is informed that while a commitment to the Gospel does not forbid the exercise of Roman citizen rights to secure a more dignified treatment in time of trouble, particularly a more dignified custody, the example of Paul advises that the rights exercised were never to be seen as a way to dissemble on one's Christian identity or the Gospel and should never harm the Christian community. A Roman reader would be aware of the truth that Christianity could negatively influence social status and legal privilege. An earnest faith might well hinder—in some circumstances foreclose entirely—the free exercise of citizen rights.

A fourth conclusion, consequent upon the third, is that ascribing a single motive to the Roman officials in Acts, either exonerating them or giving them a bad press, hardly does justice to Luke's descriptions. In fact, the analyses reveal a range of behaviour. Some Roman officials deserve a bad press. Felix' little regard for Paul's citizen status in the first instance and failure to resist social pressure and bribery, Lysias' 'creative' rendering of the facts of Paul's case, and Festus' increasing weakness in the face of social pressure all argue that Luke possesses a critical eye. However, the physical abuse and harsh custody to which Paul is subjected by Roman officials such as the Philippian two men and the Tribune in Jerusalem cannot be so categorized. When their ignorance of Paul's Roman entitlements and their employment of a deliberative process which demanded that great weight be placed upon

---

[84] Marshall, *The Acts*, 359. *Pace* F. O'Toole, 'Chapter 1. Luke's Position on Politics and Society in Luke-Acts', in *Political Issues in Luke-Acts* (Maryknoll, NY: Orbis, 1983), 8, who writes that 'Luke advocates taking full advantage of the Roman polity'.

the litigants' relative status is taken into proper account, their behaviour can only be judged understandable. It is not crassly reprobate or consciously illegal. Paul's silence comes from the constraints of religious and missionary conviction. When he discloses his citizen status, it is fitting and right to do so; it is hardly, as many would understand, because he wishes to catch out Roman officials or to embarrass them. Official sensitivity to Roman propriety is confirmed at the moment of his disclosures by historically credible expressions of shock and a proper secular 'repentance'. When Paul demands leave to plead his case before the emperor and when custodial determinations are made for him in Rome without personal interest, the result positively redounds to the praise of official Roman justice.

The penultimate conclusion is that, from his first arrest by Lysias until the end of his incarceration in Rome and excepting only a few days from Lysias' discovery of Paul's Roman citizenship to the point of his arrival in Caesarea, Paul is not just a prisoner but a prisoner in chains. Significant social/relational and missiological implications flow from this fact and these will be later considered in terms of the concepts of honour and shame.

Finally, we venture an opinion concerning the ending of Acts. We have argued that the reason for Paul's amazingly loose custody in Rome was not that he had such high status but that the trial documents contained consistent indications that there were no grounds for the Roman charges alleged and that Paul's appeal to be heard by the emperor (however it is to be construed) had been granted in the face of continued Jewish insistence that he be executed. This means that the evidence against Paul is not only weak, inconsistent and hence false from the Lukan perspective but apparently from the perspective of Roman officialdom as well. If the evidence has been properly analysed, the custody in Rome as Luke reports it and the probable material basis of the deliberations leading to that custody, notwithstanding arguments to the contrary,[85] constitute a significant and highly-placed Roman estimate of the trial's probable outcome; i.e., that Paul will be released.

---

[85]For a listing and critique of the several hypotheses as to why Acts ends as it does, including consideration of Paul's fate, see L.P. Pherigo, 'Paul's Life After the Close of Acts', *JBL* 70 (1951), 277-84; Hemer, *The Book of Acts*, 383-92.

PART 3

PAUL IN PRISON IN ACTS

CHAPTER 9

THE CONDITIONS OF LIFE IN PRISON

Modern descriptions of the relative severity or ease of Paul's custodial experiences in Acts are not typically well informed by ancient sources on prisons and imprisonment. This results in a tendency to idealize the account of Paul's custodial experiences. Such an approach flattens individual descriptions and undercuts Luke's purposes as he records that Paul must suffer (Acts 9:16) for the name and that 'prison and hardships' (δεσμὰ καὶ θλίψεις: Acts 20:23) await Paul in Jerusalem. The thrust of this chapter will be to chronicle ancient indications of the privations of life in custody.

I. The Physical Constraints of Imprisonment

The question of the impact of facilities has already been touched upon 'from the outside looking in', in the sense of discussing the process of assigning prisoners to a juridically and socially appropriate custody.[1] Our interest now is 'from the inside', looking to the prisoner's own experience.

1. Overcrowding and Lack of Basic Necessities

To assess the capacity of an ancient prison we must consider not only its size but also reports of its population. Where little of a prison structure has survived, as in the case of the upper stories of the *carcer* in Rome, no indications of capacity or what constituted overcrowding can be given. We also don't know, for example, whether the note that the philosopher Apollonius of Tyana (reign Domitian) was kept in the free prison in Rome along with about fifty other prisoners indicates overcrowding.[2] However, where substantial remains exist, as in the case of the state prison at Athens, some indication of prison conditions relative to prisoner population is possible. With a small number of prisoners, the eight cells and courtyard of the Athens prison would have served adequately; it could, however, become heavily crowded and, hence, uncomfortable.

Such factors as war and civil disturbance,[3] the enforcement of condemnatory edicts,[4] and delay in processing cases due to their volume or out of incompetence or sheer maliciousness,[5] could pack the prisons beyond capacity. This had consequences for prisoners, including unbearable heat and dehydration. The *Martyrdom of Perpetua and Felicitas* (203 AD) records: 'What a difficult time it was! With the crowd the heat was stifling'.[6] Later in this document, in a vision given to one

---

[1]*Supra,* ch. 2.
[2]Philostratus, *VA* 7.26.
[3]*Supra.* 41f.
[4]The Christian martyr literature records roundups and incarcerations of large numbers of confessors.
[5]The administrative headache of general overcrowding is evidenced in the document *PPetr.* 2:13 (3)[8] [256-253 BC and cited in MM, 143]. See also J.H.W.G. Liebescheutz, *Antioch: City and Imperial Administration in the Later Roman Empire* (Oxford: Clarendon, 1972), 112.
[6]*Mart. Perp. & Felic.* 3.6.

of the Christian prisoners, it is recounted: 'I saw Dinocrates coming out
of a dark hole, where there were very many others with him, very hot
and thirsty'.[7] The confessor Lucian (c. 250 AD) writes: 'The stifling
heat, caused by our crowded numbers, is intolerable'.[8] The air in prisons—and we may be sure that the need for security resulted in inadequate ventilation[9]—could, with overcrowding, become stale and even
dangerous. Lucian (c. 163 AD) writes of Demetrius' prison that it possessed 'stifling air (since many were confined in the same place,
cramped for room, and scarcely able to draw breath)'.[10] Such expressions as exclusion 'from drawing free breath',[11] of emerging from the
prison into the 'fresh air of justice',[12] of the soul in the body being lik-
ened to a prisoner in the jail who 'cannot even draw a breath of free
air'[13] and of prisoners being 'long deprived of the breath of our common air'[14] all acknowledge this horrible reality.

We possess few more graphic accounts of the grim consequences
of overcrowding than the description Athenian POWs in the quarry
prison of Syracuse (413 BC): Thucydides writes:

> Crowded as they were in large numbers in a deep and narrow place,
> at first the sun and the suffocating heat caused them distress, there be-
> ing no roof; while the nights that followed were, on the contrary, au-
> tumnal and cold, so that the sudden change engendered illness.
> Besides, they were so cramped for space that they had to do every-
> thing in the same place; moreover, the dead were heaped together
> upon one another, some having died from wounds or because of the
> change in temperature or like causes, so that there was a stench that
> was intolerable.[15]

Diodorus Siculus writes the following about the prison at Alba Fucens:

> This prison is a deep underground dungeon, no larger than a nine-
> couch room, dark, and noisome from the large numbers committed to
> the place, who were men under condemnation on capital charges, for

---

[7]Ibid. 7.4.
[8]H.B. Workman, Persecution in the Early Church: A Chapter in the History of Renunciation (Fernley Lectures 36; London: Charles H. Kelly, 1906), 292.
[9]See Plutarch, Phil. 19.3.
[10]Lucian, Tox. 29.
[11]Cicero, Ver. 2.5.23 (70 BC).
[12]Ibid. 2.5.160.
[13]Philo Judaeus, De ebrietate 101 (20 BC-60 AD).
[14]Cod. Theod. 9.40.22 (414 AD).
[15]Thucydides 7.87.1f.

most of this category were incarcerated there at that period. With so many shut up in such close quarters, the poor wretches were reduced to the physical appearance of brutes, and since their food and everything pertaining to their other needs was all foully commingled, a stench so terrible assailed anyone who drew near that it could scarcely be endured.[16]

If overcrowding brought stresses both physical and psychological upon the prisoner, so too did solitary confinement. Dio Cassius writes how Gallus (30 AD) was incarcerated so that 'he had no companion or servant with him, spoke to no one, and saw no one, except when he was compelled to take food'.[17] Similar arrangements were made in other cases during this period,[18] among them that of Drusus, the grandson of Tiberius, who was detained and starved to death 'in a lower room of the Palace'.[19]

We may be sure that within prisons generally, provisions for comfort in sleep were virtually non-existent. Plutarch, in his fictional account of events in the prison at Thebes (379 BC), mentions that the prisoners lay on beds, the term χάμευνα probably here indicating a kind of rough sleeping pallet near to the ground.[20] Comments regarding the philosopher Apollonius' imprisonment suggest that he had either claimed or been assigned the bed (κλίνη) on which he slept.[21] Apollonius, however, was confined in the free prison at Rome and its occupants were generally of higher status. In a harsh, poorly furnished, heavily crowded facility,[22] or set in stocks,[23] one might be forced to make do with a spot on the floor. Demetrius' experience at night of 'the clash of iron, [and] the scant sleep'[24] in the *Toxaris* (c. 163 AD) bears the marks of truth. The confessor Lucian and his cellmates at Carthage in 250 AD are described as happy 'even sleeping on the ground'.[25]

---

[16]Diodorus Siculus 31.9.2.
[17]Dio Cassius 58.3.5.
[18]*Ibid.* 58.3.6.
[19]Suetonius, *Tib.* 54.2.
[20]Plutarch, *De Gen.* 598.B. *Cf.* LSJ, 1976.
[21]Philostratus, *VA* 7.30.
[22]Lack of furnishings and/or crowding seems to be presumed in the discussion at *b. Nez. V: Sanh.* I:37b concerning whether a woman confined in a prison is able to conceive while standing.
[23]*Cf. Mart. Let. Phil. (uerso Rufini latina)* 7f. and the account of the martyrdom of Vincent cited in A.J. Mason, *The Historic Martyrs of the Primitive Church* [London: Longmans, Green, 1905], 381f. (both c. 304 AD).
[24]Lucian, *Tox.* 29.

The only mention of bedclothes in the literature consulted is of provisions made by the prisoners themselves or their helpers. The outer cloak or over-garment, was essential clothing under normal circumstances. Worn on the back during the day, it became, when taken off and wrapped around or draped over the body, a part of one's bedding, keeping out the cold of the night.[26] So also in prison, Philopoemen (182 BC), before lying down to try to sleep, wraps himself in his soldier's cloak.[27] Despite ease granted in the manner of Agrippa's keeping in the Praetorian camp at Rome (36/7 AD), his bed and bedding were inadequate. His servants therefore 'brought him garments that they pretended to sell, but, when night came, they made him a bed with the connivance of the soldiers'.[28] We must add two NT examples. The angelic command in Acts that Peter put on his cloak (Acts 12:8) *after* the chains have fallen from his wrists suggests that his cloak was before that moment serving him as bedding or a sleep covering. The request in 2 Tim. 4:13 that Timothy bring the cloak[29] left at Troas may, against other suggestions[30] and in keeping with the clear indications above, simply be intended to reflect the prisoner's need for greater warmth and comfort at night owing to want of these in his place of custody. The urgent request for Timothy to come to Paul (2 Tim. 1:4; 4:9, 21) and to bring, among other important items, Paul's cloak for·this purpose, finds additional confirmation in indications of a failure of practical assistance in the local context (2 Tim. 1:8, 15; 4:9-12, 14-16; contrast 1:16-18)[31] and the approach of winter (2 Tim. 4:21).

2. Darkness and Light

One of the abiding hallmarks of life in prison was darkness. There is ample witness to the fact that prisons generally were devoid of much natural light. The exceptionally deep Syracuse quarry, for example,

---

[25]Cyprian, *Ep.* 20.3 [Oxf., *Ep.* 21].

[26]*Cf.* Exod. 22:26f.; Deut. 24:17f.; Matt. 5:40 and the hilarious account of the obedient bedbugs in the *Apocr. Acts John* 60.

[27]Plutarch, *Phil.* 20.2.

[28]Josephus, *AJ* 18.204 [18.6.7]. *Cf.* LSJ, 1896.

[29]*Cf.* W.C.F. Anderson, 'Paenula', *DGRA*, vol. 2, 308f.

[30]See P. Trümmer, '"Mantel und Schriften" (2 Tim 4,13). Zur Interpretation einer persönlichen Notiz in den Pastoralbriefen', *BZ* 18 (1974), 193-207; M. Prior, *Paul the Letter-Writer and the Second Letter to Timothy* (JSNTS 23; Sheffield: JSOT, 1989), 153f. and 236f. nn. 43-5.

[31]But see Prior, *Paul the Letter-Writer*, 153.

was a place of oppressive darkness.[32] Philostratus observes that the philosopher Apollonius, 'when day came ... offered his prayers to the Sun, as best he could in prison';[33] apparently even in the free prison at Rome, a locale for upper class prisoners, there was minimal natural light. Tertullian, declares the prison to be a place 'full of darkness'.[34] Examples could be multiplied.

If natural light was poor in prisons generally, it was non-existent in the more secure cells. Where the prison room or cell was below ground level as the 'treasury' (θησαυρός) of Messene[35] or the *Tullianum* of Rome[36] and no artificial lighting was furnished, darkness was virtually complete. A secure cell above ground at the centre of a prison structure could be just as dark. The connection between darkness and inner cells is secure enough that at some places the expression *in tenebris* (darkness) is intended by the author as virtually synonymous with being imprisoned: *tenebrae* may be safely rendered by the word 'dungeon'.[37]

Nightfall robbed the prisoner of what little light there was in the prison. Regimens were apparently such that the prison and its occupants were secured against all exit. If the *Apocryphal Acts of Thomas* (early 3rd. cent. AD) is an indication, a part of that security was that prisoners were not permitted lights after nightfall; they were expected to bide their time in total darkness.[38] The presence of lights at night suggested prison escape or at least clandestine planning. One security measure apparently employed by wardens was to lock prisoners away in the most secure and hence darkest recesses of a prison at night. While it was convenient and minimized the need for many guards, later legislation acknowledged the practice to be cruel. An enactment in the *Theodosian Code*, dating to 320 AD, declared for the remand prisoner as follows:

---

[32]Cicero, *Ver.* 2.5.21, 23.
[33]Philostratus, *VA* 7.31.
[34]Tertullian, *Ad Martyres* 2; also *Mart. Let. Lyons & Vienne* 27f. (177 AD); *Mart. Perp. & Felic.* 3.5 (203 AD); Cyprian, *Ep.* 15.2 (250 AD = Oxf., *Ep.* 37); *ibid.* 77.3 (259 = Oxf., *Ep.* 77); *Mart. Mont. & Luc.* 4.1-3 (259 AD) *Mart. Mar. & James* 6.1, 3 (259 AD); *Mart. Das.* 5.3 (304 AD).
[35]Plutarch, *Phil.* 19.3: It 'admitted neither air nor light from outside'.
[36]Rome's death chamber, twelve feet below ground level, is often described as a place of darkness and gloom (e.g., Livy 6.17.5; 38.59.10; Sallust, *Cat.* 55.3; Ovid, *Consolatio ad Liuiam* 278). Cf. the connection of depth with darkness in the phrase εἰς οἴκημα ζοφῶδες in Heliodorus' fictional *Aeth.* 8.6.2 (220-40 BC).
[37]Cicero, *Cat.* 4.10.
[38]See *Apocr. Acts Thom.* 153.

When incarcerated he must not suffer the darkness of an inner prison, but he must be kept in good health by the enjoyment of light, and when night doubles the necessity for his guard, he shall be taken back into the vestibules of the prisons and into healthful places. When day returns, at early sunrise, he shall forthwith be led into the common light of day that he may not perish from the torments of prison....[39]

The darkest places in prisons were typically also the least healthy. While being deprived of sunlight would, over time, have definite physiological effects, far more discussion in the literature relates to the psychological impact of living in near- or total-darkness. A pagan asks certain Christian prisoners 'in a taunting voice how we were getting on with the darkness... of prison'.[40] The dark prison merits such epithets as 'foul' and 'noxious' and 'terrible'[41] because it inspires not only revulsion but sheer terror. One Christian confessor admits, 'I was terrified, as I had never before been in such a dark hole', and another relates how 'the consolation and the joy of the day removed the agony we endured at night'.[42]

Small wonder that the dark prison is identified in Christian literature as one of the devices of the Devil to erode the life and faith of the Christian[43] and that it also becomes a foil for 'light' imagery. Tertullian exhorts the confessors that prison 'is full of darkness, but ye yourselves are light'.[44] Another asks: 'Well, now pagans, do you still believe that Christians, for whom awaits the joy of eternal light [quos namet gaudium lucis aeternae], feel the torments of prison or shrink from the dungeons [lit. darkness, tenebrae] of this world?' and continues a few lines later, 'Dedicated as they are to God the Father, their brothers care for them by day, Christ by night as well'.[45] In the face of persecution, a confessor replies that 'the soldiers of Christ even in a dungeon enjoy the most brilliant light'.[46] The darkness of the prison also becomes the place of luminous visions of heaven,[47] of brilliantly clad or light-bear-

---

[39]Cod. Theod. 9.3.1 (≈ Cod. Just. 9.4.1 [353 AD]).

[40]Mart. Mar. & James 8.2-4 (259 AD).

[41]Mart. Mont. & Luc. 4.2 (259 AD); Cod. Theod. 6.29.1 (355 AD); and 9.38.6 (381 AD) respectively.

[42]Mart. Perp. & Felic. 3.5 (203 AD) and Mart. Mont. & Luc. 4.7 (259 AD) respectively.Cf. also Mart. Mar. & James 6.1 (259 AD); Mart. Mont. & Luc. 4.2 (259 AD).

[43]See Mart. Let. Lyons & Vienne 27f. (177 AD).

[44]Tertullian, Ad Martyres 2 (c. 195 AD): 'Habet tenebras, sed lumen estis ipsi'.

[45]Mart. Mar. & James 6.1 and 3 respectively (259 AD).

[46]Ibid. 8.4.

[47]Mart. Perp. & Felic. 11.4; 12.1; Mart. Mar. & James 6.6. Cf. Mart. Mont. & Luc. 4.1-3; 11.2-4.

ing angelic and divine visitors[48] and of visionary miracles which open pinched windows to allow an unimpeded view of the heavens.[49]

3. Paul's Experience of Prison in Acts

Paul's prison experience at Philippi was certainly the worst of Luke's record. After a vicious beating, Silas and he had immediately been confined in stocks in the inner cell (Acts 16:24) of the prison. Most likely, the apostles' entire stay was in near or complete darkness. Nightfall would have been all but imperceptible. The usual security precaution of denying light to prisoners at night was certainly employed, as the jailer's cry for lamps or torches (φῶτα: Acts 16:29)[50] confirms.

Difficult questions have been asked concerning Acts 16. One relates to how the other prisoners would have been able to hear Paul and Silas singing and praying. Would it not be difficult, if not impossible, for the sound to travel distinctly through the prison? If one wishes to emphasize from the Greek verb ἐπακροάομαι that the prisoners gave Paul and Silas 'their closest attention', and that the tense (imperfect) shows the missionaries to have held it throughout',[51] the need to answer this question is rendered more urgent still. Pesch improbably has Paul and Silas singing so loudly that the whole prison can hear them;[52] Haenchen suggests that the comment concerning the prisoners is a literary confirmation that the earthquake is an act of God but has no historical basis.[53]

Another problem adheres to Paul's confident assertion to the jailer, 'We are all here!' (Acts 16:28). How would Paul have known this from the inner cell? Haenchen offers that this question is better left unasked;[54] Conzelmann suggests that the words are legendary and pure theatre.[55] Where Pesch is content to state that the question is not answered by the text,[56] others predicate to Paul miraculous knowledge of the prison population, great psychological insight into how prison-

---

[48]*Mart. Mar. & James* 7.3; *Mart. Mont. & Luc.* 4.1-5.2; 7.3.

[49]*Mart. Mont. & Luc.* 8.6 (259 AD).

[50]BAGD, 871. K. Lake and H.J. Cadbury, *The Acts of the Apostles*, in *BC*, vol. 4, 198.

[51] Williams, *Acts*, 280.

[52] Pesch, *Die Apostelgeschichte*, 2, 115. *Cf.* Schille, *Die Apostelgeschichte*, 347.

[53]Haenchen, *The Acts*, 497.

[54]*Ibid., The Acts*, 497 n. 8.

[55]Conzelmann, *Acts*, 132.

[56]Pesch, *Die Apostelgeschichte*, 115.

ers would behave in an earthquake, or considerable powers of persuasion in preventing prisoners from escaping.[57] Similar solutions attach to Paul's (or Luke's) knowledge that the chains of *all* (Acts 16:26) the prisoners had been loosed.

Finally, it is often asked why the jailer did not first look around the prison to see who might have escaped and why he chose to enter the inner cell. Some suggest that this is an irrational reaction born from 'shock';[58] others, more sceptically, that the jailer's action 'belongs to the logic of edifying narration'[59] or should probably be numbered among what Krodel calls the many 'rational impossibilities'[60] of the text.

These responses, though only occasionally explicitly[61], share the belief that the other prisoners occupied different cells than Paul and Silas. But nothing in the text hinders the possibility that all shared the same inner cell. Moreover, though seldom mooted for Acts 16,[62] such practice was not without precedent in the ancient world. The jailer would have been following the practice hinted at in the provision of the *Theodosian Code* and illustrated in Lucian's *Toxaris* (cited above) of taking prisoners from other places in the prison or from the freedom of the prison yard and cramming them all together into the most secure part of the prison overnight. This would have placed all the prisoners at Acts 16 in the inner cell even if the jail possessed other cells or areas, as is likely.

That this better construes the custody arrangements in the text is seen in the natural—as opposed to the improbable and hostile—answers it generates to the problems. Crowded together in the same cell, all prisoners would easily have heard the apostles singing and praying. Paul's confident shout to the jailer that he and all the other prisoners were still 'here' (Acts 16:28) would also be much better explained. The pitch-blackness and the aftermath of earthquake would hardly have hindered the sense of movements within the cell and any traffic out of the single entrance would instantly have been known. Such a

---

[57]See, e.g., the discussion in Schille, *Die Apostelgeschichte*, 347; Krodel, *Acts*, 312.

[58]E.g., Williams, *Acts*, 281 and *cf.* I.H. Marshall, *The Acts of the Apostles* (TNTC 5; Grand Rapids: Eerdmans, 1980), 272.

[59]Haenchen, *The Acts*, 497.

[60]Krodel, *Acts*, 311.

[61]So Schneider, *Die Apostelgeschichte*, 217; Pesch, *Die Apostelgeschichte*, 116; Longenecker, 'The Acts 464.

[62]Schille, *Die Apostelgeschichte*, 347 is one. J.B. Polhill, *Acts* (NAC 26; Nashville: Broadman, 1992), 355 only incidentally mentions that the prisoners 'were all still in the cell'.

custody arrangement, moreover, would also disclose the compelling logic of the jailer's headlong rush (εἰσεπήδησεν: Acts 16:29) into the inner cell—*not* the prison generally—rather than any other cell after he had called for lights. It was in this cell that a nocturnal head count of all the prisoners in the facility would be made, whether Paul had assured the jailer that all prisoners were present and accounted for or not. Passing through the open doors of the prison to that inner cell, the jailer's distress would reach a climax when he discovered that the last and most important door also had sprung open. Finally, if the *sound* of chains falling from prisoners' limbs—or from the walls if this is what happened—had not disclosed the fact to Paul and the others, the presence of the lights in the inner cell would certainly have done so.

Jamming the prisoners into a single secure cell would frustrate escape with maximum efficiency and convenience to the jailer and his staff. It would also—beyond the agony and pain that Paul and Silas were already suffering from the beating and the stocks—have resulted in many of the conditions of inner cells discussed above. This would include stale air, stench, and stifling heat caused by overcrowding and poor ventilation, as well as general foulness, noise, and the consequent sleeplessness.

Little beyond what has already been indicated can be said concerning the physical demands of the facilities in which Paul was confined in Jerusalem and Caesarea. Though briefly treated with great harshness at the outset, the conditions of Paul's custody in Jerusalem soon became less demanding. He was confined in a dignified manner in the Fortress Antonia in senior officers' quarters and, apparently, creature comforts and reasonable requests were attended to—except in the matter of visitors. Paul's restraint in the brief first phase of his Caesarean custody, we have argued, was much more routine and unexceptional. The constraints on him in those first five days were normal; i.e., he was guarded closely and carefully by his keepers. Friends and associates were denied access to him. In the two year second phase of Paul's Caesarean custody, the conditions of his keeping were relaxed. He remained in Herod's palace, but now in the personal care of a centurion; exactly where in the palace one cannot say, except that officers' quarters would seem to have been an unlikely place. Felix' instructions strongly imply that Paul was sheltered from the worst aspects of the prison system. He was not oppressively guarded by his keeper(s) in having to answer for his every move or activity. Nor was he isolated from the care of co-religionists 'on the outside'.

What can we learn about the custody facilities in which Paul was kept aboard ship by the centurion Julius on the way to Rome? Most passengers on ancient ships 'camped on deck, living either in the open or under tiny temporary shelters. There were also steerage accommodations ... in the bowels of the ship'.[63] For prisoners in transit, however, the situation could be very different. 3 Macc. 4:10 indicates that prisoners were sometimes held below deck. Some were 'tied to the crossbeams of the ships..., and, what is more, with their eyes in complete shadow because of the thick deck just above'. They would have suffered the cruelties of darkness and perhaps suffocating heat. When bishop Felix was transported by ship from Tibuica in Africa about 303 AD, he boarded in 'heavy chains and stayed in the hold for four days, tossed about under the feet of horses. He tasted neither bread nor water, and thus fasting he came to harbour in the city of Agrigentum'.[64] The demands of security would usually have meant transport not only under a suitable guard[65] but also probably in chains.[66]

The conditions during Paul's custody aboard ship were not apparently worse than for those who guarded him. He is able to address the ship's crew, the centurion and his compatriots as well as the other passengers with ease, and he sees the play being made by certain sailors in the bow area to abandon the ship (Acts 27:10f., 21-26, 30-36). Clearly, he is kept above deck. There seems no reason to believe that Paul was kept differently on the first two sea vessels at Acts 27:2, 4f. and on the second Alexandrian grain carrier at Acts 28:11. We may conclude that he was afforded a modicum of dignity in transit. The need for security and the examples given above, however, render it likely that Paul was sent to Rome in chains. Paul's ability to hear the high-level conversations noted above may imply that he was chained to the centurion himself. No decision can be made as to how fellow-prisoners were treated.

The three days' hospitality (Acts 28:7) offered to all by the Maltese official Publius, the bed and board given by the commoners of Malta (presumably one of the many τιμαί at Acts 28:10) to Paul and his companions in the next three months[67] and the seven days' stay (Acts 28:14) in the homes of Christians at Puteoli are further indications that

---

[63]L. Casson, *Ships and Seamanship in the Ancient World* (Princeton: PUP, 1971), 181 and examples given in nn. 65f.
[64]*Mart. Felix, appendix.*
[65]*Supra*, 30.
[66]E.g., in Latin, Livy 29.19.5; 29.21.12; In Greek, Josephus, *AJ* 20.131 [20.6.2]; *BJ* 7.449 [7.11.3]

Paul, his companions, and his keepers all shared in the normal rigours of travel. Paul's transit—apart from the need for basic security and the disastrous shipwreck—was therefore not harsh. While Acts never indicates that the centurion Julius permitted additional overnight rest stops, several would have occurred along the 120 or so miles between Puteoli and Rome; perhaps as many as five, if the company travelled by foot. Either of the two stopping points mentioned at Acts 28:15—the Forum of Appius and the Three Taverns—are likely rest venues.[68] If no hospitality was on offer from Christians along the way, Julius would have billeted and fed his retinue in one of the inns or hostels of the government post.

II. Chains

The ancient literature shows some variation in the manner in which prisoners wore chains. We read of prisoners being fettered by one or both legs,[69] wearing manacles on one or both wrists,[70] and in other cases wearing chains on every limb.[71] A pattern of chaining, probably not atypical, can be found in Lucian's *Toxaris* (c. 163 AD): The wearing of a 'collar' (κλοιός) and 'manacles upon one hand' satisfied the demands of security for inmates of the prison in Egypt there described.[72] The fact that the prisoners were manacled only by one hand is explained when Demetrius pleads permission to be chained with his friend *in the same set of manacles;*[73] i.e., the prisoners were chained in pairs. At night, writes Lucian, the prisoner 'had to be fully secured by his bonds'.[74] This meant beyond the other measures—at least initial-

---

[67]*Contra* the very late tradition which identifies a certain cave on Malta as the locale of Paul's imprisonment. *Cf.* B. Schwank, 'Und so kamen wir nach Rom (Apg 28,14). Reisenotizen zu den letzten beiden Kapiteln der Apostelgeschichte', *Erbe und Auftrag* 36 (1960), 177 for discussion.

[68]*Tres Tabernae* and *Apii Forum* were stopping places about 33 and 43 miles from Rome respectively.

[69]E.g., Livy 32.26.18 (198 BC); Tertullian, *Ad Martyras* 2 (195 AD); Philostratus, *VA* 7.36 (reign of Domitian); Cyprian, *Ep.* 33.2 (250 AD = Oxf., *Ep.* 39); *ibid.* 77.3 (257 AD = Oxf., *Ep.* 77); *Mart. Let. Phil.* (c. 304-7 AD).

[70]For examples, *supra*, 30. So too Acts 12:6f.; Juvenal 16.560f. (2nd. cent. AD).

[71]E.g., Seneca, *Con.* 1.6.2 (*b. c.* 55 BC); Arrian, *Epict. Diss.* 1.29.5 (2nd. cent. AD); Heliodorus, *Aeth.* 8.9.1 (c. 220-40 AD); Cyprian, *Ep.* 76.2 (257 AD = Oxf., *Ep.* 76); Achilles Tatius, *Clit. & Leuc.* 5.23 (c. 300 AD).

[72]Lucian, *Tox.* 29.

[73]*Ibid.* 32.

ly—confinement in the stocks.[75] Elsewhere, however, we read of how numbers of prisoners were secured at night by a single length of chain which was run through their fetters.[76] The discomforts thus caused are easy to imagine. We might also mention prisoners who were compelled to wear, in addition to manacles, chains about the neck.[77]

Chains were usually fashioned from iron[78] and were of varying weight. In one of the earliest pieces of Roman legislation, the Twelve Tables, provisions in the matter of debt required that

> unless the debtor discharges the debt adjudged or unless someone offers surety for him in court the creditor shall take the debtor with him. He shall bind him either with a thong or with fetters of not less than fifteen pounds in weight, or if he wishes he shall bind him with fetters of more than this weight.[79]

On being informed that Carthaginian prisoners-of-war were threatening to overthrow the state, the officials in 198 BC were instructed that the Carthaginians be 'loaded with chains of not less than ten pounds' weight' which, the text continues, was typical of the public or state prison.[80] We are probably not wrong to assume that the 'triple sets of fetters'[81] clamped onto the limbs of the conspirators who pleaded before Nero in 65 AD were extremely weighty (30 lbs.?). The confessor Felix, it is said, boarded ship to travel to his trial wearing heavy chains.[82]

Chains, of course, found their principal objective in restricting mobility and preventing escape. The material from which they were fashioned and their weight, however, caused untold sufferings for prisoners. We get a glimpse of these sufferings in the literature. First, rough iron clamped upon sweaty limbs in the damp environment of the prison would eventually rust. Incarcerated during the time of the Roman civil war (c. 48/47 BC), Marius suffered the consequences of such effects. Lucan writes that 'the old man's flesh was corroded by

---

[74]*Ibid.* 29.

[75]*Ibid.*

[76]*Ibid.* 33.

[77]E.g., Ovid, *Con. Liv.* 273f. (11 AD).

[78]E.g., Lucan 72 (*c.* 48/7 BC); Josephus, *AJ* 18.237 [18.6.10] (37 AD); Tacitus, *Ger.* 31 (*c.* 56-115 AD).

[79]*ARS* 8—XII Tables 3.3.

[80]Livy 32.26.18. The weight of the chains in later legislation was related to the severity of the punishment. See *Dig.* 48.19.8.6.

[81]Suetonius, *Nero* 36.2.

[82]*Mart. Felix*, App.

iron fetters and the squalor of long captivity'.[83] Julius Bassus in the elder Seneca's *Controversiae*, may also refer to this effect when he speaks of his 'hands worn with shackles'.[84] The need for a man to strike the chains off of Josephus' limbs with an axe may indicate that his chains had been permanently fixed to him.[85] The alternative way of releasing him, if the chains were not unlockable, would have been to call for a smith.[86] Beyond the above troubles, prisoners could fall victim to torturous innovations if later legislation is any indication. We read in a provision of the *Theodosian Code* (320 AD) that 'the man who has been produced in court shall not be put in manacles made of iron that cleave to the bones, but in looser chains, so that there may be no torture and yet the custody may remain secure'.[87]

Second, the chains' weight could be debilitating. We read in the literature of 'the necks of kings livid with chains, and ruthless fetters entwining cruel hands',[88] of prisoners' limbs 'burdened with the weight of chains'[89] and of the heaping of irons upon the necks and arms of prisoners until they were nearly crushed.[90] The potential for chains to render limbs useless was increased where the prisoner was being deprived of sufficient nourishment. Julius Bassus in Seneca's *Controversiae* may be quoted in this respect: 'You would have seen my body clothed in rags, all my limbs burdened under chains, my eyes sunken in my emaciated state, my hands worn with shackles and useless'.[91] That weight also meant excruciating pain is attested in the conversation between a mocker and the philosopher Apollonius. The mocker asks, '"And how can your leg endure the weight of the fetters?" "I don't know," said Apollonius, "for my mind is intent upon other matters." "And yet the mind," said the other, "must attend to what causes pain."'[92] Tertullian's assertion that 'the leg does not feel

---

[83]Lucan 72f. In 257 AD, Cyprian (*Ep.* 76.2 [Oxf., *Ep.* 76]) writes of how the iron fetters stain the gold of the confessors' bodies.
[84]Seneca, *Con.* 1.6.2.
[85]Josephus, *BJ* 4.628f. [4.10.7].
[86]For what is probably more permanent chaining requiring a smith, Cyprian, *Ep.* 76.2 (257 AD = Oxf., *Ep.* 76); cf. *Apocr. Acts Paul* 5.
[87]*Cod. Theod.* 9.3.1 (= *Cod. Just.* 9.4.1 [353 AD]).
[88]Ovid, *Con. Liv.* 273f.
[89]*Cod. Theod.* 9.40.22 [414 AD].
[90]Cited in Mason, *The Historic Martyrs*, 380.
[91]Seneca, *Con.* 1.6.2.
[92]Philostratus, *VA* 7.36.

the chain when the mind is in the heavens',[93] heroic as it is, nevertheless bears testimony to the agony of being clamped in irons.

Finally, chains were noisy. Seneca writes of the rattling or creaking of chains.[94] Juvenal acknowledges this when he writes of the honour for the philosopher of having worn 'chains clanking on either arm';[95] and so too the *Martyrdom of Montanus and Lucius* which glories in the 'clanking of the chains as they were drawn over one another'.[96] With considerable realism, Lucian refers to 'the clash of iron'[97] as one of the reasons for the scanty sleep of prisoners.

Such references hardly exaggerate the rigours of wearing irons, whether light or heavy. They also illustrate how, in later legislation, slavery and low rank could be described as the punishment of bonds.[98] As the writer of the *Clementine Recognitions* indicates, 'bonds…are evil, and very evil'.[99]

III. Diet and Hygiene

Ancient prison systems were known for their neglect and abuse of prisoners in the matter of diet and hygiene. We first consider the prisoner's need for food and drink.

1. Food and Drink

The burden of securing adequate nourishment while in custody typically fell on the shoulders of the prisoner. Taubenschlag notes that this was the Graeco-Egyptian practice.[100] Roman practice appears to have been no different. A provision of the *Theodosian Code* (409 AD) presumes and reinforces the long-standing pattern even as it sets out to 'catch' those who cannot fit into it: prison wardens are to 'cause food

---

[93]Tertullian, *Ad Martyras* 2.
[94]Seneca, *Ad Lucilium Ep.* 9.9.
[95]Juvenal 6.560f. *Cf.* Tibullus 2.6.26: 'The iron clanks upon his legs [*Crura sonant ferro*]'.
[96]*Mart. Mont. & Luc.* 6.2.
[97]Lucian, *Tox.* 29.
[98]Macer cited in *Dig.* 48.19.10.
[99]*Clem. Rec.* 10.83f.
[100]R. Taubenschlag, '63. L'Emprisonnement dans le Droit Gréco-Égyptien', in *Opera Minora: II Band Spezieller Teil*, R. Taubenschlag (Warszawa: Pánstwowe Wydawnictwo Naukowe, 1959), 716.

to be supplied to those prisoners who do not have it'.[101] Outside of such provisions, ancient penal systems tended to ignore the needs of poor prisoners.

Mommsen writes that where prisoners had resources or could rely on the assistance of friends or family, they were not ordinarily restricted in the quality of their existence.[102] There was considerable variation in the type, quality and quantity of food and drink brought from outside the prison. Food could be (and usually was) quite simple, as was the bulk shipment of 'small loaves' destined for the prisoner at Crocodilopolis in Ptolemaic Egypt.[103] Provision in other circumstances could be lavish to the point of profligacy if we are to believe Athenaeus (2nd to 3rd cent. AD). He notes that the imprisoned prince of Paphlagonia, 'had the same number [i.e., 100 of each item of food] served to him, and lived on a splendid scale'.[104] Agrippa's ability to be supplied with 'his favourite viands',[105] the 'varied meals'[106] brought to Peregrinus and the 'accustomed usages' with which Pristinus 'stuffed' himself are all further examples of such provisions.[107] Water[108] and wine[109] are mentioned as liquid refreshments.

Without recourse to sufficient personal resources or such external help as described above, however, the lot of the prisoner, particularly the poor or young, was usually one of misery.[110] It meant depending upon the prison ration which, because of its lack of variety, quality and quantity, often put life in peril. In 413 BC, the Syracusans determined that Athenian prisoners-of-war kept in the prison quarry were to receive an individual daily ration of 'two cotyls of barley meal';[111] i.e., about 14 oz. of bread and one cotyl, or about a half-pint, of water to drink.[112] These rations were about half the amount of food

---

[101]Cod. Theod. 9.3.7.

[102]Mommsen, Droit Pénal, vol. 1, 356 n. 2. The official regulation or frustration of these provisions will occupy our attention later.

[103]See The letter, Sammelb. 16:12468, from a royal cultivator belonging to Karanis in Egypt, and the comments of E.G. Turner and W.E.W. Cockle, 'Complaint Against a Policeman', JEA 68 (1982), 273.

[104]Athenaeus, The Deipnosophists 4.144.F.

[105]Josephus, AJ 18.204 [18.6.7].

[106]Lucian, Peregr. 12.

[107]Tertullian, De ieiun. 12.

[108]E.g., b. Mo' ed III: Erub. 21b; Josephus, AJ 18.193 [18.6.6].

[109]E.g., Tertullian, De Ieiun. 12; Mart. Fruct. & Co. 3.2 which assume such provision.

[110]Mommsen, Droit Pénal, vol. 1, 356 n. 2.

[111]Diodorus Siculus 13.19.4. Cf. Thucydides 7.86f.

[112]Thucydides 7.87.2.

usually given to slaves and compare poorly with the 'two quarts of barley-meal for each man and a pint of wine'[113] given to the Lacedae-monians taken on the island of Sphacteria. They were probably barely enough to sustain life.[114] Diodorus Siculus, in describing the suffer-ings of the Macedonian king Perseus in the prison of Alba Fucens (167 BC), records that 'he begged succour even from men of the meanest stamp, whose food was the prison ration. They indeed ... generously gave him a portion of whatever they received'.[115] An appreciation of the pathos of the account and the extent of the prisoners' generosity depends upon an awareness that the men who pitied the king and shared food with him were far inferior in status, being common male-factors condemned to death. Moreover, they showed astonishing gen-erosity in sharing their meagre portions.[116] The Christian martyr literature records in one instance how the confessors languished on a diet of 'only bread and water'[117] and in another, how confessors expe-rienced illness and suffering 'from the prison ration and the cold wa-ter',[118] because it was 'meagre fare from the worst of skimpy prison rations'.[119] For the five days before sentence of death by starvation, the confessor Lucian 'received a morsel of bread and water by meas-ure'.[120] Later still, a similar want of provision is indicated in Athenae-us' record of the self-imposed daily rations of certain philosophers (2nd or 3rd cent. AD): '...one loaf of simple bread for each, a cup of wa-ter. That's all. It's prison fare that you tell of'.[121] The only generosity in official provision for many prisoners seems to have been the last meal before execution.[122]

The prison dole, under normal circumstances, was distributed at the same time each day.[123] It can easily be seen how, despite regularity

---

[113]*Ibid.* 5.16.1 and LCL, 179 n. 1.

[114]Diodorus Siculus, LCL, 177 n. 1.*Cf.* Plato, *Lg.* 10.909.C.

[115]Diodorus Siculus 31.9.3.

[116]See Seneca, *Con.* 9.4. *Cf.* Krauss, *Im Kerker*, 63.

[117]Lucian to Cyprian (250 AD: Oxf., *Ep.* 22.2) in Workman, *Persecution*, 292. *Cf.* Ben-son in Mason, *The Historic Martyrs*, 159.

[118]*Mart. Mont. & Luc.* 6.5 (259 AD). *Cf.* Cyprian, *Ep.* 76.2 [Oxf., *Ep.* 76 (257 AD)]; *ibid.* 21.2 [Oxf., *Ep.* 22 (250 AD)].

[119]*Ibid.* 21.12.

[120]Cyprian, *Ep.* 21.2 [Oxf., *Ep.* 22].

[121]Athenaeus, *The Deipnosophists* 4.161.A, B.

[122]If, that is, the experience of the confessors Perpetua and Felicitas (203 AD: *Mart. Perp. & Felic.* 17.1) can be generalized.

[123]*Cf.* Diodorus Siculus 13.19.4; *Mart. Perp. & Felic.* 6.1; Athenaeus, *The Deipnoso-phists* 4.161.A, B (2nd to 3rd cent. AD).

of disbursal, even the heartiest were gradually enfeebled by hunger, thirst and the illnesses which resulted from such niggardly portions.[124] Scarcely sustaining a prisoner when they were regularly dispersed, these rations could be turned into a weapon of punishment, torture or even execution when withheld by guards or wardens.

Polybius relates how Hannibal (217 BC) fed his Roman prisoners-of-war only enough to sustain life; to captured Roman allies, however, he was more generous. The objectives seem to have been to punish the Romans and to disrupt the alliance.[125] King Perseus (167 BC), whom we have already met, was denied the prison ration for seven days by the prison officials at Alba Fucens.[126] Gallus (30 AD) was tortured at Tiberius' orders by being 'compelled to take food ... of such a quality and amount as neither to afford him any satisfaction or strength nor yet to allow him to die'.[127] Tiberius similarly starved others; some, notably his grandson Drusus, he ordered starved to death.[128] The later imperial period admits to similar practices. Tertullian (c. 195 AD) lists among instances of official lowmindedness the denial of food and drink to prisoners to their physical and psychological detriment.[129] A Christian confessor in the *Martyrdom of Montanus and Lucius* (259 AD) writes of the 'daily ration, not of food but rather of deprivation and distress. For we were given no food, and this was the second day we had been fasting'.[130] Cyprian writes of the confessor Celerinus (c. 250 AD) in the nineteen days of his imprisonment, 'his flesh wasted away by the long endurance of hunger and thirst'.[131] The confessor Lucian writes in 250 AD that 'by the command of the emperor we were ordered to be put to death by hunger and thirst, and were shut up in two cells, that so [sic] they might weaken us by hunger and thirst'. He continues that six had already died, 'of whom in a few days you will hear of me as a companion'.[132] Finally, the commonness of such ploys is attested in a provision of the *Theodosian Code* which

---

[124]*Cf.* e.g., Tertullian, *De Ieiunio* 12; Lucian to Cyprian (*Ep.* 22.2) in Workman, *Persecution*, 292; *Mart. Mont. & Luc.* 6.5; 9.3; 12.2.

[125]Polybius 3.77.3f.

[126]Diodorus Siculus 31.9.3.

[127]Dio Cassius 58.3.5f.

[128]Suetonius, *Tib.* 54.2; 61.2; Tacitus, *Ann.* 6.23f.

[129]Tertullian, *De Ieiunio* 12.

[130]*Mart. Mont. & Luc.* 9.1. Cf.*Ibid.* 12.2;*Mart. Mar. & James* 8.2-4 (259 AD); Heliodorus, *Aeth.* 8.6.2. (220-40 AD).

[131]Cyprian, *Ep.* 33.2 [Oxf., *Ep.* 39].

[132]*Ibid.* 21.2 [Oxf., *Ep.* 22].

threatens punishment if 'by starvation beyond the due time or in any other way, any prison guard should enfeeble any prisoner'.[133]

There is little surprise that, due to poverty or bankruptcy resulting from the expense of compensating for inadequate prison rations, we read of prisoners using the language of the desperate to plead for official pity and intervention. One Egyptian prisoner petitions Nikanor the epimeletes in a letter of the Ptolemaic period:

> I have often explained to you in writing why I am being harshly treated in the prison, perishing from hunger for the last ten months, though I have been unjustly confined. ... I entreat you with prayers not to let me perish of hunger in prison, but to write to the dioiketes about these things, or to send me to him ... in order that I may be saved.[134]

Another Egyptian writes in 177 BC to the king and queen:

> Argeus took me away to the Big Jail in Crocodilopolis ... and I have up to now been confined already for three years lacking the necessities. Therefore, so that I may not waste away in jail, neglected, contrary to all decency, I beg you with every plea to order....[135]

The Egyptian Pais writes to Zenon (3rd cent. BC): 'It is now five months since I was arrested, and I am now bereft of everything so that I lack the necessities of life'.[136] Other examples of prisoners 'lacking the necessities' or 'wasting away' while in custody could be given.[137]

While Luke does not discuss the food and drink provided Paul by his keepers, in light of the immediately preceding discussion and what has been learned of Paul's various incarcerations, we are permitted to make a few fairly confident assertions and to draw out several implications. We will leave aside for now discussion of rations Paul might have had access to in Rome and those which Luke records were given by helpers 'from outside'.

Paul's and Silas' early experience in the Philippian jail conforms well with the worst images noted above. The reader will be aware of several things: Paul and Silas have probably had nothing to eat or

---

[133]Cod. Theod. 9.3.1 (320 AD).

[134]PPetr. 3:36a uerso.

[135]UC inv 1583 in Keenan, '12. Petition from a Prisoner', 96f. [text], 102 [translation] of ll. 9-11, 19-21.

[136]E.g., PLond. 7:2045.

[137]PPetr. 3:36a recto (n.d./BC); Lucian, Tox. 18 (2nd cent. AD). PCairZen. 3:59520 (mid 3rd cent. BC); Sammelb. 14:11639 (247 BC); PTeb. 3.1:777 (early 2nd cent. BC).

drink since the trial earlier that day. This is the measure of the jailer's official unconcern; jailers were not normally expected to feed their prisoners because this was the responsibility of the prisoner's friends or relatives. It also took place at the jailer's discretion and there can be little doubt that, if he had been asked, the jailer had forbidden access to the apostles and foreclosed any possibility of sustenance owing to the command he had received to 'guard them carefully' (Acts 16:23). This might also have reflected his personal hostility toward the apostles. When Luke notes that in the very hour of his conversion about midnight (Acts 16:25; cf. Acts 16:33), the jailer 'set a meal before them' (Acts 16:34), the reader should be astonished at the generosity and timing of the repast. A jailer would never have fed his prisoners out of his own larder, much less at such an hour. Once during the day and only for needy prisoners was the usual pattern of distribution, and the ration would certainly have been simpler and less substantial if given at all.

We have argued that the prisoner Paul would have been able to partake of officially provided food and drink at several points; notably during the entire period of his incarceration in Jerusalem and in the first phase of his Caesarean imprisonment. The generous character of Paul's detention in officers' quarters in Jerusalem—the measure, we have argued, of Claudius Lysias' distress at having abused a Roman possessing citizenship superior to his own—will not permit a claim that Paul suffered want of nourishment in the Antonia Fortress. He would have been well cared for in this respect, but the care would have come from the hands of Romans. The first five days of Paul's time in Caesarea, we have argued, were less accommodating as Felix had consigned the apostle to an ordinary type of custody. In this circumstance, isolated from the help of friends, he would have had to share in the official provision, whatever its quantity, quality and regularity. We might add that the only time on the journey to Rome when Paul had need of food from non-Jews, according to Luke, was for three months on Malta.

The fact that Paul consumed food put before him by the Philippian jailer and would have received, unless he had fasted, portions given him by his Roman keepers in Jerusalem and Caesarea and by the Gentile residents of Malta brings to the attention of ancient readers issues which are very significant to Luke; viz., the matters of Jewish-Gentile commensality and adherence to food purity regulations. For a Jew, the prison—and particularly the Gentile prison—was a place of profound uncleanness. Josephus mentions that when, in about 64 AD, he went to Rome on a mission to obtain the release of certain Jewish priests sent there in bonds on a slight and trifling charge, he found that 'even in affliction, they had not forgotten the pious practices of religion, and supported themselves on figs and nuts'.[138] The Mishnah classified together those who emerged from prisons with those who came from beyond the sea, from captivity and those who had been formally released from a ban, a vow, or who had been declared free of leprosy. All alike, it was judged, had come forth from uncleanness to cleanness.[139] Rabbi Akiba expressed profound gratitude to Rabbi Joshua for providing him with food and water in the Roman prison during the Bar Kochba revolt c. 132-35 AD. Akiba was aware of what lay in store had Rabbi Joshua failed to provide for him: 'When he came to R. Akiba the latter said to him, "Joshua, do you not know that I am an old man and my life depends on yours?"'[140] Akiba's comment establishes his punctiliousness in matters of ritual cleanness and food purity. He was apparently prepared to forego prison food and drink altogether if it was improperly prepared. Roman rations, alongside any other failings, were unclean to a Jew. Moreover, Akiba was punctilious in the matter of ritual cleanness to such an extent that he would only eat even clean food after he had washed his hands, and preferred washing to drinking when his meagre water ration was once halved.[141]

Had Paul wished to maintain such Jewish scruples in the consumption of food, whether for personal or for ministry reasons, the conditions of his keeping in Jerusalem, in the early period of his Caesarean stay, and on Malta would not have permitted it. Paul's commitment to unqualified table-fellowship with Gentiles (cf. Gal. 1:11-14), however, and his acceptance of the newly-converted jailer's offer of food at Philippi suggest that accepting Gentile fare in Jerusalem, Caesarea and Malta would not have been a problem—at least not to him. For Luke, to whom God's acceptance of the Gentiles and its demonstration through shared Jewish/Gentile meals and minimal purity requirements is of great importance (Acts 10:1-11;18; 15:1-35; 16:4), such sharing as he indicates at Philippi and as is implied elsewhere was highly significant.

Provisioned by Jewish-Christians during the two year second phase of the Caesarean incarceration, before leaving Sidon, in Puteoli,

---

[138]Josephus, *Vit*. 13f. [3].
[139]*m. Mo'ed Qat* 3.1f. Other categories of those who have moved from uncleanness to cleanness are also mentioned. Cf. *b. Nasim* I; *Yebam*. 64a; 716, 104a.
[140]*b. Mo'ed* III: *Érub.* 21b.
[141]*Ibid.*

and probably also in Rome, the issue of consuming unclean food may not necessarily have arisen.

2. Clothing and Personal Toilette

We have already seen that prisons were often unclean and lacking in good hygiene. The outrage of Apollonius' imprisonment by Verres (70 BC) is emphasized by the contrast between the prisoner's distinguished character and the squalor and filth of his environment.[142] Tertullian (c. 195 AD) writes of the 'unpleasant exhalations'[143] which waft heavily through the prison, Cyprian of 'the squalor of the dungeon and its horrors'[144] and the writer of the *Martyrdom of Montanus and Lucian* (259 AD) of how the confessor Flavian was unworthy 'to be soiled by the filth of the prison'.[145] Further contributing to the distress and unhealthy conditions was the prison officials' lack of interest in even a modicum of prisoner hygiene.

We have seen that, generally, where a prisoner had access to resources for personal provision in prison or was in a loose or non-prison custody, the prospects for maintaining a certain level of hygiene and good health might reasonably be expected. Prince Agrippa (36/7 AD) was able to purchase or receive garments which his attendants brought into the hostile environment of the Praetorian Camp in Rome.[146] An additional concession was that 'he should be permitted to bathe every day'.[147] If not completely free to him, the cost of daily visits to the public baths was minimal. Such, apparently, was a concession also granted to certain prisoners in loose custody in Tertullian's day. Tertullian decries the generous liberty of the free custody, complaining in the case of Pristinus that it put him 'under obligation, I suppose, to all the baths (as if they were better than baptism!)'.[148] Later still, the *Theodosian Code* includes a provision on security (409 AD) which presumes that prisoners were permitted occasional visits to the baths.[149]

---

[142]Cicero, *Ver.* 2.5.21.
[143]Tertullian, *Ad Martyres* 2.
[144]Cyprian [*Ep.* 47.3] in Workman, *Persecution*, 292.
[145]*Mart. Mont. & Luc.* 17.1.
[146]Josephus, *AJ* 18.204 [18.6.7].
[147]*Ibid.* 18.203 [18.6.7]. News of Tiberius' death reaches him one day as he is 'on his way to the bath'. *Ibid.* 18.228 [18.6.10].
[148]Tertullian, *De Ieiun.* 12.

Other documents, however, suggest that the possession of good quality clothing and the freedom to bathe regularly were concessions not widely granted. Even those, for example, who could obtain clothing or possessions for personal use and comfort might lose them to greedy prison officials. This is behind the provision of the *Digest* that 'someone should not be stripped when he is put in prison but [only] after his condemnation, as the deified Hadrian [117-38 AD] wrote in a rescript'.[150] The *Digest* continues that a condemned prisoner is permitted his 'old clothes'. This does not mean property generally, but 'the clothes the [condemned] is wearing or the small change in his money belt that he had for his subsistence, or rings of small worth, that is stuff which does nót exceed [the value of] five *aurei*'.[151] Even this scant dignity was not permitted certain Christian confessors in Alexandria who, after horrendous tortures about the time 304-7 AD, 'were dragged naked back to the prison'.[152]

Poorer or unassisted long-term prisoners had little chance of attending to their personal toilette. Lucan, writing of the prisoner Marius in Minturnae (87 BC), relates how 'the old man's flesh was corroded by … the squalor [*paedor*, lit.: 'dirt, filth'] of long captivity'.[153] The confessors in a vision of the *Martyrdom of Perpetua and Felicitas* (203 AD) emerge from the black hole of their confinement in a filthy condition.[154] Cyprian affirms in 250 AD how the confessors 'tread underfoot the squalor of the dungeon'[155] but, writing to believers condemned to the mines in 257 AD, recalls with breaking heart how, 'Your limbs unbathed, are foul and disfigured with filth and dirt'.[156]

If barbers' knives could be considered a danger to personal safety in other circumstances,[157] they were an even greater threat to the security and safety of prisoners. We read that only after his release from six months of custody was Agrippa's hair cut.[158] The 'long hair, all unkempt and matted'[159] of the prisoner in Lucian's *Toxaris* presumes a prohibition against haircuts, as does the following Mishnaic conces-

---

[149]*Cod. Theod.* 9.3.7.
[150]*Dig.* 48.20.2.
[151]*Dig.* 48.20.6.
[152]*Mart. Let. Phil. (Versio Rufini Latina)* 8.
[153]Lucan 72f.
[154]*Mart. Perp. & Felic.* 7.4.
[155]Cyprian, *Ep.* 15.3 (Oxf., *Ep.* 37).
[156]*Ibid.* 76.2 (Oxf., *Ep.* 76). *Cf. Mart. Mont. & Luc.* 17.1.
[157]Martial 3.74. *Cf.* Josephus, *AJ* 16.387f. [16.11.6 ≈ *BJ* 1.547-50 (1.27.5f.)].
[158]*Supra*, 32.
[159]Lucian, *Tox.* 30.

sion: 'These [alone] may cut their hair during mid-festival: he that comes ... out of prison'.[160]

Clothing worn in the filth of the prison and on bodies that might seldom if ever be washed or bathed, quickly became thoroughly soiled.[161] It also quickly deteriorated because it needed to serve as both work clothing and night-wear. The want of basic necessities noted earlier, while probably relating most urgently to food and drink, does not exclude the need for new clothing.

Perhaps no account better reveals the impact upon the clothing and hygiene of the prisoner than that which describes Demetrius' efforts to find his friend Antiphilus (c. 163 AD). After entering the prison, Demetrius 'made a long search for Antiphilus, who had become unrecognizable through his miseries. He went about examining each of the prisoners just as people do who seek out their own dead among the altered[162] bodies on battle-fields'.[163] Had Demetrius not called out Antiphilus' name, it would have taken much longer to find his friend, 'so greatly had he been changed by his dire straits'.[164] As Demetrius approached, Antiphilus 'parted his long hair, all unkempt and matted, drew it away from his face and so disclosed his identity'.[165] Demetrius tore 'his short cloak in two, put on one of the halves himself and gave the remainder to Antiphilus, after stripping from him the filthy worn-out rags that he was wearing'.[166]

The only explicit mention of clothing in a Pauline prison context occurs in Luke's account of the episode at Philippi. It may be recalled that an official beating called for the malefactor to be stripped of his clothing in order to bare his body for the lictors' rods and that it is the clothing of Paul and Silas and not that of the magistrates to which Acts 16:22 refers.[167] The despoiling would have been conducted with little regard for the apostles' clothing. If the clothes were returned and went with them into the prison at all, they would have been badly torn, giv-

---

[160]m. Mo'ed Qat 3.1.
[161]Ibid. 3.2: 'And these [alone] may wash their clothes during mid-festival: he that comes ... out of prison'.
[162]The sorry physical condition of the prisoners probably suggests the image of the battlefield; the use of the term ἕωλος can mean 'day old', 'stale', 'rotting', or 'stinking'.
[163]Lucian, Tox. 30.
[164]Ibid.
[165]Ibid.
[166]Ibid.
[167]Supra, 125.

ing their bodies—and particularly their wounds—inadequate protection from the unsavoury elements of the inner prison.

Paul's clothes may well have been ruined in Jerusalem during the abuse and mistreatment of the rioting mob (Acts 21:30-32).[168] Once in custody in the Antonia Fortress, his clothing may have suffered further deterioration. Inquisitorial flogging also called for the prisoner to be stripped of his clothing,[169] which may have taken place before Paul was actually stretched out (Acts 22:24f.). Outside of Philippi, Jerusalem, and perhaps the first phase of the Caesarean incarceration, provisions of clothing would probably have been adequate to Paul's needs. What clothing he had with him on his trip to Rome we can only guess. Had he been carefully provisioned, Paul would have had appropriate travel wear and shelter for the inclement weather of the late sailing season (Acts 27:9). Casson writes that the Roman traveller

> probably had to have more changes of clothing, as well as special wear adapted to the rigours of the road: heavy shoes or heavy sandals, broad-brimmed hat ..., and a selection of capes ...—a short light one for milder weather (the Greek *chalamys* or the Roman *lacerna*), another for rainy days (e.g. the Roman *paenula*, made of wool or leather, fitted with a hood, and reaching to the knees), still another for cold days (e.g. the *birrus*, a long wool garment with hood, rather like an Arab burnous).[170]

What of the prisoner Paul's bathing or getting his hair cut? It is likely that Herod's palace at Caesarea, built along Roman lines, would have contained, or had nearby, facilities for bathing after the Roman fashion. It would, however, be wrong to assume that a prisoner like Paul would automatically or even occasionally have had opportunity to use them. Nothing can be said concerning the Fortress Antonia or Paul's ability to attend to his personal toilette there. It is also doubtful that Paul was permitted regular hair-cuts during his time in custody in either Caesarea or Rome. The only conceivable situation in which such a risk might have been undertaken would have been an officially supervised 'cut and clean up' prior to his various 'days in court', but this is mere speculation.

---

[168]Cf. *Mart. Let. Lyons & Vienne* (177 AD).
[169]Cf. Matt. 27:24-31; Mark 15:20.
[170]L. Casson, *Travel in the Ancient World* (London: George Allen and Unwin, 1974) 176. If Paul slept on deck during his transport to Rome, he and his party may have used small tent-like shelters. Cf. Casson, *Ships*, 181.

IV. Stress, Distress and Mortality

Prison, in the ancient context, was closely associated with death because it often served as the place of execution.[171] The association with
death was further solidified by the physical and psychological distress
brought by life in custody.[172]

1. General Debility and Sickness

The writer of the *Letter of Phileas* (304-7 AD) tells how Christians who
were tortured, 'with care and a sojourn in prison recovered their health
and became even more confident'.[173] Far from praising the salutary
benefits of prison, however, this text merely indicates that prison offered a relative respite from the even worse horrors of torture. The association of prison with general debility and sickness is strong in the
literature. Pheidias (432 BC) in Athens 'was led away to prison, and
died there of sickness'[174] according to one account. The Athenian prisoners-of-war who remained in the quarry prison in Syracuse (413 BC)
'ended their lives pitiably amid the hardships of their place of confinement'.[175] Demosthenes (324 BC) escaped the state prison at Athens
'owing to the weakness of his body, which could not endure confinement'.[176] The wonder-working King Eunus was remanded to prison *c.*
132/5 BC, in which environment 'his flesh disintegrated into a mass of
lice'.[177] Philostratus tells how the philosopher Musonius (reign of Nero) 'lay in danger of death; and he would have died for all his gaoler
cared, if it had not been for the strength of his constitution'.[178] Philostratus, in recounting the imprisonment of Apollonius (reign Domitian), indicates that even in the free prison at Rome where higher class
prisoners were found, 'some of them were sick'.[179] A stay of but two
months in the holding facility of an Egyptian tax office in 228 AD was

---

[171] *Supra*, 13f.
[172] von Eisenhut, 'Die römische Gefängnisstrafe', 278.
[173] *Mart. Let. Phil.* 9.
[174] Plutarch, *Per.* 31.5.
[175] Diodorus Siculus 13.33.1.
[176] Plutarch, *Dem.* 26.2.
[177] Diodorus Siculus 34.2.23. For other such cases of what has been termed *morbus pedicularis, cf.* Herodotus 4.205; Acts 12:23; Lucian, *Pseudomantis* 59.
[178] Philostratus, *VA* 4.35.
[179] *Ibid.* 7.26.

enough for the tax-farmer Aurelius Epinicus to become seriously ill and die.[180]

The Christian martyr literature furnishes an unhappy record of the debilitation, illness, suffering and death which were so often a part of prison life.[181] One of the great injustices of imprisonment is indicated in a provision of the *Theodosian Code* (320 AD): men not proven to have committed a wrong because they have been denied due process, men who may well be innocent, are imprisoned and allowed by prison officials 'to be consumed by long wasting disease'.[182] Even the gospel of Matthew closely links sickness and imprisonment.[183]

2. Suicide

We may be sure that many who are described as perishing in prison in fact succumbed to prison conditions over time.[184] In other cases, however, it may be questioned whether the deaths were due to illness or some other cause.[185] A number of references are sufficiently general and indicate circumstances which allow that death by other means than those indicated above is possible. The jurist Marcian's finding that 'the property of those persons who die in prison ... when the outcome of the case is in doubt is not to be confiscated'[186] is an example of just such a generalizing reference to death in prison. Our interest here is the situation in which a prisoner might take his or her own life.

There was, first of all, a legal reason why a Roman might choose suicide. Roman law permitted that a citizen in danger of a capital penalty and the seizure of all property by the State might kill himself and so ensure the transfer of his estate to the legally nominated heirs. During the reign of Tiberius (*c*. 31 AD) one of the reasons why many took their own life before being convicted was so that 'their children might inherit their property, since very few estates of such as voluntarily

---

[180]*POxy*. 43:3104.
[181]E.g., *Mart. Perp. & Felic*. 11.9; 14.2f. (203 AD); Benson citing the correspondence of Cyprian in Mason, *The Historic Martyrs*, 159 (250 AD); *Mart. Mont. & Luc*. 6.5; 9.1; 14.4 (259 AD).
[182]*Cod. Theod*. 9.3.1 (≈ *Cod. Just*. 9.4.1).
[183]Matt. 25:36, 43.
[184]See Seneca, *Con*. 9.1; *cf*. Plutarch, *Cim*. 4.3; Cicero, *Ver*. 2.1.7 (70 BC); Philostratus, *VA* 8.22 (reign Domitian).
[185]Note, e.g., the descriptions of the deaths of Pheidias (432 BC: Plutarch, *Per*. 31.5), and Pleminius (194 BC: Livy 29.19.10; 29.22.9; 34.44.7f.
[186]*Dig*. 48.21.3.7.

died before their trial were confiscated', whereas 'most of the estates of those who failed to die in this manner were confiscated'.[187] As the accusers of Vibulenas Agrippa (36 AD) were closing their case against him, he took poison from under his robes and drank it. Quick-handed lictors rushed him to the prison, attempting to garrotte his near lifeless body.[188] The testamentary implications of his action may well have been in view on both sides. The same may presage Albucilla's jailing (37 AD) after an ineffectual attempt to take her own life.[189] This escape from the threat to one's estate was later granted condemned decurions and their sons while awaiting confirmation of sentence from the emperor; their testaments were not null and void until the emperor had replied.[190]

Suicide was a possible response to prison conditions too miserable and prospects of release too remote. At one place, Seneca (63-65 AD) advises that the man who seriously contemplates suicide as an option can be calmed: 'What terrors have prisons and bonds and bars for him? His way out is clear'.[191] At another place, he asks a friend in trouble, 'Do you grudge your executioner his privilege, or do you merely relieve him of his task?'[192]

Once in custody, however, the option of suicide was no longer easily available. Slips in the security of house arrest allowed Publius Vitellius (c. 31 AD), under the guise of needing a pen-knife for his writing, to attempt suicide. As 'adjournment followed adjournment, Vitellius, anxious to be rid alike of hope and fear', carried out his act. According to Tacitus he 'slightly incised an artery, and in the sickness of his heart made an end of life'.[193] Suetonius relates that 'he opened his veins with a penknife, but allowed himself to be bandaged and restored, not so much from unwillingness to die, as because of the entreaties of his friends; and he met a natural death while still in confinement'.[194] Whatever the actual circumstances of his demise, incarceration and grave uncertainty appear to have induced a state of distress which could only be escaped by suicide. Tiberius had Gallus (30 AD) closely guarded not so much 'to prevent his escape, but to pre-

---

[187]Dio Cassius 58.15.4-16.1.
[188]Tacitus, Ann. 6.40.
[189]Ibid. 6.58; Dio Cassius 58.27.4.
[190]Dig. 28.3.7. Cf. Dionysius Halicarnassensis, Ant. Rom. 11.46.3.
[191]Seneca, Ep. ad Lucilium 26.10.
[192]Ibid. 70.9. Cf. Arrian, Epict. Diss. 2.6.22.
[193]Tacitus, Ann. 6.5.8.
[194]Suetonius, Vit. 7.2.3.

vent his death'.[195] The expectation is made clear in later legislation that prison officials and guards were forbidden, on pain of severe punishment by the court, to facilitate the suicide or murder of their charges by personal neglect or hostility,[196] or by allowing weapons or poison to be brought into the prison.[197] Closure of this avenue of 'escape' only intensified the distress of prisoners. They might give way to dejection[198] or give up the struggle and refuse to take food.[199] Even then, however, guards might force-feed a prisoner.[200] It is not incredible, then, that prisoners begged a speedy death,[201] or emerged from confinement broken in body and spirit.[202]

3. The Prisoner Paul's Distress in Acts

Luke, for all he tells us of the rigours of Paul's incarcerations and sufferings, says little about how he held up physically. He also says little about Paul's emotional or psychological reactions. But then, such details concerning other individuals were not provided in Acts either. Only a few passages present themselves for consideration.

Obviously, Paul suffered considerably at the hands of the lictors in Philippi. His and Silas' beating covered their bodies with bloody welts severe enough that their cleansing was effected before any further religious or practical action was undertaken (Acts 16:33f.). The intended readers, who must certainly have been aware of the physical distress and danger caused by the apostle's wounds, are informed by Luke that, far from lapsing into depression, the apostles prayed and sang hymns to God (Acts 16:25).

Some scholars have seen in the care given by the Sidonian Christians at Acts 27:3 an indication that Paul suffered from depression or illness or needed care because he was in an invalid state.[203] The term 'provision' (ἐπιμελείας) is employed outside the NT to designate care

---

[195]Dio Cassius 58.3.5. See also Livy 39.19.2.

[196]*Dig.* 48.3.14.3-5.

[197]*Dig.* 48.3.8.

[198]Philostratus, *VA* 7.26.

[199]Lucian, *Tox.* 30.

[200]Dio Cassius 58.3.5.

[201]See Dio Cassius 58.3.6; Suetonius, *Tib.* 61.5.

[202]Cicero, *Ver.* 2.5.24.

[203] Hervey, *The Acts*, 291; R.B. Rackham, *The Acts*, 481. See R.J. Knowling, *The Acts of the Apostles*, 518, for a listing of other scholars subscribing to this view.

for the sick,[204] and a cognate term, (ἐπιμελέομαι), is used at Luke 10:34f. in such a manner. The assumption, however, would seem to be unwarranted in the present context. First, the expression by itself need not necessarily refer to such care as that claimed above.[205] Second, in other contexts where the verb 'to obtain' (Acts 27:3) occurs with 'provisions' (ἐπιμέλεια), the sense is of material assistance for sustaining life. Athenaeus, citing Poseidonius, records:

> Many persons being unable to manage themselves on account of the weakness of their intellect, give themselves voluntarily into the service of more intelligent men, in order that they may secure from them provision for their daily needs [ὅπως παρ᾽ ἐκείνων τυγχάνοντες τῆς εἰς τὰ ἀναγκαῖα ἐπιμελείας], and in turn may themselves render to their patrons, through their own labours, whatever they are capable of in the way of service.[206]

Finally, the general conditions of sea travel relevant to Acts 27:3 suggest that the practical help of food and perhaps clothing and other supplies is probably intended by the word ἐπιμελείας. Ships plying the Mediterranean could have cooking facilities—some very elaborate[207]—and it may have been that catering was available aboard larger vessels to passengers who were willing to pay. The merchant coaster on which passage is first booked by the centurion's company, however, is not likely to have had such elaborate facilities. Passengers may well have had to fend for themselves. Additionally, whereas the Caesarea to Sidon journey of some 75 miles had taken but a day (Acts 27:3), the trip from Sidon to Myra, a stretch in excess of 400 miles, would take considerably longer, especially in the uncertain wind and weather conditions of the season (Acts 27:4, 9). Food supplies would need to be sufficient for the maximum time at sea. If the preferred economical manner of travel was to live either in the open or under tiny temporary shelters, a secondary concern aboard ship might have been adequate clothing and shelter against the elements. The centurion's permission is an expression of kindness, knowing what the practical demands of such a trip might be, rather than concern that Paul was too ill to travel. Finally, the expectation that prisoners pay for their own food may well have held while prisoners were in transit as well as in prison.[208]

---

[204]LSJ, 645. BAGD, 296.
[205]The expression has the broader sense of care for physical or perhaps administrative needs as e.g., 1 Macc. 16.14; 2 Macc. 11.23; 3 Macc. 5.1.
[206]Athenaeus, *The Deipnosophists* 6.263.C, D.
[207]Casson, *Ships*, 178.

When he first met the brothers at Rome, records Luke, 'Paul thanked God and was encouraged' (Acts 28:15). Ramsay states that this phrase must indicate 'some marked frame of mind. We have already observed Paul in a similar state of depression when he was in Troas and Philippi'.[209] Depression may not be the emotional state Luke intends. 'Courage' (θάρσος) in other contexts suggests—especially at Acts 23:11 where Jesus bids the prisoner Paul to take courage[210]—that fear or anxiety are its opposite. It will be argued that Paul feared the reception he, as a prisoner, would receive from Christians and Jews in Rome.

[208]So Tajra, *The Trial of St. Paul:* 173.

[209]W.M. Ramsay, *St. Paul the Traveller,* 347.

[210]See also Josephus, *AJ* 9.55 [9.4.3]; *Mart. Pol.* 12.1; *Herm. Vis.* 3.1.5.

CHAPTER 10

PAUL'S CUSTODY IN ROME

The light two year military custody under house arrest in Rome, it was argued above, amounts to an indication of the Roman assessment of Paul's innocence and prospects for release. Paul was permitted to live in single rented accommodation, probably lodging in the near vicinity of the Castra Praetoria. This chapter will consider what this arrangement can tell us about his material means. This will necessitate a discussion of what tenement structures and life in rented accommodation generally were like in Rome at about this time as well as who rented, how much they needed to pay, what the rental conditions were, and what value they got for their money. The further issue of the reciprocal impact of Paul's being both a prisoner and a tenant will be discussed. Finally Paul's access to the public grain supply will be considered.

I. The Apartment Rental Market in Rome

One of the first facts of living in Rome was that only the privileged and aristocratic few could afford to purchase or rent private houses (*domi*). Virtually all of the nearly one million inhabitants of residential Rome lived in a room or rooms in one of the many thousands of tenement buildings in the city.[1] These structures, first mentioned about the year 456 BC, were known as *insulae*. McKay writes that

> the term *insula*, no doubt originally applied to a plot of land bounded by streets, was gradually extended to multiple dwellings which included older homes which had been subdivided into rooming-houses or *pensioni* and the larger, more commodious multi-storeyed apartment buildings.[2]

These buildings were constructed in a variety of ways. It may nevertheless be helpful to give a description of a typical structure to better appreciate the standard elements and their names as well as something of the amenities and construction. The multi-storeyed tenement building could be between three and five floors high, covering an entire plot of land surrounded on all sides by streets. In the case of the building of Diana in Ostia (see Fig. 19f.) which occupied a corner plot of 23.30 x 39.30 m., other structures faced it on the N and NW sides. The provision of a courtyard (8.80 x 5.80 m.) along the lines of the *atrium* of a private home gave light to the N and NE rooms and furnished the residents with a limited open communal area. Grander open courtyards, replete with fountains and gardens, were possible in such structures but these were not considered an efficient use of building space. The ground floor apartments, having entrances facing out to the street, were typically let out as shop-dwellings (*tabernae*).[3] Any unit of accommodation above the shop-dwelling level was known as a *cenaculum*, whether one was referring to a whole floor, a multi-floor apartment, or a small single room. It could, depending upon the plan, be accessible by stairs from the street, from the courtyard, or from both (see Fig. 20*a*,

---

[1]See B.W. Frier, 'The Rental Market in Early Imperial Rome', *JRS* 67 (1977), 27; A.G. McKay, *Houses, Villas and Palaces in the Roman World* (Aspects of Greek and Roman Life; Southampton: Thames and Hudson, 1975), 83; A.D. Clarke, 'Rome and Italy', in *The Book of Acts in Its Graeco-Roman Setting*, ed. D.W.J. Gill and C. Gempf (A1CS 2; Grand Rapids: Eerdmans/Carlisle: Paternoster, 1994), 475-78.
[2]McKay, *Houses*, 83.
[3]See J. Packer, 'Housing and Population in Imperial Ostia and Rome', *JRS* 57 (1967), 85.

b). These units were also called *cenacula meritoria* or *conducta*[4] and might possess, as an added feature, balconies.

Blocks of apartments were built by wealthy speculators. Indications are that a shrewd owner—called in law the *dominus insulae*—could earn great sums. Garnsey writes that 'from the time of his marriage to Terentia shortly before 77 BC Cicero had the use of an annual income of 80,000 sesterces in rent from apartment blocks, *insulae*, in Rome'.[5] A number of shops in Puteoli came into Cicero's hands two years before his death in 43 BC as a bequest from the banker Cluvius. Dilapidated as they were, these shops brought in an additional income of 80,000 sesterces.[6] The jurist Alfenus (*c.* 39 BC) reckons the rental of a complete block at 30,000 sesterces, the various apartments then being sublet to individuals to give 10,000 sesterces profit to the speculator.[7] The jurist Paulus (2nd to 3rd cent. AD) indicates that a similar arrangement paid 50,000 sesterces to the owner and 10,000 sesterces to the speculator.[8] The formula for such returns on investment required that one minimize building, purchase/letting and maintenance costs while maximizing tenancy and rental charges.

This had, first of all, necessary and often significant effects upon the quality of building. Fuelled by the pressing need to house an ever-growing populace, tenement construction in Rome was caught in a vicious circle that frustrated sound architectural principle and imperial action.[9] Frequent fires were a disincentive to large expenditure and careful construction with sound materials. If one built expensively and well, chances were that the neighbours hadn't and so the risk of damage remained. Building on the cheap, however, only increased the risk of fire and added the threat of structural collapse. Strabo, in his record of Rome about the year 7 BC, notes the city's hunger for timber and stones

> for the building of houses, which goes on unceasingly in consequence of the collapses and fires and repeated sales (these last, too, going on

---

[4]Suetonius, *Vit.* 7.2 (*cenacula meritoria*); Juvenal 3.234 (*meritoria*); *Dig.* 19.2.30 (*conductum*).
[5]P. Garnsey, '7: Urban Property Investment', in *Studies in Roman Property by the Cambridge University Research Seminar in Ancient History*, ed. M.I. Finley (Cambridge/London/New York/Melbourne: CUP, 1976), 126f. and sources p 190 n. 12.
[6]*Ibid.*, 126 and sources 190 n. 11.
[7]*Dig.* 19.2.30.
[8]*Ibid.* 19.2.7.
[9]*Cf.* McKay, *Houses*, 87f. and J.H. Middleton and W. Smith, 'Domus', *DGRA*, vol. 1, 666.

unceasingly); and indeed the sales are intentional collapses, as it were, since the purchasers keep tearing down the houses and building new ones, one after another, to suit their wishes.[10]

Seneca, writing in the early decades AD, asks:

What value do you set on finding lodging in a wilderness, a shelter in rain, a warm bath or a fire in cold weather? Yet I know at what price I can obtain these things when I enter an inn [deversorium]. How great a service does he do us who props up our tottering house [domus], and with unbelievable skill keeps erect a group of buildings [insulae] that are showing cracks at the bottom![11]

In another place he laments 'tenement walls crumbled and cracked and out of line'.[12] The conflagration of 64 AD did not lead to sounder construction such as is found in the Ostian apartment blocks which survive until today.[13] Instead, the same death traps continued to be erected. Juvenal (1st to 2nd cent. AD) asks cynically:

Who at cool Praeneste, or at Volsinii amid its leafy hills, was ever afraid of his house tumbling down? Who in modest Gabii, or on the sloping heights of Tivoli? But here we inhabit a city propped up for the most part by slender flute-players: for that is how the bailiff patches up the cracks in the old wall, bidding the inmates sleep at ease under a roof ready to tumble about their ears. No, no, I must live where there are no fires, no nightly alarms.[14]

Aulus Gellius (c. 123-65 AD) writes how the rhetorician Antonius Julianus and his companions, looking down from the Cispian Hill, 'saw that a block of houses [insula], built high with many storeys, had caught fire, and that now all the neighbouring buildings were burning in a mighty conflagration'. One of his companions remarked to him, 'The income from city property is great, but the dangers are far greater. But if some remedy could be devised to prevent houses in Rome from so constantly catching fire, by Jove! I would sell my country property and buy in the city'.[15]

---

[10]Strabo 5.3.7.
[11]Seneca, Ben. 6.15.7.
[12]Ibid., De ira 3.35.5.
[13]Packer, 'Housing and Population', 82.
[14]Juvenal 3.190-98.
[15]Aulus Gellius 15.1.2f.

Economy also dictated that amenities in such buildings be kept largely to a minimum. It may be taken as reasonably sure on the strength of the Ostian evidence that apartments in Rome were not heated and that upper floors had no running water.[16] McKay writes of Ostia: 'Most of the population, one must assume, lived in two rooms without benefit of formal kitchens or latrines'.[17] Rome would have been little different. Rudimentary portable stoves were employed to cook food and give some relief from the cold—hence the many fires in Rome. Private baths would also have been rare in apartment buildings, though proximity to the many public baths and amenities in Rome hardly made this a terrible inconvenience.[18]

McKay indicates that, generally, 'the higher one went, the less appealing living conditions became'.[19] The inconvenience of many flights of stairs appealed as little then as today. Martial writes: '...I live up three flights of stairs, and high ones'.[20] The summer heat was more oppressive in the upper floors and there was an increased risk of death from fire or collapse. Juvenal gives some insight in this regard when he writes with irony:

> Ucalegon below [i.e., on the ground-floor] is already shouting for wa-
> ter and shifting his chattels; smoke is pouring out of your third-floor
> attic above, but you know nothing of it; for if the alarm begins in the
> ground-floor, the last man to burn will be he who has nothing to shel-
> ter him from the rain but the tiles, where the gentle doves lay their
> eggs. Codrus possessed a bed too small for the dwarf Procula, a mar-
> ble slab adorned by six pipkins, with a small drinking cup, and a re-
> cumbent Chiron below, and an old chest containing Greek books
> whose divine lays were being gnawed by unlettered mice. Poor Cod-
> rus had nothing, it is true: but he lost that nothing....[21]

Building as high as permitted and as cheaply as possible was only part of the formula for significant capital returns. The profitability of urban apartment building was also keyed to the mix of rent level and degree of crowding that tenants could be forced to accept. Many

---

[16]See R. Meiggs, *Roman Ostia* (2nd. edn.; Oxford: Clarendon, 1973) 249. *Insulae* might have a communal water source as in the *insula* of Diana (Fig. 20a designated by 'W').
[17]McKay, *Houses*, 93. Note the *latrina* in the *insula* of Diana (Fig. 20a designated by 'L').
[18]*Cf. supra*, 216f.
[19]McKay, *Houses*, 95.
[20]Martial 1.117.7.
[21]Juvenal 3.198-208.

landlords were not adverse to renting every nook and cranny right up to the roof line. Codrus' occupancy of a garret in the Juvenal quotation above may be cited as an example. Another indication of overcrowding may be found in Juvenal's observation that 'most sick people in Rome perish for want of sleep, the illness itself having been produced by food lying undigested on a fevered stomach. For what sleep is possible in a lodging?'[22]

Although less comfortable and more dangerous, correspondingly, apartments on the higher storeys were less expensive. One might wish to have an apartment only one flight up, but such were probably not only billed as 'high-class',[23] they had a 'high-class' bill as well. In consequence we find that the highest dwelling areas housed poorer folk like Juvenal's Codrus, while the better-off lived below. Meiggs observes that 'Juvenal and Martial can look with envious eyes on the spreading mansions of wealthy patrons; they live themselves in the apartment blocks. Martial is given a small farm on the Via Nomentana; at Rome he has only a third-floor apartment'.[24]

Broadening our discussion somewhat as we consider possible options for Paul in Rome, mention should be made of rental spaces which were more accessible to the very poor in boarding houses and (wayside) inns known variously as *cauponae, deversoria, hospitia, stabula, tabernae* or *tabernae deversoriae*. These were often disreputable places peopled by individuals of dubious morals; hence, a poor second choice to the apartment blocks.

> The transient ... most often put up at an inn, and even respectable inns, the ones the Romans generally dignified by the neutral terms *hospitium* 'place for hospitality' or *deversorium* 'place for turning aside', included prostitutes among the services offered, while the kind they called *caupona* was distinctly low class: it catered to sailors and carters and slaves; its dining-room had more the atmosphere of a saloon than a restaurant; and the *caupo* (or *copo*), as one who ran a *caupona* was called, was of the same social and moral level as his establishment. Indeed, *caupones*, along with ships' captains and owners of livery stables, were the subject of special legislation, since a traveller was completely at their mercy, and the law was aware that, as a group, they were hardly noted for scrupulous honesty.[25]

---

[22]Juvenal 3.232-35.
[23]See the Pompeii rental advertisements in *RomCiv.* 2:213 [*i, ii*] of *c.* 79 AD.
[24]Meiggs, *Roman Ostia*, 237f. and citing Martial 1.117.7.
[25]Casson, *Travel*, 204.

Petronius' *Satyricon* furnishes a graphic description of the mean-ness of a seaside boarding house, its staff and its occupants.[26] The owner (*hospes*) was one M. Mannicius and it was run by a gout-plagued *procurator insulae* named Bargates (his freedman?). Other staff included cooks and scullions, building attendants, assorted slaves, and a woman who looked after the rooms, saw to meals ordered by guests, and let the guests in at night. The character Encolpius rented one of the many single rooms (*cellae*), the door of which was lockable from inside and out. The room's furnishings consisting only of a bed against the wall and a large wooden candlestick. Residents were called *hospites* or *deversitores*; if transient, they were known as *viatores*, but if more per-manent, *cauponae*.[27] Such places also existed in Rome. Casson writes:

> In the heart of Rome, just a few steps from the forum, a building has been uncovered which had more than thirty nearly identical rooms, windowless little cells—they measured as a rule a scant five to six and a half feet by six—that were entered from narrow low corridors. The place was either a cheap rooming-house or brothel. It lasted in its choice location until, along with everything else nearby, it was demol-ished to make way for the grandiose park Nero laid out around his sumptuous new palace, the Golden House.[28]

Casson continues that experienced travellers would examine the mat-tresses in such establishments carefully, 'since bedbugs were so com-mon they were known as *cauponarum aestiua animalia* "the summertime creatures of the inns"'.[29] For personal cleanliness and attending to the call of nature, the resident could make use of the *latrina*—typically next to the kitchen—or one of the many public baths or latrine facilities nearby. If a meal was desired and one did not or could not obtain or prepare it on the premises, a search had to be made for a satisfactory restaurant.[30] From what Casson indicates, such eating establishments all too commonly served simple fare and offered morally doubtful en-tertainments.[31] McKay, with an eye to both the poorer quality apart-ment- and boarding house-type accommodation, concludes:

---

[26]Petronius, *Sat.* 94-97.

[27]Frier, 'The Rental Market', 32f. gives a helpful analysis of this text.

[28]Casson, *Travel*, 208.

[29]*Ibid.* He mentions in this context the miracle of the bedbugs in *Apocr. Acts John* 60.

[30]For pictures of such establishments, *cf.* Casson, *Travel*, plates 15-17; W. Smith and W. Wayte, 'Caupona', *DGRA*, vol. 1, 388.

[31]Casson, *Travel*, 211-18.

The crushing anonymity, the loneliness and ugliness of the high-rise apartments or the run-down boarding-houses are repeatedly evidenced. Impoverished writers, Romans in depressed circumstances and immigrants were regularly sentenced to what have been called disposable cubicles for dispensable people.[32]

The final element in the profit equation for the landlord was how much he or she could charge the tenants. Indications are that the rents in Rome were grossly inflated. Suetonius writes that Julius Caesar in 45 BC 'remitted a year's rent in Rome to tenants who paid two thousand sesterces or less, and in Italy up to five hundred sesterces'.[33] The maximum concession to those normally resident in Rome may have been not only to the poorer members of Caesar's forces,[34] but to those better-off but hard-pressed as well if we consider that in 54 BC Caelius, a friend of Cicero, paid 10,000 sesterces for an apartment (*in aediculis*: lit. 'in rooms') in an apartment building on the Palatine.[35] In any event, if Caesar's maximum remittances to soldiers living in Rome and Italy were an attempt at general parity, they suggest that accommodation in the city of Rome was about four times more than anywhere else in Italy.

If rental rates did not worsen, they certainly did not improve with the passing of time. Writing in the later decades of the 1st century AD, Martial recalls to someone who aspires to live in Rome and pay his rent from fees charged for conducting cases as a rhetor, 'Atestinus and Civis each conducted cases—you know both—but neither made his full rent'.[36] He states later in his work that some tenants fell far behind in their rents: '...I have seen them, the lot that was not distrained upon for two years' rent'.[37] Juvenal observes in one place that 'it is but seldom that soldiers find their way into a garret',[38] and in another responds to the accusation of being a beggar, 'Yes, but my rent cries on me to beg; and so does my single slave-lad'.[39] He comments that 'it is

---

[32]McKay, *Houses*, 85.
[33]Suetonius, *Caes.* 38.2.
[34]Middleton and Smith, 'Domus', 665, suggest, however, that this was the usual rent paid by poor people.
[35]Cicero, *Cael.* 17, rebuffs the reproach that the rooms rented at 30,000 sesterces annually by observing that the price has been exaggerated by a factor of three because the owner wants to sell the *insula*.
[36]Martial, 3.38.5.
[37]*Ibid.* 12.32.2f.
[38]Juvenal, 10.18.
[39]*Ibid.* 9.63f.

no easy matter, anywhere, for a man to rise when poverty stands in the way of his merits: but nowhere is the effort harder than in Rome, where you must pay a big rent for a wretched lodging'.[40] A little later he caustically observes: 'If you tear yourself away from the games of the Circus, you can buy an excellent house at Sora, at Fabrateria or Frusino, for what you now pay in Rome to rent a dark garret for one year'.[41] We also begin to appreciate the hardship caused, particularly to the lower classes, after the fire of 64 AD, when Nero 'required all classes to contribute a part of their incomes, and all tenants of private houses and apartments to pay a year's rent at once to the privy purse'.[42]

Where one was too far below the poverty line to cherish any pretensions to dignity and did not want to risk sleeping rough, a room of poor quality could be secured overnight for an *as* (somewhere between 0.25 and 0.4 sesterces) in boarding house-type accommodation.[43] Martial may have similar accommodation in view when he writes: 'Whence comes your poor toga and the rent of your grimy garret? Whence is provided the farthing?'[44]

Frier has given a helpful account of how and when rent was paid in the various types of rental accommodation noted above. For leases between the principal tenants of apartments and their landlords,

> the rental contracts envisaged in the legal texts concerning *locatio conductio rei* (leasehold) of urban dwellings normally run for a year or multiples of years, and the shortest payment-period envisaged is for a full half-year payable *at the conclusion of the period.* Similar terms of lease and similar payment-periods are provided in most Egyptian leases for houses. Such a lease-form, with payment *after* use, is very favourable to the tenant and thus suggests a considerable amount of trust on the part of the landlord....[45]

Even when a tenant fell into arrears and while full payment was still a possibility, the landlord might let the tenant continue to rent 'in detention of the premises' which was an informal lien on the tenant's property.[46] Without convincing payment prospects or significant property,

[40]*Ibid.* 3.164-66.
[41]*Ibid.* 3.223-25.
[42]Suetonius, *Nero* 44.2.
[43]Petronius, 8.4.
[44]Martial, 3.30.3f. The *quadrans* (0.25 *as*) was the cost of entry to the *balneae.*
[45]Frier, 'The Rental Market', 29f.
[46]*Ibid.,* 30.

the tenant might be out on his ear or, perhaps more likely, hauled to a court of law. Frier comments that 'the evidence decidedly implies that a degree of social status was involved in taking a long-term lease of the type described above'.[47] Commercial leases for ground-floor shop/dwellings were 'perhaps in most instances also stable and long-term, rather like the leases for *cenacula*'.[48] What of the poorer folk who could only afford the upper-most storey garrets? Frier offers:

> On what terms these flats were rented is not known, but it is reasonable to suppose that in some instances the leases for them also were stable and long-term. The objection which the poor might have had to such leases is obvious: payment in a large lump sum is very burdensome for those living on near subsistence incomes. For the same reason, landlords might well have been reluctant to rent to the poor on conditions of trust similar to those they applied to tenants of *cenacula*.[49]

Frier asserts that the inn-like *deversoria* and *cauponae* of Rome, because of their transient and lower class resident clientele, would have had more or less sharply distinguishable rental arrangements from the 'apartment'; i.e., daily or short-term and continuously renewed by both parties.[50] He concludes that the different arrangements in the urban rental market were interpenetrated 'by considerations of social status and subjected to social restraint and regulation'.[51] Higher status and better prospects for payment inspired greater trust and thus encouraged longer leases of the end-paid variety; lower status and poorer material prospects engendered a distrust which, if it did not drive one into a room among the less desirable boarding houses, probably thrust one to the roof-top garrets with less favourable lease arrangements.

II. Paul's Domestic Arrangements in Rome

It remains now to fit the prisoner Paul into this context. In light of the exorbitant rental charge that would certainly have been involved, it is

---

[47]*Ibid.*
[48]*Ibid.*
[49]Frier, 'The Rental Market', 30.
[50]*Ibid.*, 34f.
[51]*Ibid.*, 35.

unlikely that Paul was able to afford a private house during his two years in Rome.[52]

'In the apartment' (Εἰς τὴν ξενίαν) at Acts 28:23 is rendered *in hospitium* in the Vg. Should we understand by this that Paul contracted to live in a board house- or *hospitium*-type accommodation? Casson writes: 'People who had to spend more than a few days in a place and had no friends or associates to offer them hospitality, nor any letters of recommendation, took hired lodgings, as St. Paul did during his stay in Rome'.[53] We have seen that such urban accommodation was rudimentary and generally quite cramped. Occupants usually slept in tiny rooms and the only large public area would probably have been the restaurant.[54] The clientele was definitely low-class, consisting of transients, rough types, and the very poor who could afford no better. Moreover, the general atmosphere and entertainments in such places catered to and encouraged immorality.

This, however, does not fit well with Luke's description of Paul's circumstances at the end of Acts. The increasing numbers of Jewish leaders Paul received and his later reception of all who came to hear him (Acts 28:17, 23, 30) suggests not only that there must have been sufficient room for such gatherings to take place but also that there was not such a low moral tone or atmosphere in the place as to violate Jewish (or Christian!) religious sensibilities or to discourage attendance. While we are not told so, Paul must surely have considered carefully the implications for his ministry of taking various types of lodging before he contracted for accommodation. Moreover, the assistance of Roman co-religionists (*cf.* Acts 28:15f.) in finding suitable accommodation—which Casson has clearly ignored—should not be ruled out. We do not know whether official restrictions influenced where Paul might stay but, safety and security being primary considerations, a rough boarding house or inn might well have been thought too dangerous. The feeling of risk might have been mutual: an owner might consider the presence of a prisoner on the premises day in and day out and chained to a soldier-guard—even if he was paying—to be a threat to 'business'. Finally, while Paul would hardly have shunned Gentile-Christian mixed meals on principle, it is highly unlikely that, given the choice, he would have hired quarters which prevented him from preparing or receiving food or that limited him to religiously

---

[52]*Contra* J.G. Gray, 'Roman Houses, in which Paul Preached the Kingdom of God', *USQR* 15 (1903/4), 310-19.
[53]Casson, *Travel*, 204.
[54]*Ibid.*, 207.

questionable food that had been questionably prepared. The above considerations render the notion that Paul chose to live in such quarters unlikely. 'Apartment' (ξενία) must therefore be taken as an informal or generic term for rental accommodation.

Many of the problems identified above for a Jewish-Christian prisoner with soldier-guard in tow and living in this type of accommodations are addressed and a closer fitness to the details of the ending of Acts is possible if one assumes that Paul lived in an apartment in one of the thousands of tenement buildings in Rome. Unlike life in the cubbyhole environment of most rooms in boarding houses, such accommodation would have given relatively more space to a prisoner occupant. It is hard to conceive of Paul as confined at night to a tiny room with a soldier-guard, or sitting by day entertaining visitors in the prurient environment of a restaurant. Much more convincing is the picture of Paul shut up with his guard in an apartment at night and, during the day, able to divide his time between his rooms and the precincts of his tenement—perhaps wandering about the courtyard if such was a part of his dwelling. He would in these living conditions, as would most of his free neighbours, have been able to prepare his own meals and not need to depend completely upon the provision of others or rely upon the questionable and probably more expensive cooked fare furnished in the local *tabernae* and *popinae*. Paul's block may, as the apartment block of Diana at Ostia (Fig. 20a), have served some of his other needs in having both a freshwater source and a public bath.

Paul's meetings with Jews and the hospitality he showed to visitors who came to him thereafter—particularly the second meeting where Luke indicates that the numbers were considerably increased (Acts 27:23)—fit much better the environment of an apartment building. Sadler's surmise that Paul had access, beyond his own quarters, to 'a large room capable of containing a considerable congregation'[55] is unrealistic because such a room would hardly have been left vacant to serve tenants or others as an occasional venue. This would have been a waste of space and money. Rather, such a room would typically have been let out for a much longer period and at a handsome price. If Paul's quarters were of too modest a size to accommodate such numbers of visitors as Acts would seem to imply, perhaps the *atrium*—of course again, if such existed in his building—could have been used without

---

[55]M.F. Sadler, *The Acts of the Apostles With Notes Critical and Practical* (1887; rpt. London: G. Bell and Sons, 1910), 501.

great disturbance to the other tenants. In fact, most tenants would probably not have been around to be disturbed. Packer writes:

> Like his Ostian counterpart, the typical citizen of Rome must have lived almost entirely outside his apartment, in the streets, shops, arcades, arenas, and baths of the city. The average Roman domicile must have served only as a place to sleep and store possessions.[56]

As well, in contrast to the boarding house environment, a tenement would not obviously have violated Jewish moral or religious sensibilities nor kept visitors away.

The only serious drawback to the adoption of this picture would seem to be the cost of this higher quality accommodation. We have seen that such accommodation—particularly second storey apartments—could be prohibitively expensive, taxing the resources of individuals who in other respects might have been considered quite comfortably well off. A prisoner on a capital charge might not inspire in the landlords much confidence in collecting an end-paid tenancy; after all, what if his case came up before the due date and things went badly? Paul's circumstance and its attendant uncertainties would probably have been reflected in a rental contract more obviously favouring the landlord. We have no idea what Paul's 'net worth' was nor do we know what prospects he had for being supported by friends. We will argue presently that serious doubt attaches to the idea that Paul would have been permitted to work at his trade. We may say at this point that, had Paul worked, he would probably have been required to rent an even higher-priced street-level *taberna* (cf. Figs. 19, 20a). We are inclined, in the light of the above-noted considerations, to think that Paul, probably for economy and perhaps out of necessity, hired a third storey or higher apartment.[57]

III. Paul and the Grain Distribution

What provisions for nourishment might Paul have had access to in Rome? As we have argued above, Paul is unlikely to have permitted himself the practical, religious and ministry risks of eating food prepared in the Roman *popinae* and *tabernae*. His food would probably have come from or through other Christians and would have been pre-

---

[56]Packer, 'Housing and Population', 87.
[57]Cf. Bruce, *The Book of Acts*, 509, who alone offers this as a possibility.

pared or at least eaten in his rooms. But where would he have obtained it and how would he have paid? It seems most likely that Paul qualified for free food rations and that he would not have felt hindered from sharing in it.

In Paul's day, it was possible for qualified recipients to receive a monthly ration of 5 *modii*—about 10 gallons—of free corn on a year-round basis. The practice, first regularly established by law in 123 BC, was known as the corn distribution or *frumentum publicum*. Rickman writes:

> Its dietetic value has been calculated at about 3,000-4,000 calories per day, a range which is not very different from modern ideals of about 3,300 calories per day for male adults. It would certainly have helped to feed some members of a man's family, but it was never in itself the whole answer even to the feeding of an individual. A man still had to find the costs of milling and baking his ration of grain as well as the means of buying vegetables, wine and other items to go with his bread.[58]

It would have reduced, to some extent, the cost of Paul's two year stay in Rome and would have gone some way toward adequate nourishment.

But could Paul, newly arrived and a prisoner under house arrest, have qualified for this public food? Information available would seem to indicate that he could. Rickman writes that 'the necessary conditions to qualify for admission to the distributions under the early Empire remained full citizenship, properly registered domicile in the city, and a specified age, a minimum of eleven years, or possibly fourteen years of age'.[59] Certainly, Paul met the third qualification. As to the first, no serious objection can be entered either to his Roman citizenship or to its quality as we have previously argued. On the point of the second qualification, Acts 28 is quite clear that Paul resided for two years in Rome in rented accommodation. In the late Republic, lists of corn recipients were drawn up on a district by district basis by both Caesar and Augustus with the cooperation and assistance not only of district magistrates but also tenement landlords.[60] If this method, or something like

---

[58]G. Rickman, *The Corn Supply of Ancient Rome* (Oxford: Clarendon, 1980), 173. See B.W. Winter, 'Acts and Food Shortages', in *The Book of Acts in Its Graeco-Roman Setting*, ed. D.W.J. Gill and C. Gempf (A1CS 2; Grand Rapids: Eerdmans/Carlisle: Paternoster, 1994), 59-78.

[59]*Ibid.* 188.

[60]*Ibid.*, 190.

it, was followed in the middle decades of the 1st century AD—and even if Paul occupied one of the least desirable rooms in one of these tenement structures—his permanent domicile could be legally established and entitlement secured.

The objection that Paul, being a prisoner under house arrest, would have been disqualified may be answered at two points. First, the fact of his being a prisoner would be immaterial to his entitlement. Seneca, at about the time of Paul's stay in Rome, wrote:

> the thief no less than the perjurer and the adulterer and everyone, without distinction of character, whose name appears on the register receives grain from the state; whatever else a man may be, he gets his dole, not because he is good, but because he is a citizen, and the good and the bad share alike.[61]

Paul, whatever people might have thought of his circumstances as a prisoner, was nevertheless a citizen. It must be remembered, moreover, that Paul was *not* a condemned person but merely a defendant being kept in light remand conditions. Second, it is probably true that being under house arrest, Paul would not have been permitted personally to travel all the way across the city from the region of the Castra Praetoria to the Porticus Minucia in the SE part of the Campus Martius where the public grain was actually distributed.[62] It would have constituted an unnecessary threat to his security and a breach of the conditions of his custody. Paul's access to free corn, however, would not necessarily in these circumstances have been frustrated. The imprisoned apostle could still have availed himself of this food by giving his corn ration ticket to an associate who would pick up his monthly allotment of 5 *modii* for him.

Having established that Paul *could* have shared in the grain distribution, we must ask further whether it is likely that Paul *would* have done so. It is at this point that a number of potential objections arise. First, Paul does indicate in both the Acts and epistles (Acts 20:33-35; 1 Cor. 9:1-18; 2 Thess. 3:6-13) a settled policy of living by the labour of his own hands. Paul was almost certainly unable to work at his trade to defray living costs in Rome on practical, financial, security and safety grounds as we shall see. Paul, we have argued, was a man of some

---

[61]Seneca, *Ben.* 4.28.2.

[62]On the Porticus Minucia as the sole distribution point in the middle decades of the 1st century AD and its location, see Rickman, *The Corn Supply*, 192-95 and his appendix entitled 'Porticus Minucia', 250-52.

means. One cannot be certain of the extent of these means. What is certain, however, is that living in the capital city of the Empire—even at a very modest level—consumed a person's resources at an alarming rate.[63] The financial constraints of his imprisonment and the pressures of an inflated cost of living open up the possibility that he would have seriously considered the free food rations as a means of defraying his costs.

A second objection is that Paul, who emphasizes that he would not be a burden to his churches, would certainly not have allowed himself to become a burden to the State. This objection depends upon certain false premises. The corn distribution, while it was free and did help the needy citizenry of Rome most of all, was not merely a poor dole. It was a right of citizens—with a few exceptions.[64] If, as we have argued previously, Paul valued his Roman citizenship so highly that he disclosed it to advantage in particular tight situations, then we can hardly assert that he would have necessarily disavowed any share in the corn distribution, a right enjoyed by as many as 200,000 or more[65] of his fellow-citizens in the capital. Moreover, indications of the unimprisoned Paul's embrace of a vigorous material independence in such NT passages as those just cited above must not be thought to preclude his pursuit of such options as might have been available and necessary in entirely different circumstances. The epistle to the Philippians illustrates the point well. There we see a prisoner who, despite real and sincere protestations of contentment in all circumstances (Phil. 4:11-13), is nevertheless obliquely solicitous of Philippian material aid (Phil. 4:10, 17f.) and properly grateful for having receiving it (Phil. 4:10, 14, 18f.).

We have not argued that Paul must have shared in the public grain distribution, but that he was entitled, had good reason to do so, and might actually have availed himself of this right. In the event, what monetary or material resources he personally possessed or had received from others toward his support would then have been helpfully preserved. He could direct these resources to the purchase of other necessities.

---

[63]*Supra*, 234-36.
[64]Rickman, *The Corn Supply*, 172.
[65]*Ibid.*, 181.

CHAPTER 11

PRISON CULTURE

Prisons of the first century were social worlds in miniature, peopled by those who were kept and their keepers. Formal and informal administrative structures and responsibilities were operative, as were various relationships between individuals and groups. In these ancient social worlds of keepers and the kept, status indicators would have generally played the same role as in the courtroom.

The author of Acts parades a whole coterie of individuals before the reader: there are prison guards, a jailer and a tribune, centurions, various kinds of soldiers, and co-prisoners. The brevity of some references to these individuals may indicate they are incidental to the author's purpose. The information is vital, nevertheless, for it contributes to the readers' appreciation of the character of the Pauline prison experience and its impact upon him and others. Where Luke does elaborate, of course, the reader's interest should be heightened.

I. Prison Personnel

Custodial arrangements for prisoners in the ancient world were varied—the product of time, tradition, and circumstances. This variability is helpfully illustrated in a discussion in the *Digest*. The jurist Callistratus qualifies individuals as those 'in bonds', those kept in public custody, by bandits, by even greater powers, or in a quarry prison.[1] Ulpian adds: '...in the same position are also those who are kept in custody by soldiers, the attendants of a magistrate, or servants of a municipality'.[2] Such variability calls for consideration of the broader spectrum of possible arrangements.

1. Administrative Structures and Personnel in Ancient Prisons

The prison at Athens and executions within it were the administrative concern of a group known as οἱ ἕνδεκα.[3] They were comprised of representatives chosen annually by lot from each of the ten tribes with the eleventh chosen to act as secretary of proceedings. They executed their charge through slaves owned by the Athenian State. Those referred to in some places as οἱ τῶν ἕνδεκα ὑπηρέται or simply οἱ ὑπηρέται[4] would have discharged the more important prison duties. Xenophon's reference to one Satyrus (404 BC) as head of this slave group when it formally processed with the Eleven suggests a hierarchical structure.[5] Satyrus also served the Eleven as executioner, preparing the hemlock and administering it to the condemned.[6] The ὑπηρέτης who regularly saw and spoke with Socrates (399 BC) in the prison and who mixed the hemlock would also then have been the chief jailer or warden over the prison[7] as would the δημόσιος who bruised the hemlock and administered it to Phocion and his companions (318 BC).[8]

Under the chief jailer, other 'assistants' served in various capacities. They were responsible to guard inmates and to put individuals

---

[1]*Dig.* 4.6.9.
[2]*Ibid.* 4.6.10.
[3]Pollux,.*Onom.* 8.102; Xenophon, *HG* 2.3.54. See also D.M. MacDowell, 'Hendeka', *OCD*, 496.
[4]Xenophon, *HG* 2.3.54; Plato, *Phd.* 116.B.
[5]Xenophon, *HG* 2.3.54.
[6]Xenophon, *HG* 2.3.55f. Further, Plato, *Phd.* 63.D, E.
[7]Plato, *Phd.* 116.B-D; 117.A, B, E.
[8]Plutarch, *Phoc.* 36.2-4.

(most often slaves) to the torture.[9] The secretary had several undersecretaries.[10] If these—or one of them at least—were numbered among the 'assistants', the clerical functions encompassed would certainly have included keeping prison records. There also appear to have been slave personnel below these assistants who attended to menial tasks, apparently even doing the bidding of prisoners. Socrates instructed a young male slave who was standing nearby to tell the chief jailer he was ready to take the hemlock.[11]

Sparta's equivalent to the Eleven was the Ephors (ἔφοροι). They too possessed certain powers to arrest, incarcerate and execute individuals and exercised these powers through public slaves, also designated 'assistants'.[12] The arrangements for the Spartan king Agis and his family (440 BC) illustrate: the slaves, as senior prison keepers, were commanded to conduct the condemned to the city prison. When both they and certain mercenaries in attendance refused to lay hands upon Agis to take him into the death chamber and strangle him, the Ephor Damochares angrily thrust the king into the cell and—apparently departing from convention—executed Agis and later his mother and grandmother with his own hands.

We read of the following administrative positions in Egyptian prisons before the Roman hegemony: wardens in Arsinoe and Kerkesouka and a warden named Paos who receive/arrest and convey prisoners to the great prison at Crocodilopolis about the mid third century BC;[13] the warden (c. 257 BC) who, it is alleged, has permitted a sailor to escape from prison;[14] and the warden of the prison at Tebtunis (early 2nd cent. BC) who accepts sureties from a prisoner but refuses his release.[15] Lower-level prison personnel are also identifiable: guards who secure the citadel of Alexandria (220/19 BC) against incursion by the revolutionary Cleomenes and his associates;[16] five prison guards posted to a facility at Philadelphia (mid 3rd cent. BC);[17] and prison guards who receive from one Apollonius (127 BC) a supply of wine.[18]

---

[9]*Ibid.* 35.1; Isocrates, *Trap.* 15f.; Demosthenes, *Nic.* 23-25.
[10]Pollux, *Onom.* 8.102. *Cf.* Isocrates, *Antid.* 237f.
[11]Plato, *Phd.* 117.A.
[12]Plutarch, *Agis* 19.5-20.4.
[13]*Sammelb.* 3:7202.17-19, 34-36; *PPetr.* 3:28 *uerso* cited in *MM*, 142; *PLille* 1:7 [= *PEnteux.* 1:84].
[14]*PCairZen.* 1:59077.
[15]*PTebt.* 3.1:777. *PColZen.* 1:58 [= *PCol.* 3:58]: Dioskourides is called 'the overseer of the prisoners [τον ἐπιστατουν των δεσμωτων]'.
[16]Plutarch, *Cleom.* 37.4-6.
[17]*PCairZen.* 2:59296.

If qualifications for taking on prison duties in Egypt[19] and the levy of taxes specifically to support prisons and prison guards[20] are any indication, Egyptian prison personnel were not necessarily or perhaps even usually slaves but rather trustworthy free locals co-opted from the population and paid to work for a specified period of time. Rome's tendency not to interfere in municipal administrative arrangements would have encouraged the continuation of this pattern of employing free locals. Lucian's *Toxaris* (c. 163 AD), if it accurately relates facts, indicates the use of slaves in larger metropolitan prisons.

Turning to Roman arrangements, we note that the municipal prison system in the city of Rome was made the responsibility of three administrators, known officially as the *triumviri* or *tresuiri capitales*, about the year 290 BC.[21] They were roughly equivalent to the Eleven of Athens and the Ephors of Sparta. Cicero describes them as minor magistrates with partial authority, having charge over the confinement of criminals and the infliction of capital punishment.[22] They were, according to Pomponius, 'the board of guardians of the jail, [who] were constituted so that when a mandatory punishment was to be carried out, it should be done by their agency'.[23] During the second Punic War (219-201 BC) the banker P. Munatius, caught taking a chaplet of flowers from a statue of Marsyas and putting it on his own head, was 'ordered by the Triumviri to be put in chains'.[24] Sosia, a slave in one of the plays of Plautus (255-184 BC) makes the comment:

> ...yet here I am strolling around all alone at this time of night! (*seems to hear something and jumps*) What if the police should lock me up in jail? To-morrow I should be taken out of that preserve closet and get served—to a rope's end [*i.e., to the *flagrum*]....[25]

Plautus' writings elsewhere contain characters who threaten to leave the names of certain individuals with the *triumviri* for their interest and action.[26]

---

[18]*PSI* 13:1315.

[19]See *BGU* 9:1828 (c. 1 BC); *POxy.* 3:580 (c. 2nd cent. AD); *PFlor* I.2^{75} (265 AD) in *MM*, 142.

[20]On guards' wages in Egypt *infra*, 259 and see *PSI* 13:1315 (250 BC).

[21]Livy, *Epit.* 11. *Cf.* Livy 9.46.3. On how they were chosen, W. Smith and A.S. Wilkins, 'Tresviri', *DGRA*, vol. 2, 868.

[22]Cicero, *Leg.* 3.6 [3.3].

[23]*Dig.* 1.2.2.30.

[24]Pliny, *Nat.* 21.9.

[25]Plautus, *Am.* 155f. *Cf.* Horace, *Epod.* 4.11f. (c. 65-68 BC).

[26]Plautus, *Aul.* 413f.; *As.* 131. *Cf.* Smith and Wilkins, 'Tresviri', 868.

This board of three appears to have had charge over both Rome's quarry prison and the prison in which was found the *Tullianum*. In 198 BC, when it was feared that the Carthaginian hostages and prisoners were plotting to do violence to the Roman State, Livy records that 'the three officials in charge of the quarry-prison'[27] were ordered to increase their vigilance. On the senate's adoption of Cato's recommendation concerning the Catilinarian conspirators in 63 BC, Cicero 'ordered the triumvirs to make the necessary preparations for the execution'.[28] Thereafter, Lentulus was personally led by Cicero to the dungeon and the praetors did the same for each of the others.[29] The executions of women convicted of capital crimes similarly fell within the remit of the *triumviri* and were carried out in the prison according to Valerius Maximus (*fl.* reign of Tiberius),[30] who notes elsewhere that they were also responsible for the crucifixion of offending slaves.[31] The elder Seneca (born *c.* 55 BC) asserts that to 'expiate wicked deeds one requires triumvirs, the place of assembly, the executioner'.[32]

Responsibility for the general safety of the city also called for the *triumviri* to patrol the streets by night, seizing disturbers of the peace and rushing to supervise the fighting of fires—hence their additional designation as the three men of the night or night-watch (*tresuiri nocturni*).[33] Acting beyond the constraints of their remit or dereliction in the discharge of their duties were chargeable offences.[34]

The details of running the prisons in the administrative care of the board of three were taken care of by public slaves (*servi publici*) under their command.[35] The three did not, apparently, personally execute those under capital sentences. Though Cicero commanded them to make the preparations to execute the Catilinarians,[36] for example, it was a slave serving the State as public executioner who did the actual deed.[37] This individual we meet elsewhere and at later times in the context of prison executions.[38] He put to death slaves and foreigners

[27]Livy 32.26.17.

[28]Sallust, *Cat.* 55.1. *Cf.* Cicero, *Catil.* 2.12.27.

[29]Sallust, *Cat.* 55.2.

[30]Valerius Maximus 5.4.7.

[31]*Ibid.* 8.4.2.

[32]Seneca, *Con.* 7.1.22. See Mommsen, *Droit Pénal*, vol. 3, 269 and n. 2.

[33]So A. Berger and B. Nicholas, 'Vigintisexviri', *OCD*, 1121. *Cf.* Livy 9.46.3.

[34]Valerius Maximus 8.1 *damn.* 5f. *Cf.* Krauss, *Im Kerker*, 71f.

[35]Hitzig, 'Carcer ', 1579. Further, Krauss, *Im Kerker*, 72f. and *cf. Mart. Agap.* 6.1 (303 AD).

[36]Sallust, *Cat.* 55.1 cited above.

[37]Plutarch, *Cic.* 22.2.

and could, when commanded, execute citizens convicted of treason. He was also responsible—probably along with other slave personnel—for putting individuals to the torture. Owing to the heinous character of his occupation, he was required to live outside the city, only entering when officially required. Intimately connected with the prison though he was, it may be doubted that he was keeper of the prison under the *triumviri*.[39] In similar fashion, the *triumviri*, while charged with administering corporal punishment, did not actually personally ply scourges on the backs of malefactors; this was the job of attendants called 'public criers' or 'heralds'.[40] They too seem to have been only occasional to the prison system at Rome.

It is not sure which prison in Rome held the philosopher Apollonius during the reign of Domitian, though his case and the description of his circumstances suggest a civilian rather than military custody.[41] The free prison where he was first incarcerated had a governor or chief jailer[42] as well as assistants and guards of various kinds.[43] The prison governor was answerable to the prefect Aelianus concerning Apollonius' treatment and received instructions and commands from Aelianus through court notaries.[44] Whether he was the same governor as the one in charge of the Roman prison in which the philosopher Musonius of Babylon was incarcerated during the reign of Nero, or was another who only held the same official position, we cannot be certain.[45]

Lictors attached to magistrates in Rome appear to have had a semi-formal connection with the Imperial capital's prisons as well. Appius Claudius (449 BC) ordered his lictors to hale to prison any Roman citizen who threatened to disobey his commands;[46] Julius Caesar (60/59 BC) had Marcus Cato dragged out of the Senate House to the jail by a lictor.[47] Lictors in Rome were also responsible at times for the execution of condemned citizens in the prison—more particularly in the *Tul-*

---

[38]E.g., Valerius Maximus 6.9.13 (*c.* 95 BC); Dio Cassius 58.11.5 (31 AD; *cf.* Suetonius, *Tib.* 61.5); Seneca, *Ad Lucilium Ep.* 70.9 (63-65 AD). *Cf.* with the first entry of this footnote Valerius Maximus 4.7.3 and Cicero, *Balb.* 11.

[39]W. Smith and A.S. Wilkins, 'Carnifex', *DGRA*, vol. 1, 366 on this and earlier comments.

[40]Horace, *Epod.* 4.12. *Cf.* Livy 26.15.3 (211 BC).

[41]Philostratus, *VA* 7.22, 28-30.

[42]*Ibid.* 7.28.

[43]*Ibid.* 9.31.

[44]*Ibid.* 7.29, 31.

[45]*Ibid.* 4.35.

[46]Dionysius Halicarnassensis, *Ant. Rom.* 11.38.3f.

[47]Suetonius, *Jul.* 20.4.

lianum. Quick-handed lictors rushed the poisoned and dying knight Vibulenus Agrippa (36 AD) to the prison 'and his throat—though he had now ceased to breathe—[was] tormented by a halter'.[48] Lictors in Rome would seem to have been occasional to the prisons at Rome and not a formal part of their administrative structure.

Lucan indicates that Marius miraculously escaped the sword of a Cimbrian lictor (?) in the prison at Minturnae about 87 BC.[49] Whether the Cimbrian fit into the prison administration is not known. Some lictors attached to the governors of certain provinces and colonies, however, appear to have been fitted into the administrative system of prisons. Cicero indicates this when he writes about one of the Sicilian governor Verres' lictors in 70 BC; 'The prison warder would come along, the governor's executioner, bringer of death and death's terrors to the allies and citizens of Rome—Sextius the lictor'.[50] Sextius' position as 'warder' can hardly be considered a menial post. He was Verres' right hand man, perhaps nominated from among Verres' own freedmen[51] for the post of senior lictor.[52] The charge in question, moreover, was the great quarry prison at Syracuse.

Sextius appears, however, to have been grafted into a well-established system having both lower- and upper-level prison personnel who followed long-standing procedures which continued despite changes in governors and their lieutenants. Cicero works this fact to advantage when he asserts that he will prove Verres' guilt by reference to both eyewitness testimony and prison records. He writes:

> ...let us have the prison record, which is carefully kept so as to show the dates on which prisoners are received, and on which they die—or are put to death. *The record is read.* You see, gentlemen, how citizens of Rome were herded into the Stone Quarries, how all these honest countrymen of yours were flung one on top of another in this place of dishonour. Look now for the footprints that indicate their departure from that place. There are none! Did all those men die there? Even were it a valid defence to say so, we should not believe him when he

---

[48]Tacitus, *Ann.* 6.40.

[49]Lucan 76-81; Plutarch, *Mar.* 39; Velleius Paterculus 2.19.3; and *infra*, 413f.

[50]Cicero, *Ver.* 2.5.118 (≈ Quintillian, *Inst.* 8.4.27). See further, Josephus, *BJ* 2.364-66 [2.16.4].

[51]*Cf.* A.H.M. Jones, 'The Roman Civil Service (Clerical and Sub-Clerical Grades)', in *Studies in Roman Government and Law*, A.H.M. Jones (Oxford: Basil Blackwell, 1960), 154; and Hitzig, 'Carcer ', 1579 who calls him Verres' personal public servant.

[52]Cicero, *Ver.* 2.5.142.

said so. But there in this same document we find written what he was too careless to notice and too ill-educated to understand, namely the word *edikaiöthësan*, the Sicilian equivalent of 'the death penalty was inflicted upon them'.[53]

These records would have been kept by clerical personnel known as *scribae* or *commentarienses*, and contained the name, homeland, date of entry and time in jail, as well as other personal data of the prisoner together with the outcome of the case. Each month the record was reviewed by the prison overseer or another competent authority. The records were updated on the basis of daily reports from assistants.[54]

While we have not mentioned clerical personnel previously except in conjunction with the Athenian secretary and undersecretaries, all civilian prisons, whatever their size, must have had some such functionary. Egyptian lists of prisoners names, one even engraved in stone, have survived.[55] Behind the outrageous remarks and behaviour of Caligula (37-41 AD) toward various prisoners stands the clear indication that extensive and careful prison records were kept.[56]

As an ever-growing city in the latter decades of the 1st century BC, Rome necessarily saw an increase in its crime rate. So too, the city's size and building practices rendered more persistent and serious the problem of fires.[57] The board of three and the relatively few slave personnel whom they utilized could not keep up with the increased demands in the earlier period. Moreover, addressing the problem by resort to the use of military forces was not a desirable option. Augustus, in response to a serious fire in 23 BC, 'established a fire-brigade of 600 slaves commanded at first by the aediles but after 7 BC (when Rome was divided into 14 *regiones* and 265 *vici*, each with four *vicomagistri*) by the *vicomagistri*'.[58] After another serious fire in 6 AD, Augustus formed a quasi-military body of seven cohorts known as the *vigiles* (watchmen) and charged them with civilian policing and fire-fighting in Rome.[59] To their leader, a knight known as the *praefectus vigilum*, de-

---

[53]*Ibid.* 2.5.147f.
[54]Krauss, *Im Kerker*, 72. *Cod.Theod.* 8.15.3; 8.15.5.2 (266, 370, 373 AD); 9.3.5. (271 AD = *Cod. Just.* 9.4.4); 9.3.6 (380 AD = *Cod. Just.* 9.4.5); Hitzig, 'Carcer', 1580 for comments upon the *commentariensis* in the later legislation.
[55]Taubenschlag, '63. L'Emprisonnement', 715 and nn. 19f. *Cf. POxy.* 43:3104.
[56]Suetonius, *Cal.* 27.1; 29.1.
[57]*Supra*, 229f.
[58]J.P.V.D. Balsdon, 'Vigiles', *OCD*, 1120.
[59]Suetonius, *Aug.* 30.1; Dio Cassius 55.26.5; 57.19.6. *Cf.* P.K. Bailey Reynolds, *The Vigiles of Imperial Rome* (London: Humphrey Milford [OUP], 1926), 13.

volved what had earlier been the triumviral oversight of these two responsibilities.[60] Bailey Reynolds writes:

> The business of extinguishing fires having formerly been a servile oc-
> cupation, he [i.e., Augustus] would not entrust it to citizens, but so
> large a force as 7,000 armed and disciplined slaves might have been a
> menace, and have caused a popular outcry, he would not tolerate
> that, but compromised by raising the brigade from freedmen. This
> also served to emphasize the non-military character of the corps, for
> recruiting for the army was still confined to citizens of free birth (ex-
> cept in great emergencies), and thus the Vigiles were of a lower stand-
> ing than the other troops, not only of the city, but of the whole army,
> including the auxiliaries.[61]

When combined with the three Urban cohorts this gave Rome a ratio
of one policeman/peacekeeper to seventy-five inhabitants.[62] Each cohort of watchmen was responsible for two regions of the city. They
were, up until about 20 AD and along with the Praetorian cohorts,
quartered in private houses; later, they were quartered in sub-stations
(*excubitoria*) throughout the city, one in each region.[63]

Policing called for prison facilities as well as individuals who
had charge of them. Bailey Reynolds notes

> two appointments to special duties of the cohort, namely OP C(A)
> and OP CO. OP CA is almost certainly Optio Carceris, as this post is
> found both in the Urban and Praetorian troops. The Vth cohort of Vig-
> iles had two in 205 [AD] and three in 210. Three would thus be the es-
> tablishment; troops are not always up to strength. The prison in
> question is obviously for offenders taken by the Vigiles in their night-
> ly patrols, and not merely military detention cells.[64]

The position of officer in charge of the prison was a junior staff post
held by NCOs. It was, according to Speidel, a little higher than its
counterpart in the urban cohorts and was roughly equivalent to being
a *beneficiarius tribuni*. An NCO career of 25 years as a watchman lead-

---

[60]Dio Cassius 55.26.4f. For a discussion of whom he was subordinate to and in
what circumstances, *cf.* Balsdon, 'Vigiles', 1120f.; Bailey Reynolds, *The Vigiles, passim*. On various officeholders, Tacitus, *Hist.* 1.46; 1.72.
[61]Bailey Reynolds, *The Vigiles*, 15.
[62]*Ibid.*, 15f.
[63]Dio Cassius 57.19.6; Suetonius, *Tib.* 37.1; and see Balsdon, 'Vigiles', 1120f.
[64]Bailey Reynolds, *The Vigiles*, 86. *Cf.* Mommsen, *Droit Pénal*, vol. 1, 370 and nn. 3f.
who discusses this officer, citing *CIL* 6:2406.

ing to honourable retirement would require, if one was posted to the duty of officer in charge, service of three to four years and as many as five other posts of similar duration.[65] Reynolds notes among the various lesser functionaries in the inscriptions a 'KARC(*erarius*), once only in 205 [AD] (unless one should read KAR for BAR in the roll of 210), who is probably responsible for the cleanliness of the prison'.[66] Lesser individuals would have discharged lesser prison or guarding responsibilities, standing in general equivalence to the standard military cohorts to which we now turn.

Already in the early Imperial period, custody—including imprisonment, prisoner transport and method of execution—began increasingly to be taken over by the military.[67] The younger Pliny, in his correspondence with the emperor Trajan (98-117 AD) writes, 'I am doubtful whether I ought to continue using the public slaves in the various towns as prison warders, as hitherto, or to put soldiers on guard-duty in the prisons'.[68] The emperor replies, 'There is no need, my dear Pliny, for more soldiers to be transferred to guard-duty in the prisons. We should continue the custom of the province and use public slaves as warders',[69] and indicates that soldiers should not be called away from active service. Confirmation that the process continued without fully overtaking the older structures[70] is found in the need, as late as Ulpian's day, to indicate the various kinds of keepers who might have charge of prisoners.[71] The encroachment of the military administration upon civilian prison establishments is, furthermore, evident in the titles of various military prison personnel; a distinction is made in some sources between those attached to the state prison and those attached to the military prison inside the legionary camp.[72]

Several grades of officers, known as *beneficiarii* because their responsibilities conferred upon them the privilege of exemption from menial work, could be connected with prison duties.[73] They were pri-

---

[65]M. Speidel, *Roman Army Studies: Volume One* (Amsterdam: J.C. Gieben, 1984), 440f., 449. Cf. D.J. Breeze, 'The Career Structure Below the Centurionate', *ANRW* II/1 (1974), 439.

[66]Bailey Reynolds, *The Vigiles*, 88, citing *CIL* 6.1057.7,4; 1058.3,7.

[67]Hitzig, 'Carcer', 1580; Arbandt *et al.*, 'Gefangenschaft', 321.

[68]Pliny, *Ep.* 10.19.

[69]*Ibid.* 10.20.

[70]The civilian prison in Carthage in 259 AD was under the authority of local magistrates but manned by soldier guards according to *Mart. Mont. & Luc.* 3.1; 4.1.

[71]*Dig.* 4.6.10 cited above. Cf. *ibid.* 4.6.10; 11.4.1.6; 47.2.52.12; 48.3.10.

[72]So Speidel, *Roman Army Studies*, 238 and G. Lopuszanski, 'La Police Romaine et les Chrétiens', *AntCl* 20 (1951), 41 citing A. von Domaszewski.

marily responsible for the preparation of cases for jurisdiction,[74] though some were also required to keep the prison accounts and prisoner records in order. One stood by the Christian martyr Pionius (249/51 AD) in the amphitheatre, received the martyr's clothing, and saw to it that the executioner crucified him in accordance with the condemnatory order.[75] Prison directors serving under the title of *optio carceris/custodiarum* can be found both among the cohorts of Rome and in the provinces. The director in charge of the military prison and its Christian occupants at Carthage was an NCO named Pudens.[76] Pudens probably organized the escort and led the confessors from the prison on the day of their death at the emperor's games; he was present at the amphitheatre, conversed with the confessors, and saw them die.[77]

Unlike watchmen, this class of officers might aspire to the centurionate level. About two years in a post such as prison director plus five more posts of similar duration in a Praetorian cohort might, with merit, lead to the rank of re-enlisted veteran or centurion. There were also two tracks for advancement among non-praetorian forces taking 13-20 and 25 years respectively. They required longer service in posts such as prison director and had less certain centurial prospects on the former track and none on the latter.[78] Lopuszanski cites examples of veterans charged with duties such as conducting inquisitorial torture, keeping the prison register, keeping a prisoner of high rank and executing a murderer.[79] We have already considered the involvement of centurions in guarding prisoners and have noted that they would have had charge of only the most serious or high ranking malefactors.[80]

The above-described prison officials would have had minor grade prison personnel at their command; turnkeys, clerks and assistants,[81] torturers, soldiers,[82] and assistants (*ministri*). These prison personnel were answerable through the normal chain of command but

---

[73]The largest and most complicated *officium* was that of the provincial zfgovernor according to Jones, 'The Roman Civil Service', 161 and nn. 62f. *Cf.* G.R. Watson, *The Roman Soldier*, 75-88.

[74]Watson, *The Roman Soldier*, 86.

[75]*Mart. Pion.* 21.1. Further *Dig.* 48.20.6 and Seneca, *De Ira* 1.18.4; *Ben.* 3.25.

[76]*Mart. Perp. & Felic.* 9.1; 16.4.

[77]*Ibid.* 18.1; 21.1, 4.

[78]Speidel, *Roman Army Studies*, 449.

[79]Lopuszanski, 'La Police romaine', 34 and n. 1 citing *CIL* 6:2755, 11:2108; *CIL* 11:19; Tacitus, *Ann.* 2.58, 68; and *idem*, *Hist.* 1.46 respectively.

[80]*Supra*, 30.

[81]Arbandt *et al.*, 'Gefangenschaft', 321; Krauss, *Im Kerker*, 72.

[82]See discussion *supra*, 30.

could be directly answerable, from least to greatest, to the chief in command.

2. Keeper-Inmate Relations: Underlying Motives

Mommsen has written that 'without doubt, the personality of the director of the prison and indeed those of his subalterns for their part... played a great role in the matter of prisoner treatment'.[83] In our chapter on prison environment the various bodily and psychological sufferings which prisoners experienced occupied our attention. These sufferings are traceable to the fact that ancient prisons were often governed by seriously troubled staff-inmate relations. The following pages explore why this was so. Why did prison personnel not make the life of prisoners less onerous? Why, in point of fact, did they frequently take steps to neglect and harm prisoners? We begin, however, by asking what motives there might have been for humanitarian behaviour toward prisoners.

Motives suggested by the literature for humane staff-inmate relations are several. First, those charged with keeping a prisoner might behave with greater civility out of a high regard for the status of that prisoner. Plutarch writes, for example, that when king Agis was brought to Sparta's state prison (240 BC), the prison assistants, despite dire threats and verbal abuse from the Ephor Damochares, 'did not dare to lay hands on Agis, and likewise that even the mercenaries who were there shrank from the deed and were loth to do it, feeling as they did that it was contrary to the laws of God and man to lay hands upon the person of a king'.[84] Macro balked when ordered by Tiberius to handcuff Agrippa, twice asking for clarification, 'partly because he was not quite sure whom he meant and partly because he would not have expected him to plan such treatment for Agrippa'.[85] Agrippa's rank and privilege were prominent in Macro's mind. Hormus, the freedman of Vespasian (69-79 AD), exercised personal discretion in obtaining for the prisoner Bassus a more honourable confinement without chains in token of his high standing.[86]

---

[83]Mommsen, *Droit Pénal*, vol. 1, 356.
[84]Plutarch, *Agis* 19.6. This same quasi-religious status consciousness stands behind the change in king Perseus' manner of incarceration; *cf.* Diodorus Siculus 31.9.2-5.
[85]Josephus, *AJ* 18.189f. [18.6.6].
[86]Tacitus, *Hist.* 3.12.

Second, and perhaps more usual, guards and keepers treated prisoners civilly because they had been so ordered. The Jewish Agrippa's military keepers were chosen because of their 'humane character'.[87] Macro had also ordered that they allow him certain privileges. In similar fashion, the philosopher Apollonius was well-treated after a time by his jailer because the praetorian prefect Aelianus had so ordered it.[88] Later Imperial legislation explicitly required prison personnel to treat their wards more humanely.[89]

Third, prison personnel might be more generous owing to religious fear of or solidarity with the prisoner. The author of the *Martyrdom of Perpetua and Felicitas* writes that Pudens, the adjutant in charge of the military prison at Carthage in 203 AD, began to show the Christian confessors in his charge great honour, 'realizing that we possessed some great power within us. And he began to allow many visitors to see us for our mutual comfort'.[90] A vision recounted in the Talmud praises a Gentile jailer who converted to Judaism as one who would share in the world to come because he protected female Jewish prisoners from being raped.[91] Philostratus relates how the philosopher Apollonius was escorted by a quaternion of guards who kept their distance owing to fear of his magical powers.[92]

Fourth, guards and keepers might be favourably disposed to prisoners out of pity and in the face of prisoners' entreaties. When in 353 BC Dion's sister and pregnant wife were cast into the prison at Syracuse, they prevailed upon the pity of their keepers. Dion's wife 'had a most wretched confinement, and gave birth in the prison to a male child, which the women ventured to rear, with the consent of their guards'.[93] Also probably the beneficiary of official pity, the Christian confessor Perpetua in 203 AD writes: '...I got permission for my baby to stay with me in prison'.[94] The classical jurists Ulpian and Modestinus acknowledge that keepers, out of pity for the prolonged binding or bad quarters of prisoners in their charge, might be moved to release them.[95] Pionius and his fellow Christian confessors in 249/50 AD were

[87]Josephus, *AJ* 18.203 [18.6.7].
[88]Philostratus, *VA* 7.28, 31.
[89]*Supra*, chapter 9 *passim*.
[90]*Mart. Perp. & Felic.* 9.1. Cf. *ibid.* 16.4 where he is later identified as a Christian.
[91]*b. Mo'ed* VII: *Ta'an.* 22a.
[92]Philostratus, *VA* 7.31.
[93]Plutarch, *Dio* 57.3.
[94]*Mart. Perp. & Felic.* 3.9.
[95]*Dig.* 16.3.7; 48.3.14.2.

allowed a more salubrious location in the prison by 'offering the guards the usual friendship'.[96]

We mention, finally, an instance where a prisoner actually embarrasses a tribune into granting several prisoners greater ease in their custody. The Christian Perpetua accuses the Tribune in charge of the camp prison at Carthage of being so cruel to her and the other confessors as to make their death at the games in honour of the Emperor Geta's birthday less enjoyable and entertaining because of their poor health. 'The officer became disturbed and grew red. So it was that he gave the order that they were to be more humanely treated'.[97]

These examples show that humanity was to be found in prison guards, but it was a rare commodity. Improvements in the quality of a prisoner's keeping seem to have been only marginal.

The greater pressure upon prison personnel was to treat prisoners harshly. Sometimes diligence engendered negative relations; that is, harsh treatment might be employed because it meant greater security while relaxed arrangements were less secure. Pity expressed in loosely keeping a prisoner or giving a prisoner freedom was considered deceitful or fraudulent at least and treasonable at most in later legislation.[98] If sympathy in prison personnel was frowned upon, so were sloth, drunkenness and other forms of negligence and, even more, connivance in an inmate's escape or shady dealings.[99] Such behaviour incurred penalties linked to the importance of the prisoner and the culpability of the keeper: fines, transfers/demotions, corporal punishment, or death could result.[100] Trajan writes to Pliny that the reliability of public slaves serving in prisons 'depends on your watchfulness and discipline. For, as you say in your letter, if we mix soldiers with public slaves the chief danger is that both sides will become careless by relying on each other'.[101]

Even those who had charge over the watchers were watched. Magistrates could bring trouble on their own heads if they released prisoners without cause; and when a prisoner was entrusted to an in-

---

[96]*Mart. Pion.* 11.5.
[97]*Mart. Perp. & Felic.* 16.4.
[98]*Dig.* 16.3.7.; 48.3.12; 48.4.4.
[99]*Ibid.* 48.3.8, 12, 14. Cf. Plutarch, *Dem.* 26.1f.; J.H.W.G. Liebeschuetz, *Antioch*, 189. On the consequences of breaches of security, Lucian, *Tox.* 31f.; Achilles Tatius, *Clit. & Leuc.* 7.1; *Dig.* 48.3.8. Mischance might be forgivable (*Dig.* 48.3.12); gullibility (Dio Cassius 76.10.3; cf. Plutarch, *De Gen.* 598.A, B), however, probably was not.
[100]*Dig.* 48.3.12, 14.
[101]Pliny, *Ep.* 10.20.

experienced guard and escaped, the blame rested with his superior.[102] Kindness in a climate with such potentially great cost to prison person- nel and administrators alike was, not surprisingly, rare.

Second, adherence to commands concerning particular prisoners inevitably engendered hostility. When the chief jailer of Athens' State prison sees to Socrates' poisoning (399 BC), he tells the philosopher, 'Socrates, I shall not find fault with you, as I do with others, for being angry and cursing me, when at the behest of the authorities, I tell them to drink the poison'.[103] One can easily imagine the measures taken by the magistrates of the Ardeans in 186 BC to keep Minius Cerrinius when they are commanded 'not only to prevent his escape but also to allow him no opportunity to commit suicide'.[104] Tiberius in 30 AD similarly commanded the praetors in regard to the custody of Gallus and certain others. In fulfilment of the command, Gallus 'had no com- panion or servant with him, spoke to no one, and saw no one, except when he was compelled to take food'.[105] Tiberius further commanded that other prisoners be denied 'not only the consolation of reading, but even the privilege of conversing and talking together'.[106] There are ex- amples of prison personnel being ordered to seriously harm prison- ers.[107] The hostility of prisoners was easily redirected from the one issuing the commands to those carrying them out.

Jailers were also expected not only to listen to the talk of the in- mate population but also to collude with government spies and *agents provocateurs* in ruses designed to entrap unconvicted inmates. Apollo- nius and his imprisoned colleague Musonius did not converse with one another on this account[108] and Philostratus indicates that at sever- al points during Apollonius' own imprisonment, spies were put in prison by the jailer for the sole purpose of doing such mischief.[109] This hardly endeared jailers to their charges or fostered trust.

Third, harsh treatment and mutual hostility arose out of the con- viction of prison personnel that inmates deserved what they suffered. Musonius of Babylon, had he not a strong constitution, would have

---

[102]*Dig.* 48.3.10; 48.3.14 *prol.*
[103]Plato, *Phd.* 116.C.
[104]Livy 39.19.2.
[105]Dio Cassius 58.3.5.
[106]Suetonius, *Tib.* 61.4.
[107]E.g., *Mart. Let. Lyons & Vienne* and other Christian martyr documents *passim. Cf.* Arbandt *et al.,* 'Gefangenschaft', 321.
[108]Philostratus, *VA* 4.46.
[109]*Ibid.* 7.27, 36f. See further on its pervasiveness, *ibid.* 4.43; Arrianus, *Epict.* 4.13.5; and *cf.* Achilles Tatius, *Clit. & Leuc.* 7.1.3f.; 7.6.5.

died 'for all his gaoler cared'.[110] Antiphilus, in Lucian's *Toxaris*, was 'regarded as the most villainous of all the malefactors that there were in the prison' by his Egyptian jailer who considered it a virtue to abuse the prisoner as he would 'gratify and avenge his god by exercising his authority over Antiphilus with a heavy hand'.[111] Superstition about the abilities of the prisoner's god also sometimes inspired abuse. The military tribune who kept the Christian Perpetua and her co-confessors confined 'treated them with extraordinary severity because on the information of certain very foolish people he became afraid that they would be spirited out of the prison by magic spells'.[112]

Guards and keepers interacted each day with society's evildoers. If they had not been chosen in the first instance because of toughness verging on cruelty,[113] they might be expected to become tough, cruel and morally bankrupt. This is exactly the thrust of Philo's comments in *De Iosepho*:

> Everyone knows how full of inhumanity and cruelty gaolers are; pitiless by nature and care-hardened by practice, they are brutalized day by day towards savagery, because they never even by chance see or say or do any kindness, but only the extremes of violence and cruelty. Just as men of well-built physique, if they add to this athletic training, grow sinewy and gain irresistible strength and unequalled robustness, it becomes doubly impervious and inaccessible to the kindly and humane emotion of pity. For even those who consort with the good are improved in character by the pleasure they take in their associates, so those who live with the bad take on some impression of their vice. Custom has a wonderful power of forcing everything into the likeness of nature. Gaolers then spend their days with footpads, thieves, burglars, men of violence and outrage, who commit rape, murder, adultery and sacrilege, and from each of these they imbibe and accumulate something of their villainy, out of which miscellaneous amalgam they produce a single body of evil, a fusion of every sort of pollution.[114]

---

[110]Philostratus, *VA* 4.35.

[111]Lucian, *Tox.* 28.

[112]*Mart. Perp. & Felic.* 16.2.

[113]Josephus, *AJ* 18.203 [18.6.7], when it indicates that the Jewish Agrippa's keepers were chosen because of their humanity, tends to prove the general rule (*cf. ibid.* 18.204 [18.6.7]).

[114]Philo, *De Ios.* 81-84. The power in the metaphor of the soul as the chief jailer of the prison of the passions in Philo's *Immut.* 111-15, depends for its effect upon this principle of corruption by association.

Prison personnel are shown in some documents to behave towards criminals in a criminal manner. King Perseus (165 BC), 'after clinging to life for two years, ...offended the barbarians who were his guards, and was prevented from sleeping until he died of it'.[115] Suetonius relates that 'since ancient usage made it impious to strangle maidens, young girls were first violated by the executioner and then strangled'.[116] Rape was presumed by the Jewish sages when a Jewish woman was imprisoned on a capital charge.[117] Later Christian authors speak of that 'lowmindedness'[118] of prison personnel which led to calculated neglect and abuse of prisoners and of keepers' actions coming from their being 'aroused and filled with the Devil'.[119]

Finally, hostility and abuse were often engendered by the overseer's lust for material gain. This was not because prison personnel were not remunerated for their services: slave and free personnel employed by the State were paid—whether in cash or in kind—out of the public coffers in both the Greek and Roman contexts. If Plato's comments concerning the Law-Wardens of the Σωφρονιστήριον can be generalized to the Eleven, the annual salary for the latter was 365 *drachmae*; one *drachma* a day.[120] It is difficult to decide whether the 12 *drachmae* insisted upon by the chief jailer of the Athenian State prison for mixing up the proper weight of hemlock for Phocion (318 BC) was a legitimate fee or simply the customary perquisite. In any event, the public slave did not budge until he got his cash.[121]

The Roman legionary forces received a basic rate of pay;[122] NCOs such as the prison director received more because of their greater responsibility.[123] The pay of praetorian guards was usually much higher; that of the urban cohorts less.[124] The watchmen quickly came to match the praetorian and urban cohort pay-scales; auxiliary forces' pay varied considerably, depending upon circumstances and favour but it was generally less than that of the legionaries.[125]

---

[115]Diodorus Siculus 31.9.5.
[116]Suetonius, *Tib.* 61.5. *Cf.* Dio Cassius 58.11.5.
[117]*b. Nez.* VII: *'Abod. Zar.* 23*a*.
[118]Tertullian, *De Ieiun.* 12.
[119]*Mart. Let. Lyons & Vienne* 27f. Further, *Mart. Pion.* 18.10.
[120]Krauss, *Im Kerker*, 50 in his discussion of Plato, *de Legib.* 10.980.A.
[121]Plutarch, *Phoc.* 36.3f.
[122]Watson, *The Roman Soldier*, 90f., on the rates of pay at different periods.
[123]*Ibid.*, 92.
[124]*Ibid.*, 97f., on the rates.
[125]*Ibid.*, 99-101.

Despite their pay—which was in some cases generous—records reveal that there was trouble with extortion and bribery. Prison personnel sold acts of benevolence or restraint from acts of violence. There was traffic in access to prisoners, swift production in court, ease from chains, ease from harsh confinement in dark places, access to (quality) food and drink, a swift and painless execution for those 'on death row', or even escape.[126] Prison personnel might be bribed by accusers to confine their opponents at law more harshly or even to cause their death[127] and when they died, their possessions were not immune from pilferage by prison personnel.[128]

Lopuszanski writes that corruption was inherent in every police organization in the Imperial period.[129] Its prevalence in the Roman armed forces sprang in part from official permission given centurions to sell furloughs. Tacitus describes the resulting distress of such officially-sanctioned corruption about the year 69 AD:

> The troops also demanded that the payments usually made to centurions to secure furloughs should be abolished, since they amounted to an annual tax on the common soldiers. A quarter of each company would be away on furlough or loafing about the camp itself, provided the soldiers paid the centurion his price, and no one cared how the burden pressed on the soldiers or how they got their money; in reality it was through highway robbery, petty thieving, and by menial occupations that the soldiers purchased rest from military service. Moreover the richest soldiers would be cruelly assigned to the most fatiguing labour until they bought relief.[130]

Such problems must have filtered down to that part of the civilian population who were unfortunate enough to wind up in prison. *Concussio*, meaning extortion with all its negative connotations, appears in the

---

[126]Cicero, *Verr.* 2.5.118 (70 BC); Lucian, *Tox.* 31 (163 AD); *Mart. Perp. & Felic.* 3.4-9 (203 AD); *Mart. Cyp.* 5.4 (257/8 AD); *Dig.* 48.3.8 (2nd/3rd cent. AD); *Cod. Theod.* 8.15.3 (364 AD); 9.2.3 (380 AD); 9.3.1 (320 AD; ≈ *Cod. Just.* 9.4.1); 9.3.6 (380 AD); 9.40.5 (364); *Apocr. Acts Thom.* 118, 151 (*c.* 250 AD); *Apocr. Acts Paul* 17f. (185-95 AD). Cf. *Mart. Pion.* 11.3-7 (249/51 AD). Further, A. Deissmann, *St. Paul: A Study in Social and Religious History,* 47f. n. 2, citing P*Petrie* 35a, b; 36a.

[127]E.g., *Cod. Theod.* 9.3.1 (320 AD; ≈ *Cod. Just.* 9.4.1); B. Baldwin, 'Crime and Criminals in Graeco-Roman Egypt', *Aeg* 43 (1963), 258f. citing P*Karan.* 421.

[128]See *Dig.* 48.20.6; 48.21.3.7. Cf. further Mark 15:24; Matt. 27:35; Luke 23:34; John 19:23f.; *Mart. Max.* 3.3; and *Mart. Pion.* 21.1.

[129]Lopuszanski, 'La Police romaine', 16.

[130]Tacitus, *Hist.* 1.46. On 'gifts' (*sportulae*) in 4th century AD Antioch, see Liebeschuetz, *Antioch,* 50 and n. 9.

prison literature;[131] but so too do words which suggest a pragmatic attitude by those who had to pay. In the *Apostolic Constitutions* all Christians are encouraged to contribute to the support of prisoners and to pay bribes for their guards, the bribes being called 'the soldiers' wages'![132] The benefits of such behaviour could be considerable; the risks, despite legislation to curb it, appear to have been worth chancing.

3. Paul and His Keepers in Acts

There is a tendency among some modern commentators to understand from Luke's record of the events at the Philippian jail, the city's status as a veteran colony, and the fact that soldiers did serve in prison systems, that the Philippian jailer was, if not a serving military person perhaps of centurial rank, then certainly a retired soldier.[133] It is further argued that he was a Roman citizen.[134]

For several reasons, however, the above picture must be questioned. First, the province of Macedonia had been from 14 AD a demilitarized province with only small units and individual soldiers detached to administrative and security responsibilities.[135] Josephus clearly indicates the administrative arrangements; the province was subservient to a proconsul having six lictors to enforce his will.[136] Second, Peterlin has argued that a retired soldier, particularly one from the higher ranks, would hardly have found such a position desirable.

---

[131]Tertullian, *De Fuga* 12; *Mart. Perp. & Felic.* 3.6. For a discussion of this term and the words διασεσμός/διασείω (*cf.* Luke 3:14), see Lopuszanski, 'La Police romaine', 6f., 16f., 38; LSJ, 411.

[132]Cited in Lopuszanski, 'La Police romaine', 39. LSJ, 1136 renders the term used here with the positive expression 'payment of wages, recompense'. *Cf.* Heb. 2:2; 10:35.

[133]A serving soldier: R.B. Rackham, *The Acts*, 288; W. Neil, *The Acts*, 184. A pensioned soldier: G.A. Krodel, *Acts*, 311; R.N. Longenecker, 'The Acts of the Apostles', 464; F.F. Bruce, *The Book of the Acts*, 315; V. Brannick, *The House Church in the Writings of Paul* (Wilmington, Delaware: Michael Glazier, 1989), 62.

[134]So, e.g., Krodel, *Acts*, 311.

[135]R.K. Sherk cited in D. Peterlin, *Paul's Letter to the Philippians in the Light of Discord in the Church* (University of Aberdeen: Unpublished PhD. Dissertation, 1992), *ad loc.* For sources on the province's passage into and out of senatorial administration, *cf.* E.B. James, 'Macedonia', *DGRG*, vol. 2, 236; B. Reicke, *The New Testament Era: The World of the Bible from 500 BC to AD 100*, tr. D.E. Green (Philadelphia: Fortress, 1968), 231.

[136]Josephus, *BJ* 2.365 [2.16.4]. *Cf. supra*, 248-50 and Cyprian, *Ep.* 15.2 [Oxf., *Ep.* 37] on the twelve *fasces* of magistrates, consuls and proconsuls.

Probably possessing a significant lump sum military pension, he would have avoided such a servile occupation and sought more lucrative and honourable pursuits.[137] Veterans, however, could struggle more than Peterlin allows; their prospects on retirement were not universally favourable: Burn found, for example, that retired veterans in Roman Africa and the Danubian provinces lived 'at some sub-standard level midway between that of free citizens and slaves, in a twilight zone of second-class citizenry'.[138] Having said this, the sensibilities that Peterlin notes—whether we are speaking of a citizen veteran, the scion of a veteran or even a free man—would probably have kept him from such an occupation. Philippi's founding as a veteran settlement, moreover, hardly requires that the jailer be a veteran. The great settlements had occurred nearly a century before.[139] Veterans could have charge of prisons, but these were re-enlisted veterans on continuing service;[140] this hardly supports the commentators' case.

More likely, the Philippian jailer was a public slave. It was noted above that in civilian contexts—excluding the quasi-military arrangements for Rome—prison personnel were commonly slaves owned by the State.[141] First, while there is no specific indication of the slave office of δεσμοφύλαξ in available extra-biblical sources for Philippi, the record attests to the significant presence of public slaves in the Philippian civic structure.[142] Second, the details of the text of Acts argue strongly that we have a typical and wholly civilian administrative context. By analogy to their provincial superior the Macedonian governor and the civilian magistrates at Rome, the Philippian civilian magistrates [duouiri] carried the administrative responsibility for malefactors and prisons.[143] Like their superiors the Macedonian governor and the civilian magistrates at Rome, they had lictors through whom they enforced their juridical will. The chain-of-command downward is also clear from Luke's account: i.e., magistrates -> lictors -> jailer -> servants. The magistrates commanded the punitive action against the apostles: the lictors[144] carried it out. Whether directly or through lic-

[137]D. Peterlin, *Paul's Letter to the Philippians in the Light of Discord in the Church.* (University of Aberdeen: Unpublished PhD. Dissertation, 1992) *ad loc.*
[138]Cited in Watson, *The Roman Soldier,* 151f.
[139]*Supra,* 116, 119f.
[140]*Supra,* 253.
[141]*Supra,* 244-50. Cf. also Peterlin, *Paul's Letter to the Philippians, ad loc.*
[142]Peterlin, *Paul's Letter to the Philippians, ad loc.*
[143]*Dig.* 47.2.52.12.
[144]*Supra,* 125 n.57.

tors, the jailer was commanded to keep the apostles securely (Acts 16:22-24). In the morning, the lictors, with orders from the magistrates, authorized the jailer to release Paul and Silas (Acts 16:35f.). The lictors were, like their counterparts in Rome, but apparently unlike the lictor Sextius in Sicily, only occasional to the prison from an administrative standpoint and evidently did not relate to anyone in the prison lower than the jailer. Against Peterlin, we need not blanch at calling the jailer the 'governor' or 'chief guardian' of the prison.[145] Though Luke calls him the 'jailer' [δεσμοφύλαξ: Acts 16:23, 27, 36] rather than some other title (e.g., chief jailer), he is certainly more than a mere guard or door-keeper. The jailer has sole responsibility for running the prison and seeing to its security and he has slave underlings who do his bidding (viz., Acts 16:29). Apart from lacking the authority to carry out executions, the Philippian jailer compares closely with the chief 'assistants' in the Athenian and Spartan context. His is a senior civic post which puts him above many of his slave peers. Indications of wealth and standing in the text (e.g., references at Acts 16:31-33 to his 'household' which may have included slaves, and to his 'house') are not at all problematic.

Before the earthquake relations between the Philippian jailer and his prisoners were not cordial. The instructions of the magistrates are that Paul and Silas be kept securely (Acts 16:23). The jailer places the apostles in the inner cell and locks their feet in stocks. Both forms of restraint, as has earlier been indicated, may be considered punitive, the expression of official hostility. So too might the jailer's disregard for their severe injuries and their need for physical sustenance.

The jailer would have known why the apostles had been incarcerated. As in other such urban institutions, the Philippian prison would have possessed a log [ratio carceris or commentarium] of all prisoners and their crimes. Even if the jailer had not been present at the trial, which seems likely,[146] he would nevertheless have known from the prison log that Paul and Silas had been punished for the crimes of fomenting civil unrest and threatening the ancient customs of the Ro-

---

[145]Peterlin, Paul's Letter to the Philippians, ad loc. So designated by Rackham, The Acts, 288; Haenchen, The Acts, 498; Krodel, Acts, 311.

[146]Pace F.F. Bruce, The Acts of the Apostles. The Greek Text with Introduction and Commentary (1951; Grand Rapids: Eerdmans, 1990), 362; A. Wikenhauser, Die Apostelgeschichte (RNT 5; 4th ed.; Regensburg: Friedrich Pustet, 1961), 190; I.H. Marshall, The Acts of the Apostles (TNTC 5; Grand Rapids: Eerdmans, 1980), 272; K. Lake and H.J. Cadbury, The Acts of the Apostles: English Translation and Commentary, in BC, vol. 4, 199.

mans by promulgating atheistic and misanthropic Jewish ἔθη. Nothing would have been entered concerning Paul's and Silas' Roman citizenship—it had not yet, as we have earlier argued, been divulged. All the jailer knew was that these were low status Jewish criminals deserving no special treatment.

The jailer's cry, 'Sirs, what must I do to be saved?' (lit.: Acts 16:30) adds conviction to the view that the jailer had not simply kept the apostles but had in fact abused them. It is true that his question does lend itself well to Paul's distinctively Christian response,[147] but it may just as easily be the expression of Gentile religious sensitivity to the numinous. Such religious terror reflects his perception that his abuses had aroused the ire of the apostles' god.[148] After the pattern of other jailers noted above, the Philippian jailer may initially have thought that he was honouring Roman custom and his own deities by abusing his charges.

If the rest of the prisoners were kept with the apostles, as has been argued, the Philippian jailer was also guilty of causing a more general suffering. The Western addition to Acts 16:30 that the jailer 'secured the rest' (τοὺς λοιποὺς ἀσφαλισάμενος) of the prisoners before dealing with the apostles is probably not original. Ramsay indicates that it may accurately reflect the picture of an 'orderly, well-disciplined character'.[149] Metzger offers, however, what he calls 'the great probability ... that after an earthquake the average Near Eastern jailer was hardly likely to exhibit such a degree of discipline'.[150] If one must choose between the two characterizations, Ramsay's and the Western glossator's carry the greater conviction. The earthquake and the jailer's subsequent conversion would hardly have made him as careless, forgetful and soft toward the other prisoners as Metzger portrays! The jailer undergoes a conversion which radically alters how he treats Paul and Silas. This will be discussed at length below.[151]

Paul's treatment at the hands of his soldier keepers in the early period of his arrest in Jerusalem was harsh; he was clapped in irons and bodily carried up the steps leading to the Fortress Antonia. His

---

[147]Not a reason automatically to designate it a later Christian reformulation. See Conzelmann, *Acts of the Apostles*, 133; Lake and Cadbury, *BC*, vol. 4, 199.

[148]E.g., Neil, *The Acts*, 185. L. Schmitz, 'Poseidon', *DGRBM*, vol. 3, 506 on earthquake and the gods.

[149]W.M. Ramsay, *St. Paul the Traveller*, 222.

[150]B.M. Metzger *et al.*, *A Textual Commentary on the Greek New Testament* (New York: UBS, 1971), 449.

[151] *Infra*, 390-92; *cf. supra*, 214-15.

treatment reaches its lowest point as he is stretched out for inquisitorial torture. This job was probably given to a specific group of soldiers whose task it was to conduct such gruesome interrogations; i.e., to those minor grade NCO's designated 'torturers' (*quaestionarii*).[152] The centurion standing nearby (Acts 22:25) is almost certainly not a casual bystander but probably the senior officer commanded to supervise and formally audit the inquiry. His response to Paul's subtle eleventh hour citizenship disclosure shows an awareness of the potentially devastating consequences that might befall his superior. By interrupting proceedings, he puts the Tribune Lysias significantly in his debt.

Paul's custodial circumstances change quite remarkably once he discloses his Roman citizenship. His lightened custody is the measure of the Tribune's embarrassment and fear at being utterly compromised. It would be seriously incorrect, however, to assert that henceforth relations between the prisoner and his keepers were amicable. This becomes plain in the account concerning Paul's nephew, the style of which Conzelmann has incorrectly described as peaceful and idyllic, containing details which are expanded for their own sake.[153] In fact, considerable tension is discernable. When told of the plot against his life, Paul calls one of the centurions in the officers' barracks and asks him to take the young messenger to the Tribune. Paul was, in virtue of his late citizen disclosure and its potentially damaging consequences to the Tribune, granted both a lighter treatment and the freedom to make reasonable requests. Some, on the basis of the imperative at Acts 23:17, infer that Paul could snap his fingers and centurions did his bidding.[154] But the verb 'asked' on the lips of the centurion (Acts 23:18) contradicts this inference and neither 'he said' (Acts 23:17) nor 'calling to' [προσκαλεσάμενος: Acts 23:17f.] can be said to support it. The imperative is better construed as an urgent request rather than a command.[155]

Furthermore, Paul does not identify his nephew or pass the information along the chain of command, but intimates to the centurion only that this is 'a lad' who 'has something to tell' the Tribune (Acts 23:17). Such secrecy reveals two things; most obviously, the information was of a highly sensitive nature; but more importantly, Paul did not trust a centurion or any other person in the Fortress apart from his nephew to convey it. Recalling that there were serious problems with

---

[152]*Supra*, 253.
[153]Conzelmann, *Acts*, 194.
[154]E.g., Haenchen, *The Acts*, 646.
[155]So Marshall, *The Acts*, 368.

corruption in every police organization in the Imperial period, it hardly strains the imagination to see in the information brought by Paul's nephew a virtual gold mine for anyone who leaked it to the right parties. Paul acts in such a way as to suggest that, despite considerations extended, the Fortress was still a hostile and potentially life-threatening place.

The Tribune's behaviour betrays the same concern. He takes the lad aside and interviews him out of earshot of other military personnel (Acts 23:19) and sternly cautions him not to tell *anyone* (Acts 23:22). Finally, he makes arrangements hastily to convey Paul to Caesarea (Acts 23:23f., 31-35). Surely in these actions the Tribune must have been concerned that his prisoner's security not be compromised either from without the Fortress or from within. Ehrhardt's comment captures well the character of Paul's Jerusalem sojourn:

> It was by no means a pleasure to be a prisoner of a Roman army unit; and those who see St Luke as an admirer of Rome on account of this description of St Paul's treatment, might reasonably be asked to do a spell of protective custody even under modern conditions.[156]

We have argued that Felix was at first unimpressed by Paul and that Paul was, in consequence, treated as 'just another prisoner'. After the judicial enquiry, Felix orders a less severe custody for Paul. He is to be kept in the personal care of a centurion—perhaps an officer of the headquarters staff—rather than a lower-ranking soldier or, for that matter, in the general care of the military prison system. The centurion is commanded to give Paul some freedom which, when negatively stated, amounts to something like a command not to guard Paul so closely that he is utterly dependent upon the centurion and his co-watchers to sanction or approve his every activity. Paul is additionally sheltered from the vagaries and debilities of the military prison system when the centurion is further commanded to hinder none of his friends from seeing to his needs. These new custodial arrangements express more of Felix' political astuteness and personal venality than any higher esteem he may now have for Paul. The venue, we have argued, probably continued to be the residence of Herod.

The fact of Paul's being a Jew in a Roman prison and in the care of non-Jewish military personnel in Caesarea—recall also the earlier military custody in Jerusalem—has not heretofore been noted. It is rel-

---

[156]A. Ehrhardt, *The Acts of the Apostles: Ten Lectures* (Manchester: MUP, 1969), 112.

evant to a proper understanding of the nature and quality of staff-inmate relations. Broughton writes that

> legionary soldiers were not regularly used in Judaea unless on special occasions. It is true that a legion was stationed at Jerusalem to keep order while the succession to Herod was being decided, and that the legions could always be called upon in case of need.[157]

By and large, however, prefects or procurators administered auxiliary forces which were locally levied and non-Roman in character. Soldiers 'were drawn, for the most part, from the inhabitants of Palestinian pagan cities, particularly Caesarea and Sebaste. The rest were supplied by Roman Syria'.[158] They were responsible to Roman officers.[159]

The populations from which these troops came were, as we have seen, generally hostile toward the Jews and particularly so in Caesarea.[160] Anti-Semitic feeling was often both heightened and acted out by the military when policing the Jewish population or enforcing unpopular Roman policies; bloodshed and suffering occurred on both sides, as the examples illustrate.[161] Luke may be short on detail in his description of Paul's Caesarean custody; the above context permits some scope for restrained inference. In the harsh earlier phase of the Caesarean imprisonment, and despite the concessions granted in the later phase, we dare not idealize the prisoner apostle's relations with his military keepers. There must have been at the least a climate of hostility, whether it found opportunity for expression or not. Recall that the Jewish prince Agrippa, despite concessions granted in the manner of his keeping from individuals at the highest official level, had to behave with utmost circumspection in the general camp environment; He even suffered at the hands of his 'humane' keepers at one point.

When it was decided that Paul should be sent on to Rome, he 'and some other prisoners were handed over to a centurion named Julius, who belonged to the Imperial Regiment' (Acts 27:1). Julius had a

---

[157]T.R.S. Broughton, 'Note 33. The Roman Army', in *BC*, vol. 5, 439 with a view to Josephus, *AJ* 19.360-66 [19.9.2].

[158]L.I. Levine, *Caesarea Under Roman Rule* (Studies in Judaism in Late Antiquity, 7; Leiden: E.J. Brill, 1975), 20.

[159]H.J. Cadbury, 'Note 26. Roman Law and the Trial of Paul', in *BC*, vol. 5, 300.

[160]*Supra*, 169f.

[161]*Cf.*, e.g., Josephus, *BJ*, 1.52 [2.3.4], 58, 63 [2.4.2f.] (≈ *AJ* 17.266 [17.10.3], 278-84 [17.10.7]); 1.547-50 [1.27.5f.] (≈ *AJ* 16.373-94 [16.11.4-7]); 2.172-74 [2.9.3] (≈ *AJ* 18.55-59 [18.3.1]); 2.223-27 [2.12.1]); 2.228-31 [2.12.2] (≈ *AJ* 20.113-17 [20.5.4]); 2.268 [2.13.7]). *Cf. ibid.*, *AJ passim*.

detail of soldiers to assist him (Acts 27:31f., 42). The search for greater precision in identifying this Julius has yielded three possibilities. Convinced that a prisoner as important as Paul would hardly have been delivered to the care of a centurion from an auxiliary cohort, the Greek phrase σπεῖρα Σεβαστή at Acts 27:1 is rendered 'troop of the Emperor' by some.[162] In addition to the problems already noted regarding the late date of the founding of the *castra peregrinorum*, whether forces quartered there were used for policing/prisoner transport or even existed in the time of Paul's troubles and the obviously interpretative character of MS *gigas*,[163] Broughton points out that 'no *cohors Caesariensium* is known'.[164] This is also admitted by Ramsay, who calls the expression 'a popular colloquial way of describing the corps of officer-couriers'.[165] But is Luke unaware of the proper military terminology?

It has been suggested that σπεῖρα Σεβαστή renders the Latin *cohors Sebastenorum* and that Julius is connected with certain Samaritan troops whom we read about in Josephus.[166] For this to be correct, it must be assumed that Luke is guilty of corrupting or at least shortening the designation because the Greek should read Σεβαστηνῶν and not Σεβαστή, a point not supported by any variants in the textual tradition. Moreover, σπεῖρα Σεβαστή is a rather exact translation of *cohors Augusta* as the Vulgate clearly shows.[167]

Lopuszanski notes that many cohorts bore next to their official name an honorific *cognomen*; for example, the *cohors I Thracum* which carried the epithet *Augusta*. But if this is the case with the troop in question its identification is virtually impossible and the appellation, which is incorrect and ambiguous, betrays the author of Acts as ignorant of the customary military terminology of reference.[168] This is but one of two possibilities. Lopuszanski offers the second when he ventures that the creation of auxiliary units by the emperor Augustus might result in

---

[162]See Ramsay, *St. Paul the Traveller*, 314f. *Cf.* Haenchen, *The Acts*, 697; Broughton, 'The Roman Army', 443f.; A.W.F. Blunt, *The Acts of the Apostles in the Revised Version* (Clarendon Bible 4; Oxford: Clarendon, 1922), 250; G.H.C. Macgregor and T.P. Ferris, *The Acts of the Apostles* in *IB*, vol. 9, 332.

[163]For those holding to this interpretation, *cf. supra*, 174-77.

[164]Broughton, 'The Roman Army', 440.

[165]Ramsay, *St. Paul the Traveller*, 315.

[166]Josephus, *BJ* 2.236 [2.12.5], who notes a cavalry troop καλουμένην Σεβαστηνῶν.

[167]D.B. Saddington, *The Development of the Roman Auxiliary Forces from Caesar to Vespasian (49 BC-AD 79)* (Harare: University of Zimbabwe, 1982), 51.

[168]Lopuszanski, 'La Police romaine', 31. The identification of *Augusta* here in Acts as an honorific title is asserted, e.g., in Conzelmann, *Acts*, 215; Haenchen, *The Acts*, 697; Wikenhauser, *Die Apostelgeschichte*, 274.

the conferral of *Augusta* as official rather than honorific title.[169] Saddington, in his recent work on the development of the Roman auxiliary forces, asserts just such a dual pattern.[170] Epigraphic evidence argues the greater likelihood of both the second possibility and its validity in explaining the designation in Acts. We find a *cohors I Augusta* levied from the Syrian population and located in Syria during the time of Quirinius (6 AD); no further titulary indications are given.[171] We also find a reference to a prefect 'of the Augustan cohort (σπείρης Αὐ[γουστῆς...)' stationed in Batanaea east of Galilee some time during the reign of Herod Agrippa II (*c.* 50-100 AD);[172] again, only the bare designation. Saddington asserts that 'the Coh. Augusta of Acts (under Nero) and the Ala Augusta of the Claudian period and the Coh. Augusta I of the Augustan period may be compared'.[173] It is a safe conclusion that Luke's identification (must we fault him for 'missing' the *numerus*, a small point if there was but one *cohors Augusta* in the vicinity?) is historically sound and sufficient for his readers.

Most soldiers in auxiliary cohorts could only hope to obtain the citizen franchise on completion of their military service. Sherwin-White points out that this could be true even for centurions.[174] He continues, however, that Julius was, in all likelihood, an older man who already possessed the Roman citizenship:

> There was good reason why an enfranchised man should prefer to be known by his *nomen* alone. It indicated and to a certain extent guaranteed his citizen status, whereas a Latin *praenomen cognomen* might be used by anybody. There is a certain formality in the use of the *nomen*.[175]

Recall as well that Claudius made it a capital offence to use the *nomen gentile* if one did not actually possess the franchise.[176] Julius is a *nomen*

---

[169]Lopuszanski, 'La Police romaine', 32.

[170]See Saddington, *The Development of the Roman Auxiliary Forces*, 173, his discussion on 'personal' regiments (*ibid.*, 147ff.), and supposed 'wrinkles' in the thesis (*ibid.*, 171-73).

[171]*ILS* 1:2683 and Saddington, *The Development of the Roman Auxiliary Forces*, 57 for discussion.

[172]*OGIS* 421 quoted in Conzelmann, *Acts*, 215. *Cf. CIL* 6:3508 cited in Broughton, 'The Roman Army', 443 and Bruce, *The Acts of the Apostles*, 511, where a *Cohors III Augusta* is indicated in Rome.

[173]Saddington, *The Development of the Roman Auxiliary Forces*, 137.

[174]A.N. Sherwin-White, *Roman Society and Roman Law in the New Testament* (Sarum Lectures 1961/2; Oxford: Clarendon, 1963), 160.

[175]*Ibid.*, 161.

gentile. Protests aside,[177] there could hardly be a better choice for supervising the transport of Paul and the others to Rome than a high ranking auxiliary soldier who also possessed citizenship. The soldiers under his command—who were almost certainly not themselves citizens—would have been chosen for proven discipline and general reliability. Whether these were regulars or NCOs we can only guess, though it would seem wasteful to send a detachment of NCOs on such an extended mission.

Luke is concerned, early in his account of the journey to Rome, to show that Julius treated Paul with some civility. Prisoners might suffer hunger and dehydration through the neglect of their keepers aboard ship, as we have seen. While berthed in Sidon, however, Julius permitted Paul to go to his friends to be materially provisioned for the extended journey. This permission, Luke indicates to his reader, was 'in kindness to Paul' (φιλανθρώπως: Acts 27:3). How Julius knew that Paul had friends in Sidon the text does not say; he may have asked Paul or he may have been petitioned. In any event, Paul is permitted to see his friends, but probably under the watchful eye of a soldier.[178]

Confinement below decks could also be the lot of prisoners transported by sea as we have discovered. The text suggests that this was not Paul's experience; he appears to have spent the journey above decks. These conditions too were in Julius' power to grant or deny and may be interpreted as an additional token of his kindness, though the text is silent on the point. We are only told that Julius was disposed to treat Paul kindly, not why. The reason might relate to Julius' appreciation that, for all the profound differences between them, on the point of Roman citizenship at least, there was a kinship between Paul and himself. The impact of concerned friends who were ready to go with him to Rome also should not be discounted.[179]

At the point of shipwreck, Luke records: 'The soldiers planned to kill the prisoners to prevent any of them from swimming away and escaping. But the centurion wanted to spare Paul's life and kept them from carrying out their plan' (Acts 27:42f.). The reader is encouraged to understand that the earlier favourable disposition of the centurion

---

[176]Suetonius, *Claud.* 25.3. Further on Roman names and the citizenship, *supra*, 84-86.

[177]We may single out Lentz, *Luke's Portrait of Paul*, 333.

[178]So Tajra, *The Trial of St. Paul*, 174; Williams, *Acts*, 429; Haenchen, *The Acts*, 698f.; Marshall, *The Acts*, 404; R. Pesch, *Die Apostelgeschichte* (EKKNT 5; Zurich: Benziger, 1986), vol. 2, 289.

[179]On Paul's travel companions, *cf. infra*, 372-78.

has undergone some development. Julius' regard for and concessions to Paul, however, did not initially extend to the acceptance of advice. He was unimpressed by Paul's pronouncements concerning the dangers of journeying from Fair Havens to Phoenix—he was more persuaded by the nautical experts (Acts 27:10f.). But eventually, Paul's continued pronouncements and warnings, the conviction and authority with which he delivered them and their prescient character as discovered in the unfolding events, apparently impressed Julius sufficiently that he acted upon Paul's counsel (Acts 27:31-38). Unlike the keepers observed above whose superstition and religion resulted in their harming inmates in their care, Julius' religious cipherings led him to protect Paul, a man clearly in close touch with his deity.[180]

Nothing is said of arrangements in the provisioning and keeping of the other prisoners on the way to Rome. It would be wrong to assume positive relations. Rather, several negative inferences arise from Luke's comment that it was out of a desire to save Paul that the centurion prevented the soldiers from killing the prisoners. First is the intention of the soldiers to kill the prisoners. The conditions of storm and shipwreck might excuse the soldiers of personal liability had any of their charges escaped. However, mitigating circumstances would have had to be successfully pleaded and if they failed to convince, punishment might well have fallen heavily upon their heads.[181] Capital punishment was a serious prospect if the soldiers were deemed derelict, especially if the prisoners had been convicted of capital crimes. Ruthless as killing the prisoners might have seemed, it may have been the more prudent and legally defensible course, particularly if ratified by a superior. Altruism and sympathy for prisoners clearly did not figure in the soldiers' deliberations.

Second, the death of all the prisoners—Paul included—was contemplated. The action, if sanctioned, would have been carried out irrespective of prisoner status or charges and without regard to whether the prisoner was a convict or simply on remand. This suggests that, while the soldiers had heard Paul address them on several occasions during the voyage and even followed his directions, they seem not to have been impressed by him as the centurion was.

Finally, all the prisoners were preserved because the centurion wished to save Paul. Had Paul not so impressed him, the centurion

---

[180]Cf. R.P.C. Hanson, *The Acts* (New Clarendon Bible; Oxford: Clarendon, 1967), 251.

[181]On the conditions of escape where guards were or were not punished, *cf. supra,* 30-31.

would have felt no compunction about sanctioning the slaughter of all
the prisoners. At the least, this implies an ambivalent attitude on the
part of the centurion toward the other prisoners.[182]

Responsibility for the transport and billeting of the prisoners and
military escorts would have fallen to the centurion and it is virtually
certain that he did this by means of requisition. In his analysis of a recently discovered inscription from the region of Sagalassos (Pisidia)
dated 18/9 AD, E.A. Judge writes that the edict

> sets out a basic pattern for the transport system which affected all
> travellers in NT times. Local communities were collectively responsi-
> ble for the transport and billeting services that were required by offi-
> cial personnel passing through their territory.[183]

The inscription limits the number of donkeys, mules and carts, and establishes the rates of hire to be paid by officials of various ranks. Similar services were also provided 'to those on military service, or who
hold a certificate [Lat.: *diplomum*], and to those who are travelling from
other provinces on military service'.[184] Among military persons, a centurion is granted the power to requisition 'a cart or three mules or six
donkeys'[185] at the minimum rate of hire. The edict concludes:

> Accommodation for all those who belong to my staff and for those on
> military service from all provinces and for the freedmen and slaves of
> the excellent leader (*Gk.* the Augustus) and their beasts ought to be
> supplied free, but without their demanding the rest (of their costs)
> free from those who are unwilling (to supply them).[186]

A *diploma* of entitlement itself, coming from Judaea, might not have
carried great authority. But Julius probably had no need of such. His
military rank as a centurion and the character of his party, under such
provisions as those of the edict noted above, would by themselves
have qualified him to requisition. Mitchell remarks that 'centurions,

---

[182]So Marshall, *The Acts*, 415; R.J. Knowling, *The Acts of the Apostles*, ed. W.R. Nicoll
(Expositor's Greek Testament 2; 1901; rpt. Grand Rapids: Eerdmans, 1983), 536.
This last observation damages the interpretation of B.H.M. Hermesdorf, 'Paulus
Vinctus', *StudCath* 29 (1954), 129.

[183]*New Docs.* vol. 1, #9, 42.

[184]*Ibid.*, *ll*.16f. *Cf.* S. Mitchell, 'Requisitioned Transport in the Roman Empire: A
New Inscription from Pisidia', *JRS* 66 (1976), 109, whose translation contemplates
only two groups.

[185]*New Docs.* vol. 1, #9, *l.* 21.

[186]*Ibid. l.* 23-25. Further on terminology, Mitchell, 'Requisitioned Transport', 127.

unless they were absconding, would also always be acting in state
service, either detached for a special mission or simply passing
through to join another unit'.[187]

Julius would have booked passage and perhaps secured food on
various ships (Acts 27:2, 6; 28:11) based upon his official entitlement.[188] Following three days of hospitality in the villa of the local
magistrate Publius (Acts 28:7),[189] the burden of housing and feeding
Julius, his soldiers and the prisoners would probably have fallen to
various members of the community.[190] The community apparently
embraced the demands of this three month long undertaking quite
cheerfully (Acts 28:10).

Difficulties are alleged in the commentaries relating to Paul's
stay with the Christians at Puteoli (Acts 28:14). The first pertains to the
prisoner's apparent freedom to seek out the Christians of the city and
accept their invitation irrespective of the centurion's agenda or prefer-
ence. Conzelmann writes that 'Paul's time was at his own disposal'
and Schille that Luke has lost Paul the prisoner from view.[191] The first
person plural aspect of the text, however, downplays the Pauline initiative; Luke and Aristarchus may have sought out and interacted with
the local Christians. It still appears, though, that accommodation arrangements were in the hands of Paul and his two companions rather
than the centurion. Second, the duration of the party's stay in Puteoli
has occasioned modern doubts regarding the account's historicity.
While a continuation and even growth in the centurion's positive attitude toward Paul (Acts 27:3, 43) is frequently given as an explanation
for the stay with Christians in Puteoli,[192] its seven day duration has
been thought to require further comment. Looking back to the sea journey, Hemer suggests that 'perhaps the element of pressure and desper-

---

[187]Mitchell, 'Requisitioned Transport', 126. Further, B.M. Rapske, 'Acts, Travel
and Shipwreck', 18-21.

[188]See Judge in *New Docs.* vol. 1, #9, 44.

[189]It seems difficult to maintain that Publius was officially bound by the same demands of requisition.

[190]F. Millar, 'The World of the *Golden Ass*', *JRS* 71 (1981), 68, notes that 'the right
not to be forced to accept official travellers was an exceptional privilege'.

[191]Conzelmann, *Acts*, 224; Schille, *Die Apostelgeschichte*, 474 respectively. *Cf.* C.J.
Hemer, *The Book of Acts in the Setting of Hellenistic History*, ed. C.H. Gempf (WUNT
49; Tübingen: J.C.B. Mohr/Paul Siebeck, 1989), 156; Longenecker, 'The Acts', 567;
Neil, *The Acts*, 256; Wikenhauser, *Die Apostelgeschichte*, 285 who note this same concern.

[192]E.g., Stählin, *Die Apostelgeschichte*, 324; Longenecker, 'The Acts', 567; Neil, *The
Acts*, 256; Macgregor and Ferris, *The Acts*, 345.

ation had been taken out of the journey with the safe arrival on Italian soil, and the soldiers were given some leave ashore in the intervals of their duties'.[193] Bruce, looking forward, suggests that 'presumably Julius had business (perhaps in his capacity as *frumentarius* corn merchant) which detained him at Puteoli for a week';[194] others have suggested that 'the centurion had to go ahead to Rome to report the arrival of his party and receive instructions about where they were to be stowed, and then return to take charge of them again'.[195] But it is doubtful that the centurion was connected with the grain trade or that he had business in Puteoli. Against the other suggestion, 'the centurion required no other instructions than those he had received in Caesarea'.[196] Haenchen's conclusion, however, that Acts 28:14a must therefore be a Lukan literary device to allow for news of Paul's arrival to reach the Roman Christians seems premature.[197]

Additional observations regarding certain aspects of the practice of requisitioning travel and accommodation are helpful to the above discussion. Despite an ever greater concern to regulate and restrict the powers of requisition, the literature and epigraphic record abounds with instances of abuse of the system in every period. Requisition was 'the most important area of contact and conflict between state and subject in the Roman Empire', according to Millar, who continues:

> the tensions thus created are reflected in a long series of complaints on the one side and of pronouncements by governors and Emperors on the other. It is surely significant that in our documentary evidence from outside Egypt far more attention is given to this issue than to that of direct taxation in cash or kind.[198]

The evident material pressures and the hostility that was often felt toward officials who had to be billeted at cost to proprietors and private individuals would have made the centurion's responsibility for seeing to his party's needs along the way a generally tension-filled and unhappy one. Might not then the sincere offer of hospitality (Acts 28:14) to the entire party[199] from a Christian community (perhaps staying in

---

[193]Hemer, *The Book of Acts*, 156. So also Hanson, *The Acts*, 253; J.V. Bartlet, *The Acts* (Century Bible [NT] 5; Edinburgh: T.C. and E.C. Clark, 1901), 376.

[194]E.g., Bruce, *The Acts of the Apostles*, 535.

[195]E.g., Williams, *Acts*, 448; Hanson, *The Acts*, 253; Knowling, *The Acts*, 544.

[196]Haenchen, *The Acts*, 719. So also Marshall, *The Acts*, 419.

[197]Haenchen, *The Acts*, 719. Schille, *Die Apostelgeschichte*, 474f., too has problems with the authenticity of Acts 28:14b.

[198]Millar, 'The World', 67f.

the home of a wealthy Christian patron?) have been a quite welcome alternative? Recalling our earlier discussion of the generally poor quality of boarding houses and wayside inns which were the standard accommodation on the roads leading to Rome,[200] such an offer would have seemed even more attractive. The centurion's evident regard for Paul, while a matter of record for Luke, need not necessarily have been the pivotal motivation behind his permission for and sharing in a 'Christian' stopover in Puteoli; the venue and offer themselves may have been sufficient reasons. Ignatius' keepers too, without being impressed by either prisoners or helpers, nevertheless accepted the kindness and favour extended *en route* to Rome.[201] Ignatius' stay in Smyrna appears to have been long enough for him to write four quite extended epistles (*Eph., Mag., Trall., Rom.*) and to send and receive various ecclesiastical delegations. His greetings to the house of Tavia and to the wife of the Procurator (or Epitropus?) with her whole house and her children there may also suggest lodging and hospitality.[202] The same Christian room and board arrangements may have been on offer and accepted at Troas (*cf.* Acts 20:4-12) as the prison detail waited for sail to Neapolis.

Several things can be said of the duration of the stay in Puteoli beyond the general observation that warm hospitality often tempts its recipients to extend their stay. First, in the apocryphal *Acts of Peter* the road from Puteoli to Rome is described as rough and flinty, making significant demands upon its travellers.[203] One might quite legitimately, therefore, wish to steel oneself for the journey by a longer initial rest stop, particularly after a recent sea voyage punctuated in its latter stage by (shipboard?) stops of three days in Syracuse and a single day in Rhegium (Acts 28:12f.). This would hardly be judged an act of military dereliction. Second, travel to Rome using the facilities of the *cursus publicus* might encourage such delay. Casson presents here perhaps too rosy a picture when he writes:

> The traveller charged with government business, and hence with the facilities of the *cursus publicus* at his disposal, had few problems: he

---

[199]The 'we' of the text does not necessarily exclude the centurion, soldiers and other prisoners.

[200]*Supra,* 177-81, 228-36. L. Casson, *Travel in the Ancient World* (London: George Allen and Unwin, 1974), 176-218, describes such accommodation and indicates that private accommodation on offer was strongly preferred.

[201]Ignatius, *Rom.* 5.1.

[202]*Ibid., Smyr.* 13.2; *Pol.* 8.2. See nn. LCL on difficulties with the text.

[203]*Apocr. Acts Pet.* 2.6.

would present his *diploma* to the nearest authorized inn and be issued an appropriate conveyance. He would consult his handlist or map for the stopping places available along his route, and at these he would eat, sleep, and pick up changes of animals and equipment until he reached his destination.[204]

As one drew nearer to Rome, the demands upon the transport and billeting facilities would have become greater and more clearly priority-orientated. Consequently, the prospect of there being 'no room in the inns' on the way to Rome was quite real, particularly for a detail of soldiers from an outlying province with not a few prisoners in tow. This would argue powerfully not only for the desirability of accepting the private hospitality on offer but also, perhaps in anticipation of a dearth of *hospitium* on the road ahead, a tendency to linger. Moreover, Julius could well have had to wait in Puteoli for vehicular transport—if he was able to procure it at all—as he and his company were 'non-priority'[205] travellers.[206]

Indications of guard/prisoner relations in Rome can be found in the statements that Paul was permitted to live by himself with the soldier guarding him (Acts 28:16) and that he preached the kingdom of God and taught about the Lord Jesus Christ unhindered (Acts 28:31). In our discussion of the custody to which Paul was assigned in Rome,[207] comments relevant to the present discussion were made which may briefly be reiterated here. Among the many indications that Paul had been assigned to a remarkably loose type of custody in Rome was the fact that he was chained to but a single soldier guard who permitted friends and interested strangers considerable freedom of access during the daylight hours. That such liberal access was not an expression of each soldier's generous and humane spirit toward Paul but had been commanded is probably reflected in the pre-eminently legal term 'unhindered' [ἀκωλύτως]; hence our description of the freedoms granted as reflecting 'official benignity'. This is not, however, to assert that the various soldiers assigned to Paul were unwilling to be or incapable of being impressed by the character or message of their prisoner.

---

[204]Casson, *Travel*, 188. He notes the possibility of pressure on the system when he indicates that 'private voyagers were officially barred from the *cursus publicus*, but, human nature being what it is, exceptions were inevitable'.

[205]See in this regard Frend, 'A Third-Century Inscription', 54.

[206]The reader is directed to our previous comments on prospective stopover and provisioning prospects for the remaining route to Rome, *supra*, 206.

[207]*Supra*, 177-82.

II. Prison Inmates

Having considered Graeco-Roman prison administrations and keeper-inmate relations and comparing these with Paul's own circumstances, we turn briefly to the matter of inmate relations in the ancient context and in the experience of Paul in Acts. As was the case in the above discussion, so too in this matter, considerable variability occurs.

1. Inmate Relations in the Extrabiblical Sources

In some characterizations, prison is 'the devil's house ... wherein he keeps his family' and the place for those who are 'hardened sinners'.[208] But this hardly means that relations between inmates were uniformly hostile; they could be remarkably positive. Consider first several instances where prisoners shared their rations with one another. Fellow prisoners of King Perseus (167 BC), 'affected by the magnitude of his misfortune, in which they shared, wept and generously gave him a portion of whatever they received'.[209] Asilius Sabinus (reign Tiberius) admitted the generosity of convicted men with whom he was incarcerated in Rome; they had given him some of their food when he begged them for a share.[210] The anonymous Christian continuator of the *Martyrdom of Montanus and Lucius* marks out the piety of one of the confessors in the following words:

> ...I need not mention his extraordinary fasting in prison: when the others took even their meagre fare from the worst sort of skimpy prison rations, Flavian alone abstained from his tiny share, preferring to be worn by frequent and voluntary fasts provided the others could be fed on his food.[211]

Another indication of positive inmate relations is intimated by one of Achilles Tatius' characters, who at one point remarks in an aside to the reader, '...in misfortune man is a creature always inquisitive to hear about another's woes; community of suffering is something of a medicine for one's own troubles'.[212] Prisoners might derive comfort by sharing their woes among themselves and giving encouragement and

---

[208]Tertullian, *Ad Mart.* 1 and Philostratus, *VA* 7.40 respectively.
[209]Diodorus Siculus 31.9.3.
[210]Seneca, *Con.* 9.4.20f.
[211]*Mart. Mont. & Luc.* 21.12.
[212]Achilles Tatius 7.2.3.

advice. In the state prison of Athens, Andocides is befriended by Timaeus who, though of less repute than himself, gives him wise counsel and helps him with a plan to extricate himself from his difficult legal position.[213] Lucian relates in the *Toxaris* how Demetrius displayed the affection which he had for Antiphilus, 'neglecting his own adversities (though he himself had fallen ill) but taking care that Antiphilus should sleep as well as possible and should suffer less distress. So they bore their discomforts more easily by sharing them with each other'.[214] The philosopher Apollonius, out of sympathy for fifty fellow-inmates in the free prison who were broken in spirit, isolated, and negatively feeding upon one another's misery, determined 'to talk to them and comfort them'.[215] Wishing that he might administer some drug to dull their misery 'lest their own feelings destroy them before Domitian can do it',[216] Apollonius encourages them as a group and also individually by his rational and philosophical assessment of their circumstances.[217] The NT apocryphal and Christian martyr literature also provides examples of imprisoned confessors encouraging one another and non-Christians alike.[218]

All was not harmonious among prisoners. Asilius Sabinus spoke sneeringly of those who kept him alive with their food in the prison; though unconvicted, he complained, he had to beg bread from 'parricides'.[219] He wished to register outrage at having to accept the generosity of men beneath him in dignity and legal predicament. Tertullian warns Christian prisoners of the dangers of spiritual defection and of dissension and squabbling among themselves in the harsh climate of the prison.[220] Previous discussion of spies and informers in prison taught us that not all were what they seemed to be. Disguised as a fellow prisoner, a spy came to Apollonius: 'In his deportment this person had a downcast air, and, as he himself admitted, looked as if he ran a great risk. He had great volubility of speech, as is usually the case with sycophants who have been chosen to draw up eight or ten informations'.[221] The words 'as is usually the case' and the use of the prisoner-

---

[213]Plutarch, *Alc.* 20.3.
[214]Lucian, *Tox.* 32.
[215]Philostratus, *VA* 7.22.
[216]*Ibid.* 7.26.
[217]*Ibid.* 7. *passim.*
[218]E.g., *Apocr. Acts Paul* 3 (c. 185-95 AD); *Apocr. Acts Thom.* 108, 125 (early 3rd cent. AD); *Mart. passim* where solidarity is very clearly evident.
[219]Seneca, *Con.* 9.4.20f.
[220]Tertullian, *Ad Martyras* 1.
[221]Philostratus, *VA* 7.28.

innocently-confiding-to-spy theme in such works as Achilles Tatius' *Leucippe and Cleitophon*[222] suggest that the practice was neither incredible nor unusual. It too provoked distrust.

A general policy requiring that the sexes be confined separately is to be found in the time of Constantine the Great.[223] Up to that time, not only are women confined,[224] they are incarcerated in the same cells as men. During the great purge of the early thirties AD under the emperor Tiberius,

> ...senators as well as knights, and women as well as men, were crowded together in the prison, and upon being condemned either paid the penalty there or were hurled down from the Capitol by the tribunes or even by the consuls, after which the bodies of all of them were cast into the Forum and later thrown into the river.[225]

In the early years of Claudius' reign,

> many men, ... and women, too, were executed at this time, some of the latter even meeting their fate in the very prison itself. And when they were to die, the women, were led in chains upon a scaffold, like captives, and their bodies, also were thrown out upon the [Gemonian] Stairway....[226]

The Christian confessors Perpetua and Felicitas were imprisoned together in 203 AD with a number of other young catechumens—both men and women.[227] Pionius and his fellow confessors—again, both men and women—were tried and imprisoned as a group c. 249/51 AD. They found themselves imprisoned with Limnus a presbyter of the Catholic Church, a Macedonian woman of Karinê, and a man named Eutychian of the sect of the Phrygians.[228]

---

[222]Achilles Tatius 7.1.3f.; 7.2.1-4; 7.6.5.

[223]Mommsen, *Droit Pénal*, vol. 1, 356f. and 357 n. 1. See *Cod. Theod.* 9.3.3 (340 AD = *Cod. Just.* 9.4.3) and discussion Arbandt et al., 'Gefangenschaft', 321; Hitzig, 'Carcer', 1580.

[224]For examples of women imprisoned without reference to the presence of male prisoners: Plutarch, *Dion* 57.3; *PCairZen.* 3:59482, 4:59601; *PEnteux.* 1:83; Pliny, *Nat.* 7.121f.; *BGU* 4:1139; Josephus, *BJ* 5.544 [5.13.1]; *Mart. Agap.* 3.7; 4.4.

[225]Dio Cassius, 58.15.3. Further, Dio Cassius 58.11.5 (cf. Suetonius, *Tib.* 61.5); 58.27.4 (cf. Tacitus, *Ann.* 6.58).

[226]Dio Cassius 60.16.1.

[227]*Mart. Perp. & Felic.* 2.1-3.

[228]*Mart. Pion. passim* but esp. 11.1f. Cf. A.J. Mason, *The Historic Martyrs of the Primitive Church* (London: Longmans, Green, 1905), 159.

While the law gave a condemned woman the temporary protection of a delay in the execution of her sentence if she was pregnant,[229] her prospects in a prison with male felons were predictably grim. The Talmudic vision of the jailer who had converted to Judaism quite vividly illustrates the female prisoner's vulnerability to sexual abuse. When asked his occupation, the jailer responds,

> I am a jailer and I keep the men and women separate and I place my bed between them so that they may not come to sin; when I see a Jewish girl upon whom the Gentiles cast their eyes I risk my life to save her. Once there was amongst us a betrothed girl upon whom the Gentiles cast their eyes. I therefore took lees of [red] wine and put them in her skirt and I told them that she was unclean.[230]

The bleak prison environment, and most inmates' equally bleak prospects, might also push Christians in the direction of immorality. Riddle in his discussion of such dangers among Christians writes that 'in the situation of Cyprian the abuse had specific reference to the sexual behavior of certain imprisoned confessors, so that Cyprian had explicitly to denounce their disgraceful sexual relationship (*Epistle* v.3; vii.5)'.[231]

2. Paul's Co-Prisoners in Acts

There are but two instances where Luke explicitly mentions Paul's fellow prisoners. The first is at Philippi. The reader discovers from the text that Silas too is a Roman citizen (Acts 16:37) and is encouraged to assume, moreover, by the way in which events unfold, that the two missionaries have a previously settled strategy of response in the face of abusive treatment. Other prisoners—all of them non-Christians—come into view as interested auditors of the apostles' prayers and hymns in the inner prison (Acts 16:25) and as transient partakers in the miraculous opening of the prison and release from bonds (Acts 16:26).

The second instance where Luke notes that Paul is in the company of other prisoners is *en route* to Rome. These prisoners had probably been collecting in Caesarea over time until there was a sufficient

---

[229]*Dig.* 48.23.4 and e.g., *Mart. Perp. & Felic.* 15.1f. (203 AD); *Mart. Agap.* 3.7 (303 AD).

[230]*b. Mo'ed* VII: *Ta'an.* 22a. Further Jewish discussion on the matter of sexual intercourse and purity in the prison context, *b. Nasim* I: *Yebam.* II.69b and II.71b; *b. Nez.* V: *Sanh.* I.37b; *b. Nez.* VII:'*Abod. Zar.* 23a; *b. Mo'ed* VII: *Ta'an.* 22a.

[231]D.W. Riddle, *The Martyrs: A Study in Social Control* (Chicago: UCP, 1931), 71.

number to warrant transport.[232] Whether Luke intended, by using
ἕτερος instead of ἄλλος at Acts 27:1, that the 'other' prisoners were of
a different kind than Paul cannot be determined. Suggestions have
been made that they, in contrast to Paul, were not Roman citizens who
had appealed,[233] or had already been condemned and destined to fill
out their lives in work projects or to be offered as entertainment at public games.[234] The prisoners are doubly indebted to Paul for their lives:
they are not only kept safe from the swords of the soldiers because of
the centurion's regard for Paul (Acts 27:42f.), Paul is also the 'salvation'
of both them and the rest of the 276 passengers (Acts 27:22-24, 34).[235]

Our consideration of inmate relations in the Graeco-Roman context opposes the assumption that when other prisoners are mentioned
in Acts they must be males. It may be that both men and women suffered side by side with the apostle at Acts 16 and 27f. and shared,
whether knowingly or not, in the benefits and blessings which companionship with the prisoner Paul conferred.

---

[232]So E.M. Blaiklock, *The Acts of the Apostles* (TNTC; Grand Rapids: Eerdmans,
1959), 189.
[233]E.g., Bruce, *The Acts of the Apostles*, 511; Neil, *The Acts*, 247.
[234]E.g., Williams, *Acts*, 428; Rackham, *The Acts*, 480; Ramsay, *St. Paul the Traveller*,
314.
[235]G.B. Miles and G. Trompf, 'Luke and Antiphon: The Theology of Acts 27-28 in
the Light of Pagan Beliefs about Divine Retribution, Pollution, and Shipwreck',
HTR 69 (1976), 264, but cf. *infra*, 340-41, 359-60.

CHAPTER 12

THE SHAME OF BONDS

The first century Mediterranean culture was dominated by honour and shame; it is thus easy to underestimate the stigma attached to incarceration and bonds. Ancient literary sources link prison with dishonour. The process of being publicly conducted there, particularly while bound, and even the wearing of chains when one was not imprisoned or prison- bound, was perceived (as was intended) to be degrading. Public exposure, irrespective of innocence or guilt, resulted in a shame that could be life-long.

Because prisoners no longer possessed their former dignity there was great social pressure to withdraw from or abandon the prisoner. This pressure was felt most keenly by close friends, associates and family members. Christians too felt it despite calls for solidarity and loving care. All this naturally harmed a prisoner's sense of self-worth. The higher a prisoner's status and the more severe the form of custody (which could include public displays), the greater the sense of shame.

The record of Paul's imprisonments reveals that he recognises the shame and fears the negative effects. The reader is left by the last verse of Acts, however, with the conviction that, far from being overcome by the shame of his circumstances, Paul overcame them.

Paul's incarcerations reflected the official assessment of his status and social worth. We have demonstrated that official deliberations were concerned primarily with the nature of the crime alleged and the status of the accused and of the accuser. We have also seen that powerful negative influences effected the ancient juridical process.

Paul's legal and social status as depicted in Acts is historically highly probable. This portrayal reflects a high degree of status dissonance or low status crystallization which could be seriously troublesome, depending upon who was assessing Paul. It is further argued that Acts discloses appropriate indications of sensitivity to status, offence and other influences as it reports how Paul went before magistrates and officials. Owing to low status crystallization reinforced by strong religious commitments, Paul came to what would have seemed to an ancient reader unnecessary grief as he passed through the social/juridical template. Significant official recalibrations on subsequent disclosures of Paul's status and citizenship did occur in Acts, resulting in somewhat improved circumstances.

There was a general public, however, who observed Paul's actual progress to imprisonment and chains or, in the case of Luke's readers, who would have known about it. It is these individuals to whom we now turn our attention as we consider the social stigma of being in bonds. Several questions posed earlier may be recalled: At the level of interpersonal relations in ministry, would not incarceration—particularly extended incarceration—constitute a massive frontal assault upon Paul's status, credibility and missionary vocation? Might co-workers, helpers, and churches—both those of his own mission and those outside of it—be moved to view differently the missionary now become a prisoner? Further, how would interested non-believers have perceived him? There is evidence that imprisonment seriously stigmatized individuals in the ancient world generally. This would have been no less the case for Paul and, as such, this carried implications for Luke.

I. Honour and Shame

Ancient Mediterranean society was governed by honour and shame.[1] Malina and Neyrey define honour as 'the positive value of a person in his or her own eyes plus the positive appreciation of that person in the eyes of his or her social group', indicating that it is 'a claim to positive worth along with the social acknowledgment of that worth by others'.[2]

The sources of honour which Malina and Neyrey identify in their model as 'ascribed' or 'acquired'[3] conform quite well with the sources of status earlier discussed in the present work.[4] 'Shame' can have an eminently positive value when it means 'sensitivity for one's own reputation and sensitivity to the opinion of others'.[5] It also has a negative value. Malina and Neyrey write:

> ...people *get shamed* (not *have* shame) when they aspire to a certain status which is denied them by public opinion. When a person realizes he is being denied the status, he is or gets shamed; he is humiliated, and stripped of honor for aspiring to a value not socially his. Honor assessments thus move from the inside (a person's claim) to the outside (public validation). Shame assessments move from the outside (public denial) to the inside (a person's recognition of the denial).[6]

Malina and Neyrey continue that honour 'like all other goods in first-century Mediterranean society, is seen to exist in limited amounts' and as such becomes the object of 'a constant social tug of war, a game of social push and shove' which they term 'challenge-riposte'.[7] Such exchanges follow a four step pattern:

> 1) a claim (often implied by action or gesture) which infringes upon the social space of its recipient;
> 2) the perception of the recipient that there is potential to dishonour his or her self-respect or self-worth;

---

[1]The reader is referred to B.J. Malina and J.H. Neyrey, 'Honor and Shame in Luke-Acts: Pivotal Values of the Mediterranean World', in *The Social World of Luke-Acts: Models for Interpretation*, ed. J.H. Neyrey (Peabody, Mass.: Hendrickson, 1991), 25-65; H. Moxnes, 'Honor, Shame, and the Outside World in Paul's Letter to the Romans', in *The Social World of Formative Christianity and Judaism: Essays in Tribute to Howard Clark Kee*, ed. J. Neusner *et al.* (Philadelphia: Fortress, 1988), 207-218, esp. 208; D.L. Daube, 'Shame Culture in Luke', in *Paul and Paulinism: Essays in Honour of C.K. Barrett*, ed. M.D. Hooker and S.G. Wilson (London: SPCK, 1982), 355-72; and B.J. Malina, *The New Testament World: Insights from Cultural Anthropology* (Atlanta: John Knox, 1981), 25-50 and the sources there cited.
[2]Malina and Neyrey, 'Honor and Shame', 25f. *Cf.* Malina, *The New Testament World*, 27f.
[3]*Cf.* Malina and Neyrey, 'Honor and Shame', 27f., 32-34.
[4]*Supra*, 56-62.
[5]Malina and Neyrey, 'Honor and Shame', 44.
[6]*Ibid.*, 45. *Cf.* Malina, *The New Testament World*, 46.
[7]Malina and Neyrey, 'Honor and Shame', 29. *Cf.* Malina, *The New Testament World*, 30 and 33. Pitt-Rivers, cited in Moxnes, 'Honor, Shame, and the Outside World', 208, refers to honour and shame providing the 'currency in which people compete for a reputation'.

3) the recipient's response to the challenge which may take the form
of a positive refusal to act (= displaying scorn, disdain or contempt),
acceptance of the message (= offering a counter-challenge) or a negative refusal to act (= giving no response) thereby accepting a loss of
reputation and hence dishonour; and finally,
4) the verdict of the watching public.[8]

A physical affront is a challenge to one's honour, an intent to dishonour. Failure to respond—or an ineffectual response—brings dishonour
and disgrace upon the one challenged, shaming him and causing him
to feel shame. Malina and Neyrey observe:

> ...publicity and witnesses are crucial for the acquisition and bestowal
> of honor. Representatives of public opinion must be present, since
> honor is all about the court of public opinion and the reputation
> which that court bestows. Literally, public praise can give life and
> public ridicule can kill.[9]

Malina and Neyrey indicate that the conflict dynamics of forensic trials, in which we have a considerable interest, can helpfully be understood in terms of labelling and deviance processing theory.
'Deviance', they write, 'refers to those behaviors and conditions assessed *to jeopardize the interests and social standing of persons who negatively label the behaviour or condition*'.[10] Those who are deviant, whether
because of 'ascribed deviant status' (what they are intrinsically) or 'acquired deviant status' (what they have done or said), are named or labelled as such. Malina and Neyrey observe that

> if the labelling process succeeds, the alleged deviant will be caught up
> in the role indicated by the label and increasingly live out the de-
> mands of the new role. The new label comes to define the person. The
> *master status* engulfs all other roles and labels.[11]

Deviance processing is summarized thus:

> 1) a group, community or society interprets some behaviour as devi-
> ant;

---

[8]Malina and Neyrey, 'Honor and Shame', 30f. *Cf.* Malina, *The New Testament World*,
30-33, 36f. and esp. 31 for a tabular display.
[9]Malina and Neyrey, 'Honor and Shame', 36.
[10]B.J. Malina and J.H. Neyrey, 'Conflict in Luke-Acts: Labelling and Deviance Theory', in *The Social World of Luke-Acts: Models for Interpretation*, ed. J.H. Neyrey (Peabody, Mass.: Hendrickson, 1991), 100.
[11]*Ibid.*, 101.

2) it defines the person who so behaves as deviant;

3) it accords the treatment considered appropriate to such deviants.[12]

The process of defining, in order to succeed, must in addition to its exclusionary function, disseminate and give broader respectability to the new definition of deviance. This is done by converting individuals to the new definition and showing how it supplements, reinforces, or makes up for a lack in the existing rules. Deviance processing includes the public process of 'retrospective interpretation'—i.e., reconstructing the deviant's other behaviours and personal biography so it is consistent with and affirmative of the new label.[13] There follows, as the final step in the labelling process, the 'status degradation ritual', where the deviant's 'old identity is destroyed and his old status degraded'.[14]

Such a socially devastating process would be vigorously resisted in first century Mediterranean culture as people were not individualistic and ambivalent but 'dyadic' or group-oriented and therefore extremely concerned about what others thought.[15] The labelling process may be interrupted by an 'alternative retrospective interpretation' according to Pfuhl which might include:

1) denial of personal responsibility for the behaviour,

2) denial that an injury has been committed,

3) denial that the victim is in fact a victim (i.e., that the victim actually warrants the injury),

4) condemnation of the condemners, and

5) appeal to higher loyalties (i.e., superior values, demands or expectations).[16]

---

[12]*Ibid.*, 102.

[13]*Ibid.*, 105f. This process results in the deviant's responsibility being affirmed, a real injury being acknowledged, the victims being affirmed, the deviant being universally condemned, and all this being ratified by a successful appeal to a higher authority (e.g., God's will, the good of the people). *Ibid.*, 106f.

[14]*Ibid.*, 107.

[15]J.H. Neyrey, 'First-Century Personality: Dyadic, Not Individualistic', in *The Social World of Luke-Acts: Models for Interpretation*, ed. J.H. Neyrey (Peabody, Mass.: Hendrickson, 1991), 72f. *Cf. supra*, 141-42 on the importance of being 'connected' in community and ch. 5 on Philippi.

[16]Cited in Malina and Neyrey, 'Conflict in Luke-Acts', 108f.

II. Imprisonment, Bonds and Shame

Prisons were naturally places to which strong associations of dishonour or shame attached in the ancient world. This stands behind the action of the ancient Athenians in calling their State prison a 'chamber' (οἴκημα); in this way they covered up its ugliness with a more kindly term.[17] When the offended citizens of Crotona condemn the house of the athlete Astylus (c. 275 BC) to become a prison, it is an act of shaming.[18] Cicero in 70 BC calls the prison at Syracuse a place of the greatest dishonour and Epictetus (c. 50-120 AD) opines that while a podium and a prison are alike places, the former is a high place and the latter low (ταπεινός).[19] Finally, Suetonius records in tones of incredulity how the fallen emperor Vitellius 'did not cease to beg that he be confined for a time, even in the prison'.[20]

1. The Shame of Imprisonment and Bonds

Imprisonment is closely associated with shame and dishonour in a number of ancient collocations of personal disasters. Cicero describes how Romans avoid, by going into exile, 'imprisonment, death, or dishonour'; Epictetus, in discussing how one might triumph over life's vicissitudes, says, 'Bring on death and you shall know; bring on hardships, bring on imprisonment, bring on disrepute, bring on condemnation'; Seneca asserts that the wise man is skilled at taming such evils as 'pain, want, disgrace, imprisonment, exile'.[21] In the concluding admonition to help the Christian in distress with whom Christ closely identifies, the writer of the *Apocryphal Acts of John* (c. 2nd-3rd cent. AD) exhorts, '...he [i.e., Christ] is at hand even now in prisons for our sakes, and in tombs, in bonds and dungeons, in reproaches and insults'.[22]

Prison is a place of dishonour pre-eminently because it is the fitting place for malefactors—for social deviants. Negative associations attach to the place and damaging connotations might be expected to attach to its occupants irrespective of their deserts.[23] This is why Lu-

---

[17]Plutarch, *Sol.* 15.2f.
[18]Pausanius, *Testimonium* 6.13.1. *Cf.* Pliny, *Nat.* 7.121 on the opposite process.
[19]Cicero, *Ver.* 2.5.148 and Arrian, *Epict.* 2.6.25 respectively.
[20]Suetonius, *Vit.* 7.17.1.
[21]Cicero (*Caec.* 100); Arrian (*Epict.* 2.1.35; *cf. ibid.* 1.4.23f.); and Seneca (*Ad Lucilium Ep.* 85.41.
[22]*Apocr. Acts John* 103.

cius Scipio's contemplated imprisonment (187 BC) was viewed as an attempt at persecution and insult[24] and why Domitian's imprisonment of Apollonius was said to have been an insult.[25]

Thrusting individuals into prison and/or bonds was publicly perceived—both officially and unofficially—to degrade their status and hence bring them into shame or disrepute. Several Athenian examples may serve as illustrations. In Antiphon's *De caedi Herodis* (*c.* 420 BC), the Mytilenean defendant Euxitheus speaks of the unparalleled illegality of his being officially denied the opportunity to furnish sureties as an alternate to imprisonment. This had been done in part, he vigorously asserts, to bring disgrace upon him.[26] Demosthenes writes (*c.* 355-353 BC) that certain malefactors should not only be fined heavily but also be imprisoned so that they live in disgrace.[27] In both examples the disgrace is said to be life-long,[28] suggesting that their imprisonment has effectively thrust them down to a permanent, socially-reprehensible 'master status'. Placing Athenian prisoners in stocks would also have exposed them to the same type of lasting public humiliation and stigma.[29]

Roman examples of the association of imprisonment and chains with lasting shame and disgrace are also easy to find. When the civil tribunes convened an assembly and fined M. Furius Camillus (390 BC) 100,000 *asses*, writes Dionysius Halicarnassensis, 'they were not unaware that his entire estate was but a small fraction of the amount of the fine, but they desired that this man who had won the most famous wars might incur disgrace by being hauled to prison by the tribunes'.[30] The action is shortly thereafter described as an indignity and an unendurable insult.[31] One of the important functions of parading malefactors to prison in chains was their exposure to unrelenting public

---

[23]E.g.: Plautus, *Captiui* 751 (*c.* 255-184 BC); Cicero, *Catil.* 1.19 (63 BC); Dio Cassius 58.11.1 (31 AD); Seneca, *Con.* 9.4.20f. (*c.* 31 AD); Suetonius, *Vit.* 7.17.1 (69 AD); Eusebius, *HE* 8.6 (reign of Diocletian) cited in H.B. Workman, *Persecution in the Early Church: A Chapter in the History of Renunciation* (Fernley Lectures 36; London: Charles H. Kelly, 1906), 292.

[24]Livy 38.59.9f. *Cf. ibid.* 38.60.6.

[25]Philostratus, *VA* 7.34.

[26]Antiphon, *De caed. Her.* 18.

[27]Demosthenes, *In Timocr.* 115.

[28]Antiphon, *De caed. Her.* 18; Demosthenes, *In Timocr.* 115. *Cf.* Diodorus Siculus 13.103.2.

[29]*Cf.* R. Whiston and W. Wayte, 'Carcer', *DGRA*, vol. 1, 362.

[30]Dionysius Halicarnassensis, *Ant. Rom.* 13.5.1.

[31]*Ibid. Cf.* the experience of Lucius Scipio, Livy 38.59.1-4, 9f.

scrutiny and resultant shame. Dio Cassius describes how Sejanus' conductors, as they led him in bonds to the prison, kept 'uncovering his head when he would fain cover it'.[32] Vitellius' conductors

> bound his arms behind his back, put a noose about his neck, and dragged him with rent garments and half-naked to the Forum. All along the Sacred Way he was greeted with mockery and abuse, his head held back by the hair, as is common with criminals, and even the point of a sword placed under his chin, so that he could not look down but must let his face be seen.[33]

Claudius ordered that the tribune Celer, following his condemnation, be 'sent back in chains to Jerusalem, with orders that he was to be delivered over to Jewish outrage: after being dragged round the city, he was then to be beheaded'.[34]

The same associations inhered where individuals were sent to Rome in chains. When the commander Bassus was first taken to Ardia in 69 AD, it was under an honourable guard (*honorata custodia*). On his arrival there he was clapped in irons by Vibennius Rufinus who was prefect of the cavalry; almost immediately, however, he was released from these bonds by Hormus, the freedman of Vespasian.[35] The contrast is clear: to be unchained is to be treated with some honour, to be chained brings public dishonour. The contrast indicated in the Latin encourages acceptance of the translation 'in honourable confinement' as a fitting rendering of ἐν φυλακῇ ἀδέσμῳ which is found in a number of places in the literature. The indication of chaining which is its opposite would then carry a concomitant shame connotation.[36]

The incongruity between the honour due to a privileged foreign royal and the shame and humiliation associated with publicly wearing chains must, in part, make Macro several times balk at the command of Tiberius to shackle Agrippa. The exchange of Agrippa's iron shackles for a gold ornamental chain of equal weight symbolically indicates the shift from shame and disgrace to honour and privilege.[37] The in-

---

[32]Dio Cassius 58.11.1.F.

[33]Suetonius, *Vit.* 7.17.1.*Cf.* Apuleius, *Met.* 3.2; Livy 26.4.15; Ovid, *Con. Liv.* 271-76.

[34]Josephus, *BJ* 2.246 [2.12.7].

[35]Tacitus, *Hist.* 3.12.

[36]Dio Cassius 36.53.3-6. *Cf. Ibid.* 20.66.2; Arrianus, *An.* 2.15.5; 7.24.2. *Cf.* A.N. Sherwin-White, *Roman Society and Roman Law in the New Testament.* (Sarum Lectures 1961/2; Oxford: Clarendon, 1963), 73 and nn. 3f. for further examples in Tacitus and Pliny.

[37]Josephus, *AJ* 18.189f. [18.6.6], 237 [18.6.10].

congruity similarly motivated a young recruit who rushed forward to lend Nero aid when he saw the emperor performing *The Frenzy of Hercules* 'in mean attire and bound with chains, as the subject required'.[38] The serious disgrace and lasting stigma attaching to those who had been made to wear bonds is clearly indicated in the way that the highborn prisoner Josephus was freed from his bonds and given the Roman franchise by the newly-made emperor Vespasian (70 AD):

> ...Titus, who was beside his father, said, 'Justice demands, father, that Josephus should lose the disgrace [ὄνειδος] along with his fetters [σίδηροι]. If instead of loosing, we sever his chains, he will be as though he had never been in bonds at all'. For such is the practice in cases where a man has been unjustly put in irons. Vespasian approving, an attendant came forward and severed the chain with an axe.[39]

The connection between bonds and shame is elsewhere indicated in the literature. In the *Controversiae*, for example, Seneca associates chains and reproach;[40] Ulpian states that a person forcibly deported or registered on a list of deportees 'shall not suffer fetters nor any other affront which is suffered by a person who had acquiesced in his sentence'.[41] Tacitus relates that among the German tribe of the Chatti, the bravest men wore an iron ring—something shameful as it was worn in token of chains—until each had freed himself of any shame by the slaughtering of an enemy.[42]

2. Perceptions of the Prisoner

We have seen that prisoners were the objects of hostility and harsh treatment within prison systems.[43] Whether convicted or not, those who became prisoners no longer possessed their former dignity in the public view and hence merited a negative perception. Plutarch writes for example, that when the condemned public informer Aristogeiton asked Phocion to come to the Athenian State prison to see him, Phocion's friends tried to dissuade him, chiding him that he ought not to see such a wicked man. Phocion replied: 'Let me go, my good men;

---

[38]Suetonius, *Nero* 6.21.3.
[39]Josephus, *BJ* 4.628f. [4.10.7]. *Cf.* Suetonius, *Ves.* 8.5.6.
[40]Seneca, *Con.* 9.1.7.
[41]*Dig.* 49.7.1.3.
[42]Tacitus, *Ger.* 31.
[43]*Supra*, chapter 6.

for where could one take greater pleasure in meeting Aristogeiton'.[44] Phocion, we may understand, is going principally to savour the prisoner's shame. Plato writes in his *Laws* that no citizen or free person is permitted to hold intercourse with certain criminals.[45] This is, in effect, communal shunning. Apollonius of Tyana, completely shorn of his hair, chained at the leg and confined among the worst felons, was abused by both the emperor and his spies by having these indignities gleefully pointed out to him.[46] Malicious individuals wishing to discredit him, writes Philostratus,

> perverted the facts, and say that he first made his defence, and only then was imprisoned, at the same time that he was also shorn; and they have forged a certain letter in the Ionic dialect, of tedious prolixity, in which they pretend that Apollonius went down on his knees to Domitian and besought him to release him of his bonds.[47]

Dio Chrysostom (40-125 AD) indicates the popular assessment of the prisoner's lack of social merit in the associations of the following passage—that individuals 'would never imagine that a beggar or a prisoner or man without repute was once king'.[48] Judas, after being cast into prison in the *Acts of Thomas* (early 3rd cent. AD), indicates a similar assessment in his prayer: '...I have become poor and needy and a stranger and a slave, despised and a prisoner and hungry and thirsty and naked and weary'.[49]

Deviance processing theory suggests that 'labels' might be attached to prisoners. Thus terms for prison and its accoutrements were applied in a derisive way.[50] In Plautus (255-184 BC), for example, such terms of abuse as 'jail guard' (*custos carceris*) and 'fetter farmer' (*catenarum colonus*) are used.[51] Cicero (63 BC) refers to Gracchus as the 'ex-convict and gaol-bird' (*ex compedibus atque ergastulo*); the English ex-

---

[44]Plutarch, *Phoc.* 10.4f.; cf. ibid., *Regum et imperatorum apophthegmata* 188.B.7.
[45]Plato, *Lg.* 10.909.A-C.
[46]Philostratus, *VA* 7.34, 36f.
[47]*Ibid.* 7.35.
[48]Dio Chrysostom, *De ser.* 1.22 [Discourse 14 (LCL)].
[49]*Apocr. Acts Thom.* 145.
[50]I. Opelt, *Die lateinischen Schimpfwörter und verwandte sprachliche Erscheinungen: Eine Typologie* (Bibliothek der klassischen Altertumswissenschaften; Heidelberg: Carl Winter, 1965), 65.
[51]Plautus, *As.* 298f. These terms are admittedly being applied by slaves to one another. See Opelt, *Die lateinischen Schimpfwörter*, 59f. and *passim* for the application of such shame words as *verbero, statua verberea, mastigia, furcifer* and *carcer* to slaves.

pression 'gaol-bird' is probably also a fitting rendering of δεσμώτης in Achilles Tatius' *Clitophon and Leucippe*.[52]

Friends and close associates experienced great pressure to withdraw from or abandon the prisoner. Euxitheus asserts that one objective of the prosecution in making him a prisoner was 'that I should undergo bodily suffering, and by reason of that bodily suffering find my friends readier to tell lies as witnesses for the prosecution than speak the truth on my behalf'.[53] The physical consequences of his imprisonment alone put incredible pressure upon Euxitheus' friends to engage in 'retrospective interpretation'. They come to see him as capable of murder; all previous biographical indications to the contrary and their friendship with him aside. Livy notes (187 BC) that, 'when Lucius Scipio was being taken to prison ... no one of his colleagues was coming to his assistance'.[54] Seneca (c. 63-65 AD) warns his reader against cultivating friendships with those self-interested individuals whom he terms 'fair-weather' friends: '...at the first rattle of the chain such a friend will desert him'.[55] The number of Apollonius of Tyana's disciples (reign of Domitian) shrank from thirty-four to eight out of fear of imprisonment and death if they followed him to Rome.[56] In the *Toxaris* (163 AD), Lucian praises Agathocles' singular commitment to his friend Deinias. Agathocles stands by him through the whole series of his troubles, even voluntarily sharing exile on Gyaros, while the rest of Deinias' friends abandon him.[57] Lucian also relates how, when Antiphilus was arrested and taken to prison,

> nobody came to his assistance; on the contrary, even his erstwhile friends turned their backs upon him on the ground that he had robbed the Anubideum and considered it an act of impiety on their own part if they had ever drunk or eaten with him. ... Poor Antiphilus therefore remained in confinement for a long time....[58]

The prisoner's household did not remain untouched by his or her lot; in fact, they too came under considerable pressure. The Mytilenean Euxitheus laments the fact that his own family is besmirched by his becoming a prisoner; the accusers 'have brought lifelong disgrace

---

[52]Cicero, *Rab. Perd.* 20 and Achilles Tatius, *Clit. & Leuc.* 8.1.3 respectively.
[53]Antiphon, *De caed. Her.* 17f.
[54]Livy 38.57.3f.
[55]Seneca, *Ad Lucilium Ep.* 9.9.
[56]Philostratus, *VA* 4.37 on their various excuses.
[57]Lucian, *Tox.* 18.
[58]*Ibid.* 28f.

on me *and my family*.[59] The father of the Christian Perpetua (203 AD) cites his shame as a reason to abandon her confession: 'Do not abandon me to be the reproach of men', he pleads.[60] One of the Christian confessors about 259 AD relates a vision in which he is met by a pagan, his own brother in the flesh, who asked 'in a taunting voice how we were getting on with the darkness and the starvation of prison'.[61] Even slaves might be tempted to show disregard or even scorn and contempt. The chained and guarded prince Agrippa apparently might have expected to receive such abuse. When, however, one of the slaves of Gaius gave him a cool draught of water at his request, Agrippa vowed:

> Sir slave, if this service of yours turns out well, when I escape from these bonds, I will lose no time in negotiating your emancipation by Gaius, for you have, in doing me service as a prisoner, omitted nothing of the respect that you accorded me in my former state.[62]

Antiphilus in Lucian's *Toxaris* is less fortunate. His slave Syrus gets him into trouble in the first place. After being imprisoned, Antiphilus' two remaining slaves, without regard for their master's former dignity and ownership of them, make off with everything in his house.[63]

The pressure to cave in and show contempt for or abandon their imprisoned fellows was also felt by the followers of Jesus from the earliest days. In the parable of the sheep and the goats commendation and condemnation are extended in part on the basis of how Jesus' followers have responded to imprisoned disciples. The king invites the sheep to share in the inheritance of his father's kingdom, in part he asserts, because 'I was in prison and you came to me' (Matt. 25:36). Asked by the sheep when they had ever done this, he responds, 'I tell you the truth, whatever you did for one of the least of these brothers of mine, you did for me' (Matt. 25:40). The king next consigns the goats to eternal punishment, in part again he says, because 'I was sick and in prison and you did not look after me' (Matt. 25:43). Asked when they had ever refused the king, he replies, 'I tell you the truth, whatever you did not do for one of the least of these, you did not do for me' (Matt. 25:45). The parable clearly asserts that the cost of abandoning the Christian prisoner, whether out of fear, contempt or shame, is an eternal one because

---

[59]Antiphon, *De caed. Her.* 18 [My italics].
[60]*Mart. Perp. & Felic.* 5.2.
[61]*Mart. Mar. & James* 8.2f.
[62]Josephus, *AJ* 18.193 [18.6.6].
[63]Lucian, *Tox.* 28.

of the king's radical identification with him. The writer to the Hebrews commends his readers for their solidarity when they might have abandoned their brothers and sisters to shame and abuse. He recalls,

> Sometimes you were publicly exposed to insult [pl. of ὀνειδισμός] and persecution [pl. of θλῖψις]; at other times you stood side by side with those who were so treated. You sympathized with those in prison and joyfully accepted the confiscation of your property, because you knew that you yourselves had better and lasting possessions. (Heb. 10:33f.)

He encourages them to continue unflinchingly in this pattern: 'Remember those in prison as if you were their fellow prisoners, and those who are mistreated as if you yourselves were suffering' (Heb. 13:3).

When Ignatius of Antioch (d. 117 AD) writes to the Smyrneans, 'May my spirit be for your life, and my bonds, which you treated neither with haughtiness nor shame. And he who is perfect hope, Jesus Christ, shall not be ashamed of you',[64] he is commending them for resisting the pressure to show contempt for or be ashamed of the prisoner. He is not dealing in hypotheticals: when he identifies the behavioural fruit of heretics to the Smyrneans, he writes: 'For love they have no care, none for the widow, none for the orphan, none for the distressed, none for the afflicted, none for the prisoner, or for him released from prison, none for the hungry or thirsty'.[65]

His letter to Polycarp carries a commendation which depends upon the prospect of a negative response to his situation: 'In all things I am devoted to you,—I and my bonds, which you loved'.[66] The writer of the *Apostolic Constitutions* (c. 300 AD) indicates that believers ought not to overlook Christians condemned to the beasts or to the mines for their confession, but rather to render them material assistance. In another place the same author advises that if prisoners 'be such as to be attested to by Christ before His Father, you ought not to be ashamed to go to them in the prisons'.[67] The thrust of these encouragements is that a faithful confession of Christ should outweigh the shame associated with the prisoner's bonds in the eyes of fellow Christians.

---

[64] Ignatius, *Smyrn.* 10.2. Cf. *ibid.* 11.1.
[65] *Ibid.* 6.2.
[66] *Ibid.*, *Pol.* 2.3.
[67] *Apostolic Constitutions* 4.9 and 5.1 respectively.

3. The Prisoner's Self-Perception

Examples exist, therefore, of pressure to pour scorn upon those who
are confined and wearing bonds. Some of our examples have indicated
that prisoners themselves were sensitive to how they were viewed.
They identify their chains as an insult and an attack on their dignity.[68]
With some pathos, Josephus records the Jewish prince Agrippa's distress at the destructiveness of bonds to his dignity: Roman officials

> led him away a prisoner in his crimson robes. The heat was intense
> and, since he had not had much wine at his meal, he was parched with
> thirst. His feelings were divided between this distress and the shock
> to his self-esteem [τὸ παρ' ἀξίαν κατελάμβανεν].[69]

Individuals might well try to avoid the shame and indignity of incarceration and bonds by taking their own lives. According to Hermip-
pus, the philosopher Anaxagoras (d. 428 BC),

> was confined in the prison pending execution; ... Pericles came for-
> ward and asked the people whether they had any fault to find with
> him in his own public career; to which they replied that they had not.
> 'Well', he continued, 'I am a pupil of Anaxagoras; do not then be car-
> ried away by slanders and put him to death. Let me prevail upon you
> to release him'. So he was released; but he could not brook the indig-
> nity he had suffered and committed suicide.[70]

The reactions of prisoners in other cases, while not as extreme,
nevertheless are just as expressive of their sense of shame. In the face
of the civil tribunes' evident desire to disgrace him by hauling him to
prison and despite his clients' and relatives' payment of the fine levied
against him, writes Dionysius Halicarnassensis, 'Camillus, feeling that
the insult was unendurable, resolved to quit the city'.[71] Individuals, if
they could not kill themselves or flee the shame and disgrace of prison
and bonds, might simply try to hide themselves. We have already noted the pitiable attempts of the prisoners Sejanus and Vitellius to cover

---

[68]Seneca, *Con.* 9.1.7; Achilles Tatius, *Clit. & Leuc.* 6.5.

[69]Josephus, *AJ* 18.192 [18.6.6]. *Cf. ibid.* 18.193 [18.6.6] where Agrippa notes his
'former state'.

[70]Diogenes Laertius, *Lives of Eminent Philosophers* 2.13. *Ibid.* 2.12-14 on various other accounts of the trial of Anaxagoras. See also E.g., Cicero, *Rep.* 3.34; Seneca, *Ad
Lucilium Ep.* 26.10; Livy 37.46.5.

[71]Dionysius Halicarnassensis, *Ant. Rom.* 13.5.1. *Cf.* the case of Demosthenes, Plutarch, *Dem.* 26.1f.

their faces from view as they were publicly conducted in bonds to prison.[72] Later Roman law was sensitive to the social stigma associated with bonds when it acknowledges that one need not have to suffer the disadvantage of being locked away in a prison to qualify for restitution; simply wearing bonds entitles one to such consideration. Ulpian opines in this regard: '...we also understand to be in bonds those who are bound in such a way that they cannot without disgrace appear in public'.[73] Clearly, the feeling of shame at the prospect of publicly appearing in bonds was so formidable that it outweighed the urge to defend oneself in the face of another who sought to do one harm.

It is a reasonable inference that the higher one's status and the greater one's dignity, the more profound would be the public stigma attached to incarceration and wearing bonds and the greater the personal sense of shame felt by the one so kept. Recalling the inverse relation diagrammatically portrayed between the status of the accused and the severity of the custody (see Fig. 9), one might venture as a general rule that public scorn would be greatest and the prisoner's personal sense of shame least tolerable when the prisoner's status was highest and the custody heaviest.

4. A Note on Nakedness, Flogging and Shame

There was also shame associated with stripping, flogging or beating individuals. Briefly, forced public nakedness was employed to shame individuals, whether it was a single action or formed part of a more extended status degradation ritual. Stripping prisoners-of-war was employed by Gelo the tyrant of Syracuse and by others as a strategy to humiliate them and excite contempt for them.[74] Garnsey notes of beating and the fine that the former punishment was regarded by the Romans 'as the more severe sanction, principally because all forms of corporal punishment were held to be degrading'.[75] Having treated crucifixion, burning alive, decapitation, sentencing to the mines and deportation to an island, Callistratus notes: 'The remaining punishments relate to a person's reputation, not to the risk of his *caput*, such as ... [being] punished by beating with rods'.[76] The social stain upon

---

[72]Dio Cassius 58.11.1.F; Suetonius, *Vit.* 7.17.1 cited above.
[73]*Dig.* 4.6.10.
[74]*Frontinus, Str.* 1.11.17f.; Plutarch, *Ages.* 9.5. *Cf.* Suetonius, *Vit.* 7.17.1; *Dig.* 48.20.2.
[75]P.D.A. Garnsey, *Social Status and Legal Privilege in the Roman Empire* (Oxford: Clarendon, 1970), 138.

those who were flogged could be, as with imprisonment, lasting. While one who had been flogged was not automatically barred from holding a high public office, indicates Callistratus, 'Nonetheless, I think it is dishonorable for people of this kind who have been subjected to flogging to be admitted to the *ordo*, and especially in those *civitates* which have plenty of men of standing'.[77] The record of the sufferings of ancient Jewish (*and* contemporary Christian) martyrs at Heb. 11:36 links closely the experience of jeers and floggings. It should also be noted that the rationale in OT Jewish law for restricting flogging to forty lashes was that, beyond this number, the malefactor would have been publicly degraded.[78] We turn now to consider the matter of shame in relation to the Roman imprisonments of Paul in Acts.

III. Paul's Imprisonments and Shame Concerns in Acts

It is clear from the sources cited above that to be a prisoner in the ancient world—whether it meant wearing bonds or simply being confined—was publicly degrading. Prisoners were shamed and insulted before the general community, their friends and family. Extended and sometimes permanent changes in relations and perceptions resulted. Their sense of self-respect could be shattered—sometimes mortally.

Would the prisoner Paul have been alive to such concerns? The answer must be 'Yes' if we have an eye to the captivity epistles of the NT. They show a deep sensitivity to the potentially destructive consequences which the shame of prison and bonds might bring upon Paul, his mission and his relationships with others. In Phil. 1:12-18 Paul addresses shame concerns. There he explains how his chains, far from being a ministry disaster, have actually served to further the gospel. The consequences of Paul's bonds upon his self-perception and the vigour of his witness comes into explicit view at Phil. 1:20: 'I eagerly expect and hope that I will in no way be ashamed, but will have sufficient courage so that now as always Christ will be exalted in my body, whether by life or by death'. The issue of the shame and social stigma attached to wearing bonds is noted several times over in 2 Timothy. We read at 2 Tim. 1:8, 'So do not be ashamed to testify about our Lord,

---

[76]*Dig.* 48.19.28.
[77]*Ibid.* 50.2.12.
[78]Deut. 25:3. The design of the scourge foreshortened public exposure. *Cf. m. Mak.* 3.12f.

or ashamed of me his prisoner'. The pastor avers at 2 Tim. 1:11f. that it is in virtue of his appointment as a herald, apostle and teacher of the gospel that he suffers: 'Yet I am not ashamed [ἀλλ'οὐκ ἀπαισχύνομαι]'. The Christian Onesiphorus, who might well have found in the prisoner's bonds a powerful reason to avoid him, is blessed at 2 Tim. 1:16: 'May the Lord show mercy to the household of Onesiphorus, because he often refreshed me and was not ashamed of my chains'. The strong association between chains and wrongdoing is also expressed at 2 Tim. 2:9: 'This is my gospel, for which I am suffering even to the point of being chained like a criminal [μέχρι δεσμῶν ὡς κακοῦργος]'. The search for similar sensitivities to the shame of imprisonment and bonds for Paul in Acts is not disappointed.

1. Philippi

Paul's imprisonment at Philippi gives a significant indication of concern for shame issues. We have argued previously that it would be reasonable to expect at Acts 16 that Paul would not allow the protection and advantage of his citizenship to compete with or damage important personal and ministry commitments. This is not to say, however, that Paul did not value his Roman citizenship. Acts 16, in fact, reveals a pragmatic and tactical employment of the citizenship which clearly indicates that he highly prized it and the dignity and advantages that it conferred upon him.[79] Just at the point of his release, Paul declares to the lictors at Acts 16:37, 'They beat us publicly without a trial, even though we are Roman citizens, and threw us into prison. And now do they want to get rid of us quietly? No! Let them come themselves and escort us out'.

There has been a significant modern misapprehension of how Paul employs his citizenship here. Tajra has asserted that

> When he pronounced the formula *ciuis Romanus sum*, Paul valorized [*sic*] his rights as a citizen to protection by invoking a whole legal disposition, the Valerian and Porcian laws and their sequels, which had been enacted precisely to protect a Roman citizen from magisterial abuse. The apostle was in fact declaring that the *Duouiri* had exceeded their legal authority by ordering the beating of a Roman citizen when this action was forbidden by the above legislation. The proclamation

---

[79]*Contra* R.J. Cassidy, *Society and Politics in the Acts of the Apostles* (Maryknoll, New York: Orbis, 1987), 102. *Cf.* the discussion of the Philippi episode *supra*, ch. 5.

ciuis Romanus sum was essentially an appellatory formula: Paul was stressing his right to appeal to a higher judicial authority for protection against the illegal action of the *Duouiri*.[80]

Tajra's description of what Paul is doing, however, cannot be correct. First, while Paul is noting—we should say emphasizing—his citizenship, it is hardly the case that he is here lodging a formal appeal. The expression ἀνθρώπους Ῥωμαίους ὑπάρχοντας is not direct enough in its context readily to translate into the formula *cives Romani sumus* (*cf.* Vg.: *homines Romanos*). Second, if Paul is lodging a formal appeal, this is the wrong time to do so as we saw earlier. Third, according to records of the *Lex Iulia*, it was against a citizen's appeal[81] that the order to punish or confine citizens in proscribed ways could be considered illegal and thus punishable. Our analysis of Acts 16 indicates that neither just before nor during his ordeal did Paul disclose his citizenship or enter an appeal. Paul apparently does not have a case if this is the burden of his protest. Having said this, however, it would be wrong to leap to the conclusion that the timing of the disclosure must be an improbable piece of Lukan apologetic.[82] It remains to ask, then, what Paul's objection consists in and whether it is legitimate. The answer to this question has two parts, one having a legal focus upon the term ἀκατάκριτος and the other keyed to the underlying motivation disclosed in the description of the actions of the magistrates and employing the important words δημόσιος and λάθρᾳ.

Perhaps the most natural way of rendering ἀκατάκριτος is 'uncondemned'.[83] Many object, however, as it is thought to imply that, had the apostles been properly condemned, they could have been flogged despite being citizens.[84] It is asserted, in consequence, that the term should be rendered 'without examination/investigation'[85] and it is argued that some legal expression like *re incognita*[86] or *indicta causa*[87]

---

[80]H.W. Tajra, *The Trial of St. Paul: A Juridical Exegesis of the Second Half of the Acts of the Apostles* (WUNT 2/35; Tübingen: J.C.B. Mohr [Paul Siebeck], 1989), 28.

[81]The reader's attention is drawn to the phrases *aduersus prouocationem* (Ulpian, *Dig.* 48.6.7) and *antea ad populum, nunc imperatorem appellantem* (Paul, *Sent.* 5.26.1) and the earlier *aduersus prouocationem* in Cicero, *Rep.* 2.31. This observation is made by Sherwin-White, *Roman Society*, 63.

[82]*Cf.* in this regard the comments of E. Haenchen, *The Acts of the Apostles: A Commentary*, ed. tr. B. Noble *et al.* (Oxford: Basil Blackwell, 1971), 503f.; H. Conzelmann, *Acts of the Apostles: A Commentary on the Acts of the Apostles*, tr. J. Limburg *et al.* (Hermeneia; tr. 2nd ed. 1972; Philadelphia: Fortress, 1987), 133; and J.C. Lentz Jr., *Luke's Portrait*, 139-70.

[83]LSJ, 48; BAGD, 29. Elsewhere in the NT only at Acts 22:25.

which does not carry the implication that citizens could be beaten, should be understood to stand behind it. Several things may be said in this regard. While ἀκατάκριτος may be construed as a loose equivalent to these Latin expressions, the problem is not thereby avoided. The problem is not in how one construes ἀκατάκριτος but in its linkage with δέρω ... δημοσίᾳ. Moreover, the Latin apparently agrees with the rendering 'uncondemned', translating ἀκατάκριτος at both places by *indemnatus*,[88] the opposite of *damnatus*.

The principal thought underlying Paul's protest appears to run as follows: Roman citizens generally expected trials to progress in an orderly fashion; i.e., with opportunity for plaintiffs to accuse and for defendants to present their side of the case *before* the magistrate declared his verdict and ordered an appropriate punishment. A punishment felt to be too severe in such an orderly context could be appealed against. Paul accuses that the Philippian magistrates, wrongly assuming the apostles' non-citizen status, have illegally foreshortened due process by moving directly from the accusation phase to the punishment phase. This stands whether ἀκατάκριτος focuses upon the failure of the broader legal process (*re incognita, indicta causa*) or the failure

---

[84]So, e.g., W.M. Ramsay, *St. Paul the Traveller and Roman Citizen* (London: Hodder and Stoughton, 1895), 224f.; R.J. Knowling, *The Acts of the Apostles*, ed. W.R. Nicoll (Expositor's Greek Testament 2; 1901; rpt. Grand Rapids: Eerdmans, 1983), 354; A.W.F. Blunt, *The Acts of the Apostles in the Revised Version* (Clarendon Bible 4; Oxford: Clarendon, 1922), 213; G.H.C. Macgregor and T.P. Ferris, *The Acts of the Apostles* (IB 9; New York: Abingdon, 1954), 224; R.B. Rackham, *The Acts of the Apostles* (Westminster Commentaries 41; 7th ed. 1913; London: Methuen, 1951), 291 n. 1.

[85]The closest similar term, ἄκριτος, can carry this sense. Cf. Plutarch, *Alc.* 20.3 and the entries in LSJ, 56; BAGD, 29.

[86]*Re incognita* carries the sense of a case 'not investigated', 'unheard' or 'untried' according to OLD, 871. The investigation may be improper because the accused is condemned *in absentia* or, if present, the accused is refused the opportunity to defend him/herself before final determination as examples from Cicero, *ND*, 2.29.73, *Caec.* 10.29, *Dom.* 8.20 and Sallust, *Jug.* 14.20 show.

[87]*Indicta causa* means something like 'without the case's having been pleaded' or 'without a hearing' according to OLD, 883. Again, the impropriety can be due to condemnation of the accused without the formality of a trial, *in absentia*, or without the opportunity of a self-defence, as Livy 38.33.2, 11; Cicero, *Phil.* 2.23.56, *Rab. Perd.* 4.12, *Ver.* 2.2.43, *Ver.* 2.5.109, *Leg.* 1.15.42; Caesar, *Gal.* 7.38; Curtius 3.12.19 illustrate.

[88]*Indemnatus* is rendered 'not found guilty in a court of law' or 'uncondemned' in OLD, 881. While perhaps not a formal juridical phrase as are *re incognita* and *indicta causa*, *indemnatus* suggests irregularity along similar lines to them as Livy 3.13.4f., 35.34.7; Cicero, *Dom.* 10.26; Sallust, *Catil.* 51.29; Seneca, *Con.* 9.2.21; and Juvenal 6.562 indicate.

of the needful penultimate step in it (*indemnatus*).[89] In short, Paul accuses that the Philippian magistrates are guilty of *serious procedural irregularities* owing to their faulty assumptions, the result being that Roman citizens had been unjustly punished.[90]

The failure to appeal and the late disclosure of citizenship might, from the magistrates' perspective, have been considered deceptive. However, the evident speed of the trial, the apparent failure to quiz defendants, and the allegation of an intention to release the apostles surreptitiously (λάθρᾳ: Acts 16:37) might be taken by interested provincial superiors to insinuate official incompetence and culpability.[91] The fact that *Roman citizens* had been ordered savagely beaten and imprisoned in such circumstances and that an objection was being lodged on the basis of that citizenship may have raised in the minds of the magistrates—whether rightly or not—the threatening spectre of prosecution under the provisions of the *Lex Iulia*. In short, Paul and Silas could have mounted an at least arguable and potentially devastating case against the magistrates (and city?)[92] had they chosen to do so.

Commentators frequently seize upon the derivable missiological benefits of Paul's citizenship disclosure. It is probably true that the manner of Paul's (and Silas') disclosure may benefit the fledgling Philippian congregation which he will soon leave;[93] it may also protect Christian missionaries who will follow[94] or preserve and foster the ad-

---

[89]Both are allowed as possibilities by G. Schille, *Die Apostelgeschichte des Lukas* (THNT 5; Berlin: Evangelische Verlagsanstalt, 1984), 424; Haenchen, *The Acts*, 633; Conzelmann, *Acts*, 189; K. Lake and H.J. Cadbury, *The Acts of the Apostles: English Translation and Commentary*, in *BC*, vol. 4, 283.

[90]The adjective 'illegal' which frequently occurs in descriptions of the magistrates' actions is too strong. 'Irregular' or 'delinquent' is perhaps more accurate.

[91]*Contra* W. Stegemann, 'War der Apostel Paulus ein römischer Bürger?' *ZNW* 78 (1987), 202f.

[92]On magistrates and cities who violated the rights of Romans, *cf. supra*, 53-55. Cf. Tajra, *The Trial of St. Paul*, 29; D.J. Williams, *Acts* (San Francisco: Harper and Row, 1985), 283; H.O.A. Keinath, 'The Contacts of the Book of Acts with Roman Political Institutions', *CTM* 1 (1930), 192; J.V. Bartlet, *The Acts* (Century Bible [NT] 5; Edinburgh: T.C. and E.C. Clark, 1901), 293; Knowling, *The Acts*, 354.

[93]See Williams, *Acts*, 283; G. Stählin, *Die Apostelgeschichte* (NTD 5; 4th ed.; Göttingen: Vandenhoeck und Ruprecht, 1970), 222; E.M. Blaiklock, *The Acts of the Apostles* (TNTC; Grand Rapids: Eerdmans, 1959), 128; I.H. Marshall, *The Acts of the Apostles* (TNTC 5; Grand Rapids: Eerdmans, 1980), 274; A. Wikenhauser, *Die Apostelgeschichte* (RNT 5; 4th ed.; Regensburg: Friedrich Pustet, 1961), 191; W. Neil, *The Acts of the Apostles* (NCB 42; London: Oliphants/Greenwood: Attic, 1973), 186; Knowling, *The Acts*, 354. D.O. Bauernfeind, *Kommentar und Studien zur Apostelgeschichte*, ed. V. Metelmann (WUNT 22; Tübingen: Mohr, 1980), 211 goes so far as to state that the claim is made on behalf of the congregation.

vance of the Gospel more generally.[95] But the words suggest a much more immediate and status-based Pauline concern. Paul's words at Acts 16:37 are pre-eminently a vigorous drive to claw back some dignity after having been deeply shamed; in terms of the mechanisms laid out at the beginning of the present chapter, they are a 'challenge-riposte' response to a profoundly devastating status degradation.

Brought before the magistrates, the apostles' clothes were torn from their backs, they were flogged severely and were marched off to the prison where they were summarily locked into stocks in the most secure cell in the prison. We have already considered this abusive treatment from the standpoint of the official juridical and social assessment and concluded that it expressed the conviction that Paul and Silas were low-status individuals safely presumed by accusation alone to be guilty of criminal behaviour; they were entirely lacking in legal and social merit.[96] The mistreatment alone would have caused them to smart deeply from the indignity and shame, and all the more so as they were Roman citizens.

But Paul also emphasizes that this had all happened to them 'publicly' (δημόσιος).[97] Witnessing their humiliation were not only the magistrates, their minions and the aggrieved owners of the slave girl, but also the Philippian crowd. We have argued previously that, far from being unruly and wild, the crowd behaves here in an orderly and articulate fashion; it observes and participates.[98] The pressure upon the magistrates to attend to the charges and act upon them is, in consequence, considerable. But so too is the resulting damage to the apostles' reputation. The crowd views Paul's and Silas' nakedness and their humiliating beating. It also witnesses their ignominious conduct to the prison, perhaps many hearing the commands given as to the manner of keeping required. Thus witnessed and endorsed by a sizable proportion of the Philippian populace—including a substantial number of fellow Romans—their degradation could not have been more complete. Whatever they might have been before, the apostles' 'master status' is now 'criminal' (κακοῦργος). They are also open to some of the other titles of abuse earlier considered. Uncontested, the shame of their

---

[94]See Marshall, *The Acts*, 274.

[95]See Stählin, *Die Apostelgeschichte*, 222; Williams, *Acts*, 283; Wikenhauser, *Die Apostelgeschichte*, 191.

[96]*Supra*, 120f.

[97]Commentators seldom discuss the significance of the δημόσιος / λάθρᾳ contrast.

[98]*Supra*, 121-123.

beating and bonds would henceforth obtrude upon all social relations in Philippi. There would be no honour for them or their message.

The incredulity of Paul's question, 'And now do they want to get rid of us quietly?' must also be understood in terms of honour and shame. The citizen Paul will brook no secret (λάθρᾳ) expulsion from the prison because this would only reinforce the formal degradation, piling insult upon insult. A release under such conditions is resisted not because it is sneaky or illegal,[99] but because it sustains and reinforces the social damage.

Paul has clearly indicated a high status deeply wounded; lying under the surface of that indication are threatening implications which would be clearly perceptible to the magistrates. But Paul does not threaten legal action; rather, he demands a significant status transaction. He insists that the magistrates 'come themselves and escort us out'. Some commentators have interpreted this as 'a visible reprobation of the magistrates' illegal conduct', 'humiliation', 'restitution', or 'reparation'.[100] These, however, ought not to be considered options to choose between, but elements in a single transaction. Paul and Silas have, because of the constraint of their religious commitments, been seriously injured socially in a status degradation process. Subsequently, Paul challenges the magistrates who are fellow Romans possessing the greatest dignity and status in the colony. By a challenge-riposte, Paul makes a significant claim upon their dignity and status by insisting that they escort Paul and Silas out of the prison *in full public view*.

Paul stages what Williams has called a 'sit-in',[101] refusing to budge from the prison until he has full satisfaction. One may recall the principled response of the poet Philoxenus (396 BC) who had been condemned to the quarries for criticizing the compositions of the tyrant Dionysius of Syracuse. Given the chance to secure his freedom if he withdrew his criticisms, he 'preferred to go back to his prison'.[102] Perhaps even closer to what Paul is here doing is Metellus' refusal to appeal to the tribunes for his release from Rome's prison (60 BC). Trusting in the leverage of his own considerable dignity, political power and popularity, Metellus remained in prison, allowing the dangerous pressure of the incongruity between his status and his treatment to

---

[99] *Contra* Bartlet, *The Acts*, 293. Cf. Tajra, *The Trial of St. Paul*, 25.

[100] So Tajra, *The Trial of St. Paul*, 28; B. Reese, 'The Apostle Paul's Exercise of His Rights as a Roman Citizen as Recorded in the Book of Acts', *EvQ* 47 (1975), 142; Haenchen, *The Acts*, 498; and Knowling, *The Acts*, 354 respectively.

[101] Williams, *Acts*, 282.

[102] Cicero, *Att.* 4.6 and Winstedt's comments [LCL] at 287 n. 2.

mount until his magisterial opponent, in humiliation, climbed down.[103] Paul's refusal to vacate the prison effectively raises pressure on the magistrates who now know that Romans, whose citizenship merits serious consideration in law and by social convention, are currently in their prison at their instigation.

Any resistance that the magistrates might have felt because of this encroachment upon their dignity is swept aside by the potentially dangerous consequences of inaction. They feel compelled to comply. This amounts to a 'negative refusal to act'—i.e., a failure to counter-challenge. When Luke records at Acts 16:39 that the magistrates 'came to appease them and escorted them from the prison', this amounts to their effective acceptance of a loss of reputation and hence their being dishonoured. In the limited economy of honour, it also amounts to an effective conferral of the magistrates' lost honour upon the apostles.[104] It will be recalled that in the challenge-riposte interchange, publicity and witnesses are crucial for the acquisition and bestowal of honour. Without the watching public, a status transaction would not occur. The prison being quite near to or abutting the *forum*,[105] the procession of magistrates humbly leading out prisoners would have been very public and those who saw it would have been pressed socially to interpret the scene before them, revising upward their earlier status 'verdict' concerning the apostles.

Before leaving the Philippi episode, some assessment of the effectiveness of the transaction must be given as it is relevant to our consideration of Paul's future prison troubles. First, Acts indicates that the apostles had made a significant but only partial gain of honour because the magistrates 'ask' (ἐρωτάω: Acts 16:39)[106] the apostles to leave the city. Such a request surely grows out of their concern at the

---

[103]When Metellus was barred from receiving friends through the prison door he planned to have an opening cut into his cell from outside. This too raised the pressure. *Cf.* Dio Cassius 37.50.1f.

[104]The fuller text of Codex Bezae at verse 39a emphasizes the magnitude of the offence and increases the currency of the status transaction (the magistrates come 'with many friends') and indicates a Roman sensitivity to the relation between 'Romanness' and *innocentia* (the apostles are acknowledged as 'righteous men'). *Cf.* B.M. Metzger *et al.*, *A Textual Commentary on the Greek New Testament* (New York: UBS, 1971), 451.

[105]*Supra*, 125f.

[106]The verb can hardly be construed to be a demand indicating expulsion (Haenchen, *The Acts*, 503, citing Mommsen; Williams, *Acts*, 283). Better, Sherwin-White, *Roman Society*, 77; F.F. Bruce, *The Book of Acts* (NICNT; 1954; rev. ed. Grand Rapids: Eerdmans, 1988), 320; Neil, *The Acts*, 186.

public confusion and upset arising from what must have seemed a radical change in magisterial behaviour. The Philippians would have been puzzled and perhaps even angered when they saw their chief magistrates openly humbling themselves and just as openly conferring honour upon those who only the day before had been universally deemed as criminals worthy of beating and bonds. The additions of the Western text regarding the magistrates' fear of popular hostility and their concern at not being able to protect the apostles[107] are at least intuitively close to the actual motivation for the request. Furthermore, Acts 16:40 indicates: 'After Paul and Silas came out of the prison, they went to Lydia's house, where they met with the brothers and encouraged them. Then they left'. The apostles will not be hurried out of the city as this would be inconsistent with the honour newly conferred upon them. They linger only long enough to make their retrieved status known to the populace and to the congregation; then they leave. Clearly, the apostles too perceive that while they have gained some benefit from the status transaction, the situation remains unstable and potentially dangerous. Only at a later time will Paul travel through Macedonia and enter Philippi (Acts 20:1-6). How long he remains in Philippi on that occasion, the text does not say.

Second, the epistles of Paul themselves attest to a considerable residual shame regarding this experience despite the status transaction. Paul, writing to the Thessalonians shortly after the Philippi disaster,[108] states, 'You know, brothers, that our visit to you was not a failure. We had previously suffered and been insulted in Philippi, as you know, but with the help of our God we dared to tell you his gospel in spite of strong opposition' (1 Thess. 2:2).[109] Paul carries a lasting sense of the social stigma of the Philippi episode, not only indicating it to the Thessalonians some time later but also disclosing to them its inhibitory potential as he first came to them. Had he not received God's

---

[107]Metzger et al., A Textual Commentary, 451. Cf. Knowling, The Acts, 354.

[108]C.J. Hemer, The Book of Acts in the Setting of Hellenistic History, ed. C.H. Gempf (WUNT 49; Tübingen: J.C.B. Mohr/Paul Siebeck, 1989), 186 speaks of a few weeks or months.

[109]Paul's attention to the residual shame at 1 Thess. 2:2 (cf. his exact recollection at 2 Cor. 6:5; 11:23-25) and Luke's description of the degradation process, the status transaction achieved through the leverage of Paul's citizenship, and the intimation of subsequent social instability and danger at Acts 16 amount to differences of emphasis rather than conflict. What Paul does not say but Luke does hardly requires that Luke dreamt it up. Cf. Stegemann, 'War der Apostel Paulus', 202f.; with somewhat less scepticism, see G. Lüdemann, Early Christianity According to the Traditions in Acts: A Commentary, tr. J. Bowden (London: SCM, 1987), 179-84.

gracious help, the dishonour, shame and feeling of failure arising from the Philippian experience would have severely affected his sense of ability to preach. Paul—again, at some distance from the time of his public humiliation in Philippi[110]—recalls to the Philippians the shame of his bonds in their city. After telling them that his present incarceration, far from being a great disaster, is actually advancing the preaching of the gospel, Paul encourages them to solidarity in suffering, reminding them at Phil. 1:29f., '...it has been granted to you on behalf of Christ not only to believe in him, but also to suffer [πάσχω] for him, since you are going through the same struggle [ἀγών] you saw I had, and now hear that I still have'. Resonances of the shame of his bonds continue.

2. Jerusalem

In order to understand the negative impact of Paul's binding at Jerusalem, one must keep in mind the circumstances of his arrest. Luke indicates at Acts 21:20-27 that, on arriving in Jerusalem, Paul is informed that a great many Jews who are zealous for the law have come to faith in Jesus. They are inclined to believe reports that Paul is teaching Jews who live among the Gentiles to abandon the law. To allay such suspicions, the church leadership recommends that Paul share in and undertake the cost of completing the Nazarite vows of four other Jews.

The information gathered on the shame of bonds permits the confident inference that when Paul is roughly seized, beaten by the Jewish mob, and then formally arrested by the Romans who bind him with two chains, his status is seriously damaged. First, Paul would feel shamed by the verbal and physical abuse and by the chaining. Paul's proud assertion of his Greek citizenship and the carefully nuanced disclosure of his Roman citizenship are attempts at shielding himself or seeking relief from the most hostile and humiliating assessments and abuses. When slapped across the mouth for declaring his innocence before the Sanhedrin, Paul instantly responds with a vigorous and abusive verbal counter-challenge (= 'riposte'),[111] only retracting it

---

[110]The reader will appreciate that the places claimed for the writing of this epistle—whether Ephesus, Caesarea or Rome—remove one progressively further in time from the events at Philippi.

[111]So Tajra, *The Trial of St. Paul*, 94, citing Jacquier. Paul would hardly have left such a slight unanswered in such familiar company.

when he is reminded of the superior status of the one who has ordered him to be struck (Acts 23:2-5).

Second, the seizure and chaining would have had a highly prejudicial effect on the perception of Paul by the many uninformed observers in the Temple area—the actions themselves would be construed as confirmation of his guilt. Paul is verbally and visually labelled a malefactor and sedition-raiser. Reports of what had happened to Paul in the Temple area would almost certainly have had the same confirmatory effect regarding Paul's guilt among the many zealous Jewish Christians, fostering hostility and the very divisions that the strategy of James and the brothers was designed to avoid.[112] Close friends, co-religionists and even members of one's household, as we have seen, could be deeply scandalized by a person's incarceration. One cannot doubt that some—perhaps even many—Jerusalem Christians felt scandalized by the accusations against Paul and his bonds. Maximum security conditions having been imposed upon Paul in the Antonia Fortress and the appearance of Paul's nephew having the earmarks of being exceptional,[113] sympathetic visitors would not have had access to him. It is, moreover, doubtful whether many would even have felt inclined to visit Paul had they been given the opportunity to do so.

3. Caesarea

Paul's extended incarceration in Caesarea in chains and quartered somewhere in Herod's official residence must also be viewed against the backdrop of the increasing violence of Jewish/Gentile conflicts. How Christians living there would have been perceived by the two belligerent communities is difficult to say. Considering the ministry emphasis and fruitfulness of such apostolic visitors to the city as Peter (Acts 10:1-11:18) and the presence of important resident members such as Philip the Evangelist (Acts 8:4-40; cf. 21:8f.), the church probably found itself uncomfortably caught in the crossfire. The pressure upon Christians to feel shame for and disassociate themselves from the apostle would have been great—recall in particular that the entire Jew-

---

[112]Luke's silence concerning what became of the Jerusalem collection probably does not tell against its acceptance. Cf. K.F. Nickle, *The Collection: A Study in Paul's Strategy* (Studies in Biblical Theology 48; London: SCM, 1966), 70f., 148-51.
[113]*Supra*, 148-49.

ish community (ἅπαν τὸ πλῆθος τῶν Ἰουδαίων: Acts 25:24) at Caesarea petitioned Festus for Paul's death.

There is further indication in the Lukan record of the Caesarean imprisonment of sensitivity to the scandal of Paul's imprisonment. When Paul declaims with rhetorical flourish to King Agrippa at Acts 26:29, 'Short time or long—I pray God that not only you but all who are listening to me today may become what I am, except for these chains', mention of chains is hardly 'in a lighter vein' or intended as a 'grim jest'.[114] Nor—one should agree with Haenchen—is the reference only 'symbolic' for imprisonment.[115] His appearance before such an august body bound with chains presents a picture of humiliation which Paul would be anxious to counteract. Standing before them as a prisoner in chains, such an unqualified wish to Agrippa and the rest would be audacious and insulting. Paul therefore makes it very clear that he wishes for his hearers the same faith that he has come to have, excepting—Paul might well again have raised his manacled wrist(s)[116]—the great loss in honour and dignity which he has had to endure.

4. En Route to Rome

Given leave to have his case referred to the Emperor, Paul is conducted to Rome under military guard and in chains. While Luke gives no explicit indication of it, the fact of Paul's being bound would necessarily have intruded itself upon the public consciousness all along the way. Two places in the record merit consideration. In the first, the Maltese apparently assume that Paul's escape from the storm vindicates him as innocent of wrongdoing despite the usual associations attaching to his being a prisoner in chains. When the snake bites him, they are convinced that he is a murderer suffering divine retribution; when he does not die from the snakebite, it is supposed that he is a god (Acts 28:1-6).[117] A much more certain indication of the prisoner's consciousness

---

[114]So, R.N. Longenecker, 'The Acts of the Apostles', in The ExpBibCom, vol. 9, 555 and C.S.C. Williams, The Acts of the Apostles (BNTC 5; London: A. and C. Black, 1964), 266 respectively.

[115]Haenchen, The Acts, 690.

[116]Cf. Acts 26:1 where Paul begins his speech with a gesture of his chain-laden right hand. The motion, is 'in the manner typical of ancient orators' according to Marshall, The Acts 390.

[117]For discussion, G.B. Miles and G. Trompf, 'Luke and Antiphon: The Theology of Acts 27-28', HTR 69 (1976), 259-67.

of the social implications of his bonds may present itself at Acts 28:15. There we read that, when the brothers at Rome came down to meet him, 'at the sight of these men Paul thanked God and was encouraged'. While a fuller discussion of this passage is reserved for later, it is clear that Paul was greatly concerned[118] that the fact of his being a prisoner could influence negatively how, if at all, the Christians in Rome would receive him. Their absence would have been a devastating indication that they were ashamed of him and his bonds.

5. Rome

Paul is permitted a very light custody in Rome though he is chained. Pauline and Lukan sensitivities concerning the social and legal damage that imprisonment and bonds might do plays a clear part in the record. At his first official meeting with the Jewish leaders in Rome, Paul asserts his innocence of all Jewish charges and gives a summary description of the circumstances of his arrest and appearance in Rome to await Caesar's disposition of his case. He concludes his address to them at Acts 28:20 by asserting, 'It is because of the hope of Israel that I am bound with this chain'. Had the term δεσμοί been used, the reader might have understood Paul to be referring to his imprisonment more generally. The same conclusion might also have been warranted had he simply used the self-designatory term δέσμιος. That ἅλυσις, a term unambiguously indicating the actual chain, is used focuses the attention of the Roman Jews (and Luke's readers) upon the most explicit physical token of Paul's imprisonment.[119] Perhaps raising his manacled hand, Paul is effectively challenging the Jews to interpret correctly the image he presents to them. The chain is not the object of shame or a reason for them to disassociate themselves from him as a wrongdoer. Rather, it is the token of his full kinship and religious solidarity with them, actually confirming that he shares in the same hope as they do.

Finally, having briefly related the conditions of his incarceration for two full years, Luke indicates the tone and character of Paul's ministry at Acts 28:31: 'Boldly and without hindrance he preached the kingdom of God and taught about the Lord Jesus Christ'. Our interest here is in the use of παρρησία (Acts 2:29; 4:13, 29, 31; 28:31; vb.: παρρησιάζομαι: Acts 9:27f.; 13:46; 14:3; 18:26; 19:8; 26:26), which has been

---

[118]*Supra*, 223f. on the word θάρσος and *infra*, 387 for the full discussion.
[119]See Knowling, *The Acts*, 548.

called one of the 'key-words' in Acts by van Unnik, who observes: 'it is the last word that resounds in our ears when we close the book'.[120]

It is of considerable relevance to this passage that a close connection exists between παρρησία/άζομαι and the insult and shame of imprisonment. The canonical Pauline epistles make such a connection. Paul, having reminded the Thessalonians of the suffering and insult (ὑβρίζω)—which can also mean 'injury'—sustained through the beating and imprisonment at Philippi, speaks of how he and his associates had the confidence (παρρησιάζομαι) to preach despite again meeting local opposition (1 Thess. 2:2). It was noted in earlier discussion of this passage that, had Paul not received God's gracious help, the shame and feeling of failure arising from the Philippian experience would have hindered his ability to preach. The form of that divinely-given help which overcame past shame and present opposition, Paul indicates, was παρρησία. At Phil. 1:20 the shame associated with Paul's imprisonment and his forthright boldness despite it (παρρησία) are again brought into close relation. van Unnik is prepared to state that 'the opposite to παρρησία clearly is "to be ashamed", of course in the tribulations and even danger of death'.[121] Concerning Paul's παρρησία to command obedience at Phm. 8, van Unnik writes, 'Paul, who according to worldly standards is far inferior to the wealthy Philemon, and is in prison, is bold enough to give orders to Philemon to do his duty, but he refrains from that right; here again the "freedom of speech" Paul enjoys is "in Christ"'.[122] Mention might also be made of the close association between imprisonment and the need for παρρησία at Eph. 6:19f.: 'Pray also for me, that whenever I open my mouth, words may be given me so that I will fearlessly [ἐν παρρησία] make known the mystery of the gospel, for which I am an ambassador in chains. Pray that I may declare it fearlessly [παρρησιάζομαι], as I should'. That παρρησία, which is God-given and not something from within the apostle himself, will overcome the negative effects of his sufferings, but particularly the shame of his bonds.[123]

---

[120]W.C. van Unnik, 'The Christian's Freedom of Speech in the New Testament', BJRL 44 (1961), 477. Further on the term in its NT contexts, cf. H. Schlier, 'παρρησία, παρρησιάζομαι', TDNT, vol. 5, 871-86; H.-C. Hahn, 'Openness, Frankness, Boldness', NIDNTT, vol. 2, 734-37.

[121]Ibid., 475.

[122]Ibid., 474, [My italics].

[123]Cf. Hahn, 'Openness', 736; van Unnik, 'The Christian's Freedom', 474f. Also van Unnik, ibid. on Eph. 3:12.

Luke records at Acts 4:13 that Peter and John, far from being cowed by their overnight imprisonment or their interrogation before the Sanhedrin demonstrate, by their fearless speech, great courage (παρρησία). The authorities remark to themselves that Peter and John, though unschooled ordinary men, had been with Jesus. When Festus interrupts Paul's defence before king Agrippa to say that he is out of his mind, Paul replies at Acts 26:26: 'What I am saying is true and reasonable. The King is familiar with these things, and I can speak freely [παρηησιάζομαι] to him'. This παρρησία of the prisoner Paul comes shortly before his self-conscious reference to his wearing chains (Acts 26:29).

The fact that Luke tells the reader in some detail about the physical conditions of Paul's Roman imprisonment at the end of Acts—including his being chained and under guard—and that these custody arrangements lasted for two full years must be taken as significant and determinative for our understanding of παρρησία at Acts 28:31. Luke is indicating to his readers that the usual shame connotations associated with chains and incarceration did not apply, being more than satisfactorily met in the provision of God. Far from withdrawing from all preaching and teaching out of the stigma of his circumstances, or perhaps holding back as he sensed himself under the scrutiny of believers and unbelievers who saw or came to see him, the prisoner Paul preached and taught not just boldly but with all boldness (μετὰ πάσης παρρησίας).

CHAPTER 13

THE PRISONER'S LIFE

The reasons for delays in trials include the volume of court business; turnover of magistrates; magisterial misbehaviour; and the dilatory actions of litigants. Paul's extended imprisonment in Caesarea was caused by the litigants' power and Felix' hunger for money. Paul's two years in Rome simply resulted from the capital's trial calendar. Paul thus spent much time in detention. Time could be spent preparing one's case, playing games or reading, writing, and engaging in philosophic or religious pursuits.

Paul's meeting with the Jewish leaders at Rome relates to case preparation. He set his position before them because he values their support. It is unlikely that he played games in prison, though he did read; and non-biblical examples of prison writing commend Caesarea and especially Rome as suitable for literary activity. Concerning religious ministrations, Acts shows that prison did not void Paul's ministry. In Philippi, he and Silas convert the jailer; in the account of the Caesarean imprisonment, Luke's emphasis falls upon the frequent witness of Paul before Felix. Paul prayed and sang, and probably celebrated the Eucharist when possible.

Acts ends strongly. Paul meets with Roman Judaism to discuss Jesus and the kingdom of God. This, as with all his Jewish preaching, meets with mixed success. With it the exclusive preaching to Judaism in Rome is completed and Paul preaches to both Jews and Gentiles. Luke closes with a picture of a prisoner whose place of confinement has become a house church.

Paul's imprisonments and bonds inevitably made a negative statement about his status and his guilt. Acts records, in the clearest possible terms, however, not only Pauline protests of innocence, but also
official assessments to the same effect. Luke's agenda must be to assert
in as many ways as records and recollections permitted that, though
charged with serious crimes, the apostle to the Gentiles was *not* a
wrongdoer. Luke also tells his readers that Paul did not claim his
rights and privileges, but sometimes voluntarily suffered abuse and
bonds, his status having on these occasions been underestimated by
officials.

Luke's readers would have been sensitive not only to matters of
guilt and innocence but also to the disqualificatory aspects of imprisonment and bonds. He needed to show that the apostle Paul continued, despite these, to be effective, appreciated, and approved. Our
discussion of Paul and his helpers will explore the means whereby
Luke showed that 'prisoner' and 'missionary' were not mutually exclusive. We shall argue that this was achieved in three ways.

First, Luke's Paul continued to be a witness to the resurrected Jesus despite the constraints of incarceration. Insofar as the ancient
sources provide a structure by which to analyse the Lukan record and
permit us to make reasoned inferences, the matter of how the prisoner
Paul occupied his time will be considered. Second it would have been
important for Luke to show, as far as the facts permitted, that Paul was
not rejected by Christians shamed by his incarceration, but was in fact
embraced and assisted in his needs and his ministry. We shall in the
next chapter treat ancient helpers and helping behaviours and set beside them what Luke says or intimates concerning the helpers and help
extended to Paul. Third, after all that could be said concerning the
above two points, certain larger questions might still have remained in
people's minds. Luke, it will be argued, indicates not only as he begins
to recount Paul's incarcerations but well before, that these experiences
actually fell within the divinely-set terms and conditions of Paul's ministry. Moreover, it will be argued that Luke shows the imprisoned missionary to be vindicated before Christian and non-Christian alike by
divine assurances and assistance at critical moments.

The present chapter, which examines the first step noted above
in Luke's strategy, deals with the complications that incarceration
brought and relates how these were addressed. Whatever else it might
mean, 'doing time' in the ancient world surely meant the disruption of
normal activities and established life patterns. Every prisoner hoped
for release on furnishing sureties or at least a rapid trial culminating in

a favourable result to minimize that disruption. However, extended custody while awaiting trial or verdict—the lot of not a few individuals met in the sources consulted—could mean the unravelling of the fabric of life 'outside'. In addition, life in prison would have been governed, as Apollonius of Tyana indicates,[1] by varying degrees of torpor and stasis.

I. Extended Incarceration and Its Reasons

Luke writes concerning Paul's time in Caesarea that 'when two years had passed, Felix was succeeded by Porcius Festus, but because Felix wanted to grant a favour to the Jews, he left Paul in prison' (Acts 24:27). Of Paul's time in Rome it is recorded, 'for two whole years Paul stayed there in his own rented house and welcomed all who came to see him' (Acts 28:30). Had Luke simply used the expression διετία, this could indicate that Paul was in prison for the period of a year plus part of another year. However, the adjective ὅλη indicates the completion of a full two year period of time.[2] Haenchen writes that 'anyone who writes thus knows (1) that a change occurred, and (2) in what it consisted'.[3] In regard to the former instance, Lake has argued from extrabiblical sources that the two years indicated at Acts 24:27, the text of which he states is 'wholly ambiguous',[4] refers to the duration of Felix' procuratorship and not to the duration of Paul's imprisonment. His argument has convinced a number of scholars. The evidence, far from compelling the reader to construe this to be a reference to Felix' early recall in 55/56 AD, rather argues more convincingly for a recall date of about 59 AD.[5] A termination of Felix' office at 55/56 AD, moreover, would make something of a nonsense of Paul's indication that Felix had been judge over the Jewish nation for many years (ἐκ πολλῶν

---

[1]Cast into a Roman prison, Apollonius conversed with the other inmates. He remarked to his disciple Damis, '...what else is there for us to do until the time comes when the despot will give me such audience as he desires?' Philostratus, VA 7.22.
[2]G. Schneider, Die Apostelgeschichte: II Teil (HTKNT 5/2; Freiburg: Herder, 1982), 420 who points to the use of ὅλη with other time indications at Acts 11:26 and Luke 5:5.
[3]Haenchen, The Acts, 724-26. The aorist of ἐμμένω is further indication of a change in Paul's condition after the two years to Knowling, 'The Acts of the Apostles', 552, who cites E.deW. Burton, Syntax of the Moods and Tenses in New Testament Greek (1898; 3rd. edn. rpt.; Edinburgh: T. and T. Clark, 1976), § 39b.
[4]K. Lake, 'Note 34. The Chronology of Acts', in BC, vol. 5, 465.
[5]Supra, 162 n.57.

ἐτῶν: Acts 24:10). Paul would hardly have risked making such a rhetorical flourish if it was so obviously untrue.[6] We take the διετία then to refer to the period of Paul's incarceration, the verb πληρόω arguing for its being a full two years in duration.

1. Extended Incarceration in the Ancient World

Macgregor writes: 'That Paul was kept waiting for a decision in his case for no less than two years [in Caesarea] has seemed incredible to some recent scholars'.[7] An incarceration of two years' duration in Rome might inspire the same reactions. But we should not be greatly surprised. The duration of imprisonment before final disposition of one's case in the ancient world could vary widely. Egyptian evidence across a considerable period of time indicates that while imprisonment might be for only a few days,[8] it could last months, or even years.[9] Some examples may also be given of extended periods of imprisonment in Greek contexts.[10] When Lucullus (72 BC) captured Cabeira and other strongholds in Asia Minor, he

> found great treasures, and many prisons, in which many Greeks and many kinsfolk of the king were confined. As they had long been given up for dead, it was not so much a rescue as it was a resurrection and a sort of second birth, for which they were indebted to the favour of Lucullus.[11]

There are also numerous Roman examples of extended imprisonment, some lasting years, before trial or final disposition.[12]

---

[6]Cf. B. Winter, 'The Importance', 505-31 and Hemer, *Acts in the Setting of Hellenistic History*, 173.

[7]G.H.C. Macgregor and T.P. Ferris, *The Acts*, 314.

[8]*PEnteux.* 1:83 (221 BC): 4 days; *PCairZen.* 3:59520 (mid 3rd cent. BC): 22 days; Taubenschlag, 'L'Emprisonnement ', 716 n. 28, notes an imprisonment of 40 days in a 3rd cent. BC document *Zen.* 59.639.

[9]Taubenschlag, 'L'Emprisonnement', 716 n. 29 citing *PSI* 4:347 (n.d.); Plutarch, *De lib. educ.* 11.F (283-246 BC).

[10]Diodorus Siculus 17.80.2 (323-328 BC) 3 years; *ibid.* 19.105.2 (316-311 BC): 5 years.

[11]Plutarch, *Luc.* 18.1.

2. The Reasons for Extended Incarceration

Reasons for delay in coming to trial in the ancient Mediterranean world and hence having to endure extended incarceration were several and varied. One was the sheer volume of court business. Lewis shows how this arose in the provinces in his discussion of judicial procedure in Roman Egypt.[13] It was the duty of the Roman governor to process annually through Egypt and conduct assizes in the thirty administrative districts. Wealthy individuals might circumvent the usually long wait by making a trip to Alexandria and attempting to arrange for a personal hearing. One who was less important, however, whether out of poverty or lack of influence, could only bide his time at home; where he was unable to furnish sureties in a serious case, he might have to await his day in court in the local lockup. Lewis shows that the volume of business to be handled at an assize was enormous.[14] A plaintiff who had not been heard might have to await the governor's next annual visit; if a petition had been received, it would be packed up and taken to Alexandria and answered in the months that followed. Often the case was simply referred back to the local officials and this 'as far as the complainant was concerned, was simply piling delay upon delay'.[15] We might add that, as the provincial capital was the central clearinghouse for cases referred from all provincial districts for determination, the court calendar there was often overwhelmed.

The pattern described above and the delays that resulted were not exceptional to Egypt; they occurred throughout the Empire. Sherwin-White indicates, for example, that 'Pliny in Bithynia-Pontus took two seasons to work through a rather small province'.[16] Moreover, what was true of the provinces was especially the case in the Imperial

---

[12]Josephus, *AJ* 18.169f. [18.6.5]; Philo, *In Flaccum* 128f. (2 years); Dio Cassius 59.6.2 (7 years); Josephus, *Vit.* 13f. [3] (4-5 years?); *b. Nez.* V: *Sanh.* I.12a; *Ber.* 16b (several years); G. Bagnani, 'Peregrinus Proteus and the Christians', *Historia* 4 (1955), 112 (2 years). The following examples from the Christian confessors may be noted: Cyprian, *Ep.* 33.2 [= Oxf., *Ep.* 39] (19 days); *Mart. Mont. & Luc.* 12.2f. (several months); *Mart. Fruct. & Co.* 2.1 (six days); Mason, *The Historic Martyrs*, 289 (2.5 years), 296 (2 years).

[13]What follows is a summary of the chapter entitled '*Insciam Legum* or The Administration of Justice' in N. Lewis, *Life in Egypt Under Roman Rule* (Oxford: Clarendon, 1983), 185-95, 227f. nn.

[14]Lewis, *Life in Egypt*, 190 citing *POxy.* 2131 and *PYale* 61.

[15]Lewis, *Life in Egypt*, 192.

[16]A.N. Sherwin-White, 'The Early Persecutions and Roman Law Again', 212.

capital which was the heart of the judicial system and ultimate reposi-
tory for referred cases. Garnsey, writes that

> there was widespread dissatisfaction at the beginning of the Princi-
> pate with the existing state of both the civil and the criminal law. The
> *ius ordinarium*, built up by the praetor through edicts, was felt to be ex-
> cessively formalistic and inflexible, and its delays were notorious; the
> criminal jury-courts, meanwhile, were slow-moving and corrupt.[17]

Tacitus' reference to Augustus' creation of the post of urban prefect to
address the slow-moving remedies of the law [(*ob*)*tarda legum auxilia*],
he suggests, 'may well contain an implied criticism of existing civil and
criminal procedures'.[18] General congestion in the court system continued to be a concern. During the reign of Claudius, writes Dio Cassius,
'the number of law-suits was now beyond all reckoning'.[19] The situation was exacerbated by later civil distress until at the beginning of
Vespasian's principate, 'lawsuit upon lawsuit had accumulated in all
the courts to an excessive degree, since those of long standing were left
unsettled through the interruption of court business and new ones had
arisen through the disorder of the times'.[20] Vespasian's various remedies were enacted out of the conviction that 'the lifetime of the litigants
would not suffice for the regular proceedings'.[21]

    Second, extended remand resulted from changes in the officiat-
ing magistrates. Two examples illustrate: In a papyrus of 10 BC, a petitioner complains to the prefect Gaius Turranius that he and several
others had been imprisoned and were on the point of being released by
Cordus, the official overseeing the case, when his term of office came
to an end. Subsequent inquiry under the oversight of his successor Bri-
son had resulted in their being left in prison.[22] Mason describes how
the confessor Pamphilus was condemned by the governor Urban at
Caesarea (307 AD). He continues: '...almost immediately after, Urban
fell into sudden disgrace with his master Maximin, and was executed
at Caesarea itself, and another governor appointed in his place. Pamphilus lay apparently forgotten in his prison for two whole years'.[23]

---

[17]P.D.A. Garnsey, *Social Status and Legal Privilege in the Roman Empire* (Oxford:
Clarendon, 1970), 65.
[18]Garnsey, *Social Status*, 92, citing Tacitus, *Ann.* 6.11.3.
[19]Dio Cassius 60.28.6.
[20]Suetonius, *Ves.* 8.10.
[21]*Ibid.* For a Greek example of extended imprisonment because of war, *cf.* Diodorus Siculus 15.8.5.
[22]*PLond.* 2:354.

Third, delay might arise out of magisterial misbehaviour. Lewis remarks that one of the ways that a prefect might attempt to speed up the judicial process was to press friends into service as judges. There was, however, a need to watch out for and warn against judicial foot-dragging. Even when judgements had been rendered, lesser officials might resist executing them.[24] Procrastination and obfuscation of the judicial process was not only a predilection of governors and lesser officials; emperors too might be guilty. Of Tiberius, Josephus writes, 'no king or tyrant was ever more given to procrastination'.[25] Nero, Suetonius tells us, followed a ponderous procedure, requiring the parties to present their case individually and privately before him. He also consulted with his advisors individually and privately, requiring that their opinions be set down in writing and submitted to him. This allowed Nero, according to Suetonius, the freedom of giving his personal decisions but representing them as majority verdicts.[26] Aelian's remark to Apollonius about awaiting Domitian's 'leisure'[27] and the philosopher's own reply also indicate that emperors would not be hurried.

Finally, delay often arose from the actions of the litigants themselves. Postponements might, on the one hand, be sought and granted for entirely legitimate reasons; for example, if there was need to see to the harvest,[28] through some inability to be present when the case was called,[29] or if time were needed to accumulate evidence.[30] Purposely dilatory tactics, on the other hand, were also prevalent. Dio Cassius notes that out of an awareness that many 'who expected to lose their cases would no longer put in an appearance', the emperor Claudius, about the year 46 AD, 'issued a proclamation announcing that he

---

[23]Mason, *The Historic Martyrs*, 296.

[24]Lewis, *Life in Egypt*, 192-94 and sources there cited. See *PCairZen.* 3:59520; *cf. Cod. Theod.* 9.3.6.

[25]Josephus, *AJ* 18.169 [18.6.5]. Further, *ibid.* 18.170 [18.6.5] remarks: 'Similarly he was negligent about hearing trials of prisoners'. The reader should recall from the discussion of imprisonment as a *poena* and place of remand that Tiberius' dilatory behaviour was not innocent.

[26]Suetonius, *Nero* 15.1. *Cf.* the comments and sources cited by J.B. Lightfoot, *Saint Paul's Epistle to the Philippians* (1913; rpt. Grand Rapids: Zondervan, 1953), 4f. and n. 4.

[27]Philostratus, *VA* 7.22.

[28]Lewis, *Life in Egypt*, 193.

[29]*Ibid.* One might also think of conditions such as those elaborated in *Dig.* 4.6 *passim.*

[30]See Tacitus, *Ann.* 13.43, 52.

would decide the cases against them by a given day even in their absence; and he strictly enforced this rule'.[31] This recourse was also taken provincially as the edicts of the Egyptian prefects Marcus Mettius Rufus (89 AD) and Titus Pactumeius Magnus (c. 189 AD) show.[32] Normally, delay injured the plaintiff by keeping him from his rights and benefited the defendant by allowing him to continue even longer in the enjoyment of the fruit of his wrong, whether real or supposed.[33] In the case of a defendant who had been imprisoned and could not obtain sureties, however, the advantage clearly fell to the plaintiffs and all the more so when they, whether legitimately or otherwise, were able to prolong their opponent's incarceration.

3. Paul's Extended Incarceration in Acts

Paul's case before Felix at Caesarea, on being prorogued, faded unresolved into the juridical background. The decision to prorogue was partially inspired by an official knowledge of the Way which belied the strength of the plaintiffs' case and by the ostensible motive of needing more information from Lysias. We have argued that the measures taken were also inspired by Felix' awareness of the damage the respective parties' status and political influence might do him as well as his propensity to venality.

If the pronouncement of adjournment effectively removed Felix from having to take immediate action which would upset the parties in the case and increase his unpopularity, extended delay further protected him from such dangers. In the absence of a citizen's appeal, such a recourse was not illegal.

The delay might have been circumvented by Paul when Felix remarked that at the same time that he was gratifying his interest in Paul's message, he 'was hoping that Paul would offer him a bribe' (Acts 24:26). If outright freedom was not for sale, perhaps a quicker trial and even a verdict in favour of Paul were. The unmistakable implication of the next phrase—*viz.*, 'when two years had passed' (Acts 24:27)—is that Paul's reaction was a principled resistance which delayed his hearing and may have prevented his release.

---

[31]Dio Cassius 60.28.6. *Cf.* Suetonius, *Cl.* 15.2.
[32]Quoted in Lewis, *Life in Egypt*, 193 and *cf. POxy.* 42:3017 (250 AD) there cited.
[33]J.M. Kelly, *Roman Litigation* (Oxford: Clarendon, 1966), 118.

Would extending the suspension of proceedings (and consequently extending Paul's imprisonment) have arisen in part, as an official delaying tactic, because of personal representations by the Jews? Though the text is silent on this specific point, the mention of Felix' doing the Jews a 'favour' (Acts 24:27) permits a fairly confident answer. We observe, first of all, that Felix took the initiative. He had fallen into trouble with the Jewish élite, alienating them at one point by suppressing disturbances in Caesarea at the cost of many Jewish lives.[34] Second, a 'favour', we are reminded by Knowling, is a deposit 'for which a due return might be expected'.[35] Felix might well have been expected to do any number of significant things to assuage Jewish hatred of him. If keeping Paul in prison was one of these ways—for Luke it is understandably a singular motive—this is remarkable. By implication, it indicates that the hatred of the Jews for Paul had such depth over time that his continued incarceration was thought by Felix to constitute a means by which he might ingratiate himself to his provincial enemies.[36] The value of Paul would hardly have been clear to Felix solely from the trial two years earlier. That Paul's continued imprisonment was such a significant 'bargaining chip' suggests that Felix had resisted more recent representations clearly hostile to Paul. This would reinforce the conviction concerning the prisoner Paul's high currency and probably keep Felix, unless bribed, from releasing him promptly.

More may be said about the 'favour'. We have seen that at the transition point between officials, prisoners might become 'lost' in the bureaucratic machinery, spending months or years longer in custody awaiting 'discovery'. This is probably not the underlying thrust of Felix' 'favour' or at least not how the Jews construed it because of their immediate efforts to have Paul executed extra-judicially when Festus arrived (Acts 25:1-5, 14-16). The 'favour' was to put an official question mark to Paul's claims of innocence by leaving him a prisoner. When exposed to Jewish accusation, there was a greatly increased prospect of his falling victim to the ignorance, magnanimity, or aggrandizing tendencies of the new appointment.

---

[34]Josephus, *AJ* 20.182 [20.8.9 ≈ *BJ* 2.270 (2.13.7)]. *Cf.* Tacitus, *Ann.* 12.54 and the discussion of political instabilities *supra*, 164f.

[35]Knowling, 'The Acts', 490 and note the examples there cited. H.W. Tajra, *The Trial of St. Paul*, 132, speaks of 'a marked nuance of reciprocity'.

[36]Marshall's reference to this action as a 'slight injustice to an unpopular individual' (*The Acts of the Apostles* [TNTC 5; Grand Rapids: Eerdmans, 1980], 382) would then be an underestimation of both the background and the transaction itself.

It is safe to assume that Paul would not have been personally known to the official in Rome who recorded the date of his arrival, the details of his case, and set the conditions of his custody. The two years of Acts 28:30, moreover, cannot represent an official interest in prolonging Paul's wait for his day in court. But do they reflect an officially set time period? The reference to a full period of two years (διετία ὅλη) is seen by some to indicate a statute of limitations on prosecutions.[37] The prisoner Lampon's two year imprisonment, it is argued, is described as μήκιστον χρόνον, meaning the 'longest time' (i.e., legally possible) rather than simply 'a very long time'.[38] Cadbury adds that the two year appeal period permitted by the Senate to Bithynians convicted by the disgraced Julius Bassus in 98 AD 'may show that such a period of grace was customary'.[39] He cites as further support an edict (*BGU* 628 *recto*) identified as Neronian which, in deference to those oppressed by long delays in settling their cases, set general time limits of nine months for those coming to Rome from transalpine locales and eighteen months for those coming from across the sea.[40]

It is doubtful that the two whole years refer to a statute of limitations. First, the context of deliberate judicial delay in the Philo text and the way μήκιστον χρόνον is normally rendered would seem to argue that the two years Lampon spent in prison awaiting trial were simply 'a very long time'.[41] Second, the *biennium* within which those convicted by Bassus might appeal their convictions is a special senatorial provision and not a general principle in law. Third, not only is the time period noted in *BGU* 628 *not* two years, there are serious problems in assigning the document to Nero's reign.[42] Finally, the notion of such a rule is undermined by the fact that the Jewish priests for whom

---

[37]In H.J. Cadbury, 'Note 26. Roman Law and the Trial of Paul', in *BC*, vol. 5, 330. The reader is directed to Cadbury's summary of the history of this view, including Ramsay's contributions to it, *ibid.*, 326 n. 1. Tajra, *The Trial of St. Paul*, 195f.; H.C. Kee and F.W. Young, *The Living World of the New Testament* (London: Darton, Longman and Todd, 1960), 303f. are more recent proponents of this view.

[38]Philo, *In Flaccum* 128f. [Eng. = 'for as long as possible']. Lake cited in Cadbury, 'Roman Law', 330.

[39]Cadbury, 'Roman Law', 332, citing Pliny, *Ep.* 10.56f.

[40]Cadbury, 'Roman Law', 333-35 See Conzelmann, *Acts*, 240f., Appendix 11 for both the text and an English translation.

[41]Sherwin-White, *Roman Society*, 116f. *Cf.* Bruce, *The Acts of the Apostles*, 541.

[42]Sherwin-White, *Roman Society*, 115. Further on the date, Tajra, *The Trial of St. Paul*, 195; F.F. Bruce, *New Testament History* (London: Thomas Nelson, 1969), 344 and *cf.* W.M. Ramsay, 'Suggestions on the History and Letters of St. Paul. 2. The Imprisonment and Supposed Trial of St. Paul in Rome: Acts 28', *Exp* VIII/5 (1913), 279-81.

Josephus sought release in 64 AD—i.e., Paul's day—had been in prison for at least four or five years.[43]

Did the Jews employ delaying tactics to harm Paul by extending his incarceration in Rome?[44] Luke does state that as late as four months after Paul's departure from Caesarea, the Jewish leaders in Rome had received no written or oral communications from Judaea against him (Acts 28:21). A four month delay in news coming from Jerusalem, however, probably only reflects the seasonal limitations of travel (cf. Acts 27:9; 28:11). Further against the notion of Jewish delaying tactics, it has been argued that the Jews pressed for resumption of proceedings against Paul during the two year Caesarean incarceration. Felix' 'favour' had encouraged them to attempt to rush Festus to *ex parte* action. Frustrated in this, they seized the opportunity immediately to litigate when it was presented to them. If the pattern above is any indication, we might expect them to have made attempts to hasten rather than delay prosecuting Paul in Rome.

We conclude that the two whole years Paul spent in Rome were due to the heavily congested Roman court calendar and that the named Jewish accusers were as much at the mercy of the grindingly slow process as the prisoner. Having said this, however, any trouble that the system's slowness did to Paul would certainly not have resulted in the plaintiffs losing any sleep.[45]

II. Prison Pastimes

Paul would have had much time on his hands because of delay. Prisoners might of course be crippled into inactivity by their troubles, as were many of those considered above; or they might try to keep active to the extent that their incarceration permitted. We turn to how prisoners occupied their time and how this might help us analyse what Luke writes concerning Paul.

---

[43]Josephus, *Vit.* 13f.[3].

[44]So Ramsay, 'Suggestions', 276. *Cf.* Lightfoot, *Saint Paul's Epistle to the Philippians*, 2f.

[45]V. Bartlet, 'Two New Testament Problems: 1. St. Paul's Fate in Rome', *Exp* VIII/5 (1913), 466.

1. Mundane Pursuits

When persons went to prison, their ability to secure a livelihood for themselves and their families and their ability to meet the demands of their employers were seriously curtailed or entirely frustrated. Amuntas writes to Zenon (mid 3rd cent. BC) asking him to intercede regarding an item on loan which has been caught up in a seizure and sale action against the property of a prisoner named Herakletas.[46] The employer Sostratos writes to Zenon that because of the imprisonment of Rhodon the guard of his hay, it has all been carried off; certain of his bee-keepers have been imprisoned and the hives have been removed elsewhere and seriously damaged.[47] The farmer Pathiophis pleads with Zenon to release his imprisoned wife who is destroying herself with worry for her children; the worry and extra burden on Pathiophis is keeping him from his work.[48] Kallisthenes pleads to be released from prison, or else goods he has put up in pledge and wine as yet unsold will be lost.[49] The prisoner Pais and his family, their resources bankrupted, throw themselves upon the mercy of Zenon because they are staring into the face of starvation and death.[50] Ignatius (98-117 AD) acknowledges the spread of disaster when he chides those who have no care 'for the prisoner, *or for him released from prison*'.[51] The provisions in Roman legislation by which persons over twenty-five obtained restitution confirm that imprisonment in the later Roman context could also lead to significant, if not complete, loss of the means to provide for self and family.[52]

Prisoners could be made to work at public projects.[53] But could they carry on their trade or business, supporting themselves and others *while in prison*? For Paul, Philippi, Jerusalem and the early phase at Caesarea would not have allowed for such a possibility. For the later Caesarean custody, Paul was materially assisted by associates (Acts 24:23). There is considerable interest in this question, however, for the

---

[46]*Sammelb.* 3:6787. Further on sequestration, *PCairZen.* 2:59275; R. Taubenschlag, *The Law of Greco-Roman Egypt in the Light of the Papyri* (New York: Herald Square, 1944), 417 and n. 37.

[47]*PCairZen.* 3:59368 [= *Sammelb.* 3:6769].

[48]*PCairZen.* 3:59482. *Cf. ibid.* 4:59601.

[49]*Ibid.* 4:59626.

[50]*PLond.* 7:2045.

[51]Ignatius, *Smyr.* 6.2. [*My italics.*]

[52]*Dig.* 4.6.*passim.*

[53]*Cf.*, e.g., Plautus, *Captivi* 722-26, 729-31 (255-184 BC); *P Col.* 3:58 (248 BC [= *PColZen.* 1:58]); Philostratus, *VA* 5.19 (reign of Nero).

time of Paul's custody in Rome at Acts 28:16-31; particularly in light of the expression ἐν ἰδίῳ μισθώματι. Whether one prefers the rendering 'at his own expense', 'on his own earnings' or, as we have argued, 'in his own hired lodging',[54] the question of how Paul covered costs remains.

A number of scholars suggest that Paul, in the easier conditions of a light military custody, was able to carry on his trade.[55] Hanson and others argue that 'it is known from Ulpian ... that a prisoner awaiting trial was allowed to pursue his trade'.[56] The text, *Dig.* 4.6.10, reads: 'In the same position are those who are kept in custody by soldiers, the attendants of a magistrate, or servants of a municipality, if they are shown not to have been able to look after their own business'.[57] The inference that Paul and other prisoners could work, however, cannot be drawn from this legal provision. An eye to the context of the provision of restitution puts the following constraints upon how the provision is to be understood: the situation in view is of legal actions from which an individual might suffer disadvantage or loss related to business or other material interests he or she holds outside the prison. Restitution is granted where it can be shown that those interests could not properly be administered from inside the prison. Looking after one's own affairs in this context might include signing legal documents, making payments, meeting contractually agreed deadlines, and generally giving timely instruction through plenipotentiaries—whether relatives, business partners, freedmen or slaves; it does not allow for a prisoner setting up a tent-making business to support himself while in custody.

Other factors already discussed also render the prospect very unlikely. First, adequate security required guards, on penalty of severe punishment, to keep their prisoners in such a way that they could neither escape nor harm themselves. If barber's knives and pen knives were a serious danger to prisoners and best kept away from them,[58]

---

[54]*Supra*, 177-82.

[55]Tajra, *The Trial of St. Paul*, 191f.; Williams, *Acts*, 452; Schille, *Die Apostelgeschichte*, 476; Schneider, *Die Apostelgeschichte*, 408 n. 30; Marshall, *The Acts*, 425; Hanson, *The Acts*, 253f.; H.J. Cadbury, 'Lexical Notes on Luke-Acts III. Luke's Interest in Lodging', *JBL* 45 (1926), 322 and nn. 31f.; Wendt and Knabenbauer cited in Knowling, 'The Acts', 552.

[56]Hanson, *The Acts*, 253f. So also, e.g., Schneider, *Die Apostelgeschichte*, 408 n. 30; Schille, *Die Apostelgeschichte*, 476; Marshall, *The Acts*, 425; Cadbury, 'Roman Law', 320.

[57]*Cf.* further on the monetary disadvantage of being 'in bonds', *Dig.* 2.11.4.1; 4.6.1.1; 22.1.23; 49.14.45.1.

[58]For a discussion of the above noted security concerns, see *supra*, 32, 217-18.

would Paul's keepers have allowed labour which required knives, awls and other sharp tools? Second, rental costs and the prospects for a prisoner renting being what they were, Paul probably occupied an economical third floor apartment in one of the thousands of tenement buildings in the capital. It is doubtful that he would have wanted or even been able to afford a street-level storefront from which business was usually conducted.[59] Recall too that the living quarters were for him *alone* (*cf.* Acts 28:16, 23, 30). Finally, Paul's imprisonment would have been inconvenient to the conduct of business to say the least. Physically, it 'would have been awkward if he was continually chained by the wrist to a soldier'.[60] And even if he had been permitted to carry on business, custom would have been negatively affected by Paul's circumstances.

We conclude that Paul could not have engaged in his trade. Ramsay has written that by appealing, 'Paul was choosing undoubtedly an expensive line of trial. All this had certainly been estimated before the decisive step was taken'.[61] We agree with Ramsay on this point and his conclusion that Paul supported himself from 'hereditary property',[62] though our rendering of ἐν ἰδίῳ μισθώματι would not foreclose the possibility of outside help from Christians living abroad or those living in Rome.

Faced with the prospect of extended incarceration, a prisoner might make legal attempts to obtain justice or immediate release. Individuals could seek redress by writing petitions:

> In Ptolemaic times we find petitions addressed by the humblest individuals to the king and queen, of which several specimens are included among the Serapeum papyri. Under the Roman rule the privilege was continued, petitions being addressed to the Prefect in place of the king, and also to the subordinate officials, especially the strategus of the nome. A petition to the latter officials seems, indeed, to have been the normal method of setting the machinery of justice in motion for the redress of an injury.[63]

---

[59]*Supra,* 229 in the general context of the discussion there.

[60]Bruce, *The Book of the Acts,* 509f.

[61]W.M. Ramsay, *St. Paul the Traveller and the Roman Citizen* (London: Hodder and Stoughton, 1895), 311f. So also Tajra, *The Trial of St. Paul,* 131, 173 who, citing J.H. Oliver, 'Greek Applications for Roman Trials', *AJP* 100 (1979), 543-58, is convinced that Paul had to pay a prescribed deposit as part of the appellatory process. It should be noted that Paul's was a criminal rather than civil/monetary case.

[62] Ramsay, *St. Paul the Traveller,* 312.

[63]*PLond.* 2:354 [p. 163].

There is, for example, the urgent letter to Nikanor the epimeletes in which the petitioner writes: 'I have *often explained to you in writing* why I am being harshly treated in the prison, perishing from hunger for the last ten months, though I have been unjustly confined'.[64] The prisoner refers to the decrees that require the epimeletes to act justly to all those in prison and concludes with a plea that this official write to the *dioketes* or even send him directly so he will not die. A similar document (177 BC) shows the same concern to detail the case and ask for intervention in securing a release.[65] A prisoner with material means might attempt to obtain release by means of baksheesh.[66] The Zenon petitions noted above are also urgent requests for release written *in extremis*.[67] Among Egyptian examples from the Roman period are the petition sent by several prisoners to the prefect Gaius Turranius *c.* 10 BC.[68]

Most surviving petitions from prisoners are not original documents. Keenan writes concerning the task of accurately rendering *UC inv.* 1583 that

> lacunae hamper the work of decipherment, as do a number of cancellations (lines 4, 5, 6, 8, 9, 13, 18) and other corrections (*cf.* app. crit. on lines 19 and 21) which, together with the general sloppiness of the handwriting, suggest our text was a draft rather than a final copy, and quite possibly left incomplete.... Additional support for this view is provided by the verso....[69]

This suggests a process: the prisoner, intent upon sending a petition, would call for a professional scribe near the prison. For a fee, the scribe took down in rough draft the relevant details, returned to his office, and rendered a finished copy. It was then reviewed and signed by the prisoner and delivered by the scribe to the appropriate official.[70]

---

[64]*PPetr.* 3:36a *verso* [*My italics.*]. The contrast drawn in A. Deissmann, *St. Paul: A Study in Social and Religious History*, 19 n. 1, between the perfect calm of Paul's prison epistles and 'the plaintive, whining letters' among which he numbers *PPetr.* 3:36a *verso*, may not be entirely fair. The Egyptian examples are intended to motivate officials; Paul's are not.

[65]Keenan, 'Petition from a Prisoner', 91-102 [= *UC inv.* 1583].

[66]Deissmann, *St. Paul*, 47f. n. 2 for examples.

[67]*PCairZen.* 2:59275; 3:59482; 4:59492, 59601, 59626; *Sammelb.* 3:6787; *PLBat.* 20:29.

[68]*PLond.* 2:354.

[69]Keenan, 'Petition from a Prisoner', 93.

[70]See E.G. Turner and W.E.W. Cockle, 'Complaint Against a Policeman', 272.

The rough drafts thereafter were discarded as scrap.[71] The petition to Gaius Turranius mentioned above, however, must be a finished copy:

> The sheet of papyrus is itself a fine one, of unusual height and width (13.25 in. x 9 in.) for a single-columned document (and that though a large part of it is left blank at the bottom), showing, with the elaborate character of the writing, that the petitioners had not spared expense to make their petition acceptable to the prefect.[72]

There is no indication in Acts that Paul sent written petitions to officials regarding his case either during the two years of his Caesarean incarceration or while a prisoner in Rome. In Caesarea he had ample opportunity to make personal representations if he so chose, but he appears not to have done so despite 'encouragements' (*cf.* Acts 24:26). The obviously less prison-like environment and brighter ministry prospects in Rome hint that any urge to legal 'pushing' was even less a priority for Paul than in Caesarea. It would probably not have helped anyway. The *process* by which prisoners made written petitions, however, may shed light upon how Paul was assisted in his non-legal writing. We shall return to this point later.

Most prisoners would eventually have to answer to the charges against them. This could occur at a jail clearance. Provincial governors were instructed to conduct jail clearances periodically to which local senators and barristers were to be invited.

> The governor would discharge those prisoners who appeared to him on a cursory examination to be innocent, and reserve the rest for a proper trial; there was, however, nothing to prevent him condemning a man on the spot if he thought his guilt manifest, and he was accordingly instructed to give due notice of a gaol clearance so that prisoners could prepare their cases and not be taken by surprise by their accusers. A proconsul could delegate the task of gaol clearing to his legate, but in the case of Roman citizens the legate was entitled only to hold a preliminary investigation, and must send up all the prisoners to the proconsul, who would normally no doubt release the ones found not guilty by his legate and try the rest.[73]

Failing this, prisoners went to court. It is probably this to which Tertullian (c. 195 AD) refers when he reminds the martyrs that they await the

---

[71]Keenan indicates that *UC inv.* 1583 has survived to the present because it was used as cartonage for mummification; a fact which tells its own story!

[72]*PLond.* 2:354 [p. 164].

[73]Jones, *The Criminal Courts*, 117f. citing *Dig.* 1.16.6.*prol*; 48.1.12; 48.18.18.9.

judge's appearance.[74] Prisoners were usually forewarned so as to be prepared. After a humiliating confinement among serious offenders, Apollonius of Tyana is released by a court official who intimates:

> The Emperor, Apollonius, releases you from these fetters by the advice of Aelian; and he permits you to take up your quarters in the prison where criminals are not bound, until the time comes for you to make your defence, but you will probably be called upon to plead your cause five days from now.[75]

Warning was not always given. On the evening of the fifth day of an earlier phase of Apollonius' imprisonment a person comes to him, takes him aside and tells him that on the next day the Emperor will give him an audience. 'I will keep your secret', Apollonius replies, 'for it is only Aelian, I think, who can know so much'.[76]

Against the eventuality of answering to the charges in the circumstances noted above, another important prison pastime was case preparation. Prison could pose serious limitations to such activity. Euxitheus (c. 420 BC) complains that one reason his opponents had him kept in prison was that this would crimp his legal preparations.[77] Apollonius' pupil Damis, wonders at the wisdom of disturbing the other prisoners 'in the preparation of their defence'.[78]

Counsel might come from within the prison or from without. Andocides (415 BC), when incarcerated at Athens, takes legal counsel from a fellow inmate named Timaeus.[79] The conversations between Apollonius and his cell mates, while philosophically edifying, may also have assisted, to some extent, in legal ways as well.[80] Cicero's hypothetical situation, in which a prisoner awaiting death drafts a will, reflects at the least the capacity of receiving legal assistance from outside the prison. While men are off to collect the accoutrements for his execution, 'some of his friends bring tablets and witnesses to the prison, they write a will naming as heirs those whom he wished; the tablets are sealed'.[81]

---

[74]Tertullian, Ad Mart. 2. Recalling 1 Cor. 6 to the martyrs, Tertullian encourages them that at the heavenly assize, they will judge the judges.
[75]Philostratus, VA 7.40.
[76]Ibid. 7.28. Cf. Mart. Perp. & Felic. 5.1; 6.1.
[77]Antiphon, Caed. Her. 18.
[78]Philostratus, VA 7.22.
[79]Plutarch, Alc. 21.3.
[80]Philostratus, VA 7 passim. Cf. Achilles Tatius, Clit. & Leuc. 7.2.1-4.
[81]Cicero, Inv. Rhet. 2.149.

A prisoner, if materially able and not physically hindered, might receive professional assistance. Apollonius is asked, '...do you not, O Apollonius, need someone to advise you how to converse with the Emperor?'[82] The questioner gives the philosopher counsel which is gratefully received.[83] The wealthy and prominent Christian Phileas (c. 304/ 7 AD) is plagued by the attempts of well-meaning advocates, against his wishes, to derail his confession, preventing his martyrdom. One of the advocates is his unbelieving brother.[84]

Paul conducted his own defence without outside help in Caesarea before Felix, Festus, and Agrippa and the gathered assembly. This reflects both a God-given confidence and the strength of his case. Jewish hiring of a rhetor and Paul's own performance during the trial before Felix tend to confirm Paul's status and his expertise in forensic discourse.[85] If this pattern of self-representation is any indication, we may conclude that Paul also conducted his own defence in Rome.

One of Paul's earliest actions in Rome was to prepare the ground for later forensic presentation. At Acts 28:17 Paul calls together the leaders of the Jews to meet with him. One important motive is Paul's concern for the potential impact of the local Jewish communities upon the outcome of his trial. Indications of their power and influence outside of the NT show this to be a legitimate and prudent action. This is case preparation of a kind. However, it does not violate Jesus' injunctions at Luke 21:14f. (cf. Luke 12:11f.) against prepared speech.[86]

The Jewish community in Rome was sizeable. Josephus asserts that 'more than eight thousand of the Jews in Rome'[87] supported the cause of a Palestinian Jewish delegation against Varus, the legate of Syria (c. 6-4 BC). Modern estimates of the total 1st century Jewish population range from 10,000 to 50,000.[88] The higher range may be more accurate if Jewish expulsion over 'Chrestus' (c. 49 AD) was confined to troublers or specific troubled communities.[89]

The leaders who came to Paul may not have been part of a centralized authority in Roman Judaism. There is no positive reference to

---

[82]Philostratus, VA 7.28.
[83]Cf. ibid. 8.6f. Apollonius undelivered written oration, included in Philostratus' account, may reflect the assistance.
[84]Mart. Phil. coll. 11-13 of PBod and 5.5.
[85]Supra, 162-63.
[86]Προμελετάω at Luke 21:14 is a biblical hapax legomenon. It is a technical expression (cf. Aristophanes, Ec. 116) indicating the preparation and rehearsing of speech and gesture prior to a formal presentation according to T.W. Manson, The Sayings of Jesus (London: SMC, 1949), 327.
[87]Josephus, BJ 2.80 [2.6.1 ≈ AJ 17.300 (17.11.1)].

a central administration and some scholars are prepared to assert that it did not exist.[90] The lack of central organization and earlier expulsion of Jewish-Christian troublers from Rome would further tend to counsel against doubt or surprise regarding the Jews' ignorance about Paul and lack of specific knowledge about the Christian αἵρεσις to which he belonged (Acts 28:21f.).

To say that the Jewish community was not centrally organized, however, is not to assert their political impotence. Cicero acknowledges the power of the local Jewish population to sway opinion against his client Flaccus (59 BC).[91] Up to 8,000 Roman Jews supported the cause of the Palestinian delegation who opposed Archelaus as sovereign in the last century BC.[92] The Emperor's finding indicates to some extent that the delegation's case had been significantly and successfully augmented by this support. Shortly thereafter, the Jews of Rome united in support of a Jew who falsely claimed to be Herod's son Alexander.[93] Despite popular Jewish acclaim, he was found out and punished.

There were also highly placed individual Jews and Jewish sympathizers in Rome. About the year 64 AD, Josephus went to secure the acquittal of certain Jewish priests sent to Rome by Felix several years before. Josephus enlisted the services of the actor Aliturus, 'who was a special favourite of Nero and of Jewish origin'.[94] Through Aliturus, Josephus continues, 'I was introduced to Poppaea, Caesar's consort, and took the earliest opportunity of soliciting her aid to secure the liberation of the priests. Having, besides this favour, received large gifts from Poppaea, I returned to my own country'.[95] Other interventions might be mentioned.[96] One ought not to forget, either, that among the forms of favour and support available through the system of patron-

---

[88]Hauser, *Strukturen*, 83 n. 67, who notes 50,000 (H. Leon; J. Juster); 40,000 (L. Goppelt); 10,000 (*EncJud*). *Cf.* R.E. Brown, 'Part Two: Rome', in *Antioch and Rome*, R.E. Brown and J.P. Meyer (Ramsey, N.J.: Paulist, 1983), 102 and R. Penna, 'Les Juifs à Rome au Temps de l'Apôtre Paul', 328, who suggest mid 1st century AD numbers of 50,000 and 20,000 respectively; A.D. Clarke, 'Rome and Italy', 466-71.

[89]*Cf.* Suetonius, *Cl.* 25.4; Dio Cassius 60.6.6 and the discussion of Brown, 'Part Two: Rome', 100-2 who argues.

[90]So Hauser, *Strukturen*, 82 and nn. 61, 63. So also more recently, Penna, 'Les Juifs', 327. Brown, 'Part Two: Rome', 101 and n. 210, agrees based upon how easily Roman Jewry was divided over 'Chrestus'.

[91]Cicero, *Flac.* 66.

[92]For a description of how the Jewish crowd took up a position in support of the fifty delegates who had come to plead at the trial, *cf.* Josephus, *BJ* 2.105 [2.7.1 ≈ *AJ* 17.330 (17.12.2)].

[93]*Ibid.*, *BJ* 2.105 [2.7.1 ≈ *AJ* 17.330f. (17.12.1)].

[94]Josephus, *Vit.*16.

age implied by such synagogue names as *Augustenses, Agrippenses* and *Uolumnenses,* were political and juridical assistance.[97]

The power of the Jewish community was quite real and Paul's concern to address himself to its leaders as early as possible was both warranted and understandable. Luke records the assertion that Paul was unjustly accused; his arrival in the Imperial capital was the result of a defensive action and was not to be construed as harmful to Roman Jewry. Their enlistment as sympathetic confederates would have been most desirable. It is therefore hardly appropriate to accuse Paul of misplaced priorities or Luke of suppressing information concerning the Roman Church at this point. Luke records a legitimate and prudent priority activity.

Though there is no indication in Luke or the canonical Pauline captivity epistles that Paul ever did so, it is a fact that prisoners might also while away the hours of incarceration by playing games. Seneca relates how the prisoner Julius Canus (reign Gaius) gallantly jested about his advantage at a game of chess as he was called to be executed.[98] Plutarch (46/7-120 AD) tells of prisoners playing 'dice or draughts with the rope hanging overhead'.[99]

Here and there in the literature prisoners are said to pass the hours of incarceration by reading or by being read to. Socrates (399 BC) is an early example.[100] The phrase *non modo studendi solacium* is probably translated too narrowly when Suetonius writes that during the reign of Tiberius 'some of those who were consigned to prison were denied *not only the consolation of reading* but also the privilege of conversing and talking together'.[101] Intellectual activity, especially of a literary kind, is intended—certainly reading, but probably writing as well. The philosopher Epictetus (reign of Domitian) contemplates the prospect of prisoners being read to,[102] and Lucian writes that among

---

[95]*Ibid.* Her strong Jewish sympathies are indicated by Josephus in another place when he writes that Poppaea was a θεοσεβής (*AJ* 20.195 [20.8.11]). *Cf.* Tacitus, *Ann.* 16.6 and the discussion there [LCL], 492f. n. *d.*

[96]For the empress Antonia on behalf of prince Agrippa see in the present work *passim* and for other examples and sources, see Cadbury, 'Roman Law', 324 and nn. 1f.

[97]*Cf.* Penna, 'Les Juifs', 328.

[98]Seneca, *Tranq.* 14.6f.

[99]Plutarch, *De sera* 554.D.

[100]Plato, *Phd.* 61.B.

[101]Suetonius, *Tib.* 61.4. [*My italics.*]

[102]Arrian, *Epict. Diss.* 2.6.27.

the ministrations of Christians to Peregrinus during his incarceration (*c.* 132-34 AD), 'sacred books of theirs were read aloud'.[103]

Did Paul read or was he read to in prison? There are no direct indications in Acts. However, prison ministry would have been significantly augmented if Paul possessed records or *logia* of Jesus and/or significant concatenations of missiologically and catechetically helpful passages from Moses and the Prophets.[104] The reader may also properly recall the urgent appeal at 2 Tim. 4:13 that a cloak be brought to the prisoner that he had left with Carpus at Troas, but also the scrolls and especially the parchments.

2. Philosophical and Religious Disciplines

In the crisis of incarceration, it might be expected that a prisoner would turn to his god in some way. Non-Christian as well as Christians inclined to prayer. Just as he was given the cup of hemlock by the chief jailer, Socrates offers a prayer to the gods.[105] The philosopher Apollonius, 'when day came ... offered his prayers to the Sun, as best he could in prison'.[106] These prayers express Apollonius' habitual religious devotion rather than representing specific requests for escape, benevolent treatment, or release.[107] To confirm his ability and encourage his distraught disciple, Apollonius miraculously removes his foot from the fetters. Damis observes: '...for without any sacrifice,—and how in prison could he have offered any?—and without a single prayer, without even a word, he quietly laughed at the fetters, and then inserted his leg in them afresh, and behaved like a prisoner once more'.[108] Damis concludes that Apollonius could do this, not because of some divine favour, but because of his divine nature.

The NT apocryphal literature gives a number of instances of prisoners' prayers. If caution is called for in citing and analysing the material actualities of prison experience described in this literature, an even greater caution is advisable in the matter of prisoners' prayers and praise. In the apocryphal *Acts of Paul* (*c.* 185-95 AD) the imprisoned apostle busies himself with prayer. His words and the events of

---

[103]Lucian, *Peregr.* 12.
[104]*Infra*, 361.
[105]Plato, *Phd.* 117.B, C.
[106]Philostratus, *VA* 7.31.
[107]*Ibid.* 7.38.
[108]*Ibid.*

his incarceration in the temple of Apollo at Sidon recall Acts 4:29 and
1 Sam. 4. After three days' fasting and in great distress, he prays, 'O
God, look down upon their threats and suffer us not to fall, and let not
our adversary strike us down, but [deliver] us by speedily bringing
down thy righteousness upon us'.[109] Apollo's image falls down and
half the temple collapses. The apostle is expelled from the city. The
apocryphal Paul next prays in a cell of the stadium at Ephesus. Two
women named Artemilla and Eubula come 'to hear the beast-fighter's
prayer'.[110] The apostle's prayers in this account apparently serve a certain edificatory or instructive function for the women. At one point, a
lion roared 'fiercely and angrily, [so that even Paul] broke off his
prayer in terror'.[111] On the Sabbath before the Lord's day on which he
is to fight the beasts, Paul prays:

> 'My God, Jesus Christ, who didst redeem me from so many evils,
> grant me that before the eyes of Artemilla and Eubula, who are thine,
> the fetters may be broken from my hands'. And as Paul thus testified
> (or: adjured God), there came in a youth very comely in grace and
> loosed Paul's bonds, the youth smiling as he did so. And straightway
> he departed.[112]

This 'release' is not actual but visionary and in token of this vision, the
apostle no longer grieves at the prospect of fighting the beasts but rejoices.

The apocryphal Acts of Andrew (c. 190 AD) describes prison conversations through the night which are either punctuated by or concluded with communal prayers. The imprisoned Andrew concludes
the sequence by uttering a commendatory or benedictory prayer for
those gathered.[113]

As the apostle Thomas goes to prison, according to the apocryphal Acts of Thomas (first half of 3rd cent. AD), he praises Jesus that he
has been made worthy of suffering, is thankful for the patience to endure false accusations, and asks for the Lord's blessing. The prayer carries such conviction and joy that the other prisoners ask his
intercessions on their behalf. The apostle obliges.[114] Thomas' prayer
for light to remove the physical darkness of the prison is answered by

---

[109] Apoc. Acts of Paul 5.
[110] Ibid. 7.
[111] Ibid.
[112] Ibid. Cf. 2 Tim. 3:11.
[113] Apocr. Acts And. Narr. 22.
[114] Apoc. Acts of Thomas, 107f.

a supernatural effulgence which only the faithful can see. Later miraculously released, he asks God to preserve the catechumens before they are anointed, baptized and given the Eucharist; returning to the prison, he asks God to reseal the miraculously opened doors.[115]

The Christian martyr literature inspires somewhat less scepticism than the NT apocrypha. Despite an obvious tendency to idealism, this literature is particularly rich in examples of prisoners' prayers, many of which have a tone of realism. Frequently, confessors pray just before death.[116] They also pray during their incarcerations. At his arrest, Polycarp asks to pray for an hour undisturbed. He astonishes his captors by praying for two hours.[117] Later confessors pray in the prison corporately and individually and are said to pray fervently, continually, and day and night.[118]

The purposes of these prison prayers vary: Polycarp prays for all whom he had ever come in contact with and the entire Catholic church; Perpetua gives thanks to the Lord that she has been separated from her pagan father, prays for her dead brother, and together with the other prisoners successfully prays that the eight months pregnant Felicitas will be delivered of her child early so as not to be denied martyrdom with them; Pionius and his co-confessors praise God for liberty to talk and to pray without hindrance; the forty martyrs of Sebastê petition God that they may obtain His eternal blessings and His kingdom presently and forever.[119] The prayers of later confessors are valued by Christians 'outside' and especially those of bishop-confessors if the clamour for Fructuosus' intercessions are any indication.[120]

Turning to the matter of song, the first and perhaps most widely celebrated secular instance of 'making music' in prison is the hymn to

---

[115]*Ibid.* 153, 156 and 161 respectively.

[116]*Mart. Pol.* 14.1-15.1 (155/57 AD); *Mart. Let. Lyons & Vienne* 2.5 (177 AD); *Mart. Carp. Pap. & Ag.* 37, 41, 46 in *Recensio Graeca*, and 4.6; 5; 6.5 in *Recensio Latina* (166/80 AD); *Mart. Pion.* 21.7f. (249-51 AD); *Mart. Con.* 6.3b-5 (249-51 AD); *Mart. Fruct.& Co.* 4.3 (259 AD); *Mart. Mont. & Luc.* 15.1-5; 17.4; 23.6 (259 AD); *Mart. Jul. Vet.* 4.4 (304 AD); *Mart. Felix* 30f. (303 AD); *Mart. Iren.* 5 (304 AD); *Mart. Crisp.* 4.2 (304 AD); *Mart. Eup.* 3.3 (*Recensio Latina*; 304 AD).

[117]*Mart. Pol.* 7.2-8.1 (155-57 AD).

[118]*Mart. Perp. & Felic.* 7.1f., 9f.; 15.3f.; 19.1 (203 AD); *Mart. Pion.* 11.7 (249-51 AD); *Mart. Mar. & James* 5.10 (259 AD); *Mart. Fruct. & Co.* 1.4 (259 AD); *Mart. Mont. & Luc.* 10.1 (308-24 AD); *Mart. Test.* 3.4 (308-24 AD). For prayer during trial *Mart. Fruct. & Co.* 2.5 (259 AD) and *cf. Mart. Con.* 5.1.

[119]*Mart. Pol.* 8.1; *Mart. Perp. & Felic.* 3.4; 7.1-10; 15.3f.; 19.1; *Mart. Pion.* 11.5-7; *Mart. Test.* 3.4 respectively.

[120]*Mart. Fruct. & Co.* 1.4.

Apollo by Socrates (399 BC).[121] Plato writes that Socrates was commanded to do this in a recurring dream.[122] Socrates thought,

> ...in case the repeated dream really meant to tell me to make this which is ordinarily called music, I ought to do so and not to disobey. For I thought it was safer not to go hence before making sure that I had done what I ought, by obeying the dream and composing verses.[123]

This was also the motivation behind his rendering one of Aesop's fables into verse.[124] Socrates, it appears, acts out of a concern—perhaps a fear—not to bring divine trouble upon himself.[125] Tibullus (c. 48-19 BC) writes that 'hope comforts, too, the slave whom stout fetters bind. The iron clanks upon his legs, but still he sings at his task'.[126] The slave's hope is either 'of finishing his task or his expectation of gaining freedom'.[127]

The apocryphal *Acts of Thomas* contains a passage in which Judas Thomas, aware of his coming demise, holds forth in God-directed speech that is highly poetic and exultatory. This may also be said of his threefold affirmation of glory to Jesus somewhat later.[128] These passages appear hymnic and thus roughly comparable to certain NT hymnic passages (see discussion below). After offering a prayer at one point during his incarceration, Thomas utters an extended gnostic psalm called The Hymn of the Pearl.[129]

D.W. Riddle asserts that, in later days, Christians in their sufferings 'received comfort and confirmation of purpose'[130] by expressing themselves in song and praise. This might occur as they went to their deaths.[131] Three instances indicate that song or praise was also offered up during imprisonment. After their hearing, the confessor Pionius

---

[121]Plato, *Phd.* 60.D. The work is called a παιάν by Epictetus, 4.4.22 and by Diogenes Laertius, 2.42.

[122]Plato, *Phd.* 60.E.

[123]*Ibid.* 61.A, B.

[124]*Ibid.* On the content of his verse, see Diogenes Laertius 2.42; Plato, *Phd.* 84.E-85.A.

[125]Epictetus turns the thrust of Socrates' ability to compose such works as an expression of equanimity in time of trial (Arrian, *Epict. Diss.* 2.6.25f.).

[126]Tibullus 2.6.25f.

[127]J. Moffatt, 'Exegetica. Acts 16:25', *Exp* VIII/7 (1914), 93f.

[128]*Apoc. Acts of Thomas*, 142 and 153 respectively. *Cf. ibid.* 165.

[129]*Apoc. Acts of Thomas*, 108-13. See the discussion and analysis of this psalm in G. Bornkamm, 'The Acts of Thomas', *Apocr.*, vol. 2, 433-37.

[130]D.W. Riddle, *The Martyrs: A Study in Social Control* (Chicago: UCP, 1931), 48.

and his companions (c. 249-51 AD) are returned to the prison rejoicing; there they continued 'to strengthen one another with psalms and prayers'.[132] Later, when cast into the inner prison, they 'praised God and kept tranquil'; when returned by the guards to more salubrious prison quarters, 'they persisted in saying: "Praise to the Lord! This has happened to us for our good".'[133]

It is quite clear from a review of the canonical captivity epistles that prayer and praise figure prominently as pastimes for the imprisoned Paul.[134] We should not be surprised, therefore, to read of several instances in Acts where Paul prays and praises God. Luke records that at about midnight Paul and Silas prayed and sang praises to God in the Philippian prison (Acts 16:25). Sadler suggests that midnight was a regular time of prayer, irrespective of circumstances.[135] For Conzelmann, however, 'the midnight hour is part of the "numinous" mood'.[136] The term 'midnight' [μεσονύκτιον] by itself is very specific, and one might be inclined, on the basis of certain other NT occurrences (e.g.: Luke 11:5; cf. Matt. 25:6; Mark 13:35), to assess Acts 16:25 as idealized and hence redactional as Conzelmann suggests. However, 'around' [κατά with the accusative] gives a more general time indication.[137] The related phrasing 'about the middle of the night' [κατὰ μέσον τῆς νυκτός: Acts 27:27] also suggests an actual rather than contrived time indication. The apostles may not have had the luxury of choosing between wakefulness and sleep. The pain of the apostles' wounds, the discomfort of their binding and the noise and heat of a crowded inner cell may have made sleep impossible.[138] Finally, the terrors of confinement in darkness suggests strongly that if there was

---

[131]*Mart. Justin & Co.* 6.1 in *Recensio B* (165 AD); *Mart. Scil.* 15-17 (180 AD); *Mart. Perp. & Felic.* 18.7 (203 AD); *Mart. Con.* 6.2 (249/51 AD: the psalm sung is Psalm 40:1); *Mart. Agap.* 7.2 (303 AD); Eusebius, *Hist. Eccl.* 8.9.5 (?).

[132]*Mart. Pion.* 18.12.

[133]*Ibid.* 11.5f.

[134]The reader is directed to the full catalogue of passages on prayer and praise in the canonical Pauline corpus in G.P. Wiles, *Paul's Intercessory Prayers: The Significance of the Intercessory Prayer Passages in the Letters of St Paul* (SNTSMS 24; Cambridge: CUP, 1974), 297-301.

[135]M.F. Sadler, *The Acts*, 311, citing Psalm 118:62 (LXX).

[136]Conzelmann, *Acts*, 132. Schneider, *Die Apostelgeschichte*, 215, describes midnight as 'die,,formgerechte" Zeit für das forgehende Beben, das Wunder der Befreiung auslöst'.

[137]M. Zerwick and M. Grosvenor, *Grammatical Analysis* , 406. Further, Moulton, *Grammar*, vol. 3, 225.

[138]*Supra*, chapter *passim* and *cf.* Lumby, *The Acts*, 210; G. Stählin, *Die Apostelgeschichte*, 221.

a logical and helpful time for petition, praise or communion with one's God, it might have been towards or about midnight.[139]

For what did the apostles pray? The text favours the notion that the apostles did not pray for deliverance from prison but expressed praise through their afflictions.[140] First, when nothing in the previous behaviour of the apostles suggests that they wished to avoid suffering or urgently desired deliverance, one would need quite explicit justification to assume that the apostles did an about face and prayed for it at Acts 16:25.[141] Second, the close relation of prayer in the text with the verb ὑμνέω[142] would also tend to argue for praise rather than petition for release.

It is difficult to say exactly what ὑμνέω (elsewhere only at Matt. 16:30; Mark 14:26; Heb. 2:12) indicates. The noun ὕμνος occurs twice in the NT at Col. 3:16 and Eph. 5:19, there standing in close relation to the terms ψαλμός and ᾠδή. Bruce doubts that the three terms designate the three types of composition in the OT Psalter (mizmorim, tephillim and shirim respectively) and counsels against pressing etymological content for meaning; nor is it likely, he continues, that they were intended as a strict tripartite classification of praise.[143] Lohse, while suggesting general distinctions between terms, essentially concurs.[144] In the case of Acts 16:25, God is praised in song. Whether the verb indicates Psalm(s) or Christian composition(s),[145] singing praises to Him is

---

[139]Supra, 199-202 and especially Mart. Mar. & James 6.1, 3 there cited. K. Lake and Cadbury, The Acts of the Apostles, in BC, vol. 4, 197, write: 'Doubtless "singing in prison" is a common detail in hagiographical accounts, but it is also a common practice for political prisoners of all kinds and at all times. It is naturally introduced into literature; but it also often really happened'.

[140]So, e.g., Williams, Acts, 280; Marshall, The Acts, 271; W. Neil, The Acts of the Apostles (NCB 42; London: Oliphants/Greenwood: Attic, 1973), 184; Th. Zahn, Die Apostelgeschichte , 578.

[141]Supra, 129-134. Contra R.I. Pervo, Profit With Delight, 23; Conzelmann, Acts, 132.

[142]Haenchen, The Acts, 497, renders the phrase προσευχόμενοι ὕμνουν τὸν θεόν 'they sing a hymn of prayer'. Sadler, The Acts, 312 asserts: 'The literal meaning is "praying, they sang hymns".' Bauernfeind, Kommentar, 210, speaks of the apostles being 'im hymnischen Gebet'.

[143]Bruce in E.K. Simpson and F.F. Bruce, The Epistles to the Ephesians and Colossians (NICNT; Grand Rapids: Eerdmans, 1957), 284 and n. 118.

[144]E. Lohse, Colossians and Philemon: A Commentary on the Epistles to the Colossians and to Philemon, tr. W.R. Poehlmann and R.J. Karris (Hermeneia; Philadelphia: Fortress, 1971), 151. Cf. Mart. Con. 6.2 (ψάλλω); Mart. Perp. & Felic. 18.7 (psallo); Mart. Justin & Co. 6.1 in Recensio B (δοξάζω); Mart. Scil. 15-7 (Deo gratias); Mart. Agap. 7.2 (ψάλλω; δοξάζω); Eusebius, HE 8.9.5 (ψάλλω; ὕμνοι; εὐχαριστίαι).

probably in view.[146] Parallels are frequently drawn to *T. Jos.* 8:5, which reads:

> Now when I was in fetters, the Egyptian was ill with grief, and she heard me, how I praised [ὑμνέω] the Lord, being in the house of darkness, and with glad voice in joy glorified [δοξάζω] my God, only because through this cause I was delivered from the Egyptian woman.

Hollander and De Jonge, however, note several important distinctions:

> Here is not only the combination ὑμνεῖν–δοξάζειν ... as a response following upon God's salvation (cf. also the use of ὅτι), but also the motif that the adversary, the one who causes the distress, hears the hymn of praise. *Cf.* Acts 16,25, but the situation described here is different: above all, Paul and Silas praise God before not after their salvation, and it is not their adversary but their fellow-prisoners who hear them singing.[147]

Paul's and Silas' praying and singing to God was a matter of personal spiritual discipline. But it is equally clear that Luke wishes the reader to understand that this behaviour was also a witness; the other inmates were carefully listening to the apostles (Acts 16:25). The joyful content of the apostles' prayers and praise to their God would stand in stark contrast to the distress, complaint and/or anxious petition which might have been expected.[148] If the prayers and hymns were praise-oriented rather than petitionary, as we have argued above, the earthquake could only be construed as an 'answer' in the sense that God affirmed the truth of his praises and vindicated his servants rather than actually granting a specific request for release.[149]

Luke records that Paul punctuated his words of encouragement and assurance to fellow passengers aboard ship by personal example: taking bread, he gave thanks to God (εὐχαρίστησεν τῷ θεῷ: Acts

---

[145]For discussion, G. Delling, 'ὕμνος, ὑμνέω, ψάλλω, ψαλμός', *TDNT*, vol. 8, 499; K.H. Bartels, 'Song, Hymn, Psalm', *NIDNTT*, vol. 3, 668-76; Bruce, *Colossians* 284 n. 119; Lohse, *Colossians and Philemon*, 151 n. 150; Sadler, *The Acts*, 312.

[146]BAGD, 836. *Cf.* Delling 'ὕμνος', 490 and 499; Stählin, *Die Apostelgeschichte*, 221; Zahn, *Die Apostelgeschichte*, 578.

[147]H.W. Hollander and M.De Jonge, *The Testaments of the Twelve Patriarchs: A Commentary* (SVTP 8; Leiden: Brill, 1985), 389. *Contra* Haenchen, *The Acts*, 498 n. 2, the correspondence is thin. The underlying purpose in the praise must surely be radically different. Joseph actually rejoices that he has been imprisoned as this removes him from Potiphar's lascivious wife. For further discussion, F.F. Bruce, 'St. Paul in Macedonia', *BJRL* 61 (1978-79), 342f.

[148]*Supra*, 288-98 and *cf.* Stählin, *Die Apostelgeschichte*, 221.

27:35), broke it and began to eat. The reader should not take this to be a celebration of the Eucharist.[150] Rather, Paul's actions are in the pattern of prayer normally enjoined upon Jews and Christians when they took their food.[151] Having said this, however, the words 'before all' [ἐνώπιον πάντων], indicate a certain witness thrust. A pacifying and encouraging quality of the prayer must certainly stand in the fact that it would recall to the passengers that the God to whom Paul now gives thanks for food is the same one to whom Paul earlier bore witness as guarantor and ultimate preserver (Acts 27:21-26).[152]

Finally, we briefly consider Paul's prayer for Publius' sick father. Requesting to see him, Paul, 'after prayer, placed his hands on him and healed him' (Acts 28:8). The linkage between prayer and the laying on of hands for healing here is unique in Luke's record.[153] While Paul is clearly the agent through whom the cure occurs, his prayer just as clearly indicates that it is not by magical or personal power, but by the gracious answer of Paul's God that Publius' father is healed.[154] Subsequent healings on Malta probably followed a similar pattern.

The above are the only explicit instances of Paul's prayers and praise as a prisoner. But they should probably be considered representative of the prisoner's habit. This assertion is supported by the frequent linking of prayer and the reception of visions in Acts.[155] When Luke relates that the prisoner Paul received a divine communication at Acts 27:23-26 and particularly the grant of his request for the safety of

---

[149]See Schneider, *Die Apostelgeschichte*, 215 and *cf.* Haenchen, *The Acts*, 497; Marshall, *The Acts*, 271. *Contra* the connections suggested by Stählin, *Die Apostelgeschichte*, 220. Further, the helpful discussion in Lake and Cadbury, *BC*, 197, on the distinction between 'religion' and 'magic'.

[150]The words may have a 'Eucharistic' quality (*cf.* Luke 22:19) and the Western text addition may suggest that Paul shared his meal with those usually comprehended by 'we'; i.e., Paul's Christian companions. But, despite the terms—one might ask what other ones could have been used?—and the Western text associations, the context clearly indicates that the eating was for sustenance and that all were being encouraged. Further, on a 'prefigured' or 'limited' Eucharist interpretation, *cf.* B. Reicke, 'Die Mahlzeit mit Paulus auf den Wellen de Mittelmeers Act. 27,33-38', *TZ* 4 (1948), 401-10 and Bruce, *The Book of Acts*, 492 and n. 86; for a 'full' Eucharistic interpretation, *cf.* G.A. Krodel, *Acts* (Minneapolis: Augsburg, 1986), 478.

[151]So, e.g., Conzelmann, *Acts*, 220; Haenchen, *The Acts*, 707 and n. 3; Lake and Cadbury, *BC*, 336. *Cf.* 1 Tim. 4:5f.

[152]See J.W. Packer, *Acts of the Apostles* (CBC 44; Cambridge: CUP, 1973), 214.

[153]The linkage is elsewhere present but for appointment to Christian office at Acts 6:6; 13:3; for the laying on of hands only and healing, Luke 4:38-40 (// Mark 1:29-34; *cf.* 16:18); 13:13. *Cf.* James 5:14-16.

[154]So R. Pesch, *Die Apostelgeschichte* (EKKNT 5; Zurich: Benziger, 1986), vol. 2, 299; Krodel, *Acts*, 481.

the other passengers aboard ship (Acts 27:24; *cf.* 3:14; 25:11, 16),[156] there is every reason to understand that this came to him during a nightly time of prayer. The communication at Acts 23:11 may arise out of a context of prayer; it may, however, be a dream.

The consumption or non-consumption of food as a matter of religious practice has already been considered to some extent.[157] Jewish prisoners committed to the Torah were concerned to abstain from foods which might ritually defile them. In the absence of clean foods they might risk death by starvation. We argued that Paul's theologically based commitment to unqualified commensality gave him liberty to consume whatever food was offered him. Acts 16:34 and 28:10 confirm this, though the years in Caesarea and Rome probably presented a choice.

The above summary relates principally to those fasts forced upon prisoners by dint of the food on offer and the religious convictions involved. What of voluntary fasts? The *Acts of Paul* (*c.* 185-95 AD) notes fasting as a discipline which the apocryphal Paul undertook with other prisoners.[158] The confessor Aemilian (259 AD), 'continuously fasted by extending his abstinence over two days, constantly repeating prayers by which his devout soul would nourish and prepare itself for the Lord's sacrament [i.e., martyrdom] on the following day'.[159] Flavian, in the same year, was given to extraordinary fasts: '...when the others took even their meagre fare from the worst of skimpy prison rations, Flavian alone abstained from his tiny share, preferring to be worn by frequent and voluntary fasts provided the others could be fed on his food'.[160]

The NT affirms fasting as a regular element of Jewish and Christian piety (*cf.* Matt.4:2; 6:16-18; 9:14-17 [// Mark 2:18-20; Luke 5:33-35]; Luke 18:12) and Luke in particular indicates that Paul himself and other Christian leaders engaged in this spiritual discipline (Acts 13:2f.).

---

[155]The linkage is observed by Luke in the experience of Peter (Acts 10:9f.; 11:5; *cf.* 12:5, 7, 12, 15), Cornelius (Acts 10:30f.; 11:13) and, importantly, Paul (Acts 9:11f.; 13:2f.; 22:17f.). See further the discussion in D.M. Crump, *Jesus the Intercessor: Prayer and Christology in Luke-Acts* (University of Aberdeen: Unpublished PhD. Dissertation, 1988), 229-48. *Cf. Mart. Perp. & Felic.* 4.1f.; 7:1-3.

[156]So Marshall, *The Acts*, 410; A. Wikenhauser, *Die Apostelgeschichte* (RNT 5: 4th ed.; Regensburg: Friedrich Pustet, 1961), 279.

[157]*Supra*, 209-216.

[158]*Apocr. Acts Paul* 5, 8.

[159]*Mart. Mar. & James* 8.1. *Cf. ibid.* 8.4; 11.4-6.

[160]*Mart. Mont. & Luc.* 21.12.

We would not then be remiss in suggesting, despite the silence of Acts, that one of the apostle's spiritual disciplines in prison was fasting.

Where there was opportunity and permission, Christian prisoners also celebrated the Eucharist. The *Apocryphal Acts of Paul* (c. 185-95 AD) indicates the possibility, performed in this case with bread and water.[161] While the use of water instead of wine may indicate limited resources, it more likely reflects ascetic commitments. The apocryphal Judas Thomas (mid 3rd cent. AD) shares the bread and the cup with recently anointed and baptized catechumens after a miraculous release from prison.[162]

Paul's practice was regular celebration of the Eucharist, which would have been limited only by the constraints of incarceration he was experiencing at any particular time. Acts 16:34 and 27:35 are not eucharistic,[163] but there would have been other times—particularly the latter phase of the Caesarean incarceration, the times when the prisoner was billeted with Christians *en route* to Rome, and during the two years in the Imperial capital—when the opportunity would have been seized.

3. Philosophical and Religious Ministrations

Direct speech and the written word were open to a prisoner intent upon conveying information to or directing or influencing others. Consideration of the literary labours of prisoners will be strictly limited as Acts records no Pauline prison epistles and no note that such were written. Our interest in this section will be limited to the mechanics, prospects, and potentials for literary activity by prisoners and what this suggests for the prisoner Paul in Acts. To wit, what is the likelihood that Paul would have been able to engage in literary labour in the circumstances of his various incarcerations? As to prisoners' speech, there is quite evidently a significant Lukan interest.

One of the earliest examples of literary activity in prison is Socrates. His metrical rendering of Aesop's fables and the hymn to Apollo were created, Plato records, on a divine command to 'make music and work at it'.[164] The compositions must have been written down; they

---

[161]*Apocr. Acts Paul* 7. *Cf. Mart. Pion.* 3.1 (249-51 AD).
[162]*Apocr. Acts Thom.* 158.
[163]Recall the discussion *supra*, 340 n.150.
[164]Plato, *Phd.* 60.D, E. *Cf. ibid.* 61.A, B; Diogenes Laertius 2.42.

were extended and sections have survived.[165] Several secular Roman examples may also be pointed out. A. Gellius writes,

> we are told of Naevius [c. 206 BC] that he wrote two plays in prison, the *Soothsayer* and the *Leon*, when by reason of his constant abuse and insults aimed at the leading men of the city, after the manner of the Greek poets, he had been imprisoned at Rome by the triumvirs.[166]

Cicero wrote of the condemned Furius [late 60's BC]: 'with death looking him in the face, while day and night his mother sat weeping by his side in the prison, he composed a written speech in his own defense'.[167] Cicero indicates it received a wide publication: '...there is no one in Sicily to-day who does not possess this speech, and read it'.[168]

During the reign of Tiberius, writes Suetonius, some of those who were consigned to prison were denied 'the consolation of literary activity'.[169] Outside of this prohibition, the freedom to write was apparently normally accorded prisoners. The accounts concerning Publius Vitellius, under house arrest c. 35 AD, imply such permission. Tacitus writes that he 'asked for a pen-knife on the ground that he wished to write'.[170] While he may have had the obligatory inkstand, a compliment of reed-pens and material upon which to write, the knife had been removed from his pen case for security. Sextius Paconianus' literary labours against the Emperor while in prison (32 AD) won him an appointment with the public executioner three years later.[171]

The philosophers Apollonius of Tyana and Musonius carried on a prison correspondence in Nero's reign. Flavius Philostratus observes that 'they did not openly converse with one another, because Musonius declined to do so, in order that both their lives might not be endangered; but they carried on a correspondence through Menippus and Damis, who went to and fro the prison'.[172]

The first literary activity of a Christian prisoner outside the NT comes from Ignatius (reign of Trajan) on his way from Syria to martyrdom in Rome. While Polycarp is clear that Ignatius' works are epistles,[173] Ignatius does not explicitly use this term.[174] With apparent

---

[165]*Cf. supra*, 335-36.
[166]Gellius 3.3.15.
[167]Cicero, *Ver.* 2.5.112.
[168]*Ibid.*
[169]See the discussion of this rendering *supra*, 332.
[170]Tacitus, *Ann.* 6.5.8. *Cf.* Suetonius, *Vit.* 7.2.3.
[171]Tacitus, *Ann.* 6.39.
[172]Philostratus, *VA* 4.46.

modesty he uses the diminutive 'booklet' [βιβλίδιον[175]].[176] Ignatius takes full credit for these compositions; time and again variations on the expression 'I write to you' occur.[177] Letters radiate out from Smyrna to the Ephesians, Magnesians, Trallians and, with a date indication (24th August) to forewarn his arrival, to the Romans.[178] From Troas, letters go out to the Philadelphians, Smyrnaeans, and the Smyrnaean bishop Polycarp.[179]

Ignatius was severely limited and completely dependent upon others to assist him both with his writings and with their delivery.[180] The Ephesian Burrhus was clearly essential to him as amanuensis.[181] Despite this assistance, Ignatius' literary labours were at the mercy of the exigencies of travel and the few military 'beasts' who have charge over its timing, progress and route. Ignatius writes to Polycarp:

> Since I could not write to all the Churches because of my sudden sailing from Troas to Neapolis, as the will of God enjoins, you shall write as one possessing the mind of God to the Churches on the road in front of me, that they also shall treat me in the same way....[182]

Passing over the late second century AD epistle attributed to Paul when a prisoner at Philippi,[183] we turn to the imprisoned Christian martyrs of later fame. In the *Martyrdom of Perpetua and Felicitas* (203 AD) it is indicated that part of the record comes from the hands of confessors in the prisons at Carthage. The compiler/continuator relates concerning Perpetua: 'Now from this point on the entire account of her ordeal is her own, according to her own ideas and in the way that she herself wrote it down'.[184] Within that account, Perpetua herself writes: 'So much for what I did up until the eve of the contest. About what

---

[173]Polycarp, *Phil.* 13.2.

[174]Ignatius, *Eph.* 12.2; *Pol.* 8.1.

[175]*Ibid., Eph.* 20.1. See BAGD, 141.

[176]Ignatius, *Rom.* 8.2; *Pol.* 7.3. See BAGD, 165.

[177]Ignatius, *Eph.* 9.2; 12.1; 21.1; *Magn.* 15.1; *Trall.* 3.3; 5.1; 12.3; *Rom.* 4.1; 7.2 [2x]; 8.3; 10.1, 3; *Phld.* 11.1; *Smyrn.* 5.3; 12.1; *Pol.* 8.1.

[178]*Ibid., Eph.* 20.1; *Magn.* 15.1; *Trall.* 12.1; 13.1; *Rom.* 10.1, 3.

[179]*Ibid., Phld.* 11.1; *Smyrn.* 12.1; *Pol.* 8.1.

[180]In the present case the delegations from various churches are the logical candidates for this task: Ignatius, *Eph.* 2.1 (Onesimus, Euplus, Fronto); *Magn.* 2.1 (Damas, Bassus, Apollonius, Zotion); *Trall.* 1.1 (Polybius); *Rom.* 10.1 (Crocus?).

[181]Ignatius, *Phld.* 11.1.

[182]*Ibid., Pol.* 8.1.

[183]*Apocr. Acts Paul* 8.3.40.

[184]*Mart. Perp. & Felic.* 2.3.

happened at the contest itself, let him write of it who will'.[185] She has writing utensils and has not yet nominated the continuator. The work and the arrangements for its preservation and continuation are Perpetua's doing. The compiler/continuator might have been a deacon or one of the many other visitors noted.[186] When the document(s) exchanged hands is also a matter of conjecture.[187]

A number of letters from the Christian confessors to Cyprian, bishop of Carthage (Decian/Valerian persecutions) survive. The earliest, a brief certificate of peace [= absolution] sent from the prison at Carthage (250 AD), reads: 'Lucian wrote this, there being present of the clergy, both an exorcist and a reader'.[188] In a letter to Lucian in the same year Celerinus laments that 'Montanus, our common brother, was coming to me from you out of the dungeon',[189] without news of how the confessors were and without mention of him or his request. Lucian replies on behalf of the confessors. Celerinus concludes by breaking off an extended greeting with the words '...and all whose names I have not written, because I am already weary'.[190] He is probably writing this letter personally; in a later letter, Cyprian who complains that 'in the name also of Aurelius, a young man who had undergone the torture, many certificates were given, written by the hand of the same Lucian, because Aurelius did not know how to write himself'.[191] Other Cyprianic prison letters might be mentioned.[192]

The *Martyrdom of Marian and James* (259 AD), it is alleged, comes from the hand of one who was initially a cellmate and fellow sufferer but was later released. He relates that 'it was their wish that their battle should be communicated to their fellow Christians through me'.[193] It is a prison writing, but not, strictly speaking, a prisoner's writing.

The *Martyrdom of Montanus and Lucius* (259 AD), in part an 'epistle of the martyrs in prison to the church at Carthage',[194] begins: '...it

---

[185]*Ibid.* 10.15.

[186]*Ibid.* 3.7; 9.1; 16.4.

[187]*Ibid.* 17.1 and 18.1 for two possibilities: at the last meal or on the day of death.

[188]Cyprian, *Ep.* 16 [Oxf., *Ep.* 23]. These certificates were highly sought after and the source of great trouble to the official religious leadership (e.g., Cyprian, *Ep.* 17 [Oxf., *Ep.* 26]).

[189]Cyprian, *Ep.* 20.1 [Oxf., *Ep.* 21].

[190]*Ibid.* 21.3 [Oxf., *Ep.* 22].

[191]*Ibid.* 22.1 [Oxf., *Ep.* 27].

[192]E.g., *ibid.* 25 [Oxf., *Ep.* 31 (250 AD)].

[193]*Mart. Marian & James* 1.3. *Cf.* 1.4: 'it was not without reason that in their close intimacy they laid upon me the task which I am about to fulfil'.

[194]*Mart. Mont. & Luc. prol.*

is by the force of this reasoning that love and a sense of obligation have urged us to write this account'.[195] A loyal witness and an historical record for posterity are its objects.

The *Letter of Phileas* appears to have been written by the bishop of Thmuis from prison in Alexandria (*c.* 303/4 AD). The only indication of his authorship is the editorial comment:

> Such were the words which this martyr, truly a lover of wisdom as well as a lover of God, sent to the brothers of his diocese before his final sentence while he was still undergoing imprisonment, and thus did he set forth what he was going through, urging them to hold firmly to their faith in Christ, even after his own death, though it was not yet accomplished.[196]

The circumstances of its commission to writing are not hinted at.

Mason informs us that the Christian Pamphylius was confined in prison for two years with many other confessors at Caesarea by the governor Urban (305 AD). Mason notes that

> his time of respite was not spent in idleness. His friends had access to him; and during that period he composed with the help of Eusebius a work in six books in defence of Origen, which he addressed to the confessors who were labouring in the mines of Palestine.[197]

The *Testament of the Forty Martyrs of Sebastê* is a circular written by imprisoned soldiers in Armenia (*c.* 308-24 AD). A document from forty individuals, it has three principal senders: Meletius, Aetius and Eutychius.[198] Of the three, Meletius is the key sender. First named in the salutation, he is also the first to send personal greetings and the first named in the list of the forty.[199] Moreover, he is responsible for the document's writing.[200] Was he the senior officer in this group?

What is the likelihood of Paul writing epistles from those places where he was a prisoner in Acts? The Philippian and Jerusalem imprisonments are unlikely locales owing to the brevity of these incarcerations, the apparent rapid unfolding of events, and the lack of an obvious purpose for writing. Serious doubts also attach to the prospect of epistolary activity *en route* to Rome. Our review of the process of

---

[195]*Ibid.* 1.
[196]*Let. Phil.* 11 in the *Textus Eusebii Graecus.*
[197]Mason, *The Historic Martyrs*, 296.
[198]*Mart. Test. prol.*
[199]*Ibid.* 3.1, 4.
[200]*Ibid.* 3.4.

writing and sending the Ignatian correspondence suggests that it was a demanding and expensive activity requiring certain conditions for its success: prisoner stopovers of some duration and sufficient numbers of helpers. Paul's journey to Rome, on all these counts, would have foreclosed or at least seriously hindered letter writing. It was largely seaborne with only brief stops along the way, the only extended stopover being on the isolated island of Malta when sailing was too dangerous anyway. The last overland leg of the journey might have furnished the right conditions for literary activity—a letter or letters with news of Paul's arrival on Italian soil. It is more likely, however, that Puteolian couriers delivered the news verbally (*cf.* Acts 28:15) to the Roman church.

Without prejudice to debate regarding the provenance of the NT captivity epistles, the mechanics, prospects, and potentials for literary activity in the extended imprisonments at Caesarea and Rome are considerable. There is more than ample scope for access to the outside through comrades at Caesarea (Acts 24:23) and the travel companions, Roman Christians and the 'all' [πάντες] at Rome (Acts 28:30). Even if the Caesarean imprisonment was more harsh, it hardly compares with the terrible prison conditions from which some prisoners considered above were able to write. Whatever things Paul may have been denied in his imprisonment, writing would not have been one of them. The remarkably easy conditions of Paul's Roman imprisonment would have been all the more conducive to letter writing: more visitors, probably easier access to writing materials—but, of course, no pen-knife!

Famous among prison discourses in antiquity are those of Socrates (399 BC).[201] Plato's account of the dialogue between Socrates and his lifelong friend Crito is one and the *Phaedo* is another. Apollonius of Tyana (reign of Domitian) also offers philosophical encouragement and comfort to fellow inmates in Rome.[202]

Noteworthy in the Jewish literature are traditions concerning the imprisoned rabbi Akiba (*c.* 132-35 AD). The Talmud relates that 'it once happened that a man submitted to *halizah* with none present but himself and herself in a prison, and when the case came before R. Akiba he declared the *halizah* valid'.[203] Two additional examples confirm the practice of consulting imprisoned rabbis to resolve disputes. The Mishnah relates that R. Hananiah of Ono brought up from prison a *Ha-*

---

[201]Seneca, *Ad Lucilium Ep.* 24.4. *Cf.* Arrian, *Epict.* 2.13.24; Plutarch, *De gen.* 607.F; *ibid., Tranq.* 466.E also noting his discussion on philosophical themes with his friends.
[202]Philostratus, *VA* 7.26-42.

lakah from R. Akiba.[204] The Talmud indicates that two men were once hired for four hundred *zuz* to go to R. Akiba in the prison to seek a legal opinion.[205]

There are several instances of preaching and teaching in the NT Apocrypha. Christian preaching for the author of the *Acts of Paul* 'is preaching of continence and of the resurrection (AThe 5). In practically every episode the motif of sexual continence plays a dominant role'.[206] Indeed, it is Paul's success in preaching the salvation of men on this theme and drawing 'them away from corruption and impurity, all pleasure and death, that they may sin no more' that lands him in prison at Iconium.[207] His disciple Thecla visits Paul in the prison. Sitting at his feet and listening to him proclaim 'the mighty acts of God', her faith is increased as she kisses his fetters.[208] When Paul is called to the judgement-seat, Thecla rolls 'herself upon the place where Paul taught as he sat in the prison'.[209]

Entering Ephesus, the apocryphal Paul is imprisoned in the stadium and condemned to fight beasts. The women Eubula and Artemilla go to the prison to hear Paul pray. Paul groans and inveighs against Artemilla's riches, beauty and finery. He tells her to turn from idols and hope in God who will deliver her and Christ who will save her. Artemilla is converted and she together with Eubula immediately ask for baptism.[210] It is later related of Paul's martyrdom at Rome that he 'did not keep silence concerning the word, but communicated it to the prefect Longus and the centurion Cestus'.[211]

The apostle/Christ figure Judas Thomas (mid-3rd cent. AD) is imprisoned for taking money to build a palace which the donor assumes will be material but which turns out to be heavenly.[212] On his

---

[203]*b. Nasim* I: *Yebam.* II:104*a. Cf. m. Yebam.* 12.5. *Halizah* was the procedure undertaken by the widowed sister-in-law to her husband's brother when he refused to be her redeemer.

[204]*m. Git.* 6.7.

[205]*b. Nasim* I: *Yebam.* II:108*b.* The need to bribe individuals—probably Gentiles-to obtain the ruling arises from the fact that it was then a capital crime to practice and teach the Jewish religion. This may explain the obtuse way in which R. Johanan ha-Sandelar obtained Akiba's ruling on *halizah. Cf. b. Nez.* V: *Sanh.* I:12*a,* though this is more properly considered literary activity.

[206]W. Schneemelcher, '3. Acts of Paul', *Apocr.,* 350. *Cf.* also *Apocr. Acts of Andrew.*

[207]*Apocr. Acts Paul* 3.17. *Ibid.* 3.15 on what the crowd shouts.

[208]*Ibid.* 3.18.

[209]*Ibid.* 3.20.

[210]*Ibid.* 7 [p. 2].

[211]*Ibid.* 11.3.

[212]*Apocr. Acts Thom.* 17-20. *Cf. ibid.* 22-24.

way to prison, Thomas encourages his owner Abban, 'Fear nothing, but only believe in the God who is preached by me, and thou shalt be freed from this world but from the age to come shalt obtain life'.[213] He also preaches a gnostically inspired gospel advocating sexual abstinence, for which he is later thrown into prison at the instigation of the husband of one of Thomas' female converts.[214] While there he encourages his fellow-prisoners.[215] Released, he converts king Misdaeus' wife, resulting once again in his imprisonment. Led off, he is followed into prison by members of the king's family.[216]

Moving to the Christian martyr literature we are on somewhat more certain ground, though here too a tendency to idealize is present. By far the most significant and extensive Christian witness borne to unbelievers is to magistrates, councils, special audiences and interested pagans in attendance at formal trials and hearings. As this falls outside the remit of the present chapter, we turn to instances where confessors actually encourage, convince or challenge within the prison.

First, confessors are fully prepared *to interact with non-Christians in the prison.* Perpetua (203 AD) receives her unbelieving father there. He tearfully pleads for her to pity his grey head, spare him public reproach, think of those in the family who are so distraught over her state, and spare them the risk of suspicion that they too are Christians. She refuses his requests, asserting confidence in God's power and providential ordering of events.[217] The day before their martyrdoms, Perpetua and the others speak to the unbelievers gathered at the prison, warning 'them of God's judgement, stressing the joy they would have in their suffering, and ridiculing'[218] their curiosity. The co-confessor Saturus declares: 'Will not tomorrow be enough for you? Why are you so eager to see something that you dislike? Our friends today will be our enemies on the morrow. But take careful note of what we look like so that you will recognize us on the day'.[219] The mob departs from the prison 'in amazement, and many of them began to believe'.[220] The prisoner Pionius and his fellow confessors (249/51 AD) receive

---

[213]*Ibid.* 21.
[214]*Ibid.* 106.
[215]*Ibid.* 108, 125.
[216]*Ibid.* 142.
[217]*Mart. Perp. & Felic.* 5.1-6. A similar visit and result occurs *ibid.* 9.2f.
[218]*Ibid.* 17.1
[219]*Ibid.* 17.2.
[220]*Ibid.* 17.3.

many unbelievers who come to persuade them to give up their faith. They are surprised to hear the answers given them.[221]

Christian confessors also bear witness to their guards. An assistant guard chides Felicitas that, suffering great pain as she now does in a premature childbirth, she should have given more serious thought to the greater suffering of being thrown to the beasts when she refused to offer sacrifice to the gods. '"What I am suffering now", she replied, "I suffer by myself. But then another will be inside me who will suffer for me, just as I shall be suffering for him".'[222] Perpetua notes that Pudens the adjutant of the prison 'began to show us great honour, realising that we possessed some great power within us'.[223] Pudens eventually becomes a Christian because of their witness.[224] Pionius and his cellmates, despite suffering in the inner prison, 'praised God and kept tranquil, offering the guards the usual friendship, so that the prison warden changed his mind and had them brought back to their former place'.[225]

Second, there were opportunities for Christian prisoners to talk with one another and with believers from outside the prison. The reader of the *Letter of the Churches of Lyons and Vienne* (177 AD) is told that some confessors,

> though tortured so severely that it seemed impossible for them to survive even if they received every sort of care, lived on in prison: deprived of human attention, they were strengthened and given power by the Lord in soul and body, and continued to encourage and exhort the others.[226]

The confessor Perpetua records that she 'tried to comfort'[227] her brother, a young catechumen also caught up in the persecution and imprisoned. Pionius and his associates rejoice that they are 'at liberty to discourse ... night and day'.[228]

How did they comfort and encourage one another? Perpetua's brother asks her to pray for a vision to discover whether she is to be condemned or freed. She does so and then in the morning relates her

---

[221]*Mart. Pion.* 12.1.
[222]*Mart. Perp. & Felic.* 15.6.
[223]*Ibid.* 9.1.
[224]*Ibid.* 16.4; 21.1-5.
[225]*Mart. Pion.* 11.5.
[226]*Mart. Let. Lyons & Vienne* 1.28.
[227]*Mart. Perp. & Felic.* 3.8.
[228]*Mart. Pion.* 11.7.

Vision of the Ladder. It confirms to them both that they will have to suffer and die.[229] The sharing of such visions occurs often in this type of literature.[230] The encouragement lies in the confirmation and assurance of a certain death and, by implication, a certain and God-pleasing witness. At other times, the challenge and encouragement is more sermonic in nature. The prisoner Pionius receives 'many Christian brethren who had been carried off by force, and they made a great lament. Indeed they were constantly in deep grief, especially those who had lived a good life in the ways of the devout'.[231] In an exhortation filled with biblical and OT apocryphal quotations and allusions, Pionius expresses grief at their dejection and challenges them to renew their trust in Christ. He laments the dissembling and betrayal which has decimated and factionalised the community.[232] The confessor Lucius, weakened by illness and the privations of imprisonment, 'would not keep silent but kept instructing his companions as much as he could'.[233] The Christian soldier Isichius challenges the imprisoned veteran Julius:

> ...fulfil your promise in joy. Take the crown which the Lord has promised to give to those who believe in him, and remember me, for I too will follow you. Give my warmest greetings to the servant of God, our brother Valentio, who has already preceded us to the Lord by his loyal confession of faith.[234]

The confessors also challenge and instruct Christian visitors in the prison. Pionius warns believers who fear prosecution of the spiritual peril of accepting Jewish invitations to visit their synagogues and warns them of the risk of losing their faith and committing blasphemy against the Holy Spirit. Jewish slanders of Jesus are to be countered. If they lack the theological wherewithal to counter Jewish argument, interaction should simply be cut off.[235] Christians come to the confessors in custody and ask, in words that recall the thief's request to Jesus, for the spiritual benefit of being 'remembered'.[236] Mason, marking the

---

[229]*Mart. Perp. & Felic.* 4.3-10.
[230]*Ibid.* 10.1-14; 11.2-13.8; *Mart. Mar. & James* 6.5-15; 7.1-4; 8.2-11; 11.1f.; 11.3-6; *Mart. Mont. & Luc.* 5.1; 7.3-6; 8.3-7; 11.3-5; 21:3-5; 21.6f.; 21.8f. Cf. *Mart. Carp. Pap. & Ag.* 39, 42 in *Recensio Graeca* and 6.1-5 in *Recensio Latina* in their different accounts of the same vision.
[231]*Mart. Pion.* 12.2.
[232]*Ibid.* 12.3-6.
[233]*Mart. Mont. & Luc.* 13.4.
[234]*Mart. Jul. Vet.* 4.2.
[235]*Mart. Pion.* 13.1-14.16.

suspicious connections with the pattern of Paul's experience in Acts, observes that in the *Martyrdom of Philip and Hermes* (c. 307/9 AD), the confessors are transferred by the Thracian governor Bassus

> to a private house adjoining the prison, where they abode, like St. Paul at Rome, with a soldier or two to keep them. Disciples and in- quirers flocked to them, and many converts were made. The numbers were so great that offence was taken, and Bassus was compelled to send them again into the prison.[237]

The confessor Saturus' Vision of the Angels and the Garden is a challenge to believers outside the prison to stop quarrelling and be rec- onciled.[238] This is, ultimately, the object of the other visions mentioned above. The confessor Montanus' words of warning to Christians, while thematically related in a number of respects to words shared and re- ceived in prison, are given at the place of execution.[239]

Luke, in what he indicates and what he implies, shows that the prisoner Paul did not allow time to slip away. We have already seen that he engaged in spiritual disciplines which had both personal and ministry benefit. The book of Acts also discloses that Paul addressed individuals—whether believers or non-believers—on evangelistic and spiritual themes during his custody.

One instance of such prison speech is at Philippi. The first ques- tion to be dealt with is how one ought to construe the jailer's urgent en- treaty, 'Sirs, what must I do to be saved?' (Acts 16:30). For some, the report of the jailer's pre-conversion speech and actions are invested with considerable if not too much 'Christian' knowledge. Paul's and Silas' prayers and hymns to God, moreover, are quite evidently un- helpful to the jailer's understanding. In the first place, we have argued, the prayers and hymns are unlikely to have been petitions for release; in the second, the text tells us that the jailer was asleep before the earth- quake (Acts 16:27). For several reasons, however, it is unwarranted to assume that the account must therefore be a creation or radical rework- ing which gets away from the author at times. We observe, first, that the jailer would have been acquainted with the apostles' Jewish iden- tity and religious 'crimes', if not as a result of his presence at the trial,

---

[237] *Mart. Fruct. & Co.* 1.4. Cf. *ibid.* 3.5f.; *Mart. Jul. Vet.* 4.2; *Mart. Mont. & Luc.* 13.5f.; Cyprian. *Ep.* 15.4 [Oxf., *Ep.* 37]; *ibid.* 24.2 [28].
[238] Mason, *The Historic Martyrs*, 337.
[239] *Mart. Perp. & Felic.* 11.2-13.8.
[239] *Mart. Mont. & Luc.* 13.6; 14.1-9. Cf. *ibid.* 13.2; 23.3f.; *Mart. Perp. & Felic.* 1.35; *Mart. Cyp.* 5.1; *Mart. Fruct. & Co.* 4.1f.

than certainly from the customary entries written into the prison register.[240] Second, the earthquake itself would easily have led to a religious response owing to pagan associations of seismic disturbances
with the action of a deity. Finally, in the context of the sight of prison
doors opened by the tremors and the implication of a mass escape, the
commanding and calming voice of Paul from within the cell (Acts
16:28) would have led the jailer to make certain causal connections between the events, the information and his two wards without having
to assume that the author has predicated to the jailer a full and therefore suspect 'Christian' knowledge.[241] These connections also probably account for the jailer's heightened estimate of the apostles' status,
evident when he addresses them as κύριοι,[242] and his request for direction concerning (τί με δεῖ ποιεῖν: Acts 16:30; cf. 2:37; 22:10; Luke
3:10, 12, 14; 10:25; 18:18) how to be 'saved' from having abused a powerful deity's two servants.[243]

However faulty and misguided the jailer's conception was, his
request for spiritual direction was immediately seized upon as an opportunity to declare the Gospel message; the apostles tell him, 'Believe
in the Lord Jesus, and you will be saved'.[244] The offer of salvation is,
moreover, extended to all those in the jailer's household (Acts
16:31).[245] Οἰκία/οἶκος ought probably not to be rendered 'family' as
the term often indicates members of the family as well as slaves.[246] The
fact that the initial declaration was followed by a more extended
speaking of 'the word of the Lord' (Acts 16:32) indicates a communal
assent and submission to the preaching which undercuts the notion of

---

[240]Supra, 263-64.

[241]Modern commentaries tend to freight discussion in the direction of a Christian
interpretation of the deity in question. The point stressed above is simply that such
a leap bears little relationship to the text. Hence too the doubts noted by A. von
Harnack, The Acts of the Apostles, tr. J.R. Wilkinson (Crown Theological Library 27;
London: Williams and Norgate/New York: G.P. Putnam's Sons, 1909), 206.

[242]Contra Schneider, Die Apostelgeschichte, 217.

[243]The point of fearing a legal penalty for dereliction of duty in allowing a prison
break and hoping to escape it, as noted by Kee and Young, The Living World of the
New Testament, 245, is already past (Acts 16:27). Moreover, the jailer's contemplated suicide may arise even at Acts 16:27 partly out of a sense of having been foiled
by a deity. Further cf. supra, 264.

[244]The following parallels in Acts may be noted to the expressions at Acts 16:31f.:
On πιστευσον ἐπὶ τὸν κύριον Ἰησοῦν: Acts 9:42; 11:17 [21]; 22:19.

[245]Cf. Acts 11:14; 18:8. Vg. uses the term domus.

[246]BAGD, 557, 560f. There is no difficulty in a highly-placed public slave possessing slaves of his own. Family arrangements, however, may have been cohabitative
rather than legal.

whole household baptism on the single faith of its head and the argument that preparation was not needed prior to baptism.[247] Baptism,
however, here as elsewhere (Acts 8:13, 35-39 [37?]; 10:43, 47f.; 11:15-17;
18:8) follows fast on the heals of faith. It is not strange, as Harnack suggests, that baptism took place at once in the prison.[248] First, the profound uncertainties of the apostles' situation argue strongly for such a
hasty arrangement. Second, the Christian martyr literature shows prison to be a not unlikely context for baptism.[249] We may add that one
ought to avoid fanciful comparisons between baptism and the washing of wounds.[250]

The jailer's final words to Paul and Silas at Acts 16:36 are, 'Go in
peace'. With roots in Judaism (e.g., LXX Judges 18:6; 2 Kings 3:21; 5:19),
this expression was clearly inherited by Christianity (e.g., Luke 7:50;
8:48; cf. Acts 15:33; Mart. Marin. 4). The words are deemed by some for
this reason to be too Christian and therefore hardly appropriate to the
newly converted jailer. Their absence in MSS D it^gig, termed a 'Western
non-interpolation' by J.H. Ropes, confirms to some that it is an anachronistic Lukan attempt to account for the jailer's conversion in a source
whose original carried not a whisper of it.[251] But is the phrase that
troublesome? The other MS evidence argues for inclusion; the words
are more extensively and earlier found. The jailer and his family had
received apostolic instruction. In another Gentile context the gospel
content is identified as a preaching of peace through Jesus Christ (Acts
10:36) and the apostles are commanded to give the peace to house-
holds that warmly receive them (Luke 10:5f.; cf. Matt. 10:13). Such a
message and such apostolic behaviour might even have called for specific instruction to new disciples in giving the peace. Thus furnished,
the Jewish Christian benediction seems quite credible on the lips of a
newly-converted Gentile jailer.[252]

It is clear from the several Pauline defence speeches that Luke
has a definite interest in demonstrating that, in fulfilment of Jesus'

---

[247]Cf. the discussion in Knowling, 'The Acts', 352 and F.J. Foakes-Jackson, The Acts
of the Apostles (MNTC 5; London: Hodder and Stoughton, 1948), 156.
[248]von Harnack, The Acts, 206.
[249]E.g., Mart. Fruct. & Co. 2.1 (259 AD). Further, Apocr. Acts Paul 7; Acts Thom. 150-
58.
[250]See the discussion of Chrysostom in Bruce, The Acts, 365 and the comments of
Knowling, 'The Acts', 352.
[251]So Ropes cited in Lake and Cadbury, BC, 200. See further the discussion in
Metzger, A Textual Commentary, 451; Haenchen, The Acts, 498 and n. 4; W. Foerster,
'εἰρήνη κτλ.', TDNT, vol. 5, 411.
[252]Contra Williams, Acts, 282.

words[253] and consistent with the pattern of earlier prominent believers,[254] Paul was brought before religious and political authorities on account of Jesus' name. By his Christ-assisted extempore witness in those situations he confounded his opponents. Paul's own life, in the latter part of Acts particularly, is the most extensive realization of Jesus' forewarning and promise. Our interest here, however, is in Paul's ministry as a prisoner in confinement. We turn, initially, to the second phase of Paul's Caesarean imprisonment to consider what is indicated and what may be inferred.

The two year confinement in Caesarea is briefly described; in fact, so much so that some commentators deem it a 'dead period' for apostolic activity which Luke gladly and quickly passes over.[255] In the estimation of more recent commentators, Caesarea was a 'tedious confinement' and 'frustrating'.[256] The modern emphasis upon the apparently unfruitful interviews with Felix at Acts 24:24-26 is an attempt to fill out the two full years. Also observing that the Jews were content with an adjournment in the proceedings because Paul's ministry was basically terminated, Hauser argues that the two years are isolated from Paul's interactions with Felix and are therefore not parallel with Acts 28:30f.[257] Cassidy speaks of a parenthetical ministry of sorts on the way to Rome and indicates that it is a *resumption* 'after a lapse of more than two years'.[258] All the above characterizations, however, may be questioned.

It is no surprise that Drusilla is mentioned. Felix' marital escapades were widely known. Tacitus, after relating how Felix 'practised every kind of cruelty and lust', relates immediately the details of his marriage to another Drusilla, the grand-daughter of Cleopatra and Antony.[259] Suetonius includes the following comment for Felix: '...he became the husband of three queens'.[260] Jewish reaction would certainly have been even more negative. The Drusilla of Acts 24:24 was the daughter of Herod Agrippa I of Judaea. Her own marital history before meeting Felix was not happy.[261] Born in 38 AD, she had been

---

[253]Luke 21:12-15; *cf.* 12:11f.; Mark 13:9-11; Matt. 10:17-20.
[254]Acts 4:8-20; 5:29-32; 7:2-53.
[255]E.g., G.T. Stokes, 'The Acts' 452f.; E.L. Hicks, 'Did St. Paul Write from Caesarea?' *Int* 6 (1909-10), 241, 243. *Cf.* Macgregor and Ferris, *The Acts,* 314.
[256]Williams, *Acts,* 393 and Neil, *The Acts,* 237 respectively.
[257]Hauser, *Strukturen,* 152.
[258]R.J. Cassidy, *Society and Politics in the Acts of the Apostles,* 126.
[259]Tacitus, *Hist.* 5.9. She was the daughter of Juba II, king of Mauretania.
[260]Suetonius, *Cl.* 28.
[261]Josephus, *AJ* 19.354 [19.9.1]; 20.137-44 [20.7.1f.].

pledged in marriage as a young child to Epiphanes. Epiphanes later broke the arrangement because he was unwilling to convert to Judaism. She was then given in marriage to king Azizus who consented to circumcision. Her marriage to him was dissolved owing to the machinations of Felix who desired her, according to Josephus, out of a strong physical passion.

While we may doubt that the interview arose between Paul and Felix at Drusilla's instigation,[262] her mention is not incidental to what follows. The reader's knowledge of the couple's state of moral compromise is probably presumed, especially when consideration is given to the content of Paul's preaching and Felix' reaction. Paul spoke about faith in Christ Jesus (Acts 24:24), discoursing on the themes of righteous acts, self-control in sexual matters and the coming judgment. The convicting power of Paul's preaching is confirmed by Felix' fear and it is worth noting that ἔμφοβος is found elsewhere in Luke's work only to describe circumstances in which individuals find themselves in the presence of angelic messengers or the risen Jesus himself (Luke 24:5, 37; Acts 10:4). Rather than leading to good works or reverence for the name (cf. Acts 10:35; 19:17), however, Felix' fear results in a swift dismissal of Paul. Felix' interest in Paul thereafter shifts decidedly in the direction of obtaining a bribe (Acts 24:26); Paul's interest in Felix remains unchanged. Luke indicates that meetings occurred often and, if extension of imprisonment was thought likely to soften Paul to the prospect of paying a bribe, until the time of Felix' recall. To describe the prisoner Paul's interview with Felix and Drusilla and interviews thereafter as occasional and unfruitful, therefore, is to miss Luke's point; viz., the prisoner's forthright, powerful and incorruptible proclamation of the gospel in the opportunities furnished.

We may safely infer that Paul's conversations with Felix were only part of a more extensive prison ministry of the spoken word having an impact outside of the place of incarceration. Felix' transaction in doing a 'favour' (Acts 24:27) for the Jews by leaving Paul in prison after two year makes very little sense unless Paul had a clear and continuing high currency in Jewish eyes and the Jews were dissatisfied with an adjournment of the proceedings.[263] Moreover, the case for Paul's considerable 'value' is reinforced first of all by the report of the Jewish ruling

---

[262]Despite the words of MS syr^hmg. Even her presence at the interview cannot automatically be presumed—at Acts 24:25 Felix is afraid. Motive might be found in Felix' administrative interest in the Way (cf. Acts 24:22) and the early influence of his venality.

[263]Supra, 320-23.

élite's immediate and vigorous hostile representations at Jerusalem and Caesarea (Acts 25:2f., 15), by Luke's note concerning the renewed assassination plot (Acts 25:3) and, very possibly, by public demonstrations in the Jewish and Gentile capitals (Acts 25:24).[264]

We contend that Paul had a high currency at the end of the two year Caesarean imprisonment because he had, in significant ways and all long, been very active. Conditions for such activity would seem to have been most favourable. First, the church at Caesarea was sympathetic to the Gentile mission.[265] Second, the church also appears to have had a stable leadership not only sympathetic but historically instrumental to the furtherance of that mission. Philip the Evangelist undertook ground-breaking work among the Gentiles (Acts 8:26-40; cf. 8:4-8). It appears from the way the narrative breaks off abruptly on his arrival in the 30's AD that he not only proclaimed the Messiah in Caesarea but also that he had settled there. In the late 50's AD, Paul and his company are put up in the house (Acts 21:8) of Philip and his four prophetess daughters.[266] We are probably dealing, at Acts 21:8-16, with a house church and a leadership group at the hub of Caesarean Christendom. Finally, Paul has a continuing connection with Caesarea; he debarks from Caesarea (Acts 9:30), sails there from Ephesus at the end of the second missionary journey (Acts 18:22) and, as noted above, stays with Philip. At the least, there was warmth and kinship in ministry between Paul and the church at Caesarea.

We concluded from Acts 24:23 that Paul was not subjected to a cripplingly close guard which kept him dependant upon his keepers to approve his every action in Herod's palace. The helpers there noted, it was suggested, would have included not only family and relatives but almost certainly supportive and friendly co-religionists. The meaning of ὑπηρετέω in that context, it was argued, must be limited to meeting the prisoner's material needs; i.e., attending to his physical sustenance and no more.[267] In what numbers visitors were permitted to Paul we cannot be sure, though the somewhat relaxed conditions of his keeping and the fact that a plural substantive is used should not be overlooked. The overall impression of Paul's custody suggests that,

---

[264]See Williams, *Acts*, 413; Krodel, *Acts*, 453; Neil, *The Acts*, 241; Macgregor and Ferris, *The Acts*, 321.
[265]L.I. Levine, *Caesarea Under Roman Rule* (Studies in Judaism in Late Antiquity 7; Leiden: Brill, 1975), 24.
[266]*Ibid.*, 25.
[267]*Supra*, 170-71.

though formal permission to engage in religious activity was not given, some kind of ministry of the spoken word could have taken place.

Philosophical and religious instruction was carried out in prison by Socrates, Apollonius, Akiba, and certain of the Christian confessors. This also occurs in the apocryphal literature. The instruction indicated in the last three instances might even be called community direction—in a few cases, community leadership. In not a few of the above examples, the conditions of imprisonment were far more forbidding and restrictive than the second phase of Paul's Caesarean incarceration. Might Paul have had such a ministry? Without prejudice to the question of the possible locale(s) of imprisonment, the canonical captivity epistles may help to answer this question. There the imprisoned apostle sends individuals,[268] presumably with news and/or instruction, and, again presumably with news and/or questions, receives[269] and summons[270] individuals. The greetings in these epistles show that Christians—both associates and members of the local churches[271]—attend the prisoner. All of this presumes the opportunity for involvement in a ministry of the spoken word.

Cassidy remarks concerning Acts 27:1ff., '...it should be noted that Luke's portrait of Paul in this section of the narrative integrates an important additional element: despite the fact that Paul is a Roman prisoner, he nevertheless engages in a form of ministry among the Gentiles'.[272] Regrettably, Cassidy makes this observation 'almost as a parenthesis', observing that Luke reports no converts and concluding that the ministry is at least an implicit resumption.[273] 'Success', however, is not an invariable Lukan criterion of significance.[274] Moreover, the Lukan indication of the prisoner's public witness—particularly at Acts 27:21-26—deserves to be seen as possessing greater significance when an eye is kept to its kinship with the more formal witness of the defence speeches, the obvious constraints imposed upon that witness by its hearers and the travel circumstances,[275] and, finally, to the fact that Luke will soon draw his work to a close.

---

[268]Eph. 6:21; Phil. 1:1; 2:19, 23, 25, 28; Col. 1:1, 7 (?); 4:7-9, 17; Phm. 12; 2 Tim. 4:12.
[269]Phil. 2:25; 4:18; Col. 1:17f.; 4:12f.; 2 Tim. 1:16-18a.
[270]2 Tim. 4:9, 11, 13; 4:11.
[271]Phil. 1:1; 4:21f.; Col. 1:1; 4:10-12, 14; Phm. 1, 23f.; 2 Tim. 4:11, 21.
[272]Cassidy, *Society and Politics*, 126.
[273]*Ibid.*
[274]The present writer recalls that such a faulty criterion has led some to judge the Areopagus speech at Acts 17:16-34 a resounding failure to be repented of.

Luke records that Paul, seeing his fellow travellers weakened by appetite long gone from seasickness and worry,[276] exhorts them to be of courage (Acts 27:22, 25; cf. 27:36). Beginning with a rather histrionic and distinctively Pauline 'I told you so' (cf. Acts 27:10),[277] Paul assures them in unconditional terms that all those aboard will be delivered, but that the ship will be lost. The basis for this is a communication Paul received the previous night from a divine messenger. Krodel remarks on the appropriateness of the description of the messenger at Acts 27:23: 'A knowledgeable reader [or Christian companions, we might add!] would understand this as a reference to an "angel-Christology". A pagan would take it to refer to a divine messenger of Paul's God'.[278] The message at Acts 27:24, a reiteration and elaboration of the message two years before (Acts 23:11), is: 'Do not be afraid, Paul. You must stand trial before Caesar; and God has graciously given you the lives of all who sail with you'.[279] The ship's company (pagans and Christians alike!) can have confidence that they will be saved from the storm because Paul's God is doing him a 'favour' (χαρίζομαι). Paul, in relating the message, voicing his own unqualified faith in God, and calling for courage, asks them, in effect, to have the same belief and confidence in his God. He concludes with what is probably a prophetic statement that they will run aground on some island (Acts 27:26).[280]

---

[275]The suitability of the speech to its pagan hearers and its extreme brevity are, quite unfairly, not permitted to answer what has been called the 'complete unreality' of the picture of the apostle speaking above the noise of the storm. Moreover, the alleged unreality is all the greater when imaginatively presented. Cf. Haenchen, *The Acts*, 704, 709; Conzelmann, *Acts*, 218; Krodel. *Acts*, 475. We may ask, finally, whether Paul must be construed to be speaking so that all 276 persons on board can hear? At Acts 27:22, Paul's reference to the earlier warning not to sail (Acts 27:10f.) may be relevant to all if the πλείονες at Acts 27:12 refers to crew and passengers, but when he remarks concerning the injury and loss that had thus far been incurred (*viz.*, Acts 27:18f.), those described as the κυβερνήτης and ναύκληρος of the ship (Acts 27:11) alone would seem to be in view.

[276]The burden of the text is not that food could not be prepared in the circumstances or that supplies had been spoiled. See Acts 27:33-36. Cf. Haenchen, *The Acts*, 704; Conzelmann, *Acts*, 218; Schneider, *Die Apostelgeschichte*, 392 n. 53; Bruce, *The Acts*, 521.

[277]So J. Munck, *The Acts of the Apostles*, rev. tr. W.F. Albright and C.S. Mann (AB 31; Garden City: Doubleday, 1967), xxxv, 250.

[278]Krodel, *Acts*, 476. So also Haenchen, *The Acts*, 715 who, while noting that the separation between θεοῦ and ἄγγελος is 'specifically Lucan', does not remark that this is the only instance in Luke-Acts of the order τοῦ θεοῦ . . ἄγγελος (cf. Luke 1:26; 12:8f. [2x]; 15:10; Acts 10:3). How can the word order then be judged 'Lucan' by Haenchen, *The Acts*, 704 and Conzelmann, *Acts*, 219?

The summons to courage is initially refused so the prisoner apostle tries again somewhat later. He bids them eat while he confidently reaffirms, by a very Jewish expression,[281] his belief that all would be completely preserved from harm (Acts 27:34). Punctuating this by his own prayer and personal example, he has success: 'They were all encouraged and ate some food themselves' (Acts 27:36; cf. v. 38a). Encouragement concerning the survival prospects of those aboard did not, however, favourably dispose the soldiers to either Paul or the other prisoners.[282] While Luke indicates that Paul's confident witness to a universal salvation from death at sea was an encouragement in prospect, reaction to its actuality (Acts 27:44)—we might well imagine that it did inspire some to a high regard for the prisoner and his god—drew no Lukan comment.

In similar fashion, what ministry of the spoken word there must certainly have been on Malta is passed over in favour of an account of the travellers' hospitable reception, of Paul's miraculous preservation from the ill-effects of snakebite and the reaction this generated, and of his well-received ministry of healing.[283] Also, while Luke records the fact of the prisoner party's seven day experience of Christian hospitality at Puteoli (Acts 28:14),[284] there is no explicit indication of a ministry of the word. Such a ministry must actually have occurred, particularly when one recalls that a Lord's day would be involved. However, no comment beyond the suggestion itself can be entered as Luke focuses upon Rome.

---

[279]If it does not actually pull completely away from the pagan thoughts and conceptions of divine retribution, pollution and shipwreck recently assumed of Luke and predicated to his ancient reader, this message certainly radically redirects them along a Christian trajectory. The pagan observer might well be understood to make such connections (cf. Acts 28:3-6); the Christian reader—and very likely the hardnosed first century Roman magistrate—would not. Cf. G.B. Miles and G. Trompf 'Luke and Antiphon: The Theology of Acts 27-28 in the Light of Pagan Beliefs about Divine Retribution, Pollution, and Shipwreck', HTR 69 (1976), 259-67; D. Ladouceur, 'Hellenistic Preconceptions of Shipwreck and Pollution as a Context for Acts 27-28', HTR 73 (1980), 435-49 [esp. 441].

[280]See C.H. Cosgrove, 'The Divine ΔΕΙ in Luke-Acts', NovT 26 (1984), 178; Haenchen, The Acts, 705 and n. 1; Williams, Acts, 437; Pesch, Die Apostelgeschichte, 291; Krodel, Acts, 477; Bruce, The Acts, 522. Cf. Acts 28:1.

[281]Cf. LXX: 1 Sam. 14:45; 2 Sam. 14:11; 1 Kings 1:52.; also found at Luke 12:6f. [≈ Matt. 10:29-31]; 21:18f.

[282]We have already considered Acts 27:31f., 42f. in some detail, supra, 271-72.

[283]See Wikenhauser, Die Apostelgeschichte, 284; Longenecker, 'The Acts', 565.

[284]For discussion, supra, 273-76.

If Luke does not explicitly indicate that the prisoner Paul was vigorously engaged in a preaching and teaching ministry on the last leg of the journey, he is absolutely transparent on the point once Paul was settled in Rome. We have in the present chapter already considered at some length Paul's first address to the leaders of the Jews at Acts 28:17-22, finding in it Luke's indication that Paul engaged in a form of case preparation.[285] Having argued this, however, it seems clear enough from the response of the Jewish leader at Acts 28:21f. that Paul said more than what Luke records at Acts 28:17b-20. He must have given some explicit indication he was a Nazarene (Acts 24:5); perhaps indicating that he worshipped the God of his fathers as a follower of the Way (called at Acts 24:14 and v. 5 a αἵρεσις). Jewish unwillingness to engage him at that moment suggests diplomacy.[286]

The Jewish leaders hardly declined to engage Paul because they needed to receive instruction from Jerusalem, for they arranged a meeting with Paul some days later. Lack of time for extended discussion, seemingly ruled out by the expression ἀπὸ πρωῒ ἕως ἑσπέρας at Acts 28:23, would not account for the reticence. A far more likely motive appears to have been Jewish feelings of theological unpreparedness. That the meeting at Acts 28:23 was vigorous and serious in the quality of engagement, lengthy and far-ranging in biblical scope and theological content (ἀπό τε τοῦ νόμου Μωϋσέως καὶ τῶν προφητῶν), inlcines one to embrace the last motive. The πλείονας (Acts 28:23) would then constitute not simply more people generally but more of those well-versed in the Jewish faith and scriptures and capable of engaging Paul's presentation critically.[287] If we have correctly understood the motive for convening a second gathering and correctly identified those described, Luke shows his readers that the prisoner's ministry through the spoken word is highly significant. Paul was preaching to many of the most knowledgeable, informed and important representatives of the Jewish population of Rome.[288] That Paul desires to convene these two meetings shows his continuing connection with and sincere concern for his fellow Jews; that he is able shows his high position in Judaism. He has the continuing respect and interest of Judaism's most exalted members and that despite being made a prisoner by the machinations of the Jerusalem Jewish leadership.[289]

---

[285]Supra, 329-32.
[286]See Neil, The Acts, 257; but cf. Bruce, The Acts, 539.
[287]Hauser, Strukturen, 83 calls the πλείονας an intensification of πρῶτοι.

The prisoner Paul's preaching labours to this exalted Jewish company drew a mixed response: 'Some were convinced by what he said, but others would not believe' (Acts 28:24). It is hard to agree with the assertion of Haenchen that 'in ἐπείθοντο there is no thought of a real conversion any more than in the similar scene at 23.9. Theoretically the Jews are not at one as regards the Christian doctrine; but in practice neither of the two groups decides for Christianity'.[290] The parallelism of the Lukan description argues against such an interpretation: First, the Jews are divided into two groups; 'some' (οἱ μέν) and 'others' (οἱ δέ). The parallelism itself mandates no conclusion that the some were only a few and that the others who were unconvinced were 'the majority'.[291] The emphasis is upon division, not proportion. Second, the former group were convinced (πείθω); the latter would not believe (ἀπιστέω). On this second point of the parallelism, Weatherly observes that the active form of πείθω

> refers to the process of Christian preaching (18:4; 19:8, 26), the result of which is 'to make a Christian' (26:28). In this context as well, the process of Paul's preaching is 'persuading' (28:23), which yields those who are 'persuaded' (28:24). Furthermore, in at least one instance in Acts, those who are 'persuaded' undoubtedly refers to believers. In Acts 17:4, some in the Thessalonian synagogue are 'persuaded' and attach themselves to Paul and Silas.[292]

---

[288]The question of what becomes of the Christians at Rome in Luke's narrative after Acts 28:14f. has received an unsatisfactory treatment. Haenchen, *The Acts*, 720, 730, for example, suggests that Luke artlessly wants a warm Roman Christian welcome for Paul while at the same time desiring to portray the apostle as the founder of Roman Christianity, preaching to Jews who know virtually nothing of the Way. F.V. Filson, 'Live Issues in the Acts', *Biblical Research* 9 (1964), 31f., gives a much more satisfactory account of Luke's activity: '...Paul was the apostolic sponsor of the gospel at Rome. In the Acts he is the one apostolic leader who comes to Rome. ... The one Apostle whom Luke places there in Rome is Paul, and Paul's preaching in Rome supplies the only apostolic warrant or sponsor whom Luke can name for that church'. See a similar pattern after earlier successful Christian preaching in Samaria (Acts 8:4-25) and at Antioch (Acts 11:19f.). This helps elaborate the Lukan concern to show Paul's ongoing relationship to Judaism (*cf.* Marshall, *The Acts*, 420), yet without trivialising information which has a critical importance in its own right. Furthermore, Jewish ignorance of the Way may be less profound than some scholars suggest. *Cf.* for discussion on this last point, Bruce, *New Testament History*, 404f. and n. 6; Williams, *Acts*, 453; Neil, *The Acts*, 257f.

[289]Stählin, *Die Apostelgeschichte*, 326.

[290]Haenchen, *The Acts*, 723f. So also Conzelmann, *Acts*, 227.

[291]*Contra* Bruce, *Book of Acts* 508.

[292]J.A. Weatherly, 'The Jews in Luke-Acts', *TynBul* 40 (1989), 110.

These individuals are later designated ἀδελφοί, they go through persecutions and for that reason, argues Weatherly, should be accounted from the Lukan perspective as genuine believers. Weatherly concludes that

> in Acts 28:24, persuasion is contrasted with unbelief. The opposite is true in Acts 14:1-2, where belief is contrasted with failure to be persuaded. Luke thus appears comfortable using either πιστεύω in the active or πείθω in the passive to indicate conversion.[293]

Finally, Weatherly asserts that the imperfect tense of πείθω cannot mean 'take heed' in a sense short of actual conversion on the assumption that the same argument would then have to hold for its parallel member (i.e., the imperfect of ἀπιστέω).[294]

Paul's preaching, therefore, generated results consistent with earlier preaching outside the prison context. In keeping with other instances in the Lukan record of a turning away from exclusive Jewish preaching in the face of a divided response (Acts 13:40-47; 18:5-8; 19:8f.), Paul, focusing upon the group that has responded negatively,[295] quotes Isa. 6:9f. (LXX) and declares for the preaching of God's salvation to the Gentiles and their willing reception of it. The prospect of an ongoing official missionary relationship to the Jewish community *qua* community is apparently ended for Paul. However, this is hardly construed by Luke as a failure from the perspective of the prisoner's preaching.

Nor does Paul, Luke reports, sink thereafter into the oblivion of a fruitless confinement in Rome. Rather, the 'two whole years' of Acts 28:30 are filled with opportunity for ministry of the spoken word. The objects of this ministry are 'all who came to see him' and we may be confident from the discussion above and the progression indicated in the text (*viz.*: the Jewish πρῶτοι at v. 17 -> πλείονας of Jewish leaders at v. 23 -> the ἔθνοι at v. 28) that πάντες refers to all indiscriminately, whether Jews or Gentiles.[296] van Unnik's general conclusion that παρ-

---

[293]*Ibid.*

[294]J.A. Weatherly, *Jewish Responsibility for the Cross in Luke-Acts* (University of Aberdeen: Unpublished PhD Thesis, 1991), 205, citing Bruce.

[295]There is no justification for using Paul's words at Acts 28:25-28 to demand that there were no conversions at Acts 28:24. See Weatherly, *Jewish Responsibility*, 209-31.

[296]So also the ancient explanatory addition in the Western text reviser. See Metzger, *A Textual Commentary*, 502. *Contra* Haenchen, *The Acts*, 726; Schille, *Die Apostelgeschichte*, 479.

ρησία in Acts 'is always mentioned in connection with preaching in the synagogue and to the Jews', ignores this immediate context as Hauser has pointed out.[297] The progression also leaves in the reader's mind a strong impression that the numbers indicated by πάντες were not small.

The ministry is described at Acts 28:31 as proclaiming the kingdom of God (*cf.* Acts 20:25)[298] and teaching the things concerning the Lord Jesus Christ (*cf.* Acts 4:18; 5:28; 5:42; 18:25).[299] These indicate a ministry that is apostolic and includes both evangelism and catechesis—the prisoner is both adding members to the Christian community and strengthening it. (The latter circumstance would then unavoidably constitute a second reference to the prisoner's ongoing positive relationship with the Roman church.) The reader is also told that the imprisoned apostle vigorously and unashamedly engaged in ministry of the spoken word in all these opportunities. We have already considered the term παρρησία, arguing that far from being cowed by the shame associations that would normally attach to a prisoner in bonds, Paul engaged all and sundry not just boldly but 'with all boldness' in God's generous provision.[300]

We would be seriously remiss in not mentioning the implication of Luke's concern to inform his readers of Paul's living arrangements in Rome. Cadbury has written that the matter of lodging and lodging arrangements are of considerable interest to Luke and that this 'is most obvious in the second half of Acts'.[301] Cadbury himself does not question that Acts 28:16 refers to Paul's accommodation, but accommodation, he argues, is not described by the words ξενία and μίσθωμα at Acts 28:23 and 30 respectively.[302] We have argued, however, that just

---

[297]W.C. van Unnik, 'The Christian's Freedom of Speech in the New Testament', *BJRL* 44 (1961), 478 [*cf.* 479f.], and Hauser, *Strukturen*, 140f. respectively.

[298]Further in conjunction with the kingdom of God, the verbs λέγω (Acts 1:3), εὐαγγελίζομαι (Acts 8:12), διαλογίζομαι/πείθω (Acts 19:8) and ἐκτίθημι/διαμαρτύρομαι (Acts 28:23).

[299]Further in conjunction with the verb διδάσκω, its object can be the word of God (Acts 15:35; 18:11). Christ, His name, or truths about Him are also the content of the action indicated by κηρύσσω (Acts 8:5; 9:20; 10:42; 19:13; *cf.* 20:20), εὐαγγελίζομαι (Acts 5:42; 15:35) and καταγγέλλω (Acts 4:2).

[300]*Supra*, 310-12. Longenecker, 'The Acts', 572f., finding in Acts 28:30f. a summary statement like those of 6:7; 9:31; 12:24; 16:5; and 19:20, suggests that it is intended to summarize the character of the apostle's prison ministry for the whole of the sixth panel; i.e., Acts 19:21-28:31. The present writer, however, sees Acts 28:30f. as summary and retrospective only to the extent of describing the two year period in Rome.

[301]Cadbury, 'Luke's Interest in Lodging', 305.

such an understanding of these two terms is called for and that Acts
28:16-31 in consequence contains both there and in the verbs of invitation, remaining, welcoming and entry, repeated references to the prisoner Paul's accommodation. Were we to agree with Cadbury's
statement that 'here of course there is an additional interest in his [i.e.,
Paul's] comparative liberty and privacy',[303] we would understate and
misrepresent the Lukan objective in mentioning Paul's place of confinement. To be sure, there is an emphasis upon Paul's considerable
freedom, but it is inextricably tied to the object which that freedom
serves—viz., the vigorous and broadly directed ministry of the spoken
word to increasingly greater numbers of individuals. As Hauser has
argued, the rented accommodation is to be seen, from the Lukan perspective, much less as the living place during the imprisonment on remand and much more as the place of preaching.[304] To say that 'Paul's
lodging becomes transformed into a kind of synagogue with Paul
functioning not as a defender but as witnessing missionary',[305] as
Krodel does, rightly emphasizes accommodation as pre-eminently the
place of preaching but is relevant only for the 'Jewish phase' (Acts
28:17-28). We contend that Luke wanted to show to his readers that *the
prisoner Paul's entire two year ministry in Rome was house church-like.*
Luke was interested in lodging, but predominantly the locales where
hospitality was extended to travelling Christian missionaries and
where Christian gatherings and ministry took place. The terms οἰκία
and οἶκος are prominent in this regard.[306] Two examples should by
specially noted: 1) the summary passage at Acts 5:42 where apostolic
ministry from house to house (κατ' οἶκον) is described using the terms
διδάσκω and εὐαγγελίζομαι, and 2) Paul's description of his ministry
to the Ephesians at Acts 20:20f. as in their houses (κατ' οἴκους) and us-

---

[302]*Ibid.*, 306.

[303]Cadbury, 'Luke's Interest in Lodging', 306.

[304]So Hauser, *Strukturen*, 155-57.

[305]Krodel, *Acts*, 497f.

[306]On οἰκία as Christian locale [with leadership connection]: Acts 9:11, 17 (Damas-
can Judas on Straight Street [Saul]); 10:6, 17, 32; 11:11 (Simon the Tanner [Peter]);
12:12 (Mary the mother of John Mark [Peter & church]; 16:32 (Philippian jailer
[Paul & Silas]); 17:5 (Thessalonian Jason [Paul & Co.]); 18:7 (Corinthian Titius Jus-
tus [Paul]). On οἶκος as Christian locale [with leadership connection]: Acts 2:2 (Jerusalem house [Twelve]); 2:46 (Jerusalem from house to house [apostles]); 5:42
(Jerusalem from house to house [apostles]); 8:3 (Jerusalem from house to house
[apostles?]); 10:22, 30; 11:12f. (Caesarean Cornelius [Peter & Co]); 16:15 (Thyatira-
ian Lydia at Philippi [Paul, Silas & Co.]; 16:34 (Philippian Jailer [Paul & Silas]);
20:20 (Ephesus house to house [Paul]); 21:8 (Caesarea [Philip, Paul & Co.]).

ing the verbs ἀναγγέλλω, διδάσκω and διαμαρτύρομαι. Paul, it has been argued by Stowers, actually preferred such a use of the house as it compensated for the many disadvantages he would otherwise have sustained.[307] He continues that when attention is paid to Paul's epistles and the Acts account shorn of special Lukan concerns, 'the private home was most likely the center of Paul's preaching activity'.[308] He did not permit himself to become fully dependent upon his hosts, however, preferring to support himself by working with his own hands.[309] The image Luke presents of a Paul in Rome living in his own rented accommodation and ministering the word to all who came to him is then an image of legitimation, freedom, and spiritual effectiveness.

It might be objected that Luke uses neither οἰκία nor οἰκος at Acts 28:16-31. But we should not expect Luke to have used either of these terms as they did not accurately represent the type of accommodation Paul occupied in Rome. Further, Luke uses other terms than οἰκία and οἰκος which show that other types of accommodation were used for Christian purposes. Of particular interest in this regard are references to the Christian use of upstairs locations (ὑπερῷον: Acts 1:13, 9:36 and 20:8). The last, which mentions an upstairs room at Troas, is most significant to the present discussion in light of the earlier findings concerning rental accommodation in Rome and their implications for the prisoner Paul's experience.[310] Located on the third floor (Acts 20:10) as we suggested Paul's Roman accommodation was, the room at Troas was almost certainly the whole or a part of a tenement-type apartment building. If its height in the structure is any indication, we would not be wrong in thinking of a lower-priced living space and a therefore less wealthy Christian renter/host.[311] From the context we know that this abode served the believers at Troas as a regular meeting place and the venue for breaking bread and teaching (Acts 20:5-12). Indication that upper storey accommodation *in Rome* was suitable to Christian meetings can be found in the interrogation of the Christian

---

[307]S.K.S. Stowers, 'Social Status, Public Speaking, and Private Teaching. The Circumstances of Paul's Preaching Activity', *NovT* 26 (1984), 68.

[308]*Ibid.*, 70.

[309]*Ibid.*

[310]*Supra*, 236-39.

[311]Was it small? The meeting place may have been a one window room (Acts 20:9) which, when the whole church (Acts 20:7) and at least ten Christian visitors (Acts 20:4-6) gathered, could become both crowded and stuffy (Acts 20:8f.).

confessor Justin (*c.* 163-68 AD). Justin says to the magistrate at one point:

> I have been living above the baths of Myrtinus for the entire period of
> my sojourn at Rome, and this is my second; and I have known no oth-
> er meeting-place but here. Anyone who wished could come to my
> abode and I would impart to him the words of truth.[312]

These several examples strengthen our contention that the Lukan description is intended to assuage any doubts in the reader's mind about
the imprisoned Paul's continuing effectiveness. By describing the
place of Paul's confinement in terms which clearly suggest that it was
a type of house church, Luke vindicates the prisoner as minister of the
spoken word. The image is certainly a most positive, forward reaching
and powerful one by any Christian reckoning.[313]

---

[312]*Mart. Justin & Co.* 3.3 in *Recensio A. Ibid.* 3.3 in *Recensio B* reads 'above the baths
of a certain Martinus son of Timiotinus'. *Cf. ibid.* 2.5 in *Recensio C.*

[313]For a thorough description of the house church and its importance to Christian
witness and community, *cf.* B.B. Blue, *In Public and In Private: The Role of the House
Church in Early Christianity* (University of Aberdeen: Unpublished PhD Thesis,
1989); *idem*, 'Acts and the House Church', in *The Book of Acts in Its Graeco-Roman
Setting*, ed. D.W.J. Gill and C. Gempf (A1CS 2; Grand Rapids:Eerdmans/Carlisle:
Paternoster, 1994), 119-222; V. Brannick, *The House Church in the Writings of Paul*
(Wilmington, Delaware: Michael Glazier, 1989) and sources therein cited.

CHAPTER 14

PAUL'S HELPERS

If, as we are frequently advised, the prisoner Paul went from victory to victory, we may be sure that he did not do it alone. Christian individuals and groups who assisted Paul when he was free to carry out his missionary labours were essential to sustaining both him and his mission during his imprisonments. This chapter discusses these Christian helpers, the nature of the help they were able to offer, and the dangers to which interest in a prisoner could expose them.

From Acts 21 to the end and encompassing a period well in excess of four years the apostle Paul was imprisoned. The *peristasis* catalogues of 2 Corinthians mention many other imprisonments (2 Cor. 6:5; 11:23) in the period before Acts 20:2a.[1] Of these, Luke records only Paul's Philippian imprisonment (Acts 16:16-40; *cf.* 1 Thes 2:2), passing over others in silence. Clearly Paul was frequently in confinement and for long periods of time. How did he cope?

It is unfortunate that this question, which presses for a practical answer, often draws a largely theological response, succumbs to triumphalist assertions concerning Paul's indomitable spirit, or simply dies in the asking. Asked again, how practically speaking, *did* he cope? The answer is that Paul received help.

Admittedly, Luke does not dwell upon the helpers of the prisoner Paul or their helping activities to any great extent. But neither does he ignore them. In this chapter, we shall examine a few helpers and the help they render Paul in the book of Acts. When analysed against the much fuller background of prison helpers and helping behaviours in the Graeco-Roman world, these Lukan snippets yield some surprising and helpful insights.

I. Kinds of Helpers

The virtue of helping a prisoner because of true friendship is mooted in a letter of Seneca, dated *c.* 63-65 AD. He argues there that friendships should not be made simply to mitigate or escape disasters such as imprisonment. 'He who regards himself only, and enters upon friendships for this reason, reckons wrongly',[2] writes Seneca. Rather, the true friend seeks out one 'by whose sick-bed he himself may sit, someone a prisoner in hostile hands whom he himself may set free'.[3]

Some friends may be motivated to help the prisoner by what we might call *affection*. The emotionally depressed prisoner Publius Vitellius (31 AD),[4] Agrippa,[5] and Antiphilus and Deinias in Lucian's *Toxaris* (*c.* 163 AD),[6] are attended by friends who show such self-disregarding affection.

---

[1]Cf. V.P. Furnish, *II Corinthians* (*AB* 32A; Garden City: Doubleday 1984), 354 on the possible interpretations of the plural 'imprisonments'.
[2]Seneca, *Ep. ad Lucilium* 9.8.
[3]*Ibid.*
[4]Suetonius, *Vit.* 7.2.3.

The solidarity of friends with the prisoner sometimes has a *political or moral aspect to it*. The 'many good men' who accompany the condemned Phocion and his compatriots to the prison in Athens (318 BC), Cleomenes and his friends (220 BC) who are all under house arrest for trying to topple the Egyptian monarchy,[7] and the body of Roman senators who accompany the younger Cato (59 BC) when he is taken to prison at Caesar's command,[8] demonstrate the interweave of friendship and political or moral solidarity.

Other helpers may be specified by reference to their *philosophical or religious solidarity with the prisoner*. The *Life of Apollonius of Tyana*, a substantial proportion of which comes by way of his companion Damis,[9] gives some insight into the friends and disciples of the philosophers. Despite the danger of prison and death, Damis willingly goes with his teacher to Rome; in Apollonius' words, 'accompanying me in all I do'.[10] The philosopher Musonius, a contemporary of Apollonius, has in his Roman imprisonment under Nero, a counterpart to Damis in the person of Menippus.[11] Apollonius demonstrates fraternity with a fellow philosopher when he writes to Musonius that he is prepared to share in the latter's imprisonment and to assist him in securing his release.[12] In Judaism there are examples in the disciples who attend to John the Baptist.[13] A fraternal relationship exists between Rabbi Joshua the gritsmaker and the imprisoned Rabbi Akiba for whom he cares.[14] Christian examples would include the disciples of the Chris-

---

[5]Josephus, *Ant*.18.204 [18.6.71]. Other friends are also permitted to visit and attend to Agrippa from what is said by Josephus (*Ibid*. 18.203 [18.6.7]). In addition to affection, there might stand political opportunism. When he returned to Jerusalem as king, Agrippa gave to Silas the command of his army in consideration of the hardships he was willing to share with Agrippa (*Ibid*.19.299 [19.6.3]).

[6]Lucian, *Tox*. 27, and 17. A.M. Harmon states that the stories, declared on oath in the text to be authentic and recent happenings, 'are the thing, and the dialogue is just a framing-tale in which to display them'. (Lucian, *Tox*. [LCL], 101).

[7]Polybius 5.39.1-5.

[8]Plutarch, *Cat.Mi*. 31.1f.; *idem*., *Caes*. 14.7. Plutarch calls the senators 'influential men' in the latter passage. The significance of the action is expressed in the words of Marcus Petreius. According to Dio Cassius 38.3.2. Petreius is said to have told Caesar as he turned to go, 'I prefer to be with Cato in prison rather than here with you'.

[9]*Cf*. G. Anderson *Philostratus: Biography and Belles Lettres in the Third Century BC* (London, Croom Helm 1986) 163, on its historical reliability.

[10] Philostratus, *VA* 7.15.

[11]*Ibid*. 4.46.

[12]*Ibid*.

[13]Matt. 11:2; 14:12. *Cf*. Mark 6:29; Luke 3:20; 7:18-24.

[14]*b. Mo'ed* III: *Erub*. 21*b*.

tian martyr Montanus (259 AD)[15] and the newly converted 'adjutant who was head of the gaol'[16] and who assisted Perpetua and Felicitas (203 AD). The Apocryphal Acts also describe the visits and ministrations of convert or disciple helpers in prisons.[17]

Finally, the helper might be owned by the prisoner or otherwise beholden to him. The slaves of Cleomenes (220 BC),[18] the slaves of the consular Paetus (42 AD),[19] and the freedmen Marsyas and Stoecheus who attend the Jewish prince Agrippa (37 AD)[20] are examples.

Looking to Acts, we find explicit reference to several individual helpers: the Philippian jailer (Acts 16:27-36) the writer of the 'we' source whom many identify as Luke (Acts 27:1ff.)[21] and Aristarchus (Acts 27:2). In the case of the Philippian jailer, we clearly have a new convert. It is remarkable that this is help *from within* the prison system. The capacity in which Luke and Aristarchus attend Paul at Acts 27:1ff., however, is variously assessed. They have been identified as Paul's friends or associates,[22] slave attendants[23] and, in the case of Aristarchus, a fellow-prisoner.[24]

Aristarchus, appearing in Acts previously in connection with the riot at Ephesus (Acts 19:29) and the Jerusalem collection (Acts 20:4), is probably the same person mentioned at Colossians 4:10 and Philemon 24. Because Paul designates him 'my fellow prisoner' at Colossians 4:10 it is assumed by some that he accompanies Paul as a fellow prisoner at Acts 27:2. This, for several reasons, is unlikely. First, we should expect in two epistles, where many of the same individuals are mentioned, that there would be some consistency in assigning epithets

---

[15]*Mart. Mont. & Luc.* 19.2.

[16]*Mart. Perp. & Felic.* 16.4.

[17]*Apocr. Acts Thom.* 10.119; 13.150-1 (first half 3rd cent. AD) *Apoc. Acts of Paul* 3.17-20 (c. 185-95 AD); *Apoc. Acts of Andrew* B.5 (c.190 AD).

[18]Polybius 5.39.1-5.

[19]Pliny, *Ep.* 3.16.

[20]Josephus, *AJ* 18.204 [18.6.7]. Josephus recounts the kindness done to Agrippa by a slave of Gaius who gave him a drink of cold water. (*Ibid.* 18.193 [18.6.6]).

[21]J.V. Bartlet, *The Acts* (CBNT 5; Edinburgh: T.C. and E.C. Clark, 1901), 368: suggests that the 'we' may include others beyond Luke and Paul.

[22]So e.g., F.F. Bruce, *The Book of Acts* (NICNT; 1954; rev. ed. Grand Rapids: Eerdmans, 1988), 478 who adds that Luke books passage as ship's doctor; R.J. Knowling, 'The Acts', 515.

[23]So W.M. Ramsay, *St. Paul the Traveller and Roman Citizen* (London: Hodder and Stoughton, 1895), 311. *Cf.* R.B. Rackham, *The Acts*, 480 and W. Neil, *The Acts of the Apostles* (NCB 42; London: Oliphants/Greenwood, Attic, 1973), 247, the latter considering it a serious possibility.

[24]So Stählin, *Die Apostelgeschichte*, 314; L. Haefeli, 'Caesarea', 55.

such as 'fellow-prisoner' if these are to be taken literally. They are not.[25] Second, there is lack of close physical proximity in the text between Aristarchus and those designated prisoners. Only after the companion(s) of the 'we' source are mentioned and distinguished (Acts 27:1) from Paul and his fellow prisoners who are placed in the charge of the centurion, and after the travel arrangements are indicated, is Aristarchus mentioned at the end of verse 2. Third, Luke writes that Aristarchus 'was with us' (Acts 27:2). This associates him with Paul and the companion(s) of the 'we' source or more generally with the entire company embarking from Caesarea. The natural inference is that he stands in a looser relation to the others.[26] Finally, the assertion that Aristarchus accompanies Paul as a prisoner raises many unanswerable questions regarding his status and offence.[27] The questions themselves further erode the notion that Aristarchus is a co-prisoner. He must, then, be accompanying Paul in some other capacity.

W.M. Ramsay has argued, 'The minimum in the way of personal attendants that was allowable for a man of respectable position was two slaves; and, as we shall see, Paul was believed to be attended by two slaves to serve him'.[28] This idea and elements of the argument in support of it have considerable currency in modern treatments of the text. Ramsay continues: 'It is hardly possible to suppose that the prisoner's friends were allowed to accompany him'[29] on the analogy of Pliny's account of the transport of the prisoner Paetus. We cite this text in its entirety:

> Scribonianus had taken up arms in Illyria against Claudius [i.e., 42 AD] but was slain. Paetus, who was of his party, was brought prisoner to Rome. When they were going to put him on board a ship, Arria besought the soldiers that she might be permitted to go with him: "Of course," said she, "you mean to give a consular, as he is, a few slaves

---

[25]Aristarchus is a 'fellow prisoner' at Col. 4:10, but a 'fellow worker' at Philm. 24. Epaphras, on the other hand, is 'one of you and a servant of Christ Jesus' at Col. 4:13, but in Philm. 23 he is identified by Paul as 'my fellow prisoner'.

[26]Cf. I.H. Marshall, *The Acts of Apostles* (TNTC 5; Grand Rapids: Eerdmans, 1980), 404 and Bartlet, *The Acts,* 368, who both suggest he may be on his way home by the same route as the others. Cf. Rackham, *The Acts,* 480.

[27]If Aristarchus is a Roman citizen, has he, like Paul, been granted leave to have his case heard in Rome? If Aristarchus is not a Roman citizen, is he travelling as a condemned prisoner? Is he destined to serve out his life in one of many Imperial public works projects or to give his life as entertainment for the Roman populace at some sporting event?

[28]Ramsay, *St. Paul the Traveller,* 311.

[29]*Ibid.,* 315f.

to wait upon him at his table and toilet; but if you will take me, I alone will perform their whole duties." This favour, however, she could not obtain; upon which she hired a small fishing-vessel, and pursued that great ship in a mere cockleshell.[30]

According to Ramsay, 'The analogy shows how Luke and Aristarchus accompanied Paul: they must have gone as his slaves, not merely performing the duties of slaves (as Arria offered to do), but actually passing as slaves'.[31]

Ramsay continues[32] that friends would hardly be permitted on such vessels as are indicated in Acts 27-28. The council held on board ship (27:11) shows the centurion to be the superior officer, thus confirming that the ship was a government vessel. The grain carriers that the centurion retained (27:6; 28:11) and that Rome so depended upon for its food supply, would hardly have been left to private enterprise. They are Imperial service vessels and, as such, the Authorized and Revised versions are hardly correct in translating ναύκληρος as 'owner' at (Acts 27:11).[33]

Against Ramsay, one cannot assume, first of all, that Paul would automatically be permitted slave attendants. Paetus' wife Arria is simply giving expression to a personal presumption based upon Paetus' consular rank. He probably gets his servants, though the text does not make this explicit. Other examples show that the privilege was not automatic, not even among royals. The son of Queen Roxanê (316 BC) is denied the company of his pages in his confinement.[34] The Jewish Prince Agrippa has freedman attendants but only because of the vigorous interventions of Antonia on his behalf.[35] In addition, servants, if permitted, would probably have to be demonstrably, i.e., by virtue of documentation, members of the prisoner's household. This could not be said of Luke or Aristarchus except by resort to a crude and unacceptable legal fiction which would certainly not have passed muster with the authorities.

Dauvillier writes that while the Egyptian ships of the Ptolemies had been bequeathed to Augustus, it does not follow that all Alexandrian grain carriers plying the waters of the Mediterranean were the

---

[30]Pliny, Ep. 3.16.
[31]Ramsay, St. Paul the Traveller, 316.
[32]Ibid. 323-25.
[33]So also NIV.
[34]Diodorus Siculus 19.52.4.
[35]Josephus, AJ 18.204 [18.6.7]. J. Rougé, 'Actes 27, 1-10', VC 14 (1960), 202.

property of the Emperor.[36] It is true, as Hemer writes, that Claudius, in response to the repeated difficulties of his time, 'developed the remarkable freighter-service from Alexandria to its peak of efficiency'.[37] He did this partly by encouraging the construction of ships—some of astonishing size.[38] Other Claudian provisions,[39] however, suggest not only that there *was* a free-merchant service independent of the government, but that it furnished such a volume of grain as to be critical to the food supply needs of Rome. If grain carriage was solely a government-run operation, such inducements as Claudius employed to encourage risk-taking would hardly be necessary.

The first ship the centurion contracts for his party is probably *not* a government vessel, but from whatActs 27:2 indicates of its port of origin and progress, it was a privately owned ship of the type of coastal trader known by the generic term *oraria navis*.[40] It would be significantly smaller than the grain freighters tracking the open waters of the Mediterranean.[41]

Once the general command is given by the government authorities at Caesarea to take Paul by sea to Rome,[42] the details of travel are left entirely to the discretion of the centurion. The route arrangements are far from the type of 'military operation from first to last' which Ramsay suggests.[43]

---

[36]J. Dauvillier, 'A propos de la venue de saint Paul à Rome. Notes sur son procès et son voyage maritime', *BLE* 61 (1960), 20.

[37]C.J. Hemer, 'First Person Narrative in Acts 27-8', 88.

[38]*Ibid.*, 89. For Thasian port usage restrictions, and the granting of personal privileges and exemptions based upon ship tonnage, see L. Casson, *Ships and Seamanship in The Ancient World* (Princeton: PUP, 1971), 171f. n. 23.

[39]Suetonius, *Cl.* 18f., writes: '... he resorted to every possible means to bring grain to Rome, even in the winter season. To the merchants he held out the certainty of profit by assuming the expense of any loss that they might suffer from storms, and offered to those who build merchant ships large bounties, adapted to the conditions of each: to a citizen exemption from the *lex Papia Poppaea*; to a Latin the rights of Roman citizenship; to women the privileges allowed mothers of four children. And all these provisions are in force today'. By 'today' we should understand the period of Suetonius' life—*i.e., c.* 69-121 AD.

[40]Casson, *Ships,* 337 n. 48. For discussion of appointments and hire, see *ibid.* 337 n. 49; Pliny, *Ep.* 10.15; *Dig.* 14.1.1.12.

[41]Casson, *Ships,* 170-73 and 337.

[42]The centurion could have been ordered to take his prisoner by land and sea as seems to have been the case with Ignatius of Antioch (Ignatius, *Rom.* 5.1).

[43]See Rougé, 'Actes 27, 1-10', 193ff. who, aside from stating that the general command does not even specify the manner of conveyance, is correct that the route taken, the ports of call, and the speed of progress are all determined by meteorological and trading, rather than military, considerations.

Roman jurisprudence demanded considerable precision when it came to specifying ship's personnel. The shipowner proper is designated the *dominus navis* (*Dig.* 14.1.1.15). *Exercitor* 'designates the person to whom all income and revenues come, even if he does not actually own the ship'.[44] The *magister navis* is the director of the expedition who, if not himself also serving as *exercitor*, is appointed by the *exercitor* (*Dig.* 14.1.1.2f.) and may stand in one of several possible relationships to him (*Dig.* 14.1.1.4). He is something more than the modern day supercargo in that he has charge 'of the whole ship'.[45] He is 'appointed to hire out the ship for the carriage of cargo, to take on passengers, or to purchase provisions, or equipment...'.[46] The terms of the *magister's* appointment are usually specified in written contract and he can legally encumber the *exercitor* only if he stays within its terms.[47]

How does the ναύκληρος of Acts 27:11 fit into this schema? Casson identifies the ναύκληρος (*nauclerus* or *navicularius* in Latin) with the *dominus* or *exercitor*, and gives examples.[48] Examples, however, can also be found where it means not 'owner' but something like expedition director.[49] Its designation alone at Acts 27:11 remains uncertain; it might mean owner, entrepreneur, *or* expedition director. Clearly, more information is needed. It is here that the centurion's role aboard ship is helpful.

All indications at Acts 27:9-12 move one away from Ramsay's thesis that the centurion ranks above the ναύκληρος and κυβερνήτης and has virtual command of the ship. We note, first of all, that the words, 'So Paul warned them, "Men,...."' (27:9f.) show Paul *himself*, rather than the centurion, convening the meeting. Moreover, his warning is general and not directed to the centurion alone. The apostle speaks from considerable personal experience, having known the favourable conditions of maritime travel (Acts *passim*) and having survived several disasters that attended unfavourable conditions (2 Cor.11:25f.). The person he must convince above all others is the κυβερνήτης (Latin *gubernator*), the steersman or pilot who has complete charge of the technical details of navigation.[50] Paul may not be speak-

---

[44]*Dig.* 14.1.1.15.
[45]*Ibid.* 14.1.1.1.
[46]*Ibid.* 14.1.1.3.
[47]*Ibid.* 14.1.1.12. *Cf. ibid.* 14.1.1.2, 5.
[48]Casson, *Ships*, 315 n.67. Casson (*ibid.* n. 69) specifies this for the ναύκληρος of the ship Paul was aboard.
[49]E.g., *PHib.* 1:39, ll.5-7; *POxy.* 1:63.
[50]Dauvillier 'A propos', 15. *Cf. Dig.* 19.2.13.2.

ing out of turn—even as a prisoner. Seneca indicates that the more careful (*cautior*) pilot consults and attends the advice of those on ship who have maritime knowledge.[51] Paul's advice, while not sought, nevertheless may carry some weight.

It is hardly possible to assert that the centurion is holding council when serious regard is taken of the words 'the majority decided' (27:12). This phrase could mean a majority of the ship's crew (Acts 27:11, 27, 30) or a majority of the 276 individuals aboard (27:37).[52] A *consilium*, on the example of 25:12, only furnishes advice to the one who makes the ultimate decision. It is not the centurion himself, but 'the majority', however construed, who decide.

Paul's 'advice', by implication, is that the cargo-laden vessel and its passengers and crew should proceed no further, but winter at Fair Havens. Both the κυβερνήτης and the ναύκληρος apparently concur with Paul in regard to wintering on Crete. However, they (and particularly the ναύκληρος as owner or operator) are concerned that the grain ship might be damaged in the exposed harbour. They wish to make for the more suitable harbour 40 miles further up coast at Phoenix.

What, then, do the words, 'But the centurion, instead of listening to what Paul said, followed the advice of the pilot and of the owner of the ship' (verse 11) mean? The possibilities available to the centurion appear to be these: he might listen to Paul and either (a) elect to remove his party from the ship and contract a carrier in the safe season, or (b) try to convince the other passengers and the crew on the ship that they should winter in Fair Havens. Alternatively, he might listen to the ναύκληρος and κυβερνήτης and vote to proceed to the harbour at Phoenix. He comes down on the side of the expertise of the κυβερνήτης and ναύκληρος; so, in consequence, must his party. The centurion would have had no choice but to winter in Fair Havens if these men had fully concurred with Paul.[53]

One cannot salvage the centurion's command of the ship by reference to his involvements at the point of shipwreck. It would be an exaggeration to say, when the centurion (on Paul's advice!) prevents the flight of the sailors by having the lifeboat cut away (Acts 27:30-2) and

---

[51]Seneca, *Ep. ad Lucilium* 14.8.
[52]So Schneider, *Die Apostelgeschichte*, 390. *Cf.* the progress of Herod and his retinue by ship from Brundisium to Alexandria as described in Philo, *In Flaccum* 5.26f.
[53]So Dauvillier, 'A propos', 21.

later co-ordinates an orderly abandonment of the foundering ship (Acts 27:43f.), that he is in charge.

The deliberations and actions of Acts 27 do not show the centurion to be the commander of the ship. He is a single voice speaking on behalf of a party of individuals over whom he has charge. The 'surprising influence of the centurion upon the authority of the professionals'[54] which some see is simply not to be found.

In what capacity do Luke and Aristarchus accompany Paul? They would be accompanying him as friends in Roman eyes; as religious associates in their own eyes. At Acts 24:23 Felix grants Paul the privilege of being attended to by 'his friends'. Nothing in the intervening text suggests that circumstances have changed. Special permission may have had to be formally granted to these friends to travel with Paul as a larger party may have caused difficulties when the centurion was contracting passage. Taking commercial vessels, they would conduct themselves as fare-paying passengers. Ramsay suggests that if Paul was perceived to have personal slaves seeing to his needs on the voyage, 'his importance in the eyes of the centurion was much enhanced'.[55] Attended by non-slave friends, however, his importance should be all the greater.

The prisoner Paul is also shown to receive help from churches. Of particular concern, however, is the meeting he has with the Roman Christians on the way to Rome. While Paul is staying with the Christians of Puteoli, word is sent to the believers in Rome that he is on his way. Coming down from Rome as far as Three Taverns and the Forum of Appius, a group identified as οἱ ἀδελφοί (28:15) meet the prisoner-apostle. Most scholars specify these individuals very generally as, a 'group' or 'number' of Christians;[56] Hervey in particular likens them to the diffuse Jewish group that met the pretender Alexander as he made his way to Rome.[57] Have they correctly identified these individuals? The evidence seems to suggest not.

Rendering assistance to the prisoner is identified as a virtue in the NT and its practice is incumbent upon all Christians. Evidence suggests that from a very early point such church help was structured. Lu-

---

[54]Hemer, 'First Person Narrative in Acts 27-8', 94.
[55]Ramsay, *St. Paul the Traveller*, 316.
[56]So, e.g., Stählin, *Die Apostlegeschichte*, 475; Longenecker, 'The Acts', 568; Bruce, *The Book of Acts*, 502.
[57]A.C. Hervey, *The Acts*, 322 cites Josephus, *Ant.* 17.330 [17.12.1]: 'So when the report about him reached as far as Rome, the whole Jewish population there went out to meet him'.

cian's description of the imprisonment of Peregrinus (c. 132-34 AD),[58] affords some insight into how help was given locally. He writes that, 'from the very break of day aged widows and orphan children could be seen waiting near the prison, while their officials even slept inside with him'.[59]

Why widows and orphans are present is not indicated by Lucian. Krauss avers that the widows are present in the official capacity of deaconesses.[60] It is much more likely, however, that their official title is in fact, 'widow'. Qualifications for enrolment of widows on the official church support list according to 1 Timothy 5:9f. included being 'over sixty' and being known for such good deeds as 'helping those in trouble'[61] and 'bringing up children'.[62] This would account for the presence of aged widows at the prison as well as that of the orphans.

Who are the 'officials' Lucian mentions? Clearly, they must be local church leaders of some sort. Several possibilities are suggested by the Christian martyr literature. There we find bishops, deacons, subdeacons and catechumens in attendance upon the imprisoned confessors.[63] This pattern of local assistance through church officials may represent a later adaptation of the relief pattern of the Jerusalem church. There, individual believers gave their resources into the charge of the apostles (Acts 4:34, 36f.; 5:1f.) who in turn disbursed them amongst the needy—at first directly (Acts 6:1f.), then later through specially qualified surrogates (Acts 6:3-6).[64]

This structure in helping—i.e., church members donate; church leaders visit and disburse help—is even more clearly indicated *where churches come to the prisoner from a distance*. Ignatius writes to the Trallians that their Bishop Polybius has visited him in Smyrna: 'I received

---

[58]See G. Bagnani, 'Peregrinus Proteus and the Christians', *Historia* 4 (1955), 112. Bagnani's article helpfully describes Peregrinus' 'Christian period'.

[59]Lucian, *Peregr.* 12.

[60]F.A.K. Krauss, *Im Kerker*, 92.

[61]The assistance rendered would be of a material nature (*cf.* 1 Tim. 5:16). G. Holtz, *Die Pastoralbriefe* (Berlin: Evangelische Verlagsanstalt, 1971), 118, suggests that the sufferer is one whose life has been touched by death, serious illness, great material loss, or persecution. *Cf.* B.M. Rapske, *The Widow in the Apostolic Church* (Vancouver: Unpublished MTh Dissertation, 1987), 209.

[62]The widows here noted are sixty years of age and have not remarried after the death of their spouses. Moreover, they can get no support from children or grandchildren as they are all alone. The objects of their child-rearing are therefore orphans. *Cf.* Rapske, *The Widow*, 207.

[63]E.g., *Mart. Perp. & Felic.* 3.7 (deacons); *Mart. Mont. & Luc.* 9.2 (bishop, sub-deacon and catechumen); *Apostolic Constitutions* 5.1.1 (bishop).

[64]For discussion see Rapske, *The Widow*, 170-73.

therefore your godly benevolence through him'.[65] He asserts that he has received the entire Ephesian congregation in the person of their Bishop Onesimus.[66] The Ephesian deacon Burrhus is also sent; apparently with instructions from his church as to how long he may stay.[67] This same Burrhus is identified to the Philadelphian church as 'sent with me by the Ephesians and Smyrnaeans as a mark of honour'.[68] The non-Christian Lucian also mentions this pattern of concerted church help at a distance in aid of Peregrinus, without mentioning the titles of the individuals in these deputations: 'Indeed people came even from the cities in Asia, sent by the Christians at their common expense, to succour and defend and encourage the hero'.[69]

Ellis has argued that, 'when used in the plural with an article, "the brothers" in Pauline literature fairly consistently refers to a relatively limited group of workers, some of whom have the Christian mission and/or ministry as their primary occupation'.[70] He continues that this can also be shown for Acts. The designation οἱ ἀδελφοί (1) depicts travel companions, sometimes distinguishing them from disciples generally,[71] (2) indicates the letter-bearing envoys to the Jewish community in Rome',[72] and (3) sets apart individuals in local churches from the general body of believers, at times associating them with the church's leadership.[73] While Ellis places our group in category (1)[74] owing to the fact that they accompany Paul *en route* to Rome, they more properly belong to category (3).

The structure of help and companionship seen in the experiences of Ignatius, Peregrinus and the later confessors adds to the conviction

---

[65] Ignatius, *Trall.* 1:2.
[66] Ignatius, *Eph.* 2:1. The same is said to the Magnesians of their bishop Damas, the presbyters Bassus and Apollonius, and also to the deacon Zotion at Ignatius, *Magn.* 2.
[67] Ignatius, *Eph.* 2:1. This text indicates that other church representatives (*viz.*, Crocus, Euplus and Fronto) are in Ignatius' company. These are mentioned once again in Ignatius, *Rom.* 10:1.
[68] Ignatius, *Phld.* 11:2.
[69] Lucian, *Peregr.* 13.
[70] E.E. Ellis, 'Paul and His Co-Workers', *NTS* 17 (1970-71), 446f. Passages leading him to this conclusion are 2 Cor. 8:18f., 23; 9:3, 5; 11:9; 12:18; 1 Cor. 16:10ff. and, particularly, 1 Cor. 16:19f.; Eph. 6:23f.; Phil. 4:21f. and Col. 4:15.
[71] Ellis, 'Paul and His Co-Workers', 447 discusses Acts 9:26f., 30. See his n. 3 for additional examples.
[72] See *ibid.*, 447 and his n. 4 for discussion of Acts 28:21.
[73] *Ibid.*, 447 and his nn. 5-7 where he discusses Acts 11:1; 12:17; 14:2; 15:23; 16:1f., 27; 21:17; 22:5.
[74] *Ibid.*, 447.

that these 'brothers' are the leaders of the church in Rome. Word is sent
to the Roman church at a distance that the apostle is on his way. In conformity with the pattern, these officials come, either at the behest of
their congregation(s) or leaders or of their own accord. We may add
that Acts 28:15 carries additional evidence, increasing confidence that
these brothers are not just a ragtag crowd but rather a formal ecclesiastical escort. Bruce writes '

> ἀπάντησις [meeting] was almost a technical term for the official wel-
> come of a visiting dignitary by a deputation which went out from the
> city to greet him and escort him for the last part of his journey; cf. the
> same use in Mt 25:6; 1 Thes 4:17 (also Cicero, *Letters to Atticus* 8.16.2;
> 16.11.6).[75]

II. Access to the Prisoner

Clement of Rome, in encouraging expressions of love to those in distress, asserts: '*so far as you can*, help those in prison...'.[76] The implication
is that Christian help might be hobbled or blocked entirely by the external constraints of prison regimens and personnel. These limitations
are also relevant to the Pauline experience in such places as Philippi
and Rome.

The outer prison gate or door was the point at which family and/
or friends had to break company with the prisoner.[77] Helpers came
there to plead for the opportunity to see the prisoner.[78] There, too,
helpers might await its opening at daybreak,[79] or even camp near it
when it was closed during the night.[80]

Extra-biblical sources suggest that normally, visits were permitted only in the daylight hours. A passage in Lucian's *Toxaris* affords a

---

[75]Bruce, *The Book of Acts*, 502.
[76]*Homil. Clement.* 3.69 [My italics.] *Cf. Apostolic Constitutions* 5.1.1.
[77]*Mart. Mont. & Luc.* 17.1f.
[78]Cicero, *Verr.* 2.5.118: 'The fathers—you see them here in court—lay crouched in
the doorway; the unhappy mothers passed the nights at the prison entrance, cut
off from the last sight of their children, begging for nothing but permission to receive with their lips their son's parting breath'. *Cf.* Lucian, *Tox.* 30; Achilles Tatius,
Clit. & Leuc. 6.14.1f.
[79]Lucian, *Peregr.* 12.
[80]*Cf.* Cicero, *Ver.* 2.5.118. According to Lucian, *Tox.* 31, Demetrius, 'slept just in
front of the prison door, where he had made a place to lie and had put down some
leaves'.

helpful indication of the typical pattern. When Demetrius of Sunium heard of his friend's incarceration, he rushed to the prison: 'At that time, however, he was not admitted, for it was evening and the keeper had long ago locked the door and gone to sleep, after directing his servants to keep watch...'.[81] He is only able to gain entry in the morning. It is to be doubted that those helping the Jewish Prince Agrippa were permitted to stay with him through the night in the praetorian camp at Rome,[82] and the witness of the NT Apocrypha and Christian martyr literature also confirms this pattern.[83] Night visits constituted a risk to the security of the prison, but access to the prisoner could, if at all, be gained by means of bribery.[84]

Discretion in regulating access to visitors and helpers was usually left in the hands of prison personnel. Access might be relatively easy,[85] particularly if the prisoner was under house arrest.[86] Even so, prison security was always a matter of concern and the most relaxed conditions could instantly be staunched.[87] Cyprian (c. 248 AD) warns

---

[81]Lucian, *Tox.* 30. Demetrius' pattern is to work as a stevedore from very early in the morning until noon. He then spends the afternoon with Antiphilus until evening when the prison is closed to visitors (*Ibid.* 31). See Plutarch, *Moralia: de genio Socratis* 598 A, B on evening time as an 'unusual hour' for officials to take action regarding prisoners. Achilles Tatius, *Clit. & Leuc.* 6.15.

[82]Josephus, *AJ* 18.204 [18.6.7] suggests that they were permitted visits. That there is much connivance in the provision of clothes for Agrippa's bedding suggests that the soldiery of the *praetorium* where Agrippa was held were generally hostile to him. Allowing the freedmen or friends to stay overnight would hardly have been possible in such a generally hostile environment.

[83]In the *Apocr. Acts Thom.* 13.154, Vazan is unable to go to Thomas at night 'for the gaolers have shut them [i.e., the doors] and gone to sleep'. The jailers later indicate, '...we shut the doors at the proper time...' (*Ibid.* 13.162). Concern for the presence of visitors and lit lamps in the prison suggests that rules have been violated (*Ibid.* 13.153). *Mart. Mont. & Luc.* 4.7: 'The consolation and the joy of the day [i.e., of brothers' visits] removed all the agony we endured at night'. *Mart. Mar.& James* 6.4: 'Dedicated as they are to God the Father, their brothers care for them by day, Christ by night as well'.

[84]The mother of Furius must certainly have bribed the prison staff in order to be with her condemned son 'day and night'. (Cicero, *Verr.* 2.5.112; *cf.* 2.5.118). Lucian, *Peregr.* 12, speaks of how the Christians' 'officials even slept inside [i.e., the prison] with him after bribing the guards'. For access at night by bribery, see also *Apocr ActsThom.* 9.118 (the bribe is ten denarii); 13.151 (363 staters); *Apocr Acts Paul* 3.18 (a silver mirror).

[85]Cyprian, *Ep.* 4.2.

[86]Tertullian, *de ieiunio* 12.

[87]Lucian, *Tox.* 32, writes that when a brigand 'died in the prison (by poison, it was thought) a close guard was instituted, and not one of those who sought admission could enter the gaol any longer'.

that prison visitors be few in number and always changing. Such careful management by the local church leadership would prevent suspicion, ill-will and the risk of being denied access.[88]

Access could, however, be very difficult. The Christian Lucian is commended by Montanus and Lucius in that he 'pierced the most stubborn obstacle of our imprisonment'.[89] While officials were open to the entreaties of the helper,[90] and could give access out of pity or respect for the prisoner,[91] a frequent means of gaining entry to the prisoner was by bribery. As we have seen, bribery could give access to the prisoner at night. It was often as necessary during the day-time. Cicero writes how the prison warder and lictor Sextus sold access as a privilege: '...every groan and pang meant a scheduled profit for him. "So much for leave to see him [i.e., the prisoner]—so much to be allowed to bring in food and clothing"—and everyone paid up'.[92] Philostratus records how, after Apollonius had been in prison two days, a stranger came to him 'and said that he had purchased the right to visit him'.[93] Such bribes could be either in cash[94] or in kind.[95] Failure to have regard for the itchy palms of prison officials might result both in hardship for the prisoner and denial of access for the helper.[96] The practice of bribery was common enough that it is recorded as part of the expense of relief in the *Apostolic Constitutions* (3rd century AD): the Christian is encouraged to 'send to him [i.e., the prisoner] from your labour and your very sweat for his sustenance, and for a reward to the soldiers, that he may be eased and be taken care of'.[97]

While access to the prisoner Paul in Acts generally seems to have been easy, this cannot be said of his experience at Philippi. There is, in fact, no access from without the prison; not from associates nor from new converts. Several factors account for this: First, the imprisonment

---

[88]Cyprian, *Ep.* 4.2.
[89]*Mart. Mont. & Luc.* 9.2.
[90]Lucian, *Tox.* 30.
[91]*Mart. Perp. & Felic.* 9. Cf. *Mart. Pion.* 11.5-7.
[92]Cicero, *Verr.* 2.5.118.
[93]Philostratus, *VA* 7.30.
[94]Lucian, *Tox.* 31; *Apocr. Acts Thom.* 9.118; 13.151.
[95]*Mart. Pion.* 11.4; *b. Mo'ed* III: *'Erub* 21*b.*
[96]*Mart. Pion.* 11.3f. Denied their share of incoming goods when the Christian prisoners refuse the helpers' generosity, the guards angrily throw them into the 'inner part of the prison'—the worst part where no one can visit.
[97]*Apostolic Constitutions* 5.1.1. G. Lopuszanski, 'Police Romaine et les Chrétiens, *Antiquité Classique* 20 (1951) 39, identifies this as bribery to obtain entry to the prisoners.

of Paul and Silas seems to be punitive and entirely uninformed by the fact of the missionaries' status as Roman citizens (Acts 16:37f.). Permission to have visitors or helpers would have constituted a mitigation of the punishment. Second, the jailer is commanded to 'guard them safely' (Acts 16:23), which he effects by putting them 'in the inner cell and... their feet in the stocks' (Acts 16:24). The ἐσώτερος which we meet in the *Martyrdom of Pionius*[98] amounts to a kind of maximum security cell. Added to this, the prison, as we have seen, could be barred to visitors at night-fall (*cf.* Acts 16:24f.). The closest that the apostles' associates or converts might get at any time during their night of incarceration would be the outer gate or door of the prison. Denied from without, however, help comes from within by the hand of the jailer and his family.

What can be gathered of Paul's confinement for two years in Rome (Acts 28:16ff.) suggests a fairly generous degree of access. Sadler's insistence that Paul must have been able to 'go anywhere, provided he had the permission of the captain of the guard, who, of course, would require that the soldier to whom he was chained should accompany him',[99] does not have sufficient regard to the evidence in the text. It indicates that individuals and groups are able to come to Paul, apparently without restriction. The progression in the record of visits to Paul suggests increasing freedom of access and increasing numbers of visitors: Rome's Jewish leaders come to Paul (Acts 28:17, 20), return for a second meeting 'in even larger numbers' (Acts 28:23); finally, 'all' (Acts 28:30) who wish can have access to him.

Though Acts predicates to Paul the activity of inviting these individuals (Acts 28:17, 20, 23), the invitations must certainly have been extended through others; *viz.*, the Roman Christians.[100] Paul's confinement in an *individual dwelling* is emphasized at several places in the text.[101] He can welcome individuals and groups into his living quarters (Acts 28:30), but they are not actually permitted to live with him. The regimen previously described seems here to be implied—i.e., free access to the prisoner during the day; enforced solitude through the night. This would afford, from the authorities' perspective, sufficient freedom for the prisoner, yet without threat to security. Paul utilizes

---

[98]*Mart. Pion.*, 11.3f.

[99]Sadler, *The Acts*, 501.

[100]We should not expect that Paul's companions—the 'we' of the travel narrative—would have sufficient information to issue invitations to the leaders of the Jewish synagogues.

[101]Acts 28:16, 23, 30.

this regimen to the maximum on the second occasion of the Jews' meeting with him when he speaks 'from morning till evening' (Acts 28:23). Evening having come and having reached an impasse in the debate, those present eventually leave Paul (Acts 28:25) presumably alone with the soldier.

The final word of Acts, which Moulton and Milligan describe as 'legal to the last',[102] may also have something to say regarding the degree of access allowed the imprisoned apostle as well as the amount of assistance that helpers could give. The word 'unhindered' (Acts 28:31) suggests the tolerance of Rome generally.[103] We would agree with Stählin in adding that it probably also has an eye to the ever-present individual soldiers[104] who guarded the apostle during the years in Rome.

III. Encouraging the Prisoner

The profound anxiety of the prisoner meant that the physical presence and verbal encouragements of helpers could be a great boost. We have already mentioned the friends of Publius Vitellius (31 AD) who, when they discover that he has opened his veins, are able to convince him of the value of continuing life in custody. He consents to be bandaged and restored and dies a natural death while in confinement.[105] Lucian's praise of true friendship emphasizes quite vigorously the virtues of physical closeness and verbal encouragement. Agathocles is praised for standing *with* his friend Deinias: 'Agathocles alone of all his friends kept with him, sailed with him to Italy, went to the trial with him, and failed him in nothing'.[106] When Deinias was sentenced to exile, Agathocles 'did not desert his comrade even then, but of his own accord sentenced himself to live in Gyaros and share his exile'.[107] Demetrius of Sunium, as a part of his daily pattern, remains with Antiphilus in the prison, consoling him.[108] When denied the usu-

---

[102]*MM*, 20.

[103]Haenchen, *The Acts*, 726; Longenecker, 573; H.J. Hauser, *Strukturen der Abschlusserzählung der Apostelgeschichte (Apg 28,16-31)* (AnBib 86; Rome: Pontifical Biblical Institute, 1979), 141.

[104]Stählin, *Die Apostlegeschichte*, 329.

[105]Suetonius, *Vit.* 7.2.3. Was he successful in his suicide attempt? See Tacitus, *Ann.* 6.5.8.

[106]Lucian, *Tox.* 18. Note the many συν- compounds in the original.

[107]*Ibid.* Note again the συν- compound.

al access, Demetrius implicates himself in his friend's alleged crime and begs, on being cast into prison, to be 'confined near Antiphilus, and in the same set of irons.[109]

The Christian martyr literature also carries such emphases. The verb *refrigerare* which often means 'to make cool', can also have the sense of comforting, relieving, or refreshing.[110] In some contexts, the refreshment consists in comestibles and similar things.[111] Other contexts, however, suggest that the refreshment has a more general character which includes emotional consolation. The adjutant in charge of the prison in which Perpetua and Felicitas, are lodged (203 AD), 'began to allow many visitors to see us for our mutual comfort'.[112] The account of Montanus and Lucius (259 AD) records: 'For a few days then we were comforted by the visits of our brethren. The consolation and the joy of the day removed all the agony we endured at night'.[113] The brothers, on hearing of the imprisonment of bishop Fructuosus (259 AD), are 'with him, comforting him and begging him, to remember them'.[114]

W. von Dobschütz helpfully summarizes the Ignatian material in this regard:

> He [i.e., Ignatius] rejoices at their escort (Phil. xi., Smyr. xii.); hurrying on before by the direct road, the Ephesians go to Rome on his behalf (Rom. x). He knows that the nearer Churches have already sent deputations, and is convinced that the people of Asia Minor can do so also—for the name of God (Phil. x). Who is ready to assist those who desire to do well (Smyr. xi. 3); the Christian does not belong to himself; he must have time for God (Polyc. vii. 3). As a matter of fact we see that the Philippians, the most remote, have asked the Smyrnaeans to represent them also, and Polycarp, either himself or through a deputation, will on a favourable opportunity make the due arrangements (Polyc. ad Phil. xiii). [115]

---

[108]Lucian, *Tox.* 31.

[109]*Ibid.*, 32.

[110]*LD*, 1548; for *refrigerium* as 'rest' or 'relief', *OLD*, 1597.

[111]E.g. *Mart. Mont. & Luc.* 9.2; *Mart. Perp. & Felic.* 16.3.

[112]*Mart. Perp. & Felic.* 9.1.

[113]*Mart. Mont. & Luc.* 4.7.

[114]*Mart. Fruct. & Co.* 1.4.

[115]W. von Dobschütz, *Christian Life in the Primitive Church* (Theological Translation Library 18; London: Williams and Norgate, 1904), 241.

It is important to Ignatius that the churches show solidarity with him and, when it comes, his sense of appreciation is expressed effusively. Where possible, physical solidarity must be shown. Less desirable but still acceptable are solidarity expressed through nominated proxies or by means of epistles. Most importantly, however, the solidarity must be formal and official, i.e., the representatives must be bishops, deacons, or other approved church officials and they must be sent by their churches and leaders.

It is to be presumed that Paul derived considerable encouragement from the physical presence of helpers during the confinements at various locations described in the book of Acts. He would have certainly been heartened by the assistance and company of associates, particularly those of the 'we' source and the Thessalonian church official Aristarchus who accompanied him as he journeyed to Rome. Paul would have counted as a rich blessing the centurion's permission to solicit benefactions and accept the hospitality of Christian groups along the way to Rome.

Of particular interest to us, however, is what is said concerning the meeting of Paul and 'the brothers' (Acts 28:15). When he saw them, Luke records, 'Paul thanked God and was encouraged'. Ramsay states that this phrase must be taken as an indication of 'some marked frame of mind. We have already observed him in a similar state of depression when he was in Troas and Philippi'.[116] Yet depression is hardly the emotional state one would expect before the taking of courage. Rather, as the term θάρσος in other contexts suggests,[117] we should expect fear and anxiety to be the logically preceding emotional states.

Coming to Rome as a prisoner, one of Paul's worst fears is to be damned by the faint support of the Christian community there. Paul's vigorous reaction is motivated not only by the presence of ἀδελφοί, but even more so by their identity. As we have previously indicated they are church leaders. In terms of the Ignatian experience, they are an encouragement not only because they show physical solidarity with the prisoner, but more so because they come to Paul formally and officially. They are, *pars pro toto*, the Roman church. Longenecker remarks that the expression of gratitude to God is specially mentioned by Luke because of its unusual fervency.[118] We might add that Luke

---

[116]Ramsay, *St. Paul the Traveller*, 347.
[117]See the context of Acts 23:11; Josephus, *Ant.* 9.55 [9.4.3]; *Mart. Pol.* 12.1; *Herm. Vis.* 3.1.5.
[118]Longenecker, 'The Acts', 568.

may have also been motivated to include this exuberant response as the logical concomitant to the discovery that the church of Rome stood with Paul in his predicament.

IV. The Risks to the Helper

Helping the prisoner could pose significant threats to the safety and well-being of the helper. Officials were often very rough characters. Consequently, helpers might be harassed out of a desire for personal gain or even for sport. The Egyptian cultivator from Karanis (c. 3rd century BC) complains that the policeman Hathoris has confiscated not only bread destined for the relief of a prisoner at the great prison of Crocodilopolis but also the cultivator's own jenny. He continues, 'I made myself scarce for fear of being marched to prison'.[119] On one occasion when Rabbi Joshua was bringing a water ration to Rabbi Akiba (132-5 AD), he was stopped by the prison keeper who said to him, '"Your water to-day is rather much; do you perhaps require it for undermining the prison?" He poured out a half of it and handed to him the other half'.[120] The part water ration was only enough for Akiba to perform the ritual hand washing before eating. He did not, after that, have water enough to drink. Here we have a clear case of bullying.

There was the additional danger of simply being too intimately associated with or sympathetic toward the prisoner or his views. The relatives of imprisoned royals were in a precarious position.[121] Fearing imprisonment and death should they follow their teacher to Rome (c. 54-68 AD), the number of Apollonius' disciples is reduced from thirty-four to eight.[122]

The helpers of the Christian confessors found that when they applied themselves zealously to care-giving, the personal risks were greater. Workman states that 'visits were allowed, possibly as the easiest way whereby the authorities could learn the names of others of the faith still at large'.[123] Origen (184/5-253/4 AD), when visiting prisoners, exposed himself to personal danger when he, with extreme boldness, saluted the imprisoned confessors with the holy kiss.[124] When

---

[119]E.G. Turner and W.E.W. Cockle, 'Complaint Against a Policeman', 273.
[120]b.Mo'ed III: 'Erub. 21b.
[121]Plutarch, Lives: Agis and Cleom. 20.2-5 on the fate of King Agis and his family.
[122]Philostratus, VA 4.37.
[123]H.B. Workman, Persecution, 293.
[124]D.W. Riddle, The Martyrs, 69f., citing Eusebius, Hist. Eccl. 6.6.3f.

Agapius and Dionysius attended to the needs of six Christian prisoners (309-10 AD), they did so with such assiduity that it attracted the attention of the officials who ordered their arrest. All eight were subsequently condemned and beheaded.[125]

There were many watchful eyes and listening ears in prisons. A chance word or act might lead not only to the prisoner's but also the helper's doom. Musonius and Apollonius did not converse directly to one another during the time that the former was imprisoned (Nero 54-68 AD) 'because Musonius declined to do so, in order that both their lives might not be endangered'.[126] Later, when Apollonius himself is imprisoned by Domitian (81-96 AD), spies are sent to him. One enters the prison in the guise of a fellow prisoner: 'In his deportment this person had a downcast air, and, as he himself admitted, looked as if he ran a great risk. He had great volubility of speech, as is usually the case with sycophants who have been chosen to draw up eight or ten informations'.[127] Later, a visitor comes to Apollonius for the ostensible purpose of helping him out of his predicament. Actually, his hope is (1) that Apollonius, 'out of sheer weariness of his imprisonment...would tell some falsehood to the detriment of his friends'[128] or (2) 'to see whether he would reproach his sovereign on account of his sufferings'.[129]

Several strategies might be used to reduce the risks and dangers to the helper. First, the helper might *resort to disguise*. Apollonius advises his disciple/helper Damis,[130]

> I do not wish that you should be a sharer of my fate through being detected by your dress, which will certainly betray you and lead to your arrest; but I would rather that you followed me in the guise of one not sworn to my philosophy, but just attached to me for the other reasons.

The Talmud recounts a vision which illustrates the advantages of such a strategy. The prophet Elijah comes to Rabbi Beroka Hoza'ah and identifies to him a man who will share in the world to come. Beroka is surprised by the fact that the man is a jailer and appears not to be a Jew: he sports no distinctive Jewish tassels on his clothing and wears the latcheted black shoes common to Gentiles. When asked, the jailer ex-

---

[125]Mason, *The Historic*, 288f. citing Eusebius, *De mart. Palaest.* 3.
[126]Philostratus, *VA* 4.46.
[127]*Ibid.* 7.28.
[128]*Ibid.* 7.36.
[129]*Ibid.*
[130]*Ibid.* 7.15.

plains that he does this 'that the Gentiles amongst whom I constantly move may not know I am a Jew'.[131] Thus disguised, he is able to render sympathetic assistance to the Jews, keeping the sexes separate and protecting Jewish women from being raped.[132]

Second, where direct speech was too dangerous, *written correspondence might be less so*. Apollonius and Musonius 'carried on a correspondence through Menippus and Damis, who went to and fro the prison'.[133] Omitting such of their letters as did not handle great themes', Philostratus includes for his readers 'the more important ones in which we get glimpses of lofty topics'.[134] The letters are obtuse and quite inoffensive from a judicial or political perspective, treating nothing of import to Musonius' case nor implicating Apollonius in any illegal action.[135]

Finally, there was no substitute, whatever other strategies were employed, for *acting and speaking prudently when in the hearing of prison officials and strangers*.

The Philippian jailer finds himself in a similar predicament to that of the jailer of the Talmudic vision as he renders care and assistance to Paul and Silas at Acts 16 in what has become an extremely anti-Jewish climate. In helping the prisoners as he did, has the jailer acted illegally? Bruce says no. 'The jailer was guilty of no dereliction of duty in thus taking two prisoners into his house, his responsibility was to produce them when called upon to do so. He had no reason to fear that they would run away and leave him in the lurch'.[136] This assertion, however, runs up against juridical texts which seem to suggest that he did act illegally and could have been charged with so doing.

Consider first the matter of the softening of Paul's confinement. Both magistrates and prison guards were accountable in law for how they kept prisoners. Laxness in the method of constraint, especially if prisoners escaped as a result, was punishable. Quoting earlier rules, Venuleius Saturninus (2nd–3rd cent. AD) writes: 'If you should estab-

---

[131]*b.Mo'ed* VII: *Ta'an.* 22*a*.
[132]*Ibid.*
[133]Philostratus, *VA* 4.46.
[134]*Ibid.*
[135]Note how Paul gives in his prison epistles (e.g., Col 4:7-9) what might be termed 'harmless details' of his circumstances. He promises, however, that those individuals whom he sends will disclose in detail the state of affairs with him.
[136]Bruce, *The Book of Acts*, 318. *Cf.* Ramsay, *St. Paul the Traveller*, 222. 'He was responsible for producing his prisoner when called for; but it was left to himself to keep them as he thought best'.

lish that any persons kept in fetters have been released by the magistrates hastily and without cause, you shall order them to be bound and shall impose a fine on those who released them'.[137] The jurist Paulus (2nd–3rd cent. AD) provides that 'if the officer in charge of a prison is bribed to keep someone in custody without chains,...he must be punished by the court; if he was ignorant of the fact, he should be removed from his post for negligence'.[138] A rescript of Hadrian (117-138 AD) to Salvius provides that 'punishment must be imposed on him who has set a prisoner at large or has knowingly kept him in such a way that the prisoner is able to escape'.[139] If prisoners escape through the drunkenness or sloth of the guard, he was 'corporally punished and transferred to inferior military duties'.[140] Callistratus (2nd–3rd century AD), in citing this Hadrianic rescript, ventures the view that the same provisions should also apply to guards who keep individuals in civilian custody.[141]

That such punitive provisions for improperly keeping prisoners existed in the NT period is indicated by the record of Agrippa's imprisonment (37 AD). Even with the special provisions allowed by the praetorian prefect Macro, Agrippa should apparently have been kept in chains. That he wasn't so kept and that this breach was a danger to the centurion who had charge of him is evident. Out of fear for his personal safety on hearing the report that Tiberius is not dead, the centurion orders 'the manacles to be put on Agrippa, though he had previously taken them off, and a stricter guard to be kept than before'.[142]

The Philippian magistrates give the jailer instructions that Paul and Silas are to be imprisoned securely (Acts 16:23). Their placement in the inner prison with feet secured in stocks constitutes his compliance with the command (Acts 16:24). Following the earthquake, he does not immediately re-shackle the apostles. Rather, the text indicates that he removes his prisoners not only from the inner prison but from the prison proper to his own house.

As Bruce and Ramsay indicate, Paul and Silas are still legally the jailer's wards. However, they are no longer in the expected or required confinement from the magistrates' perspective. This action, moreover,

---

[137]*Dig.* 48.3.10.
[138]*Ibid.* 48.3.8.
[139]*Ibid.* 48.3.12.
[140]*Ibid.*
[141]*Dig.* 48.3.12.1.
[142]Josephus, *AJ* 18.233 [18.6.10].

is a contravention of the orders given him in that it effectively softens their punishment. The Western text (Acts 16:30) apparently attempts to shelter the jailer from the charge of negligence and illegality when it adds that 'the jailer "secured the rest" of the prisoners before he addressed Paul and Silas'.[143] This, however, falls short of exonerating the jailer. Punishments similar to those mentioned above may apply to him should his actions be discovered.

The jailer may be incurring even greater risk in providing a meal for the prisoners Paul and Silas. When news came to the prisoner Agrippa that Tiberius was dead, the centurion guarding him 'joined in the rejoicing at the news because it was to Agrippa's advantage and treated him to a dinner'.[144] While they were feasting and drinking, another report came that Tiberius had not died. Josephus records that the centurion was deeply perturbed at this report 'since the penalty set for such things as he had done was death, that is, both to have dined together with a prisoner and to have rejoiced at the news of the emperor's death...'.[145] Whatever the purpose of the meal, dining with a prisoner is clearly indicated as a separate offence. When the jailer offers his prisoners hospitality, he certainly does something that is very unusual. It may also, by analogy to the Agrippa incident, constitute a chargeable offence, whether capital or otherwise.

The jailer's actions are illegal, or grossly improper at the very least. However, seen within the context of the above discussion of Christian risk-taking to help the prisoner, they take on a new light. The jailer before his conversion shows an overweaned sense of responsibility[146] in being prepared to take his own life because of the apparent escape of his prisoners; as a Christian, he casts caution and concern for legal niceties aside in his zeal to help the prisoners who have converted him. Is there need to defend him or simply praise him?

---

[143]B.M. Metzger, *A Textual Commentary on the Greek New Testament* (London/New York: UBS, 1975), 449. See the rather harsh assessment of Ramsay's positive comments on the authenticity of the Western text.

[144]Josephus, *AJ* 18.231 [18.6.10].

[145]*Ibid.* 18.232 [18.6.10].

[146]*Dig.* indicates at several places that the circumstances of escape are taken into consideration in assessing culpability and assigning punishment. Surely an act of God such as an earthquake would at least have mitigated, if not completely eliminated, any punitive consequences.

CHAPTER 15

THE PRISONER PAUL'S DIVINE
HELPER IN ACTS

Luke presents a Paul who is commissioned to suffer as a prisoner witness. This vocation of prisoner witness is affirmed by prophetic oracle and embraced by Paul. The instances of divine help to Paul in prison have a significant impact upon him and upon Luke's readers. The Philippian earthquake leads to belief and baptism. The nocturnal communication to Paul in Jerusalem asserts, first, a divine pleasure which confirms Paul's ministry. Second, it provides proleptic confirmation of an ongoing witness for Paul in Rome of a similar character. Finally, at the point of shipwreck, Jesus reassures Paul not only of his Roman destiny but more specifically, of bearing witness before the Emperor himself.

The prisoner Paul is thus affirmed and his ministry enhanced; moreover the strategic placement of the oracles at Acts 23:11 and 27:23f. not only provides a glimpse into the divine perspective on the prisoner Paul, but offers a grid through which his troubles from chapter twenty-one to the end of Acts may be interpreted. To readers of Acts, Paul is indeed the 'prisoner of the Lord'.

Luke shows that the prisoner Paul continued to witness to the resurrected Jesus. He may not always log numerical successes, but the Lukan point appears to be that, whatever the results, the prisoner seized every opportunity to preach, teach and bear witness. Luke shows, moreover, that Paul was not abandoned by Christian associates and co-religionists. Rather, numbers of unbelievers showed him regard.

But why would a preacher and teacher of the Gospel find himself in so much trouble? Why was he considered a threat to the Jerusalem Jewish establishment? Further, why would he, a Roman, be detained so often and for so long by the Roman establishment?[1] Those who possessed a Christian (or Jewish–Christian) sense of 'divine retributive logic'[2] might well ask, 'The prisoner might think himself to be for the Lord, *but is the Lord for the prisoner?'*

I. The Prisoner Within the Divine Spotlight of Mission

It was important for the Christian that suffering was neither deserved nor the material expression of divine vengeance or repudiation. Christ could not be embodied in the deserved sufferings of a prisoner (*cf.* Matt. 25:36, 40). 1 Peter 4:15f. counsels: 'If you suffer, it should not be as a murderer or thief or any other kind of criminal, or even as a meddler. However, if you suffer as a Christian, do not be ashamed, but praise God that you bear that name'. Such suffering drew the community into a moral solidarity with the sufferer, often manifested in material support. Tertullian and the later *Apostolic Constitutions* clearly indicate the criterion.[3]

1. The Ancient Sources

Socrates, at the end of Plato's *Crito*, presents the constraints under which he remains in the state prison at Athens rather than fleeing. He puts the case for staying to Crito *as though* the laws of Athens them-

---

[1]*Cf.* R.J. Cassidy, *Society and Politics in Acts*, 119f., 124, 142f.
[2]Luke 13:1-5; John 9:2, and for the expression 'retributive logic', *cf.* G.B. Miles and G. Trompf, 'Luke and Antiphon: The Theology of Acts 27-28 in the Light of Pagan Beliefs about Divine Retribution, Pollution, and Shipwreck', *HTR* 69 (1976), 259-67.
[3]Tertullian, *Apol.* 39 requires that the distress be 'for the sake of God's fellowship' and the *Apostolic Constitutions* 5.1.1 that it be 'on account of the name of Christ, and love and faith towards God'.

selves were compelling him by the logic of their argument.[4] Socrates
states: '...this is what I seem to hear, as the frenzied dervishes of Cybe-
le seem to hear the flutes, and this sound of these words re-echoes
within me and prevents my hearing any other words'.[5] He advises Crito: '...let it be, and let us act in this way, since it is in this way that God
leads us'.[6] Remaining in prison can hardly be considered a vocation
except in the very narrow sense that it preserves, at least in Socrates'
mind, the Athenian laws and the commonwealth. The conviction of divine leading appears to emerge from intuition and philosophical re-
flexion rather than revelation.

Epictetus (50-120 AD) elaborates the proposition that one ought
not to yearn for the things which are not under one's personal control.[7]
He writes that God made everyone to be happy and serene, 'giving
each man some things for his own, and others not for his own'.[8] Much
unhappiness arises, however, in not knowing what is and is not one's
own. People grieve when things and persons are removed from them
and when they are removed from things and persons. It is inappropriate in these circumstances to question Zeus' management of the uni-
verse. The good and excellent man exercises his reason. He knows
'who he is, and whence he has come, and by whom he was created'[9]
and centres his attention 'on this and this only, how he may fill his
place in an orderly fashion, and with due obedience to God'.[10] He
practices the disciplines of restraint and contentment, holding life and
its materials and relationships loosely in mind and in hand. Change
must be willingly embraced as neither good nor bad. The good and excellent man must ask, '"Who was it that has sent the order?" Our
Prince, or our General, the State, or the law of the State? "Give it to me,
then, for I must always obey the law in every particular"'[11]

In this context Epictetus observes that imprisonment is not an indictment of Zeus, a notion which can be understood in terms of the pagan theodicy noted above. Custody is but one of the myriad
eventualities which might befall a person. The prisoner is within the
divine spotlight; but so too is everyone experiencing negative or posi-

---

[4]Plato, *Cri.* 50.A, C; 54.C
[5]*Ibid.* 54.D.
[6]*Ibid.* 54.E.
[7]Arrian, *Epic.* 3.24.
[8]*Ibid.* 3.24.3.
[9]*Ibid.* 3.24.95.
[10]*Ibid.*
[11]*Ibid.* 3.24.107.

tive circumstances! The experiences typically spoken of as disasters, however, are ones in which one can play 'the part of the good and excellent man, not ostensibly but in reality'.[12] This is the context of the terms 'training', 'witness', 'appointment' and 'service' in the text. The training is the discipline of looking for blessings within oneself and not outside.[13] The philosopher's witness as messenger of Zeus here is to deliver all persons 'from their erroneous notions about good and evil, and about happiness and unhappiness... and to lead them back into themselves'.[14] The good and excellent man uses his intuition in the reversals he experiences to discover a divine intention and in this way finds an appointment to service and the opportunity to focus upon the god and to submit. This is Epictetus' sense, then, of being divinely commissioned to be a prisoner.

The dependence of Ignatius of Antioch (98-117 AD) upon the canonical Pauline self-designation, 'prisoner of Christ Jesus' (Phlm. 1, 9; Phil. 1:13; Eph. 3:1; 4:1), is quite clear. He writes that he is bound in Christ Jesus[15] or for the sake of Him;[16] that he wears the bonds of Jesus Christ;[17] that he is 'sent a prisoner from Syria for the sake of our common name and hope';[18] and that he is 'a prisoner for the Name'.[19] He claims that his bonds confer upon him spiritual insight, constitute an exhortation to believers, and encourage him to give up all desires.[20] Ignatius writes that his bonds 'are most seemly in God's sight'.[21]

Ignatius admits, however, that there is deficiency if one only wears bonds. He writes, '...though I am a prisoner for the Name, I am not yet perfect in Jesus Christ'.[22] For Ignatius, being a prisoner is at the periphery of the spotlight's beam and not the divine calling or mission; martyrdom, however, is at the centre. Time and again Ignatius voices the aspiration to die.[23] At times the image is graphically sacrificial.[24] It is what he seeks, desires and wishes;[25] what he is anxious for the Romans not to hinder out of natural affection;[26] and what he asks the churches to pray that he might experience.[27] The priority of martyr-

---

[12]*Ibid.* 3.24.110.
[13]*Ibid.* 3.24.112.
[14]C.A. Brandis, 'Epictetus', *DGRBM*, vol. 2, 32.
[15]Ignatius, *Phld.* 5.1; 7.2; *Rom.* 1.1; *Eph.* 11.2.
[16]Ignatius, *Trall.* 12.2.
[17]*Ibid.* 1.1; *Rom.* 1.1; *Phld.* 5.2; 7.2.
[18]*Ibid.*, *Eph.* 1.2.
[19]*Ibid.* 3.1.
[20]*Ibid.*, *Trall.* 5.2; 12.2; *Rom.* 4.3.
[21]*Ibid.*, *Smyrn.* 11.1; *cf. Eph.* 11.2.
[22]*Ibid.*, *Eph.* 3.1.

dom over imprisonment and bonds also stands in Polycarp's letter to the Philippians.

> I rejoice greatly with you in our Lord Jesus Christ that you have followed the pattern of true love, and have helped on their way, as opportunity was given you, those who were bound in chains [incl. Ignatius], *which become the saints*, and are the diadems of those who have been truly chosen by God and our Lord.[28]

Increasingly in the later Christian literature—apocryphal and martyrological—confession leading to martyrdom and not imprisonment is seen as the pinnacle of Christian activity, and the truly God-ordained vocation. In the *Apocryphal Acts of Thomas* (1st half 3rd cent. AD), the apostle prays in the prison, 'I praise thee, Jesus, that thou hast made me worthy not only of faith in thee, but also of suffering much for thy sake'.[29] He encourages his converts: 'Do not shrink in afflictions, neither be ye doubtful when ye see me insulted and imprisoned and dying. For in these I fulfil what has been appointed for me by the Lord'.[30]

Imprisonment in the martyr literature is clearly only the forbidding background or foil to the reception of visions. The visions are the divine encouragement to the imprisoned believers that they will attain to a successful and God-pleasing confession and martyrdom.[31] Prison is within the divine spotlight's beam, but not as ultimate vocation or mission. The compiler/continuator of the *Martyrdom of Perpetua and Felicitas* (203 AD), as he closes his description of the confessors' martyrdoms, writes: 'Truly are you called and chosen for the glory of Christ Jesus our Lord!'[32] The point can also be illustrated from Cypri-

---

[23]Dying in the jaws of the wild beasts at Rome: *ibid.*, *Phld.* 5; *Smyrn.* 11.1; *Rom.* 8.3; attaining/ attaining to God: *Magn.* 1.2; 14; *Trall.* 13.3; *Rom.* 1.2; 2.1; 9.2 (*cf. ibid.*, *Rom.* 7.1 'coming to the Father'; *Eph.* 21.2 being 'thought worthy to show the honour of God'); attaining to Jesus Christ: *Rom.* 5.3 (*cf. ibid.* 4.2 on becoming 'truly a disciple of Jesus Christ' and *Eph.* 1.2 on being enabled to be a 'true disciple').

[24]*Ibid.*, *Rom.* 2.2; 4.1.

[25]*Ibid.* 6.1, 3.

[26]*Ibid.* 1.2; 4.1.

[27]*Ibid.* 8.3; *Phld.* 5; *Smyrn.* 11.1.

[28]Polycarp, *Phil.* 1.2. [My italics].

[29]*Apocr. Acts Thom.* 107.

[30]*Ibid.* 160.

[31]*Supra*, 350f.

[32]*Mart. Perp. & Felic.* 21.11.

an's letters[33] and the later martyrs, who are 'chosen for the palm of suffering'.[34]

2. The Prisoner Paul in Luke-Acts

Of course, the prisoner Paul is nowhere mentioned in the first 'book' of Luke-Acts. Authors may, however, prepare the readers of their narratives for the forthcoming appearance of a major character . The Gospel of Luke does seem to anticipate Paul and his prison experiences in significant ways.

Entering the Gospel context inevitably opens synoptic questions. A discussion of whether Luke is altering Mark, following a pre-Markan source or both lies beyond the scope of the present work.[35] We therefore draw our focus narrowly to highlight the degree of fitness in Luke's account of Jesus' words at Luke 21:12-19 with what unfolds in Acts for Paul. That fitness will be elaborated in part on the basis of the differences in the synoptic accounts (// Mark 13:9-13; Matt. 10;17-22a).

Luke 21:12-19 is the one 'backward' step ('before all these things': Luke 21:12) into nearer future time in an account which is otherwise completely concerned with the signs of the end of the age. The passage is related as relevant to Luke's readers' own situation and does not pertain only to the past.[36] However, the conviction of the words' abiding truth and their inspirational value surely must also reside in the significant real-life demonstrations of the second part of Luke's work. From the Lukan perspective, far from having an abundant supply of 'illustrations'[37] in Acts or a 'background for interpretation'[38] of the Gospel text, readers have at the least an abundance of

---

[33]See esp. Cyprian, *Ep.* 20.1, 25.5, 37.1, 76.1 [Oxf., *Ep.* 21, 31, 12, 76].

[34]*Mart. Mar. & James* 4.7. It is recorded *ibid.* 2.3, that going through an area where a severe persecution was raging, 'they realized that their footsteps had been guided by the providence of Christ to the very spot where they would receive their crown'. Cf. *Mart. Fruct. & Co.* 1.4, *Mart. Mont. & Luc.* 17.1f and *Mart. Test. prol.* and 3.4.

[35]For discussion, see J.A. Fitzmyer, *The Gospel According to Luke (X-XXIV)* (AB 28A; London: Doubleday, 1985), vol. 2, 1324-26; I.H. Marshall, *The Gospel of Luke: A Commentary on the Greek Text* (New International Greek Testament Commentary; Exeter: Paternoster, 1978), 766f.

[36]So Marshall, *The Gospel*, 767.

[37]A. Plummer, *The Gospel According to S. Luke* (ICC; Edinburgh: T. and T. Clark, 1896), 479.

[38]Fitzmyer, *The Gospel*, 1338, who also speaks of 'illustrations' (*Ibid.*, 1340).

significant fulfilments of Jesus' prophetic words. Indeed, the indications in this Gospel text find a pre-eminent fulfilment in the experience of Paul in Acts.

Jesus says at Luke 21:12, 'They will deliver you to synagogues and prisons'. The synagogue element is fulfilled in the persecuting activity of Saul (Acts 6:9; 9:2, 21; 22:19). The words 'and prisons' are not found in the accounts of Mark or Matthew. Evans writes that these words correspond 'to the frequent reference to imprisonment in Acts'.[39] Others do experience imprisonment in the earlier chapters (Acts 4:3; 5:18-23; 8:3; [9:2, 21;] 12:4-10[40]). But Paul is the prisoner *par excellence* both in the amount of time he spends in prison and in the amount of text devoted to his prison experiences (Acts 16:23-37; 21:33-28:31).

At Luke 21:12 there is a fitting transposition of terms. Whereas the other synoptics record that the disciples will be brought before governors and kings (Matt. 10:18; Mark 13:9), Luke has 'you will be brought before kings and governors'. The other synoptics might suggest that only Gentile potentates are in view,[41] but the sense of the Lukan order is both plain and confirmed in the order of events in Acts.[42] It is a Herodian king who first interrogates/persecutes (Acts 12:1-23); then follow Roman governors (Acts 18:12; 23:33-24:27; 25:1-12 [*cf.* also the governor under Aretas at Acts 9:22-25 ≈ 2 Cor. 11:32f.?])[43], concluding with the interview before Festus and Agrippa (Acts 25:13-26:32). Except for the first passage, all of these fulfilments relate to the prisoner Paul!

The readers are told that the trouble associated with becoming prisoners—the arrests, incarcerations and interrogations—will be 'on account of my name' (Luke 21:12). Marshall writes that 'the phrase could be Lucan (*cf.* Acts 4:17f.; 5:28, 40f.; 9:15f.; 15:26; 21:13), but is based on a firm early church usage (e.g. 1 Pet. 4:14, 16; 3 Jn. 7; Rev. 2:3; Jn. 15:21)'.[44] Such suffering, arising as it does out of allegiance or loyalty to Jesus, confirms that the sufferers stand within the framework of

---

[39]C.F. Evans, *Saint Luke* (TPI New Testament Commentaries; London: SCM/Philadelphia: Trinity Press International, 1990) 741.

[40]Note that Peter asserts a willingness to go with Jesus 'to prison' and to death at Luke 22:33. There is no reference to prison at Mark 14:31 or Matt. 26:35.

[41]A. Loisy, *L'Évangile Selon Luc* (1924; rpt., Frankfurt: Minerva, 1971), 494.

[42]*Pace* Marshall, *The Gospel*, 767, who suggests that the inversion has occurred 'under catechetical influence (*cf.* 1 Pet. 2:13f.)'.

[43]BAGD, 343; Fitzmyer, *The Gospel*, 1340, writes: '..."prefects" (*hegemones*) almost certainly suggests Gentile governors'. *Contra* J. Kremer, *Lukasevangelium* (Neue Echter Bibel 3; Würzburg: Echter Verlag, 1988), 203.

the divine approval. The next verse carries the strong implication that such oppressions themselves, far from being disasters, actually furnish great opportunities. Luke records: ἀποβήσεται ὑμῖν εἰς μαρτύριον. The word ἀποβαίνω in this context, means to 'turn out' or 'lead to'.[45] L. Hartmann has argued that μαρτύριον does not indicate the act of witnessing (= μαρτυρία: Luke 22:71; Acts 22:18) but the witness borne, carrying the possibility that either 1) the persecution of Christians is the testimony which will defend them before God's throne against their enemies; or 2) if the verb is taken impersonally, that God or the Son of Man will bear witness to them.[46] Marshall indicates that 'the strong point in favour of this view is that in the NT generally μαρτύριον means "evidence, testimony", not the activity of bearing testimony'.[47] In this case, the Christian experience of such troubles clearly constitutes a kind of witness vocation. The drawback to this way of understanding the text, in Evans' estimation, is that ὑμῖν should then have followed εἰς μαρτύριον rather than preceding it. Moreover, construing the expression as the act of bearing witness better fits the instructions of Luke 21:14.[48] Jesus' words in this case would then indicate that imprisonment facilitates witness but is not an actual vocation.

At Luke 21:14, it is sternly advised that while self-defence (cf. Luke 12:11) will be called for, prepared speeches in such circumstances are to be avoided in favour of utterance which Jesus himself will give. Obedience will result in opponents being confounded (Luke 21:15). Peter and the other apostles do engage in such witness in Acts, though the verb 'defend' is not used. In contrast and excepting one instance (Acts 19:33), both ἀπολογέομαι and ἀπολογία in Acts are used exclusively to describe Pauline forensic defence (ἀπολογέομαι: Acts 24:10; 25:8; 26:1f. [2x], 24; ἀπολογία: Acts 22:1; 25:16)! Again, it is difficult to avoid the conclusion that Luke will present the prisoner Paul to his readers by this terminology as a pre-eminent fulfilment of the Lord's prophetic words.

---

[44]Marshall, The Gospel, 767. Fitzmyer, The Gospel,1340, speaks of Lukan rewording of Mark 13:9. For a discussion of Luke's use of 'the name', see S. New, 'Note 11. The Name, Baptism, and the Laying on of Hands', in BC, vol. 5, 121-40.
[45]BAGD, 88. Cf. Job 13:16 [LXX]. Interestingly, the only other NT instance of such a usage of the term arises in Paul's explanation to the Philippians that his bonds have turned out (ἀποβαίνω: Phil. 1:12) to further the advance of the Gospel.
[46]Hartman as cited in Evans, Saint Luke, 742.
[47]Marshall, The Gospel, 768. Cf. BAGD, 493.
[48]Evans, Saint Luke, 742.

We turn, finally, to Luke 21:18. Jesus says there that despite betrayal by those close to the believers, even to the death of some, and despite the general hatred of men (Luke 21:15f.), '...not a hair of your head will perish'. This verse may 1) indicate that no harm will occur to the disciples without the Father's permission; 2) be a guarantee of safety to the church as a whole but not to every Christian individually (*cf.* Luke 21:16); 3) be a guarantee of ultimate spiritual preservation; or 4) be indeterminate owing to infelicities caused by Luke's bringing disparate sources together.[49] Many follow 3).[50] However, the assertion that by standing firm believers will save themselves (Luke 21:19), when taken together with the course of the book of Acts, suggest 1) and 2). Evans observes in his discussion of this phrase the 'frequent escapes of Christians from danger through divine overruling'[51] in Acts and he cites ten or eleven examples. Paul again appears to furnish Luke with a singular fulfilment of this proverbial assurance (*cf.* 1 Sam. 14:45; 2 Sam. 14:11; 1 Kings 1:52). The saying 'not a hair of your head will perish' has its sole and closest[52] counterpart in the words of the prisoner Paul to his fellow travellers just before shipwreck—*viz.* 'for the hair of none of your heads will perish' (Acts 27:34). There the immunity from life-threatening harm is physical and extensive, being vouchsafed to the prisoner who believes and, on account of him, to all the others aboard ship.

The record of Jesus' words to Ananias at Acts 9:15f. is the first explicit indication in Acts that the Christian Paul will fulfil a divine plan that calls for suffering. The Lord tells Ananias that Paul 'is my chosen instrument'.[53] Assertions that this is a metaphor drawn from the work of the potter (Jer. 18:1-11; 22:28; Hos. 8:8; Wis. 15:7f.; and *cf.* esp. 2 Cor. 4:7) and that 'to bear the name' (βαστάσαι τὸ ὄνομα) continues this metaphor are probably too finely drawn.[54] Haenchen writes that

---

[49]So Marshall, *The Gospel*, 769.

[50]E.g., *ibid.*; Fitzmyer, *The Gospel*, 1339; E.E. Ellis, *The Gospel of Luke* (NCBC; Grand Rapids: Eerdmans/London: Marshall, Morgan and Scott, 1974), 244; A.R.C. Leaney, *The Gospel According to St. Luke* (BNTC; 2nd edn.; London: A. and C. Black, 1966), 261.

[51]C.F. Evans, *Saint Luke* (TPI New Testament Commentaries; London: SCM/Philadelphia: Trinity Press International, 1990) 745.

[52]Luke 12:7 takes a different form; *cf.* Matt. 10:30.

[53]An instance of the 'Hebraic' genitive according to Moulton, *Grammar*, vol. 2, 440; M. Zerwick, *Biblical Greek*, tr. J. Smith (Rome: Scripta Pontificii Instituti Biblici, 1963), § 40. F.F. Bruce, *The Acts of the Apostles. The Greek Text with Introduction and Commentary* (1951; Grand Rapids: Eerdmans, 1990), 238 notes: 'lit., "instrument of choice", i.e., "chosen vessel"; Lat. *uas electionis*'.

'σκεῦος signifies not only "vessel" but also "instrument" or "tool".'[55]
The emphasis is that the Lord has radically subordinated Saul to his
own exclusive use.[56]

The end to which Paul has been divinely elected has occasioned
some debate. How should one construe the phrase τοῦ βαστάσαι τὸ
ὄνομά μου ἐνώπιον? Two possibilities present themselves: 1) 'to carry
the name to' the individuals thereafter mentioned; or 2) 'to bear the
name before' those individuals.[57] The more frequently understood
sense of missionary labour as going about and preaching is predominantly in view in 1); in 2) the presentation has more to do with the missionary himself.

Lohfink has furnished five grounds for the second possibility,
the first four commending themselves quite strongly to the present
writer. He argues first, that ἐνώπιον is 'before' in the sense not of 'to'
but 'openly', 'before the eyes of', or 'in the presence of' as at Acts 19:19;
Luke 5:25; 8:47; 13:26; 23:14; 24:43 (cf. 1 Tim. 5:20).[58] Second, the expressions βαστάζειν/[περι]φέρειν τὸ ὄνομα are not unfamiliar to the Graeco-Roman and early Christian literature, supporting the notion of an
acknowledged or confessed commitment.[59] Third, Lohfink draws attention to Luke 21:12-19 (cf. 12:11f.), pointing out the connection there
between suffering and confession. The relationship between that passage and Acts 9:15f. can hardly be gainsaid; it is reasonable that a suf-
fering/confession connection therefore be seen at Acts 9:15 as well.
Fourth, Lohfink concludes that once the suffering theme is acknowledged at verse 15, the connection with verse 16 becomes clear and
there is no longer the abrupt shift of frequent remark. Γάρ is to be
translated 'namely' and verse 16 is then an explanation or clarification
of what has just been said.[60] Finally, Lohfink attempts to show the
compositional links between this understanding of 'to bear the name'
and the triple account of Paul's Damascus experience.[61]

The physical extent and breadth of the Pauline mission are implied in the sequence, ἐνώπιον ἐθνῶν τε καὶ βασιλέων υἱῶν τε Ἰσ-

---

[54]So D.J. Williams, *Acts* (San Francisco: Harper and Row, 1985), 157.

[55]Haenchen, *The Acts*, 325 n. 1, following K. Lake and H.J. Cadbury, *The Acts of the
Apostles: English Translation and Commentary* in *BC*, vol. 4, 103.

[56]Of Paul's own sense of having been divinely elected, see Rom. 1:1ff.; Gal. 1:15f.;
Eph. 3:7-13.

[57]W. Michaelis, 'πάσχω κτλ.', *TDNT*, vol. 5, 919.

[58]G. Lohfink, '«Meinen Namen zu tragen ... » (Apg 9, 15)', *BZ* 10 n.s. (1966), 110.

[59]*Ibid.*, 110f.

[60]Lohfink, 'Meinen Namen', 112f.

[61]*Ibid.*, 113-15.

ραήλ.[62] The exposition of the elements for Luke's readers will come from the account itself. Paul's mission will engage the children of Israel at home and extensively throughout the Diaspora. In those places too it will open to the Gentiles. Paul will be brought before king Herod Agrippa II (Acts 25:13-26:32) and he will ask and be promised an audience before the Roman Emperor (Acts 25:10-12, 21, 25-27; 26:32; 27:24; cf. 23:11).[63] But it is the character or distinguishing feature of the missionary activity which is explicitly asserted at Acts 9:15f.—Paul's will be a witness in many and various (ὅσα)[64] sufferings. Moreover, his sufferings are clearly not indicated to be the result of his wrongdoing.[65] Rather, in even more emphatic terms than Acts 9:15, the reader is assured that the apostle's sufferings are within the divine spotlight's beam; these *are* his mission. The personal divine superintendence in the manifold sufferings is indicated in the expression 'I will show him', the 'whatever is necessary', which we shall meet again in Luke's account, shows the dynamic, divine authorization of them,[66] and 'for my name' clearly indicates the sufferer's virtue and innocence. Thereafter, Paul's rich witness unfolds for the readers, replete with an exemplary catalogue of fulfilments of divinely ordained suffering, including the humiliating abuse and imprisonment at Philippi.

As Luke turns his attention to Paul's final journey to Jerusalem, he indicates to his readers that the beam of the spotlight is being divinely focussed in the matter of Pauline mission. Paul continues to be a suffering witness, but God ordains for him that he will become more

---

[62]The translation 'before the Gentiles and their kings and before the people of Israel' in NIV is an unhappy one in the connections it suggests. The closeness in the relation would appear to be in all the elements and not in two to the exclusion of the third. See Moulton, *Grammar*, vol. 3, 338f.; BDF, § 444.

[63]Conzelmann, *Acts*, 72: 'The reference to kings (Luke 21:12) is not unusual even in the time of the empire'.

[64]The implied antecedent is πάντα as at Acts 14:27.

[65]The present writer has reservations regarding those frequent comments in the literature which suggest that Paul's witness in suffering is somehow a repayment or an expiation for his past crimes; especially in the light of Luke 12:11f.; 21:12-19 and the Pauline preaching itself at Acts 14:22 (cf. Phil. 1:29f.; 1 Thess. 3:4). See, e.g., Bruce, *The Acts*, 238; ibid., *The Book of Acts*, 186f.; Pesch, *Die Apostelgeschichte*, vol. 1, 307; Krodel, *Acts*, 177; Haenchen, *The Acts*,324f.

[66]Cf. Acts 9:6. Cosgrove, 'The Divine ΔΕΙ in Luke-Acts', 177 n. 25, indicates of the 'must' (δεῖ) of suffering at Acts 9:16: 'As God's chosen servant Paul stands in a long line of suffering prophets (Lk. 13:34 and Acts 7:52)'. While we may agree that suffering is not a 'missionary credential' of Paul, it must be more than 'the foil for God's saving intervention' (*ibid*.). His comment earlier cited and our discussion above suggest a strong vocational aspect.

particularly *a prisoner witness.* Acts 20:22-24, midway through the fare-well address to the Ephesian elders at Miletus, gives the first preview[67] of the settled divine intention to particularize the Pauline vocation. Paul first tells the Ephesians at verse 22 that, having been compelled by the Spirit, he is going to Jerusalem. It is possible to render the expression δεδεμένος ... τῷ πνεύματι as either 1) 'bound in *my* spirit', taking the dative for the accusative of respect, or as 2) 'bound by *the* Spirit', on the assumption of an instrumental dative.[68] Most reckon that the phrase refers to the Holy Spirit. Haenchen, for example, explains that 'we cannot require the author to use the full formula "the Holy Spirit" twice in immediate succession'.[69] What Paul means when he speaks of having been bound (δεδεμόνος) is not that he considers himself already shackled or chained,[70] but that he feels a strong supernatural compulsion to go to Jerusalem.[71]

The perfect participle δεδεμένος indicates that the compelling action of the Spirit has occurred antecedently.[72] The earliest possible indication in Acts of this 'binding' is just before the Ephesian riot at Acts 19:21, but is the Pauline determination there personal or divinely inspired? Cosgrove is convinced that 'here the Roman destiny is presented as originating in Paul's own resolution, before any divine necessity relative to Rome has been announced'.[73] He cites Lake and Cadbury as supportive of this view[74] when in fact they only tentatively render the phrase, 'was inspired to purpose'.[75] Though the phrase itself will not allow certainty, the fact that δεῖ occurs there would appear to decide the case in favour of a Pauline purpose divinely inspired. Other instances of the Lukan use of this term for Paul are clearly expressions of the divine will. We have already met and briefly considered the divine δεῖ at Acts 9:16 above. The two remaining passages of interest are divine communications to the prisoner at Acts 23:11 and

---

[67]The Septuagintalism καὶ νῦν ἰδού at Acts 20:22 (*cf.* 13:11; 20:25) fixes attention upon Paul's future prospects, not his present uncertainties according to Conzelmann, *Acts*, 174.

[68]Zerwick and Grosvenor, *Grammatical Analysis*, 1: 422.

[69]Haenchen, *The Acts*, 591 n. 6. *Cf.* Bruce, *The Book of Acts*, 390 n. 47.

[70]Lake and Cadbury, *BC*, 260 allow 'in captivity to', but Haenchen, *The Acts*, 591 n. 6, describes such a rendering as 'shallow'. *Cf.* Conzelmann, *Acts*, 174.

[71]E.g., Williams, *Acts*, 349; Haenchen, *The Acts*, 591 n. 6; Neil, *The Acts*, 214; Schille, *Die Apostelgeschichte*, 402.

[72]Williams, *Acts*, 349, suggests that this had gone on 'for some time'.

[73]Cosgrove, 'The Divine ΔΕΙ', 178.

[74]*Ibid.*, 178 n. 26.

[75]Lake and Cadbury, *BC*, 244 and further discussion there.

27:24, 26 which will be discussed shortly.[76] A point missed in the literature consulted which also suggests Acts 19:21 is a case of Pauline purpose divinely inspired is the fact that, as at Acts 23:11, Rome *and* Jerusalem are linked with this necessity (δεῖ με <u>καί</u>: Acts 19:21). Luke would hardly allow or suggest to his readers that the trip to Jerusalem and Rome evolved from a human intention at Acts 19:21 into a divinely inspired necessity;[77] Luke's Paul is clearly not usually led that way (Acts 13:1-4; 14:26; 16:6-10 [cf. 15:36-40]; cf. 23:11; 27:24, 26).[78]

For all his ignorance (Acts 20:22b) of the details of what will happen to him in Jerusalem, Paul does have certain Spirit-given knowledge of the essentials of what awaits him: '...in every city the Holy Spirit warns me that prison and hardships are facing me' (Acts 20:23). Outside of Acts 19:21, which gives no indication that Paul will become a prisoner witness, there are no recorded instances of his receiving these earlier communications.[79] While it is possible that Paul received these communications directly from God,[80] it is more likely that he received them through other Christian prophets. This pattern occurs later as we shall see (Acts 21:4, 10f.) and with a similar message content to that indicated here.[81] The expression 'from city to city' (Acts 20:23)[82]

---

[76]*Cf.* also Acts 20:35 where a word of the Lord lays upon Paul the necessity of furnishing a consistent example of self-support and generosity to others. The forward-looking δεῖ in conjunction with Jesus and his mission is also highly instructive (Luke 9:22; 13:33; 17:25; 22:37; 24:7, 26; Acts 17:3).

[77]E.g.,
Acts, 349, who writes that Acts 20:22 is 'an advance in Paul's perception [i.e., from Acts 19:21] of what lay before him'.

[78]It is, moreover, a modern conceit to distinguish between Lukan reasons and the 'real reason' (so Conzelmann, *Acts*, 164) for the journey. This is despite the importance of the Collection in Paul's letters. It would be similarly wrong to assert that Acts 19:21 is nothing more than a Lukan defence of Paul against the charge that he had been led and not thrown out of Ephesus.

[79]We may rule out the suggestion of Schneider, *Die Apostelgeschichte*, 295 n. 26, that Paul may have made reasoned intuitions based upon Jewish opposition. This was in fact happening all along.

[80]Paul is himself among the prophets (Acts 13:1-4) and is led of the Spirit, receiving direction through visions. *Cf.* passages cited above in Acts on how Paul is led and also 'Chapter 5. Paul and the Phenomenon of Prophecy in the Church', in D. Hill, *New Testament Prophecy* (Marshall's Theological Library; London: Marshall, Morgan and Scott, 1979), 110-40 and 223-26 nn.

[81]Lake and Cadbury, *BC*, 260, enter a fitting caution when they suggest that the Agabus incident is 'perhaps a corroboration rather than an illustration'. It would certainly have been the fullest and most explicit indication that Paul had to that point received and therefore may not be strictly comparable.

[82]*Cf.* κατ' οἶκον: Acts 2:46; 5:42; 8:3; 20:20.

indicates that urban centres are the venues for these communications. Along the way to Miletus Paul stopped at towns and cities with Christian congregations, encouraging them and lodging and worshipping with them.[83] There, prophetic utterance would have been expected to occur.

The burden of the Holy Spirit's message to Paul is δεσμὰ καὶ θλίψεις ... μένουσιν. The Holy Spirit's communication to Paul can hardly be a warning. Διαμαρτύρομαι followed by λέγων (Acts 20:23) suggests solemn testimony or witness and carries no negative freighting.[84] A negative sense predicated to the verb here would jar with the context. Paul has indicated only two verses earlier that he has solemnly borne witness (διαμαρτύρομαι: Acts 20:21) to Jews and Greeks that they must turn to God; only one verse later, he affirms his resolve to continue with the task of solemnly testifying (διαμαρτύρομαι: Acts 20:24) to the gospel of God's grace. The whole point of verse 24, in fact, is that Paul will *not* mistake the divine communication as a warning not to go to Jerusalem. The divine spotlight is focussed so that witness will be fulfilled through incarceration and its related distresses.[85]

Paul first says at Acts 20:24, οὐδενὸς λόγου ποιοῦμαι τὴν ψυχὴν τιμίαν ἐμαυτῷ. According to Conzelmann, it

> means either 'I do not consider my life worth mention' (thus τίμιος = ἄξιος, 'worth') or we have here a mixture of two expressions: οὐδενὸς λόγον ποιοῦμαι, 'I have regard for nothing' (*cf.* variants), and 'I do not consider my life precious'.[86]

In any event, self-preservation is *not* Paul's highest priority and this is deliberately reckoned as such for the purpose of (ὡς)[87] completing or finishing his course (*cf.* Acts 13:25; 2 Tim. 4:7). The course is further ex-

---

[83] Acts 20:2f. (μαθηταί throughout Macedonia and Greece), 4 (stop-overs with congregations in Berea, Thessalonica, Derbe, as well as in Asia indicated by Paul's travel companions) 6a (Philippi), 6b-12 (Troas), 13 (overland to Assos), 14 (Mitylene), 15 (Miletus).

[84] *Cf.* BAGD, 186 which notes Heb. 2:6 as a comparable example (NIV renders the verb there as 'testify').

[85] Virtually all of the θλίψεις experienced by the apostle shortly after his arrival in Jerusalem and in the years thereafter spring from his being a prisoner witness.

[86] Conzelmann, *Acts*, 174. For further explanation of the MS tradition on this verse, *cf.* B.M. Metzger *et al.*, *A Textual Commentary on the Greek New Testament* (New York: UBS, 1971), 479.

[87] The only instance of final ὡς in the NT. *Cf.* C.F.D. Moule, *An Idiom Book of New Testament Greek* (2nd. edn.; Cambridge: CUP, 1959), 138 n. 1; Moulton, *Grammar*, vol. 3, 105; BDF, §391(3).

plained[88] as the ministry which Paul has received from the Lord Jesus to bear solemn witness to the gospel of the grace of God. What is absolutely critical here may be highlighted by putting the negative implication: For Paul to value his life—i.e., to avoid incarceration and its attendant afflictions—would be to refuse the ministry of solemn witness. Paul, in response to the multiple witness of the Spirit, willingly embraces imprisonment and its sufferings as divine calling. He asserts his willingness to stand within the spotlight as a prisoner witness.

In the twenty-first chapter of Acts, Luke indicates to his readers that the spotlight will be intensified so that Paul fulfils the vocation of a prisoner witness. Paul's seven day stop-over[89] at the port city of Tyre is spent with the Christian community.[90] In the context of this local fellowship Paul receives yet another divine portent of trouble in Jerusalem: 'Through the Spirit they urged Paul not to go to Jerusalem' (Acts 21:4). On the surface and outside of the broader context, this remark would appear to suggest that Paul has disregarded or disobeyed a divine oracle. The Spirit tells him not to go, but he does.[91] There are several reasons why such an assessment of the narrator's intention cannot be correct.

Luke has recorded at Acts 19:21 and 20:22 that Paul is under the divine imperative, not only having received mediated communications before but also as he continues his onward progress to Jerusalem. Luke appears not to see a contradiction between this divine communication and progress and what is noted at Acts 21:4. Moreover, it is hardly to be imagined that the Spirit is sending mixed signals, and that Luke ignorantly reflects the conflict, leaving it unresolved. Rather, it is more likely that we have a 'condensed'[92] version of a pattern similar to

---

[88]Schneider, *Die Apostelgeschichte*, 295 n. 31.

[89]A port call of such duration is not inconsistent with Paul's being 'in a hurry to reach Jerusalem, if possible, by the day of Pentecost' (Acts 20:16). Several reasonable explanations are given by I.H. Marshall, *The Acts of the Apostles*, 338. *Cf*. B.M. Rapske, 'Acts, Travel and Shipwreck', in *The Book of Acts In Its Graeco-Roman Setting*, A1CS 2: 14-21.

[90]Were these Tyrian believers among those Hellenists scattered during the persecution? *Cf*. Acts 11:19; 15:3.

[91]D.E. Aune, *Prophecy in Early Christianity and the Ancient Mediterranean World* (Grand Rapids: Eerdmans, 1983), 264 allows this: '...Luke understands it as a prohibition delivered by the Spirit through a prophet to Paul. Yet, in the light of Paul's "disobedience" to the oracle, ... this may be an instance in which prophetic speech is "evaluated".' Further on evaluating prophets and their oracles, *ibid*., 217-22. *Cf*. Lake and Cadbury, *BC*, 266.

[92]So Aune, *Prophecy*, 264, despite his comments *supra*, 407 n.91.

that reflected at Acts 21:10-14: i.e., a prophecy followed by Christian reaction or comment. The expression 'through the Spirit' relates to a divine communication—the readers will recall Paul's words at Acts 20:22f.—which is descriptively accurate but motivationally neutral. The expression 'not to go up to Jerusalem' represents not the divine portent itself but the personal counsel given to Paul by the Tyrian Christians. They have 1) *misunderstood* the communication as either a) warning Paul against going to Jerusalem or b) of providing a divine insight so that he might prudently avoid trouble. On the other hand, they may have 2) *understood* the communication properly and counselled disobedience.[93] The Tyrians' reception of a divine portent is clear; their counsel, while sincere, is nevertheless misguided, ill-informed and at loggerheads with the divine intention. Paul, however, interprets the motivationally neutral divine communication differently: it testifies to him of the changes which God will bring to his witness if he obeys, *not* as a warning against going to Jerusalem.

Three things, then, are clear. First, there is an unmistakable and consistent divine indication that trouble awaits Paul in Jerusalem. Second, however they interpreted the portent, the Tyrian Christians demonstrate a great love and esteem for the apostle. They are deeply concerned for his welfare (*cf.* Acts 21:5f.). Third, Paul continues to possess an undeflectable resolve to follow the Spirit's guidance in going to Jerusalem.

As he lodges with Philip the Evangelist in Caesarea, the divine intention for the manner of Paul's witness is given its most explicit and powerful expression. It is set forth in pre-eminently prophetic and particularly compelling terms. The Jerusalem prophet Agabus (*cf.* Acts 11:27-29) comes down from Judaea ostensibly to deliver a prophetic message concerning Paul. He takes Paul's belt (ζώνη),[94] binding himself with it, and says, 'The Holy Spirit says, "In this way the Jews of Jerusalem will bind the owner of this belt and will hand him over to the Gentiles"' (Acts 21:11).

The symbolic action of binding recalls OT prophetic acts.[95] Williams writes that 'the prophet was considered to set in motion a train of events culminating in the one symbolized. His act was almost "sac-

---

[93]Marshall, *The Acts*, 339 points to disobedience as a real possibility and cites Acts 26:19.

[94]A 'long cloth which was worn as a girdle, wound several times around the body', according to Haenchen, *The Acts*, 601 n. 5. *Cf.* sources therein cited and BAGD, 341.

[95]E.g., 1 Kings 11:29-39; Isa. 8:1-4; 20:2-4; Ezek. 4:1-3; 5:1-4; Jer. 13:1-11; 19:1-13; 27:1-22; Hosea 1:2.

ramental"; inspired by God, it was an act with power'.[96] The expression τάδε λέγει τὸ πνεῦμα ἅγιον is what Aune describes as 'a Christianized variant of the OT messenger formula; "thus says the Holy Spirit" is certainly a very close approximation of the familiar "thus says Yahweh", and would have had an archaic ring to it'.[97]

Such clearly OT-like prophetic action and speech in Agabus, might suggest a similar OT prophetic accuracy. Looking to Luke's description of Paul's arrest later in the account raises certain questions. Evidently, the apostle was not bound by the Jews and handed over to the Romans, but was bound *by the Romans* and *rescued from* the Jews. Grudem[98] suggests, in consequence, three possibilities in understanding the thrust of the phrase τάδε λέγει τὸ πνεῦμα ἅγιον: 1) Agabus claimed divine authority for the actual words and the minor discrepancies are not sufficient to nullify the claim;[99] 2) the words were not the very words of the Holy Spirit, only the content generally had been revealed;[100] and 3) Agabus, imitating and perhaps not understanding the nature of his prophetic gift, acted inappropriately in attempting to attain to a prophetic status he did not possess.[101] A variant of the first option seems the most appropriate understanding. One cannot really avoid the OT-like action and words of Agabus. Further, it has been suggested that the differences between the prophecy and the record of the event may arise from Luke's desire to cast the prophecy in terms reminiscent of Jesus' predictions concerning himself in service of a kind of master/servant parallelism.[102] Finally, why should the prophetic word of Acts 21:11 be held rigidly to account to the later arrest report at Acts 21:27-33 without considering the possibility that the later report, though longer and more complete, may in fact be missing certain details? It must be accounted an equal possibility that had the report been fuller than its eight verses the difficulties might actually have been resolved in the direction of the prophecy. The Pauline report

---

[96]Williams, *The Acts of the Apostles*, 237. So also Neil, *The Acts*, 217

[97]Aune, *Prophecy*, 263. Aune points out Rev. 2:7, 11, 17, 29; 3:6, 13, 22; 14:13 as markedly similar.

[98]Summarizing W. Grudem, *The Gift of Prophecy in the New Testament and Today* (Eastbourne: Kingsway, 1988), 96-102.

[99]So, e.g., Lake and Cadbury, *BC*, 268; Williams, *Acts*, 357; Marshall, *The Acts*, 340.

[100]So, e.g., Grudem, *The Gift of Prophecy*, 96 who speaks of 'a prophecy with two small mistakes'.

[101]So, e.g., Hill, *New Testament Prophecy*, 107f.

[102]See on this point Marshall, *The Acts*, 340; Williams, *Acts*, 357; Krodel, *Acts*, 395; Munck, *The Acts*, 207.

at Acts 28:17 accords well with Acts 21:11 and it appears that Luke did
not see 'inconsistencies' needing vigorous harmonization.

This prophecy is predictively strong but again motivationally
neutral, and Agabus himself apparently draws no directive corollaries
from it for Paul.[103] Paul's companions and his Caesarean hosts, however, do. Luke records at Acts 21:12, 'When we heard this, we and the
people there pleaded with Paul not to go up to Jerusalem'. The pressure upon Paul is considerable, for the 'pleaders' are not ordinary believers. Among them is Philip who is identified to the reader as one of
the Seven, an evangelist, and one peculiarly sensitive to the Spirit (Acts
6:3, 5; 8:4-40; 21:8). Philip's four unmarried daughters are themselves
prophetesses (Acts 21:9). Their mention is hardly extraneous or intended to set a mood.[104] In fact these Caesarean pleaders, because of their
sensitivity to the Spirit, prophetic renown and the frequent collegiate
functioning of prophets in the early church (Acts 11:27f.; 13:1-4; *cf.* 1
Cor. 14:29-33), would have raised pressure upon Paul to a near unbearable level if they seemed to understand that the predicted fate for Paul
was avoidable. This is, in fact, the case as Paul indicates at Acts 21:13a:
'Why are you weeping and breaking my heart?' That he is deeply
moved by the pleas is clear from the use of the rare and evocative term
συνθρύπτειν.[105] Despite the emotional blows to his resolve, Paul emphatically asserts at Acts 21:13b, 'I am ready not only to be bound, but
also to die in Jerusalem for the name of the Lord Jesus'. As at Acts
20:24, Paul here affirms that he is prepared fully to embrace the particular suffering to which he has now been called (δεθῆναι) and even
more (ἀποθανεῖν), though in the latter instance he has not been called
to do so, for the sake of Jesus.[106] In even more vivid and clear terms
than at Acts 21:4, the readers are told of the certainty of the portent, the
love and concern of the Christian community for the apostle and of
Paul's unshakeable resolve to fulfil the mandate.

Paul's companions and the Caesarean Christians—prophets and
others alike—finally give up trying to persuade Paul with the words,
'The Lord's will be done' (Acts 21:9). These words which may recall to

---

[103]The difficulties seen by Overbeck and Haenchen, *The Acts*, 602 n. 1, who cites
him, are entirely a matter of forcing the prophecy to take a 'warning off' slant. *Cf.*
Aune, *Prophecy*, 264; Bruce, *The Book of Acts* 401; Krodel, *Acts*, 394; Neil, *The Acts*,
217.

[104]Conzelmann, *Acts*, 178. *Cf.* Marshall, *The Acts*, 340 sees this as extraneous to the
text and therefore probably indicative of the use of a source.

[105]Lake and Cadbury, *BC*, 269.

[106]*Ibid.*

the readers Jesus' own prayer (Luke 22:42; cf. Mart. Pol. 7.1) are, as Conzelmann asserts, 'not an expression of resignation, but a positive affirmation of the will of God'.[107] No other expression could fix more firmly in the readers' minds the assurance that the spotlight has been intensified and that Paul, far from standing at its periphery or outside its circumference through religious or political wrongdoing or by mischance, will be a prisoner witness in accordance with the divine will. In this, the Lord leads Paul and Paul unswervingly obeys.

The foregoing analysis of the Lukan record argues for a definite nuancing of Paul's words at Acts 28:20b. Paul is indeed asserting an intimate spiritual kinship and solidarity with his Roman Jewish brethren in referring to the hope of Israel. But he cannot simply be saying that the hope of Israel has landed him in chains. Rather, it is for the sake of[108] the hope of Israel that he is made to wear the chains with all the negative and threatening implications it carries. The hope of Israel and his commitment to it have called for wearing the chains: they are therefore a means of his witness.[109] Paul is not simply a witness who has been imprisoned but one who fulfils the divine will as prisoner witness.

II. Divine Assistance and Assurance

We turn, finally, to consider the tokens of divine assistance and assurance to prisoners in the ancient literature canvassed and for Paul in the Acts. We shall not consider instances where *mediated* assistance or assurance is seen as God's work, for example in the *Martyrdom of Montanus and Lucius* where the confessors speak of the Lord's refreshment 'through our dearest brother Lucian' and certain others.[110] Our interest is in the direct or unmediated involvement of the deity with the prisoner through acts, visions, oracles and such.

---

[107]Conzelmann, *Acts*, 178. So also Schneider, *Die Apostelgeschichte*, 305; Marshall, *The Acts*, 341. *Pace* Lake and Cadbury, *BC*, 269.

[108]We take ἕνεκεν + genitive this way rather than 'because'. *Cf.* BAGD, 264.

[109]B.-J. Koet, 'Paul in Rome (Acts 28:16-31): A Farewell to Judaism?' *Bijdragen* 48 (1987), 400. See further his comments *ibid.*, 400 n. 6.

[110]*Mart. Mont. & Luc.* 9.2.

1. The Ancient Sources

The *Bacchae* of Euripides (*c.* 405 BC) is part of what was a considerable and popular body of Dionysiac material.[111] In it Dionysus, son of the god Zeus[112] and Semele, goes to Thebes in human form to establish his worship. He inspires the women of Thebes to Bacchic revelries and, as a result, angers Pentheus the king of Thebes. Pentheus orders that the women be seized and imprisoned When Dionysus himself is brought back a prisoner before Pentheus, the king's servants report:

> The captured Bacchanals thou didst put in ward,
> And in the common prison bind with chains,
> Fled to the meadows are they, loosed from bonds,
> And dance and call on Bromius the God.
> The fetters from their feet self-sundered fell;
> Doors, without mortal hand unbarred themselves.[113]

The liberation of the women—presumably by Dionysus himself, though this is not explicitly stated—serves, according to Dodds, 'no obvious purpose in the economy of the play beyond giving Pentheus the unheeded warning that the supernatural cannot be controlled by lock and key. It is introduced primarily because it is a traditional Dionysiac miracle'.[114]

A later version of the story is found in a summary of the play *Pentheus* by Pacuvius (220-132 BC). Pentheus out of jealousy sends his servants to capture Dionysus (= Father Liber). The servants bring back instead Acoetes who is one of Dionysus' followers.

> Pentheus, when he was appointing a heavier penalty for him, ordered him in the meantime to be kept fettered in prison. And when the doors of the jail had fallen open of their own accord, and Acoetes' bonds had fallen from him, Pentheus was astonished and went to Cithaeron in order to be a spectator of the rites of Father Liber.[115]

---

[111]On the antiquity of the Dionysiac literature, *cf.* L. Schmitz, 'Dionysus', *DGRBM*, vol. 1, 1046-49.

[112]Because he is a divine figure, we do not consider his own prison exploits (Euripides, *Bacch.* 604-41). For a similar reason, Apollonius of Tyana (81-96 AD; *cf.* Philostratus, *VA* 7.34, 38; 8.5, 8) may be set aside as not relevant to the present study.

[113]Euripides, *Bacch.* 443-48.

[114]E.R. Dodds, *Euripides' Bacchae: Edited with Introduction and Commentary* (2nd. edn.; Oxford: Clarendon, 1960), 132 and see his further discussion.

[115]In *Remains of Old Latin* (LCL), vol. 2, 272-75.

The purpose served by the release may be the same as Dodds has suggested above. Pentheus' curiosity eventually leads to his death at the hands of the Bacchanals. In Ovid's *Metamorphoses* (c. 1-10 AD) the Pacuvius version is apparently followed. Acoetes is captured by Pentheus and, after explaining how he came to be a follower of Dionysus,[116] torture is ordered for him.

> Straightway Acoetes, the Tyrrhenian, was dragged out and shut up in a strong dungeon. And while the slaves were getting the cruel instruments of torture ready, the iron, the fire—of their own accord the doors flew open wide; of their own accord, with no one loosing them, the chains fell from the prisoner's arms.[117]

The loosing amounts to a kind of rescue miracle. Despite the miracle, king Pentheus is unimpressed.[118]

C. Marius, in his flight from Sulla (87 BC), was captured at the Roman colony of Minturnae and thrown into prison. After a prolonged incarceration, the city magistrates ordered his execution. The executioner, however, refused. Lucan's (39-65 AD) version of the events, described as the fearful reflection of an elderly Roman who saw in Marius an historical precedent for the civil war, runs as follows:

> When power to take his hated life was granted to a foeman, naught came of it; for, in beginning the deed of slaughter, the man was palsied and let the sword slip from his strengthless hand. A great light shone in the prison darkness; he saw the awful deities that wait on crime, and he saw Marius as he was yet to be; and he heard a dreadful voice—'You are not permitted to touch that neck. Before he dies himself, Marius must, by the laws that govern the ages, bring death to many. Lay aside your useless rage'.[119]

Marius' preservation from execution is described as Fate's way of *extending* his guilty suffering. The Cimbrian executioner, if he truly wished to see his people avenged for the slaughter they had suffered at the hands of the Romans under Marius, would be wise to let his victim live. Alive, Marius would eventually slaughter many Romans and thus avenge the Cimbrians. This is 'theological' reflection or religious

---

[116]*Cf.* Ovid, *Met.* 3.572-691 with Apollodorus, *Bibl.* 3.5.3.
[117]Ovid, *Met.* 3.695-700.
[118]*Ibid.* 3.701.
[119]Lucan 2.76-83.

metaphor in explanation of both how and why Fate and/or the deities order the lives of men and nations as they do.

There is considerable variation in the other accounts of the circumstances of Marius' release. Plutarch (mid 1st cent. AD) is aware that he relates a story known in different forms.[120] In his account, Marius is under house arrest. Plutarch writes:

> ...we are told that to the soldier the eyes of Marius seemed to shoot out a strong flame, and that a loud voice issued from the shadows saying: 'Man, why dost thou dare to slay Caius Marius?' At once, then, the Barbarian fled from the room, threw his sword down on the ground, and dashed out of doors, with this one cry: 'I cannot kill Caius Marius'.[121]

Velleius Paterculus (c. 19 BC-31 AD) has the venue as the prison at Minturnae and the deed ordered of a public slave of German nationality:

> ...this man had been taken a prisoner by Marius when he was commander in the war against the Cimbri; when he recognized Marius, giving utterance with loud outcry to his indignation at the plight of this great man, he threw away his sword and fled from the prison.[122]

The *Epitome* of Livy (59 BC-17 AD) contains the following brief but entirely naturalistic assessment of the event: 'A slave of Gallic nationality was sent to kill him, but withdrew appalled by the dignity of so great a man'.[123]

In the apocryphal NT literature the Lord Jesus is called at one place the 'helper in prison' and at another the 'helper of his servants'.[124] The *Acts of Andrew* (c. 150-90 AD) is, relatively speaking, the most restrained in what it asserts concerning divine assistance and assurance. At one point Andrew exhorts the disciple Maximilla to refuse sexual relations with her husband Aegeates, 'especially since I have seen the Lord (in a vision) who said to me: "Andrew, Aegeates' father, the devil, will release you from this prison".'[125] This is a divine assurance to Andrew that he will be martyred. At another place it is said that shortly after Aegeates had decided that Andrew should die by

---

[120]Plutarch, *Mar.* 39.
[121]*Ibid.*
[122]Velleius Paterculus 2.19.3.
[123]Livy, *Epit.* 77.
[124]*Apocr. Acts Paul* 3 and *Apocr. Acts Thom.* 149 respectively.
[125]*Apocr. Acts And.* 8.

crucifixion, 'Maximilla, the Lord going before her in the form of Andrew, went with Iphidamia to the prison'.[126] Nothing, however, is
made of the relation between the apparition and the apostle whom
Maximilla then comes upon in the prison discoursing with many
Christian visitors.

Several instances of divine help are recorded in the apocryphal
Acts of Paul (c. 185-95 AD). The apostle at one point imprisoned in the
temple of Apollo at Sidon, prays that God would not allow him or his
company to suffer at the hands of the hostile inhabitants and officials.
In response to Paul's prayer God causes a section of the temple to collapse.[127] The divine response in the story is not a deliverance for when
the Sidonians return to the temple they find Paul and his company
(still in the temple?) weeping 'that they were to become a spectacle for
everyone'.[128] The trial section is not extant. The next we read, they
have left Sidon for Tyre.

Later imprisoned in Ephesus, the apocryphal Paul on the day before he is to fight the beasts prays to Jesus Christ, asking for deliverance from his chains and imprisonment so that he might baptize
Armetilla in the sea: '...there came in a youth very comely in grace and
loosed Paul's bonds, the youth smiling as he did so'.[129] Then, Paul actually leads Armetilla out of the locked prison and baptizes her in the
sea. He later miraculously returns to his prison cell.[130]

If the previous two apocryphal *Acts* are relatively restrained, the
Acts of Thomas (c. 200-50 AD) is a veritable nest of complicated indications of divine activity. These complications arise from the author's desire to emphasize the twin relationship between Thomas and Jesus, at
times leaving distinctions in identity unresolved. On the way to the
prison, the enquirer Mygdonia meets Judas Thomas coming to her pre-
ceded by a great light.[131] Asked how he has managed to escape, he replies, 'My Lord Jesus is more powerful than all powers and kings and
rulers'.[132] Anointing and baptizing her and giving her the Eucharist,
Thomas returns to the prison where he finds the doors of the prison
open and the guards all sound asleep. He exults in the tender love and
zealous care of God, concluding with the words, 'Glory be to the only-

---

[126]*Ibid.* 14. *Cf.* Acts 12:15.
[127]*Apocr. Acts Paul* 5.
[128]*Ibid.*
[129]*Ibid.* 7.
[130]A surmise. The text is very unclear as to what occurs.
[131]*Apocr. Acts Thom.* 118.
[132]*Ibid.* 119.

begotten of the Father, glory to the compassionate who was sent from his heart!'[133] At these words the guards awake in great puzzlement at the sight of prison doors opened but prisoners safely inside.

Later, the disciples Tertia, Mygdonia and Marcia come into the prison led, they presume, by Thomas who has opened the homes in which they had been locked by their husbands.[134] When Thomas hears this, he exults:

> Glory be to thee, Jesus of many forms, glory to thee who dost appear in the guise of our poor manhood! To thee be glory, who dost encourage us and strengthen us and give <joy> and comfort us, and stand by us in all our dangers and strengthen our weakness![135]

Warned by the jailer to extinguish their lamps lest they be accused to the king, the apocryphal Thomas prays that they be permitted divine illumination. '...suddenly the whole prison was as bright as the day. But while all who were in the prison slept in a deep slumber, only those who had believed in the Lord were just then awake'.[136]

When Vazan asks who will release them that he might be baptized, Thomas declares, 'Believe in Jesus, and thou shalt find the doors open!'[137] Leaving the prison ahead of Thomas and the others, Vazan comes upon his wife Mnesara near their house. She has been told by the Saviour in a vision to go to Thomas in the prison and is given a young man to lead her there. Visible to her only, the youth disappears when Thomas and the others meet up with Mnesara and Vazan. Seeing Thomas, she acknowledges him as the one whom she saw and who gave her the youthful guide.[138] Thomas does not deny the connection. Baptism, anointing and a celebration of the Eucharist then occur after which the disciples return to their house arrest. Before leaving them, Thomas first makes it clear that though he is intimate with the Saviour, he is other than the Saviour. He then prays that Jesus will reseal the doors of the house. Returning to the prison, he finds the guards quarreling and in great disturbance because the doors have all been found open, though the prisoners have not escaped.[139] At daybreak the guards complain to the king regarding the nocturnal activities and the

---

[133]*Ibid.* 122.
[134]*Ibid.* 151f.
[135]*Ibid.* 153.
[136]*Ibid.*
[137]*Ibid.* 154.
[138]*Ibid.* 154f.
[139]*Ibid.* 162.

breaches of prison security. When the king inspects the prison, he finds 'the seals as they were (before)'.[140] He upbraids the jailers for lying.

In contrast to the above, the divine assistance and assurance to imprisoned confessors in the Christian martyr literature is very restrained. Material miracles still occur, but the dominant divine help takes the form of visions of comfort and encouragement, some fifteen or so of which have already been noted and discussed in summary.[141] If there are miraculous repasts, lighted cells, releases from prison, or prison visits from martyred confessors and divine/angelic beings, these are ethereal and spiritual. The *Martyrdom of Montanus and Lucius* (259 AD) is introduced thus:

> But this suffering, dearest brothers, this privation, this period of misery [i.e., in the prison], was God's concern. For he who wished us to be tried in this way arranged that we should receive a message in the midst of our trials. Victor, a presbyter and one of our fellow martyrs, had the following vision; he was to die shortly afterwards.[142]

In the vision, Victor speaks to a child [= Christ] with a brilliantly shining face who has entered the prison. Victor and the other confessors are encouraged by the child to stand firm and the sign of Jacob is given as an assurance to them.[143] In similar fashion, the *Martyrdom of Marian and James* (259 AD) asserts that the confessors are dedicated to God the Father despite their sufferings in the prison, 'their brothers care for them by day, Christ by night as well'.[144] Christ's care takes the form of visions to Marian and Aemilian. In these, the purpose is assurance of a certain and God-pleasing confession and a subsequent heavenly welcome at their death. The direct divine assistance quite consistently looks beyond the prison to martyrdom.

2. The Prisoner Paul in Acts

Paul, as he stands before the Roman governor Festus, king Herod Agrippa and the rest of the gathered body of dignitaries in Caesarea confidently asserts, '...I have had God's help to this very day, and so I stand here and testify to small and great alike' (Acts 26:22). Our inter-

---

[140]*Ibid.*
[141]*Supra*, 350f.
[142]*Mart. Mont. & Luc.* 7.1f.
[143]*Ibid.* 7.3-11.
[144]*Mart. Mar. & James* 6.4.

est, earlier stated, is in unmediated tokens of divine assistance and assurance. Three occur for Paul in Acts at 16:26, 23:11, and 27:23f., 26.

Frequently in discussions of Acts 16, Luke is said to have laid hold of the standard motifs of prison escape literature. Pervo is a noteworthy recent advocate of this view.[145] A close examination of the ancient examples he furnishes raises serious questions concerning the way the comparisons are made. For example, when Euripides, Ovid, Pacuvius, Nonnos, and the various NT apocryphal *Acts* are compared with Luke, Acts becomes 'just another one of many' and the impression is left of Lukan dependency. Numbers, however, can be deceiving. The first four authors represent variations of a *single story* and Conzelmann's observation is worth recalling that there is no literary dependence of Luke upon Euripides which is perhaps the most celebrated example of the Dionysiac story.[146] The apocryphal *Acts*, rather than serving to demonstrate the breadth of use of some general miraculous escape motifs in the literature, are probably more realistically instances of mimicking or accentuating NT accounts in service of special agendas. In the second instance, Acts 16 is not a prison escape account. Doors are opened and bonds loosed, but the prisoners stay in the prison. It seems wrong to argue on the basis of similarities in later apocryphal, martyrological and other Christian literature a derivative quality or some such thing in Luke. There are similar elements. But if weight is improperly assigned, categories loosely drawn and directions suggested without adequate warrant there can be little confidence in the results.

The focus of the divine activity in the Philippi episode is the earthquake and its attendant material results. As the apostles were praying and singing hymns to God, 'suddenly there was such a violent earthquake that the foundations of the prison were shaken. At once all the prison doors flew open, and everybody's chains came loose' (Acts 16:26). The prayers and hymns, we argued, were not for deliverance but had a praise content. The earthquake, therefore, vindicates the truth of the prayer/hymn content—it is a divine affirmation.[147] It triggers connections in the jailer's mind which permit an effective witness

---

[145]Pervo, *Profit With Delight*, 18-24 and particularly 147 n. 15. *Cf.*, e.g., Conzelmann, *Acts*, 94; Krodel, *Acts*, 311.

[146]Conzelmann, *Acts*, 94.

[147]At Acts 4:23-31 the shaking [σαλεύω] of the foundations of the building in which the disciples pray appears to be a token of divine assent to their requests for boldness of speech, healing, and the performance of miraculous signs and wonders through the name.

leading ultimately to his and his household's conversion and baptism. The miracle facilitates mission, not escape. The witnesses may be abused and incarcerated, 'but God's word is not chained'.[148]

On two occasions—at Acts 23:11 and 27:23-26—Jesus stands near to the prisoner Paul to deliver words of assurance and assistance.[149] Aune finds in Acts 23:11 the following tripartite pattern:

> *Narrative Setting:*The following night the Lord stood near Paul [ἐ- φίστημι αὐτῷ] and said,
> *Admonition:*'Take courage [θαρσέω]!
> *Reason:*As you have testified [διαμαρτύρομαι] about me at Jerusalem, so you must also [δεῖ καί] testify [μαρτυρέω] in Rome'.[150]

The phrase ἐπιστὰς αὐτῷ and related expressions function as technical terms in the Jewish and Graeco-Roman contexts, indicating a revelatory dream experience according to Aune. It is 'apparently based on the image of someone standing beside the bed or pallet of a sleeping figure'.[151] The expression can, however, also indicate wakeful revelatory experiences as exemplified by Luke 2:9 and 24:4. Whether the Lord comes to Paul in a vision as he sleeps, or appears to him as he is praying at Acts 23:11 cannot be determined.

It may be doubted that we should take the formulaic admonition θάρσει here (Matt. 9:2, 22; 14:27 [pl.]; Mark 6:50 [pl.]; 10:49) to mean that Paul had deep apprehensions or was smitten by anxiety.[152] True, the worst fears of the church leadership and of Christian friends along Paul's way to Jerusalem had been realized shortly after he had arrived. But he had been notified clearly and several times over of the divine intention for him and had resolved to see that intention fulfilled. Paul finds himself now a prisoner in the Fortress Antonia and in a position of considerable uncertainty as to how events will unfold past this point. In this uncertainty, the Lord comes near to the prisoner. The Lord assures Paul that the divine plan for him has been fulfilled in Jerusalem and will be further fulfilled far beyond the geographical heart of Judaism.

---

[148]2 Tim. 2:9.

[149]Interestingly, the first occurrence is after Jewish official discussion of the prospect or possibility of such for Paul at Acts 23:9. For other Pauline visions, Acts 16:9; 18:9f.; 22:17; *cf.* 9:4.

[150]Adapted from Aune, *Prophecy*, 267

[151]*Ibid.*, 431 n. 133 and examples there cited. *Cf.* Acts 12:7; *New Docs.*, vol. 1, #6.

[152]So Bruce, *The Book of Acts* 430; Williams, *Acts*, 385; Haenchen, *The Acts*, 639.

In the first instance he is told, 'you have testified about me in Jerusalem'. It is doubtful that the witness referred to here relates primarily to Paul's much earlier preaching in Jerusalem at Acts 9:28f.[153] Rather, Paul's experiences and activities subsequent to his arrest a few days before are in view: specifically, his appearances before and witness[154] to the Jewish mob from the steps of the Fortress Antonia and, very briefly, the Sanhedrin (Acts 22:1-21; 22:30-23:11). The first words are an indication both of divine satisfaction at Paul's witness in Jerusalem and of the fulfilment of the prophetic indications of the divine δεῖ[155] for him in Jerusalem.

Paul is told, 'so you must also testify in Rome'. With this second mention of Rome in Acts, Paul's earlier Spirit-inspired conviction of the divine δεῖ of going to Rome (Acts 19:21) receives a direct and emphatic confirmation.[156] Cosgrove enters a necessary corrective when he cautions against notions of a rigid and inviolable determinism in the divine δεῖ. He observes that while the δεῖ is a divine 'must', there are indications in Acts that the co-operation and obedience of Paul are important.[157] There are, nevertheless, events in Acts which fall entirely beyond Paul's control and which require for fulfilment the unassisted activity of God. Luke bids his readers understand and interpret many of the ensuing events and actions through which the prisoner–witness Paul progresses—no matter how complex or convoluted—as instances of a continued divine blessing and assistance.

We have seen in Luke's gospel the prophetic assertion that Jesus' followers, among whom Paul is numbered in Acts as one of the most prominent, will become prisoner–witnesses before various authorities. Paul is assured in an increasingly detailed and explicit fashion that he is destined to stand in the divine spotlight highlighting a mission which is quintessentially that of prisoner-witness. Acts 23:11 calls for additional comment as it appears further to reinforce this mandate. The text, set in parallel terms and framed by the expression 'as ... so' (ὡς ... οὕτω), surely encourages the reader to see here more than the

---

[153]Munck, *The Acts*, 225, offers this as a possibility.

[154]Marshall, *The Acts*, 367; Williams, *Acts*, 385; Krodel, *Acts*, 429 helpfully note that the emphasis is upon witness not self-defence.

[155]Δεῖ καί would appear to reinforce the sense of divine necessity in the first element.

[156]The function of this phrase can hardly be to give the readers certainty that Paul actually did bear witness in Rome as Haenchen, *The Acts*, 639 and Schneider, *Die Apostelgeschichte*, 334 suggest.

[157]Cosgrove, 'The Divine ΔΕΙ', 178, 181, 183.

barest terms of comparison. The fact of witness is there to be sure, but so too must be the character of that witness. As Paul has been a prisoner-witness before groups and authorities in Jerusalem, so in the same way he will be a prisoner-witness in Rome.[158]

Finally, after a two year period of incarceration and now at the point of disaster at sea, the prisoner Paul discloses to his shipmates at Acts 27:23f. that he has received a divine communication having both personal and general significance.

> *Narrative Setting:*Last night an angel of the God whose I am and whom
> I serve stood beside me [παρέστη γάρ μοι] and
> said,
> *Admonition:*'Do not be afraid [μὴ φοβοῦ],
> *Address:*Paul
> *Reason:*You must [δεῖ] stand trial before Caesar;
> and [and lo: καὶ ἰδοὺ] God has graciously given you the lives of all
> who sail with you'.[159]

In form, the 'stood beside me' phrase of the narrative setting, indicating either a dream or waking oracle, and the admonition 'do not fear' are variants of the similar expressions found at Acts 23:11.[160] The personal address, writes Aune, 'is frequently found in OT oracles of assurance, but only very rarely in the Graeco-Roman oracles which have a basically similar structure'.[161]

The reason segment of the divine communication is bipartite. First, Paul is assured in no uncertain terms that he will bear witness at the very heart of the Empire. The divine δεῖ[162] here confirms the more general earlier promise of Acts 23:11 and specifies the conditions more explicitly—the prisoner will bear witness not just 'in Rome' but 'before Caesar'. The divine assurance given specifically to Paul at Acts 27:23f. is to be the hermeneutical tool with which Luke's readers interpret the remaining threats of storm, summary execution, shipwreck and snakebite which Paul experiences.[163]

---

[158]Williams, *Acts*, 385 and Munck, *The Acts*, 225f. refer to the chains and the authorities respectively.
[159]Adapted from Aune, *Prophecy*, 268.
[160]*Ibid.*, 267f.
[161]*Ibid.*, 268.
[162]Cosgrove's comments ('The Divine ΔΕΙ', 178f.) concerning human co-operation in and obedience to the divine δεῖ are once again fittingly recalled.
[163]*Contra* Miles and Trompf, 'Luke and Antiphon', 259-67.

In the second element of the reason[164] it is disclosed that Paul has apparently been praying for the preservation of his shipmates. He personally receives, along with the assurance of the divine δεῖ in his own case, the lives of all aboard ship as a 'gift' (χαρίζομαι) from the Lord. Their physical salvation is in some sense subject to his discretion as he sets contingencies in their salvation (Acts 27:31). Finally, the indication 'nevertheless, we must run aground on some island' at Acts 27:26 is further testimony to the divine provision of a certain indication (δεῖ) of the means whereby Paul and those placed in his hands will be kept from perishing at sea.

---

[164]The demonstrative particle ἰδού 'is frequently found in OT oracles of assurance', according to Aune, *Prophecy*, 268.

CHAPTER 16

CONCLUSION:
THE AUTHOR AND THE IMPRIS-
ONED MISSIONARY

In the light of the known and varied crises that imprisonment brought upon Paul and his mission, one of Luke's important objectives was to defend or justify the prisoner missionary Paul to his readers. This necessitates a discussion of what it was like in the Roman world to be put through custodial deliberations; what it was like to experience imprisonment, bonds and prison culture; and what would have been the psychological and social impact of such an experience upon relationships to individuals and the community at large 'on the outside'. Paul's own custody experiences in Acts must also be compared and analyzed. Once the ground has been cleared Luke's special interests become more readily discernible.

I. The Ancient Context and the Text of Acts

As with litigation in the courtroom, the process of going into custody shared in the general structure and ethos of ancient Mediterranean, and, in particular, Roman society. 'Going to jail' in this culture was a complex legal and social process. There were institutionalized and acceptable measures by which an individual might be officially evaluated to determine a fitting custody. If a person had committed a serious crime—i.e., a crime that was serious in itself or in terms of the high status of the one against whom it had been perpetrated—that person could expect a heavier custody; if the crime was less serious by these measures, custody might be lighter. A canvass of the literature permitted a general classification of pre-eminently prisonable offences.

Another measure by which custody was determined was the relative status of the accused and accuser. A higher status accused might garner a lighter custody, a lower status person would typically be assigned a more harsh and forbidding custody. On the other hand, a higher status accuser might expect and receive from the examining magistrate due consideration in the form of a harsher custody for the accused, whereas an accuser's lower status might impair such favourable consideration.

Notions of 'high' and 'low' in ancient estimation were discussed under the rubrics of citizen and social status. Roman citizenship, while it opened up the prospect of appeal to the people and/or their tribunes and later to the Emperor himself against summary capital punishment and such other punishments as flogging and incarceration, was certainly not an ironclad guarantee of one's coming to rights. The citizen under threat of imprisonment might have difficulty where the magistrate had little regard for the law and no fear for its consequences, where the people or their officials were hostile or timid in the face of a claim, or where the defendant's citizenship was unaugmented by sufficient additional entitlements such as wealth and 'connections'. Under these circumstances an appeal might not be made, might be delayed, or, if made, might fail.

The social status of the individual increased in importance in juridical treatments and custodial deliberations as the value of the citizenship gradually declined. Social status was measured in terms of birth credentials, social standing, offices, honours and wealth as well as the style of one's life relative to that of one's opponent. To possess both Roman citizenship and a high social status conferred the greatest advantage and ensured the most favourable custodial treatment.

When assigning custody, deliberating magistrates might be moved by favour, influence and bribery. Formally deemed unacceptable and punishable under the law, this trio of pressures often wormed its way into the process, skewing deliberations to the advantage or disadvantage of some litigants. Unchecked magisterial power and the grant of significant immunity from prosecution had a further corrupting influence upon the deliberative process.

Among the purposes custody served in the ancient world were protection and remand. For others, prison was the place to await execution, or the place where executions were carried out. Imprisonment also served as a form of magisterial coercion and increasingly in the Roman context (despite legal objections to the contrary) it became a punishment to which individuals were formally sentenced. Custodial options also varied in their severity. By Ulpian's measure the sequence, 'state prison, military custody, entrustment to sureties, and freedom on personal recognizance', denoted the general custodial options running from most to least severe. It was further determined that distinction in severity might be made within and between these categories. For example, within the state prison of Rome and its urban counterparts in other cities of the Mediterranean world there were nightmarish inner cells; between the categories of state prison and military custody there were places like the quarry prisons. Whether one was bound or not and how one was bound were additional means of distinguishing the severity. Military custody in the camp, in a home, in transit to the place of assize or execution and into exile might also vary quite considerably in degree of severity. Chaining in all these venues seems to have been the rule except for the highest status individuals and in the easiest of custodial environments. The rank and experience of military keepers was often keyed to the notoriety, importance or social distinction of the prisoner. Entrustment to the care of sureties and release on one's own recognizance in its different arrangements was much more exclusively the domain of high status individuals.

In the end the key aim for the accused was to emphasize his or her citizen- and social status to maximum personal advantage and, if not avoiding custody altogether, then at least avoiding the most personally damaging forms. The countering process also served, beyond defence, the object of doing as much damage to one's opponent as one could. After all, self-defence and doing maximum damage were also the accuser's principal objectives. While the diagram furnished in this study (Fig. 1) might suggest linearity and rigidity of analysis, in real life the process of setting custody was non-linear, dynamic and very much open to situational factors. In its basic thrust, however, the diagram sets forth ancient concerns and the process of bringing those concerns to bear.

The privations of life in custody were seen to be many and could be quite severe for prisoners in the ancient world. Overcrowding in cramped prison facilities designed exclusively in terms of security brought with it unbearable heat, dehydration, suffocating closeness, noise, reeking stench and contagion to inmates. Most prison structures were, moreover, very poorly illuminated. The daylight gloom and nightly darkness were frequent sources of distress if not outright terror. Perish the thought that one might be locked up in the complete darkness of a secure inner cell. Adequate furnishings can hardly be spoken of.

The wearing of chains and/or stocks, while securing prisoners from escaping, was an additional physical rigour. Weighty iron chains restricted prisoner mobility and were also frequently the cause of untold sufferings: rusty, they chafed and corroded the skin; too tight, they were an innovation in torture; too heavy, they would pain or even cripple their wearers; in addition they contributed, when the prisoner moved, to the general din and sleeplessness of the whole prison environment.

It was expected that prisoners would attend to their own nourishment. Those who could rely upon provisions from family, friends or contracted providers might have better prospects of staying healthy. Poverty and the need to rely upon officially provided prison rations, however, was often a recipe for disaster. The daily prison ration was more often than not severely restricted in its variety, quality and quantity. Thus dependent, one also became vulnerable to the punishment, torture or death caused by its purposeful or malicious denial by prison staff. It is small wonder that the weak and plaintive cry for help of prisoners long denied the basic necessities is not infrequently heard in the literature. Those not suitably advantaged in material wealth or provision from outside soon found that clothing long worn in the squalor of the prison turned to filthy and hardly wearable rags. Freedom to bathe regularly if at all appears to have been a special concession granted to but a few. Haircuts were unnecessary and a security risk and were therefore, outside of exceptional circumstances, not granted.

We read in the ancient prison literature, in consequence, of grinding general debility, withering illness and death. It is small wonder that those faced with the prospect of such a hellish existence tried, out of despair, to take their own lives, and equally unsurprising that among the requirements of keepers was the need both to keep their wards secure and to keep them from killing themselves.

Since Luke indicates that there were relationships between the missionary prisoner Paul, his keepers and other prisoners, it was also a matter of some interest to explore ancient prison culture, or the social world of custodians and inmates. Administrative structures and sorts of personnel in ancient prisons were variable. There were public slave-run prisons in Athens and Sparta and at Rome having a chief jailer/executioner (but a chief jailer only in Rome) and various slave subordinates serving as guards and doorkeepers, secretaries, undersecretaries and menials. The above prisons were run under the general supervision of elected citizens called the Eleven, the Ephors and the *triumviri capitales* respectively. The lictors of magistrates in Rome, while they had the power to arrest and imprison malefactors and even execute them there, appear not to have been formally connected with the prison system normally. In the provinces, however, some appear to have been grafted onto existing systems.

Rome's growth in size and lawlessness triggered the levying of a quasi-military force of 7,000 freedmen known as the *vigiles* under a Roman knight having, among other things, civilian peacekeeping responsibilities which included keeping troublemakers in holding cells within sub-stations. The pressure to move away from slave to more fully military prison-keeping arrangements is early seen in the literature and sufficiently strong to result in some organizational hybridization. In the military prison context, administration was taken care of by various *beneficiarii* while such lesser duties as turnkey and guard fell to the lower ranks.

The documents considered show both positive and negative keeper-inmate relations. Humane treatment might occur out of a high regard for the status of the prisoner, owing to orders from superiors, out of religious fear of or solidarity with the prisoner, out of pity, and even out of embarrassment. Hostility and harsh treatment might be engendered simply by the level of security officially expected, obedience to specific commands, feelings that the prisoner somehow 'deserved it', or out of greed for personal enrichment.

Relations between inmates too, could be governed by helpfulness or hostility. Positive relations might be expressed in sharing food, extending practical comfort, giving encouragement and legal advice, and, in the case of Christians, sharing and helping because of religious solidarity. Hostility resulted from status differences, irritablility and squabbling caused by failure to cope with the harsh prison environment, and distrust of prisoners who might actually be in collusion with the authorities. There was for many years no separation of the sexes in prisons. This had predictably unhappy effects.

Custody and bonds might cause great social devastation to persons because social relations were extensively driven by honour and shame concerns in the ancient Mediterranean world. Imprisonment and bonds both carried significant shame connotations. Prison and shame appear together in ancient collocations of disasters which might befall individuals. Prison is identified as a place of dishonour because of its connection with dishonourable occupants. Being publicly conducted to prison was also terribly degrading. The stigma and shame could be longlasting, even lifelong. There was great pressure upon individuals and groups who knew or were formerly associated with the prisoner to treat him or her with revulsion or simply abandon them. This pressure was felt by friends and associates, family members, and even slaves. Christians too, despite encouragements and theological warnings, might abandon a believing prisoner out of the shame associated with custody and bonds. The prisoner was also deeply affected by the loss of honour associated with such treatment. Some felt the shame and disgrace strongly enough that they would not venture out in public even if permitted. It was the same when individuals suffered the indignity of public nakedness and/or flogging.

We continue to be aware that the book of Acts has been judged by many scholars to be at best an impoverished historical record of the events it seeks to describe. Other candidate *genres* have been proffered. Doubts have been registered concerning the cost to Luke's record of a thoroughgoing treatment of it as an ancient novel. The present reader will appreciate that this issue has not been forgotten in the exegetical treatments of the Lukan record of Paul's prison experiences.

The above-noted summary of findings concerning procedures, perceptions, experiences and behaviours in the matter of imprisonment and bonds constitutes a part of the broader ancient context and it is from this context with its concerns and sensitivities that Luke-Acts gives evidence to be a document of antiquity. Moreover, it is to readers who peopled this context that Luke wrote his double work. We offer, within the limits of the present study, the observation that the ancient context informs our understanding of the canonical Acts in a number of ways which suggest that not a few of the perceived historical problems of some prison passages are in fact inadequately informed perceptions. An eye to the ancient context helpfully furnishes the modern reader with a 1st century AD-based appreciation of the events. This moves toward the resolution of a number of alleged difficulties in the direction of a greater confidence in the historical trustworthiness of the Lukan record. One might cite such examples as the discussions of the public clash of personalities under official Roman scrutiny at Philippi, the 'un-Roman' character of Paul's citizenship disclosure there, the fitness of Paul's initial indication of his Tarsian over his Roman citizenship in Jerusalem, his 'un-Roman' citizenship intimation in the Antonia Fortress, the Tribune's subsequent social/juridical damage assessment and the ambiguities of a considerably lightened custody for Paul in Jerusalem. We have indicated that the texts possess a logic which a view to the ancient context discloses. Other examples might be offered, but these should suffice to indicate the helpfulness of context to text in understanding the Lukan record of Pauline prison experiences.

II. The Missionary Prisoner Paul as Presented in Acts

What of Luke's defence of the missionary Paul in his various prison troubles? As a matter of first importance, our attention was directed to the matter of Paul's identity. Based upon an analysis of the information available, Paul in Acts, in terms of his legal status, is a Tarsian and Roman citizen and, regarding social status, possesses impeccable Jewish birth credentials, superior Pharisaic educational credentials, and significant political connections and influence. We have argued that he is thus an historically credible figure. There is, moreover, no reason to doubt that he was a man of some means who engaged in leatherworking. While his status in Acts is an eminently credible one, it is also one shot full with a status dissonance possessing explosive potential if the 'wrong' people should be assessing him. The various elements of his status—Tarsian, Roman, Jew, Pharisee and prisoner—did not rest comfortably alongside one another and the addition of the term 'Christian' hardly simplified matters.

In descriptions which are sensitive to Roman official concerns in setting custody, Luke records for his readers how Paul, possessing a dissonance-laden status as he does, is subjected initially to one harsh assessment after another. At Philippi he and Silas move silently, and from a Roman perspective unnecessarily, through a 'worst case scenario'. The earlier experience in Jerusalem is similar. The custody arrangements in Caesarea are initially of the usual harsh and close character, but improve in the second phase. However, the improvement hardly arises from magisterial virtue. Rather, while the facts of the case appear to favour Paul, the greater power of the Jerusalem élite and Paul's assumed greater vulnerability to a plea for a bribe permit only a lightened custody in the Herodian palace but no dismissal of the case. The custodial deliberation at Rome is the most purely formal and dispassionate. It also significantly favours Paul in that he is permitted to live under house arrest with light military supervision which, without prejudice to other matters, may reflect not considerations of Paul's status but the greater likelihood of his acquittal.

Luke's accounts of Paul's citizen disclosures suggest that Paul's Roman citizenship was important to him. However, the disclosures are strategy-driven. When, where, before whom and how Paul discloses his citizenship is subject to the priorities of his identity as a Jew, the integrity of his missionary message and concerns to guard the faith of his converts. Paul was faithful both because he preached and because he kept his mouth shut at times. Luke's readers would probably have picked up the emphasis upon the priority of the gospel over the rights and entitlements of one's legal and social status. Paul was prepared to suffer the shame of imprisonment and chains in the interests of an unambiguous witness.

The privations of life in custody were many and severe for ancient prisoners. Paul's and Silas' custody experience in Philippi is the worst of the Lukan record. The entire prison population had probably been thrust into the inner cell with Paul and Silas for the night, resulting in their experience of virtually all of the worst things associated with overcrowding. Paul's other imprisonments are variable in character but never apparently as bad as Philippi. Outside of his wearing bonds, Paul's travel to Rome aboard ship is neither physically harsh nor punitive in character beyond anything that the soldier-guards and other prisoners and passengers experienced.

During their Philippian imprisonment, Paul and Silas would have experienced dietary neglect. In Jerusalem and the early phase of the Caesarean custody, Paul would have had to consume Gentile food—a violation of the Torah for those with strong Jewish sensibilities but not out of keeping with his Christian liberty. Paul's clothing had been despoiled in Philippi and possibly in Jerusalem. Friends and associates may have met his need for clothing in the other prison cir-

cumstances. A regular personal toilette for Paul, in the light of our dis-
coveries, seems unlikely. Luke indicates that the prisoner Paul
possessed a generally positive frame of mind throughout his imprisonments in Acts and that he was not apparently in danger of the kind of
distress or depression which might lead to suicide. He had great concerns, but not of this kind.

That Paul probably took accommodation in a third storey apartment of a tenement building at Rome is suggested both by the general
rental conditions in Rome and the compatibility of such an arrangement with the details of Acts 28. It is a reasonable prospect that he, as
a Roman citizen, would have been entitled to and would not have felt
hindered in economizing somewhat in his living expenses in Rome by
availing himself of a rightful share in the public grain dole.

Luke's depiction of Paul's experience of prison culture in Acts is
mixed and there is no unreserved praise for Paul's keepers. The Philippian jailer—a slave governor—out of his pagan religious motivation is
at first neglectful and physically abusive in the way he keeps Paul and
Silas. He also abuses the other prisoners by cramming them into the inner cell with the two missionaries. Relations in Jerusalem are also far
from ideal. Paul's considerable wariness and secrecy in obtaining a private interview between his nephew and the Tribune indicates a climate of considerable distrust and tension in the Fortress Antonia at
Jerusalem. While it is not a matter of Lukan comment, Paul's rapid removal to Caesarea does not bring him into more amicable military sur-
roundings. The continuing deterioration in relations between Jews and
Greeks in Caesarea might have meant additional tension as the troops
guarding Paul were levied from amongst those sympathetic to the
Gentile population. While Luke shows that the centurion Julius had a
generally positive regard for the prisoner Paul, perhaps out of religious or superstitious motives, this cannot be consistently maintained
for the entire period of travel to Rome. Except for the centurion's regard for Paul, it apparently mattered little to him or the rest of the soldiers whether the other prisoners were killed at the point of shipwreck.
Christian voluntarism in the matter of provisioning and billetting Paul
and the rest of the prisoners along the way would certainly have been
welcomed by Julius as a more desirable alternative to the less happy
arrangement of requisitioning provisions and accommodation. Rome,
we argued, was a place of cool formality and officially commanded benignity.

Little is said of Paul's relations with other prisoners in Acts. We
may presume a mutually agreed upon strategy of response between

Paul and Silas owing to their apparently uniform behaviour in the face of crisis at Philippi. Non-Christian co-prisoners share in the benefits of divine acts of vindication and preservation from physical harm which are extended to the prisoner Paul as well as hearing the apostles' message at Philippi and just before being shipwrecked on Malta.

Luke indicates, in keeping with the Mediterranean culture of his day, a sensitivity to shame and honour concerns when he shows Paul exerting considerable effort to recover as much of his and Silas' lost honour as possible in Philippi by means of forcing a highly public social transaction with the magistrates. It is a challenge-riposte following upon a severe status degradation ritual. The result of the transaction is not fully successful and in fact causes social disturbance and leaves a lasting residual sense of shame in Paul as evidenced in his epistles. Luke is also careful to record other instances of shame concern. We may safely infer from the highly public attempt at Jewish lynch justice and from Paul's public binding and incarceration by the Romans, that Paul has been shamed in the eyes of many in Jerusalem. Paul is also keenly aware of the scandalous and offensive impression that he must surely be leaving in the minds of King Agrippa and the other members of the Caesarean audience when, as a man humiliated by the wearing of a chain, Paul wishes that all who have gathered to hear him might be as he is. Self-consciously, Paul wishes for his audience faith, but not a chain. On Malta, negative assumptions concerning Paul's receiving his just deserts must arise from their knowledge that he is a prisoner owing to his chains. Paul looks with concern to the reactions of the official Christian delegation from Rome who come to greet him and insists on a proper rather than a typical interpretation of the chain he wears to the Jewish leadership in Rome. Among the last words of Luke in Acts is παρρησία which stands as an antonym to shame.

In the face of such a massive negative impact—the damage of the process of going into custody, the rigours and constrictions of being in custody, and the shame/dishonour connections of being a prisoner in jail and wearing bonds—what could Luke do or say to counter the impression of disqualification and to demonstrate unequivocally Paul's continuing viability as a missionary? We have argued that Luke in fact does three things in defence of the missionary prisoner Paul:

First, Luke is concerned to show that Paul continued, despite his being a prisoner in bonds, to be an effective missionary. Of the reasons in the ancient world why there might be delay in coming to trial—1) volume of court business; 2) bureaucratic hiccoughs between magistrates; 3) magisterial misbehaviour; and 4) dilatory actions by litigants—reasons 3) and 4) seem to hold for Caesarea and 1) for Rome. Paul's delays, we saw, were neither overly long nor unusual when compared with extra-biblical examples. Among the various pastimes that the prisoner Paul could not engage in was plying his trade. He is also very unlikely to have spent time anxiously writing petitions or crafting defence speeches when an eye is had to his general behaviour in Acts and if Paul had any attention to the instruction concerning dependence upon Jesus for assistance in speech. He does, however, engage in a type of case preparation in his meeting with the Roman Jews when he sets forth before them the conditions of his arrival in Rome in the hope of receiving their acceptance and support. The Roman Jewish community can significantly help or harm him. Prisoners were also known to play games to pass the hours in prison but it is unlikely that such indications for Paul would have been mentioned as they hardly mattered to Luke's agenda. Access to Christian or other literature for Paul's own study would certainly have been welcomed by him and seems very likely to have been furnished, though Luke says nothing of such a pastime in Acts.

Prisoners, Christian and non-Christian alike, were given to individual and corporate prayer and singing which varied in duration, frequency and could occur at all times of the night or day. Luke writes that among his religious diciplines, the prisoner Paul prayed and sang. In Philippi Paul and Silas offer up prayers and hymns of praise about and to God. Their words are closely attended by other prisoners and their action is confirmed as faithful witness by a miracle. Paul's prayers before taking food aboard ship and for the healing of Publius' sick father have both a personal and a witness thrust as well. The divine communications received by Paul in Jerusalem and just before the shipwreck may arise out of a disciplined prayer life. There is no indication in Luke that the prisoner Paul fasted; moreover, Paul is not as some believe, celebrating the Eucharist with the jailer at Philippi or with his travel companions as his ship founders at sea. We may be sure on the basis of epistolary indications that the prisoner Paul would regularly have fasted and celebrated the Eucharist as there was opportunity. It is to be regretted that Luke says nothing of the prisoner Paul's literary activity. The mechanics, prospects and potential for writing letters from prison which is evident in the numerous non-NT examples cited gives confidence, however, that Paul could have written from either Caesarea or Rome without apparent difficulty.

Lukan statements concerning Paul's religious ministrations present the strongest defence of the missionary prisoner. The text and textual implication of Acts leave little doubt that the prisoner Paul is to be understood not as disqualified or compromised but as actively involved in a ministry of preaching, teaching and community direction. Seizing upon the Philippian jailer's stumbling pagan attempts at making religious connections in the event and pressing a broad appeal, the prisoners convert and baptize not only the jailer but also his entire household. The jailer's, 'Go in peace', to the prisoners is an historically credible confirmation of his conversion.

We have argued that the two year Caesarean imprisonment is far from the barren period that some make it out to be. A high-level, timely, forthright, and incorruptible witness occurs in frequent opportunities over the two years for Paul to declare the gospel to a needy Felix. The silence of the text concerning the Caesarean Christians should not be counted an indication of their abandonment of him. Rather, Paul's high 'favour' currency to the Jews argues persuasively for Paul's ongoing impact in the Caesarean Christian community to the Jews' deep annoyance and dismay. The Caesarean church's history with Gentile ministry, its Gentile inclinations and makeup, and its kinship in ministry with Paul actually argue pursuasively for a firm embrace rather than abandonment. Paul's involvement with the church may be more in the nature of community direction and hence merit less attention than the repeated evangelistic interviews with Felix.

On the journey to Rome, the only two instances where Paul's conversation has an evangelistic or witness thrust are when he delivers the divine message of encouragement to his shipmates. While this witness appears to have no lasting effect, as Luke concludes his work there can be no doubt as to the quality or character of the prisoner's continuing effectiveness in ministry. Initially put off by the leading Jews in Rome at the first meeting out of their concern to be adequately prepared to engage him theologically, Paul's second meeting is a setpiece presentation to Roman Judaism. Moreover, it generates the twofold response characteristic of earlier preachings—*viz.*, faith and unbelief. Luke is here undoubtedly asserting the prisoner's continuing ministry effectiveness. But nowhere is this effectiveness more powerfully presented than when he indicates to the readers at the close of Acts that the prisoner's place of house arrest has in effect become a house church where the ministry continues without diminution in content, vigour or willing ears to hear.

Second, Luke shows that Paul, far from inspiring the shame and revulsion of associates in ministry, co-religionists and interested pagans, is surrounded by helpers. Christian co-workers stand by the prisoner-missionary rather than taking the easier and safer route of slipping away from him. Luke and Aristarchus 'cover' Paul with what status they have and show solidarity with him as he goes to Rome. Paul's nephew braves the tense and potentially threatening military environment of the Fortress Antonia to deliver a message which, if improperly divulged, might mean his death. The Philippian jailer, a recent convert, takes great risks in attending to Paul's and Silas' bodily needs. The Roman church, moreover, embraces the prisoner apostle officially and at its highest levels of leadership, while small congregations along the way hasten him along with various expressions of love and consideration as he progresses to Rome.

Finally, Luke is at considerable pains to show that the prisoner-missionary Paul has divine approval. Paul undergoes a progressive focussing of his commission so that the sphere of his mission will be in bonds within the confines of prison cells and under house arrest. In the first part of Luke's double work, Paul is significantly anticipated as the pre-eminent fulfilment of Jesus' prophetic words concerning the experience of disciples who become prisoner-witnesses to him. A look at the book of Acts in what it relates and in the words that it uses, confirms this. Early in the book of Acts Paul is claimed by the risen Lord and made to stand within the divine spotlight of mission as his suffering witness. The readers are then told of the numerous ways in which he must fulfil his calling, including an example of imprisonment at Philippi. Then Luke tells his readers how, when Paul sets his face toward Jerusalem under the Spirit's direction, the spotlight is divinely focussed through the agency of Christian prophets in congregation after congregation: Paul will indeed do Jesus' bidding, but now more particularly as his prisoner-witness. Finally, as he nears Caesarea, the divine spotlight is intensified in a prophetically rich context which concludes with the unanimous positive affirmation that indeed, for Paul to be arrested and placed in bonds is, by the voice of Christian prophets, the Lord's will done.

Maddox writes that 'if in Luke's eyes the main thing about Paul was his mission, then the final section of Acts is disappointing, for in the last nine chapters no one is converted'.[1] Krodel asserts that 'for Luke, Paul the imprisoned, suffering witness and defender of the faith is even more important than Paul the missionary'.[2] The quotations

---

[1]R. Maddox, *The Purpose of Luke-Acts* (FRLANT 126; Göttingen: Vandenhoeck and Ruprecht, 1982), 76.
[2]G.A. Krodel, *Acts* (Minneapolis: Augsburg, 1986), 397.

clearly miss the Lukan emphasis, for the dichotomy, 'either missionary, or prisoner' is a patently false one. Paul is declared at the outset to
be destined to prosecute his missionary labour throughout Acts as suffering witness. We have a vigorously asserted synthesis. The spotlight
of God's choice of Paul to be his witness and to be involved in a ministry of suffering as he is involved in missionary labour is focussed
upon Paul at the very outset of his ministry. And if there is any change
whatsoever, it is not in the move from missionary to suffering witness,
but in the focus and intensity of the divine spotlight of God's choice
upon his life which demonstrates, to any who might doubt, that as
prisoner-witness Paul fulfils his missionary vocation. Paul is indeed
the missionary-prisoner for Luke; effective, appreciated and divinely
approved in his free doings with all the struggles that attended in the
earlier phase of his ministry as described in Acts and effective, appreciated and divinely approved in the tribulations of his bonds in the latter phase of Acts.

There were severe crises for the missionary-become-prisoner.
But through the adversity, the stigma and the shame, Paul had in the
author of Acts, above all the other human helpers who stood alongside
him, that best friend who sticks closer than a brother and who appears
to have loved him at all times (Prov. 17:17).

TABLE OF FIGURES

Republic in the British Museum (London: British Museum Publications, 1910), vol. 3, Plate XCV. 13.

Figure 11: Fasces from the Original in the Capitol at Rome. Adapted from W. Smith 'Fasces', *DGRA*, vol. 1, 826.

Figure 12: Plan of the *Forum* of Philippi. *a.* Traditional 'St. Paul's Prison', b. Building (prison?) Converted to a Cistern. Composed and adapted from M. Séve and P. Weber, 'Le Côté Nord du Forum de Philippes', *BCH* 110 (1986), 535, fig. 3 and 578f. plan C. [Not fully to scale].

Figure 13: Metal Stocks found in the Gladiators' Barracks at Pompeii. From P. Gusman, *Pompei: The City, Its Life and Art,* tr. F. Simmonds and M. Jourdain (London: William Heinemann, 1900), 153.

Figure 14: Circular Form of Metal Stocks found at Pompeii. From Gusman, *Pompei,* 153.

Figure 15: Plan Showing Relation of Fortress Antonia to Herod's Temple With Alternate Fortress Plan Inset. *a.* Temple, *b.* Court of the Priests, *c.* Court of Israel, *d.* Court of the Women, *e.* Court of the Gentiles, *f.* Stairs to Colonnades and Antonia, *g.* Fortress Antonia. Adapted from plan by L.H. Vincent in B. Mazar, 'Les Fouilles au S. et S. O. du Mont du Temple', *Le Monde de la Bible* 13 (1980), 26, fig. 33. Inset adapted from Th.A. Busink, *Der Tempel von Jerusalem von Salomo bis Herodes. Eine archäologische-historische Studie unter Berücksichtigung des westsemitischen Tempelbaus* (Leiden: Brill, 1980), vol. 2, 1179, fig. 253.

Figure 16: Variations of the Roman Scourge: *a.* Chain and Knuckle-Bones; b. Leather Thongs; *c.* Leather and Knuckle-Bones; *d.* Leather and Lead Shot. *a* and *b* from M. Greenberg, 'Scourging', *IDB,* vol. 4, 245, fig. 33. *c* and *d* from J.D. Douglas and F.F. Bruce, 'Scourging, Scourge', *IllBibDic,* vol. 3, 1403.

Figure 17: Herod's Promontory Palace: *a.* Artist's Perspective; *b.* Foundation Plan. Adapted from B. Burrell *et al.,* 'Uncovering Herod's Seaside Palace', *BAR* 193 (1993), 52.

Figure 18: Map of the City of Rome. Adapted from D.R. Dudley, *Urbs Roma: A Source Book of Classical Texts on the City and Its Monuments* (Aberdeen: Phaidon, 1967), inner leaves of cover.

Figure 19: Ostian *Insula—The Caseggiato di Diana:* Axonometric Plan. Adapted from A.G. McKay, *Houses, Villas and Palaces in the Roman World* (Aspects of Greek and Roman Life; Southampton: Thames and Hudson, 1975), 88f., ill. 34.

Figure 20: Ostian *Insula—The Caseggiato di Diana: a.* Ground Floor Plan, *b.* Floor Plan, *Piano Nobile.* Adapted from McKay, *Houses, Villas and Palaces,* 97, fig. 33f.

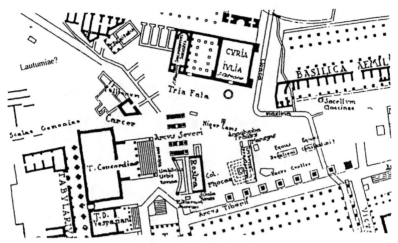

Fig. 1. Map of the Roman Forum.

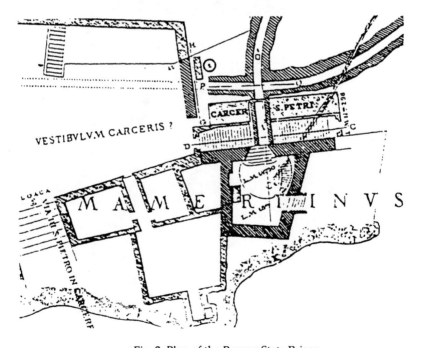

Fig. 2. Plan of the Roman State Prison.

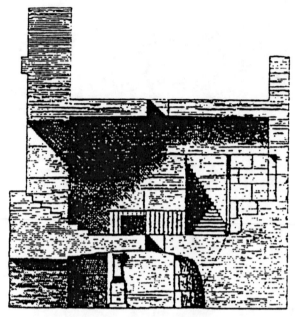

Fig. 3. Section of the Roman *Carcer* and *Tullianum*.

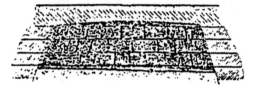

Fig. 4. Section of the *Tullianum*.

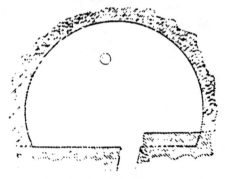

Fig. 5. Plan of the *Tullianum*.

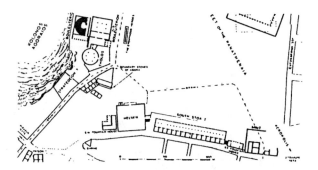

Fig. 6. Map of Part of the Athenian Agora (4th cent. BC).

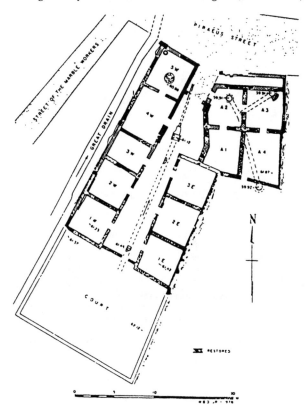

Fig. 7. Plan of the Athenian State Prison.

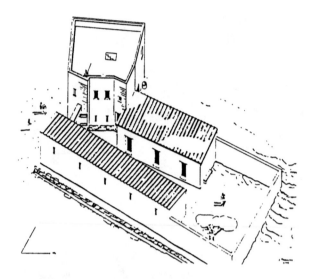

Fig. 8. Perspective of the Athenian State Prison.

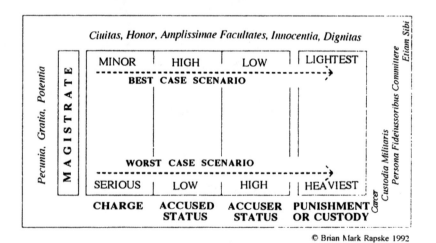

Fig. 9. Factors Influencing the Treatment of Accused Persons.

Fig. 10. Denarius (enlarged) Celebrating the Citizen-Right of *Prouocatio*

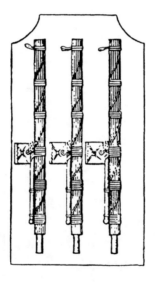

Fig. 11. Fasces from the Original in the Capitol at Rome.

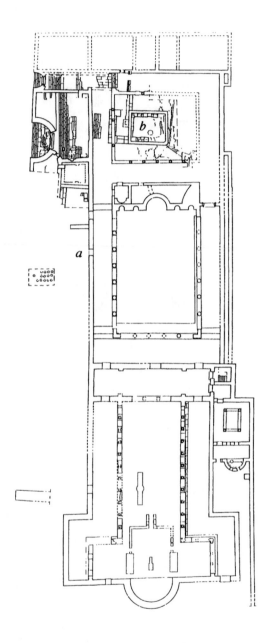

Fig. 12. Plan of the *Forum* of Philippi. *a*. Traditional "St. Paul's Prison,"
b. Building (prison?) Converted to a Cistern.

Fig. 13. Metal Stocks Found in the Gladiators' Barracks at Pompeii.

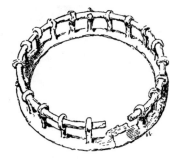

Fig. 14. Circular Form of Metal Stocks Found at Pompeii.

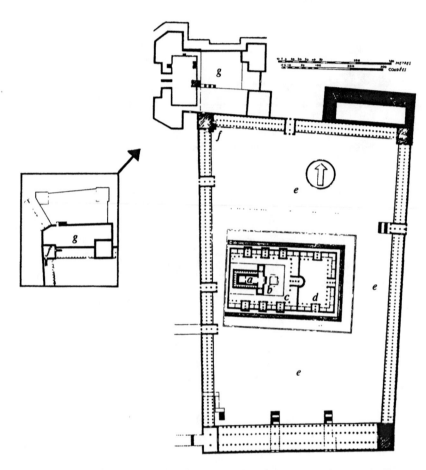

Fig. 15. Plan Showing Relation of Fortress Antonia to Herod's Temple
With Alternate Fortress Plan Inset. *a*. Temple, *b*. Court of the Priests,
c. Court of Israel, *d*. Court of the Women, *e*. Court of the Gentiles,
f. Stairs to Colonnades and Antonia, *g*. Fortress Antonia.

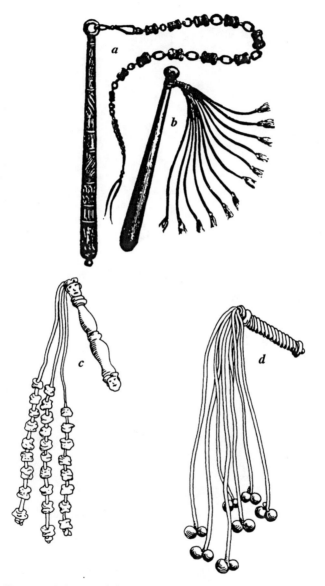

Fig. 16. Variations of the Roman Scourge: *a*. Chain and Knuckle-Bones; *b*. Leather Thongs; *c*. Leather and Knuckle-Bones; *d*. Leather and Lead Shot.

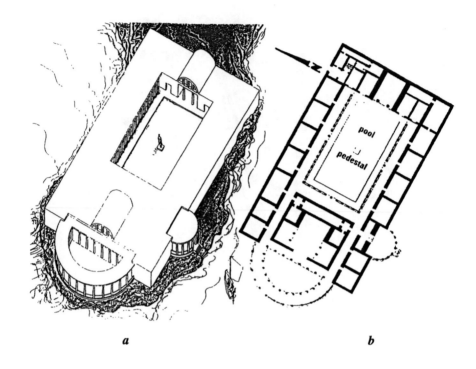

a   *b*

Fig. 17. Herod's Promontory Palace: *a*. Artist's Perspective; *b*. Foundation Plan.

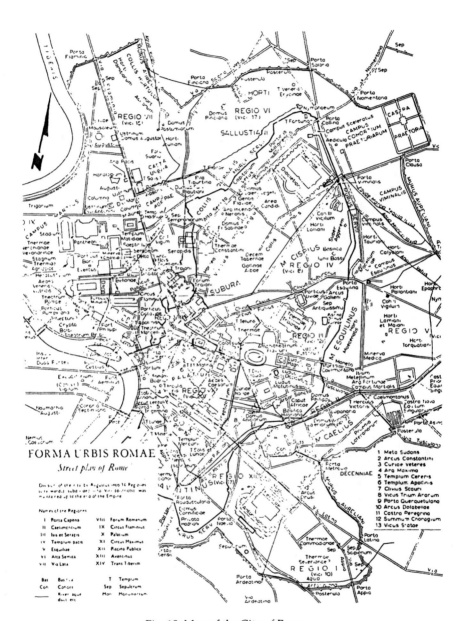

Fig. 18. Map of the City of Rome.

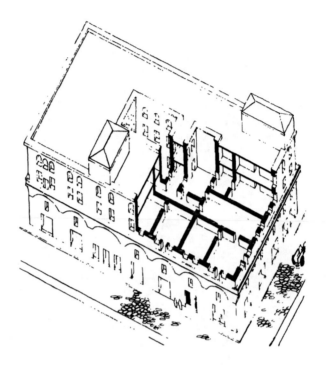

Fig. 19. Ostian *Insula - The Caseggiato di Diana*: Axonometric Plan.

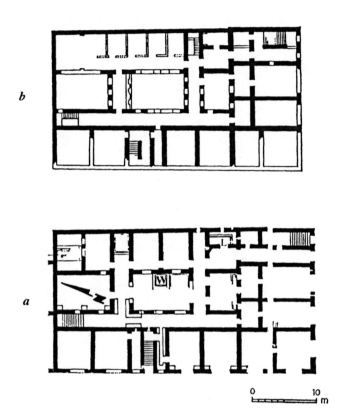

Fig. 20. Ostian *Insula* - The *Caseggiato di Diana*: *a*. Ground Floor Plan ("W"- water source, "L" = *latrina*), *b*. Floor Plane, *Piano Nobile*.

BIBLIOGRAPHY

Primary Sources and Collections

Abbott, F.F. and A.C. Johnson, ed. *Municipal Administration in the Roman Empire.* Princeton: PUP, 1926.

Aland, K. *et al.*, ed. *The Greek New Testament.* 3rd edn.; Stuttgart: UBS, 1983.

Andokides on the Mysteries. ed. D. MacDowell. Oxford: Clarendon, 1962.

The Apology of Aristides. In *Texts and Studies: Contributions to Biblical and Patristic Literature.* gen. ed. J.A. Robinson. Cambridge: CUP/London: C.J. Clay, 1893. Volume 1, number 1.

Bell, H.I. *Jews and Christians in Egypt.* Greek Papyri in the British Museum 6; London: British Museum, 1924.

Berkowitz, L., *et. al. Thesaurus Linguae Graecae: Canon of Greek Authors and Works.* 2nd ed.; New York/Oxford: OUP, 1986.

Apulei Apologia Siue Pro Se De Magia Liber: With Introduction and Commentary. ed. Butler, H.E. and A.S. Owen. Oxford: Clarendon, 1914.

The Clementine Homilies; The Apostolical Constitutions. In *Ante-Nicene Christian Library: Translations of the Writings of the Fathers Down to A.D. 325.* ed. A. Roberts and J. Donaldson. Edinburgh: T. and T. Clark, 1870. Volume 17.

The Clementine Recognitions. In *Ante-Nicene Christian Library: Translations of the Writings of the Fathers Down to A.D. 325.* ed. A. Roberts and J. Donaldson. Edinburgh: T. and T. Clark, 1867. Volume 3.

Colunga, A. and L. Turrado, ed. *Biblia Vulgata.* BAC 14; Madrid: Biblioteca de Autores Cristianos, 1985.

The Corpus of Roman Law: Volume 2--Ancient Roman Statutes. ed. tr. A.C. Johnson *et al.* Austin: University of Texas, 1961.

Deissmann, A. *Light from the Ancient East.* tr. L.R.M. Strachan. London: Hodder and Stoughton, 1927.

The Digest of Justinian. ed. T. Mommsen, P. Kreuger and A. Watson. Philadelphia: UP, 1985. 4 volumes.

Ecclesiastico: Testo ebraico con apparato critico e versioni greca, latina e siriaca. ed. F. Vattioni. Napoli: Istituto Orientale di Napoli, 1968.

Edwards, M. and S. Usher, tr. com. *Greek Orators I: Antiphon and Lysias.* Warminster, England: Aris and Phillips/Chicago: Bolchazy-Carducci, 1985.

Ehrenberg, V. and A.H.M. Jones, ed. *Documents Illustrating the Reigns of Augustus and Tiberius.* 2nd. edn.; Oxford: Clarendon, 1976.

Epstein, I., ed. *The Babylonian Talmud.* London: Soncino, 1938. 35 volumes.

Heliodorus. *Les Éthiopiques: Théagéne et Charicléa.* ed. R. M. Rattenbury *et al.* In *Collection des Universités de France: L'Association Guillaume Budé.* Paris: Les Belles Lettres, 1943. 3rd volume.

Hennecke, E., W. Schneemelcher. *New Testament Apocrypha: Volume Two-- Writings Relating to the Apostles; Apocalypses and Related Subjects.* tr. R.McL. Wilson. Philadelphia: Westminster, 1965.

Hollander, H.W. and M.De Jonge. *The Testaments of the Twelve Patriarchs: A Commentary.* SVTP 8; Leiden: Brill, 1985.

Horsley, G.H.R., ed. *New Documents Illustrating Early Christianity.* Macquarie University: Ancient History Documentary Research Centre, 1981-9. 5 volumes.

Hunt, A.S. and C.C. Edgar. *Select Papyri: Volume 2 Official Documents.* LCL; London: William Heinemann/Cambridge: HUP, 1934.

Jerome. *Lives of Illustrious Men.* In *A Select Library of Nicene and Post-Nicene Fathers of the Early Christian Church.* ed. tr. H. Wace, P. Schaff and E.C. Richardson. Oxford: James Parker/New York: Christian Literature Company, 1892. Series 2, volume 3.

Jones, A.H.M., ed. *A History of Rome Through the Fifth Century. Volume II: The Empire.* London/Melbourne: Macmillan, 1970.

Keenan, J.G. '12. Petition from a Prisoner: New Evidence on Ptolemy Philometor's Accession'. In *Collectanea Papyrologica: Texts Published in Honor of H. C. Youtie, Part One, Numbers 1-65.* ed. A.E. Hanson. Bonn: Rudolph Habelt, 1976. 91-102.

Lewis, N. and M. Reinhold, ed. tr. *Roman Civilization. Sourcebook I: The Republic.* New York: Harper and Row, 1966.

Lewis, N. and M. Reinhold, ed. tr. *Roman Civilization. Sourcebook II: The Empire.* New York: Harper and Row, 1966.

Lipsius, R.A. and M. Bonnett, ed. *Acta Apostolorvm Apocrypha.* Lipsiae: Hermannvm Mendelssohn, 1891, 1898, 1903. 3 volumes.

The Loeb Classical Library. London: William Heinemann/New York: G.P. Putnam's Sons/Cambridge, Mass.: HUP, various dates.

Meyer, P.M. *Juristische Papyri: Erklärung von Urkunden zur Einführung in die juristische Papyruskunde.* Berlin: Weidmannsche Buchhandlung, 1920.

Mitteis, L. and U. Wilcken. *Grundzüge und Chrestomathie der Papyruskunde.* Leipzig/Berlin: B.G. Teubner, 1912.

Moulton, J.H. and G.Milligan. *The Vocabulary of the Greek Testament Illustrated from the Papyri and Other Non-Literary Sources.* London: Hodder and Stoughton, 1930.

Musurillo, H. *The Acts of the Christian Martyrs: Introduction Texts and Translations.* Oxford: Clarendon, 1972.

Musurillo, H.A. *The Acts of the Pagan Martyrs: Acta Alexandrinorum.* Oxford: Clarendon, 1954.

Oehler, F., ed. *Quninti Septimii Florentis Tertulliani Quae Supersunt Omnia*. Lipsiae: T.O. Weigel, 1853. Tomus 1.

Origen. *Origen: An Exhortation to Martyrdom, Prayer First Principles: Book IV, Prologue to the Commentary on the Song of Songs, Homily XXVII on Numbers. The Classics of Western Spirituality*. tr. ed. R.A. Greer. London: SPCK, 1979.

Paulus, Julius. *Sententiae*. Cited in Riccobono, S. *et al.*, ed. *Fontes Iuris Romani Antejustiniani*. Volume 18. Florentiae: S.A.G. Barbèra, 1940. eng. tr. Scott, S.P. *The Civil Law*. (Cincinnati: Central Trust Company, 1932) volume 1.

Petronius, *The Satyricon*. ed. E.T. Sage. Century College Latin Series; New York/London: Century, 1929.

PHI Demonstration CD ROM: #1. © *The Packard Humanities Institute, University of Pennsylvania*, 1987. Contents: (1) PHI Latin Texts (partially corrected); (2) CCAT Biblical Materials, University of Pennsylvania.

PHI Demonstration CD ROM: #2. © *The Packard Humanities Institute, University of Pennsylvania*, 1988. Contents: Duke Data Bank of Documentary Papyri, Duke University.

Die Pseudoklementinen: II. Rekognitionen in Rufins Übersetzung. ed. B. Rehm. Berlin: Deutsche Akademie der Wissenschaften, 1965.

Fontes Iuris Romani Anteiustiniani. ed. S. Roccobono *et al.* Florentiae: S.A.G. Barbèra, 1940-43. 3 volumes.

Inscriptiones Latinae Selectae. ed. H. Dessau. Berolini: Apud Weidmannos, 1892-1916. 3 volumes in 5 parts.

Keenan, J.G. '12. Petition from a Prisoner: New Evidence on Ptolemy Philometor's Accession'. In *Collectanea Papyrologica: Texts Published in Honor of H.C. Youtie, Part One, Numbers 1-65*. ed. A.E. Hanson. Bonn: Rudolph Habelt, 1976. 91-102.

Rahlfs, A., ed. *Septuaginta*. Stuttgart: Deutsche Bibelstiftung, 1935. 2 volumes.

Roberts, A. and J. Donaldson, ed. *Ante-Nicene Library: Translations of the Writing of The Fathers Down to A.D. 325: Volume 11 The Writings of Tertullian - Volume 1*. Edinburgh: T. and T. Clark, 1869.

Roberts, A. and J. Donaldson, ed. *Ante-Nicene Library: Translations of the Writing of The Fathers Down to A.D. 325: Volume 18 The Writings of Tertullian - Volume 3*. Edinburgh: T. and T. Clark, 1870.

Scott, S.P. *The Civil Law*. Cincinnati: Central Trust, 1932.

Smith, R., tr. *The Greek Romances of Heliodorus, Longus and Achilles Tatius*. London: Henry G. Bohn, 1855.

Saint Cyprien Correspondance, Tome 1. tr. L. Bayard. Paris: Guillaume Budé, 1925.

The Theodosian Code and Novels and the Sirmondian Constitutions. tr. ed. C. Pharr *et al.* Princeton: PUP, 1952.

Thesaurus Linguae Graecae Pilot CD ROM #C. ©*Thesaurus Linguae Graecae*, University of California, Irvine, 1987.

Valerius Maximus. *Factorum et Dictorum Memorabilium*. ed. C. Kempf. Lipsiae: Teubner, 1888.

The Writings of Cyprian, Bishop of Carthage. In *Ante-Nicene Christian Library: Translations of the Writings of the Fathers Down to A.D. 325*. tr. R.E. Wallis. Edinburgh: T. and T. Clark, 1870. Volume 8.

Selected Bibliography

Adinolfi, M. 'San Paolo á Pozzuoli (Atti 28, 13b-14b)'. *RBib* VIII/3 (1960), 206-24.

Alexander, L. 'Luke's Preface in the Context of Greek Preface-Writing'. *NovT* 28 (1986), 48-74.

Alexander, L.C.A. 'Christians as Outsiders: Some Functions of a Political Metaphor'. Sheffield: British New Testament Conference, 13 Sept. 1991 [Lecture].

Anderson, W.C.F. 'Paenula'. *DGRA* 2:308-9

Applebaum, S. 'Chapter 8. The Legal Status of the Jewish Communities in the Diaspora'. In *Compendia*, vol. 1, 420-63.

Applebaum, S. 'Chapter 9. The Organization of the Jewish Communities in the the Diaspora'. In *Compendia*, vol. 1, 464-503.

Arbandt, S., W. Macheiner and C. Colpe. 'Gefangenschaft'. *RAC* 9 (1976), 318-45.

Ashby, T. and P.K.B. Reynolds. 'The Castra Peregrinorum'. *JRS* 13 (1923), 152-67.

Aune, D.E. 'Review of H. I. Pervo, *Profit With Delight*'. *JRel* 69 (1989), 399-400.

Aune, D.E. *Prophecy in Early Christianity and the Ancient Mediterranean World*. Grand Rapids: Eerdmans, 1983.

Avi-Yonah, M. 'The Development of the Roman Road System in Palestine'. *IEJ* 1 (1950/1), 54-60.

Bagnani, G. 'Peregrinus Proteus and the Christians'. *Historia* 4 (1955), 107-12.

Baldwin, B. 'Crime and Criminals in Graeco-Roman Egypt'. *Aeg* 43 (1963), 256-63.

Ball, W.E. *St. Paul and the Roman Law and Other Studies on the Origin of the Form of Doctrine*. Edinburgh: T. and T. Clark, 1901.

Balsdon, J.P. 'Maiestas'. *OCD*, 640-41.

Balsdon, J.P. 'Vigiles'. *OCD*, 1120-21.

Barnes, T.B. *Tertullian: A Historical and Literary Study*. 1971; rev. Oxford: Clarendon, 1985.

Barnes, T.D. 'Legislation Against the Christians'. *JRS* 58 (1968), 32-50.

Barr, D.L. and J.L. Wentling. 'The Conventions of Classical Biography and the Genre of Luke-Acts: A Preliminary Study'. In *Luke-Acts: New Perspectives from the Society of Biblical Literature Seminar*. ed. C.H. Talbert. New York: Crossroad, 1984), 63-68.

Bartels, K.H. 'Song, Hymn, Psalm'. *NIDNTT*, vol. 3, 668-76.

Bartlet, J.V. *The Acts*. Century Bible [NT] 5; Edinburgh: T.C. and E.C. Clark, 1901.

Bartlet, V. 'Two New Testament Problems. I. St. Paul's Fate at Rome'. *Expositor* VIII/5 (1913), 464-67.

Bauernfeind, D.O. *Kommentar und Studien zur Apostelgeschichte*. ed. V. Metelmann. WUNT 22; Tübingen: Mohr, 1980.

Bauman, R.A. *Impietas in Principem: A Study of Treason Against the Roman Emperor With Special Reference to the First Century A.D.* MBPAR 67; München: C.H. Beck, 1974.

Bauman, R.A. *The Crimen Maiestatis in the Roman Republic and Augustan Principate*. Johannesburg: Witwatersrand University Press, 1967.

Beare, F.W. *The Epistle to the Philippians*. BNTC; 3rd. edn., London: A and C. Black, 1973.

Benko, S. *Pagan Rome and the Early Christians*. London: B.T. Batsford, 1984.

Benoit, P. 'The Archaeological Reconstruction of the Antonia Fortress'. In *Jerusalem Revealed: Archaeology in the Holy City 1968-1974*. tr. R. Grafman. Jerusalem: Israel Exploration Society/"Shikmona" Publishing, 1975. 87-89.

Berger, A. 'Prison'. *OCD*, 731.

Berger, A. 'Vigintisexviri'. *OCD*, 1121.

Berger, A. and B. Nicholas. 'Law and Procedure, Roman'. *OCD*, 583-90.

Bertram, G. 'φυλάσσω κτλ''. *TDNT*, vol. 9, 236-44.

Betz, H.D. 'Lucian von Samosata und das Christentum'. *NovT* 3 (1959), 226-37.

Bietenhard, H. 'People, Nation, Gentiles, Crowd, City'. *NIDNTT*, vol. 2, 788-805.

Blaiklock, E.M. 'Tarsus'. *IllBibD*, vol. 3, 1519.

Blaiklock, E.M. *The Acts of the Apostles*. TNTC; Grand Rapids: Eerdmans, 1959.

Bludau, A. 'Die Militärverhältnisse in Cäsarea im apostol. Zeitalter. Zur Apostelgeschichte 10:1; 27:1'. *Theologisch-praktische Monatsschrift* 17 (1907), 136-43.

Blue, B.B. *In Public and In Private: The Role of the House Church in Early Christianity*. University of Aberdeen: Unpublished PhD Thesis, 1989.

Blunt, A.W.F. *The Acts of the Apostles in the Revised Version*. Clarendon Bible 4; Oxford: Clarendon, 1922.

Brandis, C.A. 'Epictetus'. *DGRBM*, vol. 2, 31-33.

Brannick, V. *The House Church in the Writings of Paul*. Willmington, Deleware: Michael Glazier, 1989.

Breeze, D.J. 'The Career Structure Below the Centurionate'. *ANRW* II/1 (1974), 435-51.

Brewer, E. 'Roman Citizenship and Its Bearing on the Book of Acts'. *ResQ* 4 (1960), 205-19.

Broughton, T.R.S. 'Note 33. The Roman Army'. In *BC*, vol. 5, 427-45.

Brown, R.E. and Meyer, J.P. *Antioch and Rome*. Ramsey, N.J.: Paulist, 1983.

Bruce, F.F. 'Is the Paul of Acts the Real Paul?" *BJRL* 59 (1976), 282-305.

Bruce, F.F. 'St. Paul in Macedonia'. *BJRL* 61 (1978-79), 337-54.

Bruce, F.F. *New Testament History*. London: Thomas Nelson, 1969.

Bruce, F.F. *Paul: Apostle of the Free Spirit*. Exeter: Paternoster, 1977.

Bruce, F.F. *Philippians*. New International Biblical Commentary 11; Peadoby, Mass.: Hendrickson, 1989.

Bruce, F.F. *The Acts of the Apostles: Greek Text with Introduction and Commentary*. 1952; 3rd. rev. enl. ed.; Grand Rapids: Eerdmans/Leicester: Apollos, 1990.

Bruce, F.F. *The Book of the Acts*. NICNT; 1954; rev. ed. Grand Rapids: Eerdmans, 1988.

Bruce, F.F. *The Speeches in the Acts of the Apostles*. TNTL 1942; London: Tyndale, 1942.

Brunt, P.A. 'Charges of Provincial Maladministration Under the Early Principate'. Historia 10 (1961), 189-227.

Büchsel, F. 'βαστάζω'. *TDNT*, vol. 1, 596.

Bull, R.J. 'Caesarea Maritima--The Search for Herod's City'. *BAR* 8 (1982), 24-40.

Bunbury, E.H. 'Alba Fucensis or Fucentis'. *DGRG*, vol. 1, 86-87.

Burchard, C. *Der dreizehnte Zeuge: traditions- und kompositionsgeschichtliche Untersuchungen zu Lukas' Darstellung der Frühzeit des Paulus*. FRLANT 103; Göttingen: Vandenhoeck und Ruprecht, 1970.

Burton, H.F. 'Rome in Paul's Day'. *BW* 3 (1894), 87-96.

Busink, Th. A. *Der Tempel von Jerusalem von Salomo bis Herodes. Eine archäologisch-historiche Studie unter Berücksichtigung des westsemitischen Tempelbaus. 2 Band: Von Ezechiel bis Middot.* Leiden: Brill, 1980.

Cadbury, H.J. 'Lexical Notes on Luke-Acts II: Recent Arguments for Medical Language'. *JBL* 45 (1926), 190-209.

Cadbury, H.J. 'Lexical Notes on Luke-Acts III: Luke's Interest in Lodging'. *JBL* 45 (1926), 305-22.

Cadbury, H.J. 'Note 24. Dust and Garments'. In *BC*, vol. 5, 269-277.

Cadbury, H.J. 'Note 26. Roman Law and the Trial of Paul'. In *BC*, vol. 5, 297-338.

Cadbury, H.J. *The Book of Acts in History.* London: A. and C. Black, 1955.

Camp, J.M. *The Athenian Agora: Excavations in the Heart of Classical Athens.* New Aspects of Antiquity; London: Thames and Hudson, 1986.

Campbell, R.H. 'Social Gospel'. *NIDCC*, 911-12.

Carrez, M. 'L'appel de Paul a Cesar (Ac 25,11): La double appartenance, juive et chrétienne, de la première Église d'après le livre des Actes'. *MHC* (1981), 503-10.

Carson, R.A.G. *Principal Coins of the Romans. Volume 1: The Republic c. 290-31 BC.* London: British Museum Publications, 1978.

Cassidy, R.J. and J.S. Howson. *Political Issues in Luke-Acts.* Maryknoll, New York: Orbis, 1983.

Cassidy, R.J. *Society and Politics in the Acts of the Apostles.* Maryknoll, New York: Orbis, 1987.

Casson, L. *Ships and Seamanship in the Ancient World.* Princeton: PUP, 1971.

Casson, L. *Travel in the Ancient World.* London: George Allen and Unwin, 1974.

Chilton, C.W. 'The Roman Law of Treason Under the Early Principate'. *JRS* 45 (1955), 73-81.

Clark, A.C. *The Acts of the Apostles.* Oxford: Clarendon, 1933.

Clark, G. 'The Social Status of Paul'. *ExpTim* 96 (1984-85), 110-11.

Clarke, W.K.L. 'St Luke and the Pseudepigrapha: Two Parallels'. *JTS* 15 (1913/4), 597-99.

Coleman, R.T. *Paul's Prison Life.* Southern Baptist Theological Seminary, Louisville: Unpublished PhD. Dissertation, 1939.

Colin, J. 'Une affaire de tapage nocturne devant l'empereur Auguste." *Revue Belge de Philologie et d'Historie* 44 (1966), 21-24.

Collart, P. *Phillipes, ville de Macédoine, depuis ses origines jusqu'à la fin de lépoque romaine.* 'Coll. Travaux et Mémoires. École française d'Athènes'. fasc. 5. 2 tomes. Paris: E. de Boccard, 1938.

Connolly, R.H. 'Syricisms in St. Luke'. *JTS* 37 (1936), 374-85.

Conzelmann, H. *Acts of the Apostles: A Commentary on the Acts of the Apostles.* tr. J. Limburg *et al.* Hermeneia; tr. 2nd ed. 1972; Philadelphia: Fortress, 1987.

Corbett, P.B. *Petronius.* Twayne's World Authors Series 97; New York: Twayne, 1970.

Cosgrove, C.H. 'The Divine DEI in Luke-Acts'. *NovT* 26 (1984), 186-90.

Cranfield, C.E.B. *A Critical and Exegetical Commentary on the Epistle to the Romans.* ICC; Edinburgh: T. and T. Clark, 1975. Volume 1.

Crawford, M.H. *Roman Republican Coinage.* Cambridge: CUP, 1974. Volumes 1 and 2.

Creed, J.M. *The Gospel According to St. Luke.* London: Macmillan/New York: St. Martin's, 1965.

Crisler, J. 'Caesarea World Monument'. *BAR* 8 (1982), 41.

Croix, G.E.M.de Ste. 'Why Were the Early Christians Persecuted?" *Past and Present* 26 (1963), 6-38.

Croix, G.E.M.de Ste. 'Why Were the Early Christians Persecuted?--A Rejoinder'. Past and Present 27 (1964), 28-33.

Crump, D.M. *Jesus the Intercessor: Prayer and Christology in Luke-Acts.* University of Aberdeen: Unpublished PhD Dissertation, 1988.

Dabrowski, E. 'Le prétendu procès romain de S. Paul d'après les recherches récentes'. In *Studiorum Paulinorum Congressus Internationalis Catholicus.* Volume 2. AnBib 18; Rome: 1963. 197-205.

Daube, D.L. 'Shame Culture in Luke'. In *Paul and Paulinism: Essays in Honour of C.K. Barrett.* ed. M.D. Hooker and S.G. Wilson. London: SPCK, 1982. 355-72.

Dauvillier, J. 'A propos de la venue de saint Paul à Rome. Notes sur son procès et son voyage maritime'. *BLE* 61 (1960), 3-26.

Davies, P. 'The Ending of Acts'. *ExpTim* 94 (1983), 334-38.

Davies, P. 'The Macedonian Scene of Paul's Journeys (Acts 16s et 20)'. *BA* 26 (1963), 91-106.

Davies, S. 'Review of R. I. Pervo, *Profit With Delight'. CBQ* 51 (1989), 162-64.

Davies, W.D. *Paul and Rabbinic Judaism: Some Rabbinic Elements in Pauline Theology.* 1948; rev. edn., London: SPCK, 1955.

de Visscher, F. and F. de Ruyt. 'Les Fouilles d'Alba Fucens'. *L'Antiquité Classique* 20 (1951), 72-74.

Deissmann, A. 'Zur ephesinischen Gefangenschaft des Apostels Paulus'. In *Anatolian Studies Presented to Sir W. M. Ramsay,* ed. W.H. Buckler and W.M. Calder. Manchester: MUP, 1923. 121-27.

Deissmann, A. *St. Paul: A Study in Social and Religious History.* tr. L.R.M. Strachan. London: Hodder and Stoughton, 1912.

Delebecque, É. 'L'art du conte et la faute du tribun Lysias selon les deux versions des Actes (22,20-30)'. *LTP* 40 (1984), 217-25.

Delebecque, É. 'L'embarquement de Paul, captif, à Césarée, pour Rome (*Actes des Apôtres,* 27,1-2)'. *LTP* 39 (1983), 295-302.

Delebecque, É. 'Paul entre Juifs et Romains selon les deux versions de Act. XXVIII'. RevThom 84 (1984), 83-91.

Delebecque, É. 'Saint Paul avec ou sans le tribun Lysias en 58 à Césarée (Actes XXIV,6-8). Texte court ou texte long?" *RThom* 81 (1981), 426-34.

Delebecque, É. *Les Actes des Apotres.* Collection d'etudes Anciennes; Paris: Belles Lettres, 1982.

Delebecque, É. *Les Deux Actes des Apôtres.* Etudes bibliques Nouvelle serie 6; Paris: Gabalda, 1986.

Delling, G. 'ὕμνος, ὑμνέω, ψάλλω, ψαλμός". *TDNT,* vol. 8, 489-503.

Delling, G. 'Das letzte Wort der Apostelgeschichte'. *NovT* 15 (1973), 193-204.

Derrett, J.D.M. 'Law in the New Testament: The Palm Sunday Colt'. *NT* 13 (1971), 241-58.

Dessau, H. 'Der Name des Apostels Paulus'. *Hermes* 45 (1910), 347-68.

Dibelius, M. and W.G. Kümmel. *Paul.* tr. F. Clark. London/New York/Toronto: Longmans, Green, 1953.

Dodd, C.H. 'The Mind of Paul: II," in *New Testament Studies* (1934; rpt. Manchester: MUP, 1953), 83-128.

Dodds, E.R. *Euripides Bacchae: Edited with Introduction and Commentary*. 2nd. edn.; Oxford: Clarendon, 1960.

Douglas, J.D. and F.F. Bruce. 'Scourging, Scourge'. *IllBibD*, vol. 3, 1402-3.

Drane, J. *Introducing the New Testament*. Tring: Lion, 1986.

Duncan, G.S. 'VI. The Epistles of the Imprisonment in Recent Discussion'. *ExpTim* 46 (1934/5), 293-98.

Duncan, G.S. 'Were Paul's Imprisonment Epistles Written from Ephesus?" *ExpTim* 67 (1955/6), 163-66.

Duncan, G.S. *St. Paul's Ephesian Ministry: A Reconstruction with Special Reference to the Ephesian Origin of the Imprisonment Epistles*. London: Hodder and Stoughton, 1929.

Dupont, J. '*Aequitas romana*. Notes sur *Actes* 25, 16'. *RSR* 49 (1961), 354-85.

Dupont, J. 'La conclusion des Actes et son rapport à l'ensemble de l'ouvrage de Luc'. In *Les Actes des Apôtres....* ed. J. Kremer. BETL 48; Louvain, 1979. 359-404.

Dupont, J. *Les Actes des Apôtres*. Paris: Les Éditions du Cerf, 1964.

Edersheim, E. *Sketches of Jewish Social Life in the Days of Christ*. London: Religious Tract Society, 1876.

Edmundson, G. *The Church in Rome in the First Century. An Examination of Various Controverted Questions Relating to Its History, Chronology, Literature and Traditions*. Bampton Lectures 122; London: Longmans, Green, 1913.

Edwards, R.B. 'Review of R. I. Pervo, *Profit With Delight*'. *SJT* 42 (1989), 423-24.

Egli, E. 'Das römische Militär in der Apostelgeschichte'. *ZWT* 27 (1884), 10-22.

Ehrhardt, A. *The Acts of the Apostles: Ten Lectures*. Manchester: MUP, 1969.

Ehrman, A.Z. 'Sanhedrin'. *EncJud*, vol. 14, 839-40.

Eisenhut, W.von. 'Die römische Gefängnisstrafe'. *ANRW* I/2 (1972), 268-82.

Elliger, W. *Paulus in Griechenland: Philippi, Thessaloniki, Athen, Korinth*. Stuttgarter Bibelstudien, 92/93; Stuttgart: Verlag Katholisches Bibelwerk, 1978.

Ellis, E.E. 'Paul and His Co-Workers'. *NTS* 17 (1970/1), 437-52.

Ellis, E.E. *The Gospel of Luke*. NCBC; Grand Rapids: Eerdmans/London: Marshall, Morgan and Scott, 1974.

Enslin, M. S. 'Once Again, Luke and Paul'. *ZNW* 61 (1970), 253-71.

Enslin, M. S. 'Paul and Gamaliel'. *JR* 7 (1927), 360-75.

Ernst, J. *Das Evangelium Nach Lukas*. RNT; Regensburg: Friedrich Pustet, 1977.

Eulenstein, R. 'Die wundersame Befreiung des Petrus aus Todesgefahr, Acts 12,1-23. Ein Beispiel für die philologische Analyse einer neutesamentlichen Texteinheit'. *WD* 12 (1973), 43-69.

Evans, C.F. *Saint Luke*. TPI New Testament Commentaries; London: SCM/Philadelphia: Trinity Press International, 1990.

Feldman, L.H. *Josephus and Modern Scholarship (1937-1980)*. New York/Berlin: Walter de Gruyter, 1984.

Fiebiger, H.O. 'Frumentarii'. PW, vol. 7, 122-25.

Filson, F.V. 'Live Issues in the Acts'. *BR* 9 (1964), 26-37.

Filson, F.V. 'The Journey-Motif in Luke-Acts'. In *Apostolic History and the Gospel*. ed. W.W. Gasque and R.P. Martin. Exeter: Paternoster, 1970. 68-77.

Finegan, J. *The Archeology o f the New Testament: The Mediterranean World of the Early Christian Apostles*. Boulder, Col.: Westview/London: Croom Helm, 1981.

Fitzgerald, M. 'Part II: The Ship of Saint Paul--Comparative Archaeology'. *BA* 53 (1990), 31-39.

Fitzmyer, J.A. *The Gospel According to Luke (X-XXIV)*. AB 28A; London: Doubleday, 1985.

Flather, J.H. 'Compes'. *DGRA*, vol. 1, 523.

Foakes Jackson, F.J. *Josephus and the Jews: The Religion and History of the Jews as Explained by Flavius Josephus*. 1930; rpt., Grand Rapids: Baker, 1977.

Foakes-Jackson, F.J. *The Acts of the Apostles*. MNTC 5; London: Hodder and Stoughton, 1948.

Foerster, G. 'The Early History of Caesarea'. In *The Joint Expedition to Caesarea Maritima. Vol. 1. Studies in the History of Caesarea Maritima*. Missoula, Mont.: Scholars Press, 1975. 9-22.

Foerster, W. 'εἰρήνη κτλ.'.'. *TDNT*, vol. 5, 400-20.

Forbes, C. 'Comparison, Self-Praise and Irony: Paul's Boasting and the Conventions of Hellenistic Rhetoric'. *NTS* 32 (1986), 1-30.

Frend, W.H.C. 'A Third-Century Inscription Relating to *Angereia* in Phrygia'. *JRS* 46 (1956), 46-56.

Frey, J.B. 'Le judaïsme à Rom aux premiers temps de l'Eglise." *Biblica* 12 (1931), 129-56.

Freyne, S. '4. Bandits in Galilee: A Contribution to the Study of Social Conditions in First-Century Palestine'. In *The Social World of Formative Christianity and Judaism*, Neusner *et al.* Philadelphia: Fortress, 1988. 50-68.

Frier, B.W. 'The Rental Market in Early Imperial Rome'. *JRS* 67 (1977), 27-37.

Fuller, R.H. 'Review of R. I. Pervo, *Profit With Delight*. *RelS* 15 (1989), 160.

Gabba, E. 'True History and False History in Classical Antiquity'. *JRS* 71 (1981), 50-62.

Gager, J.G. 'Chapter 4. Religion and Social Class in the Early Roman Empire'. In *The Catacombs and the Colosseum: The Roman Empire as the Setting of Primitive Christianity*. ed. S. Benko and J.J. O'Rourke. Valley Forge: Judson, 1971. 99-120.

Garland, D.E. 'The Christian's Posture Towards Marriage and Celibacy: I Corinthians 7'. *RevExp* 80 (1983), 351-62.

Garnsey, P. '7: Urban Property Investment'. In *Sudies in Roman Property by the Cambridge University Research Seminar in Ancient History*. ed. M.I. Finley. Cambridge/London/New York/Melbourne: CUP, 1976. 123-36, 190-93.

Garnsey, P. 'Adultery Trials and the Survival of the Quaestiones in the Severan Age'. *JRS* 57 (1967), 56-60.

Garnsey, P. 'Appendix: Demolition of Houses and the Law'. In *Sudies in Roman Property by the Cambridge University Research Seminar in Ancient History*. ed. M.I. Finley. Cambridge/London/New York/Melbourne: CUP, 1976. 133-36, 191-93.

Garnsey, P. 'The Criminal Jurisdiction of Governors'. *JRS* 58 (1966), 51-59.

Garnsey, P. 'The *Lex Julia* and Appeal under the Empire'. *JRS* 56 (1966), 167-89.

Garnsey, P. 'VII. Legal Privilege in the Roman Empire'. In *Studies in Ancient Society*. ed. M.I. Finley. Past and Present Series 2; London/Boston: Routledge and Kegan Paul, 1974. 141-65.

Garnsey, P. *Social Status and Legal Privilege in the Roman Empire*. Oxford: Clarendon, 1970.

Geldenhuys, J.N. *Commentary on the Gospel of Luke*. New London Commentary on the New Testament; Edinburgh/London: Marshall, Morgan and Scott, 1950.

Georgi, W. 'Pauli Reisegefährten nach Rom'. *LW* 70 (1924), 186-94.

Gilchrist, J.M. 'On What Charge was St. Paul Brought to Rome?" *ExpTim* 78 (1966/7,) 264-66.

Grand, R. 'La prison et la notion d'Emprisonnement'. *Revue Historique de Droit Français et Étranger* 19 (1940-1), 58-87.

Grandjean, S. 'La dernière page du livre des Actes'. *LC* 9 (1906), 336-49.

Grant, M. *The Army of the Caesars*. London: Weidenfeld and Nicholson, 1974.

Grant, M. *The Jews in the Roman World*. London: Weidenfeld and Nicolson, 1973.

Gray, J.G. 'Roman Houses, in which Paul Preached the Kingdom of God'. *USQR* 15 (1903-4), 310-19.

Greenberg, M. 'Scourging'. *IDB*, vol. 4, 245-46.

Greenidge, A.H.J. 'The Porcian Coins and the Porcian Laws'. *ClassRev* 11 (1897), 437-40.

Greenidge, A.H.J. *The Legal Procedure of Cicero's Time*. Oxford: Clarendon, 1901.

Grudem, W. *The Gift of Prophecy in the New Testament and Today*. Eastbourne: Kingsway, 1988.

Grueber, H.A. *Coins of the Roman Republic in the British Museum*. London: British Museum Publications [William Clowes], 1910. Volumes 2 and 3.

Grundmann, W. 'δεῖ, δέον ἐστί'.'. *TDNT*, vol. 2, 21-25.

Grundmann, W. *Cities of Vesuvius: Pompeii and Herculaneum*. New York: Macmillan, 1971.

Gundry, R.H. *A Survey of the New Testament*. Exeter: Paternoster, 1970.

Gusman, P. *Pompei: The City, Its Life and Art*. tr. F. Simmonds and M. Jourdain. London: William Heinemann, 1900.

Guthrie, D. *New Testament Introduction* Downers Grove: IVP, 1970.

Hackett, J. 'Echoes of Euripides in Acts of the Apostles?" *ITQ* 23 (1956), 218-27.

Hackett, J. 'Echoes of the *Bacchae* in Acts of the Apostles?" *ITQ* 23 (1956), 350-66.

Haefeli, L. 'Cäsarea am Meer. Topographie und Geschichte der Stadt nach Josephus und Apostelgeschichte'. *Neutestamentliche Abhandlungen* 10/5 (1923).

Haenchen, E. ' "We" in Acts and the Itinerary'. *JTC* 1 (1965), 65-99.

Haenchen, E. *The Acts of the Apostles: A Commentary*. ed. tr. B. Noble *et al.* Oxford: Basil Blackwell, 1971.

Hagner, D.A. 'Pharisees'. *ZPEB*, vol. 4, 745-52.

Hahn, H.-C. 'Openness, Frankness, Boldness'. *NIDNTT* 2:734-7.

Hansack, E. 'Er lebte ... von seinem eigenen Einkommen (Apg 28,30)'. *BZ* 19 (1975), 249-53.

Hansack, E. 'Nochmals zu Apostelgeschichte 28,30. Erwiderung auf F. Saums kritische Anmerkungen'. *BZ* 21 (1977), 118-21.

Hanson, R.P.C. *The Acts*. New Clarendon Bible; Oxford: Clarendon, 1967.

Harnack, A. *The Mission and Expansion of Christianity in the First Three Centuries*. Tr. J. Moffatt. Theological Translation Library 19. London: Williams and Norgate/New York: G. P. Putnam's Sons, 1908.

Harnack, A. von. *The Acts of the Apostles*. tr. J.R. Wilkinson. Crown Theological Library 27; London: Williams and Norgate/New York: G.P. Putnam's Sons, 1909.

Harrison, E.F. 'Acts 22:3 -- A Test Case for Luke's Reliability'. In *New Dimensions in New Testament Study*. ed. R.N. Longenecker and M.C. Tenney. Grand Rapids: Zondervan, 1974. 251-60.

Hastings, J. *The Acts of the Apostles*. 2 volumes; Speaker's Bible; Aberdeen: Speaker's Bible, 1927-28.

Hauser, H.J. *Strukturen der Abschlusserzahlung der Apostelgeschichte (Apg 28, 16-31)*. AnBib 86; Rome: Biblical Institute P., 1979.

Haverfield, F. 'On the stratjgoí of Philippi." *JTS* 1 (1899-1900), 434-35.

Hawthorne, G.F. *Philippians*. Word Biblical Commentary 43; Waco: Word, 1983.

Hemer, C.J. 'First Person Narrative in Acts 27-28'. *TynBul* 36 (1985), 79-109.

Hemer, C.J. 'Tarsus'. *ISBE*, vol. 4, 734-36.

Hemer, C.J. 'The Name of Paul." *TynBul* 36 (1985), 179-183.

Hemer, C.J. *The Book of Acts in the Setting of Hellenistic History*. ed. C.H. Gempf. WUNT 49; Tübingen: J.C.B. Mohr/Paul Siebeck, 1989.

Hengel, M. *Acts and the History of Earliest Christianity*. tr. J. Bowden. London: SCM, 1979.

Hengel, M. and C. Markschies. *The 'Hellenization' of Judaea in the First Century After Christ*. tr. J. Bowden. London: SCM/Philadelphia: Trinity Press International, 1989.

Hengel, M. *Between Jesus and Paul: Studies in the Earliest History of Christianity*. tr. J. Bowden. London: SCM, 1983.

Hermesdorf, B.H.D. 'Paulus Vinctus'. *StudCath* 29 (1954), 120-33.

Hervey, A.C. *The Acts of the Apostles*. Volume 2; Pulpit Commentary; London: Kegan Paul, Trench, 1884.

Hicks, E.L. 'Did St. Paul Write from Caesarea?" *Int* 6 (1909/10), 241-53.

Hicks, E.L. 'Philip the Evangelist and the Epistle to the Hebrews'. *Int* 5 (1908/9), 245-65.

Hill, D. *New Testament Prophecy*. Marshall's Theological Library; London: Marshall, Morgan and Scott, 1979.

Hirschfeld, N. 'Part I: The Ship of Saint Paul--Historical Background'. *BA* 53 (1990), 25-30.

Hirschfeld, O. '39. Die Sicherheitspolizei im römischen Kaiserreich (1891)'. In *Kleine Schriften von Otto Hirschfeld*. Berlin: Weidmannsche Buchhandlung, 1913. 576-612.

Hirschfeld, O. '40. Die ägyptische Polizei der römischen Kaiserzeit nach Papyrusurkunden (1892)'. In *Kleine Schriften von Otto Hirschfeld*. Berlin: Weidmannsche Buchhandlung, 1913. 576-612.

Hitchcock, F.R.M. 'The Pastorals and a Second Trial for Paul." *ExpTim* 41 (1929/30), 22-23.

Hitzig, F.H. 'Carcer 1)'. PW, vol. 3, 1576-81.

Hitzig, F.H. 'Custodia'. PW, vol. 4, 1896-99.

Hock, R.F. 'Paul's Tentmaking and the Problem of His Social Class'. *JBL* 97 (1978), 555-64.

Hock, R.F. *The Social Context of Paul's Ministry: Tentmaking and Apostleship*. Philadelphia: Fortress, 1980.

Hohlfelder, R.L. 'Caesarea Beneath the Sea'. *BAR* 8 (1982), 42-47.

Hohlfelder, R.L. *et al.* 'Sebastos, Herod's Harbour at Caesarea Maritima'. *BA* 46 (1983), 133-43.

Hollander, H.W. *Joseph as an Ethical Model in the Testaments of the Twelve Patriarchs*. SVTP 6; Leiden: Brill, 1981.

Horsley, R.A. and J.S. Hanson. *Bandits, Prophets and Messiahs: Popular Movements at the Time of Jesus*. New Voices in Biblical Studies; San Fransico: Harper and Row, 1985.

Hubbard, B.J. 'The Role of Commissioning Accounts in Acts'. In *Perspectives on Luke-Acts*. ed. C.H. Talbert. Danvilee, VA: Association of Baptist Professors of Religion/Edinburgh: T. and T. Clark, 1978. 187-98.

Hülsen, Chr. 'Carcer 2)'. PW, vol. 3, 1581-82.

Hülsen, Chr. *Das Forum Romanum Seine Geschichte und Seins Denkmäler*. Rom: Verlag von Loescher, 1904.

Hülsen, Chr. *Forum und Palatin*. München: Drei Masken Verlag, 1926.

Hultgren, A.J. 'Paul's Pre-Christian Persecutions of the Church: Their Purpose, Locale, and Nature'. *JBL* 95 (1976), 97-111.

Hunter, J.D. *Evangelicalism: The Coming Generation*. Chicago/London: CUP, 1987.

Hunter, W.A. *A Systematic and Historical Exposition of Roman Law in the Order of a Code*. 2nd. edn. rev.; London: William Maxwell and Son, 1885.

Hunter, W.A. *Introduction to Roman Law*. London: William Maxwell and Son, 1885.

Jacquier, E. *Les Actes des Apotres*. Paris, 1926.

James, E.B. 'Macedonia'. *DGRG*, vol. 2, 233-37.

Jeremias, J. ' Ἐν ἐκείνῃ τῇ ὥρᾳ, (ἐν) αὐτῇ τῇ ὥρᾳ'. ZNW42 (1949), 214-17.

Jeremias, J. 'Paulus als Hillelit'. In *Neotestamentica et Semitica: Studies in Honour of Matthew Black*. ed. E.E. Ellis and M. Wilcox. Edinburgh: T. and T. Clark, 1969. 88-94.

Jeremias, J. *Jerusalem in the Time of Jesus: An Investigation into Economic and Social Conditions During the New Testament Period*. tr. F.H. and C.H. Cave. London: SCM, 1969.

Jervell, J. *The Unknown Paul: Essays on Luke-Acts and Early Christian History*. Minneapolis: Augsburg, 1984.

Jewett, R. *Dating Paul's Life*. London: SCM, 1979. [=A *Chronology of Paul's Life*. Philadelphia: Fortress, 1979].

Johnson, L. 'The Pauline Letters from Caesarea'. *ExpTim* 68 (1956-57), 24-26.

Johnson, S.E. 'Caesarea Maritima'. *LTQ* 20 (1985), 28-32.

Jones, A.H.M. 'I Appeal Unto Caesar'. In *Studies in Roman Government and Law*. Oxford: Basil Blackwell, 1960. 51-65.

Jones, A.H.M. 'Imperial and Senatorial Jurisdiction in the Early Principate. In *Studies in Roman Government and Law*. Oxford: Basil Blackwell, 1960. 69-98. [Also in *Historia* 3 (1955), 464-88.]

Jones, A.H.M. 'The Roman Civil Service (Clerical and Sub-Clerical Grades)'. In *Studies in Roman Government and Law*. Oxford: Basil Blackwell, 1960. 151-75. [Also in *JRS* 39 (1949), 38-55.]

Jones, A.H.M. 'The Roman Civil Service (Clerical and Sub-Clerical Grades)'. *JRS* 39 (1949), 38-55.

Jones, A.H.M. *A History of Rome Through the Fifth Century. Volume I: The Republic*. The Documentary History of Western Civilization; New York: Harper, 1968.

Jones, A.H.M. *A History of Rome Through the Fifth Century. Volume II: Empire.* The Documentary History of Western Civilization; London/Melbourne: Macmillan, 1970.

Jones, A.H.M. *The Criminal Courts of the Roman Republic and Principate.* ed. J.A. Crook. Oxford: Basil Blackwell, 1972.

Jones, A.H.M. *The Greek City from Alexander to Justinian.* Oxford: Clarendon, 1940.

Jones, B.W. and R.D. Milns. *The Use of Documentary Evidence in the Study of Roman Imperial History.* Sources in Ancient History 5; Sydney: SUP, 1984.

Jones, H.S. *Companion to Roman History.* Oxford: Clarendon, 1912.

Judge, E.A. 'Cultural Conformity and Innovation in Paul: Some Clues from Contemporary Documents'. *TynBul* 35 (1984), 3-24.

Judge, E.A. 'Papyrus Documentation of Church and Community in Egypt to the Mid-Fourth Century'. *JAC* 20 (1977), 47-71.

Judge, E.A. 'St. Paul and Classical Society'. *JAC* 15 (1972), 19-36.

Judge, E.A. *Rank and Status in the World of the Caesars and St. Paul.* Broadhead Memorial Lecture 1981/University of Canterbury Publications 29; Christchurch, New Zealand: University of Canterbury, 1982.

Judge, E.A. *The Conversion of Rome.* North Ryde, Australia: Macquarie University Ancient History Association, 1980.

Judge, E.A. *The Social Pattern of Christian Groups in the First Century.* London: Tyndale, 1960.

Juster, J. *Les Juifs dans l'Empire romain. Leur condition juridique, économique et sociale.* Paris: Paul Geunthner, 1914. 2 volumes.

Kany, R. 'Der lukanische Bericht von Tod und Auferstehung Jesu aus der Sicht eines hellenistischen Romanlesers'. *NovT* 28 (1986), 75-90.

Kaye, B. 'The New Testament and Social Order'. In *Law, Morality and the Bible.* ed. B. Kaye and G. Wenham. Downers Grove: IVP, 1987.

Kee, H.C. and F.W. Young. *The Living World of the New Testament.* London: Darton, Longman and Todd, 1960.

Kee, H.C. *Understanding the New Testament.* Englewood Cliffs, NJ: Prentice-Hall, 1957.

Keinath, H.O.A. 'The Contacts of the Book of Acts with Roman Political Institutions'. *CTM* 1 (1930), 117-23, 191-9.

Kelly, J.M. *Roman Litigation.* Oxford: Clarendon, 1966.

Kelso, J.L. 'Paul's Roman Citizenship as Reflected in his Missionary Experiences and his Letters'. *BSac* 79 (1922), 173-83.

Kelso, J.L. 'The Roman Influence in the New Testament'. *BS* 79 (1922), 310-20.

Kilgallen, J.J. 'Paul Before Agrippa (Acts 26:2-23): Some Considerations'. *Bib* 69 (1988), 170-95.

Kilpatrick, G.D. 'Acts XXIII. 23 DEXIOLABOI." *JTS* 14 (1963), 393-94.

Knoch, O. *Die »Testamente« des Petrus un Paulus: Die Sicherung der apostolischen Überlieferung in der spätneutestamentlichen Zeit.* SBS 62; Stuttgart: KBW, 1973.

Knowling, R.J. *The Acts of the Apostles.* ed. W.R. Nicoll. Expositor's Greek Testament 2; 1901; rpt. Grand Rapids: Eerdmans, 1983.

Knox, W.L. *The Acts of the Apostles.* Cambridge: CUP, 1948.

Koet, B.-J. 'Paul in Rome (Acts 28:16-31): A Farewell to Judaism?" *Bijdragen* 48 (1987), 397-415.

Kraabel, A.T. 'Paganism and Judaism: The Sardis Evidence'. *Paganisme, Judaïsme, Christianisme: Mélanges Offerts à Marcel Simon*. ed. A. Benoit *et al.* Paris: E.De Boccard, 1978. 13-33.

Krauss, F.A.K. *Die Gefangenen und die Verbrecher unter dem Einfluss des Christenthums. Geschichtlicher Ueberblick, umfassend die ersten siebzehn Jahrhunderte.* Blätter für Gefängnisskunde, 25 (1889) 1-95. [Heidelberg: G. Weiss, 1889.]

Krauss, F.A.K. *Im Kerker vor und nach Christus. Schatten und Licht aus den profanen und kirchlichen Culture = und Rechtsleben vergang.* Tübingen: J.C.B. Mohr, 1895.

Kremer, J. *Lukasevangelium*. Neue Echter Bibel 3; Würzburg: Echter Verlag, 1988.

Kremer, J., ed. *Les Actes des Apotres: Traditions, Redaction, Theologie.* BETL 48; Gemloux: Duculot, 1979.

Krodel, G. A. *Acts*. Minneapolis: Augsburg, 1986.

Kunkel, W. *An Introduction to Roman Legal and Constitutional History.* tr. J.M. Kelly. Oxford: 1966.

Ladoucer, D. 'Hellenistic Preconceptions of Shipwrecks and Pollution as a Context for Acts 27-28'. *HTR* 73 (1980), 435-49.

Lake, K. 'Note 34. The Chronology of Acts'. In *BC*, vol. 5, 445-74.

Lake, K. 'Note 35. Localities in and Near Jerusalem Mentioned in Acts'. In *BC*, vol. 5, 474-86.

Lake, K. and H.J. Cadbury. *The Acts of the Apostles: English Translation and Commentary.* In *BC*, vol. 4.

Lanciani, R. *The Ruins and Excavations of Ancient Rome.* London: Macmillan, 1897.

le Gall, J. 'Notes sur les prisons de Rome à l'époque républicaine'. *MAH* 56 (1939), 60-80.

Leaney, A.R.C. *The Gospel According to St. Luke.* BNTC; 2nd edn.; London: A. and C. Black, 1966.

Leary, T.J. 'The "Aprons" of St Paul--Acts 19:12'. *JTS* n. s. 41 (1990), 527-29.

LeBlant, E. *Les Persécuteurs et les Martyrs aux Premiers Siècles de Notre `Ere.* Paris: Ernest Leroux, 1893.

Lemerle, P. *Philippes et la Macédoine orientale à lépoque chrétienne et byzantine. Recherches d'histoire et d'archéologie.* 'Bibliothèque des Écoles Françaises d'Athènes et de Rome'. fasc. 158. 2 tomes. Paris: E. de Boccard, 1945.

Lenski, G.E. 'Status Crystallization: A Non-Vertical Dimension of Social Status'. American Sociological Review 19 (1954), 405-13.

Lenski, R.C.H. *The Interpretation of the Acts of the Apostles.* 1934; rpt., Minneapolis: Augsburg, 1961.

Lentz, J.C.Jr. *Luke's Portrait of Paul.* SNTSMS 77; Cambridge: CUP, 1993.

Leon, H.J. *The Jews of Ancient Rome.* Morris Loeb Series 5; Philadelphia: Jewish Publication Society of America, 1960.

Levick, B. *Tiberius the Politician.* Aspects of Greek and Roman Life; London: Thames and Hudson, 1976.

Levine, L.I. *Caesarea Under Roman Rule.* Studies in Judaism in Late Antiquity 7; Leiden: Brill, 1975.

Lewis, N. *Life in Egypt Under Roman Rule.* Oxford: Clarendon, 1983.

Liebeschuetz, J.H.W.G. *Antioch: City and Imperial Administration in the Later Roman Empire.* Oxford: Clarendon, 1972.

Lifshitz, B. 'Césarée de Palestine, son Histoire et ses Institutions'. *ANRW* II/8 (1977), 490-518.

Lightfoot, J.B. *Saint Paul's Epistle to the Philippians.* 1913; rpt. Grand Rapids: Zondervan, 1953.

Lintott, A.W. 'Provocatio. From the Struggle of the Orders to the Principate'. *ANRW* I/2 (1972), 226-67.

Lisco, H. *Vincula Sanctorum: Ein Beitrag zur Erklärung der Gefangenschaftsbriefe des Apostels Paulus.* Berlin: Schneider/Klinsmann, 1900.

Lohfink, G. '«Meiner Namen zu tragen...» (Apg 9,15)'. *BZ* n.s. 10 (1966), 10.

Lohse, E. *Colossians and Philemon: A Commentary on the Epistles to the Colossians and to Philemon.* tr. W.R. Poehlmann and R.J. Karris. Hermeneia; Philadelphia: Fortress, 1971.

Loisy, A. *L'Évangile Selon Luc.* 1924; rpt., Frankfurt: Minerva, 1971.

Longenecker, R.N. 'The Acts of the Apostles'. Volume 9, *The Expositor's Bible Commentary.* ed. F.E. Gaebelein. Grand Rapids: Zondervan, 1981.

Lopuszanski, G. 'La Police Romaine et les Chrétiens'. *AntCl* 20 (1951), 5-46.

Lüdemann, G. *Early Christianity According to the Traditions in Acts: A Commentary.* tr. J. Bowden. London: SCM, 1987.

Lüdemann, G. *Early Christianity According to the Traditions in Acts: A Commentary.* tr. J. Bowden. London: SCM, 1989.

Luedemann, G. '8. The Acts of the Apostles as a Historical Source'. In *The Social World of Formative Christianity and Judaism.* ed. J. Neusner et al. Philadelphia: Fortress, 1988. 109-111.

Lumby, J.R. *The Acts of the Apostles With Maps, Introduction and Notes.* Cambridge Bible for Schools and Colleges, 54; 1882; rpt. Cambridge: CUP, 1904.

Maccoby, H. *Judaism in the First Century.* Issues in Religious Studies; London: Sheldon Press, 1989.

MacDowell, D.M. 'Hendeka'. *OCD,* 496.

Macgregor, G.H.C. [Intro and Exegesis] and T.P. Ferris [Exposition]. *The Acts of the Apostles.* Volume 9; Interpreter's Bible; New York: Abingdon, 1954. 1-352.

MacMullen, R. *Enemies of the Roman Order: Treason, Unrest and Alienation in the Empire.* Cambridge, Mass.: HUP/London: OUP, 1967.

MacMullen, R. *Roman Social Relations, 50 B.C. to A.D. 284.* New Haven/London: Yale University Press, 1974.

Maddox, R. *The Purpose of Luke-Acts.* FRLANT 126; Göttingen: Vandenhoeck and Ruprecht, 1982.

Maigret, J. 'Paul, prisonnier à Césarée'. *Bible et Terre Sainte* 41 (1961), 3-4.

Malina, B.J. 'Conflict in Luke-Acts: Labelling and Deviance Theory'. in *The Social World of Luke-Acts: Models for Interpretation.* ed. J.H. Neyrey. Peabody, Mass.: Hendrickson, 1991. 97-122.

Malina, B.J. 'First-Century Personality: Dyadic, Not Individualistic'. in *The Social World of Luke-Acts: Models for Interpretation.* ed. J.H. Neyrey. Peabody, Mass.: Hendrickson, 1991. 67-96.

Malina, B.J. and J.H. Neyrey. 'Honor and Shame in Luke-Acts: Pivotal Values of the Mediterranean World'. in *The Social World of Luke-Acts: Models for Interpretation.* ed. J.H. Neyrey. Peabody, Mass.: Hendrickson, 1991. 25-65.

Malina, B.J. *The New Testament World: Insights from Cultural Anthropology.* Atlanta: John Knox, 1981.

Manson, T.W. 'Sadducee and Pharisee -- The Origin and Significance of the Names'. *BJRL* 22 (1938), 144-59.

Manson, T.W. *The Sayings of Jesus*. London: SMC, 1949.

Manson, W. *The Gospel of Luke*. MNTC; London: Hodder and Stoughton, 1930.

Mantel, H. 'Sanhedrin'. *EncJud*, vol. 14, 836-39.

Marindin, G. E. 'Nervus'. *DGRA*, vol. 2, 228-29.

Marrow, S.B. '*Parrhēsia* and the New Testament'. *CBQ* 44 (1982), 431-46.

Marshall, I.H. 'Apg. 12 - ein Schlüssel zum Verständnis der Apostelgeschichte'. In Das Petrusbild in der neueren Forschung. ed. C.P. Tiede. Wuppertal, 1987. 192-220.

Marshall, I.H. *Luke: Historian and Theologian*. 1970; rev. ed., Exeter: Paternoster, 1988.

Marshall, I.H. *The Acts of the Apostles*. TNTC 5; Grand Rapids: Eerdmans, 1980.

Marshall, I.H. *The Gospel of Luke: A Commentary on the Greek Text*. New International Greek Testament Commentary; Exeter: Paternoster, 1978.

Marshall, T.H. *Citizenship and Social Class and Other Essays*. Cambridge: CUP, 1950.

Mason, A.J. *The Historic Martyrs of the Primitive Church*. London: Longmans, Green, 1905.

Mattill, A.J.Jr. 'The Value of Acts as a Source for the Study of Paul'. In *Perspectives on Luke-Acts*. ed. C.H. Talbert. Edinburgh: T. and T. Clark, 1978. 76-98.

Maxey, M. *Occupations of the Lower Classes in Roman Society*. [Chicago: CUP, 1938]. In *Two Studies on the Roman Lower Classes*. M.E. Park and M. Maxey. Roman History; New York: Arno, 1975.

Mayer-Maly, Th. 'Carcer'. In *Der Kleine Pauly*. ed. K. Ziegler and W. Sontheimer. Volume 1. Stuttgart: Alfred Druckenmüller, 1964. 1053-52.

Mazar, B. 'Les Fouilles au S. et S.O. du Mont du Temple'. *MB* 13 (1980), 20-28.

McKay, A.G. *Houses, Villas and Palaces in the Roman World*. Aspects of Greek and Roman Life; Southampton: Thames and Hudson, 1975.

McKelvey, R.J. 'Temple'. *IllBibD*, vol. 3, 1522-32.

Mealand, D.L. 'The Close of Acts and Its Hellenistic Greek Vocabulary'. *NTS* 36 (1990) 583-97.

Meeks, W.A. and R.L. Wilken. *Jews and Christians in the First Four Centuries of the Common Era*. SBLSB 13; Missoula: Scholars, 1978.

Meeks, W.A. *The First Urban Christians: The Social World of the Apostle Paul*. New Haven/London: Yale University Press, 1983.

Meiggs, R. *Roman Ostia*. 2nd. edn.; Oxford: Clarendon, 1973.

Meyer, R. and P. Katz. "ὄχλος'.'. *TDNT*, vol. 5, 582-90.

Michaelis, W. 'πάσχω κτλ'.'. *TDNT*, vol. 5, 904-39.

Michaelis, W. 'σκηνή κτλ'.'. *TDNT*, vol. 7, 393.

Michaelis, W. *Die Gefangenschaft des Paulus in Ephesus und das Itinerar des Timotheus*. NTF 1/3; Gütersloh: Schmitz, 1925.

Michel, O. 'οἶκος κτλ'.'. *TDNT*, vol. 5, 119-59.

Middleton, J.H. and W. Smith. 'Domus'. *DGRA*, vol. 1, 654-87.

Middleton, J.H. *The Remains of Ancient Rome*. London/Edinburgh: A. and C. Black, 1892. Volume 1.

Miles, G.B. and G. Trompf. 'Luke and Antiphon: The Theology of Acts 27-28 in the Light of Pagan Beliefs about Divine Retribution, Pollution, and Shipwreck'. HTR 69 (1976), 259-67.

Milgrom, J. 'Of Hems and Tassels'. BARev 9 (1983), 61-65.

Millar, F. 'Emperors at Work'. JRS 57 (1967), 9-19.

Millar, F. 'The Emperor, the Senate, and the Provinces'. JRS 56 (1966), 156-66.

Millar, F. 'The World of the Golden Ass'. JRS 71 (1981), 63-75.

Mitchell, S. 'Requisitioned Transport in the Roman Empire: A New Inscription from Pisidia'. JRS 66 (1976), 106-31 and pl. 8-10.

Mitford, T.B. 'Roman Rough Cilicia'. ANRW II/7.2 (1980), 1235

Moessner, D.P. '"The Christ Must Suffer": New Light on the Jesus-Peter, Stephen, Paul Parallels in Luke-Acts'. NovT 28 (1986), 220-56.

Moffatt, J. 'Exegetica. Acts 16:25'. Exp VIII/7 (1914), 89-96.

Mommsen, Th. 'Die Rechtsverhältnisse des Apostels Paulus'. ZNW 2 (1901), 81-96.

Mommsen, Th. Le Droit Pénal Romain. tr. J. Duquesne. Manuel des Antiquités Romaines, 17-19; Paris: Ancienne Librairie Thorin et Fils, Albert Fontemoing, 1907. [From the original Römisches Strafrecht. Leipzig: 1899.]

Mommsen, Th. Römisches Staatsrecht. Handbuch der römischen Alterthümer; Leipzig: S. Hirzel, 1887-88. 3 volumes in 5 parts.

Montefiore, C.G. The Synoptic Gospels. Library of Biblical Studies; 2nd. edn. rev.; New York: KTAV, 1968. 2 volumes.

Moore, G.F. Judaism in the First Centuries of the Christian Era: The Age of the Tannaim. Cambridge: Harvard University Press, 1927. Volume 1.

Mosley, A.W. 'Historical Reporting in the Ancient World'. NTS 12 (1965/6), 10-26.

Moxnes, H. 'Honor, Shame, and the Outside World in Paul's Letter to the Romans'. in The Social World of Formative Christianity and Judaism: Essays in Tribute to Howard Clark Kee. ed. J. Neusner et al. Philadelphia: Fortress, 1988. 207-18.

Muhlack, G. Die Parallelen von Lukas-Evangelium und Apostelgeschichte. Theologie und Wirklichkeit 8; Frankfurt am Main: Lang, 1979.

Munck, J. The Acts of the Apostles. rev. tr. W.F. Albright and C.S. Mann. AB 31; Garden City: Doubleday, 1967.

Mussies, G. 'Chapter 22. Greek in Palestine and the Diaspora'. In Compendia, vol. 2, 1040-64.

Nash, E. 'Carcer Mamertinus'. Pictorial Dictionary of Ancient Rome. London: A. Zwemmer/Tübingen: Ernst Wasmuth, 1961. 1:206-8.

Neil, W. The Acts of the Apostles. NCB 42; London: Oliphants/Greenwood: Attic, 1973.

Nestle, E. 'St. Paul's Handicraft: Acts xviii.3'. JBL 11 (1892), 205-6.

Nestle, E. 'The Aprons and Handkerchiefs of St. Paul'. ExpTim 13 (1901/2), 282.

Nestle, W. 'Ankläge an Euripides in der Apostelgeschichte'. Philologus 59 (1900), 46-57.

Neumann, K.J. 'Coercitio'. PW, vol. 4, 201-4.

Neusner, J. The Rabbinic Traditions About the Pharisees Before 70. Part 1: The Masters. Leiden: Brill, 1971.

New, S. 'Note 11. The Name, Baptism, and the Laying on of Hands'. In BC, vol. 5, 121-40.

Nickle, K.F. *The Collection: A Study in Paul's Strategy.* Studies in Bibilical Theology 48; London: SCM, 1966.

Nippel, W. 'Policing Rome'. *JRS* 74 (1984), 20-29.

Nock, A.D. *Essays on Religion and the Ancient World.* ed. Z. Steward. Oxford: Clarendon, 1972. Volume 2.

O'Reilly, L. *Word and Sign in the Acts of the Apostles: A Study in Lucan Theology.* Analecta Gregoriana 243; Roma: Editrice Pontificia U. Gregoriana, 1987.

Oliver, J.H. 'Greek Applications for Roman Trials'. *AJP* 100 (1979), 543-58.

Opelt, I. *Die lateinischen Schimpfwörter und verwandte sprachliche Erscheinungen: Eine Typologie.* Bibliothek der klassischen Altertumswissenschaften; Heidelberg: Carl Winter, 1965.

Orr, R.W. 'Paul's Voyage and Shipwreck'. *EvQ* 35 (1963), 103f.

Packer, J. 'Housing and Population in Imperial Ostia and Rome'. *JRS* 57 (1967), 80-95.

Packer, J.W. *Acts of the Apostles.* CBC 44; Cambridge: CUP, 1973.

Paton, L.B. 'Jerusalem in Bible Times. 12. Jerusalem in New Testament Times'. *The Biblical World* 30 (1907), 407-17.

Penna, A. 'La due prigionie romane di S. Paolo'. *RivistB* 9 (1961), 193-208.

Penna, R. 'Les Juifs à Rome au Temps de l'Apôtre Paul'. *NTS* 28 (1982), 321-347.

Perry, B.E. *The Ancient Romances: A Literary-Historical Account of Their Origins.* Sather Classical Lectures 37; Berkley/Los Angeles: UCP, 1967.

Pervo, R.I. *Profit With Delight: The Literary Genre of the Acts of the Apostles.* Philadelphia: Fortress, 1987.

Pesch, R. *Die Apostelgeschichte.* EKKNT 5; Zurich: Benziger, 1986. 2 volumes.

Peterlin, D. *Paul's Letter to the Philippians in the Light of Discord in the Church.* University of Aberdeen: Unpublished PhD. Dissertation, 1992.

Pfister, F. 'Die zweimalige römische Gefangenschaft und die spanische Reise des Apostles Paulus und der Schluss der Apostelgeschichte'. *ZNW* 14 (1913), 216-21.

Pherigo, L.P. 'Paul's Life After the Close of Acts'. *JBL* 70 (1951), 277-84.

Piana, G.La. 'Foreign Groups in Rome During the First Centuries of the Empire'. HTR 20 (1927), 383-403.

Pitch, A.S. 'Sharp Eyes Find Ancient Treasure on the Beach'. *BAR* 7 (1981), 48-51.

Platner, S.B. and T. Ashby. *A Topographical Dictionary of Ancient Rome.* Oxford: OUP/London: Umphrey Milford, 1929.

Plooij, D. 'Acts 28:14, 16'. *ExpTim* 24 (1912-3), 186.

Plumacher, E. *Lukas als hellenistischer Schriftsteller: Studien zur Apostelgeschichte.* SUNT 9; Göttingen: Vandenhoeck und Ruprecht, 1972.

Plummer, A. *The Gospel According to S. Luke.* ICC; Edinburgh: T. and T. Clark, 1896.

Pokor'ny, P. 'Die Romfahrt des Paulus und der antike Roman'. *ZNW* 64 (1973), 233-44.

Polhill, J.B. *Acts.* NAC 26; Nashville: Broadman, 1992.

Praeder, S. 'Acts 27:1-28:16: Sea Voyages in Ancient Literature and the Theology of Luke-Acts." *CBQ* 46 (1984), 683-706.

Prior, M. *Paul the Letter-Writer and the Second Letter to Timothy.* JSNTS suppl. ser. 23; Sheffield: JSOT, 1989.

Quinn, J.D. 'Seven Times He Wore Chains (1 Clem 5,6)'. *JBL* 97 (1978), 574-76.

Quinn, J.D. 'The Last Volume of Luke: The Relation of Luke-Acts to the Pastoral Epistles'. In *Perspectives in Luke-Acts*. ed. C.H. Talbert. Danville, Virginia: Association of Baptist Professors of Religion/Edinburgh: T. and T. Clark, 1978.

Rabello, A.M. 'The Legal Condition of the Jews in the Roman Empire'. *ANRW* II/13 (1980), 662-762.

Raber, R. 'Coercitio'. *KP*, vol. 1, 1240-41.

Rackham, R.B. *The Acts of the Apostles*. Westminster Commentaries 41; 7th ed. 1913; London: Methuen, 1951.

Radl, W. 'Befreiung aus dem Gefängnis. Die Darstellung eines biblischen Grundthemas in Apg 12'. *BZ* 27 (1983), 81-96.

Radl, W. *Paulus und Jesus im Lukanischen Doppelwerk: Untersuchungen zu Parallelmotiven im Lukasevangelium und in der Apostelgeschichte*. Europaische Hochschulschriften Reihe 23: Theologie 49; Bern: Lang, 1975.

Räisänen, H. *Paul and the Law*. WUNT 29; Tübingen: J.C.B. Mohr [Paul Siebeck], 1983.

Rajak, T. 'Was there a Roman Charter for the Jews?" *JRS* 74 (1984), 107-23.

Ramsay, W.M. 'Cornelius and the Italic Cohort'. *Expositor* V/4 (1896), 194-201.

Ramsay, W.M. 'Notes: The Philippians and Their Magistrates'. *JTS* 1 (1899-1900), 114-16.

Ramsay, W.M. 'Suggestions on the History and Letters of St. Paul. 2. The Imprisonment and Supposed Trial of St. Paul in Rome: Acts 28'. *Expositor* VIII/5 (1913), 264-84.

Ramsay, W.M. 'Tarsus'. *Expositor* VII/1 (1906), 258-77, 353-69, 453-70.

Ramsay, W.M. 'Tarsus'. *Expositor* VII/2 (1906), 29-47, 135-160, 268-288, 365-384.

Ramsay, W.M. *St. Paul the Traveller and the Roman Citizen*. London: Hodder and Stoughton, 1895.

Ramsay, W.M. *The Cities of Saint Paul: Their Influence on His Life and Thought*. Dale Memorial Lectures. London: Hodder and Stoughton, 1907.

Rapske, B. *The Widow in the Apostolic Church*. Regent College, Vancouver: Unpublished MTh Dissertation, 1987.

Rapske, B.M. 'The Importance of Helpers to the Imprisoned Paul in the Book of Acts'. *TynBul* 42.1 (1991), 3-30.

Redalie, Y. 'Conversion ou Liberation? Notes sur Actes 16,11-40'. *Bulletin du Centre Protestant d'Études* 26 (1974), 7-17.

Reese, B. 'The Apostle Paul's Exercise of His Rights as a Roman Citizen as Recorded in the Book of Acts'. *EvQ* 47 (1975), 138-45.

Reicke, B. 'Chapter 19. Caesarea, Rome, and the Captivity Epistles'. In *Apostolic History and the Gospel: Biblical and Historical Essays presented to F.F. Bruce on his 60th Birthday*. ed. W.W. Gasque and R.P. Martin. Exeter: Paternoster, 1970. 277-86.

Reicke, B. 'Die Mahlzeit mit Paulus auf den Wellen de Mittelmeers Act. 27,33-38'. *TZ* 4 (1948), 401-10.

Reicke, B. *The New Testament Era: The World of the Bible from 500 BC to AD 100*. tr. D.E. Green. Philadelphia: Fortress, 1968.

Reifenberg, A. 'Caesarea: A Study in the Decline of a Town'. *IEJ* 1 (1950/1), 20-32 and pl. viii-xvi.

Reitzenstein, R. *Hellenistic Mystery-Religions: Their Basic Ideas and Significance.* tr. J.E. Steely. Pittsburgh Theological Monograph Series 15; 3rd ed. 1926; Pittsburgh: Pickwick, 1978.

Rengstorf, K.H. 'ἀποστέλλω (πέμπω), κτλ'.'. *TDNT,* vol. 1, 398-447.

Reynolds, P.K. Bailey. *The Vigiles of Imperial Rome.* London: Humphrey Milford [OUP], 1926.

Reynolds, P.K.B. 'The Troops Quartered in the Castra Peregrinorum'. *JRS* 13 (1923), 168-89.

Rich, A., J.H. Flather and L.C. Purser. 'Balneae'. *DGRA,* vol. 1, 266-84.

Richardson, L.Jr. *Pompeii: An Architectural History.* Baltimore/London: Johns Hopkins,University Press, 1988.

Rickman, G. *The Corn Supply of Ancient Rome.* Oxford: Clarendon, 1980.

Riddle, D.W. *The Martyrs: A Study in Social Control.* Chicago: UCP, 1931.

Rivoira, G.T. *Rokman Architecture and its Principles of Construction Under the Empire.* tr. G. McH. Rushforth. Oxford: Clarendon, 1925.

Roetzel, C.J. *The World that Shaped the New Testament.* Atlanta: John Knox Press/London: SCM, 1985.

Rogers, R.S. 'Treason in the Early Empire'. *JRS* 49 (1959), 90-94.

Rogers, R.S. *Criminal Trials and Criminal Legislation Under Tiberius.* Middletown, Conn: American Philological Association, 1935.

Rokeah, D. *Jew, Pagans and Christians in Conflict.* SPB 33; Jerusalem: Magnes/Leiden: Brill, 1982.

Roloff, Jurgen. *Die Apostelgeschichte.* NTD 5; 17th ed.; Göttingen: Vandenhoeck und Ruprecht, 1981.

Rongy, H. 'Act. 27.1-10'. *VC* 14 (1960), 193-203.

Rongy, H. 'La finale des Actes devant la critique récente'. *Revue Ecclésiastique de Liége* 17 (1926), 273-83.

Roth, C. *et al.,* ed. 'Gamaliel, Rabban'. *EncJud,* vol. 7,295-99.

Roth, H.L. *Ancient Egyptian and Greek Looms.* Bankfield Museum Notes 2/2; Halifax: F. King and Sons, 1913.

Rougé, J. 'Actes 27:1-10'. *VC* 14 (1960), 193-203.

Rowlingson, D.T. 'Paul's Ephesian Ministry: An Evaluation of the Evidence'. *ATR* 32 (1950), 1-7.

Roxan, M.M. *Roman Military Diplomas 1954-1977.* Occasional Publication # 2; London: University of London Institute of Archaeology, 1978.

Runciman, W.G. 'Class, Status and Power?" In *Social Stratification.* ed. J.A. Jackson. Sociological Studies 1; Cambridge: CUP, 1968. 25-61.

Saddington, D.B. *The Developmnet of the Roman Auxiliary Forces from Caesar to Vespasian (49 BC-AD 79).* Harare: University of Zimbabwe, 1982.

Sadler, M.F. *The Acts of the Apostles With Notes Critical and Practical.* 1887; rpt. London: G. Bell and Sons, 1910.

Safrai, S.M. 'Chapter 7. Jewish Self-Government'. In *Compendia,* vol. 1, 377-419.

Safrai, S.M. 'Chapter 18. The Synagogue'. In *Compendia,* vol. 2, 908-44.

Safrai, S.M. *et al.,* ed. *Compendia Rerum Iudicarum ad Nouum Testamentum: The Jewish People in the First Century: Historical Geography, Political History, Social, Cultural and Religious Life and Institutions.* Assen: Van Gorcum, 1974, 1976. 2 volumes.

Salmon, E.T. *Roman Colonization Under the Republic.* Aspects of Greek and Roman Life; London: Thames and Hudson, 1969.

Sanders, H.A. 'The Birth Certificate of a Roman Citizen'. *CP* 22 (1927), 409-13

Sanders, J.T. 'Chapter 10. The Pharisees in Luke-Acts'. In *The Living Text: Essays in Honor of Ernest W. Saunders*. ed. D.E. Groh and R. Jewett. Lanham/New York/London: University Press of America, 1985. 141-188.

Sandmel, S. 'Parallelomania'. *JBL* 81 (1962), 1-13.

Saum, F. '«Er lebte ... von seinem eigenen Einkommen» (Apg 28,30)'. *BZ* 20 (1976), 226-29.

Schalit, A. 'Zu AG 25,9." *ASTI* 6 (1968), 106-13.

Schierling, S.P. and M.J. Schierling. 'The Influence of the Ancient Romances on Acts of the the Apostles'. *ClassBul* 54 (1978), 81-88.

Schille, G. *Die Apostelgeschichte des Lukas.* THNT 5; Berlin: Evangelische Verlagsanstalt, 1984.

Schlatter, A. *Die Apostelgeschichte.* Stuttgart: Clawer, 1962.

Schlier, H. 'παρρησία, παρρησιάζομαι'.'. *TDNT,* vol. 5, 871-86.

Schmid, J. *Zeit und Ort der paulinischen Gefangenschaftsbriefe.* Freiburg im Bresgau: Herder, 1931.

Schmitz, L. 'Dionysus'. *DGRBM,* vol. 1, 1046-49.

Schmitz, L. 'Poseidon'. *DGRBM,* vol. 3, 505-7.

Schneider, G. *Die Apostelgeschichte: I Teil.* HTKNT 5/1; Freiburg: Herder, 1980.

Schneider, G. *Die Apostelgeschichte: II Teil.* HTKNT 5/2; Freiburg: Herder, 1982.

Schulz, F. 'Roman Registers of Births and Birth Certificates'. *JRS* 32 (1942), 78-91.

Schulz, F. 'Roman Registers of Births and Birth Certificates: Part II'. *JRS* 33 (1943), 55-64.

Schürer, E. *The History of the Jewish People in the Age of Jesus Christ (175 BC-AD 135).* ed. tr. rev. G. Vermes *et al.* Edinburgh: T. and T. Clark, 1973-86. 3 volumes.

Schwank, B. 'Und so kamen wir nach Rom (Apg 28,14). 'Reisenotizen zu den letzten beiden Kapiteln der Apostelgeschichte'. *Erbe und Auftrag* 36 (1960), 169-93.

Schwartz, D.R. 'The Accusation and the Accusers at Philippi (Acts 16, 20-21)'. *Bib* 65 (1984), 357-63.

Schweizer, E. *The Good News According to Luke.* tr. D. E. Green. London: SPCK, 1984.

Scott, S.P. *The Civil Law.* Cincinnati: Central Trust Company, 1932. Volume 1.

Scramuzza, V.M. 'Note 25. The Policy of the Early Roman Emperors Towards Judaism'. In *BC,* vol. 5, 277-97.

Scroggie, W.G. *Paul's Prison Prayers.* London: Marshall Bros., 1922.

Seager, A.R. and A.T. Kraabel. 'IX. The Synagogue and the Jewish Community'. In Sardis From Prehistoric to Roman Times: Results of the Archaeological Exploration of Sardis 1958-75. ed. G.M.A. Hanfmann. Cambridge/London: Harvard UP, 1983. 168-91, 281-85.

Séve, M. and P. Weber. 'Le Côté du Forum de Philippes'. *BCH* 110 (1986), 531-81.

Shaw, B.D. 'Bandits in the Roman Empire'. *Past and Present* 105 (1984), 3-52.

Sherwin-White, A.N. 'The Early Persecutions and Roman Law Again'. *JTS* ns 3 (1952), 199-213.

Sherwin-White, A.N. 'Why Were the Early Christians Persecuted?--An Amendment'. *Past and Present* 27 (1964), 23-27.

Sherwin-White, A.N. *Roman Society and Roman Law in the New Testament.* Sarum Lectures 1961/2; Oxford: Clarendon, 1963.

Sherwin-White, A.N. *The Roman Citizenship*. 2nd edn.; Oxford: Clarendon, 1973.

Sihler, E.G. 'St. Paul and the Lex Julia de Vi'. *TQ* 18 (1914), 23-31.

Simpson, E.K.and F.F. Bruce. *The Epistles to the Ephesians and Colossians*. NICNT; Grand Rapids: Eerdmans, 1957.

Smith, J. *The Voyage and Shipwreck of St. Paul*. London: Longmans, Green, 1880.

Smith, W. 'Fasces'. *DGRA*, vol. 1, 826-27.

Smith, W. 'ἐνδεχα, ὁι'. *DGRA*, vol. 2, 942.

Smith, W. and A. S. Wilkins. 'Carnifex'. *DGRA*, vol. 1, 366.

Smith, W. and A. S. Wilkins. 'Tresviri'. *DGRA*, vol. 2, 868-69.

Smith, W. and W. Wayte. 'Caupona'. *DGRA*, vol. 1, 387-88.

Songer, H.S. 'Paul's Mission to Jerusalem: Acts 20-28'. *RevExp* 71 (1974), 499-510.

Souter, A. 'Interpretations of Certain New Testament Passages." *Exp* VIII/8 (1914), 94-96.

Speidel, M. *Roman Army Studies: Volume One*. Amsterdam: J.C. Gieben, 1984.

Spitta, F. 'Die zweimalige römische Gefangenschaft des Paulus'. in his *Zur Geschichte und Literatur des Urchristentums*. Band I. Göttingen: Vandenhoeck und Ruprecht, 1893. 1-108.

Springer, E. 'Der Prozess des Apostels Paulus'. *Preussische Jahrbücher* 218 (1929) 182-96.

Stagg, F. 'The Unhindered Gospel'. *RevExp* 71 (1974), 451-62.

Stählin, G. 'ξένος κτλ'.'. *TDNT*, vol. 5, 1-37.

Stählin, G. *Die Apostelgeschichte*. NTD 5; 4th ed.; Göttingen: Vandenhoeck und Ruprecht, 1970.

Stambaugh, J.E. and D.L. Balch. *The New Testament in Its Social Environment*. Library of Early Christianity 2; Philadelphia: Westminster, 1986.

Stegemann, W. 'War der Apostel Paulus ein römischer Bürger?" *ZNW* 78 (1987), 200-29.

Steinsaltz, A. *The Essential Talmud*. tr. Chaya Galai. London: Weidenfeld and Nicolson, 1976.

Stern, M. 'Chapter 6. The Province of Judaea'. In *Compendia*, vol. 1, 308-76.

Stern, M. 'Chapter 24: The Jews in Greek and Latin Literature'. In *Compendia*, vol. 1, 1101-59.

Stewart, R.A. 'Judicial Procedure in New Testament Times'. *EvQ* 47 (1975), 94-109.

Stokes, G.T. 'The Acts of the Apostles'. *The Expositor's Bible*. 2 volumes. ed. W.R. Nicoll. new edn.; London: Hodder and Stoughton, 1915.

Stowers, S.K. 'Social Status, Public Speaking, and Private Teaching. The Circumstances of Paul's Preaching Activity'. *NovT* 26 (1984), 59-82.

Strachan-Davidson, J.L. *Problems of the Roman Criminal Law*. Volume 1. Oxford: Clarendon, 1912.

Strobel, A. 'Passa-Symbolik und Passa-Wunder in Acts. XII.3ff'. *NTS* 4 (1957/8), 210-15.

Stubbe, E. 'Gefangenenfürsorge/Gefangenenseelsorge'. *TRE* 12 (1984), 144-48.

Sullivan, R.D. 'The Dynasty of Judaea in the First Century'. *ANRW* II/8 (1977), 296-354.

Tajra, H.W. 'L'appel à César: séparation d'avec le Christianisme?" *ETR* 56 (1981), 593-98.

Tajra, H.W. *The Trial of St. Paul: A Juridical Exegesis of the Second Half of the Acts of the Apostles*. WUNT 2/35; Tübingen: J.C.B. Mohr (Paul Siebeck), 1989.

Tarn, W.W. and Griffith, G.T. *Hellenistic Civilization*. 3rd edn.; London: Edward Arnold, 1952.

Taubenschlag, R. '63. L'Emprisonnement dans le Droit Gréco-Égyptien'. *Opera Minora: II Band Spezieller Teil*. Warszawa: Pánstwowe Wydawnictwo Naukowe, 1959. 713-719.

Taubenschlag, R. '64. Le Procès de l'Apôtre Paul en Lumière des Papyri'. *Opera Minora: II Band Spezieller Teil*. Warszawa: Pánstwowe Wydawnictwo Naukowe, 1959. 721-26.

Taubenschlag, R. *The Law of Greco-Roman Egypt in the Light of the Papyri 332 B.C.-640 A.D.* New York: Herald Square, 1944.

Täubler, A. 'Relatio ad principem'. *Klio* 17 (1920/21), 98-101.

Tcherikover, V. *Hellenistic Civilization and the Jews*. tr. S. Applebaum. Philadelphia: Jewish Publication Society of America/Jerusalem: Magnes, 1961.

Thompson, H.A. *The Athenian Agora: A Guide to the Excavation and Museum*. 1954; 3rd edn., Athens: American School of Classical Studies at Athens, 1976.

Tiedtke, E. and H.-G. Link. 'δεῖ'. In *NIDNTT*, vol. 2, 662-69.

Trebilco, P.R. 'Paul and Silas--'Servants of the Most High God' (Acts 16.16-18)." *JSNT* 36 (1989), 51-73.

Trebilco, P.R. *Jewish Communities in Asia Minor*. SNTSMS 69; Cambridge/New York/Melbourne: CUP, 1991.

Trompf, G.W. 'On Why Luke Declined to Recount the Death of Paul: Acts 27-28 and Beyond'. In *Luke-Acts: New Perspectives from the SBL Seminar*. ed. C.H. Talbert. New York: SBL, 1984. 225-39.

Trümmer, P. "Mantel und Schriften' (2 Tim 4,13). Zur Interpretation einer persönlichen Notiz in den Pastoralbriefen'. *BZ* 18 (1974), 193-207.

Turner, E.G. 'Tiberius Julius Alexander'. *JRS* 44 (1954), 54-64.

Turner, E.G. and W.E.W. Cockle. 'Complaint Against a Policeman'. *JEA* 68 (1982), 272.

Van der Horst, P.W. 'Chariton and the New Testament. A Contribution to the Corpus Hellenisticum'. *NovT* 25 (1983), 348-55.

van den Bergh, G.C.J.J. '*Custodiam Praestare:* Custodia-Liability or Liability for Failing Custodia?' *Tijdschrift voor Rechtsgeschiedenis* 43 (1975), 59-72. [English Title: The Legal History Review.]

van Unnik, W.C. 'Die Anklage Gegen die Apostel in Philippi'. In *Sparsa Collecta: The Collected Essays of W.C. van Unnik, Part I*. Supplements to *Novum Testamentum* 29; Leiden: Brill, 1973. 374-385.

van Unnik, W.C. 'Luke's Second Book and the Rules of Hellenistic Historiography'. In *Les Actes des Apôtres: Traditions, Rédaction, Théologie*. ed. J. Kremer. Gembloux: J. Duculot/Leuven: LUP, 1979. 37-61.

van Unnik, W.C. 'Once Again: Tarsus or Jerusalem'. In *Sparsa Collecta: The Collected Essays of W. C. van Unnik, Part I*. Supplements to *Novum Testamentum*, 29; Leiden: Brill, 1973. 321-327.

van Unnik, W.C. 'The Christian's Freedom of Speech in the New Testament'. *BJRL* 44 (1961), 466-88.

van Unnik, W.C. *Tarsus or Jerusalem: The City of Paul's Youth*. tr. G. Ogg. London: Epworth, 1962.

Vielhauer, P. 'On the "Paulinism" of Acts'. In *Studies in Luke-Acts*. ed. L.E. Keck and J.L. Martyn. Nashville/New York: Abingdon, 1966. 33-50.

Vincent, H. and F.-M. Abel. *Jérusalem Nouvelle.* 'Jérusalem. Recherches de topographie, d'archéologie et d'histoire." Tome 2. Paris: J. Gabalda, 1914/22/26.

Vögeli, A. 'Lukas und Euripides'. *TZ* 9 (1953), 415-38.

von Harnack, A. *Militia Christi. The Christian Religion and the Military in the First Three Centuries.* intr. D.McI. Gracie. 1905; rpt. Philadelphia: Fortress, 1981.

Walaskay, P.W. *'And So We Came to Rome," The Political Perspective of St Luke.* SNTSMS 49; CUP, 1983.

Wallace, S.LeR. *Taxation in Egypt from Augustus to Diocletian.* 1938; rpt., New York: Greenwood, 1969.

Walton, C.S. 'Oriental Senators in the Service of Rome: A Study of Imperial Policy Down to the Death of Marcus Aurelius'. *JRS* 19 (1929), 38-66.

Watson, G.R. *The Roman Soldier.* Aspects of Greek and Roman Life; London: Thames and Hudson, 1969.

Weatherly, J.A. 'The Jews in Luke-Acts'. *TynBul* 40 (1989), 107-17.

Weatherly, J.A. *Jewish Responsibility for the Cross in Luke-Acts.* University of Aberdeen: Unpublished PhD Dissertation, 1991.

Weinreich, O. 'Gebet und Wunder: Türöffnung im Wunder-, Prodigien-, und Zauberglauben der Antike, des Judentums und Christentums: Genethliakon Wilhelm Schmid zum Siebzigsten Geburtstag am 24 Februar 1929 ...'. *Tübinger Beiträge zur Altertumswissenschaft* 5 (1929), 200-464. [Stuttgart: W. Kohlhammer, 1929.]

Weiser, A. *Die Apostelgeschichte: Kapitel 1-12.* Okumenischer Taschenbuch Kommentar zum Neuen Testament 5/1; Gutersloher Taschenbucher 507; Gutersloh: Mohn, 1981.

Weiser, A. *Die Apostelgeschichte: Kapitel 13-28.* Okumenischer Taschenbuch Kommentar zum Neuen Testament 5/2; Gutersloher Taschenbucher 508; Gutersloh: Mohn, 1985.

Weiss, H.F. 'Φαρισαῖος'.'. *TDNT*, vol. 9, 11-48.

Welch, C.H. *Acts 13 or 28?...* Banstead, Surrey, England: Berean Publishing Trust, 1957.

Wellhausen, J. 'Noten zur Apostelgeschichte'. *Nachrichten von der königlichen Gesellschaft der Wissenschaften zu Göttingen. Philologisch-historische Klasse.* 1907. 1-21.

Westbury-Jones, J. *Roman and Christian Imperialism.* 1939; rpt., New York/London: Kennikat, 1971.

Whiston, R. and W. Wayte. 'Carcer'. *DGRA*, vol. 1, 362-63.

White, W. 'Gamaliel'. *ZPEB*, vol. 2, 649.

Whittaker, M. *Jews and Christians: Greco-Roman Views.* Cambridge Commentaries on Writings of the Jewish and Christian World 6; Cambridge: CUP, 1984.

Whittuck, E.A. 'Custodia'. *DGRA*, vol. 1, 589.

Whittuck, E.A. 'Familia'. *DGRA*, vol. 1, 824-25.

Wiefel, W. 'The Jewish Community in Ancient Rome and the Origins of Roman Christianity'. In *The Romans Debate.* ed. K.P. Donfried. Minneapolis: Augsburg, 1977. 100-19.

Wikenhauser, A. *Die Apostelgeschichte.* RNT 5; 4th ed.; Regensburg: Friedrich Pustet, 1961.

Wiles, G.P. *Paul's Intercessory Prayers: The Significance of the Intercessory Prayer Passages in the Letters of St Paul.* SNTSMS 24; Cambridge: CUP, 1974.

Williams, C.B. 'The Caesarean Imprisonment of Paul'. *The Biblical World* 34 (1909), 271-80.

Williams, C.S.C. *The Acts of the Apostles*. BNTC 5; London: A. and C. Black, 1964.

Williams, D.J. *Acts*. San Francisco: Harper and Row, 1985.

Williams, R.R. *The Acts of the Apostles*. Torch Bible Commentaries; London: SCN, 1953.

Wilson, S.G. *The Gentiles and the Gentile Mission in Luke-Acts*. SNTSMS 23; Cambridge: CUP, 1973.

Winter, B. 'The Importance of the *Captatio Beneuolentiae* in the Speeches of Tertullus and Paul in Acts 24:1-21'. *JTS* 42 (1991), 505-31.

Workman, H.B. *Persecution in the Early Church: A Chapter in the History of Renunciation*. Fernley Lectures 36; London: Charles H. Kelly, 1906.

Yamauchi, E. *The Archaeology of New Testament Cities in Western Asia Minor*. Glasgow: Pickering and Inglis, 1980.

Yates, J. and W. Wayte. 'Flagrum'. *DGRA*, vol. 1, 864.

Zahn, Th. 'Zur Lebensgeschichte des Apostels Paulus.' *NKZ* 15 (1904), 23-34.

Zahn, Th. *Die Apostelgeschichte des Lucas*. KNT 5.1/2; Leipzig: A. Deichert [Werner Scholl], 1919, 1921.

Zeller, E. 'Klassische Parallelen zu neutestamentlichen Stellen'. *ZWT* 10 (1867), 198-208.

INDEX OF MODERN AUTHORS

INDEX OF ANCIENT SOURCES

Ulpian
  Cod. Theod.
    9.2.2 39
  Dig.
    1.18.13 15
    1.18.13f. 10
    3.1.1.4 64
    3.3.19 68
    4.3.11.1 57
    4.8.31 66
    11.5.1.4 22
    26.10.3.17 22
    28.3.7 13
    47.2.52.12 25
    48.2.7.prol. 148
    48.2.7.1 148
    48.3.1 11 21
        39 41
        47
    48.3.3 11 39
        41
    48.3.5 12
    48.6.7 51 52
        300
    48.19.8.9 18
    48.19.8.13 18
    48.19.35 18
    48.22.6.1f. 13

Valerius Maximus
  2.7.15 49
  4.7.3 248
  5.4.7 247
  5f 247
  6.9.13 14 248
  8.1 247
  8.4.2 247
Varro
  L.
    5.151 21 24
Velleius Paterculus
  2.19.3 249 414
Vitruvius
  5.2.1 21

Xenophon
  An.
    1.2.23 74
    1.2.26 73

INDEX OF BIBLICAL REFERENCES

OLD TESTAMENT

NEW TESTAMENT

INDEX OF SUBJECTS

Printed in the United States
78793LV00005B/27